Lecture Notes in Computer Science 2315

Edited by G. Goos, J. Hartmanis, and J. van Leeuwen

Springer
Berlin
Heidelberg
New York
Barcelona
Hong Kong
London
Milan
Paris
Tokyo

Farhad Arbab   Carolyn Talcott (Eds.)

Coordination
Models and Languages

5th International Conference, COORDINATION 2002
York, UK, April 8-11, 2002
Proceedings

 Springer

Series Editors

Gerhard Goos, Karlsruhe University, Germany
Juris Hartmanis, Cornell University, NY, USA
Jan van Leeuwen, Utrecht University, The Netherlands

Volume Editors

Farhad Arbab
Centre for Mathematics and Computer Science
Software Engineering Department
Kruislaan 413, 1098 SJ Amsterdam, The Netherlands
E-mail: farhad.arbab@cwi.nl

Carolyn Talcott
SRI International
333 Ravenswood Ave., Menlo Park, CA 94025, USA
E-mail: clt@cs.stanford.edu

Cataloging-in-Publication Data applied for

Die Deutsche Bibliothek - CIP-Einheitsaufnahme

Coordination models and languages : 5th international conference,
coordination 2002, York, UK, April 8 - 11, 2002 ; proceedings / Farhad Arbab ;
Carolyn Talcott (ed.). - Berlin ; Heidelberg ; New York ; Barcelona ; Hong Kong ;
London ; Milan ; Paris ; Tokyo : Springer, 2002
    (Lecture notes in computer science ; Vol. 2315)
    ISBN 3-540-43410-0

CR Subject Classification (1998):D.1.3, C.2.4, F.1.2, D.2.4, I.2.11

ISSN 0302-9743
ISBN 3-540-43410-0 Springer-Verlag Berlin Heidelberg New York

Springer-Verlag Berlin Heidelberg New York
a member of BertelsmannSpringer Science+Business Media GmbH

http://www.springer.de

© Springer-Verlag Berlin Heidelberg 2002
Printed in Germany

Typesetting: Camera-ready by author, data conversion by PTP-Berlin, Stefan Sossna
Printed on acid-free paper   SPIN 10846610   06/3142   5 4 3 2 1 0

Preface

This volume contains the proceedings of the Fifth International Conference on Coordination Models and Languages (Coordination 2002), held in York, UK, 8–11 April 2002. Coordination models and languages close the conceptual gap between the cooperation model used by the constituent parts of an application and the lower-level communication model used in its implementation. Coordination-based methods provide a clean separation between individual software components and their interactions within their overall software organization. This separation, together with the higher-level abstractions offered by coordination models and languages, improve software productivity, enhance maintainability, advocate modularity, promote reusability, and lead to software organizations and architectures that are more tractable and more amenable to verification and global analysis.

Coordination is relevant in design, development, debugging, maintenance, and reuse of all complex concurrent and distributed systems. Specifically, coordination becomes paramount in the context of open systems, systems with mobile entities, and dynamically re-configurable evolving systems. Moreover, coordination models and languages focus on such key issues in Component Based Software Engineering as specification, interaction, and dynamic composition of components.

A total of 55 papers were submitted to this conference. Following the high quality standards of review and selection in this conference series, each submission was read by at least one of the two program co-chairs and carefully reviewed by at least three anonymous referees. All review results were then considered and extensively discussed in the program committee for the final selection. A total of 18 submissions were accepted as regular papers and 14 others as short papers. We were fortunate to have Perdita Stevens, Edinburgh University, Jim Waldo, Sun Microsystems, Inc., and Michael Wooldridge, University of Liverpool as invited speakers.

The conference was organized in cooperation with the ACM Special Interest Group on Software Engineering (SIGSOFT). This volume and the conference would not have been possible without the contributions of all authors, the evaluation work of the program committee, and the careful review of the anonymous referees. We are grateful to them all for their intellectual contributions. Special thanks to Freek Burger for his help in managing our electronic submission and evaluation process and in preparation of these proceedings. Last but not least, we acknowledge the support of the University of York, and especially thank Alan Wood for chairing the local organization of this conference.

February 2002

Farhad Arbab
Carolyn Talcott

Steering Committee

Farhad Arbab   CWI, The Netherlands
Paolo Ciancarini   U. Bologna, Italy
Chris Hankin   Imperial College, London, UK
George Papadopoulos   U. Cyprus, Cyprus
António Porto   New U. Lisbon, Portugal
Gruia-Catalin Roman   Washington U. Saint Luis, USA
Robert Tolksdorf   T.U. Berlin, Germany
Alexander Wolf   U. Colorado, Bolder, USA

Program Committee

Farhad Arbab   CWI, Amsterdam, The Netherlands, co-chair
Carolyn Talcott   SRI Int., Menlo Park, CA, USA, co-chair

Gul Agha   U. Illinois, Urbana-Champaign, USA
Lubomir Bic   U. California, Irvine, USA
Marcello Dønøuıguc   U. Leiden, The Netherlands
Rocco De Nicola   U. Firenze, Italy
GianLuigi Ferrari   U. Pisa, Italy
José Luiz Fiadeiro   U. Lisbon, Portugal
Roberto Gorrieri   U. Bologna, Italy
Tom Henzinger   U. California, Berkeley, USA
Paola Inverardi   U. l'Aquila, Italy
Jean-Marie Jacquet   U. Namur, Belgium
Shmuel Katz   The Technion, Israel
Joost Kok   U. Leiden, The Netherlands
Naftaly Minsky   Rutgers U., USA
Oscar Nierstrasz   U. Berne, Switzerland
Rick Schlichting   AT&T Labs-Research, USA
Katia Sycara   Carnegie Mellon U., USA
Alan Wood   U. York, UK

Organizing Chair

Alan Wood   University of York, UK

Referees

Xuhui Ao

Paolo Baldan

Lorenzo Bettini

Maurizio Bonuccelli

Andrea Bracciali

Michele Bugliesi

Po-Hao Chang

Michel Chaudron

Claudio Sacerdoti Coen

Dario Colazzo

Pierpaolo Degano

Michael B. Dillencourt

Yevgeniy Gendelman

Joseph Giampapa

Marcelo Glusman

Yukun Gou

Luuk Groenewegen

Juan Guillen Scholten

Matti Hiltunen

Mihail Ionescu

Nadeem Jamali

Myeong-Wuk Jang

Amalia Katz

Hairong Kuang

Nirman Kumar

Charles Lakos

Brent Langley

Antóia Lopes

Michele Loreti

R. Lucchi

Kirill Mechitov

A. Montresor

Henry Muccini

Koji Noguchi

Susanna Pelagatti

Luigia Petre

Rosario Pugliese

Iris Reinhartz-Berger

Giovanni Russello

Assaf Schuster

Laura Semini

Koushik Sen

Constantine Serban

Michel Wermelinger

G. Zavattaro

Reza Ziaei

Table of Contents

Playing Games with Software Design

Perdita Stevens

Division of Informatics, University of Edinburgh

Modern software development processes openly acknowledge what software designers have always whispered: software design is not done as a monolithic phase between analysis and implementation. Rather, the process of designing software is incremental, experimental, often concurrent, and interleaved with other activities. It is a game, in the sense that it involves strategising, exploring options, balancing objectives - and in the sense that it can be fun to do in groups!

At the same time the market for software design tools has expanded and become more competitive, largely because of the emergence of the Unified Modelling Language as dominant design notation. Yet these two thematic changes in the community's view of software design, embodied in methodologies and tools respectively, do not yet seem to be harmonious. The current generation of software design tools supports the recording and verification of design better than it supports design itself. The tools are neither players in the design game, nor reliable referees.

Is this a problem, and does it have anything to do with coordination? I will argue that the answers to both questions are Yes, and will support what I say with particular reference to designing frameworks and product-line architectures. The talk reflects work in progress.

F. Arbab and C. Talcott (Eds.): COORDINATION 2002, LNCS 2315, p. 1, 2002.

Coordination and System Design in a Network-Centric Age

Jim Waldo

Sun Microsystems, Inc.

While the slogan "the Network is the Computer" has been around for over a decade, few in the computer industry (including those who used the slogan) actually believed it. At best, the slogan has been interpreted as meaning that the network is an important way to connect computers. But there has been a hard and fast line in system design between the computer and the network that is used to connect different computers, allowing those computers to share data and, at some high level, coordinate to perform some common function. Rather than the network being the computer, the network has marked the border between computers.

There are good reasons for using the network as the demarcation line between one computer and the next. The assumptions that can be made about a homogeneous context within a particular computer cannot be made from one computer to the next. Different data formats, binary representations, and instruction sets are not possible within a single machine, but are both common and possible on machines joined by a network. More importantly, the use of the network introduces failure modes and latencies which are not found within a single machine. While there have been many attempts to build distributed system infrastructures that attempt to make the building of software running on multiple computers separated by a network look just like software that is constructed for a single machine, there are also powerful arguments to the effect that such attempts are doomed.

We might simply resign ourselves to the current state of affairs if it were not for other pressures that are coming to bear. The need for systems to scale and change over time is increasing more rapidly than our ability to scale and change single, contained systems. Our reliance on these systems is increasing, making it less and less acceptable for the systems either to fail or to be halted for a period of time for upgrades. The coming of pervasive computing, in which networks of computing elements, embedded in devices that we do not think of as computers, will increase both the scale of networks and our reliance on them.

The standard ways in which we have built distributed systems are not sufficient for the building of large scale, highly reliable, evolving, always-available systems. To meet the challenges of building such systems will require that we approach distributed computing in a new way, a way that will adopt and adapt many of the techniques that have been used in the coordination community for some time.

F. Arbab and C. Talcott (Eds.): COORDINATION 2002, LNCS 2315, pp. 2–3, 2002.

In this talk, I will describe an experiment in building an infrastructure for these kinds of distributed systems. The experiment, embodied in the Jini(tm) networking technology, relies on coordination mechanisms such as associative lookup and loose coupling through Linda-like tuple spaces to build highly adaptive and reliable systems out of various hardware and software components. After discussing the technology and why it was designed in the way it was, I will turn to some of the things we have learned as a result of the experiment, concluding with some discussion of the directions we plan on taking in the building of our next iteration of the technology.

Time, Knowledge, and Cooperation: Alternating-Time Temporal Epistemic Logic and Its Applications

Michael Wooldridge[1] and Wiebe van der Hoek[2]

[1] University of Liverpool, UK
[2] University of Utrecht, The Netherlands

Branching-time temporal logics have proved to be an extraordinarily successful tool in the formal specification and verification of distributed systems. Much of this recent success stems from the tractability of the model checking problem for the branching time logic CTL. Several successful verification tools (of which SMV is the best known) have been implemented that allow designers to verify that systems satisfy requirements expressed in CTL. Recently, CTL was generalised by Alur, Henzinger, and Kupferman in a logic known as "Alternating-time Temporal Logic" (ATL). The key insight in ATL is that the path quantifiers of CTL could be replaced by "cooperation modalities", of the form $<< G >>$, where G is a set of agents. The intended interpretation of an ATL formula $<< G >> \phi$ is that the agents G can cooperate to ensure that ϕ holds (equivalently, that G have a winning strategy for ϕ). It turns out that the resulting logic very naturally generalises and extends CTL. In this talk, I will discuss extensions to ATL with *knowledge modalities*, of the kind made popular by the work of Fagin, Halpern, Moses, and Vardi. Combining these knowledge modalities with ATL, it becomes possible to express such properties as "group G can cooperate to bring about ϕ iff it is common knowledge in G that ψ". The resulting logic — Alternating-time Temporal Epistemic Logic (ATEL) — has a range of applications, which will be discussed in the talk. In addition, I will relate some preliminary experiments with ATEL model checking, which shares the tractability property of its ancestor CTL.

F. Arbab and C. Talcott (Eds.): COORDINATION 2002, LNCS 2315, p. 4, 2002.
© Springer-Verlag Berlin Heidelberg 2002

Coordination for Orchestration

Luis F. Andrade[1,2], Jose L. Fiadeiro[1,3], Joao Gouveia[2],
Georgios Koutsoukos[2], and Michael Wermelinger[1,4]

[1] ATX Software S.A.,
Alameda António Sérgio 7 - 1 C,
2795-023 Linda-a-Velha, Portugal
landrade@atxsoftware.com

[2] OBLOG Software S.A., Alameda António Sérgio 7 - 1 A
2795-023 Linda-a-Velha, Portugal
{jgouveia,gkoutsoukos}@oblog.pt

[3] Department of Informatics, Faculty of Sciences, University of Lisbon
Campo Grande, 1749-016 Lisboa, Portugal
jose@fiadeiro.org

[4] Dep. of Informatics, Fac. Sciences and Technology, New University of Lisbon
2829-516 Monte da Caparica, Portugal
mw@di.fct.unl.pt

Abstract. Based on the identification of some shortcomings of object-oriented methodology and technology to address the challenges of supporting the engineering and deployment of Web Services, we suggest that alternative approaches can be found in what we call "coordination methodology and technologies" - a set of modelling primitives, design principles, design patterns, and analysis techniques that we have been developing for supporting the construction and evolution of complex software systems that need to operate in very volatile and dynamic environments.

1 On the Challenges Raised by Web Services Architectures

In the literature, "Web Services" in general are being promoted as a technology for "dynamic -business", the next generation of the Internet "culture" in which a shift is made from B2C to B2B. This shift puts an emphasis on program-to-program interaction, which is quite different from the user-to-program interaction that characterised (thin) clients interacting with business applications in the B2C model. In particular, initiatives that were typical of the user side, like "searching" (although not necessarily "surfing"...), have now to be performed on the business side, which means supported by software. Readings on the technologies that have been made available in the past few months will normally emphasise this shift from client-to-server, static, linear interaction to dynamic, mobile and unpredictable interactions between machines operating on a network, and identify it as one of the challenges that needs to be met in full for the architecture to impose itself in its full potential.

F. Arbab and C. Talcott (Eds.): COORDINATION 2002, LNCS 2315, pp. 5–13, 2002.
© Springer-Verlag Berlin Heidelberg 2002

Web Services have been often characterised as "self-contained, modular applications that can be described, published, located, and invoked over a network, generally the Web" [1]. Building applications (in fact, new services that can themselves be published) is a dynamic process that consists in locating services that provide the basic functionalities that are required, and "orchestrating" them, i.e. establishing collaborations between them, so that the desired global properties of the application can emerge from their joint behaviour. Hence, this new architecture is often characterised by three fundamental aspects for which support is required: *publishing* services so that they can be used by other services; *finding* services that meet required properties; and *binding* to services after they are located to achieve the required integration.

The models that have been proposed in the meanwhile, namely the Service Oriented Architectures based on publish/find/bind, address these issues directly in terms of technological solutions that can be supported immediately, at varying levels, by open source software. However, in order to understand what exactly is necessary to support the engineering and deployment of Web Services, and, hence, what is still required in terms of research and development effort, we have to characterise exactly what this new architecture is about and how it relates to the software development methodologies and supporting technologies that are available today.

That current technologies have severe shortcomings is there for everybody to see. In the own words of Microsoft [2]:

> *"With the integration and communication infrastructures complete our applications can now "speak" to other applications over the Internet, but we don't have a good mechanism for telling them when and how to say it. We have no way of representing the process. Today the "process" is spread throughout the implementation code of every participant involved in the process. This mechanism for representing the process of business interactions is fragile, prone to ambiguities, does not cross organizational boundaries well, and does not scale. The larger the process gets and the more participants that are involved, the more static the process is and the harder it is to propagate changes and new players into the process."*

The goal of this paper is, precisely, to address these shortcomings. Because of their widespread use in industry, and the fact that a trend seems to be already imposing itself, we start by taking a close look to what object-orientation has to offer to come to the conclusion that there are key issues in services that are beyond its grasp. We then suggest that what is missing in object-orientation can actually be found in the "coordination" realm. Finally, we set up a research agenda on "coordination for orchestration".

2   Why Object-Oriented Techniques Cannot Address Them

The question of determining how exactly object-oriented techniques can contribute to the engineering of Web Services is a fair one. It reflects a (legitimate) concern for the investments that have been made already on object-oriented technologies. It must be made clear to people and, especially, to the companies that want to be part of the New Economy, what kind of investments this new generation of architectures for the Web requires before it becomes obsolete. This is particularly so because Web Services are often presented as a "logical" evolution of, on the one hand, object-oriented analysis and design and, on the other hand, of "components" as geared to the deployment of e-business solutions.

In this paper, we would like to disagree with this "evolutionary" view. Not that we do not consider Web Services as the "next step" in what has been the "evolution" of Software Engineering in the Internet age. What we contend is that this step is itself a simple "evolution" of existing concepts and techniques. We believe that the move from object to service oriented systems is a true shift of paradigms, one that should be fully, and formally, characterised so that both methodologies and supporting technologies can be developed to take maximum profit of its potential.

The main reason for our disagreement is precisely the fact that the shift from objects/components to services is reflected fundamentally on the interactions - what in the terminology of Web Services is usually associated with "orchestration". The view exposed in section 1 is of systems that are in a continuous process of reconfiguration due to the fact that services need to establish, dynamically, the collaborations that allow them to provide the functionalities that are being requested by some other service. Hence, Web Services require flexible architectures in which collaborations can be established and changed dynamically and reactively. For this purpose, interactions cannot be hardwired in the code that implements the services. If collaborations are not modelled directly as first-class entities that can be manipulated by a process of dynamic reconfiguration, the overhead that just-in-time integration and other operational aspects of this new architecture represent will not lead to the levels of agility that are required for the paradigm to impose itself.

However, traditionally, interactions in OO are based on *identities*, in the sense that, through clientship, objects interact by invoking the methods of specific objects (instances) to get something specific done. This implies that any change on the collaborations that an object maintains with other objects needs to be performed at the level of the code that implements that object and, possibly, of the objects with which the new collaborations are established.

On the contrary, interactions in the service-oriented approach should be based on the description of what needs to be done, thus decoupling the "what one wants to be done" from "who does it". This translates directly to the familiar characterisation of Web Services as "late binding" or, better, "just-in-time binding". It is as if collaborations in OO where shifted from instance-to-instance to instance-to-interface, albeit with a more expressive notion of interface. Hence, the first conclusion that we would like to draw is that Web Services are, indeed, beyond OO methodology and technology, especially in what concerns the support that needs to be provided for establishing and managing interactions. Clientship and other OO means of establishing interactions among objects lead to systems that are too tightly coupled for the kind of dynamics required by the Web.

3 How "Coordination" Can Contribute to "Service Orchestration"

The second conclusion that we can draw from the discussion on the limitations of object-oriented approaches is that "coordination" technologies, as we have been developing around the notion of "coordination contract", seem to play a fundamental role in enabling service-oriented architectures, namely in what concerns the "orchestration infrastructure" [1] [2] i.e. what supports the dynamic aspects of the paradigm - the "process" and "interaction" aspects. These technologies are based on the separation between what in systems is concerned with the computations that are responsible for the functionality of the services that they offer and the mechanisms that coordinate the way components interact, a paradigm that has been developed in the context of so-called Coordination Languages and Models [8].

Our own contribution [5] has been directed to making this paradigm usable in the development of a new generation of information systems that exhibit the levels of agility required to operate in contexts of highly volatile business requirements and continuous change in the way they need to support organisational structures and strategies. For this purpose, we brought together concepts and techniques from Software Architectures (the notion of connector [3]), Parallel Program Design (the notion of superposition [10]), and Distributed Systems (techniques for supporting dynamic reconfiguration [12]) that are now integrated in a collection of semantic primitives that support the modelling of systems that are flexible and more amenable to change. In particular, these primitives allow, precisely, for the kind of "just-in-time" binding required by Web Services to be performed in a non-intrusive, compositional way. The technology that we have been promoting supports dynamic configuration, which is exactly what is required for this form of binding.

The underlying methodology of "coordination-based" development is also essential for service-oriented systems in the sense that it externalises interactions as connectors (coordination contracts) that can be dynamically superposed on system components, i.e. at run-time, without interruption of "normal business", and encourages developers to identify dependencies between components in terms of *services* rather than identities. The notion of component that we assume is the more general one that has been popularised in [15] by which we mean "a unit of composition with contractually specified interfaces and explicit context dependencies only". The identification of the components to which coordination contracts are applicable is made through "coordination interfaces" that identify the properties that they need to exhibit rather than the classes to which they have to belong

To illustrate the kind of approach that we have in mind, consider the case of the services that financial institutions have been making available in recent times through what we could call a "flexible package" - the ability to coordinate deposits and debits between two accounts, typically a checking and a savings account, so that the balance of one of the accounts is maintained between an agreed minimal and maximal amount by making automatic transfers to and from the other account. The service that is offered is the detection of the situations in which the transfers are required and their execution in a transactional mode. Because this behaviour should be published as a service that customer applications looking for flexible account management should be able to bind to, the following aspects should be ensured.

In the first place, the service cannot be offered for specific accounts. A "binding process" should be responsible for instantiating, at execution time, the service to the relevant components. Nor should it be offered for specific object classes: the service itself should be able to be described independently of the technology used by the components to which it will be bound. Instead, it is the find/bind process that should be able to make the adaptation that is needed between the technologies used for implementing the service and the ones used by the components to which it is going to be bound. This adaptation can itself be the subject of an independent publish/find/bind process that takes place at another level of abstraction, or be offered for default combinations by the service itself. This is important to enable the implementation of the service itself to evolve, say in order to take advantage of new technologies, without compromising the bindings that have been made.

Hence, in our approach, the description of the applications to which the service can be bound is made of what we call *coordination interfaces*. For instance, in the case of the flexible package, two coordination interfaces are required: one catering for the account whose balance is going to be managed, typically a checking account, and the other for the "savings" account. The trigger/reaction mode of coordination that our approach supports requires that each coordination interface identifies which events produced during system execution are required to be detected as triggers for the service to react, and which operations must be made available for the reaction to superpose the required effects.

The nature of triggers and operations can vary. Typical events that constitute triggers are calls for operations/methods of instance components, and typical operations are those made public through their APIs. Another class of events that we have found useful as triggers is the observation of changes taking place in the system. For such changes to be detected, components must make available methods through which the required observations can be made (something that the mechanism of find/bind must check), and a detection mechanism must be made available in the implementation platform to enable such changes to be effectively monitored (something that is not universally provided).

The two coordination interfaces that we have in mind can be described as follows:

```
coordination interface savings-account
import types money;
operations
    balance():money;
    debit(a:money)  post balance(a) = old balance()-a
    credit(a:money)  post balance(a) = old balance()+a
end
```

Notice how the properties of the operations that are required are specified in an abstract way in terms of pre and post-conditions.

```
coordination interface checking-account
import types money;
triggers balance():money;
operations
    balance():money;
    debit(a:money)  post balance(a) = old balance()-a
    credit(a:money)  post balance(a) = old balance()+a
end
```

The difference between the two interfaces lies in the inclusion of the trigger in the checking-account. This is because it is changes on the balance of checking account that will the trigger the service to react. More specifically, we are requiring from the component that will be bound to this interface that it makes changes in the balance to be detected by the flexible-package service.

The second important requirement is that the service itself be described only on the basis of these coordination interfaces and its own operations, and in terms of the properties that it ensures when it is bound to components that comply with the interfaces. This description can be made in terms of what we call a "coordination law":

```
coordination law flexible-package
interfaces c:checking-account, s:savings-account
attributes minimum,maximum:money
rules
    when c.balance()<minimum
    do   s.debit(min(s.balance(),maximum-c.balance()))
         and c.credit(min(s.balance(),maximum-c.balance()))
    when c.balance()>maximum
    do   c.debit(c.balance()-maximum)
         and s.credit(c.balance()-maximum)
end contract
```

Each coordination rule in the law identifies, under "when", a trigger and, under "do", the reaction to be performed on occurrence of the trigger. In the cases at hand, these reactions define sets of actions that we call the *synchronisation sets* associated with the rules. As already mentioned, the reactions are executed as transactions, which means that the synchronisation sets are executed atomically. In what concerns the language in which the reactions are defined, we normally use an abstract notation for defining the synchronisation set as above.

When the interfaces are bound to specific components, their behaviour is coordinated by an instance of the law, establishing what we call a "coordination contract". [4]. The behaviour specified through the rules is superposed on the behaviour of the components without requiring the code that implements them to be changed.

We need to stress the fact that coordination interfaces are defined so as to state *requirements* placed by laws on the entities that can be subjected to its rules and not as a declaration of features or properties that entities offer to be coordinated. This means that coordination interfaces should restrict themselves to what is essential for the definition of given laws and hence, in the extreme, can be local to the laws themselves. However, for the sake of reusability and simplification of the binding process, it is useful to externalise coordination interfaces from the laws in the context of which they are defined, and establish a hierarchy between them that is consistent with the compliance relationship in the sense that a component that complies with a given interface also complies with any ancestor of that interface or, that any binder of the component for that interface will also serve as a binder for any ancestor. Hence, in a sense, coordination interfaces fulfil the role of representations of abstract business entities in the sense that the hierarchy of interfaces will, ultimately, provide a taxonomy of all the business uses that are made of entities in the application domain.

Given this, we insist that, as a methodological principle, the definition of coordination interfaces should be driven by the modelling of the business services as coordination laws and not by the modelling of the entities of the business domain as it is usual in object-oriented and other traditional "product"-oriented approaches. In this sense, it makes no sense to define a coordination interface for accounts in general but, instead, and in the extreme, as many interfaces as the business services that apply to accounts require (something that is evolutionary in nature because it is as impossible to predict how an information system will evolve as for how the business of an organisation will grow). Ultimately, these will identify all the usages that the specific business makes of the notion of Account in a "service-oriented" perspective. As business evolves, new coordination interfaces are defined and placed in the hierarchy. In a product-oriented notion of interface, each such change in the business rules would require a change in the account interface, which is against the spirit of "agility-enhancer" that web services are supposed to deliver.

4   Concluding Remarks

Our main goal in this paper was to show that, in order to supply a methodology and associated technologies that can support Web Service Engineering, we should be looking more in the direction of "coordination" than "object-orientation". We hope that the examples were clear enough to illustrate how the modelling primitives that we have developed around the notion of "coordination contracts" [4] can be used for supporting an "orchestration infrastructure", namely for representing business interactions in a way that makes them independent of their application to specific components of systems.

We should add that these primitives have a mathematical semantics defined over a categorical framework [7]. A micro-architecture based on the use of design patterns has also been developed that allow their usage over typical environments for component-based development [9]. This micro-architecture has been deployed for Java components in what we call the "Coordination Development Environment" - a prototype of a tool supporting the methodology that is freely available from http://www.atxsoftware.com.

This means that we have gone already a long way into the definition of a framework that can support the engineering of web services at the business level. However, it is clear that we have not reached the end! There are a number of issues that need to be addressed before that.

The main ones are related to the classification of services and the binding processes. The former present challenges that are more localised and "technological" in nature; basically, there are classification mechanisms available "in the market", e.g. those based on the UDDI [1], and lots of room for improvement! On the side of the binding mechanisms, there seems to be more scope for methodological work because it addresses the fabric of the paradigm itself. This is one of the areas in which we will be investing for the coming times! The categorical framework is ideal for formalising binding mechanisms but the nature of the process itself has to be better understood in the first place, namely in what concerns the levels of adaptability with which they need to endow the "orchestration" process.

Another important research direction concerns the extension of the coordination technologies that we presented to address distribution and mobility. This is work that is starting now in collaboration with IEI/CNR and the Universities of Munich, Pisa and Florence. Finally, we are also engaged in integrating these solutions within the UML [6] for which we have the collaboration of a team of researchers coordinated by Ana Moreira.

References

[1] Web Services architecture overview – the next stage of evolution for e-business, IBM Research 2000
[2] *BizTalk Orchestration – a new technology for orchestrating business interactions*, Microsoft Research 2000
[3] R. Allen and D. Garlan, "A Formal Basis for Architectural Connectors", ACM TOSEM, 6(3), 1997, 213–249.
[4] L.F. Andrade and J.L. Fiadeiro, "Interconnecting Objects via Contracts", in *UML'99 – Beyond the Standard*, R. France and B. Rumpe (eds), LNCS 1723, Springer Verlag 1999, 566–583.
[5] L.F. Andrade and J.L. Fiadeiro, "Coordination Technologies for Managing Information System Evolution", in Proc. CAISE'01, K.Dittrich, A.Geppert and M.Norrie (eds), LNCS 2068, Springer-Verlag 2001, 374-387.
[6] G. Booch, J. Rumbaugh and I. Jacobson, *The Unified Modeling Language User Guide*, Addison-Wesley 1998.
[7] J.L. Fiadeiro and A. Lopes, "Algebraic Semantics of Coordination, or what is in a signature?", in *AMAST'98*, A.Haeberer (ed), Springer-Verlag 1999.
[8] D. Gelernter and N. Carriero, "Coordination Languages and their Significance", Communications ACM 35, 2, pp. 97–107, 1992
[9] J. Gouveia, G. Koutsoukos, L. Andrade and J. Fiadeiro, "Tool Support for Coordination-Based Software Evolution", in *Technology of Object-Oriented Languages and Systems – TOOLS 38*, W.Pree (ed), IEEE Computer Society Press 2001, 184–196.
[10] S. Katz, "A Superimposition Control Construct for Distributed Systems", ACM TOPLAS 15(2), 1993, 337–356.
[11] H. Kilov and J. Ross, *Information Modeling: an Object-oriented Approach*, Prentice-Hall 1994.

[12] J. Kramer. "Configuration Programming – A Framework for the Development of Distributable Systems", Proc. CompEuro'90, pp. 374–384, IEEE, 1990.

[13] B. Meyer, "Applying Design by Contract", *IEEE Computer*, Oct.1992, 40–51.

[14] D. Notkin, D. Garlan, W. Griswold and K. Sullivan, "Adding Implicit Invocation to Languages: Three Approaches", in *Object Technologies for Advanced Software*, S. Nishio and A. Yonezawa (editors), LNCS 742, Springer-Verlag 1993, 489–510.

[15] C. Szyperski, *Component Software: Beyond Object-Oriented Programming*, Addison Wesley 1998.

Concurrent Semantics for the Web Services Specification Language DAML-S

Anupriya Ankolekar[1], Frank Huch[2], and Katia Sycara[1]

[1] Carnegie Mellon University, Pittsburgh PA 15213, USA
{anupriya,katia}@cs.cmu.edu,
[2] Christian-Albrechts-University of Kiel, 24118 Kiel, Germany
fhu@informatik.uni-kiel.de

Abstract. The DARPA Agent Markup Language ontology for Services (DAML-S) enables the description of Web-based services, such that they can be discovered, accessed and composed dynamically by intelligent software agents and other Web services, thereby facilitating the coordination between distributed, heterogeneous systems on the Web. We propose a formalised syntax and an initial reference semantics for DAML-S.

Keywords: DAML-S, Web services, concurrent semantics, agents

1 Introduction

The DARPA Agent Markup Language Services ontology (DAML-S) is being developed for the specification of Web services, such that they can be dynamically discovered, invoked and composed with the help of existing Web services. DAML-S, defined through DAML+OIL, an ontology definition language with additional semantic inferencing capabilities, provides a number of constructs or DAML+OIL classes to describe the properties and capabilities of Web services. DAML-S will be used by Web service providers to markup their offerings, by service requester agents to describe the desired services, as well as by planning agents to compose complex new services from existing simpler services. Other approaches to the specification of Web services from the industry are UDDI, WSDL, WSFL and XLANG, which address different aspects of Web service description provided by DAML-S. Furthermore, DAML-S is unique in that, due to its foundations in DAML+OIL, it provides markup that can be semantically meaningful for intelligent agents.

Although DAML-S is intended primarily for Web-based services, the basic framework can be extended to facilitate the coordination and interoperability, more generally, of systems in heterogeneous, dynamic environments. In this paper, we propose an interleaving, strict operational semantics for DAML-S[1] informally described in [1].

---

[1] DAML-S is currently under development and the language described here is the DAML-S Draft Release 0.5 (May 2001).

F. Arbab and C. Talcott (Eds.): COORDINATION 2002, LNCS 2315, pp. 14–21, 2002.

The development of a reference semantics for DAML-S brings any ambiguities about the language specification to the fore so that they can be addressed and resolved. It can also provide the basis for the future DAML-S execution model. Furthermore, having a formal semantics is the first step towards developing techniques for automated verification of functional and non-functional properties of the DAML-S execution model. The formalisation of other Web standards would make it easier to compare and contrast their capabilities and better understand the strengths and weaknesses of various approaches.

In this paper, we model a core subset of DAML-S, referred to as *DAML-S Core*. Every service defined in DAML-S can be transformed into a functionally equivalent service definition in DAML-S Core stripped of additional attributes that aid in service discovery or any quality-of-service parameters. The next section, Section 2, presents the DAML-S ontologies and the process model of a service. Section 3 discusses some of the issues involved in developing a formal model for DAML-S and presents the syntax of DAML-S Core. Finally, a formal semantics for DAML-S Core is given in Section 4.

2   The DAML-S Ontology

The DAML-S ontology consists of three parts: a *service profile*, a *process model* and a *service grounding*. The service profile of a particular Web service would enable a service-requesting agent to determine whether the service meets its requirements. The profile is essentially a summary of the service, specifying the input expected, the output returned, the precondition to and the effect of its successful execution. The process model of a service describes the internal structure of a service in terms of its subprocesses and their execution flow. It provides a detailed specification of how another agent can interact with the service. Each process within the process model could itself be a service, in which case, the enclosing service is referred to as a *complex* service, built up from simpler, atomic services. The service grounding describes how the service can be accessed, in particular which communication protocols the service understands, which ports can receive which messages and so forth.

In this paper, we will only be considering the service process model, since it primarily determines the semantics of the service's execution. The formalisation proposed here will however form the basis for an execution model and provide inputs for the definition of the service grounding. The inputs, outputs and effects of a process can be instances of any class in DAML+OIL. The preconditions are instances of class Condition. There are a number of additional constructs to specify the control flow within a process model: Sequence, Split, Split+Join, If-Then-Else, Repeat-While, Repeat-Until. The execution of a service requires communication, interaction between the participants in a service transaction. The DAML-S constructs for communication will be described in the future service grounding. Since modelling the communication within a service transaction is essential to describing the execution semantics of a service described in DAML-S, we define a set of what we consider basic communication primitives, for example, for the sending and receiving of messages.

3   Modelling DAML-S Core

The DAML-S class `Process` and its subclasses, representing agents, are modelled as functions. DAML-S agents essentially take in inputs and return outputs, exhibiting simple function-like behaviour. A Web page, for example, is an extremely simple agent which has no input and as output, merely some HTML content. The input to a `Process` is not restricted and could be a `Process` itself, resulting in a 'higher-order' agent, offering meta-level functionality. A simple example of a higher-order service is an agent that, when given a task and an environment of existing services, locates a service to perform the task, invokes the service and returns the result. The functionality of the agent thus depends on the set of services in the world that it takes as input.

Furthermore, agents can be composed together. This composition itself represents an agent with its own inputs and outputs. The composition could be sequential, dependent on a conditional or defined as a loop. The composition could also be concurrent, where the agents can interact with each other, representing relatively complex, distributed applications, such as chat systems.

DAML-S classes are defined through DAML+OIL, an ontology definition language. DAML+OIL, owing to its foundations in RDF Schema, provides a typing mechanism for Web resources [8] [9], such as Web pages, people, document types and abstract concepts. The difference between a DAML+OIL class and a class in a typical object-oriented programming language is that DAML+OIL classes are meant primarily for data modelling and contain no methods. Subclass relationships are defined through the property `rdfs:subClassOf`. We model classes in DAML-S as type expressions and subclasses as subtypes. Modelling other properties with arbitrary semantics does not significantly affect the type system or the functional behaviour of DAML-S agents and are therefore not considered further. More formally,

Definition 1 (Type Expressions). A type expression $\tau \in \mathcal{T}$ is either a type variable $\alpha \in \mathcal{V}$ or the application, $(T\tau_1 \cdots \tau_n)$, of an n-ary type constructor $T \in \mathcal{F}$ to the type expressions $\tau_1, \ldots, \tau_n$.

Type constructors in $\mathcal{F}$ are determined by DAML-S Core classes, such as `List`, `Book` and `Process`. In addition to these, DAML-S Core has a predefined functional type constructor $\rightarrow$, for which, following convention, we will use the infix notation. All type constructors bind to the right, i.e. $\tau_1 \rightarrow \tau_2 \rightarrow \tau_3$ is read as $(\tau_1 \rightarrow (\tau_2- > \tau_3))$.

Type expressions build the term algebra $T_{\mathcal{F}}(\mathcal{V})$. DAML-S agents can be polymorphic with respect to their input and output, for example an agent which duplicates input of arbitrary type. Polymorphic types are type expressions containing type variables. The expression $a \rightarrow b$, for instance, is a polymorphic type with type variables a and b, which can be instantiated with concrete types. The substitution $[a/\text{integer}, b/\text{boolean}]$ applied to $a \rightarrow b$ results in the type $\text{integer} \rightarrow \text{boolean}$. Identical type variables in a type expression indicate identical types. For the formalisation of polymorphism, we use *type schemas*, in which all free type variables are bound: $\forall \alpha_1, \ldots, \alpha_n.\tau$, where τ is a type and $\alpha_1, \ldots, \alpha_n$ are the generic variables in τ.

Although DAML-S Core agents can be functionally simple, they derive much of their useful behaviour from their ability to execute concurrently and interact with one another. The communication an agent is engaged in is a side-effect of its functional execution. Communication side-effects can be incorporated into the functional description of agents with the help of the IO monad. Monads were introduced from category theory to describe programming language computations, actions with side-effects, as opposed to purely functional evaluations. The IO monad, introduced in Concurrent Haskell [7], describes actions with communication side-effects.

The IO monad is essentially a triple, consisting of a unary type constructor IO and two functions, return and (>>=). A value of type IO a is an I/O action, that when performed, can engage in some communication before resulting in a value of type a. The application return v represents an agent that performs no IO and simply returns the value v. The function (>>=) represents the sequential composition of two agents. Thus, action1 >>= action2 represents an agent that first performs action1 and then action2. Consider the type of (>>=): $\forall a,b.\text{IO } a \to (a \to \text{IO } b) \to \text{IO } b$. First, an action of type IO a is performed. The result of this becomes input for the second action of type $a \to \text{IO } b$. The subsequent execution of this action results in a final value of type IO b. The expression on the right-hand side of (>>=) must necessarily be a unary function that takes an argument of type a and returns an action of type IO b.

Although the communication an agent is engaged in can be expressed with the IO monad, we still need to describe the means through which communication between multiple agents takes place. We model communication between agents with *ports* [6], a buffer in which messages can be inserted at one end and retrieved sequentially at the other. In contrast to the *channel* mechanism of Concurrent Haskell, only one agent can read from a port, although several agents can write to it. The agent that can read from a port is considered to own the port. Since we need to be able to type messages that are passed through ports, each agent is modelled as having multiple ports of several different types. This conceptualisation of ports is also close to the UNIX port concept and is therefore a natural model for communication between distributed Web applications. Agents and services are modelled as communicating asynchronously. Due to the unreliable nature of the Web, distributed applications for the Web are often designed to communicate asynchronously.

Definition 2 (DAML-S Core Expressions). *Let* Var^τ *denote the set of variables of type* τ. *The set of* DAML-S Core *expressions over* Σ, $Exp(\Sigma)$, *is defined in Table 1. The set of expressions of type* τ *is denoted by* $Exp(\Sigma)^\tau$.

Definition 3 (DAML-S Core Agents). *Let* $x_i \in Var^{\tau_i}$, x_i *pairwise different and* $e \in Exp(\Sigma)^\tau$. *A DAML-S service definition then has the following form*

$$s \; x_1 \cdots x_n := e$$

$s \in \mathcal{S}$ *is said to have type* $\tau_1 \to \cdots \to \tau_n \to \tau$. $\mathcal{S}$ *denotes the set of services.*

In the definition of $Exp(\Sigma)$ in Table 1, we use partial application and the curried form of function application. For a function that takes two arguments, we use the curried type $\tau_1 \to \tau_2 \to \tau_3$ instead of $(\tau_1, \tau_2) \to \tau_3$.

Table 1. DAML-S Core Expressions

Σ	$\Sigma \subseteq Exp(\Sigma)$
var	$Var^\tau \subseteq Exp(\Sigma)^\tau$
abs	$\backslash x \rightarrow e \in Exp(\Sigma)^{\tau_1 \rightarrow \tau_2}$ for $x \in Var^{\tau_1}$, $e \in Exp(\Sigma)^{\tau_2}$
appl	$(e_1\ e_2) \in Exp(\Sigma)^{\tau_2}$ for $e_1 \in Exp(\Sigma)^{\tau_1 \rightarrow \tau_2}$, $e_2 \in Exp(\Sigma)^{\tau_1}$
cond	cond $e\ e_1\ e_2 \in Exp(\Sigma)^{\text{IO}\ \tau}$ for $e \in Exp(\Sigma)^{\text{boolean}}$, $e_1, e_2 \in Exp(\Sigma)^{\text{IO}\ \tau}$
return	return $e \in Exp(\Sigma)^{\text{IO}\ \tau}$ for $e \in Exp(\Sigma)^\tau$
seq	$e_1 \mathrel{>>=} e_2 \in Exp(\Sigma)^{\text{IO}\ \tau_2}$ for $e_1 \in Exp(\Sigma)^{\text{IO}\ \tau_1}$, $e_2 \in Exp(\Sigma)^{\tau_1 \rightarrow \text{IO}\ \tau_2}$
send	$e_1 ! e_2 \in Exp(\Sigma)^{\text{IO}\ ()}$ for $e_1 \in Exp(\Sigma)^{\text{Port}\ \tau}$, $e_2 \in Exp(\Sigma)^\tau$
rec	$e? \in Exp(\Sigma)^{\text{IO}\ \tau}$ for $e \in Exp(\Sigma)^{\text{Port}\ \tau}$
port	newPort$\tau \in Exp(\Sigma)^{\text{IO Port}\ \tau}$ for $\tau \in \mathcal{T}$
spawn	spawn $e \in Exp(\Sigma)^{\text{IO}\ \tau \rightarrow \text{IO}\ ()}$ for $e \in Exp(\Sigma)^{\text{IO}\ \tau}$
choice	choice $e_1\ e_2 \in Exp(\Sigma)^{\text{IO}\ \tau}$ for $e_1, e_2 \in Exp(\Sigma)^{\text{IO}\ \tau}$
serv	$s\ e_1 \cdots e_n \in Exp(\Sigma)^\tau$ for $e_i \in Exp(\Sigma)^{\tau_i}$, $s \in \mathcal{S}^{\tau_1 \rightarrow \cdots \rightarrow \tau_n \rightarrow \tau}$

Port references are constructed with a unary type constructor $\text{Port} \in \mathcal{F}$. A send operation takes as argument a destination port and a message and sends the message to the port, resulting in an I/O action that returns no value. Similarly, a receive operation takes as argument a port on which it is expecting a message and returns the first message received on the port. It thus performs an I/O action and returns a message. To be well-typed, the type of the message and the port must match. The spawn service takes an expression, an I/O action, as argument and spawns a new agent to evaluate the expression, which may not contain any free variables. The choice operator takes two I/O actions as arguments, makes a non-deterministic choice between the two and returns it as the result. For the application of choice to be well-typed, both its arguments must have the same type, since either one of them could be returned as the result.

4   Semantics of DAML-S

The semantics of DAML-S has been informally described in [1]. In this section, we describe a formal operational semantics of Core DAML-S. Our semantics is based on the operational semantics for Erlang [2] and Concurrent Haskell [7] programs, inspired by the structural operational semantics of CCS and the π-calculus.

In a Σ-Interpretation $\mathcal{A} = (A, \alpha)$, A is a T-sorted set of concrete values and α an interpretation function that maps each symbol in Ω, the set of all constructors defined through DAML+OIL, to a function over A. In particular, A includes functional values, i.e. functions.

Definition 4 (State). *A state of execution within DAML-S Core is defined as a finite set of agents: State* $:= \mathcal{P}_{fin}(Agent)$

An agent is a pair (e, φ), *where* $e \in Exp(\Sigma)$ *is the DAML-S Core expression being evaluated and* φ *is a partial function, mapping port references onto actual ports:*

$$Agent := Exp(\Sigma) \times \{\varphi \mid \varphi : \text{PortRef} \longrightarrow \text{Port}_\tau^{\mathfrak{A}}\}$$

for all τ, *where* $\text{Port}_\tau^{\mathfrak{A}} := (A^\tau)^*$ *and* PortRef *is an infinite set of globally known unique port references, disjoint with* A. *Since no two agents can have a common port, the domains of their port functions* φ *are also disjoint.*

Definition 5 (Evaluation Context). *The set of evaluation contexts* $\mathcal{EC}$ *[10] for DAML-S Core is defined by the context-free grammar*

$$E := [] \mid \phi(v_1, \ldots, v_i, E, e_{i+2}, e_n) \mid (E\ e) \mid (v\ E) \mid E \gg= e$$

for $v \in A$, $e, e_1, e_2 \in Exp(\Sigma)$, $\phi \in \Omega \cup \mathcal{S} \backslash \{\text{spawn}, \text{choice}\}$.

Definition 6 (Operational Semantics). *The* operational semantics *of* DAML-S is $\longrightarrow \subset$ State $\times$ State *is defined in Tables 2 and 3. For* $(s, s') \subset$ $\longrightarrow$ *we write* $s \longrightarrow s'$, *denoting that state* s *can transition into state* s'.

The application of a defined service is essentially the same as the application rule, except that the arguments to s must be evaluated to values, before they can be substituted into e. In a [SEQ], if the left-hand side of $\gg=$ returns a value v, then v is fed as argument to the expression e on the right-hand side. That is, the output of the left-hand side of $\gg=$ is input to e.

Evaluating **spawn** e results in a new parallel agent being created, which evaluates e and has no ports, thus φ is empty. Creating a new port with port descriptor p involves extending the domain of φ with p and setting its initial value to be the empty word ϵ. The port descriptor p is returned to the creating agent.

Table 2. Semantics of DAML-S Core - I

(FUNC)	$\phi \in \Omega$
	$\Pi, (E[\phi v_1 \cdots v_n], \varphi) \longrightarrow \Pi, (E[\phi_{\mathfrak{A}} v_1 \cdots v_n], \varphi)$
(APPL)	$free(u) \cap bound(e) = \emptyset$
	$\Pi, (E[(\backslash x \rightarrow e)\ u)], \varphi) \longrightarrow \Pi, (E[e[x/u]], \varphi)$
(CONV)	y is a fresh free variable
	$\Pi, (E[\backslash x \rightarrow e], \varphi) \longrightarrow \Pi, (E[\backslash y \rightarrow e[x/y]], \varphi)$
(SERV)	$sx_1 \cdots x_n := e \in \mathcal{S}$
	$\Pi, (E[sv_1 \cdots v_n], \varphi) \longrightarrow \Pi, (E[e'[x_1/v_1, \ldots, x_n/v_n]], \varphi)$

The evaluation of a receive expression p? retrieves and returns the first value of p. The port descriptor mapping φ is modified to reflect the fact that the first message of p has been extracted. Similarly, the evaluation of a send expression, $p!v$, results in v being appended to the word at p. Since port descriptors are globally unique, there will only be one such p in the system.

The rules for (COND-FALSE) and (CHOICE-RIGHT) are similar to the rules for (COND-TRUE) and (CHOICE-LEFT) given in Table 3. If the condition b evaluates to True, then the second argument e_1 is evaluated next, else if the condition b evaluates to False, the third argument e_2 is evaluated next. For a choice expression e_1+e_2, if the expression on the left e_1 can be evaluated, then it is evaluated. Similarly, the right-hand side e_2 is evaluated, if it can be evaluated. However, the choice of which one is evaluated is made non-deterministically.

Table 3. Semantics of DAML-S Core - II

$$\text{(SEQ)} \quad \frac{\quad}{\Pi, (E[\texttt{return } v \texttt{ >>= } e], \varphi) \longrightarrow \Pi, (E[(e\ v)], \varphi)}$$

$$\text{(SPAWN)} \quad \frac{\quad}{\Pi, (E[\texttt{spawn } e], \varphi) \longrightarrow \Pi, (E[\texttt{return } ()], \varphi), (e, \emptyset)}$$

$$\text{(PORT)} \quad \frac{p \text{ new PortRef} \quad \varphi'(x) = \begin{cases} \epsilon & \text{if } x = p; \\ \varphi(x) & \text{otherwise.} \end{cases}}{\Pi, (E[\texttt{newPort } \tau], \varphi) \longrightarrow \Pi, (E[\texttt{return } p], \varphi')}$$

$$\text{(REC)} \quad \frac{p \in Dom(\varphi) \quad \varphi(p) = v \cdot w \quad \varphi'(x) = \begin{cases} w & \text{if } x = p; \\ \varphi(x) & \text{otherwise.} \end{cases}}{\Pi, (E[p?], \varphi) \longrightarrow \Pi, (E[\texttt{return } v], \varphi')}$$

$$\text{(SEND)} \quad \frac{p \in Dom(\varphi_2) \quad \varphi_2(p) = w \quad \varphi_2'(x) = \begin{cases} w \cdot v & \text{if } x = p; \\ \varphi_2(x) & \text{otherwise.} \end{cases}}{\Pi, (E[p!v], \varphi_1), (e, \varphi_2) \longrightarrow \Pi, (E[\texttt{return } ()], \varphi_1), (e, \varphi_2')}$$

$$\text{(COND-TRUE)} \quad \frac{\quad}{\Pi, (E[\texttt{cond True } e_1\ e_2], \varphi) \longrightarrow \Pi, (E[e_1], \varphi)}$$

$$\text{(CHOICE-LEFT)} \quad \frac{\Pi, (E[e_1], \varphi) \longrightarrow \Pi', (E[e_1'], \varphi')}{\Pi, (E[\texttt{choice } e_1\ e_2], \varphi) \longrightarrow \Pi', (E[e_1'], \varphi')}$$

5   Conclusions

We have presented a formal syntax and semantics for the Web services specification language DAML-S. Having a reference semantics for DAML-S during its design phase helps inform its further development, bringing out ambiguities and clarification issues. It can also form a basis for the future DAML-S execution model. With a formal semantics facilitates the construction of automatic tools to assist in the specification of Web services. Techniques to automatically verify properties of Web service specifications can also be explored with the foundation of a formal semantics. Since DAML-S is still evolving, the semantics needs to be constantly updated to keep up with current specifications of the language.

References

1. The DAML Services Coalition. DAML-S: Semantic Markup For Web Services. In Proceedings of the International Semantic Web Workshop, 2001
2. Frank Huch. Verification of Erlang Programs using Abstract Interpretation and Model Checking. ACM International Conference of Functional Programming 1999.
3. Tackling the awkward squad: monadic input/output, concurrency, exceptions, and foreign calls in Haskell. November 2000.
   http://research.microsoft.com/Users/simonpj/papers/marktoberdorf.htm
4. Simon Peyton Jones and John Hughes, editors. Haskell 98: A Non-strict, Purely Functional Language http://www.haskell.org/onlinereport/
5. Philip Wadler. Monads for functional programming. In J. Jeuring and E. Meijer, editors, *Advanced Functional Programming*, Springer Verlag, LNCS 925, 1995.
6. Frank Huch and Ulrich Norbisrath. Distributed Programming in Haskell with Ports. Lecture Notes in Computer Science, Vol. 2011, 2000.
7. Simon Peyton Jones and Andrew Gordon and Sigbjorn Finne. Concurrent Haskell. POPL '96: The 23rd ACM SIGPLAN-SIGACT Symposium on Principles of Programming Languages. St. Petersburg Beach, Florida, pg. 295–308, 1996.
8. Annotated DAML+OIL Ontology Markup
   http://www.daml.org/2001/03/daml+oil-walkthru.html
9. Dan Brickley and R. V. Guha. *Resource Description Framework (RDF) Schema Specification 1.0*, W3C Candidate Recommendation 27 March 2000.
   http://www.w3c.org/TR/rdf-schema/
10. Matthias Felleisen and Daniel P. Friedman and Eugene E. Kohlbecker and Bruce Duba. A syntactic theory of sequential control. Theoretical Computer Science, Vol. 52, No. 3, pg. 205–237, 1987.

Coordination through Channel Composition

Farhad Arbab[1] and Farhad Mavaddat[2]

[1] CWI, Amsterdam, The Netherlands
farhad@cwi.nl

[2] University of Waterloo, Ontario, Canada
fmavadda@math.uwaterloo.ca

Abstract. $P\epsilon\omega$ is a channel-based exogenous coordination model wherein complex coordinators, called *connectors* are compositionally built out of simpler ones. The simplest connectors in $P\epsilon\omega$ are a set of *channels* with well-defined behavior supplied by users. $P\epsilon\omega$ can be used as a language for coordination of concurrent processes, or as a "glue language" for compositional construction of connectors that orchestrate component instances in a component-based system. The emphasis in $P\epsilon\omega$ is on connectors and their composition only, not on the entities that connect to, communicate, and cooperate through these connectors. Each connector in $P\epsilon\omega$ imposes a specific coordination pattern on the entities (e.g., components) that perform I/O operations through that connector, without the knowledge of those entities.

Channel composition in $P\epsilon\omega$ is a very powerful mechanism for construction of connectors. In this paper, we demonstrate the expressive power of connector composition in $P\epsilon\omega$ through a number of examples. We show that exogenous coordination patterns that can be expressed as (meta-level) regular expressions over I/O operations can be composed in $P\epsilon\omega$ out of a small set of only five primitive channel types.

1 Introduction

A channel is a point-to-point medium of communication with its own unique identity and two distinct ends. Channels can be used as the only primitive constructs in communication models for concurrent systems. Like the primitive constructs in other communication models, channels provide the basic temporal and spatial decouplings of the parties in a communication, which are essential for explicit coordination. Channel-based communication models are "complete" in the sense that they can easily model the primitives of other communication models (e.g., message passing, shared spaces, or remote procedure calls). Furthermore, channel-based models have some inherent advantages over other communication models, especially for concurrent systems that are distributed, mobile, and/or whose architectures and communication topologies dynamically change while they run.

The characteristics of channel-based models are attractive from the point of view of coordination. Dataflow models, Kahn networks [11], and Petri-nets can

F. Arbab and C. Talcott (Eds.): COORDINATION 2002, LNCS 2315, pp. 22–39, 2002.

be viewed as specialized channel-based models that incorporate certain basic
constructs for primitive coordination. IWIM [1] is an example of a more elaborate
coordination model based on channels, and Manifold [2,7] is an incarnation of
IWIM as a real coordination programming language. A common strand running
through these models is a notion that is called "exogenous coordination" in
IWIM. This is the concept of "coordination from outside" the entities whose
actions are coordinated. Exogenous coordination is already present, albeit in a
primitive form, in dataflow models: unbeknownst to a node, its internal activity
is coordinated (or, in this primitive instance, merely synchronized) with the rest
of the network by the virtue of the input/output operations that it performs.
IWIM and Manifold allow much more sophisticated exogenous coordination of
active entities in a system.

$P\epsilon\omega$ is a channel-based model for exogenous coordination [5,3]. The name
$P\epsilon\omega$ is pronounced "rhe-oh" and comes from the Greek word $\rho\epsilon\omega$ which means
"*[I] flow*" (as water in streams). $P\epsilon\omega$ is based on a calculus of channels wherein
complex connectors are constructed through composition of simpler ones, the
simplest connectors being an arbitrary set of channels with well-defined behavior.
$P\epsilon\omega$ can be used as the "glue code" in Component Based Software Engineering,
where a system is compositionally constructed out of components that interact
and cooperate with each other anonymously through $P\epsilon\omega$ connectors.

Our work on $P\epsilon\omega$ builds upon the IWIM model of coordination and the
coordination language Manifold, and extends our earlier work on components [4,
9,6]. A concrete incarnation of mobile channels to support our formal model
for component-based systems is presented in [12]. Generalization of data-flow
networks for describing dynamically reconfigurable or mobile networks has also
been studied in [8] and [10] for a different notion of observables using the model
of stream functions.

In this paper, we demonstrate the expressive power of $P\epsilon\omega$ through a number of examples. We show that exogenous coordination patterns that can be
expressed as (meta-level) regular expressions over I/O operations can be composed in $P\epsilon\omega$ out of a small set of only five primitive channel types.

The rest of this paper is organized as follows. The basic concepts used in this
paper are introduced in Section 2. $P\epsilon\omega$ expects the set of operations described
in Section 3 to be defined for all channels. The concept of connectors in $P\epsilon\omega$ and
its operations on them are defined in Section 4. Section 5 contains illustrative
examples of some useful channel types, some of which are used in our connector
examples later in this paper. The semantics of flow of data in $P\epsilon\omega$ through
connectors is intuitively described in Section 6. The sequence of examples in
Section 7 constructively show the expressiveness of $P\epsilon\omega$. Our concluding remarks
and future work are in Section 8.

2   Basic Concepts

$P\epsilon\omega$ is a coordination model and as such has little to say about the computational entities whose activities it coordinates. Without loss of generality, we refer

to these entities as *component instances* in $P\epsilon\omega$. Each component instance has its own unique identity. From the point of view of $P\epsilon\omega$, a system consists of a number of component instances executing at one or more locations, communicating through *connectors* that coordinate their activities. Each **connector**, in turn, is constructed compositionally out of channels.

A **component instance**, p, is a non-empty set of active entities (e.g., processes, agents, threads, actors, etc.) whose only means of communication with the entities outside of this set is through input/output operations that they perform on a (dynamic) set of channel ends that are *connected* to p. The communication among the active entities inside a component instance, and the mechanisms used for this communication, are of no interest. What is of interest is only the inter-component-instance communication which takes place exclusively through channels that comprise $P\epsilon\omega$ connectors. Indeed, the constituents inside a component instance may themselves be other component instances that are connected by $P\epsilon\omega$ connectors.

A **component** is a software implementation whose instances can be executed on physical or logical devices. Thus, a component is an abstract type that describes the properties of its instances.

A physical or logical device where an active entity executes is called a **location**. Examples of a location include a Java virtual machine; a multi-threaded Unix process; a machine, e.g., as identified by an IP address; etc. A component instance may itself be distributed, in the sense that its constituents may be executing at different locations (in which case, this too is an internal detail of the component instance to which $P\epsilon\omega$ is oblivious). Nevertheless, there is always a unique location associated with every (distributed) component instance, indicating where that component instance is (nominally) located. There can be zero or more component instances executing at a given location, and component instances may migrate from one location to another while they execute (mobility). As far as $P\epsilon\omega$ is concerned, the significance of a location is that inter-component communication may be cheaper among component instances that reside at the same location.

The only medium of communication between two component instances is a **channel**, which represents an atomic connector in $P\epsilon\omega$. Channels are dynamically created and discarded in $P\epsilon\omega$. A **pattern** is permanently associated with every channel at its creation time as its **filter**. The filter of a channel restricts the set of data values that can flow through that channel. To simplify our presentation, we ignore channel filters in this paper.

Each channel in $P\epsilon\omega$ has two directed ends: source and sink, with their own identities, through which components refer to and manipulate that channel and the data it carries[1]. A **source** end accepts data into its channel. A **sink** end dispenses data out of its channel. Like other values, channel end identifiers can be spread within or among component instances by copying, parameter passing,

---

[1] Channel identifiers are not directly used in $P\epsilon\omega$; The entities inside component instances refer only to channel-end identifiers, which internally refer to the identifiers of their respective channels.

or through writing/reading them to/from channel ends. This way, channel ends created in an active entity within one component instance can become known in other active entities in the same or another component instance.

A channel end that is known to a component instance can be used by any of the entities inside that component instance. Some $P\epsilon\omega$ operations can be performed by (entities inside) a component instance on a channel end, only if the channel end is connected to that component instance. The identity of a channel-end may be known to zero or more component instance, but each channel end can be **connected** to at most one component instance at any given time.

Both components and channels are assumed to be **mobile** in $P\epsilon\omega$. A component instance may move from one location to another during its lifetime. When this happens, the channel ends connected to this component instance move together with it to the new location, preserving the topology of channel connections. Furthermore, a channel end connected to a component instance may be disconnected from that component instance, and connected to another component instance at the same or a different location. This second form of mobility, changes the topology of channel connections. In this paper, we do not elaborate on the implications of mobility on implementations of $P\epsilon\omega$.

3   Primitive Operations on Channels

Strictly speaking, $P\epsilon\omega$ does not "provide" channels; rather, it expects the availability of a set of channel types provided by "users" and provides a compositional model for building connectors out of those channels. As such, $P\epsilon\omega$ expects a number of primitive operations to be defined on all channel types it knows of. Table 1 is a summary of these primitive operations. Those beginning with an underscore are to be used internally by $P\epsilon\omega$ only; (entities inside) component instances are not allowed to perform these operations directly.

The first column of Table 1 gives the syntax of the operations, where:

- [...] indicates optional parameters.
- chantype designates a channel type, see Tables 3 and 4.
- filter is a pattern used to filter the values allowed in the channel.
- cev stands for a source or sink channel-end-variable.
- t indicates a time-out value greater than or equal to 0. When no time-out is specified for an operation, it defaults to ∞. Expiration of its time-out causes an operation to fail and return with an appropriate error.
- conds is a Boolean expression of primitive conditions on channel ends such as _connected(cev), _disconnected(cev), _empty(cev), _full(cev), etc.
- inp is a sink of a channel, from which data items can be obtained.
- outp is the source of a channel, into which data items can be written.
- v is a variable from/into which a data item is to be transferred into/from the specified channel end.
- pat is a pattern that must match with a data item for it to be transferable to v.

An operation returns with a result that indicates failure if it does not succeed within its specified time-out period.

The second column in Table 1 indicates whether a connection between the component instance and the channel end is a prerequisite for the operation. Clearly, this is irrelevant for the create operation. The operations _forget, _connect, _disconnect, and the conditions in _wait can specify any channel end irrespective of whether or not it is connected to the component instance involved. The operations _read, _write, and _take, on the other hand, fail if the active entities that perform them reside in component instances that are not connected to the channel ends involved in these operations.

Table 1. Primitive channel operations

Operation	Con.	Description
create(chantype[, filter])	-	Creates a channel with the wildcard (*) or the specified filter; it returns the identifiers of its two channel ends.
_forget(cev)	N	changes cev such that it no longer refers to the channel end it designates.
_move(cev, loc)	Y	moves cev to the location loc.
_connect([t,] cev)	N	Connects the channel end cev to the component instance that contains the entity that performs this operation.
_disconnect(cev)	N	Disconnects the channel end cev from the component instance that contains the entity that performs this operation.
_wait([t,] conds)	N	Suspends the active entity that performs this operation, waiting for the conditions specified in conds to become true.
_read([t,] inp[, v[, pat]])	Y	Suspends the entity that performs this operation, until a value that can match with pat, is available for reading from the sink channel end inp into the variable v. The _read operation is non-destructive: the value is copied from the channel into the variable, but the original remains intact.
_take([t,] inp[, v[, pat]])	Y	This is the destructive variant of _read: the channel loses the value that is read.
_write([t,] outp, v)	Y	Suspends the entity that performs this operation, until it succeeds to write the value of the variable v to the source channel end outp.

– create creates a channel and returns its pair of channel ends. The ends of a newly created channel are not initially connected to any component instance.

There is no explicit operation in $P\epsilon\omega$ to delete a channel. In practice, useless channels that can no longer be referred to by any component instance may be garbage collected.

- _forget changes cev such that it no longer refers to the channel end it designates. This contributes to the eligibility of a channel as a candidate for garbage collection.

- _move moves cev to the specified location. The only consequence of moving a channel end is that it may allow more efficient access to the channel end and the data content of the channel by subsequent channel operations performed by the active entities at the new location.

- _connect succeeds when the specified channel end is connected to the component instance that contains the active entity performing it. Pending connect requests on the same channel end are granted on a first-come-first-serve basis.

- _disconnect succeeds when the specified channel end is disconnected from the component instance that contains the active entity performing it. Disconnecting a channel end pre-empts and retracts all _read, _take, and _write operations that may be pending on that channel end; as far as these operations are concerned, it is as if the channel end were not connected to the component instance in the first place.

- _wait succeeds when its condition expression is true.

- _read succeeds when a data item that matches with the specified pattern pat is available for reading, through the sink end inp, into the specified variable v. If no explicit pattern is specified, the default wild-card pattern * is assumed. When no variable is specified, no actual reading takes place, but the operation succeeds when a suitable data item is available for reading. Observe that the _read operation is non-destructive, i.e., the data item is only copied but not removed from the channel.

- _take is the destructive version of _read, i.e., the data item is actually removed from the channel. When no variable is specified as the destination in a _take operation, the operation succeeds when a suitable data item is available for taking and it is removed through the specified channel end.

- _write succeeds when the content of the specified variable either (1) does not match with the filter of the channel to which the source outp belongs, or (2) it matches the channel filter and is consumed by the channel.

4   Connectors

A **connector** is a set of channel ends and their connecting channels organized as a graph of **nodes** and **edges** such that:

- Every channel end coincides on exactly one node.
- Zero or more channel ends coincide on every node.
- There is an edge between two (not necessarily distinct) nodes if and only if there is a channel whose ends coincide on those nodes.

We use $x \mapsto N$ to denote that the channel end x coincides on the node N, and the function $Node(x)$ to designate the unique node on which the channel end x coincides. For a node N, we define $Src(N) = \{x \mid x \mapsto N \wedge x$ is a source channel end$\}$ to be the set of source channel ends that coincide on N. Analogously, $Snk(N) = \{x \mid x \mapsto N \wedge x$ is a sink channel end$\}$ is the set of sink channel ends that coincide on N.

A node N is called a **source node** if $Src(N) \neq \emptyset \wedge Snk(N) = \emptyset$. Analogously, N is called a **sink node** if $Src(N) = \emptyset \wedge Snk(N) \neq \emptyset$. A node N is called a **mixed node** if $Src(N) \neq \emptyset \wedge Snk(N) \neq \emptyset$.

Observe that the graph representing a connector is *not* directed. However, for each channel end x_c of a channel c, we use the directionality of x_c to assign a *local direction in the neighborhood of* $Node(x_c)$ to the edge that represents c. For the end x_c of a channel c, the local direction of the edge representing c in the neighborhood of $Node(x_c)$ is presented as an arrow that emanates from $Node(x_c)$ if x_c is a sink, and points to $Node(x_c)$ if x_c is a source. By definition, every channel represents a (simple) connector.

The **create** operation in Table 1 inherently deals with channels and channel ends and as such has no counterpart for nodes. Table 2 shows the counterparts of the rest of the operations in Table 1 that work on nodes instead of channel ends.

The names of the operations in Table 2 do not have underscore prefixes: they are meant to be used in components. As in Table 1, the second column in Table 2 shows whether the connectivity (of all channel ends coincident on a node) is a prerequisite for each operation. The **connect** and **disconnect** operations atomically connect and disconnect all channel ends that coincide on their node arguments to their respective component instances. Only source and sink nodes (not mixed nodes) can be connected to component instances.

A **read**, **take**, or **write** operation performed by (an active entity inside) a component instance becomes and remains *pending* (on that node or its subsequent heirs, as described below) until either its time-out expires, or the conditions are right for the execution of its corresponding channel end operation(s). Intuitively, **read** and **take** operations nondeterministically obtain one of the suitable values available from the sink channel ends that coincide on their respective nodes. The **write** operation, on the other hand, atomically replicates its value and writes a copy to every source channel end that coincides on its node argument. The precise semantics of **read**, **take**, and **write**, as well as the semantics of mixed nodes, depend on the properties of the channels that coincide on the involved nodes.

When a node is disconnected from a component instance, all **read**, **take**, and **write** operations pending on that node are pre-empted and retracted; as far as these operations are concerned, it is as if the node were never connected to that component instance.

The **nconds** in **wait** is a Boolean combination of primitive node conditions, which are the counterparts of the primitive channel end conditions of **_wait** in Table 1. For every primitive condition on a channel end x, e.g., **_connected(x)**, _disconnected(x), _empty(x), _full(x), etc., $P\epsilon\omega$ defines two corresponding primitive conditions on a node N, e.g., connected(N) and connectedAll(N), disconnected(N) and disconnectedAll(N), empty(N) and emptyAll(N), full(N) and fullAll(N), etc. A primitive node condition without the All suffix is true for a node N when its corresponding channel end condition is true for some channel end x $\mapsto$ N. Analogously, a primitive node condition that ends with the suffix All, is true for a node N when its corresponding channel end condition is true for all channel ends x $\mapsto$ N.

Table 2. Node operations in $P\epsilon\omega$

Operation	Con.	Description
forget(N)	N	This operation atomically performs the set of operations _forget(x), $\forall x \mapsto$ N.
move(N, loc)	Y	This operation atomically performs the set of operations _move$(x,$ loc$)$, $\forall x \mapsto$ N.
connect([t,] N)	N	If N is not a mixed node, this operation atomically performs the set of operations connect([t,], w), $\forall x \mapsto$ N.
disconnect(N)	N	This operation atomically performs the set of operations _disconnect(x), $\forall x \mapsto$ N.
wait([t,] nconds)	N	This operation succeeds when the condition expression nconds becomes true.
read([t,] N[, v[, pat]])	Y	If N is a sink node connected to the component instance, this operation succeeds when a value compatible with pat is non-destructively read from any one of the channel ends $x \mapsto$ N into the variable v.
take([t,] N[, v[, pat]])	Y	If N is a sink node connected to the component instance, this operation succeeds when a value compatible with pat is taken from any one of the channel ends $x \mapsto$ N into the variable v.
write([t,] N, v)	Y	If N is a source node connected to the component instance, this operation succeeds when a copy of the value v is written to all channel ends $x \mapsto$ N atomically.
join(N$_1$, N$_2$)	Y	If at least one of the nodes N$_1$ and N$_2$ is connected to the component instance, this operation destructively merges the two nodes N$_1$ and N$_2$ into a new node (i.e., N$_1$ and N$_2$ no longer exist after the join).
split(N[, quoin])	N	This operation produces a new node N$'$ and splits the set of channel ends $x \mapsto$ N between the two nodes N and N$'$ as prescribed by the set of edges specified in quoin.
hide(N)	N	This operation hides the node N such that it cannot be used in any other operation.

The composition operation join(N_1, N_2) succeeds only if at least one of the two nodes N_1 and N_2 is connected to the component instance, p, containing the active entity that performs this operation. The effect of join is the (destructive) merge of the two nodes N_1 and N_2 into a new node, N; i.e., all channel ends that previously coincided on either N_1 or N_2, now coincide on the one and the same node, N. If N_1 and N_2 are both connected to p and N is not a mixed node, then p remains connected to (all channel ends coincident on) N; otherwise, p is disconnected from (all channel ends coincident on) N. In other words, p may lose its previous connection to the channel ends coincident on N_1, N_2, or both, or it may retain its previous connection to all of them by remaining connected to the common heir of the two nodes, N.

When p loses its previous connection with any of the nodes N_1 and N_2, all read, take, and write operations pending on that node are retracted. Otherwise, all operations pending on N_1 and N_2 become pending on their common heir, N. Specifically, observe that if, e.g., N_1 is connected to p and N_2 is connected to another component instance, q, then a join(N_1, N_2) performed by an active entity inside p does *not* disrupt any operation (issued by an active entity inside q) that may be pending on N_2.

A split operation performed on a node N produces a new node N' and divides the set of channel ends that coincide on N between the two nodes N and N'. We do not use split in this paper.

The hide(N) operation is an important abstraction mechanism in $P\epsilon\omega$: hiding a node N ensures that N can no longer be used in any other operation (by any active entity in any component instance). This guarantees that the topology of channels coincident on N can no longer be modified by anyone. The operations in Table 2 work only on non-hidden nodes. They all fail with an appropriate error if any of their node arguments is hidden.

For convenience, we extend the operations in Table 2 to also accept channel ends as abbreviations for nodes: a channel end x appearing in place of a node N in any of the operations in Table 2, or in any of the primitive node conditions in a wait, stands for the node $Node(x)$. This has the practical advantage of alleviating the need for components to deal with nodes explicitly as separate entities. The components know and manipulate only channel ends. They are created by the create function in Table 1, and are passed as arguments to the operations in Table 2, where they actually represent the nodes that they coincide on, rather than specific channel ends. This makes components immune to the dynamic creation and destruction of the nodes whose coincident channel ends they use, while third parties perform join and split operations on those nodes.

5   Channel Types

$P\epsilon\omega$ assumes the availability of an arbitrary set of channel types, each with its well-defined behavior. A channel is called **synchronous** if it delays the success of the appropriate pairs of operations on its two ends such that they can succeed only simultaneously; otherwise, it is called **asynchronous**. An asynchronous channel may have a bounded or an unbounded buffer (to hold the data items it has already consumed through its source, but not yet dispensed through its sink) and may or may not impose a certain order on the delivery of its contents. A **lossy** channel may deliver only a subset of the data items that it receives, and lose the rest.

Table 3. Examples of synchronous channel types

Type	Description
Sync	has a source and a sink. The pair of I/O operations on its two ends can succeed only simultaneously.
SyncDrain	has two source ends. The pair of I/O operations on its two ends can succeed only simultaneously. All data items written to this channel are lost.
SyncSpout	has two sink ends. The pair of I/O operations on its two ends can succeed only simultaneously. Each sink of this channel acts as an unbounded source of data items that match with the channel filter. Data items are produced in a nondeterministic order. The data items taken out of the two sinks of this channel are not related to each other.
LossySync	has a source and a sink. The source end always accepts all data items that match the filter of the channel. If there is no matching I/O operation on the sink end of the channel at the time that a data item is accepted, then the data item is lost; otherwise, the channel transfers the data item exactly the same as a Sync channel, and the I/O operation at the sink end succeeds.

Although every channel in $P\epsilon\omega$ has exactly two ends, they may or may not be of different types. Thus, a channel may have a source and a sink end, two source ends, or two sink ends. The behavior of a channel may depend on such parameters as its filter, its synchronizing properties, the number of its source and sink ends, the size of its buffer, its ordering scheme, its loss policy, etc.

While $P\epsilon\omega$ assumes no particular fixed set of channel types, it is reasonable to expect that a certain number of commonly used channel types will be available in all implementations and applications of $P\epsilon\omega$. Tables 3 and 4 show a non-exhaustive set of interesting channel types and their properties. A few of these channel types are used further in this paper as the building blocks for more complex connectors to demonstrate the expressiveness of $P\epsilon\omega$.

The Sync, FIFO, and FIFOn channel types represent the typical synchronous, unbounded asynchronous, and bounded asynchronous channels.

A SyncDrain channel allows write operations on its opposite ends to succeed simultaneously, thus, synchronizing them. A SyncSpout channel is an unbounded source of data items that match with the channel filter, and can be taken from its opposite ends only simultaneously in some nondeterministic order.

AsyncDrain and AsyncSpout are analogous to SyncDrain and SyncSpout, respectively, except that they guarantee that the two operations on their opposite ends never succeed simultaneously.

Table 4. Examples of asynchronous channel types

Type	Description
FIFO	has a source and a sink, and an unbounded buffer. The source end always accepts all data items that match the filter of the channel. The accepted data items are kept in the internal FIFO buffer of the channel. The appropriate operations on the sink end of the channel obtain the contents of the buffer in the FIFO order.
FIFOn	is the bounded version of FIFO with the channel buffer capacity of n data items.
AsyncDrain	has two source ends. The channel guarantees that two operations on its two ends never succeed simultaneously. The channel is *fair* by alternating between its two ends and giving each a chance to obtain a data item into the channel. All data items written to this channel are lost.
AsyncSpout	has two sink ends. The channel guarantees that two operations on its two ends never succeed simultaneously. The channel is *fair* by alternating between its two ends and giving each a chance to dispose a data item out of the channel. The values obtained from the two ends of the channel are not related to each other.
ShiftFIFOn	is the lossy version of FIFOn, where the arrival of a data item when the channel buffer is full, triggers the loss of the oldest data item in the buffer, to make room for the new arrival.
LossyFIFOn	is the lossy version of FIFOn, where all newly arrived data items when the channel buffer is full, are lost.

An important class of channel types are the so-called lossy channels. These are the channels that do not necessarily deliver through their sinks every data item that they consume through their sources. A channel can be lossy because when its bounded capacity becomes full, it follows a policy to, e.g., drop the new arrivals (overflow policy) or the oldest arrivals (shift policy).

ShiftFIFOn is a bounded capacity FIFO channel that loses the oldest data item in its buffer when its capacity is full and a new data item is to be written to the channel. Thus, (up to) the last n arrived data items are kept in its channel buffer. A LossyFIFOn channel, on the other hand, loses the newly arrived data items when its capacity is full.

An asynchronous channel may be lossy because it requires an expiration date for every data item it consumes, and loses any data item that remains in its buffer beyond its expiration date. Other channels may be lossy because they implement other policies to drop some of the data items they consume.

A LossySync channel behaves the same as a Sync channel, except that a write operation on its source always succeeds immediately. If a compatible read or take operation is already pending on the sink of a LossySync channel, then the written data item is transferred to the pending operation and both succeed. Otherwise, the write operation succeeds and the data item is lost.

6 Dataflow through Nodes

The (active entities inside) component instances can write data values to source nodes and read/take them from sink nodes, using the node operations defined in Table 2. Generally, everything flows in $P\epsilon\omega$ from source nodes through channels and mixed nodes down to sink nodes. Some data items get lost in the flow, and some settle as sediments in certain channels for a while before they flow through, if ever. It is the composition of channels into connectors, together with the node operations read, take, and write, that yield this intuitive behavior in $P\epsilon\omega$. In this section, we give an informal description of the semantics of mixed nodes and the read, take, and write operations on sink and source nodes.

$P\epsilon\omega$ is not directly aware of the behavior of any particular channel. It merely expects every channel type to provide a "reasonable implementation" of the operations in Table 1. The set of operations in Table 1, thus, describes the **common behavior** of all channels in $P\epsilon\omega$. However, these operations are not sufficient for $P\epsilon\omega$ to "know" and be able to use a channel; for that, $P\epsilon\omega$ expects every channel to provide a few more operations through which the relevant aspects of its state and behavior can be inquired and controlled. For instance, $P\epsilon\omega$ expects to be able to *lock* a channel to preserve its state. More relevant to our presentation here, it expects a channel c to provide the inquiry functions $\text{offers}(y_c, p)$ and $\text{takes}(x_c, d)$ on its source x_c and sink y_c. Through $\text{offers}(y_c, p)$ $P\epsilon\omega$ expects to obtain the multi-set of values that may be assigned to a variable v in a $\_\text{take}(0, y_c, v, p)$. $P\epsilon\omega$ expects $\text{takes}(x_c, d)$ to be true for a data item d if d matches with the filter of c and the state of c allows a $\_\text{write}(0, x_c, d)$ to succeed. The semantics of a mixed node is defined in terms of the offers and takes functions for the channel ends that coincide on that node. Intuitively, a mixed node "pumps" the data items in the multi-sets of the offers of its coincident sink channel ends through to its coincident source channel ends that can take them.

For instance, if c is a FIFO channel then $\text{offers}(y_c, *)$ is empty if the buffer of c is empty, and a singleton (containing the first data element to be taken), otherwise. The predicate $\text{takes}(x_c, d)$ is true for any data item d that is allowed by the filter of c to enter this channel. In contrast, if c is a FIFOn channel, then $\text{takes}(x_c, d)$ is true for any data item d, as long as the number of data items in the (bounded) buffer of c is less than n.

The utility of channel composition can be demonstrated through a number of simple examples. For convenience, we represent a channel by the pair of its source and sink ends, i.e., ab represents the channel whose source and sink ends are, respectively, a, and b. Two channels, ab and cd can be joined in one of the three configurations shown in Figures 1.a-c. Assuming both channels are of type FIFO, it is easy to see that the configuration in Figure 1.a allows the contents of ab to flow through the common node on which b and c coincide into cd at some nondeterministic pace. Observe that write can be performed only on a, and d can be used only to read or take values; no write, read, or take can be performed on the (mixed) node where b and c coincide. Effectively, such a composition of two FIFO channels is equivalent to a single FIFO channel.

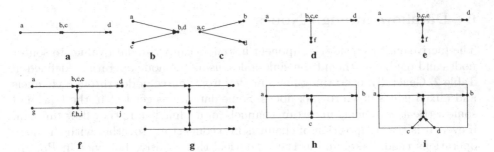

Fig. 1. Examples of channel composition and connectors

The configuration of channels in Figure 1.b allows `write` operations on a and c, and `read` or `take` operations on b and d; the channel ends b and d can be used interchangeably, because $Node(b) = Node(d)$. A `read` or `take` from this common node delivers a value out of ab or cd, chosen nondeterministically, if both are non-empty.

The configuration of channels in Figure 1.c allows `write` operations on a and c, wherein the two channel ends are interchangeable, and `read` or `take` operations on b and d. A `write` on $Node(a)$ succeeds only if both channels are capable of consuming a copy of the written data. If they are both of type FIFO, of course, all writes succeed. However, if even one is not prepared to consume the data, the write suspends.

The significance of the "replication on write" property in $P\epsilon\omega$ can be seen in the composition of the three channels ab, cd, and ef in the configuration of Figure 1.d. Assume ab and cd are of type FIFO and ef is of type Sync. The configuration in Figure 1.d, then, shows one of the most basic forms of exogenous coordination: the number of data items that flow from ab to cd is the same as the number of `take` operations that succeed on f. Compared to the configuration in Figure 1.a, what we have in Figure 1.d is a connector where an entity connected to f can count and regulate the flow of data between the two channels ab and cd by the number of `take` operations it performs on f. The entity that regulates and/or counts the number of data items through f need not know anything about the entities that write to a and/or `take` from d, and the latter two entities need not know anything about the fact that they are communicating with each other, or the fact that the volume of their communication is regulated and/or measured.

The composition of channels in Figure 1.e is identical to the one in Figure 1.d, except that now ef is of type SyncDrain. The functionality of this configuration of channels is identical to that of the one in Figure 1.d, except that now `write` (rather than `take`) operations on f regulate the flow.

We can use this fact to construct a barrier synchronization connector, as in Figure 1.f. Here, the SyncDrain channel ef ensures that a data item passes from ab to cd only simultaneously with the passing of a data item from gh to ij (and vice versa). If the four channels ab, cd, gh, and ij are all of type Sync, our connector directly synchronizes `write`/`take` pairs on the pairs of channels a and d, and g and j. This simple barrier synchronization connector can be trivially extended to any number of pairs, as shown in Figure 1.g.

Figure 1.h shows the same configuration as in Figure 1.e. The enclosing box in Figure 1.h introduces our graphical notation for presenting the encapsulation abstraction effect of the **hide** operation in $P\epsilon\omega$. The box conveys that a **hide** operation has been performed on all nodes inside the box (in this case, just the one that corresponds to the common node of the channel ends b, c, and e in Figure 1.e). As such, the topology inside the box is immutable, and can be abstracted away: the whole box can be used as a "connector component" that provides only the connection points on its boundary. In this case, assuming that the channels connected to a and b are of type **Sync**, the behavior of the connector can be described as "every **write** to c enables the transfer of a data item from a to b.

Through parameterization, the configuration and the functionality of such connector components can be adjusted to fit the occasion. For instance, Figure 1.i shows a variant of the connector in Figure 1.h, where a **write** to either c or d enables the transfer of a data item from a to b.

7 Expressiveness

The connector in Figure 2.a consists of three channels: ab, ac, and bc. The channels ab and ac are **SyncDrain** and **Sync**, respectively. The channel bc is of type **FIFO1**. Consider the behavior of this connector, assuming a number of eager producers and consumers are to perform **write** and **take** operations on the three nodes of this connector.

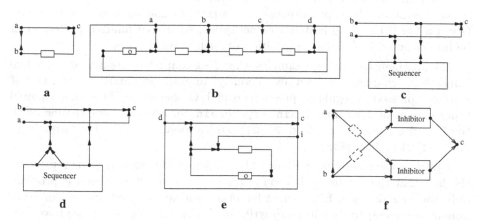

Fig. 2. Connectors for more complex coordination

The nodes a and b can be used in **write** operations only; and the node c can be used only in **take** operations. A **write** on either a or b will remain pending at least until there is a **write** on both of these nodes; it is only then that both of these operations can succeed simultaneously (because of the SyncDrain ab). For a write on a to succeed, there must be a matching take on c, at which time the value written to a is transferred and consumed by the take on c. Simultaneously, the value written to b is transferred into the FIFO1 channel bc (which is initially empty, and thus can consume and hold one data item). As long as this data item remains in bc, no other write operation can succeed on a or b; the only possible transition is for another take on c to consume the contents of the bc channel. Once this happens, we return to the initial state and the cycle can repeat itself.

The behavior of this connector can be seen as imposing an order on the flow of the data items written to a and b: the sequence of data items obtained by successive take operations on c consists of the first data item written to a, followed by the first data item written to b, followed by the second data item written to a, followed by the second data item written to b, etc. We can summarize the behavior of our connector as $c = (ab)*$, meaning the sequence of values that appear through c consists of zero or more repetitions of the pairs of values written to a and b, in that order. Observe that the a and the b in the expression $(ab)*$ do not represent specific values; rather, they refer to the write operations performed on their respective nodes, irrespective of the actual data items that they write. In other words, we may consider the expression $(ab)*$ not as a regular expression over values, but rather as a meta-level regular expression over the I/O operations that produce (isomorphic) sequences of values.

The producers and consumers connected to the nodes a, b, and c, are completely unaware of the fact that our connector coordinates them through their innocent take and write operations to impose this specific ordering on them. This interesting coordination protocol emerges due to the composition of the specific channels that comprise this connector in $P\epsilon\omega$. It is natural at this point to wonder about the expressiveness of the composition paradigm of $P\epsilon\omega$, i.e., Given a (small) set of primitive channel types, what coordination patterns can be implemented in $P\epsilon\omega$ by composition of such channel types?

We now demonstrate, by examples, that $P\epsilon\omega$ connectors composed out of five simple basic channel types can (exogenously) impose coordination patterns that can be expressed as regular expressions over I/O operations. These five channel types consist of Sync, SyncDrain, AsyncDrain, an asynchronous channel with the bounded capacity of 1 (e.g., FIFO1), and a lossy version of the latter (e.g., ShiftFIFO1 or LossyFIFO1).

Consider the connector in Figure 2.b. As before, the enclosing box represents the fact that the details of this connector are abstracted away and it provides only the four nodes a, b, c, and d for other entities (connectors and/or component instances) to (in this case) write to. Inside this connector, we have four SyncDrain and four FIFO1 channels connected together. The first (leftmost) FIFO1 channel is initialized to have a data item in its buffer, as indicated by the presence of the symbol "o" in the box representing its buffer. The actual value of this data item is irrelevant. The write operations on the nodes a, b, c, and d can succeed only in the strict left to right order. This connector implements a generic sequencing protocol: we can parameterize this connector to have as many nodes as we want, simply by inserting more (or fewer) SyncDrain and FIFO1 channel pairs, as required. What we have here is a generic *sequencer* connector.

Figure 2.c shows a simple example of the utility of our sequencer. The connector in this figure consists of a two-node sequencer, plus a pair of Sync channels and a SyncDrain channel connecting each of the nodes of the sequencer to the nodes a and c, and b and c, respectively. The connector in Figure 2.c is another connector for the coordination pattern expressed as $c = (ab)*$. However, there is a subtle difference between the connectors in Figures 2.a and c: the one in Figure 2.a never allows a write to a succeed without a matching write to b, whereas the one in Figure 2.c allows a write to a succeed (if "its turn has come") regardless of the availability of a value on b.

It takes little effort to see that the connector in Figure 2.d corresponds to the meta-regular expression $c = (aab)*$. Figures 2.c and d show how easily we can construct connectors that correspond to the Kleen-closure of any "meta-word" using a sequencer of the appropriate size. To have the expressive power of regular expressions, we need the "or" as well.

The connector in Figure 2.e is an *inhibitor*: values written to d flow freely through to c, until some value is written to i, after which the flow stops for good.

Our "or" selector can now be constructed out of two inhibitors and two LossyFIFO1 channels, plus some other connector for nondeterministic choice. The connector in Figure 2.f is a particular instance of such an "or" connector. The channel connecting the nodes a and b in this connector is an AsyncDrain. It implements a nondeterministic choice between a and b if both have a value to offer, and otherwise it selects whichever one arrives first. Each of the nodes a and b is connected to the inhibitor node of the inhibitor connector that regulates the flow of the values from the other node to c. Thus, if a value arrives on a before any value arrives on b, this connector will block the flow of b to c for good and we have $c = a*$. Symmetrically, we have $c = b*$, and we can thus write, in general, $c = (a|b)*$.

8   Conclusion

$P\epsilon\omega$ is an exogenous coordination model wherein complex coordinators, called connectors, are constructed by composing simpler ones. The simplest connectors correspond to a set of channels supplied to $P\epsilon\omega$. So long as these channels comply with a non-restrictive set of requirements defined by $P\epsilon\omega$, the semantics of $P\epsilon\omega$ operations, especially its composition, is independent of the specific behavior of channels. These requirements define the generic aspects of the behavior of channels that $P\epsilon\omega$ cares about, ignoring the details of their specific behavior. The composition of channels into complex connectors in $P\epsilon\omega$ relates their specific semantics to each other in a manner that is independent of their specific semantics.

As a coordination model, $P\epsilon\omega$ has much in common with IWIM. IWIM deals with processes and channels. $P\epsilon\omega$ abstracts away from processes and deals only with channels. $P\epsilon\omega$ is about channel composition which can be regarded as defining specialized IWIM manager processes.

There are two senses of mobility in $P\epsilon\omega$: 1) *logical mobility* which changes the topology of channel connections through `connect` and `disconnect` operations; and 2) *physical mobility* through `move` which may affect the efficiency of certain operations, but is otherwise irrelevant. $P\epsilon\omega$ shares mobility and channels as basic concepts with π-calculus. However, unlike π-calculus, $P\epsilon\omega$ is not concerned with the actual processes that communicate through channels; the concern in $P\epsilon\omega$ is on composition of channels into connectors, which has no direct equivalent in π-calculus.

The semantics of composition of connectors in $P\epsilon\omega$ and their resulting coordination protocols can be explained and understood intuitively because of their strong correspondence to a metaphor of physical flow of data through channels. This metaphor naturally lends itself to an intuitive graphical representation of connectors and their composition that strongly resembles (asynchronous) electronic circuit diagrams. $P\epsilon\omega$ connector diagrams can be used as the "glue code" that supports and coordinates inter-component communication in a component based system. As such, drawing $P\epsilon\omega$ connector diagrams constitutes a visual programming paradigm for coordination and component composition.

Connector composition in $P\epsilon\omega$ is very flexible and powerful. Our examples in this paper demonstrate that exogenous coordination protocols that can be expressed as regular expressions over I/O operations correspond to $P\epsilon\omega$ connectors composed out of a small set of only five primitive channel types.

Our on-going work on $P\epsilon\omega$ consists of the formalization of its semantics, development of logics for reasoning about connectors, and completion of its current implementation to support composition of component based software systems in Java. Adaptation of a coherent graphical notation for representation of channels is also on our list as a first step toward a visual paradigm for construction of connectors.

References

1. F. Arbab. The IWIM model for coordination of concurrent activities. In Paolo Ciancarini and Chris Hankin, editors, *Coordination Languages and Models*, volume 1061 of *Lecture Notes in Computer Science*, pages 34–56. Springer-Verlag, April 1996.
2. F. Arbab. Manifold version 2: Language reference manual. Technical report, Centrum voor Wiskunde en Informatica, Kruislaan 413, 1098 SJ Amsterdam, The Netherlands, 1996. Available online http://www.cwi.nl/ftp/manifold/refman.ps.Z.
3. F. Arbab. A channel-based coordination model for component composition. Technical Report SEN-R0203, Centrum voor Wiskunde en Informatica, Kruislaan 413, 1098 SJ Amsterdam, The Netherlands, 2001.
4. F. Arbab, F.S. de Boer, and M.M. Bonsangue. A coordination language for mobile components. In *Proc. ACM SAC'00*, 2000.

5. Farhad Arbab. Coordination of mobile components. In Ugo Montanari and Vladimiro Sassone, editors, *Electronic Notes in Theoretical Computer Science*, volume 54. Elsevier Science Publishers, 2001.

6. Farhad Arbab, F. S. de Boer, and M. M. Bonsangue. A logical interface description language for components. In Antonio Porto and Gruia-Catalin Roman, editors, *Coordination Languages and Models: Proc. Coordination 2000*, volume 1906 of *Lecture Notes in Computer Science*, pages 249–266. Springer-Verlag, September 2000.

7. M.M. Bonsangue, F. Arbab, J.W. de Bakker, J.J.M.M. Rutten, A. Scutellá, and G. Zavattaro. A transition system semantics for the control-driven coordination language manifold. *Theoretical Computer Science*, 240:3–47, 2000.

8. M. Broy. Equations for describing dynamic nets of communicating systems. In *Proc. 5th COMPASS workshop*, volume 906 of *Lecture Notes in Computer Science*, pages 170–187. Springer-Verlag, 1995.

9. F. S. de Boer and M. M. Bonsangue. A compositional model for confluent dynamic data-flow networks. In M. Nielsen and B. Rovan, editors, *Proc. International Symposium of the Mathematical Foundations of Computer Science (MFCS)*, volume 1893 of *Lecture Notes in Computer Science*, pages 212–221. Springer-Verlag, August-September 2000.

10. R. Grosu and K. Stoelen. A model for mobile point-to-point data-flow networks without channel sharing. *Lecture Notes in Computer Science*, 1101:504–??, 1996.

11. G. Kahn. The semantics of a simple language for parallel programming. In J. L. Rosenfeld, editor, *Information Processing '74: Proceedings of the IFIP Congress*, pages 471–475. North-Holland, New York, NY, 1974

10. Juan Guillen Scholten. Mocha! A model for distributed Mobile Channels. Master's thesis, Leiden University, May 2001.

Exogenous and Endogenous Extensions of Architectural Types

Marco Bernardo and Francesco Franzè

Università di Urbino - Italy
Centro per l'Applicazione delle Scienze e Tecnologie dell'Informazione

Abstract. The problem of formalizing architectural styles has been recently tackled with the introduction of the concept of architectural type. The internal behavior of the system components can vary from instance to instance of an architectural type in a controlled way, which preserves the absence of deadlock related architectural mismatches proved via the architectural compatibility and interoperability checks. In this paper we extend the notion of architectural type by permitting a controlled variability of the component topology as well. This is achieved by means of two kinds of topological extensions: exogenous and endogenous. An exogenous extension consists of attaching a set of new topology compliant components to a set of already existing components. An endogenous extension consists of replacing a set of already existing components with a set of new topology compliant components. We show that such a variability of the topology is still manageable from the analysis viewpoint.

1 Introduction

An important goal of the software architecture discipline [9,10] is the creation of an established and shared understanding of the common forms of software design. Starting from the user requirements, the designer should be able to identify a suitable organizational style, in order to capitalize on codified principles and experience to specify, analyze, plan, and monitor the construction of a software system with high levels of efficiency and confidence. An architectural style defines a family of software systems having a common vocabulary of components as well as a common topology and set of contraints on the interactions among the components. Since an architectural style encompasses an entire family of software systems, it is desirable to formalize the concept of architectural style both to have a precise definition of the system family and to study the architectural properties common to all the systems of the family. This is not a trivial task because there are at least two degrees of freedom: variability of the component topology and variability of the component internal behavior.

Some papers have appeared in the literature that address the formalization of the architectural styles. In [1] a formal framework based on Z has been provided for precisely defining architectural styles and analyzing within and between different architectural styles. This is accomplished by means of a small set of mappings from the syntactic domain of architectural descriptions to the

F. Arbab and C. Talcott (Eds.): COORDINATION 2002, LNCS 2315, pp. 40–55, 2002.

semantic domain of architectural meaning, following the standard denotational approach developed for programming languages. In [6] a syntactic theory of software architecture has been presented that is based on set theory, regular expressions, and context free grammars. Architectural styles have been categorized through the typing of the nodes and the connections in the diagrammatic syntax as well as a pattern matching mechanism. In [8] architectural styles have been represented as logical theories and a method has been introduced for the stepwise refinement of an abstract architecture into a relatively correct lower level one. In [3] a process algebraic approach is adopted. In such an approach the description of an architectural style via WRIGHT [2] comprises the definition of component and connector types with a fixed internal behavior as well as topological constraints, whereas the component and connector instances and the related attachments are separately specified in the configurations of the style, so that the set of component and connector instances and the related attachments can vary from configuration to configuration. Also in [4] a process algebraic approach is adopted. An intermediate abstraction called architectural type is introduced, which denotes a set of software architectures with the same topology that differ for the internal behavior of their architectural elements and satisfy the same architectural compatibility and interoperability properties [5].

The purpose of this paper is to make the notion of architectural type of [4] closer to the notion of architectural style through a controlled variability of the topology that preserves the properties of [5]. We propose two kinds of topological extensions: exogenous and endogenous. An exogenous extension consists of attaching a set of new topology compliant components to a set of already existing components. An endogenous extension instead consists of replacing a set of already existing components with a set of new topology compliant components. Besides giving rise to scalable architectural specifications, we show that such a controlled variability of the topology is still manageable from the analysis viewpoint, as the absence of deadlock related architectural mismatches proved via the architectural compatibility and interoperability checks scales w.r.t. the number of new components for all the exogenous extensions as well as for all the endogenous extensions satisfying a certain contraint. Finally, we prove that the endogenous extensions are more expressive than the exogenous ones.

This paper is organized as follows. In Sect. 2 we recall syntax, semantics, and architectural checks for PADL, a process algebra based ADL for the description of architectural types. In Sect. 3 and 4 we enrich PADL with exogenous and endogenous extensions, respectively, and we investigate the scalability of the architectural checks. Finally, in Sect. 5 we discuss some future work.

2   PADL: A Process Algebra Based ADL

In this section we recall the syntax, the semantics, and the architectural checks for PADL, a process algebra based ADL for the compositional, graphical, and hierarchical modeling of architectural types. For a complete presentation and comparisons with related work, the reader is referred to [4,5].

The set of process terms of the process algebra PA on which PADL is based is generated by the following syntax

$$E ::= \underline{0} \mid a.E \mid E/L \mid E[\varphi] \mid E + E \mid E \|_S E \mid A$$

where a belongs to a set Act of actions including a distinguished action τ for unobservable activities, $L, S \subseteq Act - \{\tau\}$, φ belongs to a set $ARFun$ of action relabeling functions preserving observability (i.e., $\varphi^{-1}(\tau) = \{\tau\}$), and A belongs to a set $Const$ of constants each possessing a (possibly recursive) defining equation of the form $A \stackrel{\triangle}{=} E$. In the syntax above, "$\underline{0}$" is the term that cannot execute any action. Term $a.E$ can execute action a and then behaves as term E. Term E/L behaves as term E with each executed action a turned into τ whenever $a \in L$. Term $E[\varphi]$ behaves as term E with each executed action a turned into $\varphi(a)$. Term $E_1 + E_2$ behaves as either term E_1 or term E_2 depending on whether an action of E_1 or an action of E_2 is executed. Term $E_1 \|_S E_2$ asynchronously executes actions of E_1 or E_2 not belonging to S and synchronously executes equal actions of E_1 and E_2 belonging to S. The action prefix operator and the alternative composition operator are called dynamic operators, whereas the hiding operator, the relabeling operator, and the parallel composition operator are called static operators. A term is called sequential if it is composed of dynamic operators only. The notion of equivalence that we consider for PA is the weak bisimulation equivalence [7], denoted $\approx_B$, which captures the ability of two terms to simulate each other behaviors up to τ actions.

A description in PADL represents an architectural type (AT). Each AT is defined as a function of its architectural element types (AETs) and its architectural topology. An AET is defined as a function of its behavior, specified either as a family of PA sequential terms or through an invocation of a previously defined AT, and its interactions, specified as a set of PA actions. The architectural topology is specified through the declaration of a fixed set of architectural element instances (AEIs), a fixed set of architectural interactions (AIs) given by some interactions of the AEIs that act as interfaces for the whole AT, and a fixed set of directed architectural attachments (DAAs) among the interactions of the AEIs. Every interaction is declared to be an input interaction or an output interaction and the DAAs must respect such a classification: every DAA must involve an output interaction and an input interaction of two different AEIs. Every interaction that is not an AI must be involved in at least one DAA. In order to allow for multi AEI synchronizations, every interaction can be involved in several DAAs, provided that no autosynchronization arises, i.e. no chain of DAAs is created that starts from an interaction of an AEI and terminates on an interaction of the same AEI.

We show in Table 1 a PADL textual description for a pipe-filter system. The system is composed of three identical filters and one pipe. Each filter acts as a service center of capacity two that is subject to failures and subsequent repairs. For each item processed by the upstream filter, the pipe forwards it to one of the two downstream filters according to the availability of free positions in their buffers. If both have free positions, the choice is resolved nondeterministically.

The same system is depicted in Fig. 1 through the PADL graphical notation, which is based on flow graphs [7].

Table 1. Textual description of *PipeFilter*

archi_type	PipeFilter
archi_elem_types	
elem_type	*FilterT*
behavior	$Filter \overset{\Delta}{=} accept\_item.Filter' +$
	$\qquad fail.repair.Filter$
	$Filter' \overset{\Delta}{=} accept\_item.Filter'' +$
	$\qquad serve\_item.Filter +$
	$\qquad fail.repair.Filter'$
	$Filter'' \overset{\Delta}{=} serve\_item.Filter' +$
	$\qquad fail.repair.Filter''$
interactions	**input** *accept_item*
	output *serve_item*
elem_type	*PipeT*
behavior	$Pipe \overset{\Delta}{=} accept\_item.(forward\_item_1.Pipe +$
	$\qquad\qquad forward\_item_2.Pipe)$
interactions	**input** *accept_item*
	output *forward_item$_1$*
	output *forward_item$_2$*
archi_topology	
archi_elem_instances	$F_0, F_1, F_2 : FilterT$
	$P : PipeT$
archi_interactions	**input** $F_0.accept\_item$
	output $F_1.serve\_item, F_2.serve\_item$
archi_attachments	**from** $F_0.serve\_item$ **to** $P.accept\_item$
	from $P.forward\_item_1$ **to** $F_1.accept\_item$
	from $P.forward\_item_2$ **to** $F_2.accept\_item$
end	

The semantics of a PADL specification is given by translation into PA in two steps. In the first step, the semantics of all the instances of each AET is defined to be the behavior of the AET projected onto its interactions.

Definition 1. *Given a PADL specification, let C be an AET with behavior E and interaction set $\mathcal{I}$. The semantics of C and its instances is defined by*

$$[\![C]\!] = E/(Act - \{\tau\} - \mathcal{I}) \qquad \blacksquare$$

In our pipe-filter example we have

$$[\![FilterT]\!] = [\![F_0]\!] = [\![F_1]\!] = [\![F_2]\!] = Filter/\{fail, repair\}$$
$$[\![PipeT]\!] = \qquad [\![P]\!] \qquad = Pipe$$

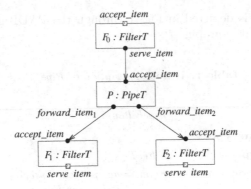

Fig. 1. Flow graph of *PipeFilter*

In the second step, the semantics of an AT is obtained by composing in parallel the semantics of its AEIs according to the specified DAAs. In our pipe-filter example we have

$$\llbracket PipeFilter \rrbracket = \llbracket F_0 \rrbracket [serve\_item \mapsto a] \,\|_\emptyset$$
$$\llbracket F_1 \rrbracket [accept\_item \mapsto a_1] \,\|_\emptyset$$
$$\llbracket F_2 \rrbracket [accept\_item \mapsto a_2] \,\|_{\{a,a_1,a_2\}}$$
$$\llbracket P \rrbracket [accept\_item \mapsto a,$$
$$forward\_item_1 \mapsto a_1, forward\_item_2 \mapsto a_2]$$

where the use of the relabeling operator is necessary to make the AEIs interact. In general, let $C_1, \ldots, C_n$ be AEIs of an AT, with interaction sets $\mathcal{I}_{C_1}, \ldots, \mathcal{I}_{C_n}$ containing the AI sets $\mathcal{AI}_{C_1}, \ldots, \mathcal{AI}_{C_n}$, respectively. Let i, j, k range over $\{1, \ldots, n\}$. We say that $C_i.a_1$ is connected to $C_j.a_2$ iff either there is a DAA between them, or there exists an interaction a_3 of C_k such that $C_i.a_1$ is connected to $C_k.a_3$ and there is a DAA between $C_k.a_3$ and $C_j.a_2$. We say that a subset of interactions of $C_1, \ldots, C_n$ is connected iff they are pairwise connected via DAAs involving interactions of $C_1, \ldots, C_n$ only and the subset is maximal. Since the actions of a connected subset of interactions must be identically relabeled in order to result in a synchronization at the semantic level, denoted by $\mathcal{I}_{C_i;C_1,\ldots,C_n} \subseteq \mathcal{I}_{C_i}$ the subset of interactions of C_i attached to $C_1, \ldots, C_n$, let $\mathcal{S}(C_1, \ldots, C_n)$ be a set of as many fresh actions as there are connected subsets of interactions among the considered AEIs, let $\varphi_{C_i;C_1,\ldots,C_n} : \mathcal{I}_{C_i;C_1,\ldots,C_n} \longrightarrow \mathcal{S}(C_1, \ldots, C_n)$ be injective relabeling functions such that $\varphi_{C_i;C_1,\ldots,C_n}(a_1) = \varphi_{C_j;C_1,\ldots,C_n}(a_2)$ iff $C_i.a_1$ is connected to $C_j.a_2$, and let $\mathcal{S}(C_i; C_1, \ldots, C_n) = \varphi_{C_i;C_1,\ldots,C_n}(\mathcal{I}_{C_i;C_1,\ldots,C_n})$ and $\mathcal{S}(C_i, C_j; C_1, \ldots, C_n) = \mathcal{S}(C_i; C_1, \ldots, C_n) \cap \mathcal{S}(C_j; C_1, \ldots, C_n)$.

Definition 2. Let $C_1, \ldots, C_n$ be AEIs of an AT. The closed and the open interacting semantics of C_i restricted to $C_1, \ldots, C_n$ are defined by

$$\llbracket C_i \rrbracket^c_{C_1,\ldots,C_n} = \llbracket C_i \rrbracket \,/\, (Act - \{\tau\} - \mathcal{I}_{C_i;C_1,\ldots,C_n}) \qquad [\varphi_{C_i;C_1,\ldots,C_n}]$$
$$\llbracket C_i \rrbracket^o_{C_1,\ldots,C_n} = \llbracket C_i \rrbracket \,/\, (Act - \{\tau\} - (\mathcal{I}_{C_i;C_1,\ldots,C_n} \cup \mathcal{AI}_{C_i})) \,[\varphi_{C_i;C_1,\ldots,C_n}] \quad \blacksquare$$

Definition 3. *Let $C_1, \ldots, C_n$ be AEIs of an AT. The closed and the open interacting semantics of the set of AEIs are defined by*

$$[\![C_1, \ldots, C_n]\!]^c = [\![C_1]\!]^c_{C_1, \ldots, C_n} \parallel_{\mathcal{S}(C_1, C_2; C_1, \ldots, C_n)}$$
$$[\![C_2]\!]^c_{C_1, \ldots, C_n} \parallel_{\mathcal{S}(C_1, C_3; C_1, \ldots, C_n) \cup \mathcal{S}(C_2, C_3; C_1, \ldots, C_n)} \cdots$$
$$\cdots \parallel_{\cup_{i=1}^{n-1} \mathcal{S}(C_i, C_n; C_1, \ldots, C_n)} [\![C_n]\!]^c_{C_1, \ldots, C_n}$$

$$[\![C_1, \ldots, C_n]\!]^o = [\![C_1]\!]^o_{C_1, \ldots, C_n} \parallel_{\mathcal{S}(C_1, C_2; C_1, \ldots, C_n)}$$
$$[\![C_2]\!]^o_{C_1, \ldots, C_n} \parallel_{\mathcal{S}(C_1, C_3; C_1, \ldots, C_n) \cup \mathcal{S}(C_2, C_3; C_1, \ldots, C_n)} \cdots$$
$$\cdots \parallel_{\cup_{i=1}^{n-1} \mathcal{S}(C_i, C_n; C_1, \ldots, C_n)} [\![C_n]\!]^o_{C_1, \ldots, C_n} \qquad \blacksquare$$

Definition 4. *The semantics of an AT $\mathcal{A}$ with AEIs $C_1, \ldots, C_n$ is defined by*

$$[\![\mathcal{A}]\!] = [\![C_1, \ldots, C_n]\!]^o \qquad \blacksquare$$

A PADL description represents a family of software architectures called an AT. An instance of an AT can be obtained by invoking the AT and passing actual behavior preserving AETs and actual names for the AIs, whereas it is not possible to pass an actual topology. This restriction allows us to efficiently check whether an AT invocation conforms to an AT definition.

Definition 5. *Let $\mathcal{A}(\mathcal{C}'_1, \ldots, \mathcal{C}'_m; a'_1, \ldots, a'_l)$ be an invocation of the AT $\mathcal{A}$ defined with formal AETs $\mathcal{C}_1, \ldots, \mathcal{C}_m$ and AIs $a_1, \ldots, a_l$. $\mathcal{C}'_i$ is said to conform to $\mathcal{C}_i$ iff there exist an injective relabeling function φ'_i for the interactions of $\mathcal{C}'_i$ and an injective relabeling function φ_i for the interactions of $\mathcal{C}_i$ such that*

$$[\![\mathcal{C}'_i]\!][\varphi'_i] \approx_B [\![\mathcal{C}_i]\!][\varphi_i] \qquad \blacksquare$$

Definition 6. *Let $\mathcal{A}(\mathcal{C}'_1, \ldots, \mathcal{C}'_m; a'_1, \ldots, a'_l)$ be an invocation of the AT $\mathcal{A}$ defined with formal AETs $\mathcal{C}_1, \ldots, \mathcal{C}_m$ and AIs $a_1, \ldots, a_l$. If $\mathcal{C}'_i$ conforms to $\mathcal{C}_i$ for all $i = 1, \ldots, m$, then the semantics of the AT invocation is defined by*

$$[\![\mathcal{A}(\mathcal{C}'_1, \ldots, \mathcal{C}'_m; a'_1, \ldots, a'_l)]\!] = [\![\mathcal{A}]\!][a_1 \mapsto a'_1, \ldots, a_l \mapsto a'_l] \qquad \blacksquare$$

Theorem 1. *Let $\mathcal{A}(\mathcal{C}'_1, \ldots, \mathcal{C}'_m; a'_1, \ldots, a'_l)$ be an invocation of the AT $\mathcal{A}$ defined with formal AETs $\mathcal{C}_1, \ldots, \mathcal{C}_m$ and AIs $a_1, \ldots, a_l$ and let $C'_1, \ldots, C'_n$ be the AEIs of the AT invocation. If $\mathcal{C}'_i$ conforms to $\mathcal{C}_i$ for all $i = 1, \ldots, m$, then there exist an injective relabeling function φ' for the interactions of the AT invocation and an injective relabeling function φ for the interactions of the AT definition such that $[\![C'_1, \ldots, C'_n]\!]^o[\varphi'] \approx_B [\![\mathcal{A}]\!][\varphi]$.* $\qquad \blacksquare$

PADL is equipped with two checks for the detection of architectural mismatches resulting in deadlocks when combining deadlock free AEIs. The first check (compatibility) is concerned with the well formedness of acyclic ATs, while the second check (interoperability) is concerned with the well formedness of sets of AEIs forming a cycle. Both checks are preserved by conformity.

Definition 7. *Given an acyclic AT, let $C_1, \ldots, C_n$ be the AEIs attached to AEI K. C_i is said to be compatible with K iff*

$$[\![K]\!]^c_{K, C_1, \ldots, C_n} \parallel_{\mathcal{S}(K; K, C_1, \ldots, C_n)} [\![C_i]\!]^c_{K, C_1, \ldots, C_n} \approx_B [\![K]\!]^c_{K, C_1, \ldots, C_n} \qquad \blacksquare$$

Theorem 2. *Given an acyclic AT, let $C_1, \ldots, C_n$ be the AEIs attached to AEI K. If $[\![K]\!]^c_{K,C_1,\ldots,C_n}$ is deadlock free and C_i is compatible with K for all $i = 1, \ldots, n$, then*

$$[\![K; C_1, \ldots, C_n]\!] = [\![K]\!]^c_{K,C_1,\ldots,C_n} \parallel_{\mathcal{S}(K;K,C_1,\ldots,C_n)}$$
$$[\![C_1]\!]^c_{K,C_1,\ldots,C_n} \parallel_{\mathcal{S}(K;K,C_1,\ldots,C_n)} \cdots$$
$$\cdots \parallel_{\mathcal{S}(K;K,C_1,\ldots,C_n)} [\![C_n]\!]^c_{K,C_1,\ldots,C_n}$$

is deadlock free.   ∎

Corollary 1. *Given an acyclic AT, if every restricted closed interacting semantics of each AEI is deadlock free and every AEI is compatible with each AEI attached to it, then the AT is deadlock free.*   ∎

Definition 8. *Given an AT, let $C_1, \ldots, C_n$ be AEIs forming a cycle. C_i is said to interoperate with $C_1, \ldots, C_{i-1}, C_{i+1}, \ldots, C_n$ iff*

$$[\![C_1, \ldots, C_n]\!]^c / (Act - \{\tau\} - \mathcal{S}(C_i; C_1, \ldots, C_n)) \approx_B [\![C_i]\!]^c_{C_1,\ldots,C_n} \qquad ∎$$

Theorem 3. *Given an AT, let $C_1, \ldots, C_n$ be AEIs forming a cycle. If there exists C_i such that $[\![C_i]\!]^c_{C_1,\ldots,C_n}$ is deadlock free and C_i interoperates with $C_1, \ldots, C_{i-1}, C_{i+1}, \ldots, C_n$, then $[\![C_1, \ldots, C_n]\!]^c$ is deadlock free.*   ∎

Theorem 4. *Let $\mathcal{A}(C'_1, \ldots, C'_m; a'_1, \ldots, a'_l)$ be an invocation of the AT $\mathcal{A}$ defined with formal AETs $C_1, \ldots, C_m$ and AIs $a_1, \ldots, a_l$. If C'_i conforms to C_i for all $i = 1, \ldots, m$, then the AT invocation and the AT definition have the same compatibility and interoperability properties.*   ∎

3 Exogenous Extensions

The instances of an AT can differ for the internal behavior of their AETs. However, it is desirable to have some form of variability in the topology as well. As an example, consider the pipe-filter system of Sect. 2. Every instance of such an AT can admit a single pipe connected to one upstream filter and two downstream filters, whereas it would be desirable to be able to express by means of that AT any pipe-filter system with an arbitrary number of filters and pipes, such that every pipe is connected to one upstream filter and two downstream filters. E.g., the flow graph in Fig. 2 should be considered as a legal extension of the flow graph in Fig. 1. The idea is that, since the AIs of an AT are the frontier of the whole AT, it is reasonable to extend the AT at some of its AIs in a way that follows the prescribed topology. This cannot be done at a simple interaction because every simple interaction must occur in at least one DAA, hence it cannot be free.

An exogenous extension of an AT can take place only at a set $K_1, \ldots, K_n$ of AEIs having one or more AIs and consists of attaching a set of new AEIs to one or more AIs of each of $K_1, \ldots, K_n$ in a controlled way. By controlled way we mean that the addendum topologically conforms to the AT, i.e.:

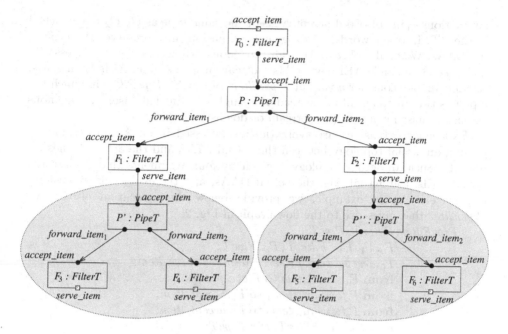

Fig ? Flow graph of an exogenous extension of *PipeFilter*

1. For each AEI C in the addendum, there is a corresponding AEI $corr(C)$ in the AT such that C has the same type as $corr(C)$ and an interaction a of C is simple/architectural iff the corresponding interaction a of $corr(C)$ is simple/architectural. Every AI in the addendum must be equal to one of the AIs of $K_1, \ldots, K_n$ involved in the extension.

2. For each AEI C and for each simple interaction a of C in the addendum, there are an AEI C' and a DAA from $C.a$ ($C'.a'$) to $C'.a'$ ($C.a$) in the addendum iff there is a DAA from $corr(C).a$ ($corr(C').a'$) to $corr(C').a'$ ($corr(C).a$) in the AT.

3. For each AEI K_i, $1 \le i \le n$, there is an AEI K_i' with the same type as K_i in the AT such that, for each AI a of K_i, there are an AEI C' in the addendum and a DAA from $K_i.a$ ($C'.a'$) to $C'.a'$ ($K_i.a$) iff there is a DAA from $K_i'.a$ ($corr(C').a'$) to $corr(C').a'$ ($K_i'.a$) in the AT, in which case the AI a of K_i is made simple.

The first constraint makes sure that no instances of new AETs are present in the addendum and that only the AIs of $K_1, \ldots, K_n$ involved in the extension propagate to the addendum. The second constraint guarantees that the addendum follows the same topological pattern prescribed by the AT. The third constraint ensures that the DAAs between the involved AEIs on the frontier of the AT and the addendum is consistent with the topological pattern prescribed by the AT. As can be noted, an exogenous extension never introduces a DAA between two interactions a_1, a_2 of two different AEIs C_1, C_2 of the addendum if no two interactions a_1, a_2 of two different AEIs of the same type as C_1, C_2 are attached in the AT. In other words, an exogenous extension fully preserves the type of the DAAs. We finally observe that an exogenous extension does not necessarily take place at a single AEI having AIs, but can involve several AEIs having AIs. As an example, consider a variant *PipeFilter'* of the AT *PipeFilter* in which the pipe has two upstream filters instead of a single one. In that case, an exogenous extension must involve both upstream or downstream filters.

Exogenous extensions are syntactically expressed in an AT invocation by passing an actual topology between the actual AETs and the actual names for the AIs. Such an actual topology is given by four arguments that declare the actual AEIs, the actual AIs, the actual DAAs, and the exogenous extensions, respectively. As an example, we provide below the invocation of the AT *PipeFilter* that gives rise to the flow graph in Fig. 2:

> $PipeFilter(FilterT, PipeT;$
>> $F_0, F_1, F_2 : FilterT, P : PipeT;$
>> $F_0.accept\_item, F_1.serve\_item, F_2.serve\_item;$
>> **from** $F_0.serve\_item$ **to** $P.accept\_item,$
>> **from** $P.forward\_item_1$ **to** $F_1.accept\_item,$
>> **from** $P.forward\_item_2$ **to** $F_2.accept\_item;$
>> **exo**$(F_3, F_4 : FilterT, P' : PipeT;$
>>> **subst** $F_3.serve\_item, F_4.serve\_item$ **for** $F_1.serve\_item;$
>>> **from** $F_1.serve\_item$ **to** $P'.accept\_item,$
>>> **from** $P'.forward\_item_1$ **to** $F_3.accept\_item,$
>>> **from** $P'.forward\_item_2$ **to** $F_4.accept\_item;$
>>>),
>> **exo**$(F_5, F_6 : FilterT, P'' : PipeT;$
>>> **subst** $F_5.serve\_item, F_6.serve\_item$ **for** $F_2.serve\_item;$
>>> **from** $F_2.serve\_item$ **to** $P''.accept\_item,$
>>> **from** $P''.forward\_item_1$ **to** $F_5.accept\_item,$
>>> **from** $P''.forward\_item_2$ **to** $F_6.accept\_item;$
>>>);
>> $accept, serve, serve, serve, serve)$

An AT invocation has the following six semicolon separated arguments:

1. The first argument is the list of actual AETs, which must conform to the corresponding formal AETs as established in Def. 5. In the invocation above, the actual AETs coincide with the formal AETs.
2. The second argument is the list of actual AEIs, whose number and types must match the number and types of the corresponding formal AEIs. In the invocation above, the actual AEIs coincide with the formal AETs.
3. The third argument is the list of actual prefixed AIs, whose number and prefixes must match the number and prefixes of the corresponding formal AIs. In the invocation above, the actual AIs coincide with the formal AIs.
4. The fourth argument is the list of actual DAAs, whose number and directions must match the number and directions of the corresponding formal DAAs. In the invocation above, the actual DAAs coincide with the formal DAAs.

5. The fifth argument is the list of exogenous extensions. Each exogenous extension has the following four semicolon separated arguments:

   a) The first argument is the list of additional AEIs, whose types must occur in the list of actual AETs of the AT invocation. The number and types of such additional AEIs must allow the topological pattern prescribed by the AT to be preserved. In the invocation above, both exogenous extensions declare two additional instances of *FilterT* and one additional instance of *PipeT*.

   b) The second argument is the list of substitutions of prefixed additional AIs for previously declared prefixed AIs, where all the prefixes/interactions in a substitution must be of the same type/equal and an AI can be replaced only once in an AT invocation thus becoming a simple interaction. Such substitutions must follow the topological pattern prescribed by the AT. In the invocation above, both exogenous extensions substitute the two *serve_item* interactions of the two additional instances of *FilterT* for the *serve_item* interaction of one of the two original downstream instances of *FilterT*.

   c) The third argument is the list of additional DAAs, which must connect the replaced AIs with the interactions of the additional AEIs as well as the additional AEIs with themselves. Such DAAs must follow the topological pattern prescribed by the AT. In the invocation above, both exogenous extensions declare three DAAs. one from one of the two original downstream instances of *FilterT* to the additional instance of *PipeT*, one from the additional instance of *PipeT* to one of the two additional instances of *FilterT*, and one from the additional instance of *PipeT* to the other additional instance of *FilterT*.

   d) The fourth argument is the list of exogenous extensions to the current exogenous extension, i.e. those exogenous extensions that can take place at the AIs declared in the substitutions of the current exogenous extension. In the invocation above, both exogenous extensions declare no nested exogenous extension. A nested exogenous extension would be declared if e.g. F_3 in Fig. 2 were attached to an instance of *PipeT* attached in turn to two downstream instances of *FilterT*.

6. The sixth argument is the list of actual names for the AIs, whose number must match the number of AIs declared in the third argument according to their possibly nested substitutions. In the invocation above, we have five AIs with the last four equally renamed, which means that the software component whose behavior is given by the AT invocation has just two interactions.

We finally investigate whether the compatibility and interoperability results proved on an AT scale to all of its exogenous extensions. In the case of the architectural compatibility check, which is concerned with acyclic ATs, we always get the desired scalability from an AT to all of its exogenous extensions provided that no cycles are introduced. Note that cycles can be introduced in an acyclic AT when performing an exogenous extension, as is the case with *PipeFilter'*.

Theorem 5. *Given an acyclic AT, let $C_1, \ldots, C_n$ be the AEIs attached to AEI K. If $[\![K]\!]^c_{K,C_1,\ldots,C_n}$ is deadlock free, C_i is compatible with K for all $i = 1, \ldots, n$, and every further AEI that can be attached to K through an acyclic exogenous extension is compatible with K, then $[\![K; C_1, \ldots, C_n]\!]$ and all of its acyclic exogenous extensions involving K are deadlock free.*

Proof. *The first part of the result stems directly from Thm. 2. The second part of the result is trivial if K has no AIs. If K has AIs and an arbitrary acyclic exogenous extension involves some of them, then the corresponding acyclic exogenous extension of $[\![K; C_1, \ldots, C_n]\!]$ is deadlock free by virtue of Thm. 2, because C_i is compatible with K for all $i = 1, \ldots, n$ and every AEI attached to K in the acyclic exogenous extension is compatible with K by hypothesis.* ■

Corollary 2. *Given an acyclic AT, if every restricted closed interacting semantics of each AEI is deadlock free and every AEI is compatible with each AEI attached to it, then the AT and all of its acyclic exogenous extensions are deadlock free.*

Proof. *It follows from the theorem above and the three constraints that establish that any addendum must topologically conform to the AT. In particular, we observe that the third constraint provides the additional information required by the theorem above about the satisfaction of the compatibility condition on the frontier of K.* ■

In the case of the architectural interoperability check, which is concerned with cyclic ATs, we obtain the desired scalability (for individual cycles) from an AT to all of its exogenous extensions, because attaching an addendum to one or more AEIs in the cycle does not alter the interoperability of the AEIs within the cycle.

Theorem 6. *Given an AT, let $C_1, \ldots, C_n$ be AEIs forming a cycle. If there exists C_i such that $[\![C_i]\!]^c_{C_1,\ldots,C_n}$ is deadlock free and C_i interoperates with $C_1, \ldots, C_{i-1}, C_{i+1}, \ldots, C_n$, then $[\![C_1, \ldots, C_n]\!]^c$ is deadlock free even in the presence of an exogenous extension involving some of $C_1, \ldots, C_n$.* ■

As an example of application of the architectural checks above, let us consider the AT *PipeFilter*. It is easy to see that F_0, F_1, F_2 are all compatible with P, hence we can conclude by Thm. 2 that $[\![PipeFilter]\!]$ is deadlock free. Let us now consider the exogenous extension of *PipeFilter* depicted in Fig. 2. By applying Thm. 5 to F_1 and F_2, we obtain that $[\![F_1; P, P']\!]$ and $[\![F_2; P, P'']\!]$ are deadlock free. By subsequently applying Cor. 2, we further obtain that every exogenous extension of *PipeFilter* is deadlock free, hence so is in particular the one in Fig. 2.

4   Endogenous Extensions

Besides exogenous extensions, there are other desirable forms of variability in the topology of an AT. As an example, let us consider Table 2, which provides a

Table 2. Textual description of *Ring*

archi_type	*Ring*
archi_elem_types	
elem_type	*InitStationT*
behavior	*InitStation* $\stackrel{\Delta}{=}$ *start.InitStation''*
	InitStation' $\stackrel{\Delta}{=}$ *receive.process.InitStation''*
	InitStation'' $\stackrel{\Delta}{=}$ *send.InitStation'*
interactions	**input** *receive*
	output *send*
elem_type	*StationT*
behavior	*Station* $\stackrel{\Delta}{=}$ *receive.process.send.Station*
interactions	**input** *receive*
	output *send*
archi_topology	
archi_elem_instances	*IS* : *InitStationT*
	S_1, S_2, S_3 : *StationT*
archi_interactions	
archi_attachments	**from** *IS.send* **to** S_1*.receive*
	from S_1*.send* **to** S_2 *receive*
	from S_2*.send* **to** S_3 *receive*
	from S_3*.send* **to** *IS.receive*
end	

PADL description of a ring of stations each following the same protocol: wait for a message from the previous station in the ring, process the received message, and send the processed message to the next station in the ring. Since such a protocol guarantees that only one station can transmit at a given instant, the protocol can be considered as an abstraction of the IEEE 802.5 standard medium access control protocol for local area networks known as token ring. One of the stations is designated to be the initial one, in the sense that it is the first station allowed to send a message. The PADL description in Table 2 declares one instance of the initial station and three instances of the normal station. Every instance of the AT *Ring* can thus admit a single initial station and three normal stations connected to form a ring, whereas it would be desirable to be able to express by means of that AT any ring system with an arbitrary number of normal stations. E.g., the flow graph in Fig. 3 should be considered as a legal extension of the AT *Ring*. The idea is that of replacing a set of AEIs with a set of new AEIs following the topology prescribed by the AT. In this case, we consider the frontier of the AT w.r.t. one of the replaced AEIs to be the set of interactions previously attached to the simple interactions of the replaced AEI. On the other hand, all the replacing AEIs that will be attached to the frontier of the AT w.r.t. one of the replaced AEIs must be of the same type as the replaced AEI.

An endogenous extension of an AT can take place at a set $K_1, \ldots, K_n$ of AEIs, with K_i attached to $K_{i,1}, \ldots, K_{i,n_i}$ for all $i = 1, \ldots, n$, and consists of substituting a set S of AEIs for $K_1, \ldots, K_n$ in a controlled way. By controlled way we mean that S topologically conforms to the AT, i.e.:

1. For each AEI C in S, there is a corresponding AEI $corr(C)$ in the AT such that C has the same type as $corr(C)$ and an interaction a of C is simple/architectural iff the corresponding interaction a of $corr(C)$ is simple/architectural. Every AI in S must be equal to one of the AIs of $K_1, \ldots, K_n$.

2. For each AEI C and for each simple interaction a of C in S, there are an AEI C' and a DAA from $C.a$ $(C'.a')$ to $C'.a'$ $(C.a)$ in S iff there is a DAA from $corr(C).a$ $(corr(C').a')$ to $corr(C').a'$ $(corr(C).a)$ in the AT.

3. For each AEI $K_{i,j}$, $1 \leq i \leq n$, $1 \leq j \leq n_i$, and for each interaction a of $K_{i,j}$ attached to an interaction a' of K_i in the AT, there are an AEI C' with the same type as K_i in S and a DAA from $K_{i,j}.a$ $(C'.a')$ to $C'.a'$ $(K_{i,j}.a)$. If $C'.a'$ is an AI, it is made simple.

The three constraints above are similar to those for the exogenous extensions. The only difference is in the third constraint, which is now simpler because of the requirement that C' has the same type as K_i.

Similarly to exogenous extensions, when invoking an AT the endogenous extensions are syntactically expressed through four additional arguments for the actual topology. As an example, we provide below the invocation of the AT *Ring* that gives rise to the flow graph in Fig. 3:

$Ring(InitStationT, StationT;$

$\qquad IS : InitStationT, S_1, S_2, S_3 : StationT;$

$\qquad ;$

$\qquad$ **from** $IS.send$ **to** $S_1.receive,$

$\qquad$ **from** $S_1.send$ **to** $S_2.receive,$

$\qquad$ **from** $S_2.send$ **to** $S_3.receive,$

$\qquad$ **from** $S_3.send$ **to** $IS.receive;$

$\qquad$ **endo(subst** $S_2', S_2'' : StationT$ **for** $S_2 : StationT;$

$\qquad\qquad ;$

$\qquad\qquad$ **from** $S_1.send$ **to** $S_2'.receive,$

$\qquad\qquad$ **from** $S_2'.send$ **to** $S_2''.receive,$

$\qquad\qquad$ **from** $S_2''.send$ **to** $S_3.receive;$

$\qquad\qquad$);

$)$

The fifth argument above is the list of endogenous extensions, which can be interleaved with the exogenous extensions. Each endogenous extension has the following four semicolon separated arguments:

1. The first argument is the substitution of new AEIs for previously declared AEIs, where the types of the replacing AEIs must occur in the list of actual AETs of the AT invocation and an AEI can be replaced only once in an AT invocation. The number and types of such replacing AEIs must allow the

topological pattern prescribed by the AT to be preserved. In the invocation above, S_2' and S_2'' substitute for S_2.

2. The second argument is the list of substitutions of prefixed additional AIs for previously declared AIs of the replaced AEIs that consequently become simple, where all the prefixes/interactions in a substitution must be of the same type/equal. Such substitutions must follow the topological pattern prescribed by the AT. In the invocation above, there are no AI substitutions as there are no AIs.

3. The third argument is the list of DAAs. Some of them replaces the DAAs involving the replaced AEIs (see those from S_1 to S_2' and from S_2'' to S_3), while the others are new DAAs connecting the replacing AEIs (see the one from S_2' to S_2''). Such DAAs must follow the topological pattern prescribed by the AT.

4. The fourth argument is the list of endogenous/exogenous extensions to the current exogenous extension, i.e. those extensions that can take place at the AEIs/AIs declared in the substitutions of the current endogenous extension. In the invocation above, there are no nested extensions.

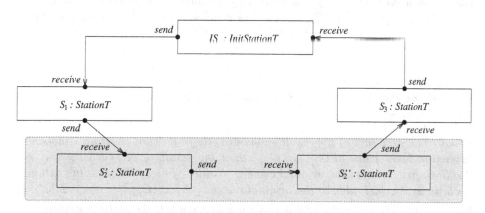

Fig. 3. Flow graph of an endogenous extension of *Ring*

We finally investigate whether the compatibility and interoperability results proved on an AT scale to all of its endogenous extensions. In the case of the architectural compatibility check, which is concerned with acyclic ATs, we always get the desired scalability from an AT to all of its endogenous extensions provided that no cycles are introduced. Note that cycles can be introduced in an acyclic AT when performing an endogenous extension, as is the case with *PipeFilter'* if we perform an endogenous extension at both downstream filters.

Theorem 7. *Given an acyclic AT, let $C_1, \ldots, C_n$ be the AEIs attached to AEI K. If $[\![K]\!]^c_{K,C_1,\ldots,C_n}$ is deadlock free and C_i is compatible with K for all $i = 1, \ldots, n$, then $[\![K; C_1, \ldots, C_n]\!]$ and all of its acyclic endogenous extensions taking place at some among $C_1, \ldots, C_n$ are deadlock free.*

Proof. The first part of the result stems directly from Thm. 2. Suppose now that an endogenous extension takes place at $C_{i_1}, \ldots, C_{i_m}$ with $1 \leq i_1, \ldots, i_m \leq n$. Since for each i_j the new AEI C'_{i_j} attached to K in place of C_{i_j} must be of the same type as C_{i_j}, the second part of the result follows by virtue of Thm. 2. ∎

Corollary 3. *Given an acyclic AT, if every restricted closed interacting semantics of each AEI is deadlock free and every AEI is compatible with each AEI attached to it, then the AT and all of its acyclic endogenous extensions are deadlock free.*

Proof. It follows from the theorem above and the three constraints that establish that any replacing set of AEIs must topologically conform to the AT. ∎

In the case of the architectural interoperability check, which is concerned with cyclic ATs, we obtain the desired scalability (for individual cycles) from an AT only to those of its endogenous extensions such that the set of replacing AEIs is weakly bisimilar to the set of replaced AEIs.

Theorem 8. *Given an AT, let $C_1, \ldots, C_n$ be AEIs forming a cycle. If there exists C_i such that $[\![C_i]\!]^{\mathrm{c}}_{C_1, \ldots, C_n}$ is deadlock free and C_i interoperates with $C_1, \ldots, C_{i-1}, C_{i+1}, \ldots, C_n$, then $[\![C_1, \ldots, C_n]\!]^{\mathrm{c}}$ is deadlock free and so is each of its endogenous extensions substituting $C'_1, \ldots, C'_{m'}$ for $C_{j_1}, \ldots, C_{j_m}$, with $1 \leq j_1, \ldots, j_m \leq n$, such that, denoted by $\mathcal{I}'$ the set of simple interactions of $C'_1, \ldots, C'_{m'}$ that are not attached to the interactions of the AEIs formerly attached to $C_{j_1}, \ldots, C_{j_m}$, there exist two relabelings φ and φ', which may not be injective only on the AIs of $C'_1, \ldots, C'_{m'}$, such that $[\![C'_1, \ldots, C'_{m'}]\!]^{\mathrm{c}}_{C'_1, \ldots, C'_{m'}} / \mathcal{I}'[\varphi'] \approx_{\mathrm{B}} [\![C_{j_1}, \ldots, C_{j_m}]\!]^{\mathrm{c}}_{C_1, \ldots, C_n}[\varphi].$*

Proof. The first part of the result stems directly from Thm. 3. If an endogenous extension takes place at $C_{j_1}, \ldots, C_{j_m}$, then the resulting extended cycle is still deadlock free, because the original cycle is deadlock free by Thm. 3, the extended cycle is weakly bisimilar to the original one as $[\![C'_1, \ldots, C'_{m'}]\!]^{\mathrm{c}}_{C'_1, \ldots, C'_{m'}} / \mathcal{I}'[\varphi'] \approx_{\mathrm{B}}$ $[\![C_{j_1}, \ldots, C_{j_m}]\!]^{\mathrm{c}}_{C_1, \ldots, C_n}[\varphi]$ and $\approx_{\mathrm{B}}$ is a congruence w.r.t. the static operators, and $\approx_{\mathrm{B}}$ preserves deadlock freedom. ∎

As an example of application of the architectural checks above, let us consider the AT *Ring*. It is easy to see that each of IS, S_1, S_2, S_3 is deadlock free and interoperates with the others, hence we get from Thm. 3 that $[\![Ring]\!]$ is deadlock free. Let us now consider the endogenous extension of *Ring* depicted in Fig. 3. Since $[\![S'_2, S''_2]\!]^{\mathrm{c}}_{S'_2, S''_2}$ is weakly bisimilar to $[\![S_2]\!]^{\mathrm{c}}_{IS, S_1, S_2, S_3}$ up to relabeling when the interactions in the DAAs between S'_2 and S''_2 are hidden, from Thm. 8 we obtain that the endogenous extension of *Ring* in Fig. 3 is deadlock free.

We conclude by observing the endogenous extensions are more expressive than the exogenous ones.

Theorem 9. *Given an AT, each of its exogenous extensions has an associated endogenous extension such that the two corresponding invocations of the AT result in the same instance of the AT.*

Proof. Given an arbitrary exogenous extension of the AT, its associated endogenous extension takes place at the AEIs whose AIs are involved in the exogenous extension, and it is obtained by considering as set of new AEIs the same new AEIs as the exogenous extension together with, for each AEI whose AIs are involved in the exogenous extension, a new AEI of the same type. ∎

5 Conclusion

In this paper we have enriched the notion of AT of [4] by introducing the capability of expressing exogenous and endogenous extensions of the topology, in such a way that the architectural checks of [5] scale w.r.t. the number of additional software components for all the exogenous extensions as well as for all the endogenous extensions satisfying a certain contraint. Finally, we have proved that the endogenous extensions are more expressive than the exogenous ones.

As far as future work is concerned, first we would like to investigate whether information can be gained about the interoperability of cycles that are generated when performing an exogenous extension on an AT, starting from the compatibility of the involved AEIs of the AT. Second, we would like to study whether the additional constraint for the interoperability result in the case of endogenous extensions can be weakened. Third, we would like to compare our approach to topological extensions with graph grammar based approaches.

References

1. G.D. Abowd, R. Allen, D. Garlan, *"Formalizing Style to Understand Descriptions of Software Architecture"*, in ACM Trans. on Software Engineering and Methodology 4:319-364, 1995
2. R. Allen, D. Garlan, *"A Formal Basis for Architectural Connection"*, in ACM Trans. on Software Engineering and Methodology 6:213-249, 1997
3. R. Allen, D. Garlan, *"A Case Study in Architectural Modelling: The AEGIS System"*, in Proc. of IWSSD-8, 1998
4. M. Bernardo, P. Ciancarini, L. Donatiello, *"On the Formalization of Architectural Types with Process Algebras"*, in Proc. of FSE-8, 2000
5. M. Bernardo, P. Ciancarini, L. Donatiello, *"Detecting Architectural Mismatches in Process Algebraic Descriptions of Software Systems"*, in Proc. of WICSA 2001
6. T.R. Dean, J.R. Cordy, *"A Syntactic Theory of Software Architecture"*, in IEEE Trans. on Software Engineering 21:302-313, 1995
7. R. Milner, *"Communication and Concurrency"*, Prentice Hall, 1989
8. M. Moriconi, X. Qian, R.A. Riemenschneider, *"Correct Architecture Refinement"*, in IEEE Trans. on Software Engineering 21:356-372, 1995
9. D.E. Perry, A.L. Wolf, *"Foundations for the Study of Software Architecture"*, in ACM SIGSOFT Software Engineering Notes 17:40-52, 1992
10. M. Shaw, D. Garlan, *"Software Architecture: Perspectives on an Emerging Discipline"*, Prentice Hall, 1996

Coordinating Mobile Object-Oriented Code*

Lorenzo Bettini[1], Viviana Bono[2], and Betti Venneri[1]

[1] Dipartimento di Sistemi e Informatica, Università di Firenze,
{bettini,venneri}@dsi.unifi.it
[2] Dipartimento di Informatica, Università di Torino, bono@di.unito.it

Abstract. Standard class-based inheritance mechanisms, which are often used to implement distributed systems, do not seem to scale well to a distributed context with mobility. In this paper, a *mixin*-based approach is proposed for structuring mobile object-oriented code and it is shown to fit in the dynamic and open nature of a mobile code scenario. We introduce MoMi (Mobile Mixins), a coordination language for mobile processes that communicate and exchange object-oriented code in a distributed context. MoMi is equipped with a type system, based on polymorphism by subtyping, in order to guarantee *safe* code communications.

1 Introduction

Internet provides technologies that allow the transmission of resources and services among computers distributed geographically in wide area networks. The growing use of a network as a primary environment for developing, distributing and running programs requires new supporting infrastructures. A possible answer to these requirements is the use of *mobile code* [26,11] and in particular of *mobile agents* [20,19,28], which are software objects consisting of data and code that can autonomously migrate to a remote computer and execute automatically on arrival.

On the other hand, the object-oriented paradigm has become established as a well suited technology for designing and implementing large software systems. In particular it provides a high degree of modularity, then of flexibility and reusability, so that it is widely used also in distributed contexts (see, e.g., Java [2] and CORBA [23]).

The new scenario arising from mobility puts at test the *flexibility* of object-oriented code in a wider framework. Object-oriented components are often developed by different providers and may be downloaded on demand for being dynamically assembled with local applications. As a consequence, they have to be strongly adaptive to any local execution environment, so that they can be dynamically reconfigured in several ways: downloaded code can be specialized by locally defined operations, conversely, locally developed software can be extended with new operations available from the downloaded code.

---

* This work has been partially supported by EU within the FET - Global Computing initiative, project MIKADO IST-2001-32222, DART project IST-2001-33477 and by MIUR project NAPOLI. The funding bodies are not responsible for any use that might be made of the results presented here.

F. Arbab and C. Talcott (Eds.): COORDINATION 2002, LNCS 2315, pp. 56–71, 2002.
© Springer-Verlag Berlin Heidelberg 2002

Hence a coordination language allowing to program object-oriented components as mobile processes should provide specific mechanisms for coordinating not only the transmission, but also the local dynamic reconfiguration of object-oriented code.

In this paper we address the above issue in the specific context of class-based languages, that "form the main stream of object-oriented programming" [1]. We propose to use a new *mixin*-based approach for structuring mobile object-oriented code, as an alternative to standard inheritance mechanisms (Section 2). A *mixin* (a class definition parameterized over the superclass) can be viewed as a function that takes a class as a parameter and derives a new subclass from it. The same mixin can be applied to many classes (the operation is known as *mixin application*), obtaining a family of subclasses with the same set of methods added and/or redefined. A subclass can be implemented before its superclass has been implemented; thus mixins remove the dependence of the subclass on the superclass, enabling dynamic development of class hierarchies. Mixins have become a focus of active research both in the software engineering [27,25,14] and programming language design [7,21,15] communities. In our approach, we use mixins and mixin application as the coordination mechanism for assembling mobile components in a flexible and safe way.

The paper proposes a formal calculus, MoMi, that integrates the mixin technology (relying on the calculus of [6]) into a core coordination language for mobile processes in a distributed context, where the main features of both components coexist in a uniform way. MoMi can be seen as a kernel language for programming and coordinating network services that allow remote communication with transmission of object-oriented code and dynamic reconfiguration of class hierarchies. The calculus is equipped with a type system, based on polymorphism by subtyping. We focus our attention on the subtyping relation on mixins, which comes out to be the main tool for coordinating the composition of local and mobile code in a safe way. The mobile code enjoys the benefits deriving from being statically type-checked and remote communications use static types "dynamically" to coordinate themselves (see Section 4).

The paper is structured as follows. In Section 2 we motivate our approach by investigating scenarios of object-oriented mobile code. In Section 3 we define the calculus MoMi whose operational semantics is given in Section 4. The type system of MoMi is presented in Section 5. In Section 6 we show an implementation of an example scenario in MoMi. Section 7 concludes the paper and discusses some related works and future directions.

2   Mobility and Object-Oriented Code

In this section we discuss two different scenarios, where an object-oriented application is received from (sent to) a remote site. In this setting we can assume that the application consists of a piece of code A that moves to a remote site, where it will be composed with a local piece of code B. These scenarios may take place during the development of an object-oriented software system in a distributed context with mobility.

Scenario 1. The local programmer may need to dynamically download classes in order to complete his own class hierarchy, without triggering off a chain reaction of changes over the whole system. For instance, he may want the downloaded class A to be a child class of a local class B. This generally happens in *frameworks* [17]: classes of the framework provide the general architecture of an application (playing the role of the local software), and classes that use the framework have to specialize them in order to provide specific implementations. The downloaded class may want to use operations that depend on the specific site (e.g. system calls); thus the local base class has to provide generic operations and the mobile code becomes a derived class containing methods that can exploit these generic operations.

Scenario 2. The site that downloads the class A for local execution may want to redefine some, possibly critical, operations that remote code may execute. This way access to some sensitive local resources is not granted to untrusted code (for example, some destructive "read" operations should be redefined as non-destructive ones in order to avoid that non-trusted code erases information). Thus the downloaded class A is seen, in this scenario, as a base class, that is locally specialized in a derived class B.

Summarizing, in **1** the base class is the local code while in **2** the base class is the mobile code. These scenarios are typical object-oriented compositions seen in a distributed mobile context. A major requirement is that composing local code with remote code should not affect existing code in a massive way. Namely, both components and client classes should not be modified nor recompiled.

Standard mechanisms of class extension and code specialization would solve these design problems only in a static and local context, but they do not scale well to a distributed context with mobile code. The standard inheritance operation is essentially static in that it fixes the inheritance hierarchy, i.e., it binds derived classes to their parent classes once for all. If such a hierarchy has to be changed, the program must be modified and then recompiled. This is quite unacceptable in a distributed mobile scenario, since it would be against its underlying dynamic nature. Indeed, what we are looking for is a mechanism for providing a dynamic reconfiguration of the inheritance relation between classes, not only a dynamic implementation of some operations.

Let us go back and look in more details at the above scenarios. We could think of implementing a kind of dynamic inheritance for specifying at run-time the inheritance relation between classes without modifying their code. Such a technique could solve the difficulty raised by scenario **1**. However dynamic inheritance is not useful for solving scenario **2**, that would require a not so clear dynamic definition of the base class. Another solution would be releasing the requirement of not affecting the existing code, and allowing to modify the code of the local class (i.e. the local hierarchy). This could solve the second scenario, but not the first one that would require access to foreign source code. We are also convinced that the two scenarios should be dealt with by the same mechanism, allowing to dynamically use the same code in different environments, either as a base class for deriving new classes, or as derived class for being "adopted" by a parent class. We remark that a solution based on *delegation* could help solving these problems. However delegation would destroy at least the dynamic binding and the reusability of the whole system [4].

Summarizing, mobile object-oriented code needs to be much more flexible than locally developed applications. To this aim we propose a new solution which is based on a mixin approach and we show that it enables to achieve the sought dynamic flexibility. Indeed, mixin-based inheritance is more oriented to the concept of "completion" than to that of extendibility/specialization. Mixins are incomplete class specifications, parameterized over superclasses, thus the inheritance relation between a derived and a base class is not established through a declaration (e.g., like **extends** in Java), instead it can be coordinated by the operation of *mixin application*, that takes place during the execution of a program, and it is not in its declaration part.

The novelty of our approach is the smooth integration of mobile code with mixins, a powerful tool for implementing reusable class hierarchies, that originated in a classical object-oriented setting as an alternative to class-based inheritance. The above examples hint that the usual class inheritance would not scale that harmoniously to the mobile and distributed context.

3   MoMi: Mobile Mixin Calculus

In this section we present the kernel calculus MoMi, aiming at coordinating distributed and mobile processes that exchange object-oriented code and reuse it in several execution environments. Following motivations discussed in the previous section, object-oriented code is structured via mixins. The mixin-based component is integrated with a core distributed and mobile calculus, where we abstract a few main features for representing distribution, communication and mobility of processes. This way MoMi is intended to represent a general framework for integrating object-oriented features in several calculi for mobility, such as, e.g., KLAIM [12] and *DJoin* [16]. Before presenting our calculus we briefly recall the main features of the calculus of mixins of [6].

3.1   Object-Oriented Expressions

The object-oriented core of our language is based on the mixin calculus of [6], whose syntax is shown in Table 1. For the sake of clarity the syntax is slightly different from the one presented in [6], since some of its details are not necessary for our purposes. We recall here the features of the mixin calculus that are pertinent to MoMi.

The mixin calculus is fundamentally class-based and it takes a

Table 1. Syntax of the mixin core calculus.

$$
\begin{aligned}
exp ::= {}& x \mid \lambda x.exp \mid exp_1\ exp_2 \mid fix \\
\mid {}& \mathsf{ref}x \mid \mathsf{deref}x \mid x := exp \\
\mid {}& \{x_i = exp_i\}^{i \in I} \mid exp \Leftarrow x \mid \mathsf{new}\ exp \\
\mid {}& \mathsf{class}\langle exp_g, [m_i]^{i \in Meth}\rangle \\
\mid {}& \mathsf{mixin} \\
& \quad \mathsf{method}\ m_j = exp_{m_j};^{(j \in New)} \\
& \quad \mathsf{redefine}\ m_k = exp_{m_k};^{(k \in Redef)} \\
& \quad \mathsf{constructor}\ exp_c; \\
& \quad \mathsf{end} \\
\mid {}& exp_1 \diamond exp_2
\end{aligned}
$$

standard calculus of functions, records, and imperative features and adds new constructs to support classes and mixins. It relies on the Wright-Felleisen idea of *store* [29], called *heap* here, in order to evaluate imperative side effects. There are four expressions involving classes: class, mixin, ◇ (mixin application), and new. A class can be created by mixin application (via the ◇ operator), and objects (that are records) can be created by class instantiation (using new). Finally, we define the root of the class hierarchy, class *Object*, as a predefined class. The root class is necessary so that all other classes can be treated uniformly, as it is the only class that is not obtained as a result of mixin application.

Table 2. Two mixins.

let A =	let B =
mixin	mixin
method m_1 = ... n() ...	method n = ...
redefine m_2 = ... next() ...	method m_2 = ...
constructor c;	constructor d;
end	end

A mixin essentially is an abstract class that is parameterized over a super class. Let us consider the mixin A in Table 2. Each mixin consists of four parts: methods *defined* in the mixins, like m_1; *expected* methods, like n, that must be provided by the superclass, during the completion of the mixin; *redefined* methods, like m_2, where *next* can be used to access the implementation of m_2 in the superclass. a *constructor* that takes care of initializing the fields of the mixin (left implicit here).

If we now consider the mixin B in Table 2, then the application $A◇(B◇Object)$ will construct a class, which is a subclass of B, that can be instantiated and used:

let C = A ◇ (B ◇ *Object*) in (new C)⇐ m_1()

An example follows in Table 3, to show how mixins work in practice (the syntax is further simplified in the example). We define a mixin Encrypted that implements encryption functionality on top of any stream class. Note that the class to which the mixin is applied may have more methods than expected by the mixin. For example, Encrypted can be applied to Socket ◇ *Object*, even though Socket ◇ *Object* has other methods besides *read* and *write*.

Table 3. Example of mixin usage.

let FileStream =	let Socket =
mixin	mixin
method write = ...	method write = ...
method read = ...	method read = ...
...	method hostname = ...
end in	method portnumber = ...
	...
	end in
let Encrypted =	
mixin	
redefine write = ... next (encrypt(data, key));	
redefine read = ... decrypt(next (), key);	
constructor (key, arg) = ...	
end in ...	

From the definition of Encrypted, the type system of the mixin calculus infers the constraints that must be satisfied by any class to which Encrypted is applied. The class must contain *write* and *read* methods whose types must be supertypes of those given to *write* and *read*, respectively, in the definition of Encrypted.

To create an encrypted stream class, one must apply the Encrypted mixin to an existing stream class. For example, Encrypted ◇ FileStream ◇ *Object* is an encrypted file class. The power of mixins can be seen when we apply `Encrypted` to a family of different streams. For example, we can construct `Encrypted` ◇ `Socket` ◇ *Object*, which is a class that encrypts data communicated over a network. In addition to single inheritance, we can express many uses of multiple inheritance by applying more than one mixin to a class. For example, `PGPSign` ◇ `UUEncode` ◇ `Encrypt` ◇ `Compress` ◇ `FileStream` ◇ *Object* produces a class of files that are compressed, then encrypted, then uuencoded, then signed.

3.2 MoMi Syntax

We consider a very simple distributed calculus similar to CCS [22], enriched with localities. This is widely inspired by KLAIM [12], in the sense that physical nodes are explicitly denoted as localities. The calculus is higher-order in that processes can be exchanged as first-entity data, and since we are interested in mobility of code this is a meaningful choice.

A node is denoted by its locality, ℓ, and by the processes P running on it. Informally, the semantics of send(P, ℓ) is that of sending (the code of) process P to a process at locality ℓ waiting for it by means of a receive. This calculus is synchronous in that both sender and receiver are blocked until the communication occurs. However, switching to an asynchronous version would be straightforward.

The syntax of the MoMi calculus (Table 4) is obtained by combining this distributed calculus with the expressions of the mixin calculus: object-oriented expressions are seen as special processes. Process *exp* cannot be followed by any continuation process: this is a syntactic simplification that does not harm the expressive power, but it helps in having a simpler operational semantics (see Section 4). On the other hand, the construct let $x = exp$ in P, which can only occur as last action in a pro-

Table 4. MoMi Syntax (see Table 1 for *exp* syntax).

$P ::=$ **nil**	(null process)
$\mid a.P$	(action prefixing)
$\mid P_1 \mid P_2$	(parallel comp.)
$\mid X$	(process variable)
$\mid exp$	(OO expression)
$\mid$ let $x = exp$ in P	(let)
$a ::=$ send(P, ℓ)	(send)
$\mid$ receive$(id : \tau)$	(receive)
$N ::= \ell :: P$	(node)
$\mid N_1 \parallel N_2$	(net composition)

cess, allows to pass to the sub-process P the results of an object-oriented computation. The receive action specifies, together with the formal parameter name, the type of the expected actual parameter. In Section 5 a type system is introduced in order to assign a type to each well-behaved process. Only the free identifiers that are arguments of receives are explicitly typed by the programmer. In the processes receive$(id : \tau).P$ and let $x = exp$ in P, receive and let act as binders for, respectively, *id* and x in the process P.

3.3 Mixin Mobility in Action

We present in the following two simple examples showing mobility of mixins in action. They represent a *remote evaluation* and a *code-on-demand* [11] situation, respectively. Let us observe that both situations can be seen as examples of mobile agents as well. A more complex example is presented in Section 6.

Example 1. Let **agent** represent the type of a mixin defining a mobile agent that has to print some data by using the local printer on any remote site where it is shipped for execution. Obviously, since the *print* operation highly depends on the execution site (even only because of the printer drivers), it is sensible to leave such method to be defined. The mixin can be applied, on the remote site, to a local class *printer* which will provide the specific implementation of the *print* method in the following way:

$$\ell_1 :: \ldots | \text{ send}(my\_agent, \ell_2) \|$$
$$\ell_2 :: \ldots | \text{ receive}(mob\_agent : \textbf{agent}).$$
$$\text{let } PrinterAgent = mob\_agent \diamond printer \diamond Object \text{ in}$$
$$(\text{new } PrinterAgent) \Leftarrow start()$$

Example 2. Let **agent** be a class defining a mobile agent that has to access the file system of a remote site. If the remote site wants to execute this agent while restricting the access to its own file system, it can locally define a mixin *restricted*, redefining the methods accessing the file system according to specific restrictions. Then the arriving agent can be composed with the local mixin in the following way.

$$\ell_1 :: \ldots | \text{ send}(my\_agent, \ell_2) \|$$
$$\ell_2 :: \ldots | \text{ receive}(mob\_agent : \textbf{agent}).$$
$$\text{let } RestrictedAgent = restricted \diamond mob\_agent \diamond Object \text{ in}$$
$$(\text{new } RestrictedAgent) \Leftarrow start()$$

This example can also be seen as an implementation of a "sandbox".

The above examples highlight how an object-oriented expression (mob_agent) can be used by the receiver site both as a mixin (Example 1) and as a base class[1] (Example 2). Indeed, without any change to the code of the examples, one could also dynamically construct a class such as **restricted** $\diamond$ **mob_agent** $\diamond$ **printer** $\diamond$ *Object*. It is important to remark that in these examples we assume that the code sent (argument of **send**) and the code expected (argument of **receive**) are "compatible". This will be guaranteed by the type matching of the actual parameter and of the formal one in the communication rule (see Table 6).

4   Operational Semantics

The operational semantics of the MoMi calculus is centered around the distributed calculus, that allows distributed processes to communicate and exchange data (i.e. processes) by means of **send** and **receive**. The semantics of the object-oriented expressions is omitted here since it is basically the same of the one presented in [6]. The reduction of an *exp* is denoted by $\rightarrow$ (its closure is $\twoheadrightarrow$) and will produce an *answer* of the form $h.v$, where h is the heap obtained by evaluating the side effects present in *exp*, and v is the value obtained by evaluating *exp*.

---

[1] Every mixin can be formally made into a class by applying it to the empty top class *Object*, as explained before.

Table 5. Congruence laws

$$N_1 \parallel N_2 = N_2 \parallel N_1$$
$$(N_1 \parallel N_2) \parallel N_3 = N_1 \parallel (N_2 \parallel N_3)$$
$$\ell :: P = \ell :: P \mid \mathbf{nil}$$
$$\ell :: (P_1 \mid P_2) = \ell :: P_1 \parallel \ell :: P_2$$

The semantics for MoMi's distributed part is based on structural congruence and reduction relations. Reduction represents individual computation steps, and is defined in terms of structural congruence. The structural congruence $\equiv$ (defined as the least congruence relation closed under the rules in Table 5) allows the rearrangement of the syntactic structure of a term so that reduction rules may be applied.

Reduction rules are displayed in Table 6. The crucial rule is (*comm*) that allows to communicate code among different sites. Code exchanged during a communication is a process that is not evaluated, and this is consistent with the higher-order nature of send and receive. The substitution $Q[P/id]$ is to be considered as a *name-capture-avoid substitution* (and so will be all substitutions from now on).

Table 6. Distributed operational semantics

$$\dfrac{\vdash \tau_1 <: \tau_2}{N \parallel \ell_1 :: \mathsf{send}(P^{\tau_1}, \ell_2).P' \parallel \ell_2 :: \mathsf{receive}(id : \tau_2).Q \rightarrowtail N \parallel \ell_1 :: P' \parallel \ell_2 :: Q[P^{\tau_1}/id]} \quad (comm)$$

$$\dfrac{exp \twoheadrightarrow h.v}{N \parallel \ell :: exp \rightarrowtail N \parallel \ell :: \mathbf{nil}} \quad (atom)$$

$$\dfrac{exp \twoheadrightarrow h.v}{N \parallel \ell :: \mathsf{let}\ x = exp\ \mathsf{in}\ P \rightarrowtail N \parallel \ell :: P[h.v/x]} \quad (let)$$

$$\dfrac{N \equiv N_1 \quad N_1 \rightarrowtail N_2 \quad N_2 \equiv N'}{N \rightarrowtail N'} \quad (net)$$

The key idea of this rule relies on the dynamic checking of the type of the actual parameter in order to guarantee a safe communication of code. Namely, the argument of a send is a process P annotated with its type τ_1, which is produced by the static analysis of process P[2]. In Section 5 we will present a type system that allows to check whether a process is typeable, so that only well-typed processes will be evaluated. Moreover, this static type analysis is assumed to produce an annotated version of the process to be evaluated, where every send's argument is annotated with its type. The (*comm*) rule uses this type information, delivered together with P, in order to dynamically check that the received item P is compliant with the formal argument (of type τ_2) by subtyping (as shown in Section 5.2). Conversely, the type τ_2 has been previously used to statically type check the continuation Q, on site ℓ_2, where id is possibly used. We would like to stress that, except for the dynamic checking required during the communication, type analysis of processes is totally static and performed in each site independently. Thus type safety of the communication results from

---

[2] Similarly, Java bytecode contains type information, used both by the classloader and the bytecode verifier.

the (static) type soundness of local and mobile code, with no need of further re-compilation and type-checking.

Finally, we require that a process, in order to be executed on a site, must be closed (i.e. without free variables), so it must be well-typed under $\Gamma = \emptyset$. It is easy to verify that if a process P is closed, for any $\mathsf{send}(P', \ell)$ occurring in P, the free variables of P' are bound by an outer let or by an outer $\mathsf{receive}$. This implies that exchanged code is closed, as expected, when a send is executed.

Any time an *exp* is met (rules (*exp*) and (*let*)), this is reduced under the rules of the operational semantics of the mixin calculus. The rule for evaluating (*let*) says that *exp* is evaluated and then the resulting value is replaced for x in P. As a consequence, one can use the let construct to send evaluated code. In this case the code will be implicitly delivered together with its heap (containing the results of evaluating the side effects present in *exp*), according to reduction rules for object-oriented expressions as defined in [6] (see Section 3.1). Thus, all the heap references will be known also at the destination site. This is typical of mobile code and mobile agent systems, where the state is transmitted together with the code. Rule (*net*) is standard for the evolution of nets.

5 Typing

In this section we present the type system for the MoMi calculus. At this stage we are not interested in typing processes in details, so a process starting with an action will simply have the constant type action. A process like $\mathsf{receive}(X : \mathsf{action}).X$ means that it is willing to receive any process starting with an action and to execute it.

5.1 Type Rules

We extend the type assignment system of [6] with rules to type processes. Here we concentrate on the typing of processes, classes and mixins.

Type syntax is defined in Table 7, where ι is a constant type; $\to$ is the functional type operator; τ ref is the type of locations containing a value of type τ; $\{x_i : \tau_i\}^{i \in I}$ is a record type; and $I, J, K \subset \mathbb{N}$. A class type, $\mathsf{class}\langle \gamma, \sigma \rangle$ includes the type γ of the argument

Table 7. Syntax of types.

$$\tau ::= \iota \mid \tau_1 \to \tau_2 \mid \tau \text{ ref} \mid \{x_i : \tau_i\}^{i \in I}$$
$$\mid \mathsf{class}\langle \gamma, \sigma \rangle$$
$$\mid \mathsf{mixin}\langle \gamma_b, \gamma_d, \sigma_{exp}, \sigma_{old}, \sigma_{new}, \sigma_{red} \rangle$$
$$\mid \mathsf{action}$$

of the class generator, and the type σ of *self*, consisting of a record type $\{m_i : \tau_{m_i}\}^{i \in I}$. In class and mixin types, γ_- is the type of the argument of a generator, and σ_- is a record type. action is the above mentioned special constant type.

Table 8 illustrates the shape of mixin types. Notice that mixin methods make typing assumptions about methods of the superclass to which the mixin will be applied. We refer to these types as *expected* types since the actual superclass methods may have different types. The exact relationship between the types expected by the mixin and the actual types of the superclass methods is formalized below in the rule for mixin application. We mark types that come from the *superclass* with ↑ and those that will be redefined or added in the *mixin* (which acts as the subclass) with ↓.

Table 8. The mixin type.

$$\text{mixin}\langle \gamma_b, \gamma_d, \sigma_{exp}, \sigma_{old}, \sigma_{new}, \sigma_{red}\rangle$$

$$\text{where} \quad \begin{aligned} &\sigma_{exp} = \{m_i : \tau_{m_i}^{\uparrow}\}^{i\in I}, \sigma_{old} = \{m_k : \tau_{m_k}^{\uparrow}\}^{k\in K}, \\ &\sigma_{new} = \{m_j : \tau_{m_j}^{\downarrow}\}^{j\in J}, \sigma_{red} = \{m_k : \tau_{m_k}^{\downarrow}\}^{k\in K} \\ &m_i, \tau_{m_i}^{\uparrow}, \tau_{m_k}^{\uparrow} \text{ are inferred from method bodies} \end{aligned}$$

Both new and redefined methods in the mixin may call superclass methods (i.e. methods that are expected to be supported by any class to which the mixin will be applied). We refer to these methods as m_i. Their types $\tau_{m_i}^{\uparrow}$ are inferred from the mixin definition. The mixin type encodes the following information about the mixin:

- γ_b is the expected argument type of the superclass generator.
- γ_d is the argument type of the mixin generator.
- $\sigma_{exp} = \{m_i : \tau_{m_i}^{\uparrow}\}^{i\in I}$, $\sigma_{old} = \{m_k : \tau_{m_k}^{\uparrow}\}^{k\in K}$ are the expected types of the methods that must be supported by any class to which the mixin is applied. m_i are the methods that are not redefined by the mixin but still expected to be supported by the superclass since they are called by other mixin methods, and $\tau_{m_k}^{\uparrow}$ are the types assumed for the old bodies of the methods redefined in the mixin.
- $\sigma_{new} = \{m_j : \tau_{m_j}^{\downarrow}\}^{j\in J}$, $\sigma_{red} = \{m_k : \tau_{m_k}^{\downarrow}\}^{k\in K}$ are the types of mixin methods (new and redefined, respectively).

For further details we refer the reader to [6]. The type system of the calculus of mixins is extended with rules in Table 9. The rule (*send*) basically states that a process performing a send is well-typed if both its argument and the continuation are well typed. For typing a process performing a receive we type the continuation with the information about the type of *id* (rule (*receive*)). The form for rule (*let*) is standard (first the type of the *exp* is inferred and then P is typed considering this information). For parallel composition (rule (*comp*)) we require that both processes have the same type[3].

Table 9. Type rules for processes.

$$\frac{}{\Gamma, id:\tau \vdash id:\tau} \; (proj)$$

$$\frac{\Gamma \vdash P : \tau \quad \Gamma \vdash P' : \tau'}{\Gamma \vdash \text{send}(P, \ell).P' : \text{action}} \; (send) \qquad \frac{\Gamma, id:\tau \vdash P : \tau'}{\Gamma \vdash \text{receive}(id : \tau).P : \text{action}} \; (receive)$$

$$\frac{\Gamma \vdash P_1 : \text{action} \quad \Gamma \vdash P_2 : \text{action}}{\Gamma \vdash (P_1 \mid P_2) : \text{action}} \; (comp) \qquad \frac{\Gamma \vdash exp : \tau \quad \Gamma, x:\tau \vdash P : \tau'}{\Gamma \vdash \text{let } x = exp \text{ in } P : \tau'} \; (let)$$

---

[3] At this stage, it is meaningful to consider only parallel composition of processes that perform actions, so we require both P_1 and P_2 to have an action type.

In order to facilitate the understanding of the type system of the MoMI calculus, we report in Table 10 the type rule for mixin application, taken from [6].

Table 10. Rule for mixin application.

$$
\frac{
\begin{array}{l}
\Gamma \vdash exp_1 : \mathsf{mixin}\langle \gamma_b, \gamma_d, \sigma_{exp}, \sigma_{old}, \sigma_{new}, \sigma_{red} \rangle \\
\Gamma \vdash exp_2 : \mathsf{class}\langle \gamma_c, \sigma_b \rangle \\
\Gamma \vdash \sigma_d <: \sigma_b <: (\sigma_{exp} \cup \sigma_{old}) \\
\Gamma \vdash \gamma_b <: \gamma_c
\end{array}
}{
\Gamma \vdash exp_1 \diamond exp_2 : \mathsf{class}\langle \gamma_d, \sigma_d \rangle
} \ (mixin\ app)
$$

$$
\text{where} \quad
\begin{array}{ll}
\sigma_{exp} = \{m_i : \tau_{m_i}^\uparrow\}, & \sigma_{old} = \{m_k : \tau_{m_k}^\uparrow\} \\
\sigma_{new} = \{m_j : \tau_{m_j}^\downarrow\}, & \sigma_{red} = \{m_k : \tau_{m_k}^\downarrow\} \\
\sigma_b = \{m_k : \tau_{m_k}, m_i : \tau_{m_i}, m_l : \tau_{m_l}\} \\
\sigma_d = \{m_i : \tau_{m_i}, m_l : \tau_{m_l}, m_j : \tau_{m_j}^\downarrow, m_k : \tau_{m_k}^\downarrow\}
\end{array}
$$

In the rule definition, σ_b contains the type signatures of all methods supported by the superclass to which the mixin is applied. In particular, m_k are the superclass methods redefined by the mixin, m_i are the superclass methods called by the mixin methods but not redefined, and m_l are the superclass methods not mentioned in the mixin definition at all. Note that the superclass may have more methods than required by the mixin constraint.

Type σ_d contains the signatures of all methods supported by the subclass created as a result of mixin application. Methods $m_{i,l}$ are inherited directly from the superclass, methods m_k are redefined by the mixin, and methods m_j are the new methods added by the mixin. We are guaranteed that methods m_j are not present in the superclass by the construction of σ_b and σ_d: σ_d is defined so that it contains all the labels of σ_b plus labels m_j.

The premises of the rule are as follows:

– The $\sigma_d <: \sigma_b$ constraint requires that the types of the methods redefined by the mixin (m_k) be subtypes of the superclass methods with the same name. This ensures that all calls to the redefined methods in m_i and m_l (methods inherited intact from the superclass) are type-safe.
– The $\sigma_b <: (\sigma_{exp} \cup \sigma_{old})$ constraint requires that the actual types of the superclass methods m_i and m_k be subtypes of the expected types assumed when typing the mixin definition.
– The $\gamma_b <: \gamma_c$ constraint requires that the actual argument type of the superclass generator be a supertype of the type assumed when typing the mixin definition. Since class generators are functions, their argument types are in contravariant position, so this justifies the supertype requirement.

In the type of the class created as a result of mixin application, γ_d is the argument type of the generator, and σ_d (see above) is the type of objects that will be instantiated from the class.

Finally, let us remark that rules of Tables 9 and 10 are syntax-driven, so they can define an algorithm for deciding whether a given process P, on a site

ℓ, is typeable. In particular, since we require P to be closed, then typability of P means that $\emptyset \vdash P : \tau$, where each subterm of P is assigned a type (even when τ is action). Thus the reconstruction of the deduction $\emptyset \vdash P : \tau$ allows to statically decorate any send's argument, occurring in P, by its type, as required by (*comm*) rule in the semantics (Table 6). For instance, let $x = exp$ in $send(x, \ell)$ has type action, and its compiled version is let $x = exp$ in $send(x^{\tau_1}, \ell)$ if exp has type τ_1.

5.2   Subtyping Relation

The main novelty of the MoMi type system is the extension of the subtyping relation to class and mixin types. In [6], subtyping exists only at the object level, to keep the inheritance and the subtyping hierarchies completely separated. Here, the key idea is to deal with classes and mixins as polymorphic entities that are exchanged among distributed sites. So we extend the subtyping relation to classes and mixins, in order to achieve more flexibility in the communication. Observe that, from the formal point of view, we have chosen to use subtyping in type matching at communication time, instead of explicitly define a *subsumption* rule in the type system. Namely, any term of type τ is implicitly assumed to have also any type greater than τ. So, in particular, in the rule (*comm*), the formal parameter of a *receive*, which is explicitly typed, matches with any received item whose type is a subtype of the one expected.

The starting point is the basic system of subtyping for arrow and ref types and other standard subtyping rules (they can be found in [6]). Concerning record types, we use the standard width subtyping. This is not a crucial simplification[4] with respect to the more complete width-depth subtyping, which would require more technicalities to be dealt with, technicalities that are not within the purpose of this paper. Width-depth subtyping on records is introduced in a forthcoming foundational work on MoMi's type system.

The subtype relation concerning mixins and classes is in Table 11. In the rule ($<:$ *mixin*) the subtype can define more new methods and require less methods, but it cannot override more methods ($|\sigma|$ is the number of methods in σ); the contravariance of the mixin (subclass) generator parameter is as expected ($\gamma_d <: \gamma'_d$), while for the superclass generator parameter covariance is required ($\gamma'_b <: \gamma_b$).

Table 11. Subtype relation for classes and mixins.

$$\frac{\Gamma \vdash \gamma <: \gamma' \quad \Gamma \vdash \sigma' <: \sigma}{\Gamma \vdash class\langle\gamma', \sigma'\rangle <: class\langle\gamma, \sigma\rangle} \quad (<: \ class)$$

$$\frac{\Gamma \vdash \sigma'_{new} <: \sigma_{new} \quad |\sigma'_{red}| = |\sigma_{red}| \quad \Gamma \vdash \sigma'_{red} <: \sigma_{red}}{\Gamma \vdash \sigma_{exp} <: \sigma'_{exp} \quad |\sigma_{old}| = |\sigma'_{old}| \quad \Gamma \vdash \sigma_{old} <: \sigma'_{old}} \\ \frac{\Gamma \vdash \gamma'_b <: \gamma_b \qquad \Gamma \vdash \gamma_d <: \gamma'_d}{\Gamma \vdash mixin\langle\gamma'_b, \gamma'_d, \sigma'_{exp}, \sigma'_{old}, \sigma'_{new}, \sigma'_{red}\rangle <: mixin\langle\gamma_b, \gamma_d, \sigma_{exp}, \sigma_{old}, \sigma_{new}, \sigma_{red}\rangle} \quad (<: \ mixin)$$

---

[4] This is typical, for instance, of popular languages such as C++ and Java.

The new subtype relation on mixins is consistent with <: constraints of the rule for mixin application (Table 10); thus the type system guarantees that what is statically type-checked on a site can be communicated to a different site without producing run-time errors when executed, as long as the above constraints are respected. Conversely, local code remains well typed even when remote code is merged in it, via a well typed communication. Thus, polymorphism by subtyping for classes and mixins guarantees type-safe communications, in the sense that errors like "message-not-understood" cannot occur, without requiring to type check neither the whole system nor the local code again.

6   A Scenario for Mixin Mobility

We will use here a slightly simplified syntax: (i) we will list the methods' parameters in between "()" instead of using explicit λ-abstractions; (ii) $exp_1; exp_2$ is interpreted as $(\lambda x. exp_2) exp_1$, $x \notin FV(exp_2)$, in a call-by-value semantics.

The example is about a client and a server, executing on two different nodes, that want to communicate, e.g., by means of a common protocol. They both use a *Socket* to this aim, however the server is willing to abstract from the implementation of such socket, by allowing the client to provide a custom implementation. This can be useful, for instance, because the client may decide to use a customized socket; in this example the client implements a socket that sends and receives compressed data (alternatively it could implement a *multicast* socket, or even a combination of the two). However, the code sent by the client may rely on some low-level system calls, that may be different on the server's site: indeed, the two sites may run different operating systems and have different architectures. These low-level system calls are then to be provided by each site (the client's and the server's sites). The customized socket of the client is then a mixin requiring the existence of such system calls, that will be provided by two different (yet compliant) superclasses, one resident on each site. The code executed in the two nodes (client and server) is in Listing 1.

Both ZipSocket and Socket rely on a superclass that provides (at least) methods write_to_net and read_from_net. The client, in its site, completes its mixin ZipSocket with NetChannel that provides these two methods for writing data on the net, by using its operating system low-level system calls. Sending the class ZipSocket ◇ NetChannel directly to the server may be nonsense, since the server may use a different operating system (or a different version of the same operating system). Instead, only the mixin ZipSocket is sent to the remote server. In the server this mixin will be received as a Socket mixin (and this succeeds since ZipSocket <: Socket) and it will be completed with NetFile, which corresponds to the NetChannel of the client. The server will then use such socket independently from the particular client's implementation. Notice that the use of subtyping in the communication (instead of a simpler type equality) completely relieves the receiver (and especially its programmer) from the real complete interface of the clients' code.

Let us now consider an alternative implementation of the same scenario, in order to show other features of MoMi: suppose that on the client ZipSocket is written like in Listing 2 on the left. In this case the class does not rely on write_to_net and read_from_net (instead it expects the superclass to provide

```
client:: let ZipSocket =                         server:: let Socket =
  mixin                                            mixin
    method zip = ...                                 method write = write to net(data)
    method unzip = ...                               method read  = read from net()
    method write = write to net(zip(data))         end in
    method read  = unzip(read from net())        let NetFile =
  end in                                           mixin
let NetChannel =                                     method write to net =
  mixin                                               // <send through the net>
    method send =                                   method read from net =
      // <send through the net>                       // <receive from the net>
    method receive =                                end in
      // <receive from the net>                   (
    method write to net = send(data)                receive( sock : Socket ).
    method read from net = receive()                let client channel = ref new
  end in                                             (sock ◊ (NetFile ◊ Object)) in
let channel = ref new                              (
  (ZipSocket ◊ (NetChannel ◊ Object)) in            (deref client channel)⇐read() ;
(                                                    (deref client channel)⇐write("welcome")
  send( ZipSocket, server ).                       )
  ( (deref channel)⇐write("hello") ;             )
    (deref channel)⇐read() )
)
```

Listing 1: Example code for client and server communication.

methods `write` and `read` that the mixin redefines), and thus it is not a subtype of `Socket` in the server. In the server, the code would be like in Listing 2 on the right. Since also `Channel` relies on a super class that provides `write` and `read`, we have that `ZipSocket` <: `Channel`. So the server receives a `ZipSocket` (as a `Channel`) that it completes with `Socket` completed, in turn, with `NetFile`.

```
                                                 Channel =
                                                   mixin
                                                     redefine write = next(data)
                                                     redefine read  = next()
ZipSocket =                                        end
  mixin                                            ...
    method zip = ...                             receive( chan : Channel ).
    method unzip = ...                           let client channel =
    redefine write = next(zip(data))               ref new (chan ◊
    redefine read  = unzip(next())                   (Socket ◊ (NetFile ◊ Object))) in
  end                                            (
                                                   (deref client channel)⇐read() ;
                                                   (deref client channel)⇐write("welcome")
                                                 )
```

Listing 2: An alternative implementation.

Finally, as hinted in Section 3.1, other implementations of such a socket can be created, simply by using more than one mixin, such as `UUEncode`, `Encrypt`, and so on.

7 Conclusions and Related Work

In the literature, there are several proposals of combining objects with processes and/or mobile agents. *Obliq* [9] is a lexically-scoped language providing distributed object-oriented computation. Mobile code maintains network references and provides transparent access to remote resources. In [8], a general model for integrating object-oriented features in calculi of mobile agents is presented: agents are extended with method definitions and constructs for remote method invocations. Other works, such as, e.g., [5,24,18] do not deal explicitly with mobile distributed code. In our calculus no remote method call functionality is considered, and, instead of formalizing remote procedure calls (like most of the above mentioned approaches), MoMI provides the introduction of safe and scalable distribution of object-oriented code, in a calculus where communication and coordination facilities are already provided.

MoMI results from the integration of two calculi, a simple coordination language for mobile code and the mixin calculus of [6]. Since it looks like in MoMI the two core calculi cooperate quite smoothly, this gives us some confidence about the modularity of this approach, so this is meant as a first step towards a general framework to experiment the mixin-based approach also with other different mobile calculi, such as the *DJoin* [16], the Ambient Calculus [10], and in particular KLAIM [12]. The type system of MoMI is currently being extended and completely formalized in order to prove main properties such as subject-reduction and type safety.

We are also designing a mixin-oriented version of KLAIM (and we are planning to extend its implementation, X-KLAIM [3], along the same line). The type system presented in this paper can be modified in order to refine action types, so that finer types can be assigned to processes, e.g. according to the capability-based type system for access control developed for KLAIM [13].

Acknowledgments. We thank Rocco De Nicola and the anonymous referees for helpful suggestions. We are very grateful to Luca Cardelli for pointing out crucial questions in the early version of the paper.

References

1. M. Abadi and L. Cardelli. *A Theory of Objects*. Springer, 1996.
2. K. Arnold, J. Gosling, and D. Holmes. *The Java Programming Language*. Addison-Wesley, 3rd edition, 2000.
3. L. Bettini, R. De Nicola, G. Ferrari, and R. Pugliese. Interactive Mobile Agents in X-KLAIM. In P. Ciancarini and R. Tolksdorf, editors, *Proc. of the 7th Int. IEEE Workshops on Enabling Technologies: Infrastructure for Collaborative Enterprises (WETICE)*, pages 110–115. IEEE Computer Society Press, 1998.
4. L. Bettini, M. Loreti, and B. Venneri. On Multiple Inheritance in Java. In *Proc. of TOOLS EASTERN EUROPE, Emerging Technologies, Emerging Markets*, 2002. To appear.
5. P. D. Blasio and K. Fisher. A Calculus for Concurrent Objects. In U. Montanari and V. Sassone, editors, *CONCUR '96: Concurrency Theory, 7th Int. Conf.*, volume 1119 of *LNCS*, pages 655–670. Springer, 1996.
6. V. Bono, A. Patel, and V. Shmatikov. A Core Calculus of Classes and Mixins. In R. Guerraoui, editor, *Proceedings ECOOP'99*, number 1628 in LCNS, pages 43–66. Springer-Verlag, 1999.
7. G. Bracha and W. Cook. Mixin-based inheritance. In *Proc. OOPSLA '90*, pages 303–311, 1990.
8. M. Bugliesi and G. Castagna. Mobile Objects. In *Proc. of FOOL*, 2000.

9. L. Cardelli. A Language with Distributed Scope. *Computing Systems*, 8(1):27–59, 1995.
10. L. Cardelli and A. Gordon. Mobile ambients. In *Foundations of Software Science and Computation Structures (FoSSaCS'98)*, number 1378 in LNCS, pages 140–155. Springer, 1998.
11. A. Carzaniga, G. Picco, and G. Vigna. Designing Distributed Applications with Mobile Code Paradigms. In R. Taylor, editor, *Proc. of the 19th Int. Conf. on Software Engineering (ICSE '97)*, pages 22–33. ACM Press, 1997.
12. R. De Nicola, G. Ferrari, and R. Pugliese. KLAIM: a Kernel Language for Agents Interaction and Mobility. *IEEE Transactions on Software Engineering*, 24(5):315–330, 1998.
13. R. De Nicola, G. Ferrari, R. Pugliese, and B. Venneri. Types for Access Control. *Theoretical Computer Science*, 240(1):215–254, 2000.
14. R. Findler and M. Flatt. Modular object-oriented programming with units and mixins. In *Proc. ICFP '98*, pages 94–104, 1998.
15. M. Flatt, S. Krishnamurthi, and M. Felleisen. Classes and mixins. In *Proc. POPL '98*, pages 171–183, 1998.
16. C. Fournet, G. Gonthier, J. J. Levy, L. Maranget, and D. Remy. A Calculus of Mobile Agents. In U. Montanari and V. Sassone, editors, *Proc. of 7th Int. Conf. on Concurrency Theory (CONCUR'96)*, volume 1119 of *LNCS*, pages 406–421. Springer-Verlag, 1996.
17. E. Gamma, R. Helm, R. Johnson, and J. Vlissides. *Design Patterns: Elements of Reusable Object-Oriented Software*. Addison-Wesley, 1995.
18. A. D. Gordon and P. D. Hankin. A Concurrent Object Calculus: Reduction and Typing. In U. Nestmann and B. C. Pierce, editors, *Proc. of HLCL '98: High-Level Concurrent Languages*, volume 16.3 of *ENTCS*. Elsevier, 1998.
19. C. Harrison, D. Chess, and A. Kershenbaum. Mobile agents: Are they a good idea? Research Report 19887, IBM Research Division, 1994.
20. F. Knabe. An overview of mobile agent programming. In *Proceedings of the Fifth LOMAPS workshop on Analysis and Verification of Multiple - Agent Languages*, number 1192 in LNCS. Springer-Verlag, 1996.
21. M. V. Limberghen and T. Mens. Encapsulation and composition as orthogonal operators on mixins: a solution to multiple inheritance problems. *Object Oriented Systems*, 3(1):1–30, 1996.
22. R. Milner. *Communication and Concurrency*. Prentice Hall, 1989.
23. Object Management Group. Corba: Architecture and specification. http://www.omg.org, 1998.
24. B. C. Pierce and D. N. Turner. Concurrent Objects in a Process Calculus. In T. Ito and A. Yonezawa, editors, *Proc. Theory and Practice of Parallel Programming (TPPP 94)*, volume 907 of *LNCS*, pages 187–215. Springer, 1995.
25. Y. Smaragdakis and D. Batory. Implementing layered designs with mixin layers. In *Proc. ECOOP '98*, pages 550–570, 1998.
26. T. Thorn. Programming Languages for Mobile Code. *ACM Computing Surveys*, 29(3):213–239, 1997. Also Technical Report 1083, University of Rennes IRISA.
27. M. VanHilst and D. Notkin. Using role components to implement collaboration-based designs. In *Proc. OOPSLA '96*, pages 359–369, 1996.
28. J. E. White. Mobile Agents. In J. Bradshaw, editor, *Software Agents*. AAAI Press and MIT Press, 1996.
29. A. Wright and M. Felleisen. A syntactic approach to type soundness. *Information and Computation*, 115(1):38–94, 1994.

Formalizing Properties of Mobile Agent Systems*

Lorenzo Bettini, Rocco De Nicola, and Michele Loreti

Dipartimento di Sistemi e Informatica, Università di Firenze
{bettini,denicola,loreti}@dsi.unifi.it

Abstract. The wide-spreading of Internet has stimulated the introduction of new programming paradigms and languages that model interactions among hosts by means of mobile agents, and that are centered
around the notions of location awareness. In this paper we show how to
use formal tools, specifically a modal logic, for formalizing properties for
mobile agent systems. We concentrate on one of these new languages,
KLAIM, and we use it to specify a system that permits maintaining the
software installed on several heterogeneous computers distributed over a
network by taking advantage of the mobile agent paradigm.

1 Introduction

The diffusion of Internet has called for new programming paradigms and languages to model interactions among hosts by means of *mobile code* [24,8]. Mobile
code is software that can be sent to remote sites and executed on arrival. A particular example of mobile code is represented by *mobile agents* [15,13,26]; these
are programs that can migrate to different sites. Mobile agents have been advertised as an emerging technology/paradigm that provides means to design and
maintain distributed systems more easily [16].

For this class of programs, like for other formalisms, it is crucial to have
tools for establishing key properties like deadlock freeness, liveness and correctness with respect to given specifications. However for network aware programs
it is also appealing to establish other important properties like resource allocation, access to resources, information disclosure. Formal tools for expressing and
proving the above mentioned properties are definitely needed.

In this paper, we describe how to prove properties of a system of mobile
agents that permits maintaining the software installed on several heterogeneous
computers distributed over a network. The applications are installed and updated only on the central server; clients download the applications from the
server, and install them locally on their computers. When a new release of an
application is installed on the server, some agents are scattered along the network

---

* This work has been partially supported by EU within the FET – Global Computing initiative, project AGILE IST-2001-32747 and by MIUR project NAPOLI. The
funding bodies are not responsible for any use that might be made of the results
presented here.

to update the application on the clients. In particular we will use the language KLAIM (*Kernel Language for Agent Interaction and Mobility*) [9] for specifying such system; We then formally specify some properties of the system through a modal logic designed for our language.

In [2] we show a prototype implementation of this distributed update system in X-KLAIM (a programming language that implements KLAIM's features) and we investigate such system from the design point of view, emphasizing the features of the mobile agent paradigm that enable an easy development and management of a distributed computer networks. Here we are interested in the formalization of distributed applications that use mobile agents; the system for software update of [2] turns out to be a good starting point for this aim: it employs mobile agents, in a distributed context, that use some specific communication protocols in order to perform their tasks.

The rest of the paper is organized as follows: Section 2 briefly introduces KLAIM, Section 3 describes the system for software maintenance via mobile agents and a possible implementation in KLAIM. In Section 4 the logic for KLAIM is presented and in Section 5 we describe some properties of the system through our modal logic. Section 6 concludes the paper.

2   The Language KLAIM

KLAIM[1] (*Kernel Language for Agent Interaction and Mobility*), is inspired by the Linda coordination model [12,7], hence it relies on the concept of *tuple space*. A tuple space is a multiset of *tuples*; these are containers of information items (called *fields*). There can be *actual fields* (i.e. expressions, processes, localities, constants, identifiers) and *formal fields* (i.e. variables). Syntactically, a formal field is denoted with !*ide*, where *ide* is an identifier.

Pattern-matching is used to select tuples in a tuple space: two tuples match if they have the same number of fields and corresponding fields match: a formal field matches any value of the same type, and two actual fields match only if they are identical (but two formals never match). For instance, tuple ("foo", "bar", 100 + 200) matches with ("foo", "bar", !*Val*). After matching, the variable of a formal field gets the value of the matched field: in the previous example, after matching, *Val* (an integer variable) will contain the integer value 300.

In Linda there is only one global shared tuple space; KLAIM extends Linda by handling multiple distributed tuple spaces. Tuple spaces are placed on *nodes* that are part of a *net*. Each node contains a single tuple space and processes in execution; a node can be accessed through its *address*. There are two kinds of addresses: *Physical localities* (also called *sites*) are the identifiers through which nodes can be uniquely identified within a net; *Logical localities* are symbolic names for nodes. A reserved logical locality, self, can be used by processes to refer to their execution node. Physical localities have an absolute meaning and can be thought of as IP addresses, while logical localities have a relative

---

[1] The requirements and the design philosophy of the language are presented in [9]; an implementation of KLAIM, X-KLAIM, is described in [1].

meaning depending on the node where they are interpreted; they can be thought of as aliases for network resources. Logical localities are associated to physical localities through *allocation environments*, represented as partial functions. Each node has its own environment that, in particular, associates self to the site of the node.

The syntax of KLAIM processes is reported in Table 1. In the rest of this section we will briefly comment upon this (we refer the interested reader to [9] for a detailed description of the language). In particular, hereafter, we will use the following syntactic categories:

- s is a physical locality,
- l is a logical locality,
- u is a locality variable,
- x is a value variable,
- e is a value expression (built up from values and value variables, by using a set of operators, not shown here),
- A is a parameterized process identifier; parameters can be of three different types: process, locality and value,
- X is a process variable,
- ℓ will denote both localities and locality variables,
- et is an evaluated tuple,
- $\widetilde{\cdot}$ represents a sequence of elements.

Table 1. KLAIM Process Syntax

$$
\begin{array}{lll}
P ::= & \mathbf{nil} & \text{(null process)} \\
& |\ act.P & \text{(action prefixing)} \\
& |\ P_1 \mid P_2 & \text{(parallel composition)} \\
& |\ P_1 + P_2 & \text{(nondet. choice)} \\
& |\ X & \text{(process variable)} \\
& |\ A\langle \widetilde{P}, \widetilde{\ell}, \widetilde{e}\rangle & \text{(process invocation)} \\
act ::= & \mathbf{out}(t)@\ell \mid \mathbf{in}(t)@\ell \mid \mathbf{read}(t)@\ell \mid \mathbf{eval}(P)@\ell \mid \mathbf{newloc}(u) \\
t ::= & f \mid f,t \\
f ::= & e \mid P \mid \ell \mid !x \mid !X \mid !u
\end{array}
$$

KLAIM processes may run concurrently, both at the same node or at different nodes, and can perform five basic operations over nodes. $\mathbf{in}(t)@\ell$ evaluates the tuple t and looks for a matching tuple t' in the tuple space located at ℓ. Whenever the matching tuple t' is found, it is removed from the tuple space. The corresponding values of t' are then assigned to the formal fields of t and the operation terminates. If no matching tuple is found, the operation is suspended until one is available. **read**$(t)@\ell$ differs from **in**$(t)@\ell$ only because the tuple t', selected by pattern-matching, is not removed from the tuple space located at ℓ. **out**$(t)@\ell$ adds the tuple resulting from the evaluation of t to the tuple space located at ℓ. **eval**$(P)@\ell$ spawns process P for execution at node ℓ. **newloc**(u) creates a new node in the net and binds its site to u. The node can be considered a "private" node that can be accessed by the other nodes only if the creator communicates the value of variable u, which is the only means to access the fresh node.

KLAIM is higher order in that processes can be exchanged as primary class data. While **eval**$(P)@\ell$ spawns a process for (remote) evaluation at ℓ, processes sent with an **out** have to be explicitly retrieved at the destination site. The receiver can then execute the received process locally, as in the following process: **in**$(!X)@$self.X. Alternatively it can spawn it for parallel execution possibly at other sites: **in**$(!X)@$self.**eval**$(X)@\ell_1$.**eval**$(X)@\ell_2.P'$.

During tuple evaluation, expressions are computed and logical localities are translated into physical ones. Evaluating a process implies substituting it with its *closure* (i.e. the process together with the environment of the node where the evaluation is taking place). The difference between operation **out**$(P)@\ell$ and **eval**$(P)@\ell$ is that **out** adds the closure of P to the tuple space located at ℓ, while **eval** sends P, not its closure, for execution at ℓ. Therefore, if node s_1 performs an **out** of P to node s_2, when P is executed at s_2, self will actually refer to s_1. This means that *static scoping* is used. On the contrary, if s_1 spawns P at s_2 with **eval**, no closure is sent: P will refer to s_2 when using self and *dynamic scoping* is used.

Finally, KLAIM processes can be built from the basic operations by using standard operators borrowed from process algebras [19]. Namely,

- **nil** stands for the process that cannot perform any action,
- *act*.P stands for the process that first executes action *act* and then behaves like P,
- $P_1 \mid P_2$ stands for the parallel composition of P_1 and P_2,
- $P_1 + P_2$ stands for the nondeterministic composition of P_1 and P_2 (only one of them will be executed).

Process identifiers are used in recursive process definitions. It is assumed that each process identifier A has a single defining equation $A(\widetilde{X}, \widetilde{u}, \widetilde{x}) \stackrel{def}{=} P$, where all free variables in P are contained in $\{\widetilde{X}, \widetilde{u}, \widetilde{x}\}$.

A KLAIM labeled operational semantics has been presented in [10,11]. In this semantics labels carry information about the action performed in the net. The formal syntax of labels is defined as follows:

$$a ::= \mathbf{o}(s_1, et, s_2) \mid \mathbf{i}(s_1, et, s_2) \mid \mathbf{r}(s_1, et, s_2) \mid \mathbf{e}(s_1, P, s_2) \mid \mathbf{n}(s_1, -, s_2)$$

A label represents the intended operation and has the form $\mathbf{x}(s_1, arg, s_2)$, where $\mathbf{x}$ is the operation (**o**, **i**, **r**, **e**, **n** respectively represent **out**, **in**, **read**, **eval**, **newloc**), s_1 is the (source) node performing the action, s_2 is the target node, and arg is the argument of $\mathbf{x}$. For instance, $\mathbf{r}(s_1, t, s_2)$ represents operation **read**$(t)@s_2$ performed at s_1.

3   The System for Software Update

We would like to consider a system for software update with applications in-stalled on a centralized server; clients will subscribe at this server for updates. Upon subscription the client will get the most recent release of the requested applications. Subscription may require a registration and possibly a payment, but we are not addressing these issues, which can be easily added to the system. The delivery of an application and of new releases are made by means of mobile agents, which will migrate to the client's site, and will install all needed modules.

When the update agent arrives at the client's site, the installation of the new release may have to wait for approval by the client; for instance the client could disable the update while that application is already running. The agent will wait for approval before updating the application, and this waiting takes place locally at the client's site. Rather than waiting, the client may decide to disconnect from the server; indeed another advantage of mobile agents is the easy implementation of *disconnected operations* [23]. Moreover, during the update, the agent might have to perform many tasks; this could be harder to implement if this had to take place over the network rather than locally. The main steps for subscription and update are depicted in Figure 1.

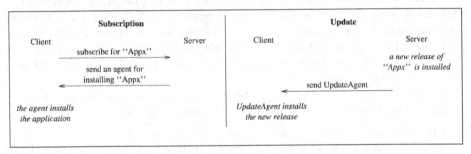

Fig. 1. Subscription and Update

3.1   A Prototype Implementation of the Software Update System

In the implementation in KLAIM, clients will communicate to the server, upon subscribing for an application, the physical locality of a private node, where the server will send agents for execution. This locality is private in the sense that it is created by the clients (with a **newloc**), and it is known only to the creator and to all the sites to which it is communicated. This private site is similar to a *place* in *Telescript*[2] [25], i.e. a private locality where agents can safely communicate, without interferences from the external world.

The code of process *RegisterApp*, that the client uses to register itself on the server for a specific application, is shown in Listing 1. This process takes as argument the localities where the server and the client reside (respectively *AppServer* and *MyLoc*) and the application's name that the client wants to

---

[2] *Telescript* is one of the first programming languages for mobile agents.

register for. The **eval**(*RegisterAgent*⟨...⟩)@*AppServer* is considered as a remote invocation, since *RegisterAgent* (Listing 2) is defined only on the server.

```
RegisterApp(AppServer, MyLoc, AppName) =
    newloc(PrivateLoc).
    eval(RegisterAgent⟨MyLoc, PrivateLoc, AppName⟩)@AppServer.
    (in(true)@PrivateLoc.P₁
    +
    in(false)@PrivateLoc.P₂)
```

Listing 1: The process that registers the client at the server

```
RegisterAgent(ClientLoc, PrivateLoc, AppName) =
    (read(AppName)@ClientDB.
     in(AppName, !ClientNum)@ClientDB.
     out(ClientNum + 1, ClientLoc, PrivateLoc, AppName)@ClientDB.
     out(AppName, ClientNum + 1)@ClientDB.
     out(true)@PrivateLoc.nil)
    +
    (out(false)@PrivateLoc.nil)
```

Listing 2: The remote process that registers a client at the server

The process *RegisterAgent* takes as argument the client's locality (*ClientLoc*), the private locality that the client and the server use to communicate (*PrivateLoc*) and the name of an application (*AppName*). *ClientDB* is a logical locality that is mapped, on the server, to a private physical locality which is known only to the server. It is used to register all the clients and to store information about them (e.g. the applications they subscribed to). Moreover the complete list of applications supplied by the server is stored there.

Since this locality is not known to the other clients, the server is sure that a client is not able to know the applications installed in another client, and that clients cannot interfere with each other. The secrecy of this locality is obtained by exploiting the locality evaluation mechanism provided by KLAIM: the clients cannot access the code of *RegisterAgent*, and thus the locality name *ClientDB* is unknown to them. That locality will only be mapped to a physical locality dynamically (at run time), through the allocation environment of the server, which is unaccessible by the other nodes. Moreover every client communicates a private locality to the server. Since that locality is known only to the client and to the server, they can use it to communicate privately. It is assumed, of course, that a client trusts the server, and that the latter will not communicate private localities to other clients.

RegisterAgent tries to find the application requested by the client, and if it succeeds it stores information about the client (updating *ClientDB*) and communicates to the client that the operation succeeded. Otherwise it communicates the failure to the client. All the communications with the client are performed through the private locality of the client, so that no interference with other clients will take place.

The client executes the process *RunApplication*, shown in Listing 3, that checks for the availability of new updates, provided by the update agents (shown later). This process receives an update through the tuple

$$(\text{``Update''}, AppName, !App)$$

at the private locality, and notifies the update agent that the update can be performed, by means of the tuple ("UpdateOK", *AppName*). Then, in case a previous version of the application is running, it stops it, it waits for the application to terminate, and it executes the new version. These operations are performed by interacting with the application through the tuples ("running", *AppName*), ("terminate", *AppName*) and ("terminated", *AppName*). Notice that the application has the opportunity of releasing all the resources before terminating. Alternatively it would be possible to modify such a process in order to only record that a new version is available and use such a new version the next time the application is started. The updating procedure can also be postponed by delaying the tuple ("UpdateOK", *AppName*).

```
RunApplication(AppName, PrivateLoc) =
    in("Update", AppName, !App)@PrivateLoc.
    out("UpdateOK", AppName)@PrivateLoc.
    ((in("running", AppName)@PrivateLoc.
        out("terminate", AppName)@PrivateLoc.
        in("terminated", AppName)@PrivateLoc.
        eval(App)@PrivateLoc.nil)
    +
    (in("stopped", AppName)@PrivateLoc.
        eval(App)@PrivateLoc.nil))
```

Listing 3: The process executed by the client that checks for new updates.

When the client wants to launch the application, it issues the command **eval**(*App*)@*Loc*, where *Loc* is the locality where the application *App* will be executed, in this case *PrivateLoc*.

3.2   The Update Agents

When a new release of an application is installed on the server, by inspecting *ClientDB*, the server will be able to know all the clients that have to be updated, and an update agent is spawned on every such client's site (Listing 4). *CheckUpdate* takes as parameters the application to update (*AppName*) and the agent that will take care of the update (*agent*). Thus *CheckUpdate* is parameterized not only over the application's name but also over the agent that updates software on the clients. The latter can be instantiated with any update agent; here we provide two examples of update agents (Listing 5 and 6).

Upon arrival at the client's site, the update agent (Listing 5) notifies its presence, so that it can be granted permission to update the software. After updating the application, the agent also records that a new version is installed in this node, and then notifies the server that this client has the new version.

```
CheckUpdate(AppName, agent) =
    out(AppName, "update in progress")@ClientDB.
    in(AppName, !ClientNum)@ClientDB.
    out(AppName, "updating", ClientNum)@ClientDB.
    eval(Iterator⟨AppName, agent, 0⟩)@self.
    in(AppName, "updated")@ClientDB.
    in(AppName, "update in progress")@ClientDB.
    out(AppName, !ClientNum)@ClientDB.nil

Iterator(AppName, agent, ClientNum) =
    (in(ClientNum, !ClientLoc, !PrivateLoc, AppName)@ClientDB.
        eval(agent)@PrivateLoc.
        out(ClientNum, ClientLoc, PrivateLoc, AppName)@ClientDB.
        Iterator⟨AppName, agent, ClientNum + 1⟩)
    +
    (in(AppName, "updating", ClientNum)@ClientDB.
        out(AppName, "updated")@ClientDB.nil)
```

Listing 4: The process for spawning an agent on every registered agent.

```
UpdateAgent(AppName, App, server) =
    out("Update", AppName, App)@self.
    in("UpdateOK", AppName)@self.
    out("updated", AppName, self)@server.nil
```

Listing 5: A first example of update agent.

Since *CheckUpdate* is parameterized over the update agent, when updating an application requires more complex operations, a more involved update agent can be used. Indeed the whole system relies on a specific protocol, but the processes that execute it could easily be changed, as long as they execute the same protocol. For instance the new release of an application may have to rely on some other application or module, which the client is unaware of (so it couldn't have registered for it); in that case the update agent could provide the client with the additional modules as well. In Listing 6 another update agent is shown that installs an additional module, before installing the application itself.

```
UpdateAgent2(AppName, App, App2, server) =
    out("Module", App2)@self.
    out("Update", AppName, App)@self.
    in("UpdateOK", AppName)@self.
    out("updated", AppName, self)@server.nil
```

Listing 6: Another update agent that also installs an additional module.

What we have shown here is only a simplified version of update agents; in a real application these agents will perform some more complex operations, but the architecture of the system remains the same.

Moreover such system is flexible in many other parts: for instance the application server, instead of spawning an agent to each client site, could spawn a single "itinerant" agent that visits every client performing the installation.

This could be made if the application server manages a local subnet, where the connections are more reliable, and it is unlikely that an agent gets stuck in some client's computer.

4   The Logic for KLAIM

An advantage of using a programming language based on a formal description, like KLAIM, is the possibility of building and using formal tools for verifying system properties. In this section, we show how to use one of these tools for assessing properties of our application.

Properties of KLAIM systems can be specified by using the modal logic introduced in [11]. This logic draws inspiration from Hennessy-Milner Logic [14] where dynamic properties of CCS processes are captured by making use of modal operators, $\langle\rangle$ and $[]$, indexed over a set of labels denoting basic actions of processes. The modal logic for KLAIM is also equipped with a complete and sound proof system that permits verifying whether a KLAIM net satisfies a given formula.

In the KLAIM logic, $\langle\rangle$ and $[]$ are indexed with predicates that will be interpreted over labels (denoted by A), and used to single out subsets of the set of possible labels. Label predicates are defined in terms of specific predicates (denoted by pp and tp) that permit characterizing properties of processes and tuples that are sent to or retrieved from nodes.

To characterize state properties of KLAIM programs, namely the presence of a tuple in a specific tuple space, specific basic state formulae have been introduced.

We let $\mathcal{L}^*$ be the set of logic formulae defined by the following grammar:

$$\phi ::= \mathbf{tt} \mid \mathbf{ff} \mid tp@s \mid tp@u \mid \langle A\rangle\phi \mid [A]\phi \mid \kappa \mid \nu\kappa.\phi \mid \mu\kappa.\phi \mid \phi \vee \phi \mid \phi \wedge \phi \mid \neg\phi$$

The basic components are

- A, an abstraction of transition labels and
- tp, which specifies properties of tuple components and uses predicates for processes (pp) and localities (sp).

If N is a net and ϕ a logic formula, we can define the concept of *satisfiability of ϕ by N*, $N \models \phi$. Every net N satisfies $\mathbf{tt}$ while none satisfies $\mathbf{ff}$. A net N satisfies $\phi_1 \wedge \phi_2$ if and only if N satisfies both ϕ_1 and ϕ_2, while N satisfies $\phi_1 \vee \phi_2$ if N satisfies ϕ_1 or ϕ_2. N satisfies $tp@s$ if there is a tuple t in the tuple space of the node s and t satisfies tp (see below). A net N satisfies $\neg\phi$ if it does not satisfy ϕ.

We have to spend more words about satisfiability of recursion formulae $\nu\kappa.\phi$ and $\mu\kappa.\phi$. Let ϕ be a formula, we define formulae ϕ_i and $\widetilde{\phi}_i$ as follows:

$$\phi_0 = \mathbf{tt} \qquad \phi_{i+1} = \phi[\phi_i/\kappa] \qquad \widetilde{\phi}_0 = \mathbf{ff} \qquad \widetilde{\phi}_{i+1} = \phi[\widetilde{\phi}_i/\kappa]$$

A net N satisfies $\nu\kappa.\phi$ if and only if, for every i, N satisfies ϕ_i. Conversely N satisfies $\mu\kappa.\phi$ if and only if there exists i such that N satisfies $\widetilde{\phi}_i$. Usually we use ν recursion for *stable* properties (i.e. that always hold), while μ will be used for *eventually* properties (i.e. that will be true sometime in the future).

Dynamic properties of nets are specified by using formulae $\langle A \rangle \phi$ and $[\Lambda]\phi$. Label predicates will be interpreted in terms of sets of pairs (a, δ) where a is a transition label while δ is a substitution. The *interpretation* of Λ is denoted by $[\![A]\!]$. We say that (a, δ) *satisfies* A if $(a, \delta) \in [\![A]\!]$.

A net N satisfies $\langle A \rangle \phi$ if it evolves to a net N' via a label a such that: there exists δ such that $(a, \delta) \in [\![A]\!]$ and N' satisfies $\phi\{\delta\}$. Conversely a net N satisfies $[A]\phi$ if, and only if, for every net N', to which N evolves via transition with an action a for which there exists δ such that $(a, \delta) \in [\![A]\!]$, N' satisfies $\phi\{\delta\}$.

The label predicates A, are formally defined as follows:

$$A ::= \circ \mid \alpha \mid A_1 \cup A_2 \mid A_1 - A_2 \mid A_1 \cap A_2 \mid \texttt{Src}(\tilde{s}) \mid \texttt{Trg}(\tilde{s})$$

$$\alpha ::= \texttt{O}(\texttt{sl}_1, \texttt{tp}, \texttt{sl}_2) \mid \texttt{I}(\texttt{sl}_1, \texttt{tp}, \texttt{sl}_2) \mid \texttt{R}(\texttt{sl}_1, \texttt{tp}, \texttt{sl}_2)$$

$$::= \texttt{E}(\texttt{sl}_1, \texttt{pp}, \texttt{sl}_2) \mid \texttt{N}(\texttt{sl}_1, -, \texttt{sl}_2)$$

$$\texttt{sl} ::= u \mid ?u \mid s$$

The basic label predicates are $\circ$ and *abstract actions*, that we denote by α. Abstract actions have the same structure of transition labels. However their source and target can be a site, locality variables or quantifications over physical localities ($?u$). Moreover, abstract actions have tuple predicates $\texttt{tp}$ and process predicates $\texttt{pp}$, instead of tuples and processes, as arguments. A pair of the form (a, δ), where a is a transition label and δ is a substitution, satisfies an abstract action α if a and α have the same structure, and δ unifies their quantified parameters (i.e. $?u$). For instance, if $P : \texttt{pp}$ then $(e(s_1, P, s_2), [s_1/u_1])$ satisfies $\texttt{E}(?u_1, \texttt{pp}, s_2)$. Every pair $(a, \emptyset)$ satisfies $\circ$, while $(a, \emptyset)$ satisfies $\texttt{Src}(\tilde{s})$ (resp. $\texttt{Trg}(\tilde{s})$) if the source (resp. the target) of a is in $\tilde{s}$.

Label predicates are composed by using $\cap$, $\cup$ and $-$, where:

- $(a, \delta) \in [\![A_1 \cup A_2]\!]$ if $(a, \delta) \in [\![A_i]\!]$ $(i \in \{1, 2\})$;
- $(a, \delta) \in [\![A_1 \cap A_2]\!]$ if there exist δ_1 and δ_2 such that $(a, \delta_i) \in [\![A_i]\!]$ $(i \in \{1, 2\})$ and $\delta = \delta_1 \cdot \delta_2$;
- $(a, \delta) \in [\![A_1 - A_2]\!]$ if there exists $(a, \delta) \in [\![A_1]\!]$ and for all δ' $(a, \delta') \notin [\![A_2]\!]$.

Process predicates permit specifying the accesses to resources of the net (tuples and sites) that processes are able to perform and their casual dependencies. One can specify properties like "first read and then use the acquired information". For tuples, instead, predicates characterize tuple patterns by specifying properties of each field. *Tuple predicates* are defined below:

$$\texttt{tp} ::= \texttt{1}_t \mid \texttt{1}_v \mid \texttt{sp} \mid !u \mid !X \mid \texttt{pp} \mid \texttt{tp}, \texttt{tp}.$$

Basically a tuple predicate can be: a *formal* ($!u$ or $!X$), a generic tuple $\texttt{1}_t$, a generic value $\texttt{1}_v$, a locality predicate $\texttt{sp}$ or a process predicate $\texttt{pp}$. Notice that by using $\texttt{1}_t$ and $\texttt{1}_v$ one can specify templates for tuples, for instance $(\texttt{1}_t, \texttt{1}_t)$ represents a tuple with at least two fields. Conversely, formals can be used for specifying the retrieving of data (localities and processes).

The syntax of *locality predicates* is defined as follows:

$$sp ::= 1_s \mid s \mid u \mid l$$

where 1_s is used for a generic locality, s and l refer to a specific physical or logical locality, respectively, and u is a locality variable used for specifying the actual use of an acquired localities. A tuple t satisfies tp if every field of t satisfies the corresponding field predicate in tp.

Process predicates are defined as follows:

$$pp ::= 1_P \mid ap \to pp \mid pp \land pp \mid X$$

$$ap ::= i(tp)@sp \mid r(tp)@sp \mid o(tp)@sp \mid e(pp)@sp \mid n(u)$$

We use 1_P for a generic process, $pp_1 \land pp_2$ for the set of processes that *satisfy* pp_1 and pp_2 and $ap \to pp$ for the set of processes that, at some point of their computation, can perform an action that satisfies ap and then evolve in processes that satisfy pp. There is an action predicate ap for every basic KLAIM action. Finally, X is a process variable that can be used for denoting the actual use of acquired processes.

Process predicates can be thought of as types that reflect the possible accesses that a process might perform along its computation and they carry information also about the possible use of acquired resources. This will allow us to specify sophisticated properties on process capabilities. For instance we can specify the set of processes that, after reading the name of a locality from a generic site, spawn a process to the read locality:

$$i(!u)@1_s \to e(1_P)@u \to 1_P$$

P : pp and t : tp are used to indicate that P and t satisfy, respectively, pp and tp. Conversely $\neg P$: pp and $\neg t$: tp indicate that P and t do not satisfy pp and tp.

In [11] a sound, complete and decidable proof system has been introduced for verifying the satisfiability of predicates by processes and tuples. To simplify the analysis of KLAIM systems the framework KLAIML [18] can be used. KLAIML, implemented in OCaml [17], consists of three components:

- an environment, klaimlrun, for simulating KLAIM systems,
- an automatic prover, klaimlprover, for testing the satisfaction of a formula by a net and
- an OCaml top level, klaimltop, that permits directly using the KLAIM library implemented for OCaml.

klaimlrun permits both executing KLAIM *programs* and generating reachable graphs. However, since these graphs could be infinite, a user *driven* generation is possible. klaimlprover, after loading a net N and a formula ϕ, tests the satisfaction of ϕ by N. Whenever a successful or an unsuccessful proof is found, the actual tree structure of the proof is exhibited. The user can navigate the proof and visualize sequents and applied rules. A time-out can be established for the proof search. In that case *partial proofs* could be visualized and the user can interactively decide to continue along the search.

5 System's Properties

In this section, we will show how, by using the logic for KLAIM, we can specify properties for the proposed system. First, we show how to ensure that the server always replies to every request by the clients. Then we formalize a key property: if a client is registered for an application then it will always receive the new updates in the correct order. Finally we show how to express the deadlock freedom of the system. Due to lack of space we just present the formulae and skip their satisfiability proofs that are somehow mechanic.

5.1 Server's Replies

The first property that we want to guarantee is that every time a client asks for a new application, the server always replies, either positively or negatively. A client asks for a new application by calling a process on the server site. This process, as we saw in Section 3, either registers the client for the requested application and then returns a positive result, or a negative result is returned. More formally, the property we want to specify is the following: *"for every site u_1 that, after the creation of a new locality u_2, evaluates a registering process at the site AppServer, u_1 will receive either a positive or a negative result"*.

First, we have to represent the event *"u_1 creates a new node u_2"*. This can be done by using the label predicate:

$$N(?u_1, -, ?u_2)$$

that, when it is used inside the modal operator [ ], permits expressing *"for every node u_1 that creates a site u_2"*.

Let u_1 be a generic client and let u_2 be the private locality that it uses to communicate with the server. When u_1 asks for the application *App*, it has to evaluate at the server a process satisfying the following predicate

$$pp = (o(\text{true})@u_2 \rightarrow 1_P) \wedge (o(\text{false})@u_2 \rightarrow 1_P)$$

This predicate is satisfied by every process that sends a negative or positive results to the client. Notice that such a process can also perform other internal operations. Moreover, we observe that other predicates may be satisfied by such a process, but the predicate described above is the one that guarantees that a client will always receive a response (either positive or negative). Hence, the event *"u_1 evaluates a registering process at the site AppServer"* is expressed by the modality:

$$[E(u_1, pp, AppServer)]$$

where the abstract action $E(u_1, \text{pp}, AppServer)$ denotes the evaluation of a process satisfying pp, from u_1, at $AppServer$.

Finally, the property "*AppServer will eventually send either the tuple* (true) *or the tuple* (false) *to* u_2" is specified by the formula ϕ defined as follows:

$$
\begin{aligned}
\phi = & \\
\mu\kappa.(& \\
& \langle O(AppServer, \text{true}, u_2)\rangle \text{tt} \\
& \vee \\
& \langle O(AppServer, \text{false}, u_2)\rangle \text{tt} \\
& \vee \\
& [\circ]\kappa \\
&)
\end{aligned}
$$

By composing the specifications above, we express the intended properties by using the following formula:

$$
\begin{aligned}
\nu\kappa_1. & \\
[N(?u_1, -, ?u_2)] & \\
(\nu\kappa_2. & \\
& [E(u_1, \text{pp}, AppServer)]\phi \\
& \wedge \\
& [\circ - E(u_1, \text{pp}, AppServer)]\kappa_2 \\
) & \\
\wedge & \\
[\circ - N(?u_1, -, ?u_2)]\kappa_1 &
\end{aligned}
$$

This formula states that every time a site u_1 creates a new node u_2 and evaluates a registering agent at the site $AppServer$, u_1 will eventually receive either a positive or a negative result.

5.2   Clients' Registration

Another important property for our system is that every registered client will receive all the updates by respecting the generation ordering.

First of all, we have to notice that there is a new update for the application *App* when the tuple (*App*, "update in progress") is inserted in the tuple space of the node named *AppServer_DB*. *AppServer_DB* is the physical locality corresponding to the logical locality *ClientDB* in the allocation environment of the node *AppServer*. Hence, the event "*a new update is available for the application App*" can be expressed by using the following label predicate:

$$
A_1 = O(AppServer, (App, \text{"update in progress"}), AppServer\_DB)
$$

On the other hand, a client u_1, registered for the application *App*, that uses the private locality u_2, will receive the new update when an update agent is evaluated at u_2. An update agent is a process that has to satisfy the following predicate:

$$\texttt{pp} = \texttt{o}(\text{``Update''}, App, 1_P)@\texttt{self} \rightarrow \texttt{i}(\text{``UpdateOK''}, App)@\texttt{self} \rightarrow 1_P$$

Notice that both the agents presented in Section 3.2 satisfy the predicate pp. The event "*a new update for App is sent to u_2*" is expressed by the label predicate:

$$A_2 = \mathrm{E}(AppServer, \texttt{pp}, u_2)$$

The property "*a registered client u_1 will receive every new update in the correct order*" can be thought of as "*the event A_1 does not take place before A_2*" and expressed by:

$$\phi_1 = \mu\kappa.[A_1]\mathbf{ff} \wedge (\langle A_2 \rangle \mathbf{tt} \vee [\circ - (A_1 \cup A_2)]\kappa)$$

Moreover, we have to notice that a client located at u_1, that uses u_2 for private communication, is registered for an application App if and only if in the tuple space of the site $AppServer\_DB$ there exists the tuple

$$(v, u_1, u_2, App)$$

for some value v. In other words, if the system satisfies the formula:

$$\langle 1_v, u_1, u_2, App \rangle @ClientDB$$

The whole property can be formalized as follows:

$$
\begin{aligned}
\nu\kappa_1. &\\
&([\mathrm{N}(?u_1, -, ?u_2)] \\
&\quad \nu\kappa_2. \\
&\qquad (\neg \langle 1_v, u_1, u_2, App \rangle @ClientDB \vee [A_1]\phi_1) \\
&\qquad \wedge \\
&\qquad [\circ]\kappa_2) \\
&\wedge \\
&[\circ]\kappa_1
\end{aligned}
$$

5.3   Deadlock Freedom

Finally we specify deadlock freedom. For this task we use the label predicate $\circ$ which is satisfied by every transition label. Hence formula $\langle \circ \rangle \mathbf{tt}$ is satisfied by every net which can execute some actions.

Deadlock freedom for our system can be checked by verifying whether the formula:

$$\phi_{df} = \nu\kappa.\langle \circ \rangle \mathbf{tt} \wedge [\circ]\kappa$$

is satisfied. Indeed a system satisfies ϕ_{df} if it can evolve and every net to which it evolves satisfies ϕ_{df}.

6   Conclusions

We have described a prototype system for software update in a network, by exploiting mobile agent technology, and we have shown how to effectively use formal tools and logics for reasoning about mobile agent based distributed systems.

The logic used in this paper is a variant of Hennessy-Milner Logic [14] enriched with state formulae and more refined action predicates which permit reasoning about properties of KLAIM systems. There are a few papers that have tackled the problem of defining a logic for process calculi with primitives for mobility. They have considered definitions of logics for π−calculus [20,21,22,3] and Mobile Ambients [4,5,6].

In the modal logic for Ambient [5], specific modalities are introduced for reasoning about "spatial distribution" of resources. These, in our approach, are rendered by means of label predicates, state formulae, and classical modal operators $\langle \rangle$ and $[]$. An advantage of this combination is that it permits naturally expressing "dynamic properties" that depend on the locality where they take place (for instance, "a tuple satisfying tp is retrieved from s_1 by s_2"). This kind of properties cannot be specified by using [5,6].

References

1. L. Bettini, R. De Nicola, G. Ferrari, and R. Pugliese. Interactive Mobile Agents in X-KLAIM. In P. Ciancarini and R. Tolksdorf, editors, *Proc. of the 7th Int. IEEE Workshops on Enabling Technologies: Infrastructure for Collaborative Enterprises (WETICE)*, pages 110–115. IEEE Computer Society Press, 1998.
2. L. Bettini, R. De Nicola, and M. Loreti. Software Update via Mobile Agent Based Programming. In *Proc. of ACM SAC 2002, Special Track on Agents, Interactions, Mobility, and Systems*. ACM Press, 2002. To appear.
3. L. Caires and L. Cardelli. A Spatial Logic for Concurrency (Part I). In *proceeding of TACS2001*, 2001. to appear.
4. L. Cardelli and A. D. Gordon. Mobile Ambients. In M. Nivat, editor, *Foundations of Software Science and Computation Structures (FoSSaCS'98)*, volume 1378 of *LNCS*, pages 140–155. Springer, 1998.
5. L. Cardelli and A. D. Gordon. Anytime, Anywhere: Modal Logics for Mobile Ambients. In *27th Annual Symposium on Principles of Programming Languages (POPL) (Boston, MA)*. ACM, 2000.
6. L. Cardelli and A. D. Gordon. Logical Properties of Name Restriction. In *proceeding of TLCA'01*, volume 2044 of *Lecure Note in Computer Science*. Springer, 2001.
7. N. Carriero and D. Gelernter. Linda in Context. *Comm. of the ACM*, 32(4):444–458, 1989.
8. A. Carzaniga, G. Picco, and G. Vigna. Designing Distributed Applications with Mobile Code Paradigms. In R. Taylor, editor, *Proc. of the 19th Int. Conf. on Software Engineering (ICSE '97)*, pages 22–33. ACM Press, 1997.
9. R. De Nicola, G. Ferrari, and R. Pugliese. KLAIM: a Kernel Language for Agents Interaction and Mobility. *IEEE Transactions on Software Engineering*, 24(5):315–330, 1998.
10. R. De Nicola and M. Loreti. A Modal Logic for KLAIM. In T. Rus, editor, *Proc of Algebraic Methodology and Software Technology, 8th Int. Conf. AMAST 2000*, number 1816 in LNCS, pages 339–354. Springer, 2000.

11. R. De Nicola and M. Loreti. A Modal Logic for Mobile Agents. Technical report, Dipartimento di Sistemi ed Informatica, Università degli Studi di Firenze, 2001. available at http://music.dsi.unifi.it/.
12. D. Gelernter. Generative Communication in Linda. *ACM Transactions on Programming Languages and Systems*, 7(1):80–112, 1985.
13. C. Harrison, D. Chess, and A. Kershenbaum. Mobile agents: Are they a good idea? Research Report 19887, IBM Research Division, 1994.
14. M. Hennessy and R. Milner. Algebraic Laws for Nondeterminism and Concurrency. *Journal of the ACM*, 32(1):137–161, Jan. 1985.
15. F. Knabe. An overview of mobile agent programming. In *Proceedings of the Fifth LOMAPS workshop on Analysis and Verification of Multiple - Agent Languages*, number 1192 in LNCS. Springer-Verlag, 1996.
16. D. Lange and M. Oshima. Seven good reasons for mobile agents. *Communications of the ACM*, 42(3):88–89, March 1999.
17. X. Leroy, D. Rémy, J. Vouillon, and D. Doligez. The Objective Caml system, documentation and user's guide. http://caml.inria.fr/ocaml/htmlman/, 1999.
18. M. Loreti. *Languages and Logics for Network Aware Programming*. PhD thesis, Università di Siena, 2002. Available at http://music.dsi.unifi.it.
19. R. Milner. *Communication and Concurrency*. Prentice Hall, 1989.
20. R. Milner, J. Parrow, and D. Walker. A calculus of mobile processes, Part I. LFCS Report Series ECS-LFCS-89-85, University of Edinburgh, June 1989.
21. R. Milner, J. Parrow, and D. Walker. A calculus of mobile processes, Part II. LFCS Report Series ECS-LFCS-89-86, University of Edinburgh, June 1989.
22. R. Milner, J. Parrow, and D. Walker. Modal logics for mobile processes. *Theoretical Computer Science*, 114:140–171, 1993.
23. A. Park and P. Reichl. Personal Disconnected Operations with Mobile Agents. In *Proc. of 3rd Workshop on Personal Wireless Communications, PWC'98*, 1998.
24. T. Thorn. Programming Languages for Mobile Code. *ACM Computing Surveys*, 29(3):213–239, 1997. Also Technical Report 1083, University of Rennes IRISA.
25. J. E. White. Telescript Technology: The Foundation for the Electronic Marketplace. White paper, General Magic, Inc., Mountain View, CA, 1994.
26. J. E. White. Mobile Agents. In J. Bradshaw, editor, *Software Agents*. AAAI Press and MIT Press, 1996.

Dynamically Adapting the Behaviour of Software Components

Andrea Bracciali[1], Antonio Brogi[1], and Carlos Canal[2]

[1] Dipartimento di Informatica, Università di Pisa, Italy
[2] Depto. Lenguajes y Ciencias de la Computación, Universidad de Málaga, Spain

Abstract. Available component-oriented platforms address software interoperability only at the signature level, while they do not provide suitable mechanisms for adapting components with mismatching interaction behaviour. This paper presents a methodology for automatically developing adaptors capable of solving behaviour mismatches between heterogeneous components. These adaptors are generated from abstract specifications of the intended connection between the components, by taking into account both signature interfaces and component behaviours.

1 Introduction

The ability to reuse existing software has always been a major concern of software engineering. In particular, the so-called component-based software development focusses on reusing and integrating heterogeneous software parts, as currently supported by several component-oriented platforms like CORBA, COM, JavaBeans, or .NET.

A serious limitation of the available platforms is that they do not provide suitable means to describe and reason on the concurrent behaviour of interacting components [14]. Indeed, while these platforms provide convenient ways to describe signatures via interface description languages (IDLs), they offer a quite limited and low-level support to describe the concurrent behaviour of components.

Several proposals [10] have been put forward to enhance component interfaces with a description of their concurrent behaviour [1,2,3,12]. Indeed, the availability of a formal description of component behaviour is the basis for verifying properties of systems consisting of large numbers of heterogeneous components. For instance, one may wish to check whether two components are compatible, that is, whether their interaction may lead or not to a deadlock.

Our objective is to address the problem of dynamically constructing adaptors capable of overcoming existing mismatches between heterogeneous components that may be separately developed. We will illustrate a methodology to derive an adaptor starting from the protocols of the components involved and from a high-level partial specification of their intended connection. The three main aspects of the methodology are the following:

F. Arbab and C. Talcott (Eds.): COORDINATION 2002, LNCS 2315, pp. 88–95, 2002.

- *Component interfaces.* Each component has a *signature* interface — in the style of traditional IDLs — which specifies the methods it provides and requires, together with type information on their parameters. Components also have a *behaviour* interface which describes their actual behaviour, that is, the order in which the methods in the signature interface are invoked. Behaviour interfaces are expressed in a subset of π-calculus [13], a process algebra which has proved to be specially suited for the specification of dynamic and evolving systems.
- *Adaptor specification.* A high-level specification of an adaptor is expressed by means of a simple notation indicating the adaptation needed for the interoperation of two components with mismatching behaviour. The specification simply states some correspondences between actions and parameters of the two components, abstracting from many behavioural concerns.
- *Adaptor derivation.* Finally, an automatic procedure deploys, if possible, the abstract description into an adaptor which lets the components interoperate in terms of their behaviour protocols. The deployed adaptor ensures successful execution, while keeping disjoint the name spaces of the components so that their interaction will occur only through the adaptor.

Our work is motivated by the ever-increasing attention devoted to developing extensively interacting distributed systems, consisting of large numbers of heterogeneous components. Most importantly, we think that constructing adaptors dynamically will be a must for the next generation of nomadic applications consisting of wireless mobile computing devices that will need to require services from different hosts at different times. The following scenario concretely relates our work to this perspective:

1. A component P gets in the vicinity of a context C of interacting components. P gets from C its signature interface, describing the services that C provides;
2. Then, P sends to C its interaction protocol, together with a proposal of connection in the form of a *mapping* between the interface of C and its own.
3. The context C, given this connection proposal, the protocol of P, and its own protocol, constructs an adaptor to be used for their interoperation.

In this paper we will focus on the notation to be used in step (2) for specifying the mapping, and on the adaptor construction procedure of step (3). The (semantical) problem of defining the mapping for two given components is at present under strong investigation, (e.g. the use of XML as "Universal Data Fromat" in the .NET framework), but it is out of the scope for this paper.

The mapping in step (2) is only a partial specification of the intended connection. It focusses on the mediation between the different languages spoken by P and C. Thus, it refers to signature interfaces, abstracting from the actual protocols of P and C represented by their behaviour interfaces. On the contrary, in step (3) protocols are considered in order to develop automatically an adaptor satisfying both the mapping and the behaviour interfaces.

In the rest of this paper, Sect. 2 shows how component behaviour can be described by means of finite interaction patterns. Sect. 3 introduces a notation for the specification of mappings, while Sect. 4 presents an algorithm for the generation of adaptors. Finally, Sect. 5 discusses related works and some concluding remarks.

2   Interface Description

In our approach, the interface of a software element (either a single component or a full context) is described by a set of *roles*, each one devoted to a specific aspect of the behaviour of the component.

Roles consist of both a signature and a behaviour interface description. The signature declares a set of input and output actions, representing the methods that the component offers and invokes, the values or exceptions returned, etc.

With respect to the behaviour, it is specified by a finite interaction pattern. The language we use for describing these patterns is a sugared subset of the synchronous π-calculus. Since the calculus allows link names to be sent and received as values, it has proved to be a very expressive notation for describing software applications with changing topologies (as open systems are). The set of behaviour expressions is defined as follows:

```
E ::= 0  |  a. E  |  (x)E  |  E || E'  |  E + E'

a ::= x?(d)  |  x!(d)  |  tau
```

where 0 represents inaction, input and output actions are respectively represented by x?(d) and x!(d), and internal actions are denoted by tau. Restrictions — like (x)E — represent the creation of a new link name x in an expression E. The parallel (not synchronizing) operator is represented by '||' inside roles, while the operator '|' is used for general parallel composition. Finally, '.' and '+' denote the standard prefix and choice operators.

Notice that behaviour expressions do not contain recursion, since they are intended to specify finite fragments of interaction. Intuitively speaking, an interaction pattern describes only the essential aspects of the interactive behaviour that a component may (repeatedly) show to its environment.

The special characteristics of mobility of the π-calculus allow the creation and transmission of link names which can be later used for communication. This determines that the interfaces of π-calculus processes are not fixed beforehand (like in other process algebras or in object-oriented environments), but instead they can be extended by link-passing. Consider, for instance, the pattern C below representing a server waiting for some query:

```
C = query?(quest,ret). ( tau. ret!(fact). 0 + tau. exception!(). 0 )
```

Initially, the signature of C consists of actions query? and exception!, link names which are public in the role. However, after performing the query? action, the interface is enlarged with an output action ret! to be performed through the link name received in action query?, and which was not known beforehand. We use the operator '>' (read as "before") for representing these changing interfaces, stating causal dependencies between action names without showing the details of the corresponding protocols. Hence the signature interface of C will be written as:

```
I_C = { query?(Data quest, Link ret) > ret!(Data fact);
        exception!(); }
```

3   Connection Specification

The intended connection between a component and a context is represented by a mapping between the signature interfaces of both elements. The specification is partial in the sense that mappings do not deal with behavioural concerns but they rather address problems like name translation and parameter reordering between two signature interfaces.

A mapping is a finite set of rules of the form $\alpha_1, \ldots, \alpha_m <> \beta_1, \ldots, \beta_n$. The left term refers to component actions, and the right one to context actions. Each term may contain one or several actions. The names of action parameters are used to describe reordering, remembering, and even synthesis of links and data during the adaptation process, indicating how data would be transmitted from one element to the other. Moreover, a rule may map some actions to **none**, indicating that there is no corresponding action for them. When executed, these actions will be "absorbed" by the adaptor when necessary, but not retransmitted.

For instance, consider a component Q that sends requests for printing a number of copies of a document by means of an action `printc!(doc,n)`, and another component R that features a printing service by accepting requests in two steps —one for setting the number of copies, and one for actually printing the document. Their signature interfaces are, respectively:

```
I_Q = { printc!(Data doc, Data n); }     I_R = { setCopies?(Data copies);
                                                 print?(Data doc); }
```

A suitable mapping for connecting Q and R is:

```
M = { none              <> setCopies?(n);
      printc!(doc,n) <> print?(doc); }
```

which indicates that the action `setCopies?` in R does not have a correspondent in Q. The example also shows that the scope of parameter names is not just a rule, but the whole mapping, and that any value received by the adaptor may be used later for matching an action in a different rule.

Notice also that mappings define matchings between actions, as represented in the signature interfaces. In the example above, the mapping does not indicate whether R requires to set the number of copies for each printing request, or whether an initial set is enough for printing a given number of copies of several documents. However, a correct adaptor would be developed in both situations, according to the actual behaviour of the two components (not shown here), which are used for generating the adaptor.

Consider now a component P described by the role:

```
Iₚ = { request!(Data q);        P = request!(q).reply?(a).0
       reply?(Data a); }
```

In order to connect P to the context C described in the previous section, we will write the mapping:

```
M = { request!(q)      <> query?(q,reply);
      reply?(fact)     <> reply!(fact);
      reply?(REFUSED)  <> exception!() }
```

The first rule resolves name mismatching, mapping **request!** to **query?**. Moreover it implicitly states that the **reply** channel used by P corresponds to the return link that C expects for its parameter **ret** in action **query?**. In fact, when dealing with mobility we must take into account that links appearing in the signature interface after the operator '>' refer to parameters which are instantiated in the mapping rules. Hence, further reference to these links must be renamed consequently, as shown in the second rule, where the action **ret!** of C is referred to as **reply!**. Finally, the third rule states that the context action **exception!** is also mapped to **reply?**. Notice how a constant value REFUSAL is used, allowing P to distinguish between real answers and service refusals.

4 Adaptors

Given two roles P and C and a mapping M that specifies the intended connections between them, the construction of a mediating component, called *adaptor*, can be done automatically. Because of space limitations, in this section we only sketch the algorithm and show an example of its application. Intuitively, the goal of the algorithm is to build a process A such that:

1. P|A|C is successful (i.e., all traces lead to success), and
2. A satisfies the given mapping M, that is, all the action correspondences and data dependencies specified by M are respected in any trace of P|A|C.

The algorithm incrementally builds the adaptor A by trying to eliminate progressively all the possible deadlocks that may occur in the evolution of P|A|C, letting P and C interoperate according to M. Informally, a deadlock is removed by expanding A with an action α by means of which the adaptor synchronises with either P or C. The algorithm is non-deterministic, since action α is non-deterministically chosen among those that P or C are ready to synchronise with.

The algorithm returns, if any, one of the possible adaptors for P and C. Notice that all the adaptors returned by the algorithm are correct (P|A|C is successful) and satisfy M. It is worth noting that the algorithm is a variant of the one we developed for checking the correctness of open contexts of components [2].

In order to produce adaptors that satisfy the given mapping, the algorithm traces the evolution of P|A|C by means of the following data structures:

- The set $\mathcal{D}$ of data acquired by matching output actions of P or C. It is used to enforce that the adaptor sends data only after receiving them.

– The set $\mathcal{F}$ of actions to be eventually matched by the adaptor. If an action occurring in a mapping rule is matched, all the other actions in the same rule must be eventually matched, and they are hence recorded in $\mathcal{F}$.
– The set $\mathcal{L}$ of link correspondences is used to guarantee the separation of name spaces between P and C.

The construction of the adaptor is a iterative process whcih starts from an initially inactive adaptor. At each iteration, the algorithm:

– Chooses an action α so as to match a dual action $\overline{\alpha}$ on which P or C is blocked. Note that not all actions $\overline{\alpha}$ can be matched by the adaptor, since it must respect the constraints of M.
– For each choosable α, the algorithm spawns an instance of itself, relative to A appropriately expanded with α. If there are no triggerable actions, then the instance *fails*.

Each instance terminates when the derivation tree of P|A|C does not contain deadlocks. If the set $\mathcal{F}$ of actions to be matched is empty, then the instance terminates successfully, and it returns the completed adaptor. Otherwise, it fails. The overall algorithm fails if all its instances fail. Otherwise, it non-deterministically returns one of the adaptors found.

Let us consider again the client/server system whose intended connection was specified in Sect. 3. Starting form A = 0, the system P|A|C is clearly deadlocked on actions request!(q) and query!(quest,ret), respectively of P and C. Of these actions, A can only match the first one, since it is not able at the moment to provide the data required for the second. Hence, the adaptor is expanded to A = request?(q). 0. As a consequence of this first step, $\mathcal{D} = \{q\}$ is updated with the data received by A, while, according to the first rule of M, the action query!(q,reply) is stored in the set $\mathcal{F}$ of actions to be eventually fired.

After A and P have synchronised on request, there is only one deadlock state that A can eliminate, matching query?(quest,ret) of C with query!(q,reply) which is taken from the set $\mathcal{F}$. However A must take care of keeping separate the link names of the two roles. In order to do that, A creates a new link, say reply', for sending it to C. The link relation reply–reply' is stored in $\mathcal{L}$, while A is expanded to:

A = request?(q). (reply') query!(q,reply'). 0

and action query!(q,reply) is removed from $\mathcal{F}$ (which now is empty), since it has been executed.

P|A|C offers now two triggerable actions: reply'!(s) and exception!(), and A can match both of them. Two (eventually successful) instances of the algorithm are spawned. Following the first one, the construction continues by extending A with the actions reply'?(s) and reply!(s). Observe how the relation between reply and reply' stored in $\mathcal{L}$ is used while applying the second rule of the mapping. On the other hand, the second instance of the algorithm extends A with actions exception?() and reply!(REFUSED), by applying the third rule in the mapping. In both cases the roles of P and C terminate. Summing up, A has been extended to:

```
A = request?(q). (reply') query!(q,reply').
    ( reply'?(s). reply!(s). 0 + exception?(). reply!(REFUSED). 0  )
```

It is easy to verify that now P|A|C does not contain deadlocks, but only two successful traces. The set $\mathcal{F}$ is empty, and hence the algorithm terminates successfully returning A. Notice that the name spaces of P and C are still separated, and hence they are not able to interact without using the adaptor. This ensures that their connection will respect the specification represented by the mapping.

5   Concluding Remarks

Several authors have proposed to extend current IDLs in order to deal with behavioural aspects of component interfaces. Some proposals use finite state machines to describe the behaviour of components, e.g [12,15], exploiting their simplicity in supporting an efficient verification of protocol compatibility. On the other hand, this simplicity is a severe expressiveness bound for modelling complex open distributed systems. Process algebras feature more expressive descriptions and analysis of concurrent systems, and support system simulation and formal derivation of safety and liveness properties [1]. In particular the usefulness of π-calculus has been illustrated for describing component models like COM [7] and CORBA [9], and architecture description languages like Darwin [11] and LEDA [4]. However, the main drawback of using process algebras is related to the inherent complexity of the analysis. In order to manage this complexity, previous work of the authors has described the use of modular and partial specifications, by projecting behaviour both over space (roles) [4] and over time (finite interaction patterns) [2]. In the present work we use a combination of both approaches.

A general discussion of the issues of component interconnection, mismatch and adaptation is reported in [6,8], while formal approaches to detecting interaction mismatches are presented for instance in [1,4,5]. The problem of software adaptation was specifically addressed by the work of Yellin and Strom [15], which constitutes the starting point for our work. They use finite state grammars to specify component behaviour, to define a relation of compatibility, and to (semi)automatically generate adaptors. Some significant limitations of their work are related with the expressiveness of the notation used, which, for instance, does not allow the representation of internal choices, parallel compositions or process creation. Furthermore, the architecture described is static, and does not deal with issues such as reorganizing the communication topology of systems. In addition, the asymmetric meaning they give to input and output actions makes it necessary the use of *ex-machina* arbitrators for controlling system evolution.

The results presented in this paper lay a foundation for the automatic development of adaptors capable of solving behavioural mismatches between heterogeneous interacting components. An interesting direction for future work is the formal verification of properties of the generated adaptor, such as security properties, as suggested in [12,15]. In practice, such a verification would allow a context to check that its invariant properties are preserved after accepting a new component, and it would also allow the joining component to check that its minimal connection requirements will be fullfilled by the proposed adaptor. Our future activities will also be devoted to develop a user-friendly environment to facilitate experimenting the proposed methodology on real CBSE applications. In this perspective, we are planning to optimize the performance of the algorithm described in Sect. 4 by applying finite model-checking techniques. We are also investigating a similarity-based hierarchy of adaptors so as to fully automize the selection of the adaptor returned by the algorithm.

References

1. R. Allen and D. Garlan. A formal basis for architectural connection. *ACM Trans. on Software Engineering and Methodology*, 6(3):213–49, July 1997.
2. A. Bracciali, A. Brogi, and F. Turini. Coordinating interaction patterns. In *ACM Symposium on Applied Computing (SAC'2001)*. ACM Press, 2001.
3. C. Canal et al. Extending corba interfaces with protocols. *Computer Journal*, 44(5):448–462, 2001.
4. C. Canal, E. Pimentel, and J. M. Troya. Specification and refinement of dynamic software architectures. In *Software Architecture*, pages 107 126. Kluwer Academic Publishers, 1000.
5. D. Compare, P. Inverardi, and A. L. Wolf. Uncovering architectural mismatch in component behavior. *Science of Computer Programming*, 33(2):101–131, 1999.
6. S. Ducasse and T. Richner. Executable connectors: Towards reusable design elements. In *ACM Foundations of Software Engineering (ESEC/FSE'97)*, number 1301 in LNCS. Springer Verlag, 1997.
7. L. M. G. Feijs. Modelling Microsof COM using π-calculus. In *Formal Methods'99*, number 1709 in LNCS, pages 1343–1363. Springer Verlag, 1999.
8. D. Garlan, R. Allen, and J. Ockerbloom. Architectural mismatch: Why reuse is so hard. *IEEE Software*, 12(6):17–26, 1995.
9. M. Gaspari and G. Zavattaro. A process algebraic specification of the new asynchronous CORBA messaging service. In *Proceedings of ECOOP 99*, number 1628 in LNCS, pages 495–518. Springer, 1999.
10. G. T. Leavens and M. Staraman, editors. *Foundations of Component-Based Systems*. Cambridge University Press, 2000.
11. J. Magee, S. Eisenbach, and J. Kramer. Modeling darwin in the π-calculus. In *Theory and Practice in Distributed Systems*, number 938 in LNCS, pages 133–152. Springer Verlag, 1995.
12. J. Magee, J. Kramer, and D. Giannakopoulou. Behaviour analysis of software architectures. In *Software Architecture*, pages 35–49. Kluwer Academic Pub., 1999.
13. R. Milner, J. Parrow, and D. Walker. A calculus of mobile processes. *Journal of Information and Computation*, 100:1–77, 1992.
14. A. Vallecillo, J. Hernández, and J. M. Troya. New issues in object interoperability. In *Object-Oriented Technology: ECOOP 2000 Workshop Reader*, number 1964 in LNCS, pages 256–269. Springer Verlag, 2000.
15. D. M. Yellin and R. E. Strom. Protocol specifications and components adaptors. *ACM Trans. on Programming Languages and Systems*, 19(2):292–333, March 1997.

An Associative Broadcast Based Coordination Model for Distributed Processes

James C. Browne, Kevin Kane, and Hongxia Tian

Department of Computer Sciences
The University of Texas at Austin
Austin, TX 78712-1188
{browne,kane,htian}@cs.utexas.edu

Abstract. We define and describe a model for coordination of distributed processes or components based on associative broadcast. Associative broadcast encapsulates processes with an associative interface. The associative interface includes a profile, which specifies the current state of the component. Each message is sent with a conditional expression (selector), which evaluates to true for specific instances of profiles. Messages are broadcast but are received by only those processes where the selector of the message evaluates to true when matched with the profile of the component. Each component dynamically specifies its profile and selectors to conform to a coordination protocol. Components can, depending on their local state, enter or leave a coordinating set without affecting the other members of the set. Associative broadcast is defined and described. A formulation of associative broadcast implementing coordination among a dynamic set of distributed processes is defined and described. Distributed mutual exclusion is formulated in associative broadcast as an illustration.

1   Introduction

This paper presents a coordination model based on a special form of broadcast communication - associative broadcast [5,6], gives distributed mutual exclusion as an example and reports results of experimental evaluation of execution behavior. Broadcast enables coordination based on every process in an interacting set locally maintaining common state necessary for collective decision procedures. Associative broadcast enables targeting of messages to processes in specific states and enables each process to select the properties of messages it will receive. Separation of message filtering from computation decreases the execution cost of coordination using broadcast and allows for specialization to specific algorithm requirements.

Broadcast-based coordination enables coordination over dynamic sets and preserves anonymity similarly to tuple space methods. It enables transparent distribution and replication for fault-tolerance. Associative broadcast enables fully distributed and fully symmetric coordination.

There has been relatively little research on coordination models and languages based on broadcast communication [7,19]. Yet many computer networks intrinsically provide a broadcast capability (Ethernet, FDDI, MAN, wireless networks based on

F. Arbab and C. Talcott (Eds.): COORDINATION 2002, LNCS 2315, pp. 96-110, 2002.
© Springer-Verlag Berlin Heidelberg 2002

cellular communication, satellite transmissions, etc.). Coordination of distributed components and processes using broadcast is thus becoming of greater interest.

Practical broadcast-based coordination systems are most readily formulated using reliable broadcast. Most computer networks, however, provide only a datagram broadcast service but do not yet provide a reliable broadcast capability. There are, however, many algorithms for implementation of reliable broadcast. These algorithms are sufficiently simple and efficient that they are readily incorporated into network interfaces and/or operating systems. The coordination model given in this paper is based on reliable broadcast and reliable associative broadcast in particular.

The associative broadcast coordination model has been implemented as a runtime system composed of Java classes. Several distributed coordination problems such as distributed mutual exclusion and distributed readers and writers with replication and distributed versions of computational algorithms such as determination of planar convex hulls and linear solvers have been used to test and evaluate the implementation. An interface definition language for encapsulating components has been defined and a compiler for this interface definition language is in development.

The remainder of this section defines associative broadcast. Section 2 defines associative interactions and specifies coordination and composition in associative interactions. Section 3 illustrates coordination in associative interactions with an algorithm for distributed mutual exclusion and reports execution behavior for the mutual exclusion algorithm and the distributed readers and writers algorithm.

We use process and component interchangeably in what follows except where confusion might result.

1.1   Associative Broadcast – Overview

Associative broadcast is so-called because the model is similar to content-addressing of associative memory. A target set specification travels with each message that is broadcast onto the network. The target set is determined for each message by the set of local recipients whose local states match that of the target specification. Therefore, the sender does not need to know the identities of the targets in order to broadcast a message; the cardinality of the target set is completely transparent to the sender, even when the set is empty.

Descriptive Names. Associative communication is based on *descriptive* names. *Descriptive* names carry information about the status of objects to which they are bound. They associate meanings with object identifiers and therefore reflect the current state of an object via these identifiers.

Domains and Attributes. Interacting processes have *a priori* agreement on the set of attributes, which will appear in the profiles of components and the selectors of messages and the meanings of that set of attributes.

Profiles. Descriptive names are implemented as profiles. A profile is a table of attributes and attribute type/value pairs, which describe the state of a process or object.

Selectors. The target set of receivers for each message is determined by a selector, which is an expression in propositional logic over the attribute domain.

Messages. A message consists of a selector and content. The content of a message is implementation dependent. Coordination and composition require that the message specify an action to be executed by the receiving components.

Message Receipt. The selector of each broadcast message is locally matched with the profile of each object in the broadcast domain. Messages are received only by those components whose profiles cause the selector of the message to evaluate to true. Matching of a selector to a component profile is atomic with respect to a profile's modification. It is therefore possible for a sender's target set to change during transmission if a profile is changed, but the matching criteria will not change for a component once matching begins. Matching is done locally and asynchronously upon "arrival" of the message.

1.2   Coordination and Composition under Associative Broadcast

Coordination is formulated by defining profiles, messages and protocols. The execution model is a partially synchronous [20] receive/action (state machine) model. A component receives a message and takes some action (possibly null) in response to the message. An algorithm or computation is specified by:

1. A set of attributes in which the profiles and selectors are specified.
2. A set of rules for binding of the states of components to specifications of profiles.
3. A set of protocols by which interactions are executed including specification of message types, the selectors to accompany each instance of a message type, the allowed sequences of messages and the responses to each instance of a message type which is received.
4. A state machine which implements the coordination protocols is interfaced to each process or component.
5. An initial state for each component.

Each component executes in conformance to the rules and protocols. There is no coordinator or global control state. Coordination and thus control is fully distributed and fully symmetric. The set of components which is interacting and coordinating can be dynamic. A component can enter a coordination set by setting an appropriate profile and (possibly) following some initialization protocol.

1.3   Composition as Coordination and Vice Versa

Composition is usually defined in terms of binding invocations of a method or procedure by one component to a method or procedure in an implementing component. Composition may, although the mechanisms differ, occur at compile time, at link/load time and at run time (RPC is runtime composition). Composition is intrinsic to runtime associative interactions. Each associative message may result in binding of a message to a component or set of components. Each binding of the message results in the execution of an action. Associative naming and binding can be used as a compilation process to select an initial set of bindings among components prior to runtime. A compiler which uses associative interfaces to compose programs implementing performance models from components has been reported [10]. The associative model of interaction integrates coordination and composition.

2   Coordination/Composition in Associative Broadcast

It is useful to position associative broadcast with respect to naming and communication models before describing the specific instance of associative interactions that we have implemented as a coordination and composition model.

2.1   Naming Models and Communication Models

Bayerdorffer [5] has developed a lattice taxonomy of name models and characterized the models of communication which can be implemented in a given model of names. The lattice taxonomy is defined with proportion of name models as axes. It is shown in [5] that direct implementation of fully distributed, fully symmetric, minimal communication algorithms among dynamic set of entities requires a model of names at the top of the lattice.

Associative broadcast is at the top of the lattice taxonomy of naming systems [5,6] and thus supports *direct* implementation of fully symmetric and fully distributed algorithms for managing membership in dynamic sets. Linda [18] and its derivatives are the only other implemented communication mechanisms known to us corresponding to the highest point of the name lattice taxonomy.

2.2   A Coordination-Oriented Implementation of Associative Interactions

The associative interfaces for composition and coordination defined and described in this paper extend associative *communication* to associative *interaction*. An interaction has the dictionary definition of a mutually agreed upon action conducted by two or more parties. An associative interface for implementation of coordination and composition has two elements: an *accepts* interface and a *requests* interface. *Accepts* and *requests* interfaces are extensions of associative broadcast to include specifications for the actions which should result from a successful match of a profile.

An *accepts* interface specifies the set of interactions in which a component is willing to participate. The *accepts* interface for a component is a set of three-tuples (profile, transaction, protocol). Multiple members of the set may be associated with each instance of a component model and new instances instantiated at runtime.

A profile is a set of attribute/value pairs.

A transaction [13] specifies the type, functionality and parameters of a unit of work to be executed. A transaction may have an identity and a state which may persist across execution sites. The arguments of a transaction are typed in the invocations as well as in the declaration. In the present implementation, only simple transactions are supported. Complex transactions that persist across multiple component interactions are planned for future work.

A protocol defines the sequence of simple interactions necessary to complete the interaction specified by the profile. The most basic protocol is data-flow, which is sending a message and continuing execution, and is already in use. More complex interaction protocols such as call-return and persistent transactions, are planned but not yet implemented.

The *requests* interface specifies the set of interactions which a component must initiate if it is to complete the interactions which it has agreed to *accept*. The *requests* interface is a set of three-tuples (selector, transaction, protocol). Multiple members of the set may be associated with each instance of an object and new instances instantiated at runtime.

A selector is a conditional expression over the attributes of the objects in its domain and the other domains with which it has interactions.

The conditional expression of a selector is a template with slots for attribute name/value pairs specified in the profiles of other object instances. A selector is said to match a profile whenever the conditional expression of the selector evaluates to true when the attribute values from the profile are inserted into or compared with the slots in the selector expression.

The informal syntax of *accepts* and *requests* interfaces is:

Accepts <unique name> {profile([attribute/value pairs]);transaction= transaction specification; protocol = protocol specification}

Requests <unique name> {selector(conditional expression over attributes);transaction = transaction specification; protocol = protocol specification}

2.3   Requirements for Implementation of Associative Broadcast Based Coordination

The two requirements for implementation of coordination based on associative broadcast are timed reliable broadcast and a mechanism for attaining consensus.

Timed Reliable Broadcast. Effective implementation of associative broadcast-based coordination requires reliable broadcast with bounded time delivery of messages. Ideally reliable broadcast would be implemented at the network or operating system levels. We have implemented reliable broadcast as a service built upon UDP and TCP/IP as a layer of the application using the algorithm of Kaashoek [14].

Consensus/Synchronization. Since coordination is fully distributed, a mechanism for reaching consensus on the common state necessary to make a decision is required. The mechanism must be based on the common state provided by associative broadcast communication. The algorithms given here use collision detection modeled after collision detection in broadcast media such as Ethernet to implement consensus.

2.4   Implementation and Applications

A runtime system implementing coordination among dynamic sets of distributed processes has been implemented as a set of Java classes. The processes which are coordinated are Java programs executing on a network of workstations. The coordination system has been tested and evaluated for performance with several manually coded applications. The applications which have been developed and tested include distributed mutual exclusion, readers and writers with replicated data objects, determination of a convex hull for a set of points in the plane, and some parallel linear algebra algorithms. A compiler which automates generation of associative coordination from declarative specifications of accepts and requests interfaces is under development.

2.5   Properties of Associative Broadcast Coordination

Coordination is independent of process location within a broadcast domain. Coordination extends over dynamic sets of processes. Coordination decisions do not depend upon stable group properties. Coordination is through consensus and is fully distributed.

3   Distributed Mutual Exclusion in Associative Broadcast

Distributed mutual exclusion for a passive resource is the most basic form of coordination for a distributed set of interacting components. Because formulation of coordination in associative broadcast will be unfamiliar to most readers we use distributed mutual exclusion to illustrate coordination in associative broadcast. The algorithm is an adaptation of Ricart and Agrawala's algorithm [17].

The algorithm is symmetric and fully distributed. It is a replicated state algorithm where state information is used to generate a global virtual sequence. Each task maintains a queue of requests, including a local request if one is extant, ordered by request sequence number. When local request has the smallest sequence number of any request in the queue then the task knows it can safely access the shared resource. Occurrence of multiple requests with identical sequence numbers can occur and correspond to a collision among packets in a packet broadcast network. Collisions are resolved by back-off and retry. Detection of a collision is observation in a local queue of multiple requests with the same sequence number. Back-off is deletion of those requests and re-issue of the local request after a suitable delay with sequence number. An informal proof of correctness is given as Appendix A.

Definitions

Shared Resource. An entity to which exclusive access is periodically required by a set of tasks.

Task. An interacting entity. Tasks have state variables: a unique identifier, a local sequence number (LSN), the highest known sequence number (HKSN) and a queue of requests for access to the shared resource. Tasks cycle through the states, "local processing," "requesting" and "holding." In the state "local processing" the tasks are executing without access to the shared resource. In the "holding" state the task is utilizing the shared resource. The "requesting" state occurs when the task requests exclusive access to the shared resource and is waiting for its turn for exclusive access. Tasks communicate through associative broadcast.

Messages. The messages types are: join, request done, and cancel. A "join" message has as its content the unique id of the joining process. The "request" message has as its content the sequence number of the request. A "done" message has as its content the sequence number of the access which was just completed. A "cancel" message causes a task to remove the corresponding request from its local request queue.

Network. The network is a broadcast media with a known maximum latency. Reliable delivery of messages and ordered delivery of messages among source-sink pairs is assumed. There is a known upper bound on time for delivery of messages.

3.1   Basic Algorithm

Let us for the time being, assume that a set of interacting tasks has been created and initialized. Each task is initialized with a unique ID, its state as "local processing" its local sequence number to zero and its highest known sequence number to zero. Each process maintains its profile to reflect its current state. The profile after initialization is: State = "local processing." The specification of the algorithm is a state machine which an action associated with receipt of each message.

If a task in the "local processing" state receives a "request" messages it enters them in its local queue of requests and updates its HKSN. If a task in the "local processing" state receives a "done" message it removes the request corresponding to this done message from its request queue. (In fact it can remove all requests with sequence numbers less than the sequence number in a given done message but this circumstance should not occur with reliable message delivery.)

A task will eventually request exclusive access to the shared resource. The steps in the algorithm to request mutual exclusion are:

1. The task sets its profile to "requesting," adds one to its current HKSN, sets its local sequence number to the HKSN and broadcasts a message with a selector which will evaluate to true for all tasks. The message content is its unique id and the sequence number for the request.
2. The task then places its own request on its local queue of requests and sets an interval timer for twice the maximum network latency.
3. During the delay the local task accepts "request" and "done" messages. As it receives "done" messages it removes the corresponding requests from the request queue. If it receives request messages during the delay period then it adds them to the request queue and, if necessary, updates its HKSN.
4. If, at the end of the delay period, there are multiple entries in the request queue with identical sequence numbers then the task will associatively broadcast a cancel

message for its local request, select a delay from a random distribution with a mean of the network latency and reissue its request using the current highest known sequence number.

5. If at the end of the delay period there are requests with lower sequence numbers in the queue then the task waits for "done" messages for these requests.

6. Whenever its SN is less than the SN of any request on the request queue then the task will set its state to "holding" and access the shared resource.

7. When it completes access to the shared resource the task will set its state to "local processing", broadcast a "done" message with a selector which will evaluate to true for profiles with state = "requesting" or "local processing" and delete its own request from the local queue.

3.2   Task Entry Algorithm

The interacting set may be dynamically created and extended. A task initializes itself and joins the interacting set by:

1. Choosing a unique identifier,

2. Setting its state to "initializing", its local sequence number to null and its highest known sequence number to null,

3. Sending out a "hello request" to all the nodes whose state is "requesting" or "local processing", which causes those nodes to send a "hello reply" which contains a boolean indicating whether or not the resource is in use, and if it is, the request from its local queue with the highest sequence number.

4. For twice the network latency, the node monitors for new request messages and hello replies and adds appropriate entries to its local requests queue. Then, it changes its state to "local processing" and is ready to execute.

The hello algorithm will not necessarily give the initializing node a complete picture of the shared requests queue; however by learning the requests with the highest sequence number, it learns about the last requests that must complete. Then, any future "done" or "cancel" messages it receives will either be for lower-numbered requests which it can safely ignore, since the higher-numbered requests are still pending, or will be for those higher-numbered requests it knows about, and it can process those messages as usual.

3.3   Task Exit Algorithm

A task can exit the interacting set at any time so long as it is in the "local processing" state.

3.4   Task Failure

1. If a task fails while in local processing mode that is the same as leaving the set voluntarily.

2. If a task fails while in the "requesting" or "holding" states then the algorithm must be extended to include an "are you alive?" message which can be sent to the owner of the sequence number of a request which has stayed in the request queue for a time longer than an appropriate threshold. If there is no response to the "Are you alive?" message within three network latencies then a "cancel" message for that request is sent by the discovering task. Multiple "cancel" messages for a given request will not cause an error.

3.5   Experimental Results

The number of messages to make a decision should be constant except when excessive back-off is generated by heavy network traffic. The algorithm has been run with up to 64 tasks competing for the resource The average number of broadcast messages to obtain mutual exclusion was about 2.5 independent of the number of tasks competing.   The fault-tolerance properties have also been confirmed experimentally. Similar results have been obtained for the other applications. For distributed readers and writers the data objects were replicated 2 and 4 times. The number of processes reading and writing was again up to 64, each on a separate workstation on a network. The average number of messages was about Nx2.5 where N is the number of *data object* replicas.

4   Related Work – Relationship of Associative Communication and Coordination to Other Models of Communication and Coordination

The possible spectrum of related work is quite broad. Splice [7] is a coordination model and language which directly makes use of broadcast.   It is enlightening to position associative broadcast coordination in the context of a recent survey of coordination models and languages by Papadopoulos and Arbab [15]. Papadopoulos and Arbab suggest that models of coordination can be approximately classified as data-driven or control driven.   Data-driven coordination models are structured by Shared Dataspaces, usually implemented as tuple spaces. Processes or components coordinate by putting or getting data from the Shared Dataspace. Linda [10] and its derivatives and enhancements are the prototypical data-driven coordination models and languages. Papadopoulos and Arbab [15] define control-driven coordination languages as follows.

> "In control-driven or process-oriented coordination languages, the coordinated framework evolves by means of observing state changes in processes and, possibly, broadcast of events. Contrary to the case of the data-driven family where coordinators directly handle and examine data values, here processes (whether coordinating or computational ones) are treated as black boxes; data handled within a process is of no concern to the environment of the process. Processes communicate with their environment by means of clearly defined interfaces, usually referred to as input or output

ports. Producer-consumer relationships are formed by means of setting up stream or channel connections between output ports of producers and input ports of consumers. By nature, these connections are point-to-point, although limited broadcasting functionality is usually allowed by forming 1-n relationships between a producer and n consumers and vice versa."

Coordination formulated under associative interactions does not, at first glance, classify cleanly as data-driven or control-driven. There is no shared dataspace and while there are messages there are neither ports nor channels.

Analogies can be made with both the shared dataspace (tuple space) based coordination models and the control-driven coordination models.

The data of a process or component is the content of a tuple. The profile contains the match variables of a tuple. Selectors play the role of tuple templates. Each process or component which is activated by a selector/tuple match may send messages as a result of the action it executes which may bind it to other components. Thus associative broadcast interactions can viewed as being based on implementation of a distributed tuple space with active linked tuples.

Each component can be viewed as a process with multiple entry points defined by its transactions. A profile implicitly defines a set of typed input ports. A selector defines a typed output port. Matching of selectors to profiles (and transactions) establishes a transient channel between two components. Thus the formulation of coordination in associative broadcast can be viewed as implementing coordination among a dynamically structured set of interacting processes.

Other than Splice those coordination models and languages which seem most similar include those which provide for dynamic creation of processes [3] and those based on distributed tuple spaces [16], those based upon distributed tuple spaces of active objects in particular, and those concerned with mobile agents [4].

5   Summary and Future Research

This paper has presented a coordination model based upon associative broadcast. The model has been implemented. Experiments with distributed algorithms implemented in the associative broadcast model have demonstrated efficient and robust coordination over dynamic sets of distributed processes.

We are currently implementing a compiler for a simple specification language for associative interfaces. The compiler will facilitate development of more complex applications and enable a richer set of experiments. We are also extending the coordination model to include runtime generation of data flow graphs and transparent replication of components to enhance fault tolerance. We are also extending the formal model of associative broadcast developed by Bayerdorffer [5] to include the extensions enabling distributed process coordination.

Acknowledgements. This research was supported by the State of Texas Coordinating Board for Higher Education under TARP grant 003658-0508-1999.

References

1. X. Ao, N. Minsky, T. Nguyen, V. Ungureanu Law-Governed Communities Over the Internet In Proc. of Coordination' 2000: Fourth International Conference on Coordination Models and Languages, LNCS, No. 1906, pages 133-147, Springer-Verlag, September 2000, Limassol Cyprus.
2. F. Arbab, F.S. de Boer, and M.M. Bonsangue. A logical interface description language for components. Proceedings of the Second International Conference on Coordination Models and Languages (COORDINATION), LNCS, 2000.
3. F. Arbab, I. Herman, and P. Spilling, "An Overview of Manifold and its Implementation", in: Concurrency: Practice and Experience, 5(1993).
4. F. Arbab, F.S. de Boer, and M.M. Bonsangue. A coordination language for mobile components. In Proceedings of the 2000 ACM Symposium on Applied Computing, SAC2000, 2000.
5. B.Bayerdorffer, "Associative Broadcast and the Communication Semantics of Naming in Concurrent Systems", PhD. dissertation, Dept.of Computer Sciences, Univ. of Texas at Austin. Dec. 1993
6. Bayerdorffer, B.,"Distributed Programming with Associative Broadcast", Proceedings of the Twenty-eighth Hawaii International Conference on System Sciences, January 1995.
7. M. Boasson "Control System Software" IEEE Trans. Automatic Control, 38(7):1094-1107 (1993).
8. F.S. de Boer and M. Bonsangue. "A compositional model for confluent dynamic data-flow networks" In *Proceedings of the International Symposium of the Mathematical Foundations of Computer Science (MFCS)*, LNCS, 2000.
9. F.S. de Boer and M. Bonsangue. A compositional model for confluent dynamic data-flow networks. In Proceedings of the International Symposium of the Mathematical Foundations of Computer Science (MFCS), LNCS, 2000.
10. J.C Browne, E. Berger and A. Dube, "Compositional Development of Performance Models in POEMS" *International Journal of High Performance Computing and it Applications* 14,pp.283-292, 2000.
11. M. Broy "Equations for Describing Dynamic Nets of Communicating Systems," in Proc. 5th COMPASS Workshop, Volume 906, LNCS, pp170-187, 1995.
12. L. Cardelli and A. Gordon "Mobile Ambients" in M. Nivat, editor, "Foundations of Software Science and Computational Structures, Volume 1378 of LNCS, pp.140-155,Springer-Verlag (1998).
13. J. Gray and A. Reuter. *Transaction Processing : Concepts and Techniques*. Morgan Kaufmann Publishers, 1993.
14. Kaashoek, M. F., Tanenbaum, A. S., Hummel, S. F., and Bal, H. E. *An Efficient Reliable Broadcast Protocol*. ACM SIGOPS Operating Systems Review 23, 4 (Oct. 1989).
15. G. A. Papadopoulos and F. Arbab "Coordination Models and Languages", in Advances in Computers, Academic Press, August 1998, Vol. 46: The Engineering of Large Systems.
16. A. Rowston and A. Wood "An Efficient Distributed Tuple Space Implementation for Networks of Workstations" In L.Bouge, P Fraigniaud, A. Mignotte and Y. Robert, editors, Europar'96, volume 1123 of LNCS pp.510-513, Springer Verlag, 1996.
17. G. Ricart and A. Agrawala "An Optimal Algorithm for Mutual Exclusion in Computer Networks" Comm.ACM 24(1)(Jan 1981), pp.9-17
18. D. Gelertner. "Generative communication in Linda." ACM Trans. Prog. Lang. Sys., 7(1):80-- 112, 1985.

19. M.M. Bonsangue, J.N. Kok, and G. Zavattaro. *Comparing coordination models based on shared distributed replicated data.* In Proceedings of the 1999 ACM Symposium on Applied Computing; Special Track on Coordination Models, Languages and Applications, ACM press, 1999.
20. C. Dwork, N. Lynch, and L. Stockmeyer. *Consensus in the presence of partial synchrony.* Journal of the ACM, 35(2):288--323, April 1988.

Appendix A: Informal Proof of Correctness of Distributed Associative Mutual Exclusion

Definitions

A *requests queue is* a finite ordered list of tuples (i, s) where i is a unique node identification number and s is a monotonically increasing sequence number. The requests queue is ordered according to the function $\oplus$, which is defined as: $(i_1, s_1) \oplus (i_2, s_2) \to ((s_1 \neq s_2) \to (s_1 < s_2) \land (s_1 = s_2) \to (i_1 < i_2))$. Note that we assume all the identifiers i are unique, so this is a total ordering. In basic terms, the requests queue is first ordered by the sequence number and, in the case of ties, is ordered by the identification number. Realize that the basic definition allows for duplication of sequence numbers.

A mutual exclusion process is *requesting* or is in the *requesting state* if it either is waiting to possess the resource after successfully negotiating a sequence number and place in the global requests queue, or currently possesses the resource. When requesting, a mutual exclusion process has a local sequence number S.

A mutual exclusion process is *negotiating* if it is attempting to enter the requesting state but is still in the conflict negotiation stage. This differs from the requesting state in that the process does not yet have a sequence number S.

Assumptions

The correct execution of this algorithm rests on a few significant but realistic assumptions. To keep the algorithm simple we leave these details to the design of the underlying network layers and the behavior of the application utilizing our mutual exclusion technique.

Assumption 1. *Reliable delivery of all messages within a known time bound.*

The literature contains many algorithms for reliable delivery of broadcast or multicast messages. Although there can be no absolute guarantee of delivery in most networks, messages are delivered in a timely manner except in cases of extreme network dysfunction. Since our nodes are all in the same broadcast domain, we presume that they are fairly closely connected, and therefore the likelihood of such an extreme disruption is remote.

Assumption 2. *Each process follows the prescribed protocol - or, in other words, we have no Byzantine faults.*

We assume that none of the nodes are intentionally attempting to disrupt or violate the protocol. Therefore we restrict our analysis of the fault-tolerance to consider only faults induced in the normal course of the operation of the algorithm.

Assumption 3. *Each process holds the resource for a bounded time.*

In any mutual exclusion situation, if a process (or a thread, or whatever the unit of execution stream is) holds a lock forever, clearly no others will be able to proceed. Therefore the algorithm is only useful if we assume that each process will acquire the resource, use it, and eventually release it so that others may proceed.

Assumption 4. *When a node is in the negotiation phase, it will collide with other nodes a bounded number of times.*

For our algorithm to behave correctly, we must assert that eventually, any node that is attempting to request will eventually successfully negotiate a unique sequence number for itself. This is similar to Ethernet - while it is not absolutely true that all collisions will be resolved, the probability of collisions not resolving is very small.

Theorem

Theorem 1. *A process which follows the Mutual Exclusion protocol and attempts to request the resource will receive exclusive use of the resource within a bounded amount of time.*

To assert this, we need the help of the following lemmas.

Lemma 1. *If two or more nodes attempt to request with the same sequence number S, S will never be used by a node in the requesting state.*

Corollary. A node in the requesting state always uses a unique sequence number S.

Lemma Proof. Suppose a set of nodes $i_1, ..., i_k$ attempt to request with the same sequence number S. Since we assume no malicious processes, all processes sent their requests before receiving any of the others' requests - otherwise they would have selected a different sequence number.

Since we assume a time bound on message delivery, and the Mutual Exclusion algorithm waits at least this long during the negotiation phase, each node will receive the requests before concluding the negotiation phase. Since these requests will arrive during the negotiation phase, each node will decide S has been collided on, and decide not to use it. Since these nodes are the only nodes that used S, S will never be used.

Lemma 2. *A node attempting to request will eventually enter the requesting state with a unique sequence number S.*

Lemma Proof. This is a direct consequence of Lemma 1. After the number of times it collides, the next attempt will not collide, and the sequence number used at that time will be S.

Lemma 3. *If a node requests with sequence number S, and verifies that no other node uses S while it is requesting, no other node uses S over the entire execution of the mutual exclusion system.*

Lemma Proof. Let the node in question be node i. Consider the following times another node j might try to use S:

1. **j enters the requesting state with S before i attempts to.** In this case, j successfully completed the negotiation phase and acquired S. This implies that i advanced its highest known sequence number past S. This contradicts the definition of a mutual exclusion process, that states that S is monotonically increasing, and therefore i would not have selected S.

2. **j attempts to enter the requesting state with S while i attempts to enter the requesting state.** In this case, i and j would have collided. This is contradictory to the assumption that i is in the requesting state, which implies a successful conclusion of the negotiation process.

3. **j attempts to enter the requesting state with S while i is requesting with S.** This is contradictory to the assumption that i verified that no other nodes used S while it was requesting.

4. **j attempts to enter the requesting state with S after i requests with S.** Since i completed its request with S, j received the appropriate messages to cause it to monotonically increase its highest known sequence number beyond S. Since we have assumed no Byzantine faults, j would not select S, and so this cannot happen.

Theorem Proof. Let i be a node in the Mutual Exclusion network, and suppose it attempts to request to use the resource at some time t.

By Lemma 2, i will successfully negotiate a unique sequence number. Let that number be S_i.

Since we assume no Byzantine faults, a node j with sequence number S_j will only have access to the resource if S_j is minimal across all current requests.

We must consider two cases.

1. **S_i is minimal.** i therefore immediately has exclusive access to the resource with no time delay from its request.

2. S_i **is not minimal.** In this case there is at least one request pending with a lower sequence number. Let $\langle\ (k_1, S_{k1}, S_{kj}, \Delta_{k1}),..., (k_m, S_{km}, \Delta_{km}), (i, S_i, \Delta_i)\ \rangle$ be the part of the request queue with lower or equal sequence numbers, where k_j is a node, S_{kj} is that node's sequence number, and Δ_{kj} is the time the node will execute while holding the resource.

Note that by the Corollary and Lemma 3, each S_{km} is unique. We don't necessarily know what each Δ_{km} is, but by Assumption 3, it does exist.

Therefore, it will take $\sum_{s=1}^{m} \Delta_{ks}$ time units for all previous requests to be serviced. At that point, process i will have the lowest sequence number. Any other processes with pending requests will have higher sequence numbers, and therefore process i will have exclusive use of the resource, with the above time delay.

State- and Event-Based Reactive Programming in Shared Dataspaces

Nadia Busi[1], Antony Rowstron[2], and Gianluigi Zavattaro[1]

[1] Dipartimento di Scienze dell'Informazione, Università di Bologna,
Piazza di Porta S. Donato 5, I-40127 Bologna, Italy.
{busi,zavattar}@cs.unibo.it
[2] Microsoft Research, 7 J J Thomson Avenue, Cambridge, CB3 0FB
antr@microsoft.com

Abstract. The traditional Linda programming style, based on the introduction and consumption of data from a common repository, seems not adequate for highly dynamic applications in which it is important to observe modification of the environment which occur quickly. On the other hand, reactive programming seems more appropriate for this kind of applications. In this paper we consider some approaches recently presented in the literature for embedding reactive programming in shared dataspaces, we present a possible classification for these approaches, and we perform a rigorous investigation of their relative advantages and disadvantages.

1 Introduction

The development of Linda-like coordination languages [Gel85] for use over wide-area networks has driven the consideration of new primitives being added to allow new styles of coordination. One set of such primitives are those that allow reactive-programming, essentially allowing a program to be notified on the insertion of tuples into particular tuples spaces, or dataspaces. Examples of Linda-like coordination languages including such primitives are JavaSpaces [W+98], TSpaces [WMLF98] and WCL [Row98].

One interesting observation is that the primitives incorporated within the coordination languages, whilst all aiming to provide support for reactive programming, have different (informal) semantics. Indeed, it is possible to classify the primitives incorporated as being: (1) state-based, (2) event based, and (3) hybrid.

In this paper we provide a formal semantics to be used to compare the expressive power and the interchangeability of these reactive mechanisms, where by interchageability we mean the possibility to substitute one mechanism in place of the others without affecting the internal behaviour of the coordinated components.

For each of the classes we consider a typical coordination primitive, for clarity we assume there is a single dataspace:

F. Arbab and C. Talcott (Eds.): COORDINATION 2002, LNCS 2315, pp. 111–124, 2002.

(1) $forEach(a, P)$: spawns an instance of process P for each occurrence of a currently in the dataspace;

(2) $notify(a, P)$: produces a listener, that we denote with $on(a, P)$, which will spawn an instance of P each time a new a is produced;

(3) $monitor(a, P)$: spawns an instance of process P for each occurrence of a currently in the dataspace, and produces a listener $on(a, P)$ which will spawn an instance of P each time a new a is produced.

Furthermore, for event-based mechanisms we consider a $dereg(a, P)$ primitive which removes one occurrence of listener $on(a, P)$.

The primitive $notify$ has been proposed as a coordination operations by JavaSpaces [W+98], $monitor$ has been introduced for the first time by one of the authors in WCL [Row98], while $forEach$ is an adaptation to our context of the so-called `copy-collect` operation [RW98]: this primitive, proposed as a solution for the typical multiple-read problem of Linda, has the ability to atomically copy all the data satisfying a certain pattern from one dataspace to another.

In this paper we demonstrate that the three approaches are equivalent by showing how each of the approaches can be reproduced in terms of the others. However, only some of these translations are adequate for open environments (new components may be introduced in the system at run time and therefore dynamically); in particular, the mapping from the state- to the event-based approach and vice versa are valid only for closed applications (where the components involved in the system are a priori known and therefore statically).

In Section 2 we further motivate the introduction of reactive primitives. In Section 3 we present a process calculus used to perform a rigorous investigation of the three reactive primitives; the results of this comparison are reported in Section 4. Finally, Section 5 contains some conclusive remarks.

2   Reactive Programming in Shared Dataspaces

In order to demonstrate why reactive programming primitives are attractive in Linda-like coordination languages, let us consider some of the functionality of a simple instant messenger type tool: the functionalities that allows a user to display a list of "buddies" and their current status (e.g., in meeting, at lunch, busy and so forth).

Each user runs a *buddy list agent* which enables them to signal to other users what their current status is, and to observe the status of the other users. A user can change their state by pressing buttons on the buddy list agent. Although this example is simple, it demonstrates the power of reactive programming.

A simple way to create the buddy list agent is to create a shared dataspace into which the buddy list agents place tuples representing their status. Whenever a user starts a buddy list agent, it inserts a status tuple into the shared dataspace, containing the user's name and their initial status. When a user changes their status in the buddy list agent, the agent removes their status tuple and inserts a new tuple with the user's name and their new status. When the agent starts, a list of all users with a status tuple is displayed, also showing their current status. As other users change their states, these changes are reflected on all the users buddy lists.

The state tuples in the shared dataspace at any one time represent the *global status* of (most of) the users and a buddy list agent can examine these tuples to determine who is currently available and their status. This means the application does not involve a centralised coordinator. It should be noted that the tuple space does not necessarily contain the entire global state because tuples are removed to be updated. Therefore, if a buddy list agent is updating their user's status tuple, the user will not be represented by a tuple in the tuple space.

The implementation of such a scheme using the standard Linda primitives is not easy, requiring shared counters and so forth. However, reactive programming primitives should be able to enable this programming style.

So, let us consider how the monitor primitive can be used in this example. When a buddy list agent is started it performs a *monitor* on the shared tuple space. This has the effect of returning all the current state tuples and any ones that are inserted in future. In the description of the buddy list agent it was described how it is possible for the shared dataspace not to contain all state tuples as one or more of the agents may be updating their status tuple. However, this does not matter because any agent updating their status tuple will reinsert the status tuple. When this occurs the *monitor* primitive will consider the inserted tuple and return it. When a buddy list agent receives the tuple it is able to check the users name locally and discover whether the tuple represents the status of as yet unseen user or if it is an update of an existing user's status.

The monitor primitive was introduced in WCL [Row98]. It explicitly returns the tuples that match the template in the dataspace, as well as tuples subsequently inserted (until a *dereg* is performed). JavaSpaces, in contrast, provides a *notify* primitive which *does not* return tuples that are already in the tuple space which match the template, simply tuples inserted subsequently[1]. This has several side effects, one is that the *notify* primitive can not be used in the same way as the *monitor* primitive in the buddy list example. From a programmer's perspective, the issue is how to ensure that each status tuple is read once. If all matching tuples in the dataspace are retrieved prior issuing the *notify* primitive (for example using a *forEach* primitive), a tuple can be inserted once the *forEach* has completed but before the *notify* has been started, and therefore, be missed. Alternatively, if the *notify* is issued first, and after a *forEach* is performed, a single tuple can be returned twice (and there is no explicit ordering). Therefore, from a programmers perspective the use of a monitor appears more powerful and flexible.

---

[1] It actually returns a notification that a tuple has been inserted not the tuple, and the process must explicitly retrieve the new tuple.

3 The Calculus

In this section, we introduce a process calculus based on the Linda coordination primitives plus the reactive mechanisms discussed in the Introduction,

By borrowing typical techniques from the tradition of process calculi for concurrency (e.g., Milner's CCS [Mil89]), an agent is described as a term of an algebra where the basic actions are typical Linda coordination primitives or one of the considered reactive based coordination operations.

To be general, we consider a denumerable set of names for data, called $Data$, ranged over by a, b, ... The set $Prog$ of programs, ranged over by P, P', ..., is the set of terms generated by the following grammar:

$$P \quad ::= \quad \mathbf{0} \mid \mu.P \mid \langle a \rangle \mid on(a, P) \mid K \mid P|P$$

$$\mu \quad ::= \quad out(a) \mid in(a) \mid rd(a) \mid$$
$$forEach(a, P) \mid notify(a, P) \mid monitor(a, P) \mid dereg(a, P)$$

where μ denotes an instance of one of the possible coordination primitives, and K stands for a generic element of a set $Name$ of program names; we assume that all program name occurrences are equipped with a corresponding (guarded) defining equation of the form $K = P$. Program names are used to support recursive definitions as, for example, in the term $Ren_{ab} = in(a).out(b).Ren_{ab}$, which represents a program able to repeatedly rename messages of the kind a in messages of the kind b.

A term P is the parallel composition (we use the standard parallel composition operator $|$) of the active programs, plus the data which are currently available in the data repository, and terms which denote listeners used for the modeling of event-based reactive programming. Term $\mathbf{0}$ represents a program that can do nothing. Term $\mu.P$ is a program that can do the action μ and after behaves like P. The term $\langle a \rangle$ denotes an instance of datum a which is currently available for $rd(a)$ and $in(a)$ operations; on the other hand, $on(a, P)$ represents a listener responsible to activate a new instance of program P each time a new occurrence of datum a is produced.

In the following we will exploit a structural congruence relation in order to equate terms which represents the same system even if they are syntactically different. Let $equiv$ be the least congruence relation satisfying:

$$P|Q \equiv Q|P \quad P|(Q|R) \equiv (P|Q)|R$$
$$P|\mathbf{0} \equiv P \quad P \equiv K \quad \text{if } P = K$$

In the following we will reason upto structural congruence, i.e., we will not make any distinction between P and Q whenever $P \equiv Q$.

We use the following notation: $P \notin R$ (to indicate that P is not a subterm of program R), $\prod_n P$ (to denote the parallel composition of n instances of program P), and $\prod_i P_i$ (to denote the parallel composition of the indexed programs P_i).

The operational semantics is defined by the transition relation $(Prog, \longrightarrow)$ defined as the least relation satisfying the axioms and rules reported in Table 1.

Table 1. The operational semantics.

$$in(a).P|\langle a\rangle|R \longrightarrow P|R$$

$$rd(a).P|\langle a\rangle|R \longrightarrow P|\langle a\rangle|R$$

$$forEach(a,P).Q|\prod_n\langle a\rangle|R \longrightarrow Q|\prod_n P|\prod_n\langle a\rangle|R \qquad \langle a\rangle \notin R$$

$$notify(a,P).Q|R \longrightarrow Q|on(a,P)|R$$

$$monitor(a,P).Q|\prod_n\langle a\rangle|R \longrightarrow Q|\prod_n P|on(a,P)|\prod_n\langle a\rangle|R \ \langle a\rangle \notin R$$

$$dereg(a,P).Q|on(a,P)|R \longrightarrow Q|R$$

$$out(a).P|\prod_i on(a,P_i)|R \longrightarrow P|\langle a\rangle|\prod_i P_i|\prod_i on(a,P_i)|R \quad \begin{array}{l}\text{for any } S,\\ on(a,S)\notin R\end{array}$$

In the following we denote by $P \longrightarrow^* P'$ the fact that either $P \equiv P'$ or there exist $P_0 \ldots P_n$ such that $P_0 \equiv P$, $P_n \equiv P'$, and $P_i \longrightarrow P_{i+1}$ (for $0 \leq i < n$).

The first two axioms deal with the $in(a)$ and $rd(a)$ coordination operations: both operations require the presence of a term $\langle a\rangle$; in the second case the result of the execution of the operation is that this term is consumed.

The third axioms describe the $forEach(a,P)$ operation: the result of its execution is the spawning of a new process P for each instance of $\langle a\rangle$ (observe that this is ensured by the side condition $\langle a\rangle \notin R$). The result of the execution of the $notify(a,P)$ operation is the spawning of the listener $on(a,P)$. The $monitor(a,P)$ primitive combines the two above operations: a new process P is spawned for each instance of $\langle a\rangle$ and a new listener $on(a,P)$ is produced.

The $dereg(a,P)$ requires the presence of a listener $on(a,P)$, and this term is removed as effect of the execution of this operation.

The $out(a)$ operation produces a new term $\langle a\rangle$; moreover, for each listener $on(a,P)$ in the environment, a new program P is spawned (observe that this is ensured by the side condition: for any S, $on(a,S) \notin R$).

In the following we will focus on three variants of the calculus, in which only one among the three reactive primitives $forEach$, $notify$, and $monitor$ is considered. The three calculi are denoted with $L[forEach]$, $L[notify]$, and $L[monitor]$, respectively. We will also consider a fourth subcalculus in which both the $notify$ and the $forEach$ operations are considered: this calculus is denoted by $L[forEach, notify]$.

4   Comparing the Reactive Mechanisms

In this section we compare the expressive power of the different reactive mechanisms by investigating the encodability of one mechanism in terms of the others. We will show that in general, for each pair of calculi there exists an encoding function from the first calculus to the second.

Two kinds of encodings are used: one adequate for closed systems only, and one suitable for open systems too. In the first case, indeed, it is necessary to assume that all the programs involved in the system are a priori known; on the other hand, the second class of encodings does not make this kind of assumption.

To be more precise, we state that an encoding function $[\![\,]\!]$ from one calculus to another is *open* if the following costraints are satisfied:

$$[\![P]\!] = [\![P]\!] \mid \textstyle\prod_{n(P)} R_a$$
$$[\![P|Q]\!] = [\![P]\!] \mid [\![Q]\!]$$

where $n(P)$ denotes the set of names of data which occur in the program P, and R_a denotes a program (depending on the considered encoding) used to manage the name a occurring inside P.

We refer to this class of encodings as "open" because the addition of a new program Q in parallel with P does not require to recompute the overall encoding of P; indeed, given P, its encoding $[\![P]\!]$ and a program Q to be added in parallel with P, we have that the new encoding

$$[\![P|Q]\!] = [\![P]\!] \mid [\![Q]\!] \mid \textstyle\prod_{n(P)\cup n(Q)} R_a = [\![P]\!] \mid [\![Q]\!] \mid \textstyle\prod_{n(Q)\setminus n(P)} R_a$$

can be obtained simply by adding new programs in parallel with the initial encoding $[\![P]\!]$

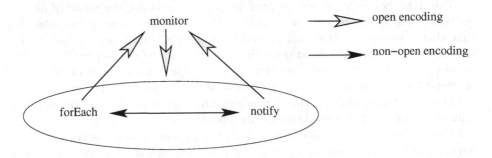

Fig. 1. Summary of the encodings.

The results presented in the rest of this section are summarized in Figure 1. In Subsection 4.1 (resp. 4.2) we show the existence of an open encoding of L[notify] (resp. L[forEach]) in L[monitor]. This means that the *monitor* primitive is expressive enough to model both the *notify* and the *forEach* operations. We show the existence of an open encoding of L[monitor] in L[forEach,notify] in Subsection 4.3.

As far as static systems are concerned, also the *notify* and the *forEach* primitives are interchangeable: we show the existence of non–open encodings of L[notify] in L[forEach] (and vice versa) in Subsection 4.4 (resp. 4.5). By composing each of these encodings with the open encoding of the *monitor* primitive in the language containing both the *notify* and the *forEach* operations, we obtain a non–open encoding of L[monitor] in L[notify] (and in L[forEach]).

4.1   Encoding L[notify] in L[monitor]

In this section we show that it is possible to model the event-based reactive mechanism of the *notify* primitive using the *monitor* operation.

The hybrid approach of the *monitor* primitive observes all the data already available at the instant in which the operation is performed, as also the future incoming entries. On the other hand, the *notify* operation observes only the incoming entries. In order to overcome this difference, for each datum $\langle a \rangle$ we exploit an auxiliary datum $\langle a' \rangle$; this kind of data are produced and subsequently removed every time an $out(a)$ operation is performed. In this way the auxiliary data $\langle a' \rangle$ are not persistent in the dataspace, but they are stored only temporarily.

When we need to model a $notify(a, P)$ operation, we use $monitor(a', P)$ which observes the auxiliary data only; as these data are not persistent, only subsequent productions will be observed.

Formally, the encoding function is defined as $[\![P]\!] = [P]$ where $[P]$ is inductively defined as follows:

$$[\mathbf{0}] = \mathbf{0} \qquad\qquad\qquad [\langle a \rangle] = \langle a \rangle$$
$$[on(a, P)] = monitor(a', [P]) \qquad [K] = K'$$
$$[P|Q] = [P]\|[Q] \qquad\qquad [\mu.P] = \mu.[P] \quad \mu \neq notify(a, Q), out(a)$$
$$[notify(a, P).Q] = monitor(a', [P]).[Q]$$
$$[out(a).P] = out(a').in(a').out(a).[P]$$

where, for each program name K in $L[notify]$ with definition $K = P$, we assume the existence of a corresponding K' in $L[monitor]$ with definition $K' = [P]$. Moreover, we assume that for each encoding $[\![P]\!]$ the auxiliary names a' are different from each of the names of data occurring in P.

This encoding satisfies the above contraints; thus it is open. Moreover, we have that it is also homomorphic with respect to the parallel operation, i.e., $[\![P|Q]\!] = [\![P]\!]\|[\![Q]\!]$. In the terminology of [dBP91] this property is called modularity with respect to the parallel composition operator.

The correctness of this encoding is formally stated by the following theorem which states that, given a program P of $L[notify]$, each computation step of P can be simulated by $[\![P]\!]$, and that each computation of $[\![P]\!]$ can be extended in such a way that it corresponds to an equivalent computation of P. Due to space limit we do not report the proof of this theorem (as also the proofs of the theorems in the following sections).

Theorem 1. *Given a program P of $L[notify]$ we have that:*

- *if $P \longrightarrow P'$ then $[\![P]\!] \longrightarrow^+ [\![P']\!]$;*
- *if $[\![P]\!] \longrightarrow^+ Q$ then there exists P' such that $Q \longrightarrow^* [\![P']\!]$ and $P \longrightarrow^+ P'$.*

An interesting property of this encoding concerns the use of the auxiliary names a'. As stated above, data $\langle a' \rangle$ are produced (and subsequently removed) simply to notify the execution of $out(a)$ operations. Observe that this production and subsequent consumption operations could be executed in interleaving with other operations performed by concurrent processes. As an example consider the encoding $[\![notify(a, P)|out(a)]\!] = monitor(a', [\![P]\!])|out(a').in(a').out(a)$. Consider now the computation of the encoding in which first $\langle a' \rangle$ is produced and consumed, after the *monitor* operation is performed, and finally, the $out(a)$ primitive is executed.

This computation is particularly of interest because no reaction is activated even if the output of $\langle a \rangle$ is executed after the execution of the program representing the $notify(a, P)$ process. However, this is not a problem for the encoding because this particular computation corresponds to the computation of the initial program in which the *notify* operation is executed only after the output of $\langle a \rangle$.

4.2   Encoding L[forEach] in L[monitor]

Now we concentrate on the modeling of the state-based primitive *forEach* using the hybrid approach adopted by *monitor*. The difference between the two operations is that *monitor* observes not only the data already available, but is also activates a listener which observes the future incoming entries. This difference can be covered simply by removing this listener immediately after its activation: following this approach, a *forEach* operation is modeled by a *monitor* primitive followed by a *dereg*. Formally, the new encoding can be defined as follows

$$[\![P]\!] = [\![P]\!]| \prod_{a\in n(P)} \langle lock_a \rangle$$

where $[\![P]\!]$ is inductively defined as above, with only two non-trivial cases

$$[\![forEach(a, P).Q]\!] = in(lock_a).monitor(a, [\![P]\!]).$$
$$dereg(a, [\![P]\!]).out(lock_a).[\![Q]\!]$$
$$[\![out(a).P]\!] \qquad = in(lock_a).out(a).out(lock_a).[\![P]\!]$$

where we assume that for each encoding $[\![P]\!]$ the auxiliary names $lock_a$ are all distinct from the names a occurring inside P.

Also in this case the correctness of the encoding is stated by a theorem similar to Theorem 1; the difference here is in the fact that we have to consider also the data $\langle lock_a \rangle$.

Theorem 2. *Given a program P of $L[forEach]$ we have that:*

- *if $P \longrightarrow P'$ then $[\![P]\!] \longrightarrow^+ [\![P']\!]| \prod_{a\in n(P)\backslash n(P')} \langle lock_a \rangle$;*
- *if $[\![P]\!] \longrightarrow^+ Q$ then there exists P' such that $P \longrightarrow^+ P'$ and $Q \longrightarrow^* [\![P']\!]| \prod_{a\in n(P)\backslash n(P')} \langle lock_a \rangle$.*

The encoding exploits, for each name of datum a occurring in the source program P, the auxiliar datum $\langle lock_a \rangle$, to implement mutual exclusion between the execution of the programs corresponding to the output operation $out(a)$ and the reactive operations $forEach(a)$. Mutual exclusion is achieved simply by forcing the withdrawal (and subsequent release) of the datum $\langle lock_a \rangle$ before (and after) each sequence of critical operations to be executed in mutual exclusion.

This locking policy is necessary in order to ensure that the listener produced by the execution of a $monitor(a)$ operation is deregistered before a subsequent output operation $out(a)$ is performed (e.g., by some other concurrent process).

Consider, as an example, the encoding of $\langle a \rangle | forEach(a, out(a))$ if we do not use mutual exclusion. In this case the target program becomes

$$\langle a \rangle | monitor(a, out(a)).dereg(a, out(a))$$

This program could activate an infinite computation in the case the $dereg$ operation is delayed indefinitely: this could happen if a loop is activated in which first the reaction $out(a)$ is executed, and after the listener $on(a, out(a))$ reacts by spawning a new instance of $out(a)$. On the other hand, the source program $\langle a \rangle | forEach(a, out(a))$ has no infinite computation.

Observe that the locking policy involves only operations on the same name; the concurrent execution of operations modeling an $out(a)$ and a $forEach(b, P)$ primitive, for example, is allowed because the two operations consider the two distinct data $\langle lock_a \rangle$ and $\langle lock_b \rangle$, respectively. Finally, observe that the encoding is open even if it is not modular.

4.2   Encoding of L[monitor] in L[forEach,notify]

In this section we investigate the possibility to model the hybrid approach exploiting both the state- and the event-based approaches. Intuitively, this can be done simply by modeling the $monitor$ operation with a $forEach$ immediately followed by a $notify$ operation.

Following this approach, we react to the data currently present in the repository as also to those data which will be introduced subsequently. The unique problem that may happen, occurs if new interesting data are produced between the execution of the $forEach$ and the $notify$ operations; in this case, the produced instance of the datum does not activate the expected reaction. To avoid this problem we could exploit a locking policy similar to the one adopted in the previous subsection.

Formally, we define the new encoding as

$$[\![P]\!] = [\![P]\!] | \prod_{a \in n(P)} \langle lock_a \rangle$$

where $[\![P]\!]$ is inductively defined as above, with only three significant cases

$$[\![monitor(a, P).Q]\!] = in(lock_a).forEach(a, [\![P]\!]).$$
$$notify(a, [\![P]\!]).out(lock_a).[\![Q]\!]$$
$$[\![on(a, P)]\!] \quad\quad = on(a, [\![P]\!])$$
$$[\![out(a).P]\!] \quad\quad = in(lock_a).out(a).out(lock_a).[\![P]\!]$$

where we assume that for each encoding $[\![P]\!]$ the auxiliary names $lock_a$ are all distinct from the names a occurring inside P.

The correctness of this encoding is a consequence of a theorem corresponding to Theorem 2 where the language $L[monitor]$ is considered instead of $L[forEach]$. This encoding exploits a locking policy which avoid the concurrent execution of operations representing *monitor* and *out* operations executed on the same name a: these operations must be executed in mutual exclusion in order to avoid that some events are not observed (then some reactions could be lost).

As an example of undesired computation consider $out(a)|monitor(a, LOOP)$, where $LOOP$ is any program which performs an infinite computation. This program has only infinite computations as it is ensured that the reaction $LOOP$ is activated, both in the case that $out(a)$ is executed before *monitor* and in the case it is executed after. Consider now the encoding of this program in the case the locking policy is not adopted:

$$out(a)|forEach(a, [\![LOOP]\!]).notify(a, [\![LOOP]\!])$$

This second program has at least one finite computation; indeed consider the case in which $out(a)$ is scheduled exactly between the execution of the *forEach* and the *notify* operations.

One could think to solve this problem simply by changing the order of the two reactive operations obtaining the new encoding:

$$out(a)|notify(a, [\![LOOP]\!]).forEach(a, [\![LOOP]\!])$$

This new program has only infinite computations; however, it could activate the undesired computation in which two reactions are activated in the case the $out(a)$ operation is executed in interleaving with the two reactive primitives.

Also in this case, the locking policy involves only concurrent operations performed on the same name. Similarly to the previous subsection, the encoding is open even if not modular.

4.4   Encoding L[notify] in L[forEach]

In the previous subsections we have formally proved the intuitive result that the hybrid paradigm is powerful enough to model both the event- and the state-based reactive approaches; moreover, we showed that the *notify* and the *forEach* primitives permit to emulate the hybrid *monitor* operation (at the price of introducing some locking mechanism). It is also interesting to observe that all the encodings that we have presented are suitable for open applications.

In this section we start the investigation of the modeling of the event-based approach using the state-based one. The interesting result is that even if an encoding exists, it is not suitable for open applications; namely, it does not satisfy the constraints we have fixed for open encodings. The problem is that the encoding that we present requires the a priori knowledge of all the possible programs that will be executed in the system. This is against the basic requirements of open applications in which we usually assume that there exist components of the system which are added at run-time.

The encoding is based on the idea that listeners can be represented by auxiliary data; namely, for each possible listener $on(a, P_{a_i})$ we use an auxiliary datum $\langle a_i \rangle$ which is introduced in the dataspace. Whenever an output operation $out(a)$ is performed, the presence of these auxiliary data $\langle a_i \rangle$ is checked, and for each of them the corresponding reaction is activated; this operation can be obtained simply by executing a sequence of operations $forEach(a_i, P_{a_i})$ for all possible reactions P_{a_i}. The drawback of this approach is that it is necessary to know a priori all the possible reactions P_{a_i} which could be involved.

Formally, let P be a program of $L[notify]$ to be encoded in $L[forEach]$; for each name a occurring in P, i.e., $a \in n(P)$, we denote with $ONP(a)$ the programs $P_{a_1}, \ldots, P_{a_l}$ which could be the possible reactions associated to a in P, i.e., all those programs P_a appearing in operations $notify(a, P_a)$ or terms $on(a, P_a)$. For each of the programs $P_{a_i} \in ONP(a)$, we consider an auxiliary name a_i and a program name K_{a_i}. With ONP we denote the function which associates to each $a \in n(P)$ the programs in $ONP(a)$.

The encoding is defined as follows

$$[\![P]\!] = [\![P]\!]_{ONP} | \prod_{a \in n(P)} \langle lock_a \rangle$$

where $[\![P]\!]_{ONP}$ is inductively defined with only three non-trivial cases

$$[\![notify(a, P_{a_i}).Q]\!]_{ONP} = in(lock_a).out(a_i).out(lock_a).[\![Q]\!]_{ONP}$$
$$[\![on(a, P_{a_i})]\!]_{ONP} = \langle a_i \rangle$$
$$[\![out(a).P]\!]_{ONP} = in(lock_a).forEach(a_1, K_{a_1}).forEach(a_2, K_{a_2})\ldots$$
$$forEach(a, K_{a_l}).out(a).out(lock_a).[\![P]\!]_{ONP}$$
$$\text{if } ONP(a) - P_{a_1}\ldots P_{a_l}$$

where we assume that for each encoding $[\![P]\!]$ the auxiliary names $lock_a$ are all distinct from the names a occurring inside P, and that the program names K_{a_i} are all distinct from the other program names K occurring in P. For each of this program name K_{a_i}, with $P_{a_i} \in ONP(a)$, we consider the following definition $K_{a_i} = [\![P_{a_i}]\!]_{ONP}$.

The program names K_{a_i} are used to model the corresponding reactions P_{a_i}. This approach is necessary, e.g., to model programs of $L[notify]$, see for example $notify(a, out(a)).out(a)$, which have an infinite behaviour even if they are not recursively defined. This cannot happen in $L[forEach]$ where only recursively defined programs could give rise to infinite computations. As an example, consider the following program corresponding to $[\![notify(a, out(a)).out(a)]\!]$ which exploit a recursive definition for the program name K_{a_1}:

$$in(lock_a).out(a_1).out(lock_a).in(lock_a).forEach(a_1, K_{a_1}).out(lock_a)$$
$$K_{a_1} = in(lock_a).forEach(a_1, K_{a_1}).out(lock_a)$$

It is worth noting that this encoding does not satisfy the constraints we have fixed for open encodings; this because the inner encoding function $[\![\ ]\!]$ depends on the initial term considered by the outer encoding $[\![\ ]\!]$. For example, encoding P

in parallel with Q is usually different from encoding P in parallel with a different program R.

In this case, the theorem proving the correctness of the encoding should be rephrased in order to manage the new kind of non-open encoding.

Theorem 3. *Given a program P of $L[notify]$ we have that:*

- *if $P \longrightarrow P'$ then $[\![P]\!] \longrightarrow^{+} [\![P']\!]_{ON_P} | \prod_{a \in n(P)} \langle lock_a \rangle;$*
- *if $[\![P]\!] \longrightarrow^{+} Q$ then there exists P' such that $P \longrightarrow^{+} P'$ and $Q \longrightarrow^{*} [\![P']\!]_{ON_P} | \prod_{a \in n(P)} \langle lock_a \rangle.$*

Also this encoding adopts mutual exclusion among the execution of operations performed on the same name. In order to undertand the importance of this locking policy consider the program $notify(a, notify(a, LOOP)).out(a)$ in which it is ensured that only one reaction can be activated (i.e., $LOOP$ cannot be activated). On the other hand, if we consider its encoding without the locking policy we obtain

$$out(a_1).forEach(a_1, K_{a_1}).forEach(a_2, K_{a_2}).out(a)$$
$$K_{a_1} = out(a_2)$$
$$K_{a_2} = LOOP'$$

where $LOOP'$ is the encoding of $LOOP$. This program could give rise to an undesired infinite computation in the case the first reaction K_{a_1} is executed in interleaving with the two $forEach$ operations.

4.5   Encoding L[forEach] in L[notify]

In this section we consider the problem of encoding the state-based reactive programming approach in the event-based one. Also in this case we show that the encoding exists, but it is not suitable for open applications.

The idea on which the encoding is based is to associate to each datum $\langle a \rangle$ a group of listeners $on(a_i, P_{a_i})$, one for each possible reaction P_{a_i}. In this context, if we want to model the execution of a $forEach(a, P_i)$ operation it is sufficient to produce a datum $\langle a_i \rangle$: as reaction to the production of this datum a number of reactions P_i, corresponding to the number of occurrences of the listener $on(a_i, P_{a_i})$, corresponding to the number of occurrences of $\langle a \rangle$, are activated.

Formally, let P be a program of $L[forEach]$ that we want to encode in $L[notify]$; for each name a occurring in P, i.e., $a \in n(P)$, we denote with $RE_P(a)$ the programs $P_{a_1}, \ldots, P_{a_l}$ which could be the possible reactions associated to a in P, i.e., all those programs P_a appearing in operations $forEach(a, P_a)$. For each of the programs $P_{a_i} \in RE_P(a)$, we consider an auxiliary name a_i and a program name K_{a_i}. With RE_P we denote the function which associates to each $a \in n(P)$ the programs in $RE_P(a)$.

The encoding is defined as follows

$$[\![P]\!] = [\![P]\!]_{RE_P} | \prod_{a \in n(P)} \langle lock_a \rangle$$

where $[\![P]\!]_{RE_P}$ is inductively defined with only the following non-trivial cases

$$[\![\langle a\rangle]\!]_{RE_P} \qquad\qquad = \langle a\rangle|on(a_1,K_{a_1})|on(a_2,K_{a_2})|\ldots|on(a_l,K_{a_l})$$
$$\text{if } RE_P(a) = P_{a_1}\ldots P_{a_l}$$
$$[\![out(a).P]\!]_{RE_P} \qquad = in(lock_a).notify(a_1,K_{a_1}).notify(a_2,K_{a_2})\ldots$$
$$notify(a_l,K_{a_l}).out(lock_a).out(a).[\![P]\!]_{RE_P}$$
$$\text{if } RE_P(a) = P_{a_1}\ldots P_{a_l}$$
$$[\![forEach(a,P_{a_i}).Q]\!]_{RE_P} = in(lock_a).out(a_i).out(lock_a).[\![Q]\!]_{RE_P}$$
$$[\![in(a).P]\!]_{RE_P} \qquad = in(a).in(lock_a).dereg(a_1,K_{a_1}).dereg(a_2,K_{a_2})\ldots$$
$$dereg(a_l,K_{a_l}).out(lock_a).[\![P]\!]_{RE_P}$$
$$\text{if } RE_P(a) = P_{a_1}\ldots P_{a_l}$$

where we assume that for each encoding $[\![P]\!]$ the auxiliary names $lock_a$ are all distinct from the names a occurring inside P, and that the program names K_{a_i} are all distinct from the other program names K occurring in P. For each of these program names K_{a_i}, with $P_{a_i} \in RE_P(a)$, we consider the following definition $K_{a_i} = [\![P_{a_i}]\!]_{RE_P}$. For the same reasons discussed in the previous subsection, also this encoding is not open.

The theorem proving the correctness of the encoding should be rephrased as follows.

Theorem 4. *Given a program P of $L[forEach]$ we have that:*

- *if $P \longrightarrow P'$ then $[\![P]\!] \longrightarrow^+ [\![P']\!]_{RE_P} | \prod_{a\in n(P)}\langle lock_a\rangle$;*
- *if $[\![P]\!] \longrightarrow^+ Q$ then there exists P' such that $P \longrightarrow^+ P'$ and $Q \longrightarrow^* [\![P']\!]_{RE_P} | \prod_{a\in n(P)}\langle lock_a\rangle$.*

Also this encoding adopts mutual exclusion among the execution of operations performed on the same name. In order to understand the importance of this locking policy consider the program $out(a)|forEach(a,forEach(a,LOOP))$; observe that if this program activates the first reaction, then also the second one will be executed (in this case the program has an infinite computation).

Consider now the corresponding encoding in the case we do not exploit the locking policy. There are two possible reactions associated to the datum $\langle a\rangle$ that we denote with $P_{a_1} = forEach(a,LOOP)$ and $P_{a_2} = LOOP$. The encoding is

$$notify(a_1,K_{a_1}).notify(a_2,K_{a_2}).out(a)|out(a_1)$$
$$K_{a_1} = out(a_2)$$
$$K_{a_2} = LOOP'$$

where $LOOP'$ is the encoding of $LOOP$. This program could give rise to an undesired computation in which only the first reaction is activated; consider the computation in which the first $notify$ is executed, after the datum $\langle a_1\rangle$ is produced, the reaction K_{a_1} is activated, and finally $\langle a_2\rangle$ is produced without producing any reaction (because the second $notify$ operation has not been executed yet). In this case even if the first reaction is activated the overall computation in finite.

5 Conclusion

In this paper we have investigated three possible primitives for reactive programming to be embedded to Linda-like languages: *forEach* (reactions depend on the current state of the repository), *notify* (reactions depends on the future output operations), and *monitor* (which combines both the kind of reactions).

We have showed that the three approaches are interchangeable: namely, we have presented a possible way to translate any application developed following an approach, in an equivalent one based on a different kind of reactive mechanism. The interesting fact is that some of the translations are not adequate for open applications, this because they require to know a priori all the possible programs involved in the system. The lesson we have learned is that the *monitor* operation appears as the more powerful because it permits to model the other two primitives in a more flexible way.

Putting together the results proved in this paper and in a previous paper [BZ00] investigating the *notify* primitive only, we obtain the interesting result that there exists a significant gap of expressiveness between a reactive Linda (Linda extended with at least one of the three reactive primitives) and the basic Linda (with only input, output, and read operations). Indeed, in [BZ00] two of the authors proved that a process calculus with only *in* and *out* operations is not Turing-powerful, while it becomes (weakly) Turing-powerful in the case the *notify* operation is added to the calculus. In this paper we showed that *notify* can be modeled also with *monitor* and *forEach*, thus the same expressiveness result holds also for these reactive primitives.

References

[BZ00]   N. Busi and G. Zavattaro. On the Expressivenes of Event Notification in Data-Driven Coordination Languages. In *Proc. of ESOP 2000*, volume 1782 of *Lecture Notes in Computer Science*, pages 41–55. Springer-Verlag, Berlin, 2000.

[dBP91]   F.S. de Boer and C. Palamidessi. Embedding as a Tool for Language Comparison: On the CSP Hierarchy. In *Proc. of CONCUR'91*, volume 527, pages 127–141. Springer-Verlag, Berlin, 1991.

[Gel85]   D. Gelernter. Generative Communication in Linda. *ACM Transactions on Programming Languages and Systems*, 7(1):80–112, 1985.

[Mil89]   R. Milner. *Communication and Concurrency*. Prentice-Hall, 1989.

[Row98]   A. Rowstron. WCL: A web co-ordination language. *World Wide Web Journal*, 1(3):167–179, 1998.

[RW98]   A. Rowstron and A. Wood. Solving the Linda multiple **rd** problem using the **copy-collect** primitive. *Science of Computer Programming*, 31(2-3):335–358, 1998.

[W+98]   J. Waldo et al. Javaspace specification - 1.0. Technical report, Sun Microsystems, March 1998.

[WMLF98]   P. Wyckoff, S. McLaughry, T. Lehman, and D. Ford. T spaces. *IBM Systems Journal*, 37(3):454–474, 1998.

Integrating Two Organizational Systems through Communication Genres

Carlos J. Costa[1], Pedro Antunes[2], and João Ferreira Dias[3]

[1] ISCTE, Dep. Ciências e Tecnologias de Informação, Avenida das Forças Armadas,
1649-026 Lisboa, Portugal
carlos.costa@iscte.pt

[2] Dep. Informatica, Faculdade de Ciências, Universidade de Lisboa, Bloco C5 - Piso 1 -
Campo Grande - 1700 Lisboa, Portugal
paa@di.fc.ul.pt

[3] ISCTE, Dep. Ciências de Gestão, Avenida das Forças Armadas,
1649-026 Lisboa, Portugal
fdias@iscte.pt

Abstract. This paper describes the integration of two different types of support to the coordination of organizational activities. On the one hand, we have network-based Electronic Meeting Systems (EMS) supporting a cooperative coordination effort. On the other hand, we find Personal Digital Assistants (PDA), supporting the individual effort to coordinate. Considering that organizational efficiency and effectiveness requires a high level of fluidity between individual and cooperative coordination efforts, the problem then is how to bring together EMS and PDA. In this paper, we propose a conceptual framework to tackle this problem based on the concept of communication genre and genre system. We also describe a software system we developed to link EMS and PDA. This system was experimented in an organizational environment. The paper concludes with an evaluation of the methodology and proposed solution.

1 Introduction

A critical issue to team performance is lack of coordination. According to some authors, coordination can be classified as impersonal or by feedback [13]. Impersonal coordination is exemplified by the use of plans, schedules, procedures and workflow systems. Coordination by feedback is illustrated by two significant examples: one-to-one communication and group meetings.

PDA are becoming important tools in the support to impersonal coordination within organizations [6], focusing on the support to organizational information such as "to-do" lists and schedules, possibly the most widely used PDA tools.

In the situation discussed in this paper we explore the PDA support to coordination by feedback, focusing on group meetings rather than one-to-one communication. Our main scenario is a meeting room where people meet face-to-face, use any desktop

F. Arbab and C. Talcott (Eds.): COORDINATION 2002, LNCS 2315, pp. 125-132, 2002.

computers available in the room and bring their own PDA as well. This scenario emphasizes the importance of the link between PDA and the EMS installed in the room. This scenario emerged from extensive usage of electronic meeting rooms and empirical recognition that EMS lack mechanisms to integrate "team meeting data" with "personal data."

The EMS/PDA link presents an important problem though: the exchanged information must have the right purpose and shape to be understood by the people using both systems. In this paper we propose a conceptual framework to tackle this problem and describe our implementation of a system linking EMS and PDA in the scenario broadly described above. The system was experimented by an organization, thus drawing some preliminary results also presented in this paper.

2 Overview

PDA can play an important role in a meeting environment. In this context, three specific scenarios may be identified: (i) As individual recording tools of meeting topics, decisions, etc. This functionality is supported by tools like MeetingLog (palmedikal.tipchi.com) or MeetingManager (www.thinkingbytes.com); (ii) As communication devices between meeting participants [7]; (iii) As private spaces used in combination with public spaces such as shared whiteboards [12], [5].

All these scenarios are adequate when there is no EMS available in the meeting room. The EMS has been characterized as a combination of tools allowing users to communicate, deliberate and manage common information in a concerted group effort [9]. EMS highlight some important limitations of PDA, like weak user interface, compared to the EMS, limited support to meeting tasks and processes and barriers to group interactions due to limited richness of the medium.

On the other hand, PDA also bring about some important limitations of EMS. EMS must produce information that is adequate to the limitations of the PDA medium. EMS must discriminate useful from useless information in an automatic way, but this is a very difficult task, considering the informal nature and semantic richness of meeting data. EMS must produce information tailored to the particular needs of the eventual recipients, rather than just producing historical data.

One approach to overcome these problems relies on human intervention – the meeting facilitator. The facilitator is able to specify an adequate level of information richness, preserving process and task information as well as contextual cues of the meeting. This approach makes the meeting facilitator a critical resource in EMS. It benefits the meeting process and outcomes but, unfortunately, also causes significant problems to EMS. In fact, it has been suggested that the human facilitator causes EMS to be self-extinguishing [2].

Several researchers proposed an increased sophistication of the automated solutions to overcome these problems. For instance, Report Browsers allow people tailoring their views over meeting results, zooming in or out specific data to display details or have a high-level view of meeting information [8]. This kind of approach also explores the collaborative development of organizational memory [3].

Another possibility to ponder is to make report production an explicit meeting task. One example of this approach is the Expert Session Analyzer[1].

Considering our goals, this last approach seems to us better suited to integrate EMS and PDA, fundamentally because it requires less PDA functionality and avoids facilitators' interventions. Clearly, one possible drawback of the approach is the additional effort requested to meeting participants.

3 Conceptual Approach

Having in mind the considerations done in the last section, we will now delineate a conceptual approach to tailor report production during meetings and integrate them with PDA. The approach is based on the concept of genre.

The concept of genre was imported from the literature and recently generalized to the organizational context ([10], [11] and [9]) and the Internet infrastructure [4]. A genre of organizational communication is an institutionalized communicative action. it also has a particular social purpose and a recognizable form, entailing recognition and action. According to [11], a meeting is a collection of four genres: logistics; agenda; the meeting itself; and the report. To this collection we added the context genre, sometimes necessary to explain actions and decisions taken in meetings.

Associated to genres we find the notion of genre system. Genre systems are the glue linking several genres together and giving insight over the way communities of practice communicate and structure work. This view over work structures is very different from other approaches, e.g. enterprise modeling, which emphasize work procedures and processes. Fundamentally, the former highlights emergent work structures while the later describes formal structures and regulated workflow.

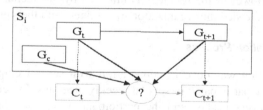

Fig. 1. Proposed approach

The conceptual approach is graphically presented in Figure 1. Our proposal is that the information associated with genre systems (Si) may contribute to create a "translator" between different communication artifacts (Ct and Ct+1) such as the ones managed by EMS and PDA. Each genre system supplies a set of clues explaining the linkage between Ct and Ct+1. Associated to each genre (Cc, Gt and Gt+1) there are specific purposes, forms, places and times where the genres may occur, as well as specific people that participate in the genre system [11].

The translation mechanism can be tailored to the specific organizational context and user needs because there is additional information behind, provided by genres. Of course, this approach has one important implication: it requires a process of genre elicitation. Such a process can be implemented through ethnographic techniques, analyzing the communication artifacts used by a community of people, identifying genres systems and then building up the corresponding translation tools. Or in can be implemented in a much longer process, where the specific community of people builds up their own set of genres and translators with the support from the EMS.

4 Using the Approach

In this section we describe a practical application of the proposed approach. The target organization was a small financial consulting and accountancy company. Both the types of structure (small, flat) and core business (independent consultancy) of this company stress the role of meetings as primary coordination mechanisms.

The Organizational Context

The target organization was already accustomed with several technologies to support coordination. Web Chat, Net-Meeting and e-mail are frequently used to support one-to-one coordination. An EMS (GroupSystems, www.ventana.com) was used on an experimental basis to coordinate the group. However, some cultural factors contributed to an unenthusiastic view of this technology. In fact, the employees, especially accountants and consultants considered that the technology imposed too many boundaries to meetings. The target organization also assessed the possibility of using workflow tools. However, the restrictions imposed by this technology to a small and informal structure, leaded the organization to continue with the same situation.

The Genre Elicitation Process

The genre elicitation was done in cooperation with several employees. In order to obtain the data, we participated in several weekly meetings. In general, those meeting were performed every Friday, and the participants were two senior consultants and one accountant. It was observed that this organization used paper and pen to write the conclusions from the meeting. Typically, after the meetings, they wrote the results in "to do" lists and calendars supported by PC and PDA. All employees have PDA, but one of the consultants uses Psion while the others use PalmOS devices.

Among several situations that were discussed with the employees, the following meeting genre systems were identified: process definition meeting (PDM), planning meeting (PM) and briefing (B).

After identifying the above genres, the related genre systems were analyzed in detail, identifying the purpose, expected outcomes, participants, structure, format and media used.

Table 1. The meeting genre system.

	Agenda	Logistics	Meeting	Context	Report
PDM	There is no formal agenda.	Decision about date and time, in an informal base	Purpose: Clarify an important organisational process. Typical phases: - Generate task list; - Identification of processes	Context information includes: - Task list - Process description	Process description
PM	Has just one item: "Planning activities"	Decision about date and time, in an informal base	Purpose: allocate tasks to each person, and guarantee that a process will be executed	Task list is used as support to the planning process	Outcomes are individual: - List of tasks; - Event in the calendar of each person
B	The "official agenda" has just one item: "Briefing"	Decision about date and time, in an informal base	Typical items: - Analyse what was done and what was not concluded - Discussion - Re-scheduling	Each participant should take notes about what she/he has done or not before the meeting	Individual Outcomes: - List of tasks that each person should do - Event in personal calendar

Artifacts Used to Support Genre Systems

Once again, the specification of artifacts that could best suit the needs of the target organization was done cooperatively; through EMS meetings (we used GroupSystems). In order to support genres, the following artifacts were selected:

– The agenda should be supported by a "topic list," both available and synchronized in a web page and a PDA;

– Logistics may be supported by e-mail;

– The meeting genre should be supported by a simple cooperative tool allowing participants to edit topics, comments, tasks and actions;

– Context information should be imported by EMS;

– Meeting reports, consisting of "topic lists," "to-do lists" and calendars, should be available in a web page and downloaded to PDA.

The Prototype

The prototype was developed after analyzing actual communication genres and artifacts. Basically, the prototype consists of a cooperative tool, allowing participants to edit topics, comments, tasks and actions, were implemented with Internet technology and a relational database. The cooperative tool runs on the Xitami (imatix.com) web server. The topic and to-do lists were implemented on the PDA using Tom Dyas' DataBase (pilot-db.sourceforge.net). The to-do list has the following fields: Task,

Due Date, Fixed Date, Complete, State, Notes, Responsible. The native Date Book from the Palm Pilot provides support calendaring information.

We also developed the EMS/PDA translation mechanisms for the data types cited above. These translation mechanisms were implemented with Perl script. These mechanisms operate the following way: (i) Identify the translation context, i.e. if the genre system is a process definition, planning or briefing; (ii)Identify the corresponding genre, expected purpose and form; (iii) Apply a parsing rule, according to the genre and context and load parsed data in the appropriate PDA file or web page.

5 Evaluation

In what concerns the prototype evaluation, two dimensions were considered: an evaluation of the conceptual approach, and an evaluation of the solution proposed to the organization participating in the research work. Considering the first dimension, we will comment each one of the previously mentioned topics.

The firs topic, the organizational context of the problem, highlights a traditionally difficult situation in the field of ISD, concerning wicked problems since neither the problems nor solutions are sufficiently known to drive IS analysis and design. The use of the genre concept, related to the meeting situation, was useful to clarify the organization context of the problem.

Obtaining requirements for this type of system is also troubling. Generally these work situations are not well documented. In addition, the perspectives are also very personal and people avoid sharing strategic data. Finally, the participation of an observer (the analyst) in meetings may also be seen with suspicion. The adoption of a cooperative elicitation process was very useful and efficient however.

In what concerns the selection of artifacts and tools to support communication genres, our approach was to ponder with the users the adoption of tools that were already being used in the organizational context. This phase was especially useful to help users know the potentialities and limitations of the available software systems. It was only at this phase that a formal list of requirements started to be clarified.

The last topic concerns the computer support to communication genres. In this stage, small prototypes were developed and integrated. Each one of the features offered by the prototypes was discussed and evaluated by the users. For instance, we proposed a complex parsing mechanism to convert EMS/PDA data, but the users rejected this solution because they did not find it necessary or useful. Offering a combo box to specify parsing rules was considered much more useful.

Summarizing, to what concerns the conceptual approach, it was found that the use of the communication genres and genre systems contributes to clarify the system development process. The concepts of genre and genre system allowed us to use a language close to the user, necessary to the participatory process. The users adopted the genre view and even discussed the possibility of applying the concept to other software tools. For instance, some more enthusiastic users suggested using genres to categorize chat data and e-mail messages.

In what concerns the solution proposed to the organization, it is not only important to analyze the final solution but, specially, the evolution of the attitude towards EMS. We noticed that the organizational attitude towards EMS and PDA changed with the project. In fact, the initial attitudes were very different. PDA had good acceptance but, when the project started, its use in meetings was declining. Prior experiments with EMS generated strong resistance. The experience with our prototype allowed a rebirth of the enthusiasm towards PDA and reduced the resistance towards EMS.

The adopted EMS, although adjusted to the needs, could have more functionality. The use of a touch screen and electronic whiteboard (like the Smart Board from Smart technologies, Inc.) was suggested, as well as a more refined user interface, reducing keyboard usage, which is very disruptive in meetings. The kind of meetings that we analyzed must be fast paced. The use of a voice modality to input data in the system was also suggested, especially to the discussion phase.

Some users also suggested the use of SMS to spread meeting results.

The users thought that the simplicity of the EMS/PDA conversion mechanism is adequate to the expectations they have when using PDA. Some users even recommended that the syntax be kept as simple as it is.

Finally, the users suggested increasing the use of PDA in meetings, to support some particular tasks. One task that was pointed out was voting (the target organization has to vote on some occasions). However, to what concerns activities that require text editing, the use of the PDA was considered not useful.

6 Conclusion

This paper brings together EMS and PDA, thus bridging the gap between different organizational coordination mechanisms, in particular impersonal coordination and group meetings. PDA have an important role in the support to individual plans and schedules, but its link with team meeting data is still low.

The conceptual approach proposed in this paper is based on the notion of genre. The genre perspective, originally employed to index literary work, has been adapted to the organizational context to analyze organizational communication, work patterns and structures. We used genres to add context and insight to the artifacts exchanged by EMS and PDA in a meeting situation. Associated with genres, we find purposes, people involved, work patterns and structures. These attributes afford tailoring the EMS/PDA data conversion mechanisms to the specific users' needs and expectations.

The paper describes the application of the EMS/PDA conversion mechanism to an organization in the accountancy field. This work was accomplished with the cooperation of several employees of the organization. The employees had also the opportunity to experiment the developed prototype. As a consequence of the evaluation, it was verified that the weaknesses of the prototype were not related to primary functionalities but with user interface features considered by the users as "not so important." Considering the project results, the project increased users' enthusiasm towards PDA usage and reduced the prior resistance towards EMS usage.

Acknowledgments. This paper was partially supported by the Portuguese Foundation for Science and technology, Project POSI/CHS/33127/99.

References

1. Aiken, M., Motiwalla, L., Sheng, O., Nunamaker, J.: ESP: An Expert System for Pre-Session Group Decision Support Systems Planning. Proceedings of the Twenty-Third Hawaii International Conference on System Sciences. Hawaii. January (1990) 279-286
2. Briggs, R., Nunamaker, J., Tobey, D.: The Technology Transition Model: A Key to Self-Sustaining and Growing Communities of GSS Users. Proceedings of the 34th Hawaii International Conference on System Sciences, Hawaii (2001)
3. Conklin, E.J.: Capturing Organizational Memory. In: Coleman, D. (ed.) Proceeding of GroupWare. Morgan Kaufman, San Mateo. CA (1992) 133-137
4. Crowston, K., Williams, M. : The Effects of Linking on Genres of Web Documents. Proceedings of the 32nd Hawaii International Conference on System Sciences. Maui, Hawaii, January (1999)
5. Greenberg, S., Boyle, M., LaBerge, J.: PDAs and Shared Public Displays: Making Personal Information Public, and Public Information Personal. Personal Technologies, Vol. 3, No.1, March. Elsevier.(1999) 54-64
6. Lewis, B.: Personal digital assistants could sneak into the office and become the next PCs", InfoWorld, Dec, Vol. 19 (1997) 38-49
7. Myers, B.: The Pebbles Project: Using PCs and Hand-held Computers Together; Demonstration Extended Abstract. Proceedings CHI'2000: Human Factors in Computing Systems. The Hague. The Netherlands, (2000) 14-15
8. Nunamaker, J., Dennis, A., Valacich, J., Vogel, D. , George, J.: Electronic meeting systems to support group work. Communications of the ACM. Vol. 34 No.7 (1991) 40-61
9. Nunamaker, J., Briggs, R., Mittleman, D., Vogel, D., Balthazard, P.: Lessons from a dozen years of group support systems research: A discussion of lab and field findings. Journal of Management Information Systems. Vol. 13 No.3 (1997)
10. Orlikowski, W., Yates, J.: Genre Repertoire: The Structuring of Communicative Practice in Organizations. Administrative Science Quarterly. Vol. 39 (1994) 547-574
11. Orlikowski, W., Yates, J.: Genre Systems: Structuring Interaction through Communicative Norms. CCS WP 205. Sloan MIT WP 4030. July (1998)
12. Roseman, M., Greenberg, S.: Building Real Time Groupware with GroupKit, A Groupware Toolkit. ACM Transactions on Computer Human Interaction. Vol. 3 No.1. ACM Press, March (1996) 66-106
13. Van de Ven, A., Delbecq, A.: Determinants of Coordination Modes Within Organisations. American Sociological Review. No. 41 (1976) 322-338

OpenCoLaS a Coordination Framework for CoLaS Dialects

Juan Carlos Cruz

Software Composition Group, University of Berne – Switzerland
cruz@iam.unibe.ch

Abstract. An important family of existing coordination models and languages is based on the idea of trapping the messages exchanged by the coordinated entities and by the specification of rules governing the coordination. No model, including our CoLaS coordination model, justifies clearly the reason of their coordination rules. Why these rules and not others? Are they all necessary? These are questions that remain still open. In order to try to provide an answer, in particular for the CoLaS model, we propose in this paper OpenCoLaS, a framework for building CoLaS coordination dialects. The OpenCoLaS framework allows to experiment with the definition of coordination rules.

1. Introduction

CoLaS is a coordination model and language for distributed active objects based on the notion of Coordination Groups. A Coordination Group is an entity that specifies, controls and enforces coordination between groups of distributed active objects. A Coordination Group specifies the Roles that distributed active objects may play in the group and the set of Coordination Rules that govern the coordination of the group. Since our first presentation of CoLaS in [1] the coordination model has changed significantly. These changes concern mainly the Coordination Rules: new rules have been introduced, some others have disappeared. These changes were motivated by the goal of obtaining a clearer separation of coordination and computation in the model. Questions such as "Why these rules and not others ?", "Are all these rules necessary?" appear all the time and remain still open. In order to try to provide answers, we propose in this paper to define OpenCoLaS, a framework to experiment with the specification of the CoLaS model. Our idea is to "open" the CoLaS model and language in a way that allows to modify and to introduce new Coordination Rules. By opening the CoLaS model we will be able to experiment with its specification.

This paper is organized in the following way: Section 2 introduces shortly the current version of the CoLaS coordination model and language; section 3 shows an example of the use of CoLaS: The Electronic Vote [4]; section 4 introduces the OpenCoLaS framework; and finally section 5 sets out some reflections on the CoLaS model related to the open questions mentioned before and presents some related work.

F. Arbab and C. Talcott (Eds.): COORDINATION 2002, LNCS 2315, pp. 133-140, 2002.
© Springer-Verlag Berlin Heidelberg 2002

2. The CoLaS Coordination Model and Language

The CoLaS coordination model and language [1][2] is composed of two kinds of entities: the Coordination Groups and the Coordination Group Participants (Participants in the following).

2.1   The Participants

Participants in CoLaS are atomic distributed active objects (distributed objects in the following). They are active objects because they are concurrent objects that have control over concurrent method invocations. They are distributed because physically they may run on different processors or machines. And they are atomic because they process invocations atomically.

2.2   Coordination Groups

Coordination Groups (CGs in the following) are entities that specify, control and enforce the coordination of a group of Participants. The primary tasks of CGs are: (1) to enforce cooperation actions between Participants, (2) to synchronize the occurrence of Participants' actions, and (3) to enforce proactive actions (in the following proactions) in Participants based on the coordination state.

Coordination Specification
A CG is composed of three elements: the Roles Specification, the Coordination State, and the Coordination Rules.

- *The Roles Specification:* defines the Roles that Participants may play in the group. A Role identifies abstractly a set of Participants sharing the same coordination behavior (i.e. same Coordination Rules).

- *The Coordination State*: defines general information needed for the coordination of the group. It concerns information like whether a given action has occurred or not in the system (i.e. historical information), etc. The Coordination State is specified by defining variables.

- *The Coordination Rules*: define the rules governing the coordination of the CG. We define 4 kinds of Coordination Rules in CoLas:

Cooperation Rules define cooperation actions between participants. They specify actions that Participants should do when they receive specific method invocations. Participants react to these method invocations only during the time they play the Role. Cooperation Rules have the form: <Role> defineBehavior: <Message> as: [<Coordination Actions>]. The <Coordination Actions> include actions that manipulate the coordination state and method invocations to Participants.

Synchronization Rules define synchronization constraints on method invocations received by Participants. The Synchronization Rules have the form:

<Role> ignore: <Message> if: [<Synchronization Conditions>] and <Role> disable: <Message> do: [<Coordination Actions>]. In the ignore rule the method invocation <Message> received is ignored if the <Synchronization Conditions> hold. The <Synchronization Conditions> are conditions referring to the Coordination State or conditions referring to the arguments of the method invocations. In the disable rule the method invocation received is disabled (processed later) and the <Coordination Actions> executed. The <Coordination Actions> are the same that in the Cooperation Rules.

Interception Rules define actions that modify the Coordination State at different moments during the handling of the method invocations by the Participants. Interception Rules have the form <Role> <Message> <Interception Point> do: <State Actions>. There are three different kinds of interceptions (InterceptAtArrival, InterceptBeforeExecution, and InterceptAfter Execution) according to the moment at which the method invocation <Message> should be intercepted. The <State Actions> are actions that modify the Coordination State.

Proactive Rules define actions that should be executed by the CG based on the coordination state, and independently of the method invocations received by the Participants. Proactive Rules have the form Proaction conditions: <Proaction Conditions> do: <Coordination Actions>. The <Proaction Conditions> are conditions referring the Coordination State. The <Coordination Actions> are the same as in the Cooperation Rules. The evaluation of the Proactive Rules is done non-deterministically by the CG.

3. An Example – The Electronic Vote

To introduce the current version of the CoLaS model we will use the same example we used in the presentation of the original CoLaS coordination model [1]: The Electronic Vote (originally introduced in [4]). We have selected this example because it will help us to compare Coordination Rules between the original model and the current CoLaS model.

Coordination Specification
The Electronic Vote Coordination Group defines a unique role Voters (Fig. 1, line 1). Every participant of the role Voters should at least be able to respond to the opinion: invocation request (Fig. 1, line 2). Eight Coordination Rules govern the coordination of the group: rules 1, 2, 3 and 4 specify cooperation rules; rules 5 and 6 interception rules; and rules 7 and 8 synchronization rules.

Rule 1 (line 8) *Rule 2* (line 12) *Rule 3* (line 15) *Rule 4* (line 21) :define The Electronic Vote protocol. The vote process starts with a startVote: message is sent by a Participant, the startVote: behavior (rule 1) defines that a message voteOn:initiator: is sent to all the Participants of the Voters role. The voteOn:initiator: behavior (rule 2) defines that each voter according to his or her opinion sends a message vote: to the initiator of the vote process. The vote:

behavior (rule 3) defines the counting of the received votes. Finally the **stopVote:** behavior (rule 4) defines that the result of the vote process is sent to all the voters when the initiator decides to stop the period of vote.

```
1 adminVote defineRoles: #(Voters).
2 Voters defineInterface: #(opinion:).
3
4 adminVote defineVariables:#(voteInProgress=false, votePeriodExpired=false).
5 adminVote defineVariables: #(numYes=0, numNot=0).
6 Voters defineVariables: #(hasVoted=false).
7.
8 [1] Voters defineBehavior: 'startVote: anIssue' as:
9   [group voteInProgress: true.
10   Voters voteOn: anIssue initiator: receiver ].
11
12 [2] Voters defineBehavior: 'voteOn: anIssue initiator: aVoter' as:
13   [aVoter vote: (self opinion: anIssue) ].
14
15 [3] Voters defineBehavior: 'vote: aVote' as:
16   [aVote = 'Yes'
17     ifTrue: [ group incrVariable: #numYes ]
18     ifFalse: [ group incrVariable: #numNot ].
19   sender hasVoted: true.]
20
21 [4] Voters defineBehavior: 'stopVote' as:
22   [group numYes >= group NumNot
23     ifTrue: [ Voters voteResult: 'Yes' ]
24     ifFalse: [ Voters voteResult: 'Not' ].
25
26 [5] Voters interceptBeforeExecution: 'stopVote' do:
27   [group votePeriodExpired: true ].
28
29 [6] Voters interceptAfterExecution: 'stopVote' do:
30   [group voteInProgress: false.
31   group votePeriodExpired: false ].
32
33 [7] Voters ignore: 'vote: aVote' if:
34   [group votePeriodExpired || sender hasVoted ]
35
36 [8] Voters disable: 'startVote: anIssue' do:
37   [group voteInProgress ]
```

Fig. 1. The Electronic Vote in CoLaS.

Rule 5 (line 26) and *Rule 6* (line 29) define Interception Rules. They specify actions on the Coordination State. Rule 5 specifies that the vote period is closed before the execution of the **stopVote:** message. Rule 6 defines that a new vote process may start after the execution of the **stopVote:** message.

Rule 7 (line 33) defines that votes received after the end of the period of vote or votes received from Participants that have already voted are ignored.

Rule 8 (line 36) defines that new requests for starting a vote process are disabled (processed later) if there is actually one vote process ocurring in the system.

Pseudo-Variables

There are three pseudo-variables that can be used within the CGs. They are: group, receiver, and sender. The group variable refers to the CG (lines 9, 17, 18, 22, 27, 30, 31, 34 and 37). The sender pseudo-variable refers to the Participant that sent the message (line 34), and the receiver pseudo-variable refers to the Participant handling the message (line 10).

4. The OpenCoLaS Framework

OpenCoLaS is a framework that allows to specify Coordination Rules for CoLaS like coordination models. The OpenCoLaS framework defines an abstract class named CoordinationRule as the root of all possible Coordination Rules. There are two possible types of Coordination Rules (abstract subclasses of CoordinationRule): Reactive Coordination Rules (ReactiveCoordinationRule) and Proactive Coordination Rules (ProactiveCoordinationRule).

4.1 Reactive Coordination Rules

Reactive Coordination Rules specify actions that should be triggered on method invocation requests received by the Participants. The ReactiveCoordinationRule class offers an instance creation method defineRule: <RuleName> semantic: <Rule Semantic Actions> used to create concrete Reactive Coordination rules. The <Rule Semantic Actions> define actions over a received method invocation request: it is possible to define a new method invocation with new argument values, or to transform the method invocation in a special NoMessage method invocation that indicates that the received method invocation should not continue to be processed. The <Rule Semantic Actions> actions also specify actions on the participant's messages mailbox (a mailbox is the place where method invocations are stored in Participants when they can not process them): like to remove a method invocation from the mailbox or to include a method invocation into the mailbox. To refer to the received method invocation and to the messages mailbox in the <Rule Semantic Actions>, there are two simple accessor methods: message and mailbox. Finally, the last action of the <Rule Semantic Actions> actions should always be to return a method invocation: the same received, a new, or a NoMessage method invocation.
The ReactiveCoordinationRule offers a second creation method defineRule: <RuleName> without a semantics, in this case the semantic by default corresponds to a return the same received method invocation. To illustrate the specification of Reactive Coordination Rules in the OpenCoLaS framework we use the CoLaS coordination model. In the CoLaS coordination model we have 5 types of rules that depend for their application on the method invocations received by the Participants. They are: Ignore, Disable, InterceptAtArrival, InterceptBeforeExcecution, and InterceptAfterExecution. Fig. 2 illustrates the way in which the CoLaS Reactive Coordination Rules are specified in the OpenCoLaS framework.

```
1  [1] ReactiveCoordinationRule
2      defineRule: #Ignore
3      semantic: [^NoMessage new ].
4
5  [2] ReactiveCoordinationRule
6      defineRule: #Disable
7      semantic: [self mailbox put: self message.
8                 ^NoMessage new ].
9
10 [3] ReactiveCoordinationRule
11     defineRule:#InterceptAtArrival
12
13 [4] ReactiveCoordinationRule
14     defineRule: #InterceptBeforeExecution
15
17 [5] ReactiveCoordinationRule
18     defineRule: #InterceptAfterExecution
```

Fig. 2. CoLaS Reactive Coordination Rules in OpenCoLaS.

Ignore (line 1): the Ignore rule specifies the return of a **NoMessage** message. The method invocation should not continue to be processed.

Disable (line 5): the Disable rule specifies that the method invocation received should be put into the participant's messages mailbox and thus processed later. The return of a **NoMessage** indicates that the method invocation should not continue to be processed.

InterceptAtArrival (line 10), *InterceptBeforeExecution* (line 13) and *InterceptAfterExecution* (line 17): specify that no action should be done on the received invocation request message.

```
1  [5] InterceptBeforeExecution
2      message: 'stopVote'
3      actions: [group votePeriodExpired: true ]
4      entryPoint: OpenCoLaS AtAccept ]
5
6  [6] InterceptAfterExecution
7      message: 'stopVote'
8      actions: [group voteInProgress: false.
9              group votePeriodExpired: false]
10     entryPoint: OpenCoLaS AtComplete ]
11
12 [7] Ignore
13     message:'vote: aVote'
14     conditions: [ group votePeriodExpired || sender hasVoted ]
15     entryPoint: OpenCoLaS AtReceive
16
17 [8] Disable
18     message: 'startVote: anIssue'
19     actions: [ group voteInProgress ]
20     entryPoint: OpenCoLaS AtAccept.
```

Fig. 3. Creation of CoLaS Reactive Coordination Rules in OpenCoLaS

In order to complete the specification of the CoLaS reactive rules it is necessary to specify during the creation of the rule instances: the <Reaction Message> to which the rule is supposed to react (**message:**), the <Coordination Conditions> that determine the applicability of the rule (**conditions:**), the <Coordination Actions> that should be executed when the rule is applied (**actions:**), and the <Entry Point> at which the rule should be verified (**entryPoint:**). The OpenCoLaS framework specifies four different entry points: **AtReceive, AtAccept, AtSend** and **AtComplete**.

The OpenCoLaS framework specifies default values for the <Coordination Conditions> and the <Coordination Actions>. For the <Coordination Conditions> a block [true] that always validates, and for <Coordination Actions> an empty block [] with no actions to be executed. Fig.3 illustrates the way in which CoLaS rule instances are created in OpenCoLaS for the Electronic Vote example.

The different <Entry Point> (Fig 4.) correspond to 4 different moments during the internal processing of method invocations requests by the Participants: **AtReceive** (when the method invocation arrives to the object), **AtAccept** (when the method invocation is selected from the messages mailbox and just before it is executed), **AtSend** (when a method invocation is sent to another object and actually before it has been received by the other object), and **AtComplete** (after the method invocation has been executed).

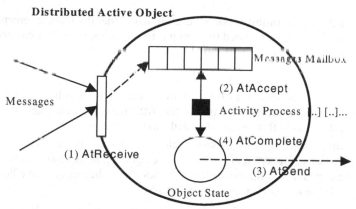

Fig. 4. OpenCoLaS <Entry Point>s.

4.2 Proactive Coordination Rules

Proactive Coordination Rules specify actions that should be triggered based on the Coordination State. The **ProactiveCoordinationRule** class in the OpenCoLaS framework offers an instance creation method **defineRule:** <RuleName> to create subclasses of Proactive Coordination rules. During the creation of Proactive Coordination Rules instances it is necessary to specify: the <Coordination Conditions> that determine the applicability of the rule (**conditions:**), and the <Coordination Actions> the actions that should be executed when the rule is applied (**actions:**). In CoLaS the evaluation and enforcement of the Proactive Coordination

Rules is done by the CG. Fig. 5 illustrates the way in which the CoLaS Proactive Coordination Rules are specified in the OpenCoLaS framework.

```
1 [1] ProactiveCoordinationRule
2    defineRule: #Proaction
3
4 [2] Proaction
5    conditions: [group votePeriodExpired ]
6    actions: [group numYes >= group NumNot
7             ifTrue: [ Voters voteResult: 'Yes' ]
8             ifFalse: [ Voters voteResult: 'Not' ]. ]
9             group votePeriodExpired: false ]
```

Fig. 5. CoLaS Proactive Coordination Rules in OpenCoLaS.

Rule 2 (line 4) defines that when the vote period expires the result of the vote should be sent to all the Voters.

5. Conclusions and Related Work

One of the main results of this work is the conclusion that the three Interception Rules specified in CoLaS can be reduced to a unique Interception Rule. We can see in Fig. 2 that the three Interception rules specified have the same <Rule Semantic Actions> and the same <Coordination Actions>. The only difference between the three rules is that they are evaluated at different entry points. We can conclude that a unique InterceptAt rule is necessary in the CoLaS model. It is possible to include a new Interception Rule to intercept messages at the AtSend entry point, actually in CoLaS there is not Interception Rule associated with this entry point.

Concerning Proactive Coordination Rules we arrived at the conclusion that the two Proactive rules: Always and Once in the original CoLaS model were not cleanly defined. The semantics of the two rules were not clear, they could have been reduced to one as we did in the current version of CoLaS.

The most important related work are Synchronizers [3] and Moses [4]. For a complete CoLaS related work refer to [1][2]. Concerning OpenCoLaS there is not much work on meta coordination models (particularly in object oriented coordination models). From our point of view meta coordination models should constitute a field of research on its own in the coordination area.

References

1. J.C.Cruz and S. Ducasse, *A Group Based Approach for Coordinating Active Objects*, Coordination'99, LNCS 1594, Springer Verlag, pp. 355-370.
2. J.C.Cruz, CORODS: a Coordination Programming System for Open Distributed Systems, Languages and Models of Objects' 2001, L'object vol. 7, no. 1-2/2001.
3. S. Frolund, Coordinating Distributed Objects, MIT Press, 1996.
4. N.Minsky and V. Ungureanu, *Regulated Coordination in Open Distributed Systems*, COORDINATION'97, LNCS 1282, Springer-Verlag, 1997, pp. 81-97.

Coordination in a Reflective Architecture Description Language*

Carlos E. Cuesta[1], Pablo de la Fuente[1], Manuel Barrio-Solórzano[1], and
Encarnación Beato[2]

[1] Universidad de Valladolid, Valladolid 47011, Spain
{cecuesta,pfuente,mbarrio}@infor.uva.es
[2] Universidad Pontificia de Salamanca, Salamanca 37002, Spain
ebeato@upsa.es

Abstract. Software Architecture studies the structure of software systems, as described by Architecture Description Languages (ADLs). When these capture structures of *change*, they are comparable to Coordination Languages. Previous work suggests that the combination with Reflection concepts renders a general framework for the description of such evolving structures. This paper describes a reflective ADL named $\mathcal{PiLar}$ designed to provide such a framework. It consists of a *structural* part, which describes the static skeleton, and a *dynamic* part, which defines patterns of change. The major novelty is the *reification* relationship, which structures a description in several meta-layers, such that the architecture is able to reason and act upon itself. The paper includes a complete $\mathcal{PiLar}$ example, to show the language's use and some of its most relevant features. It describes a Tuple Space model, illustrating the analogy with existing Coordination Models. We conclude by emphasizing $\mathcal{PiLar}$'s generality and applicability.

1 Introduction

Research in Software Architecture and Coordination Theory is bound to converge. Their origins and purpose are quite different, yet they show some significant similarities, and use comparable concepts. This is even more apparent in their respective linguistic representations: Coordination and Architecture Description Languages (ADLs) play often analogous roles, and sometimes even the same one [8,10] is used in both contexts.

Linguistically, a system's architecture is described as the complex composition of independent pieces named *components*. An ADL provides the means to join together these components, conceived as previously unrelated atomic entities. When this structure can evolve, we speak of *Dynamic Architecture*. Similarly, Coordination is about managing dependencies between concurrent agents. We can compare these agents to components; and then their dependencies comprise a dynamic architecture. Of course there are differences of emphasis, but quite often the analogy works perfectly.

Languages in both fields provide a wide range of solutions for the description of dynamic structures; a common scheme is required to compare different alternatives. Our

---

* This work has been partially sponsored by the Spanish Comission of Science and Technology through the CICYT Project TEL99-0335-C04-04, and by the Autonomous Government of Castilla and León through the Project JCYL VA61/00B.

F. Arbab and C. Talcott (Eds.): COORDINATION 2002, LNCS 2315, pp. 141–148, 2002.

previous work [7] uses the notion of *Reflection* as an unifying concept. Using this idea, we defined the reflective architectural framework MARMOL; but it still lacked a *linguistic* counterpart.

This paper describes such counterpart. We define here a reflective ADL named $\mathcal{P}i\mathcal{L}ar$ (*"PiLar is a Language for architectural description"*) loosely based on the MARMOL framework. This will allow us to effectively test reflective notions in an architectural setting, by using them as a part of a system's description. The language has been equipped with formal concurrent semantics –based on the π-calculus–, in the spirit of existing work combining architecture and process algebras [1,3,4], and was designed to combine reflection and most interesting constructions from other ADLS, maintaining applicability while providing the greatest generality.

Our purpose with $\mathcal{P}i\mathcal{L}ar$ is twofold. First, it is mainly intended to serve as *the* language to describe *other* Coordination models and Dynamic Architectures; so it should be expressive enough to define any known dynamic abstraction. Second, it is also meant to be useful as a standalone, dynamic ADL, able to specify evolving structures; as such, it needs to show a comfortable notation.

In the following sections we review the basic concepts of reflection, to later describe the syntax of our ADL, divided in a *Structural Language* and a *Dynamic Language*. Special attention is paid to the concept of *reification*, which provides the reflective structure, and concurrent semantics are briefly outlined. To clarify concepts, we examine an example, consisting of a specification of the TupleSpace Model; this way, the proposal of $\mathcal{P}i\mathcal{L}ar$ as a coordination language is substantiated.

2   Reflection in Architecture

The concept of Reflection has already a long history [9] and has been used in many areas, such as artificial intelligence, object-orientation or programming; but the combination with Software Architecture has only been proposed recently [6,7]. Reflection is defined as *"the capability of a system to reason and act upon itself"* [9]. The concept has many implications, but here we will consider it just inside Software Architecture. Our previous work in the MARMOL framework has already determined which notions are considered of interest to the field. The resulting model has a high expressive power, as proven by a comparison with the structure of dynamic ADLs and Coordination Languages: each one of them has a reflective equivalent [7].

Reflection divides an architecture in two: the part which is controlled and the part which controls. These are respectively named *base-level* and *meta-level*. The meta-level can be described as the context in which the base-level is defined; this defines a causal connection between them, expressed as a *reification* link. Each level is also divided in components. A normal, base-level component is named an *avatar*, and is reified by one or more *meta-components* in the meta-level. Components in the meta-level could be reified themselves, hence defining another level (a *meta-meta-level*). There's no limit to this process, which implicitly divides an specification in several meta-layers. Details about the resulting model can be obtained from [7].

Thus reification is the main concept to introduce in $\mathcal{P}i\mathcal{L}ar$. This is done in section 4.

3   Structural Language

There are two different concerns in any dynamic ADL: the description of the static structure and the characterization of patterns of evolution. To provide the separation of concerns, $\mathcal{P}i\mathcal{L}ar$ itself is divided in two parts: a *Structural Language* describing the static skeleton of systems, and a *Dynamic Language*, defining the rules to make it change. In this section we briefly sketch the syntax of the former, which stems naturally from the concurrent semantics, but has been designed to be similar to other ADLs'.

There's just one kind of element: the **component**, defined as a basic compositional unit, encapsulated and defined by one or more segmented interfaces, and present in a configuration through one or several *instances*. Hence it defines a type, and it is also known as *archtype*. It may be either *primitive* or *composite*. In the second case, the composition of several mutually interacting instances is hidden behind an interface, shaping a *component hierarchy*, typical of architectural description.

In $\mathcal{P}i\mathcal{L}ar$, a component definition has four parts, none of them strictly mandatory: *interfaces*, *configurations*, *reifications* and *constraints*. The latter two are described in sections 4 and 5; the other two are summarized below.

An **interface** is a logically coherent aggregation of *ports*, which are in turn defined as the component's interaction points, expressing both services and requirements. When just the interfaces are specified, we have a *primitive component*. A **configuration** defines a *composite component*. It consists of a set of component *instances*, interacting through bindings or attachments, defining a complete subsystem.

There are four kinds of **instance** declarations in $\mathcal{P}i\mathcal{L}ar$, namely *typed* instances, *arrays* of instances, *parameterized* components and *reified types*. The first is the most basic case: it defines a single instance of an archtype. The second is the usual *array* declaration of an indexed set of instances. *Parameterized* components support for the definition of generic abstractions. Finally, *reified types* refers to the use of types as instances in the meta-level, as we explain later (see section 4).

On the other side, there are three kinds of **bindings** in $\mathcal{P}i\mathcal{L}ar$, namely *links*, and *hierarchic* and *typed* bindings. They are very closely related. **Links** are simply attachments, describing a direct connection between two ports at the same level. **Hierarchic** bindings are nearly identical: but they connect ports in different levels, thus *exporting* them. **Typed bindings** are meant to provide complex connections. Their types are declared just like primitive components. They have an explicit *name*, and are declared with an argument: the set of ports to connect. Combined with reification, they acquire a great expressive power and, as explained in [7], can also be considered as *meta-level connectors*. We won't focus on this in this paper, but anyway the specification of section 6 includes a simple example.

The language, like other ADLs [10], has also support for *conditional* and *iterative* constructs; and it allows even *recursive* component definitions.

4   Reification

Reification is the only reflective notion we need to introduce in the language, as stated in section 2. It's a structural concept, but it's also important for dynamism, as it defines how constraints will be combined.

In $\mathcal{P}i\mathcal{L}ar$, like in MARMOL, reification expresses a bidirectional relationship: it can be seen as a link between an *avatar* (base-component) and a *meta-component*. Using it, a meta-component has access to the internal details of the avatar it *reflects* in; an avatar abstractions' are *reified* as meta-components.

Reification is a many-to-many relationship: a meta-component can reflect in many avatars; an avatar can be reified by many meta-components. There are two kinds of components in a meta-level: those which directly reflect in an avatar (*meta-components*) and those which don't (*meta-level components*). A meta-level component interacts with meta-components at its level; thus it can affect also the behaviour of avatars [7].

Reification in $\mathcal{P}i\mathcal{L}ar$ can be either *explicit* or *implicit*. Explicit reification uses a specific syntax, namely a \reify construct; this can be found in a structural definition, composing the section for reifications, but also within dynamic constraints. The link can receive a name, hence making it possible to dynamically modify it later.

Implicit reification simply consists of usual declarations: when an instance C of an archtype T is created, not only a component C, but also a *meta-component* T is declared. Hence, *every declared archtype can be used anytime as a meta-component*. Apart from that, implicit and explicit reification have exactly the same meaning.

Combined with primitives of the Dynamic Language, this provides the language with a great power. Given that meta-components have access to internal details of avatars, dynamism, as many other interesting abstractions, is easily expressed.

5   Dynamic Language

Behaviour in $\mathcal{P}i\mathcal{L}ar$ is provided by a number of rules, scattered throughout component definitions in the \constraint section. They are then bound to an already defined structural skeleton, where they ensure properties and react to situations.

A process algebraic syntax is a natural choice [1,3,4] for the Dynamic Language. Control constructs are then directly inspired by those of CCS [11], which is consistent with our π-calculus semantics, but easier to use. There are two notations for $\mathcal{P}i\mathcal{L}ar$. The first one is purely algebraic, and is compact but complex. The second resembles a programming language, and is more readable. We only use the latter in this paper.

A **constraint** consists on one or several rule definitions, forming a modular sub-system. The first one defines how they are combined and triggered. They describe how interactions are managed. Definitions may be *recursive*, and this is a way to express repetition. The other is *replication* (\bang), which creates a new copy of a finite process each time its first action is triggered.

There are two atomic actions: *sending* ($c!(x)$) and *receiving* ($c?(x)$). The second one *waits* for a message, and thus is usually used as the *guard* (triggering event) of a process. Interaction points are ports and internal channels: to access them hierarchically, we use the well-known *dot notation* ($Agent1.rd$). Actions are combined by *parallel composition*, separated by the | symbol, or form a *sequence*, marked by the ; symbol. Parenthesis can be freely used. Control structures are also allowed here, hence we have convenient iterative and conditional constructs.

Channels in a constraint are always *private*, except when they are specifically exported by declaring them as *ports* in the structural definition. Besides, there is an *ex-*

Table 1. Most important reflective primitives in $\mathcal{P}i\mathcal{L}ar$

Keyword	Notation	Global Meaning
avatar	α	Reference to the avatar to which the constraint is applied.
self	γ	Reference to the component in which the constraint is defined.
avatarSet	$\Sigma\alpha$	Set of all of the avatars reflected by this meta-component.
portSet	$\Sigma\pi(a)$	Set of all the (public) ports in a component a.
new	$\nu(a:t)$	Creates a new avatar a of type t (if specified).
del	δa	Destroys (deletes) an entity a (a reification or an avatar).
reify	$\rho N(a:m)$	Creates a reification N between avatar a and meta-component m.
findr	$\phi N(a:m)$	Finds a reification link between avatar a and meta-component m.

trusion (**alias**) and a *hiding* (**hide**) construct to explicitly expose and restrict names when required. *Bindings* can be considered as the sharing of channels: when two ports are connected ($a = b$), data sent in one of them are received in the other, and vice versa. On the other hand, *typed bindings* are just like any other component definition: given their constraints, they are translated as processes.

The basic Dynamic Language is just that: we only need to consider the support for *reification*, which is provided by means of several reflective primitives. The most interesting among them are summarized in Table 1. We should have in mind that these primitives are declared in an archtype, so they must be considered *inside* a meta-component, which limits their scope. This means that a meta-component can *create* or *destroy* avatars, but only those already under its control. A constraint is enforced by a meta-component and must be obeyed by all of its avatars. It should be read as a rule situated at the meta-level, where **avatar** is each one of the reflected components.

This structure defines a very dynamic framework. A meta-component not only rules, but also *creates* and *destroys* avatars. This is true also for reified bindings, thus making possible to *link* and *unlink* components. A meta-component can trigger internal changes in response to base (or meta) events, and induce external reactions by communication with other meta-level components. This way, an event in an avatar can affect itself, all components of its kind, or even several components of several kinds. But this is when we deal with just *one* meta-level: when we consider further levels, even meta-components themselves are subject to change.

5.1 Brief Note about Semantics

$\mathcal{P}i\mathcal{L}ar$ semantics conceives an architecture as a set of concurrent processes, communicating by means of named channels, in which each component is a process. We consider that concurrency is both natural and essential in the description of systems. We also believe that, linguistically, the key aspect in an architectural description is the management of *names*, a global term to include ports, instances, archtypes and links. For this reason, the π-calculus [12] has been the perfect tool to specify $\mathcal{P}i\mathcal{L}ar$'s formal semantics.

$\mathcal{P}i\mathcal{L}ar$'s semantics is then given by translation of an architectural description to a π-calculus algebraic specification. There's no space here to comment this translation in detail, but we'll give some overall indications. There is a direct correlation between architectural and process-algebraic concepts. Composition and interaction are basic notions in both fiels. Encapsulation is provided by name restriction. Ports are channels, and attachments are created by communication of ports; configurations correspond to topologies, and constraints are obviously translated as process definitions. Finally, we should consider the translation of reification. This is perhaps more complex, but it has been tackled with a standard *interposition* mechanism.

6   *PiLar* as a Coordination Language

PiLar is meant to be expressive enough to describe even the architecture of Coordination models; then, the example in Fig. 1 has been chosen to show the way it could deal with such a model. Specifically, it describes an architecture simulating the basic TupleSpace paradigm. For the sake of brevity, just the original Linda model [5] is considered: thus we have a single, flat tuplespace and the primitives **in**, **rd**, and **out**.

The description could be simpler, but we have designed it to show some significant *PiLar* features, such as the way reification works and its relevance; the structure of meta-levels; the difference between meta-components and meta-level components, or how a meta-level connector looks like.

First, we can see there are five component definitions. Two of these (*System*, *SysTS*) are composite components. The other three (*Store*, *Triple*, *AgTS*) are primitive ones: just their interfaces are described. We sketch the intended meanings for these below.

Store. Describes an interface to an ideal data store; for example, a database system. It receives requests for storing, deleting and locating some information.

AgTS. The archtype of any agent inside a tuplespace. The three ports have the usual meaning of the corresponding Linda primitives.

Triple. Defines a three-tier connection, which receives a query at *res*, looks for an answer through *get*, and provides it through both *res* and *dele*.

The starting point to deduce the structure is the **base-level:** tag. It states which components are in the base level, which is the lowest one in the hierarchy. In the Figure, this level consists of *System*, which is in turn a composite of *Agent1* and *Agent2*, instances of *AgTS*. The composite is extremely simple: no ports are exported, no bindings are made; both agents are just "standing there".

But their archtype *AgTS* is also a meta-component. Even more, it is an *active* meta-entity, as it uses the **self** keyword. There are then two components in the base level, reified by *one* component in the meta-level. All of them have three ports, which are completely unrelated. However, we are interested in this particular case in having these ports connected, so constraints are used to impose this. The four rules state that *AgTS* captures every message in every avatar, and sends it through its own ports.

It is obvious then that *AgTS* interacts with other components in the meta-level. Looking at our other composite (*SysTS*) we can see the configuration contains an instance named *AgTS*. That's the archtype used as a (meta-level) component, what we termed a *reified type* in section 3. Thus, the composite *SysTS* is a meta-level component, as it contains *AgTS*, which is a meta-component.

```
deftype Tuple = { hd, data }           \component AgTS (
                                       ( port in_:Tuple |
\base-level : ( System )                 port rd: Tuple |
                                         port out:Tuple )
\component System (                    \constraint (
 \config (                             TP def= ( OP | RP | IP )
  Agent1:AgTS |                        OP def= \bang ( avatar.out?T;
  Agent2:AgTS ))                          self.out!T )
                                       RP def= \bang ( avatar.rd?A;
\component SysTS (                        self.rd!A; self.rd?T
 \config (                               avatar.rd!T )
  DB:Store | AgTS |                    IP def= \bang ( avatar.in_?A;
  \bind (                                 self.in_!A; self.in_?T
  AgTS.out = DB.insert |                  avatar.in_!T )
  AgTS.rd = DB.query |                 ))
  L1:Triple( DB.query |
     DB.delete | AgTS.in_ ))           \component Triple (
 ))                                    ( port get | port dele |
                                         port res )
\component Store (                     \constraint (
 ( port insert | port query |          \bang ( res?Q; get!Q; get?A;
   port delete ))                       ( res!A | dele!A ) )))
```

Fig. 1. Tuplespace Model: a *PiLar* example specification

In fact, it *is* the whole meta-level, and it consists of two components: *AgTS* itself and a store, *DB*. Two of their ports are simply linked, while others are engaged in a three-tier binding *L1* of type *Triple*. We have enough information to deduce the outcoming behaviour: tuples sent in *out* are inserted in the store, *rd* receives a query (anti-tuple) and returns the result, and *in_* does the same, but erasing the used (read) tuple from the store. The whole system's behaviour is then already described.

Thinking about *Triple*, we can see it is actually a *meta-meta*-level component, reifying binding *L1*. But the constraint just uses avatar names, so it's not really an active meta-entity. Anyway, it serves as a *meta-level connector*, enforcing a certain communication protocol. This is a very simple exhibit; a dynamic variant could make use of other meta-meta-level entities, as desired.

To sum up, the system has three levels. The base level consists of a composite module *System* of two agents, *Agent1* and *Agent2* of type *AgTS*, which don't know each other. The meta-level consists of a composite *SysTS* of two components, a store *DB* of type *Store* and the reified type *AgTS*. The former is a meta-level component, while the latter is a meta-component for the agents; and they are connected by two links and a typed binding –of type *Triple*–. Finally, the meta-meta-level contains the two remaining types: *Store* and *Triple*. Both are inactive, so they can be safely ignored.

With this example, our main purpose was to show the use of the language and how a coordination model can be described with it. The key point is that the behaviour of agents and their coordination remain separated, at different levels in the architecture.

7   Conclusions and Future Work

In [7], we compare the reflective model of MARMOL with existing work in Coordination and Dynamic Architecture, and show the relationship between them in general terms. Future work on $\mathcal{P}i\mathcal{L}ar$ includes a detailed comparison of the different approaches, with much more detail and from a linguistic point of view. The combination of Architecture and Reflection is a recent idea [6,7] and its consequences have still to be explored.

The example in this paper just give a taste of $\mathcal{P}i\mathcal{L}ar$'s flexibility. The concept of *meta-component* makes possible to cope with many architectural abstractions in a common framework. Our notion of *reification* can be compared to a form of control-driven coordination, specially when considering concurrent semantics. Because of this, a detailed comparison with control-driven models such as IWIM [2] is being carried out.

The development of $\mathcal{P}i\mathcal{L}ar$ continues. The formal definition of its semantics into the untyped π-calculus is almost finished; the work on Turner's polymorphic π-calculus, which would provide it with a consistent type system, has already begun. The language might seem complex, but actually it isn't more difficult to use than Wright or Rapide. Reification appears just when it's strictly required, and in turn it offers an useful tool for the description and comparison of different dynamic ADLs.

References

1. Robert Allen. *A Formal Approach to Software Architecture*. PhD thesis, School of Computer Science, Carnegie Mellon University, May 1997. Technical report CMU-CS-97-144.
2. Farhad Arbab. The IWIM Model for Coordination of Concurrent Activities. In Paolo Ciancarini and Chris Hankin, editors, *Coordination Languages and Models*, volume 1061 of *Lecture Notes in Computer Science*, pages 24–56, Cesena, Italia, April 1996. Springer Verlag.
3. Marco Bernardo, Paolo Ciancarini, and Lorenzo Donatiello. Detecting Architectural Mismatches in Process Algebraic Descriptions of Software Systems. In *Second Working IEEE/IFIP Conference on Software Architecture*, August 2001. IEEE Press.
4. Carlos Canal, Ernesto Pimentel, and José María Troya. Specification and Refinement of Dynamic Software Architectures. In *Software Architecture*, pages 107–126. Kluwer, 1999.
5. Nicholas Carriero and David Gelernter. How to Write Parallel Programs: a Guide to the Perplexed. *ACM Computing Surveys*, 21(3):323–357, 1986.
6. Walter Cazzola, Andrea Savigni, Andrea Sosio, and Francesco Tisato. Architectural Reflection: Bridging the Gap Between a Running System and its Architectural Specification. In *6th Reengineering Forum (REF'98)*, pages 12–1–12–6. IEEE, March 1998.
7. Carlos E. Cuesta, Pablo de la Fuente, Manuel Barrio-Solórzano, and Encarnación Beato. Dynamic Coordination Architecture through the use of Reflection. In *16th ACM Symposium on Applied Computing (SAC2001)*, pages 134–140, March 2001. ACM Press.
8. David C. Luckham and James Vera. An Event-Based Architecture Definition Language. *IEEE Transactions on Software Engineering*, 21(9):717–734, September 1995.
9. Pattie Maes. Concepts and Experiments in Computational Reflection. In Norman Meyrowitz, editor, *OOPSLA'87 Conference Proceedings*, pages 147–155. ACM Press, December 1987.
10. Jeff Magee and Jeff Kramer. Dynamic Structure in Software Architectures. *Software Engineering Notes*, 21(6):3–14, November 1996.
11. Robin Milner. *Communication and Concurrency*. Prentice-Hall, 1989.
12. Robin Milner. *Communicating and Mobile Systems: the Pi-Calculus*. CUP, June 1999.

Coordinating Software Evolution via Two-Tier Programming

Amnon H. Eden[1] and Jens Jahnke[2]

[1]Dept. of Computer Science, Concordia University, Montreal, Canada
eden@acm.org

[2]Dept. of Computer Science, University of Victoria, Victoria, Canada
jens@acm.org

Abstract. Progress in the *science of programming* is reflected by the evolution of programming languages. We propose that the next step in this evolution is a more comprehensive kind of programs: To redefine the way programs are perceived and, consequently, to redefine what constitutes the activity of *programming*. Rather than treating architectural specifications as separate, we argue that they need be treated *as part of the program*. Thus, a program is specified through two tightly integrated representations:

1. *Intentional tier*: A generic ("abstract") representation of design and architectural properties (constraints) of the program which, in conformance with the *principle of least constraint* [15], is phrased in generic terms.

2. *Extensional tier*: The second specification layer which consists of the traditional source code.

As software evolves continuously, our approach stresses the relevance of the design and architectural specifications throughout the evolution of a program.

1 Abstraction

The prime weakness of contemporary software is its complexity. It is agreed that, predominantly, complexity arises from the sheer size of most software systems [11]. Complexity hinders readability, maintenance, and scalability, and it obstructs the growth and sophistication of software technology.

Complexity is handled by abstraction techniques that were gradually recognized and subsequently integrated into the programming discipline of programming.

We distinguish two distinct types of *abstraction* processes:

1. "Zooming Out": This process aims at defining coarser, larger-grained units of processing (*components* and *connectors* in the terminology by Garlan and Shaw [10]).
2. "Parameterization": The generalization of design constructs in terms that apply across programs. An example is the definition of *design patterns* [9].

F. Arbab and C. Talcott (Eds.): COORDINATION 2002, LNCS 2315, pp. 149–157, 2002.
© Springer-Verlag Berlin Heidelberg 2002

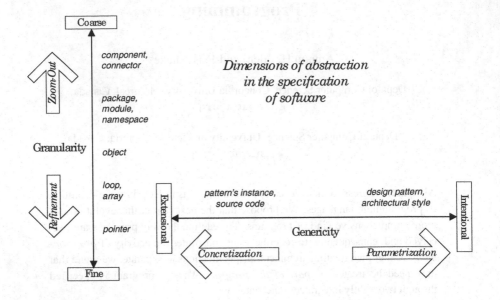

Fig. 1. An illustration of the dimensions of *abstraction*.

1.1 *Abstraction* Quod *Zooming-Out*

Many modern languages allow direct representation of computational abstractions. Initially (as in languages like Fortran and Algol), very basic control and data abstractions were introduced, such as loops and arrays. More recent programming languages (such as object-oriented languages) support further, more elaborated abstraction mechanisms, such as *encapsulation*, *information hiding*, *synchronization*, and *polymorphism*.

As a result of further evolution of programming languages, few modern language allow first-class representation of architectural concepts. For example, several languages support the division of programs into modular units (e.g., C++ namespace, Java™ package), although these specifications are typically dispersed in different places in the source code. Other examples for language support in architectural concepts appear in Table 1.

Abstraction can be characterized as an evolutionary process whose goal is to allow us to achieve a "zoom-out" perspective on programs by directly representing constructs of lower granularity as native constructs of the language. A complex program can be rendered more comprehensible if we draw a "roadmap" or "bird's-eye view" thereof, which consists only of a small number of "coarse" abstraction units. This approach is represented by the vertical axis in Figure 1.

Table 1. Intentionally-defined concepts vs. programming languages constructs supporting extensional manifestations of the same concept.

Intentional concept or architectural property	*Extensional representation* as built-in lingual constructs	
"Module" (architectural component) [10]	♦ namespace ♦ package ♦ Module	♦ C++ ♦ Java™, Ada95 ♦ Modula3
"Remote procedure call" (architectural connector) [10]	RMI (*Remote Object Invocation*)	Java™
"Pipe" (architectural connector) [10]	Standard input/ output/error; streams	C++
Prototype pattern [6]	♦ deep_copy ♦ deep_clone	♦ Smalltalk ♦ Eiffel

Nonetheless, despite advances in software design and architecture (e.g., [5, 9, 10, 13]), present programming languages do not solve the problem of architectural erosion and software maintenance of time. And why is that? We strongly believe that a key answer to this question can be based on the following observation:

Abstractions specified by any programming language are, while coarser, always *extensional*, with respect to the design or the architecture of the program itself. Architectural specifications, however, are given in intentional terms, as demonstrated below. Consequently, the original intentional specifications of program are lost over time (because they are not part of the program), and, hence, its architecture erodes.

1.2 *Abstraction* **Quod** *Parameterization*

A separate process of abstraction aims at factoring out recurring motifs in different programs. Unlike the coarse units of computation that arise from *abstraction* quod *zooming out*, recurring motifs may be observed at *any* scale. To allow grouping of similar phenomena under one expression, the specification of these motifs must be parameterized, meaning, that the descriptions must be given in *intentional* terms.

Typical examples for *parameterized* or *intentional specifications* are of *architectural styles* [10] and *design patterns* [9]. Below, we distinguish between *intentional* and *extensional* specifications and demonstrate our observation.

A definition is *intentional* if it defines a group in terms of properties of its members, whereas *extensional* definition simply enumerates the members that fall under the said category. As non-finite sets cannot be defined via the enumeration of their members, they must be defined intentionally.

For example, some *types*, such as "rational" or "real", represent intentional concepts (ignoring the real-life constraints on machine representations), while other types, such as "enumeration types", are defined by enumerating the possible values.

Consider also the analogy to *relational databases*: The extension of a database consists of various tables and records. In contrast, the database *schema* defines the tables and their interrelations in an intentional form.

Speaking of the desired properties of an ideal specification language for software architecture [15], Perry and Wolf write implied that architectural styles are expected to have intentional specifications: "We want a means of supporting a 'principle of least constraint' to be able to express only those constraints in the architecture that are necessary at the architectural level of the system description".

Formally, intentional expressions incorporate variables that range over unbounded domains, while extensional definitions must consist entirely of constants. In the next section we demonstrate in more detail different levels of parameterization.

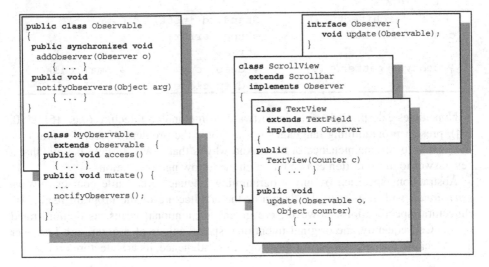

```
public class Observable
{
  public synchronized void
    addObserver(Observer o)
      { ... }
  public void
    notifyObservers(Object arg)
      { ... }
}

    class MyObservable
      extends Observable  {
    public void access()
      { ... }
    public void mutate() {
      ...
      notifyObservers();
    }
    }
```

```
intrface Observer {
    void update(Observable);
}

class ScrollView
  extends Scrollbar
  implements Observer
{
    class TextView
      extends TextField
      implements Observer
    {
    public
      TextView(Counter c)
        { ... }

    public void
      update(Observable o,
        Object counter)
          { ... }
    }
}
```

Fig. 2. Extensional specification of (an instance of) the *Observer* pattern [2]

2   Case Study: The *Observer* Pattern

In this section, we demonstrate intentional specifications using LePUS [7; 6], a formal specification language for O-O design and architecture. LePUS formulae allow us to express structural constraints, but they can also be used to capture and convey a coherent picture of the structure of programs, libraries, and frameworks [8]. LePUS formulae are given either symbolically or visually. Below, we use the symbolic version and explain the interpretation of each formula in broad terms.

Example: The MVC "usage pattern" in Swing. The designers of the Java™ *Swing* class library tell us [2, 14] that *Swing* supports what they call "The MVC usage pattern", or the "MVC Architecture" (*Model View Controller*). The concept described is generic, as it is useful in various contexts. In favour of supporting the (unlimited number of possible) implementation of the pattern, the library provides the complete implementation of classes Observer and Observable (Fig. 2), and describe (using the example in Fig. 2 and some natural language) how the remainder should be implemented. A precise and complete specification of the "usage pattern", however, need be parameterized, such as the following:

$$model \; : \; \mathbb{C} \qquad\qquad\qquad\qquad\qquad\qquad\qquad\qquad (1)$$
$$Mutators,\, Accessors \;\; : \mathrm{P}\,(\mathbb{F})$$

Inherit(model, Observable*)*

DefinedIn $^\rightarrow$*(Mutators,model)*

DefinedIn $^\rightarrow$*(Accessors,model)*

Invoke $^\rightarrow$*(Mutators,* notifyObservers*)*

(Some class *model* should inherit from the specific class Observable, and define one set of functions *Accessors*, and another set of functions called *Mutators*, such that each "mutator" must call the specific method notifyObservers.)

$$Views \; : \mathrm{P}\,(\mathbb{C}) \qquad\qquad\qquad\qquad\qquad\qquad\qquad (2)$$
$$Update \; : \mathrm{P}\,(\mathbb{F})$$

Inherit $^\rightarrow$*(View s,* Observer*)*

DefinedIn $^\leftrightarrow$*(Update Views)*

SameSignature $^\cdot$*(Update,* update*)*

Invoke $^\rightarrow$*(Update,Accessors)*

(a set of classes *Views* should each inherit from Observer and override the method update with a method that calls one or more *Accessor*.)

Equation 1 generalizes the class MyObservable by replacing the constant with the variable *model*. Equation 2 generalizes ScrollView and TextView into any number of classes that satisfy the said constraints. Note that constants are distinguished from variables by via fixed typeface.

In conclusion, the MVC "usage pattern" is specified in a combination of extensional terms (constants) and intentional terms (variables that range over non-finite sets).

Example: The Observer pattern. As "design patterns capture the ... structures of solutions that occur repeatedly when producing applications in a particular context" [5], the *Observer* pattern [9] is even more abstract than Swing's "usage pattern. Accordingly, the formal specification of the *Observer* pattern, given in Equation 3, consists solely of variables.

Since LePUS formulae are defined in mathematical logic, we can prove formally that Swing's *usage pattern* is a specialization of the *Observer*. A detailed proof of this relation can be found in [8].

$$model, observable, observer \; : \mathbb{C} \tag{3}$$
$$Views \; : \; \mathbb{P}\,\mathbb{C})$$
$$notifyObservers \; : \; \mathbb{F}$$
$$Mutators, Accessors, \quad Update \; : \; \mathbb{P}\,(\mathbb{F})$$

Inherit(model,Observable)
DefinedIn(notifyObservers,observable)
DefinedIn $\rightarrow$ (Mutators,mode l)
DefinedIn $\rightarrow$ (Accessors,model)
Invoke $\rightarrow$ (Mutators, notifyObservers)
Inherit $\rightarrow$ (Views,observer)
DefinedIn(update,observer)
DefinedIn $\leftrightarrow$ (Update,Views)
SameSignature $\rightarrow$ (Update,update)
Invoke $\rightarrow$ (Update,Accessors)

Source Code is the Extensional Specification. We have demonstrated that design and architectural properties can only be specified intentionally. Thus, while contemporary programming languages have evolved to support increasing abstractions quod "zooming-out" and deliver native constructs representing coarser, more complicated abstractions of data and control, in terms of *design* or *architectural properties*, they only support extensional expressions. For example, one may use Java™ to define classes TextView and ScrollView in a way that conforms to the design decisions (namely, that each inherits from Observer and overrides update with a method that implements a function call to an accessor.) However, programming languages do not support the *intentional* specification of this design decision, i.e., in the form that is expressed in Equation 2, (for example, by naming a set of properties that are true with respect to any *View* class.)

To resolve this difficulty, one may suggest extending programming languages so as to allow such intentional specifications. Below we explain why this has not been done and propose a different solution.

3   Programming for Evolution

In this section we discuss the relevance of design and architectural specifications beyond the initial phases of software development.

How is software developed? Research in the pragmatics of software development [3] lead to the following conclusions:

1. That software is developed in an incremental, evolutionary process, which may not conform to the waterfall [17] sequence.
2. That, in particular, at different times during the development process, development may follow both bottom-up and top-down approaches.

3. That, in particular, software is in a state of constant flux as a result of other factors, such as, rapid changes in hardware, and frequent modifications to the requirements.

In light of the non-linear nature of the development process, the use of two distinct levels of abstraction often leads to *architectural drift* and *architectural erosion* [15] and, obvious questions arise, such as:

1. *Top-down integration:* How to maintain the validity of the source code when changes are made to the architectural specifications?
2. *Bottom-up integration:* How to maintain the validity of the architectural specifications when changes are made to the source code?

4   Two-Tier Programming

Research in the specification of architectural properties [1; 18; 12] and design models [7; 15; 3] have addressed the need to render design and architectural specifications well defined, or even formal. Some research was made in the construction of tools that validate architectural specifications [13].

We, however, advocate a different, more comprehensive approach: We suggest to redefine the way programs are perceived and, consequently, to redefine what constitutes the activity of *programming*. Rather than treating architectural specifications as separate, we argue that they need be treated *as part of the program*.

More specifically, *Two-Tier Programming* is a programming approach that takes place in two levels of abstraction (quod *parameterization*):

♦ At the *extensional tier* we use the programming language to define concrete elements of the program, such as *loops, procedures, classes*, and so forth, as well as coarser constructions such as *pipes* and *remote procedure calls*, depending on the language used.
♦ At the *intentional tier* we use an *architectural specification language*, i.e., a language that allows for adequately parameterized specifications, to express local and global constraints that characterize the program in intentional terms.

Consider the analogy of *relational databases* (Section 1): It is unreasonable to discard the database's schema except in the rare case where the database is never expected to change. Similarly, one who expects a program to evolve must maintain its intentional specifications as integral part thereof.

Several complications arise from this approach. Such a programming paradigm should allow us not only to maintain simultaneous multiple representations but also to preserve their consistency throughout the program's evolution. We examine the requirements arising from the coordination endeavour.

4.1   Functional Requirements

A programming environment that supports two-tier programming need follow these requirements:

1. Maintain two representations for a program:

   ♦ Intentional tier: Maintain a collection of intentional expressions that are relevant to this specific program.

     For example, a programmer can decide to *apply* the *Observer* pattern and add `TextView`, `MyObservable` (Fig. 2). As a first step, s/he "applies" the expression given in Equations 1 and 2, which adapts the very general pattern to the specific needs of the classes `TextView` and `ScrollView`.

   ♦ Extensional tier: Maintain the source code implementation of the program in textual form and allow for the usual activities that contemporary programming involves, such as compilation, debugging, etc.

2. Maintain a library of intentional specifications: Support the specification of abstract architectural and design motifs (such as *styles* and *patterns*) in their generic form. These expressions must be maintained in a suitable "storage" so that they can be retrieved, modified, and *applied*.

   For example, such a library should be able to store a representation of the *Observer* pattern in its generic form (Equation 3).

3. Maintain and support an *association function*: An auxiliary database should associate symbols appearing inside intentional expressions with elements of the extensional tier. Associations allow the tool to detect potential violations of the intentional specification due to modifications made to the source code.

   For example, if a representation of Equation 2 is incorporated in the intentional tier, the set variable *Views* must be associated with the classes `TextView` and `ScrollView`.

4. Extended compilation: We extend the original interpretation of *compilation* to include the process that coordinates changes made in either tier:

   ♦ Bottom-up: When a "unit of change" to the source code is complete, it can be separately "compiled" in the original sense. To complete the operation, test whether the change violates constraints whose variables were associated with the affected extensions.

     – If no violation is detected: Support *reverse engineering* so as to reflect the changes that were made in the architectural representation, if any. In such case, we say the compilation process has completed.

     – If a constraint is violated by the change: Indicate where the violation has occurred and sever the affected association. The program is left in an "invalid state", which can be compared to the source code written in an ordinary programming language and which was edited but cannot be compiled.

   ♦ Top-down: When a "unit of change" to the intentional tier is complete, support *forward engineering* so change the extensional tier.

Acknowledgements. This research was supported in part by a grant from the Natural Sciences and Engineering Research Council of Canada (NSERC).

References

1. R. Allen, D. Garlan. "A Formal Basis For Architectural Connection." *ACM Transactions on Software Engineering and Methodology*, Vol. 6, No. 3, July 1997, pp. 213-249.
2. J. Coker (1997). "Keeping Objects In Sync." In: *Java Developer Connection*, http://java.sun.com
3. J. Bosch. "Relations as Object Model Components." *Journal of Programming Languages*, Vol. 4, No. 1, 1996, pp. 39-61.
4. E. R. Comer. 1997. "Alternative Software Life Cycle Models." In *Software Engineering*, Dorfman, Merlin; Thayer, Richard, pp. 404-414. Piscataway, NJ: IEEE Computer Society Press.
5. J. Coplien, D. Schmidt, eds. (1995). *Pattern Languages of Program Design*. Reading, MA: Addison-Wesley.
6. A. H. Eden. "LePUS: A Formal Specification Language of Object Oriented Design and Architecture." *2002 NSF Design, Service, and Manufacturing Grantees and Research Conference*, Jan. 7-10, 2002, San Juan, Puerto Rico.
7. A. H. Eden, Y. Hirshfeld. "Principles in Formal Specification of Object Oriented Architectures." *CASCON 2001*, November 5-8, 2001. Toronto, Canada.
8. A. H. Eden (2002). "LePUS: A Visual Formalism for Object-Oriented Architectures." *The 6th World Conference on Integrated Design and Process Technology*. Pasadena, California, June 26—30, 2002.
9. E. Gamma, R. Helm, R. Johnson, J. Vlissides (1994). *Design Patterns: Elements of Reusable Object Oriented Software*. Addison-Wesley.
10. D. Garlan, M. Shaw (1993). "An Introduction to Software Architecture." In V. Ambriola, G. Tortora, eds., *Advances in Software Engineering and Knowledge Engineering*, Vol. 2, pp. 1-39. New Jersey: World Scientific Publishing Company.
11. W. W. Gibbs (1994). "Software's Chronic Crisis." *Scientific American*, Vol. 271, No. 3, pp. 86-95.
12. D. C. Luckham, J. J. Kenney, L. M. Augustin, J. Vera, D. Bryan, W. Mann. "Specification and Analysis of System Architecture Using Rapide." *IEEE Transactions on Software Engineering*, Special Issue on Software Architecture, Vol. 21, No. 4, pp. 336-355, April 1995.
13. N. Medvidovic, R. N. Taylor (1997). "A Framework for Classifying and Comparing Architecture Description Languages". In *Proceedings of the Sixth European Software Engineering Conference*, together with *Fifth ACM SIGSOFT Symposium on the Foundations of Software Engineering*, Zurich, Switzerland, September 22-25, 1997, pp. 60-76.
14. MegaLang Institute. "Fundamentals of JFC/Swing, Part II". http://java.sun.com
15. M. O'Cinnéide, P. Nixon. "A Methodology for the Automated Introduction of Design Patterns." *Proceedings of the IEEE International Conference on Software Maintenance*, 30 August - 3 September, 1999.
16. D. E. Perry, A. L. Wolf (1992). "Foundation for the Study of Software Architecture". ACM SIGSOFT *Software Engineering Notes*, 17 (4), pp. 40-52.
17. W. W. Royce (1970). "Managing the Development of Large Software Systems: Concepts and Techniques." *1970 WESCON Technical Papers*, Vol. 14, Western Electronic Show and Convention.
18. M. Shaw, D. Garlan (1995). "Formulations and Formalisms in Software Architecture," chap. in *Computer Science Today, Lecture Notes in Computer Science Vol. 1000*. Berlin: Springer-Verlag.

Criteria for the Analysis of Coordination in Multi-agent Applications

Rejane Frozza[1,2]* and Luis Otávio Alvares[2]*

[1] Laboratoire LEIBNIZ-IMAG - 46, Avenue Felix Viallet
38031 Grenoble, France
rejane.frozza@imag.fr
[2] Instituto de Informática, UFRGS – Av. Bento Gonçalves, 9500
91501-970 Porto Alegre, Brazil
alvares@inf.ufrgs.br

Abstract. In computer science, distributed artificial intelligence is deeply involved with the problem of coordination. The coordination of agents has been approached in several applications because when well applied, it contributes to an efficient execution of activities by agents. Thus, it is an important issue to be analyzed in a society of agents. In this work, a detailed study of the characteristics and existing coordination mechanisms that involve the operation of agents in a multi-agent environment has been carried out. Thus, criteria for the comparison of different agent coordination approaches were proposed, and the use of these criteria in some applications is shown. These criteria can help in the analysis of the operation and use of an agents' coordination mechanism in a multi-agent system. A previous analysis can highlight interesting aspects of a system in relation to coordination.

1 Introduction

Multi-Agent Systems are involved with the coordination problem, trying to design coordination mechanisms for groups of artificial agents. Thus, an effective coordination among agents that operate in a multi-agent environment contribute to the improvement of quality of solutions achieved by agents and to a better operation of agents in performing tasks.

Coordination can be defined as the act of managing dependencies among activities [1]. These dependencies can increase as a consequence of activities to be executed in a same environment.

The coordination of actions taken by agents can help avoid problems such as: agents solving the same subproblem, causing redundancy; an agent solving a problem where the result of its task will be obsolete; agents trying to use the same resources at the same time; and agents waiting for events that will not take place.

---

* CAPES fellow and Student at UFRGS (Brazil), on leave at LEIBNIZ.
* Professor at UFRGS (Brazil).

F. Arbab and C. Talcott (Eds.): COORDINATION 2002, LNCS 2315, pp. 158-165, 2002.
© Springer-Verlag Berlin Heidelberg 2002

Thus, analyzing the coordination solution to be used in an application can help design more efficient and robust multi-agent systems and lead designers to discuss the quality of coordinated actions executed by agents. In order to carry out an analysis, criteria that allow to characterize elements related to coordination are required.

This paper is organized as follows: Section 2 presents coordination mechanisms for agents considered in this study. Section 3 presents the applications used to compare coordination approaches. Section 4 presents the criteria used to analyze coordination in agent systems, together with the constructed comparative table. Finally, conclusions are presented.

2 Coordination Mechanisms

Several applications in multi-agent systems can use different action coordination mechanisms in order to contribute to the improvement in the quality of solutions achieved by agents and to enhance the performance of agents in task solving.

Several works have been developed showing different coordination mechanisms. Some of them can be found in [2, 3, 4, 5]. We could see that authors have different opinions on what could be considered a coordination mechanism. This shows that further studies should be carried out, adding to the current interesting ideas in order to better characterize coordination mechanisms for agents.

In the context of this work, Ferber's classification [2] was used. Ferber describes four action coordination mechanisms: synchronization, planning, reactivity and regulation. This choice has to do with the fact that his classification approaches coordination mechanisms also commonly found in nature and human organizations.

Each of these mechanisms are briefly described as follows:

- *Synchronization*: synchronization can generate simultaneity of several actions and check whether operation results are coherent. Synchronizing several actions is defining the way of chaining these actions so that they are performed at the determined time;
- *Planning*: it is based on three phases namely, determining the set of actions to be performed to achieve an overall common goal, generating a set of plans; synchronizing/coordinating plans; choosing one of the generated plans for execution. Plans chosen can be reviewed during execution;
- *Reactivity*: it is based on the behavior of reactive agents. Reactive coordination consists of the agent's reaction to changes that occur in its local environment and the adaptation of its actions to the actions taken by other agents;
- *Regulation*: this is a method based on social laws or conventions used to ensure immediate coordination. The principle of this method is the use of behavioral rules designed to eliminate possible conflicts. For example, assigning priority rules to vehicles on an intersection in order to prevent a crash (conflict).

3 Coordination Approaches in Some Applications

Some applications that make use of different coordination approaches have been selected as practical examples where such criteria for coordination analysis have been used. Later, on Section 4, these approaches related with the coordination mechanisms presented by Ferber [2] will be shown.

Next, each coordination approach is listed with a brief description of its operation. Detailed information can be found on Table 1.

- *Coalition Formation* [6]: coalition is defined as a group of agents that decide to cooperate in order to perform a common task. Agents may determine the importance of the tasks to be performed and participate in more than one coalition. The agents that are coalition members get a reward when they complete the requested task;
- *Look-Ahead* [7]: this is designed to enhance the overall visibility of agents and provide information for decision-making, since agents need to coordinate their actions constantly in order to complete their tasks and improve system performance. Each task is completed by the execution of operations by the agents;
- *Focal Points* [8]: the idea is that agents should use coordination for human interactions without communication, approaching Focal Points as a heuristic for coordination in real environments. A successful example in the use of this approach is in the coordination of common choices among agents in simulations (two agents choose the same object in an environment without communication);
- *Communication of Evaluations* [9]: an agent, with the knowledge of a given domain, will direct the other agents, that are independent from this domain, through signals that reflect the evaluation of the coordination of its own actions and of those of the other agents;
- *Payoff Matrix* [10]: coordination requires an agent to acknowledge the environment current status and to model the actions of other agents in order to decide its own behavior (action). There is no communication among agents and the recursive modeling method is used;
- *GPGP* (Generalized Partial Global Planning) [11, 12]: this is a set of coordination mechanisms that operate linked to an agent architecture and with a local task scheduler where agents can communicate among themselves and plan their actions.

4 Analysis and Comparison Criteria Used for Coordination

In order to analyze the elements involved in coordination in practical cases, characteristics have been proposed to make comparisons among different coordination approaches, showing their differences and similarities.

4.1 Analysis Criteria Proposed

Next is a list of criteria initially proposed from studies performed, which can be analyzed in coordinated systems and that have been used to make comparisons:
- *Predictivity*: ability to determine the future status of the environment and agents. This can provide the necessary knowledge of the environment and of the capabilities of agents;
- *Adaptability*: ability to adapt to unexpected events or situations; useful for applications in evolutive contexts and to provide freedom of action to agents;
- *Action control*: this can be either centralized (a single agent holds the knowledge of a given problem and assigns tasks to the other agents) or distributed (any agent of the society can stablish rules from its knowledge);
- *Communication mode*: the way in which agents get to know actions and other agents. This can be done through interaction, perception, without communication or direct communication;
- *Conflicts*: these are either avoided or not by the coordination method; they are either approached or not;
- *Information exchange*: information handled and exchanged among agents in order for coordination to be made; this is useful for applications that deal with the development of action plans;
- *Agents*: characteristic of agents involved (homogeneous[1] or heterogeneous[2]); capabilities of the agents;
- *Applications they are designed to*: they can either adapt to any domain (a characteristic that tends to be less effective) or to certain specific domains;
- *Advantages* of the coordination approach used;
- *Disadvantages* of the coordination approach used.

These criteria have been proposed in order to help designers of multi-agent systems choose agent coordination mechanisms to be used in the domain of the application in question. Due to the characteristics and the objective of the application to be developed, a previous analysis of the issues involved in the coordination can contribute to a better performance of agents in the solution of their tasks.

4.2 Comparison among Coordination Approaches

Table 1 shows the comparison table, taking into account predetermined criteria, in order to show the applicability of these criteria. The criteria defined are at the qualitative level.

The objective of the comparative table is to allow the listing of characteristics (represented by the criteria) in each coordination approach used as a solution in multi-agent applications. Thus, it helps in the previous selection of a multi-agent coordination mechanism in system modeling.

---

[1] Homogeneous agents have the same internal structure (goals, knowledge and actions).
[2] Heterogeneous agents have different goals, knowledge and actions.

Table 1. Comparison of Different Coordination Approaches

Coordination Approaches	Characteristics (Criteria)			
	Predictivity	*Adaptability*	*Action Control*	*Communication Mode*
Coalition Formation	not occur	agents adapt to constantly changing tasks	distributed among agents	direct among agents (through messages)
Look-Ahead	occurs	agents base their actions on future predictions	distributed among agents	direct among agents (through messages)
Focal Points	not occur	not approached	centralized	without communication
Communication of Evaluations	not occur	attempt by domain-independent agents to operate in unknown environments	distributed among agents	sending of signals (scalar values)
Payoff Matrix	occurs in relation to agents' actions	agents base their actions on future predictions	centralized	without communication
GPGP	not occur	not approached	distributed among agents	can vary, for example *blackboard*

Coordination Approaches	Characteristics (Criteria)			
	Conflicts	*Information Exchange*	*Agents*	*Applications*
Coalition Formation	with strategy to solve conflicts	it occurs to develop plans	heterogeneous (in terms of interface, task and information)	dynamic environments with large amounts of information
Look-Ahead	not approached	it occurs to decide on their actions	strongly coupled[3]; homogeneous; make decisions	scheduling problems and real time
Focal Points	not approached	not occur	does not specify	common choice problems; simulations
Communication of Evaluations	not approached	it occurs on the evaluation of agents' behavior	heterogeneous (domain dependent and independent), with ability to communicate and evaluate environment situations	designed to simple applications with a limited number of possible actions
Payoff Matrix	not approached	not occur	homogeneous; decision-making ability	systems that involve decision-making to minimize damage
GPGP	negotiation is approached in coordination relationships	it occurs to perform task scheduling	homogeneous; they have certain beliefs and action planning ability	different applications that involve task scheduling

---

[3] Agents are strongly coupled because there are precedence restrictions among operations (that make up a task) and each agent can execute only one operation at a time.

	Characteristics (Criteria)	
Coordination Approaches	*Advantages*	*Disadvantages*
Coalition Formation	attempt to increase execution efficiency in group tasks; uses the idea of reward to agents	the number of possible coalitions among agents grow exponentially and has to be evaluated
Look-Ahead	solution for coordination in task allocation problems; agents decide actions in real time	time spent on action prevision; approaches only task execution in a sequential order
Focal Points	tries to model the naturalness and intuitiveness of solutions found in the world; minimizes communication costs	difficulty of agents having the abilities to identify focal points
Communication of Evaluations	works with a group of agents that operate in an useful way in different domains; enables agents that do not know the domain as whole to choose their actions	does not explore the issue of learning from evaluation signals; loss of expression of situations, reducing evaluation signals to scalar values
Payoff Matrix	attempt of an emerging coordination; minimizes communication costs; quality in decision making	time spend on action prediction when in real time environments; each application has its specific attributes that will be taken into account in the decision making process
GPGP	the use of coordination mechanisms is independent	the time spent choosing and ordering actions (generation of plans) can affect system performance in dynamic environments

Each multi-agent system has its own specific characteristic in relation to agents, actions, to the communication mode among other things that can influence the performance of the coordination mechanism used.

4.3 Relationship among Coordination Mechanisms and Approaches

Next, we present the relationship among the coordination mechanisms studied (synchronization, planning, reactivity and regulation [2]) and the coordination approaches used in practical cases shown in this section. Additionally, other techniques to perform coordination are added, thus complementing the approached mechanisms.

• *Coalition Formation*: it approaches coordination by planning and coordination by synchronization;
• *Look-Ahead*: it approaches reactive coordination (it is based on the action-perception behavior) and coordination by regulation (using priority rules for the selection of the activities to be executed by the agents);
• *Focal Points*: it approaches coordination without communication;
• *Communication of Evaluations*: it approaches coordination through the sending of signals of evaluation of agents' behavior and coordination by synchronization;
• *Payoff Matrix*: it approaches coordination without communication and reactive coordination (it is based on the action-perception behavior and on the emerging coordination behavior);

- *GPGP*: it approaches coordination by planning and has a mechanism to schedule tasks (synchronization).

We can see that coordination mechanisms can be combined or associated with other problem solving techniques in order to achieve efficiency in action execution in a coordinated way by the agents involved.

From the comparison table we can analyze that:

- With the coordination without communication approach, the selection of the actions to be executed by the agents depend on the knowledge obtained through the functions of the payoff matrices of the other agents and the use of the focal points approach;
- With the coordination with communication approach, information exchanged among agents are the basis for the coordination to take place efficiently;
- Few forms of coordination are concerned with conflict resolution, which is a factor that may happen and negatively influence the agent operation and task resolution;
- The coordination mechanisms and approaches presented here do not approach the learning issue. Learning is a tendency that may bring benefits to the coordinated operation of agents, particularly in dynamic environments where the time to decision making of actions to be executed may affect performance and results of the system.

5 Conclusion

The search of systems with a satisfactory behavior, combined with the complex nature of the interaction among agents, justifies the need to use and develop sophisticated mechanisms for the coordination of the activities performed by agents.

Coordination is something implicit in human activities. And when these activities are simulated by computer or when systems have to provide results that will be applied to real situations, coordination influences the process of agents in search of goals.

When we think about the application of coordination in an agent system, many difficulties emerge in terms of specifying what is required so that this coordination is useful. This involves to make a decision relative to the coordination mechanism to be used as a function of the agents, the domain and proposed goals; which agents should coordinate among themselves, taking their activities into account; and the resolution of other issues involved, such as the cost of information exchange among agents and conflicts that may emerge.

Therefore, having a set of criteria available to analyze mechanisms for agent coordination in the design of a system benefits its behavior. Additionally, it enables us to analyze coordination in different multi-agent systems.

Thus, this work raised some issues to be researched and used in agent coordination. The aim is to improve the performance of multi-agent systems, achieving quality in the activities performed by the agents through the proper use of a coordination mechanism for the application in question.

References

1. Malone, Thomas W.; Crowston, Kevin. The Interdisciplinary Study of Coordination. ACM Computing Surveys, v.26, n.1., p.87-119. [S.l.:s.n], march 1994
2. Ferber, Jacques. Les Systèmes Multi-Agents (Vers une intelligence collective). p.421-486; chapitre 8. Paris:InterEditions, 1995
3. Jennings, Nick R.. Coordination Techniques for Distributed Artificial Intelligence. Foundations of Distributed Artificial Intelligence. O'Hare, G.M.P. and Jennings, N.R. (Eds.). p. 187-210, chapter 6. [S.l]:John Wiley & Sons, 1996
4. Nwana, Hyacinth; Jennings, Nick. Coordination in Software Agent Systems. In: Britsh Telecon Technology Journal, v.14, n.4, p.79-88. Proceedings ... [S.l]:[s.n], 1996
5. Ossowski, Sasha. Co-ordination in Artificial Agent Societies (Social Structure and Its Implications for Autonomous Problem-Solving Agents). Berlin:Springer, 1999. (Lecture Notes in Artificial Intelligence 1535)
6. Shehory, Onn M.; Sycara, Katia; Jha, Somesh. Multi-Agent Coordination Through Coalition Formation. In: Intelligent Agents IV, Agent Theories, Architectures and Languages (ATAL'97), 4., 1997, p.143-154. A. Rao, M. Singh and M. Wooldridge (Eds.) Proceedings... Rhode Island: Springer Verlag, 1997. (Lecture Notes in Artificial Intelligence 1365)
7. Liu, Jyi-Shane; Sycara, Katia P. Multiagent Coordination in Tightly Coupled Task Scheduling. Readings in Agents. Michael N. Huhns and Munindar P. Singh (Eds.). p. 164-171; chapter 2. San Francisco: Morgan Kaufmann Publishers, 1998
8. Fenster, Maier; Kraus, Sarit. Coordination Without Communication: Experimental Validation of Focal Point Techniques. Readings in Agents. Michael N. Huhns and Munindar P. Singh (Eds.). p. 380-386; chapter 4. San Francisco: Morgan Kaufmann Publishers, 1998
9. Jong, Edwin de. Multi-Agent Coordination by Communication of Evaluations .In: European Workshop Modeling Autonomous Agents in a Multi-Agent World (MAAMAW97), 8., 1997. Proceedings ... Magnus Bonan and Walter Van de Velde (Eds.). Berlin: Springer Verlag, 1997
10. Noh, Sanguk; Gmyrasiewicz, Piotr J. Multiagent Coordination in Antiair Defense: A Case Study. In: European Workshop Modeling Autonomous Agents in a Multi-Agent World (MAAMAW97), 8, 1997. Magnus Bonan and Walter Van de Velde (Eds.). Proceedings... Berlin: Springer Verlag, 1997
11. Decker, Keith S.; Lesser, Victor R. Designing a Family of Coordination Algorithms. Readings in Agents. Michael N. Huhns and Munindar P. Singh (Eds.). p. 450-457; chapter 4. San Francisco: Morgan Kaufmann Publishers, 1998
12. Decker, Keith S.; Lesser, Victor R. Generalizing the partial global planning algorithm. In: International Journal of Intelligent and Cooperative Information Systems. v.1; n.2; p.233-248. Proceedings... [S.l.:s.n.], 1992

Towards a Colimit-Based Semantics for Visual Programming

Jeremy Gibbons

University of Oxford

Abstract. Software architects such as Garlan and Katz promote the separation of *computation* from *coordination*. They encourage the study of *connectors* as first-class entities, and *superposition* of connectors onto components as a paradigm for component-oriented programming. We demonstrate that this is a good model for what *visual programming tools* like IBM's VisualAge actually do. Moreover, Fiadeiro and Maibaum's categorical semantics of parallel programs is applicable to this model, so we can make progress towards a formal semantics of visual programming.

1 Introduction

There are signs that the popularity of pure object-oriented programming is receding, to be replaced by component-oriented programming [16]. One motivation for this trend is the desire for gaphical tools to support visual assembly by third parties of independently-developed software components. The code generated by such visual programming tools has the kind of architecture promoted by researchers such as Garlan [1] and Katz [9], who argue for the separation of actual computational behaviour from the coordination of these computations.

Their approach encourages the study of connectors as first-class entities, and superposition of connectors onto components as a paradigm for application assembly. Moreover, Fiadeiro and Maibaum's colimit-based categorical semantics of parallel programs [3], a descendant of Goguen's General Systems Theory [5], is applicable to this paradigm, so we can put the two together to make progress towards a formal semantics of visual programming.

In this paper we build on the above-mentioned existing work on superposition and on colimit-based semantics of system assemblies. Our contributions are two-fold: to show that superposition is a good model of the action of visual programming tools such as IBM's VisualAge, and to make the first steps in applying the colimit approach to semantics to superposition of coordinators.

The remainder of the paper is structured as follows. In Section 2 we motivate the movement from object-oriented to component-oriented and visual programming, and describe how visual programming tools operate, with the help of a simple example. In Section 3 we outline the components-and-connectors approach to software architecture, and summarize Goguen's General System Theory, and Maibaum and Fiadeiro's development of it as a model of concurrent systems. Although we are not yet at a stage to apply this theory directly to arbitrary software components, we provide in Section 4 a simplified illustration in terms of concurrent processes.

F. Arbab and C. Talcott (Eds.): COORDINATION 2002, LNCS 2315, pp. 166–173, 2002.

2   Components and Visual Programming

Object-oriented programming is losing its shine: despite its undoubted benefits, we are coming to the realization that it is not a silver bullet for the problems of software construction. In particular, *inheritance breaks encapsulation* [14]: in order reliably to define a subclass, one needs to see not just the public interface but also the private implementation of the superclass, and so a revision of the latter, even without changing its public interface, may break the former.

This observation has led some [16] to propose *component-oriented programming* as an improvement on object-oriented programming. The emphasis is on *object composition* rather than *class inheritance*, and *delegation* rather than *overriding*. This avoids the problem of broken encapsulation alluded to above, and paves the way for a programming methodology based on *third-party assembly* of *black box* components. Assemblers need only know the public interface of a component, not its private implementation.

2.1   Visual Assembly of Components

This in turn allows component assembly without looking at code at all. Assemblers can literally treat components as black boxes, placed on a canvas and connected by lines. Supporting software can interpret the lines as connections between operations in the component interfaces, and can automatically generate the coordinating code.

This is exactly what visual programming tools like IBM's VisualAge for Java [7] do. The details differ from tool to tool, but the idea is fairly consistent. There will be a *palette* of computational components, and a *canvas* on which these components can be dropped. Two components are connected by dragging a rubber band line from one and dropping it on the other; this connection corresponds to some code, which is generated automatically by the tool. The possible interpretations of a 'connection' will depend on the underlying language, but typically they all boil down to the invocation of some method on the target component, given some suitable triggering condition on the source component.

The Java language [6], and in particular the JavaBeans coding specification [10], was specifically designed to permit this kind of component assembly without stepping outside the language. Reflection can be used on compiled Java code to determine what methods are supported, but the Java class libraries were constructed in such a way as to avoid having to do this wherever possible. The code generated by the tool is source-level Java, which can be examined and if necessary modified afterwards.

2.2   A 'Counter' Example

To illustrate, consider a little Java applet providing a counter. It consists of three components: a button that can be pressed, a counter that is incremented on button presses, and a label that displays the value of the counter. One may expect to find these three components in a software component library. A visual assembly tool can automatically generate two new classes: an *event adapter* class, whose instances have a method to be called on button presses that will step the counter, and a *property binder* class, whose instances have a method to be called on counter value changes that will update the label. In addition, the tool will generate one more class, with a main method than instantiates the other five classes and hooks up the instances appropriately. This is illustrated in Figure 1.

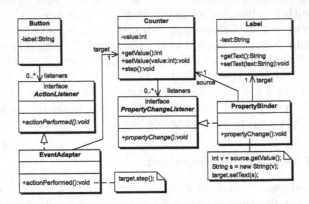

Fig. 1. The class structure of the counter applet

2.3   But What Does It Mean?

Visual programming tools like IBM's VisualAge, Borland's JBuilder, Microsoft's Visual C++ and so on usually provide only informal descriptions of the meaning of the gestures by which programs are assembled; it can be difficult to predict what the outcome of a particular series of gestures will be. Usually the outcome is in fact a source-level program, albeit not necessarily a pretty one; so one can in principle discover the meaning after the fact by examining this generated code — but that doesn't help much with predictability. Without precise, and preferably formal, descriptions of outcomes, no analysis of the visual assembly as a construction in its own right is possible, and programming is reduced to a trial-and-error process, or at best a 'black art'.

It would be much better to have a formal semantics of the visual assembly as a construction in its own right. As the construction is a diagrammatic entity, this strongly suggests a categorical semantics: category theory provides a denotational semantics for diagrams. (This is in contrast to formalisms such as graph grammars, which specify a syntax for diagrams, and graph rewriting, which provides an operational semantics.) It turns out that one can give a clean, simple semantics of such a visual construction as the *colimit* of a *diagram* of components and connectors; we show how in the remainder of the paper.

We envisage that components in the component library will come provided with their semantics, and that coordination is achieved through a small, fixed collection of (customizable) connectors, each again with its own (parametrized)

semantics. Program assembly is a matter of constructing a diagram of components and connectors, as described below. The semantics of the construction is
the colimit of the diagram.

3   Connectors and Superposition

As software systems become larger and more complex, the difficult problems
and the focus of interest migrate from the small-scale algorithmic aspects of individual components to the large-scale organizational aspects of the system as
a whole — the *software architecture* [13]. As a step towards formalizing software architectures, Allen and Garlan [1] propose the separation of *computation*
(sequential, single-threaded algorithmic activities) from *coordination* (the glue
that binds computations together), and the study of the *connectors* by which
coordination is achieved as first-class entities in their own right.

In this proposal, Allen and Garlan were following in the footsteps of a similar journey made a few years earlier by Katz [9], who had proposed *superimposition* or *superposition* of connectors (for coordination) onto components (for
computation) as a paradigm for distributed computing. The parallels between
large-scale software architecture and distributed computing should come as no
surprise: in both fields, the components from which a system is assembled are
of a fundamentally different character than the system itself, and the developer
is concerned with complex behaviour emerging from the interactions between
(relatively) simple independent units.

According to this view, the 'counter' application developed in Section 2.2
consists of three *components* (the button, the counter itself, and the label) coordinated by superposing two *connectors* (the event adapter and the property
binder). The components came 'off the shelf'; the connectors were generated
automatically by the visual programming tool from gestures made by the as-
sembler. In order to generate this code, the tool needs to know nothing about
the components beyond their publicly-advertised interfaces. (Note that there is
essentially no inheritance in the system; everything is achieved through object
composition, as suggested by Szyperski [16].)

3.1   Categorical Semantics of Superposition

Fiadeiro and Maibaum [3] provide a semantics for Allen and Garlan's notion of
connector, building on Goguen's categorical *General Systems Theory* [5]. Goguen
based this on the following slogan:

> *given a category of widgets, the operation of putting a system of widgets
> together to form a super-widget corresponds to taking a colimit of the
> diagram of widgets that shows how to interconnect them.*

We believe that this approach can be taken to give a precise semantics for Java
applications assembled from JavaBeans, and for similar visual program development methods. We cannot yet justify this belief, though; for one thing, we
would have to identify a category of JavaBeans, and this is still a subject of

much research (see for example [8], and other work from the LOOP project). What we can do is illustrate the approach in a simpler setting, and trust that the reader will accept at least that the approach is worth exploring.

In the remainder of Section 3, we explain the General Systems Theory slogan in the context of superposition. In Section 4, we illustrate its application to the superposition of simple processes.

3.2 Superposition via Colimits

In this section we present formal definitions of the categorical definitions leading up to colimits. We have tried to present these in as elementary a manner as possible, so in some cases the definitions are non-standard, although equivalent to the standard definitions. (For example, the usual definition of a diagram in a category $\mathcal{C}$ is as a functor from an indexing category to $\mathcal{C}$; the definition given here avoids having first to define functors.) Space considerations preclude us from going into too much detail, so we summarize briskly; for more detail, see a standard text on category theory, such as [12].

A *category* consists of collections of *objects* and *arrows*, each arrow between two objects. For each object, there is an *identity arrow* from that object to itself. Two arrows that meet (the target of the first is the source of the second) may be *composed*; composition is associative and identity arrows are units.

A *diagram* in a category consists of a subcollection of the objects and of the arrows, for which both endpoints of each included arrow are included. A *cocone* of a diagram with objects A_i and arrows f_k consists of an object X and arrows $g_i : A_i \rightarrow X$ coherent with the f_k — that is, $g_i = f_k \, ; g_j$ for each $f_k : A_i \rightarrow A_j$. A *colimit* of a diagram is a cocone through which any other cocone uniquely factorizes; that is, a cocone (X, g) such that for any other cocone (Y, h), there is a unique arrow $\alpha : X \rightarrow Y$ such that $g_i ; \alpha = h_i$ for every object A_i. Intuitively, colimits capture least upper bounds.

We will be concerned with categories in which the objects are components, and the arrows embeddings of smaller components into larger ones. Two components are synchronized by embedding both in a common super-component. A diagram of components models a system composed from those components, and the arrows in the diagram indicate the synchronizing interconnections between the components. A colimit of a diagram is the least common extension of all the components in the diagram, or equivalently, the minimal system synchronizing all the components; Goguen's slogan of General Systems Theory dictates that this is the appropriate meaning of the individual compositions.

4   A Simplified Example of the Categorical Semantics

In order to complete our plan to provide a categorical semantics for visual programming (for instance, visual composition of JavaBeans), we first need to choose a category in which JavaBeans are objects. As observed above, the right such choice is still an open question. We postpone that choice to further research, and resort here to a rather simpler setting: instead of JavaBeans, we will consider *traced processes*. (This illustration is based on [3].)

4.1   Traced Processes

Consider processes of the form $Toggle = step \rightsquigarrow step, rollover \rightsquigarrow Toggle$. The intention is that at each time step, a process in a particular state engages in some actions and moves into a different state. At some time steps, the process may engage in no actions (and stay in the same state).

A process or component C may be modelled as a pair $\langle \Sigma_C, T_C \rangle$, where Σ_C is the alphabet (a set), and T_C is the set of traces (a set of streams of finite subsets of Σ_C). The events in each trace are subsets rather than elements of the alphabet in order to capture absent and simultaneous actions. Trace sets are *closed under stalling*: whenever $\langle s_0, s_1, \ldots \rangle$ is in T_C, so also is $\langle s_0, s_1, \ldots, s_i, \{ \}, s_{i+1}, \ldots \rangle$, for each value of i.

For example, the component $Toggle$ has alphabet $\Sigma_{Toggle} = \{step, rollover\}$, and a trace set T_{Toggle} that consists of all possible stallings of the basic trace $\langle \{step\}, \{step, rollover\}, \{step\}, \{step, rollover\}, \ldots \rangle$. (From now on, we'll abbreviate '$step$' to 's' and '$rollover$' to 'r'.)

We define the category *TProc* to have traced processes as objects, and *embeddings between processes* as arrows. An embedding is a witness as to how one process is *simulated by* another. Intuitively, a process C is embedded within, or simulated by, a process D if, by renaming some of the actions of D and ignoring the others, it is possible to make D look like C; the embedding is simply the renaming function.

Formally, the arrow $f : \langle \Sigma_c, T_c \rangle \rightarrow \langle \Sigma_D, T_D \rangle$ is a partial function f from Σ_D to Σ_C such that,

for every trace $t' \in T_D$, there exists a trace $t \in T_C$ such that, for every event $t'_n = \{d_1, \ldots, d_m\}$ of t', the corresponding event t_n of t is the set of actions $\{c \in \Sigma_C \mid \exists i . 1 \leq i \leq m \wedge d_i \in \mathrm{dom} f \wedge f\, d_i = c\}$, the image of t'_n under f.

For example, consider the simpler process $Clock = tick \rightsquigarrow Clock$, with alphabet $\Sigma_{Clock} = \{tick\}$, and trace set T_{Clock} all stallings of $\langle \{tick\}, \{tick\}, \ldots \rangle$. (From now on, we'll abbreviate '$tick$' to 't'.) The process $Clock$ is simulated by the process $Toggle$, if (for example) one looks only at the r actions of the latter and thinks of them as t actions. So the category *TProc* contains a morphism $f : Clock \rightarrow Toggle$, where the function f from Σ_{Toggle} to Σ_{Clock} is the one-point function $\{r \mapsto t\}$.

4.2   Assembling Components

It is well-known that toggles can be chained to make asynchronous counters. The rollover event r of one toggle should be coordinated with the step event s of the next.

In the spirit of superposition, this *coordination* should be coordinated by a separate *connector*. In this case, the right connector to use is just *Clock*; it acts as a *channel* between the two toggles, or an *adapter* between their interfaces. This is captured by the diagram in Figure 2(a).

What does this collection of boxes and lines mean? Just the colimit of the diagram, as illustrated in Figure 2(b). We claim that the colimit of the

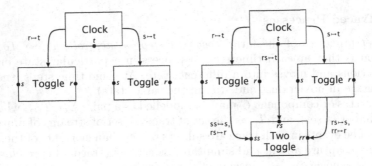

Fig. 2. (a) Interconnection of toggles; (b) Colimit of toggle system

connection diagram in Figure 2(a) is the process *TwoToggle*, with alphabet $\Sigma_{TwoToggle} = \{ss, rs, rr\}$, and trace set $T_{TwoToggle}$ all stallings of the basic trace $\langle\{ss\}, \{ss, rs\}, \{ss\}, \{ss, rs, rr\}, \ldots\rangle$. This is indeed the least common extension of the three connected components, and it does indeed model the two-bit counter formed from two chained one-bit counters.

5   Conclusion

It is probably clear from the above presentation that these are very preliminary ideas — more of a research proposal than a research report. There are many questions still to be answered and directions in which to explore, including:

- What standard process algebra (as opposed to the home-grown one used here) is best suited to describing the kinds of connection involved in visual program assembly?
- Is the corresponding category actually *finitely cocomplete*, which is to say, does every diagram of interconnected components possess a colimit and hence a meaning? Perhaps some healthiness conditions need to be placed on the diagram in order to guarantee the existence of the colimit.
- What is a suitable category for visually-composed components, such as Java-Beans?
- Although this approach was originally envisioned as simply providing a semantics for visual program assembly, can it in fact provide more? For example, the colimit approach has been used in systems such as the *SpecWare* program synthesis tool [15], in which it captures the notion of 'completion of theories'; SpecWare can automatically construct colimits. Can this construction form the basis of a visual programming tool?
- Other applications of the approach can be envisaged. For example, one problem in the use of *design patterns* [4] is that of tracing the instantiation of the design pattern through the development of a piece of software [2]. Superposition can perhaps capture the sense in which a design pattern is 'a component of' a software system, in which case there is hope of formally recording this information throughout the development process.

References

1. R. Allen and D. Garlan. A formal basis for architectural connection. *ACM Transactions on Software Engineering Methodology*, 6(3), 1997.
2. S. Bünnig, P. Forbrig, R. Lämmel, and N. Seemann. A programming language for design patterns. In *Arbeitstagung Programmiersprachen*, Paderborn, October 1999.
3. J. L. Fiadeiro and T.S.E. Maibaum. Categorical semantics of parallel program design. *Science of Computer Programming*, 28(2–3):111–138, 1997.
4. E. Gamma, R. Helm, R. Johnson, and J. Vlissides. *Design Patterns: Elements of Reusable Object-Oriented Software*. Addison-Wesley, 1995.
5. J.A. Goguen. Categorical foundations of general systems theory. In F. Pichler and R. Trappl, editors, *Advances in Cybernetics and Systems Research*, pages 121–130. Transcripta, 1973.
6. J. Gosling, B. Joy, and G. Steele. *Java Language Specification*. Addison-Wesley, 1996.
7. IBM. VisualAge for Java. http://www.ibm.com/software/ad/vajava.
8. B. Jacobs. Objects and classes, coalgebraically. In B. Freitag, C. B. Jones, C. Lengauer, and H.-J. Schek, editors, *Object-Orientation with Parallelism and Persistence*, pages 83–103. Kluwer, 1996.
9. S. Katz. A superimposition control construct for distributed systems. *ACM Transactions on Programming Languages and Systems*, 15(2):337–356, 1993.
10. Sun Microsystems. JavaBeans specification. http://java.sun.com/products/javabeans/docs/spec.html, 1997.
11. I. Mikhajlov and E. Sekerinski. A study of the Fragile Base Class problem. In *European Conference on Object-Oriented Programming*, pages 355–382, 1998.
12. B.C. Pierce. *Basic Category Theory for Computer Science*. MIT Press, 1991.
13. M. Shaw and D. Garlan. *Software Architecture: Perspectives on an Emerging Discipline*. Prentice-Hall, 1996.
14. A. Snyder. Encapsulation and inheritance in object-oriented programming languages. In M. Meyrowitz, editor, *Object-Oriented Programming, Systems, Languages and Applications*, pages 38–45, 1986. SIGPLAN Notices 21(11).
15. Y. V. Srinivas and R. Jüllig. SpecWare: Formal support for composing software. In Bernhard Möller, editor, *LNCS 947: Mathematics of Program Construction*. Springer-Verlag, 1995.
16. Clemens Szyperski. *Component Software: Beyond Object-Oriented Programming*. Addison-Wesley, 1998.

The Cost of Communication Protocols and Coordination Languages in Embedded Systems

Kees G.W. Goossens and Om Prakash Gangwal

Philips Research Laboratories, Eindhoven, The Netherlands
{Kees.Goossens,O.P.Gangwal}@philips.com

Abstract. We investigate the use of communication protocols and co-ordination languages (henceforth interaction languages) for high-volume consumer electronics products in the multimedia application domain. Interaction languages are used to reduce the cost of designing a product by introducing structure and abstraction, by being application-domain specific, and by enabling re-use. They can also reduce the manufacturing cost which includes the cost of using the interaction language, the implementation cost of the interaction language, and its running cost.
We classify services that can be offered by an interaction language and their impact on the cost of designing. Choices that can be made in their implementations are also categorised, and their impact on the manufacturing cost is shown. This is illustrated by three existing interaction languages: C-HEAP, Arachne, and STM.
We conclude first that the type of services offered by an interaction language must match the application domain. Furthermore, implementation choices are constrained by the underlying system architecture as well as the services to be offered. Finally, an interaction language with fewer services minimises the manufacturing cost but increases the cost of designing, and vice versa. The cost of designing and the manufacturing cost both contribute to the cost of the final product, which is to be minimised. These costs must be balanced when designing an interaction language.

1 Introduction

In this paper we consider the role of communication protocols and coordination languages[1] in high-volume consumer products in the multimedia application domain. There are two salient points. The multimedia application domain deals with complex systems, which can be easier to design using appropriate interaction language [24]. Moreover, high-volume production of consumer products requires a focus on system cost, which interaction languages can help to reduce. We elaborate both in turn below.

First, the multimedia application domain has its own characteristics. Multimedia processing entails huge amounts of computation and communication due

---

[1] To avoid repetition of the long phrase "communication protocol and coordination language" we write interaction language. We leave open whether the communication protocol and the coordination language are strictly separated or not [3].

F. Arbab and C. Talcott (Eds.): COORDINATION 2002, LNCS 2315, pp. 174–190, 2002.

to the high data rates (throughput) of digital video, and the large number of operations per video sample. Furthermore, the processing must obey real-time constraints because data rates are externally imposed. Applications are increasingly complex and dynamic in their behaviour, and the design and implementation of multimedia systems is therefore challenging [28]. The use of interaction languages structures the design process (how do we come to a design) and the design itself (the software and hardware components and their interaction).

Second, our applications are implemented as embedded systems (or devices) for the high-volume consumer electronics market. This means that the cost of the device is very important. The cost of a consumer device can be split into two parts: the cost of an individual device (*the manufacturing cost*, including material costs and manufacturing tests), and the so-called non-recurring engineering costs (*the cost of designing* the system). Table 1 shows these costs and their subdivisions, which we explain below.

Table 1. Factors contributing to the device cost.

cost of	with contributions from	amortised over
designing	abstraction, structuring, decomposition	design method
	tailoring to application domain	application domain
	re use	product families & design method
manufacturing	cost of use of interaction language	design
	interaction language implementation cost	design
	running cost	design

To reduce the cost of designing, the design process must be better structured [13], using abstraction and compositionality. The design of individual products can be eased through the use of interaction languages appropriate to that application domain [24]. At a higher level, product families (multiple products with common features) can benefit from re-use of existing systems to create derivatives, and standardisation of the design process, through promotion of platforms, through the use of interaction languages, and so on. It may be argued that in high-volume product runs non-recurring engineering costs are not important because they are amortised over many devices. However, improving the design process reduces the so-called time to market, which can have a large impact on the number of products sold. The amortisation column of Table 1 indicates the largest scope in which the contributions mentioned in the second column are effective. For example, the use of abstraction, structuring, and decomposition in a design method benefits all designs made with that method. Hence the cost of developing an abstract, structured, compositional interaction language is amortised over all these designs.

We relate the cost of a single device to the manufacturing cost, which is to be minimised by using an appropriate interaction language. This cost is composed of the cost of the implementation using the interaction language (the *cost of use of interaction language*), the cost of the implementation of the interaction language itself (the *interaction language implementation cost*), and the cost of using the interaction language in an implementation (the *running cost*). All these costs are paid per design.[2]

In the remainder of this paper we use the terminology of the ISO OSI reference model [8], where an interaction language offers *services* to its users, implemented by a peer-to-peer *protocol* that uses the services of lower layers. Further terminology: *designing* (or: to design) leads to a single *implementation* or *design* that when *manufactured* leads to a *device* or *product*. A design is therefore the blueprint for the tangible device. A *product family* contains designs that have common characteristics, and are perhaps *derived* from each other, through a re-use strategy or otherwise [29].

In Section 2 we classify the services provided by interaction languages and how these affect the cost of designing.

In Section 3 we observe that the same service can be implemented in different ways and we classify implementation choices and their impact on manufacturing costs.

We show how different interaction language choices, in terms of services and implementations, lead to different costs by means of three running examples. All three interaction languages address the limited amount of memory that is available to applications in (embedded) systems in the multimedia domain. Still their solutions, i.e. services and costs, are different: C-HEAP [15] implements local memory management at a low implementation cost using an explicit claim/release mechanism, Arachne [16] implements global memory management across communication channels at a higher implementation cost using an explicit claim/release mechanism, and space-time memory (STM) [25] implements global memory management with a shared data space and garbage collection.

In Section 4 we conclude that varying the balance between the cost of designing and the manufacturing cost results in different ways of designing, different interaction languages, and different designs. They can be judged only by the cost of the final products.

2   Services Offered by Interaction Languages

In this section we look at the influence of the application domain on the services that an interaction language must offer. In Section 2.1, these services are divided in coordination or configuration services, communication services, and inspection services. Some general properties of services are then defined and demonstrated in the running examples in Section 2.2 and 2.3 respectively. Finally, in Section 2.4 we examine the cost (or better: advantage) of using interaction languages in the design of embedded systems.

---

[2] The cost of getting to an implementation of the interaction language is amortised over the design method, which is included in the re-use part of the cost of designing.

2.1 Classification of Services

The services that an interaction language offers must match the applications for which it is used. For example, automotive applications are control dominated and must be robust (cannot lose events). In video surveillance applications data collection and compression may be very lossy and computation and storage must be minimised, whereas in medical applications data integrity is essential and computation and storage costs are subservient. As stated in the introduction, we focus on multimedia applications that typically deal with high data rates (e.g. high-resolution digital video) and many computations per datum. The massive number of operations that must be performed per second can only be performed in parallel. Instruction-level parallelism (e.g. by using VLIW architectures), single-instruction multiple-data (SIMD), and task-level parallelism (TLP) can be used to obtain the desired performance. Multimedia applications often consist in streams of data processed by filters (scaling, decoding, encoding, transcoding, mixing, interleaving, etc.) that are composed according to the currently required functionality. This fits the TLP programming model of a number of concurrent tasks flexibly composed by an application manager depending on the user requirements [5]. Now, the resources that are available in the system are limited because we deal with embedded systems. The quality of service delivered to the user should be optimal using these limited resources. Tasks must be coordinated and parameterized dynamically according data rates vary in the system (e.g. variable bit rate MPEG), and also to obey the fickle user.

To address these different aspects we distinguish three kind of services. The composition and interaction of tasks is regulated by an application manager, which uses configuration or *coordination services*. The tasks operating on data use *communication services* to obtain access to input data and pass results to other tasks. Both tasks and the application manager can use *inspection services* to interrogate their environment, for example to check for the availability of data or the absence of deadlock in a task graph.

Configuration or Coordination Services

During execution, a system traverses a series of configurations (or steady states). A configuration is composed of different entities, such as tasks or components, channels or connections, ports, and tokens. Tokens are memory regions used for data storage and/or communication. Tokens are gathered in collections such as channels or pools. Components and channels can be connected in a topology using ports, and tokens are associated to channels or perhaps more generally to token pools. Systems can be generically described in many ways; we do not intend to do so here, but refer to e.g. [3,2,29,27].

Configuration services enable the construction and modification of a configuration of the system. Entities must be created, destroyed, or modified (e.g. started, suspended, stopped, moved, flushed), and their interaction specified or modified (e.g. event triggers, changing the task graph). The computation and communication entities must be distributed over the limited resources of an embedded system. Entities are bound to (associated with) resources identified by their type, location, or name. For example, tasks are bound to processors, and tokens to memory regions. Similarly, mobile agents are bound more elaborately by a security profile that includes credits for computation and communication, an area to roam (LAN, WAN, virtual private network, anywhere) [6], and so on. The coordination of entities and resources, usually by an application manager, is essential for embedded systems that usually have hard real-time constraints, and always have limited resources.

Reconfiguration is the transition between two configurations. Defining the transition behaviour of entities is not easy [17]. We must define when, with whom, and how a reconfiguration takes place and what its effects on entities and their state are. *When* relates to time or location in the control or data flow; *whom* can vary from a single entity (local, autonomous reconfiguration) to everyone (global reconfiguration); *how* can mean a master-slave relationship between entities (e.g. a single quality-of-service manager plus rest of system) or cooperative via negotiation. The effect of reconfiguration can be visible (a disconnected or dangling channel) or not (suspended without warning or consent).

The difference between configuration and reconfiguration is not always sharply defined. For example, task scheduling on a programmable processor is seen as reconfiguration if it needs to be explicitly requested, otherwise it is part of the steady state. Pre-emptive scheduling of tasks is a service that is implicit, whereas explicit user-initiated suspension or thread switching could be classified as a reconfiguration service or a steady-state (communication) service. Another example is memory management. It can be implemented pervasively (like garbage collection in STM or Linda [22]), offered at the coordination level (global memory management in Arachne, local memory management in C-HEAP), or as explicitly managed shared memory [20] using communication services.

Steady-State or Communication Services

Interaction languages exist to allow entities to exchange data and synchronise in a given configuration. Data transfer services vary in the way data is accessed (message passing, shared data) and the structure of the transmission medium (does it lose or duplicate data, how is data identified and addressed, is there an underlying structuring of the data). Examples are shared memory with a load/store interface, Bonita [26] with values in a shared data space, JavaSpaces [14] with objects and associated methods or triggers in shared medium, point-to-point FIFO message-passing [19], broadcast events, and so forth.

As soon as multiple entities execute autonomously, their synchronisation becomes germane. Communication primitives often combine data transfer and synchronisation [10]. Their separation, however, allows the granularity of data communication (perhaps imposed by the communication medium) to be different from the granularity of synchronisation (which is natural to the component) [15,16]. Synchronisation can be synchronous (performed at the same instant, synchronous hand-over, rendez-vous, two threads of control coincide) or asynchronous (at different points in time) [2,11]. Asynchronous communication decouples the operation of components, and therefore requires storage of values or objects. The structure of the communication medium then becomes important. A component can fully commit to a synchronisation (blocking, i.e. for all time under all conditions) or commit conditionally. Conditions can include a deadline before which the synchronisation must take place, the amount or type of data that the other party must produce or consume [14], and so on. Multiple concurrent or dependent synchronisations can be useful, such as the two forks a hungry philosopher claims simultaneously (cf. the dependent transactions of [21]).

There may be a single coordinating task not computing on data (a boot task or quality-of-service manager) or there may be many tasks doing both (e.g. a collaborative agent-based interaction). However, the coordination and communication services are probably best separated so that a task can be designated either as a data-processing or coordinating task. Multiple coordinating tasks are best avoided as unforeseen or unwanted interactions easily arise.

Inspection Services

In a given configuration a component may want to observe and analyse the state of performance of the system. This information can be used to manage resources and to regulate the quality of the service, by reconfiguring the system if needed. The inspection services must match the reconfiguration services; it is probably not useful to observe that which cannot be steered.

At the coordinating level, activity of components could be used to detect starvation, deadlock, etc. At the component level tasks may wish to observe the state of other components before they want to engage in communication or synchronisation, or the state of the communication medium to ensure the presence of sufficient data to commence processing.

2.2   General Properties

Interaction languages and coordination languages have some general properties that we mention briefly.

Global versus Local

A global service, such as memory management or scheduling, takes into account all relevant information in the system. Globality is usually used to obtain optimal resource usage system wide. Global services are cost effective only when the use of resources varies over different parts of the system. A global software approach for buffer sharing over channels is presented in the context of embedded systems in [23].

Static versus Dynamic

Decisions can be taken for the life time of the system (static), for the duration of a configuration (dynamic), or be continually under review (more dynamic). Examples of decisions are binding of memory to channels, and binding of processes to processors. Lowering the frequency of decision-taking will usually result in less overhead. Dynamic decision-taking is worthwhile for designs where the average and worst-case resource use differ much. An example of a memory manager for dynamic data structures (but not communication) for embedded systems is presented in [9].

Global dynamic services can move resources to parts of the system where they are needed most, which can result in optimal resource throughout all configurations (Table 2). On the other hand, local static services may not be optimal, but are simplest to implement. We return to their relative merits in Figure 2(C) of Section 3.4.

Table 2. Some examples of interactions of service choices.

combination of service choices	consequences
global & dynamic	optimal throughout all configurations
global & static	optimal at start of each configuration
local & dynamic	not useful
local & static	not optimal, simple & fast

2.3   Three Running Examples

We consider three interaction languages in the application domain of signal-processing. STM [25] is for use in the so-called Smart Kiosk, produced in low volumes with limited cost restriction, whereas Arachne [16], and C-HEAP [15] are meant for embedded systems in the high-volume consumer market with a cost focus. Although their basic services are more or less equal, they optimise different properties: the structure of the communication medium and the scope of the memory management.

STM allows reconfiguration of tasks and channels at any point by any task (creation and destruction, as well as changes in topology). The communication medium is based on message passing (synchronisation and data transfer are combined) to random-access channels. Specifying a channel at a virtual-time, data can be written only once, but read several times. Reading and writing take place at any time in a time window to enable pervasive memory management by garbage collection. There are no inspection services.

Arachne supports autonomous reconfiguration by any of its components at any time. Tasks are static, but channels can be created or emptied at any time by any task. Empty tokens can be added or removed from the system at any time. The communication medium is a shared memory organised in FIFO multicast, narrowcast, and merged channels for full tokens, and pools (sets) for empty tokens. Synchronisation for empty and full tokens is independent of data transfer to and from these tokens. Synchronous token hand-over is also supported. Token management is global. Inspection services include checking the amount of data (space) in a channel (pool), the activity on communication ports, and examining the interconnection of tasks.

C-HEAP supports reconfiguration initiated by a single master (the application manager) reacted to by multiple slaves (the tasks) at predetermined points in their control flows. Tasks and channels can be created, destroyed, (re)started, suspended, resumed, and stopped. The communication medium is a shared memory organised in FIFO channels for full and empty tokens. Synchronisation for empty and full tokens is independent of data transfer to and from these tokens. Token management is per channel, i.e. local. Inspection services are limited to the checking of the amount of full or empty tokens in a channel.

For more or less the same application domain, STM offers the highest level of services, in terms of reconfiguration and abstraction of data communication, followed by Arachne, and then C-HEAP.

2.4   Services and the Cost of Designing

Using appropriate interaction languages the *cost of designing* embedded systems can be lowered in three ways (recall Table 1).

First, large or complex systems like today's multimedia products benefit from a structured and compositional design method. Interaction languages can help by separating component design from communication design (computation versus communication and coordination [3]). This separation of concerns enables hierarchical and divide-and-conquer design methods. In general, more abstract interaction languages relieve designers of detailed working out of an implementation (e.g. a message-passing instead of shared-memory architecture), leading to a reduction of the design time (but perhaps at higher implementation costs, as we shall see later). Shortening the design time is an essential prerequisite for reducing the time to market.

Second, an interaction language tuned to an application domain enables a natural, and hence efficient, description of the design at hand. For example, it depends on the application domain whether sampling of incoming data may be lossy (the data rate is higher than the sampling rate, e.g. Splice [4]) or duplicative (the sampling rate is higher than the data rate), or a combination of both. Thus we see that C-HEAP and Arachne support only lossless FIFO channels, whereas STM offers random-access data channels for more sophisticated subsampling.

Third, interaction languages and (especially) coordination languages can facilitate re-use of (parts of) designs in different products [1,29]. Design for re-use may lead to a higher design cost for lead products, but derivative products should be cheaper to design [13].

In Figure 1 we show a possible trade-off of the level of abstraction or services of an interaction language against the cost of designing a system using that interaction language. The conclusion that an interaction language lowers the cost of system design by being sufficiently abstract, by offering the appropriate

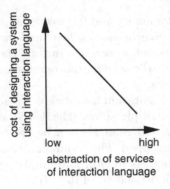

Fig. 1. Services versus cost of designing.

services for the application domain, and enabling re-use is trite by itself, but must be balanced by the manufacturing costs of the design resulting from the use of the interaction language. Care must be taken that the interaction language offering perfect services is not too expensive for its intended use (also argued in [12]). We return to this trade off in Section 3.4.

3   Implementation of Interaction Language Services

The design of high-volume consumer products is driven by cost in two ways. The first, as we saw in Section 2, is the cost of designing a system (with as major component the time to market). In this section we focus on the second, the cost of a single device. We commence by classifying the ways in which an interaction language can be implemented, in Section 3.1. Naturally, the services that an interaction language offers influence the implementation choices, as will constraints on the implementation architectures (such as re-use of existing hardware and software components, platforms, etc.). These ideas are described in Section 3.2 and illustrated using the running examples in Section 3.3. In Section 3.4 the manufacturing cost is then broken down and examined in detail. The next section (Section 4) then combines services and the cost of designing of Section 2, and implementations and the manufacturing cost of this section.

3.1   A Classification of Interaction Language Implementations

Implementations of an interaction language can be classified at a high level along a number of axes. An implementation has varying cost depending on the choices taken but the cost is also related to the match with the services that are to be offered by the interaction language.

Centralised versus Distributed

A centralised implementation of an interaction language concentrates all functionality in one place. It may therefore be easier to make than a distributed implementation because all coordination, communication, and inspection services converge on a single server. A single server avoids interference, synchronisation and consistency problems for shared data and control, and for services such as reconfiguration. The main disadvantage is its fundamentally non-scalable nature, resulting in lower reconfiguration, data, and synchronisation rates.

Hardware versus Software

Multimedia systems require both efficiency and flexibility. Embedded systems therefore contain heterogeneous components of varying flexibility and performance (CPUs, VLIWs, application-specific instruction-set processors (ASIP), dedicated and programmable hardware blocks, etc.). Interaction languages must be implemented efficiently on all these components (i.e. in hardware and in software) to provide transparent communication. C-HEAP, one of our running examples, has been implemented in software on programmable components such as MIPS, ARM, and ASIP, and in a dedicated hardware block [24].

Emulated versus Native

An interaction language can provide all its services as an integral part of the language. Usually such *native* implementations of the services are efficient because optimisations across services are possible. Alternatively, a basic set of services can be implemented natively, while the remainder is *emulated*, i.e. provided as a library or a layered protocol [12]. An example is the coherent shared-memory service [7], which can be implemented natively (in hardware) or emulated (in software on a non-coherent shared-memory service). Naturally, emulated services tend to be implemented in software, and native services in hardware or software, depending on the component they are used by (Table 3).

Table 3. Some examples of interactions of implementation choices

combination of implementation choices	consequences
emulated & software	flexible, slower
emulated & hardware	difficult to achieve
native & software	rigid, but upgradable, slower
native & hardware	rigid, faster

3.2   Interaction Language Implementations: A Compromise of Services and Architecture

An interaction language implementation must obviously match the services that are supported. Table 4 shows some combinations of services and implementations. Some choices reinforce each other, while others cannot be usefully combined. Global services tend to have a centralised implementation; they are harder

Table 4. Some examples of interactions of service and implementation choices.

combination of service and implementation choices	consequences
global & centralised	not scalable, slower & optimal (possibly)
global & distributed	not scalable, fast & optimal
local & centralised	not useful
local & distributed	scalable & fast, but not optimal
dynamic & software	best resource utilisation, but slow
dynamic & hardware	same, but hard to achieve
static & software	less useful
static & hardware	fastest, but worst resource utilisation

to implement when information is distributed in the system. Local services can be distributed more easily, and can result in scalable implementations. Global services that have a distributed implementation are possible (e.g. global synchronisation using a token ring) but still lack scalability. Services are often more easily implemented in software, but at a lower performance than hardware. Moreover, the more dynamic a service, the higher the rate at which decisions are taken. The ideal situation consists in a dynamic hardware implementation. This is often hard to achieve, and dynamic software and static hardware are compromises (the requirements of the service are opposed by the implementation).

The architecture of the system is also important in the implementation of the services. For example, if the underlying architecture is based on message passing then a shared-memory service is expensive to implement. The reverse may be easier, but is still not necessarily very efficient.

An interaction language must balance services offered, to suit an application, and the implementation cost of those services, to fit an underlying architecture. Rightly or wrongly, in embedded systems the latter often is given more consideration. This may lead to a lower manufacturing cost, but almost certainly to a higher cost of designing.

3.3   Examples Continued

As shown in Section 3.1, different implementations of the same service are possible. Using the examples of Section 2.3, we show that implementations and services of interaction language are related, and lead to different costs. We now describe why STM, C-HEAP, and Arachne are implemented in the way they are, and the consequences regarding the manufacturing cost.

STM is implemented in software to support distributed garbage collection. It is based on a multiple-address-space distributed message-passing architecture to support clusters of symmetric multiprocessors. It assumes the provision of atomic operations (e.g. read-modify-write) by the underlying architecture. Latency to services is higher (approximately 20000 cycles). Data is often copied in message-passing architectures; this can be avoided using shared memory, like in C-HEAP.

C-HEAP uses a distributed implementation to provide local memory management services. Services are fairly static: reallocation of memory, for example, is possible only by reconfiguring explicitly. A single-address-space (distributed) shared-memory architecture reduces data copying to minimise resources (buffer sizes and bus load). No atomic operations (such as read-modify-write) are required, to ease implementation. All the services offered by the interaction language are native, and are transparent across hardware and software. The combined result of these choices is that the latency to execute services is low (approximately 30-100 cycles). There are several software and hardware implementations of the interaction language. Local memory management may be pessimistic when buffers are needed for different channels at different times. Global memory management, like that performed in Arachne, aims to address this.

Arachne uses a centralised allocation administration to facilitate global memory management. It uses single-address-space (distributed) shared-memory architecture for the reasons mentioned before. All the services are native, and are transparent across hardware and software. Services are executed with medium latency (approximately 100-3000 cycles). There are hardware and software implementations of the interaction language.

We see that the implementation of each interaction language matches the type of services: C-HEAP's local static services & distributed implementation, Arachne's global dynamic services & centralised implementation. STM's global services are offered on a symmetric multiprocessor platform and are therefore emulated in software. The implementation choices of each interaction language are reflected in its manufacturing cost. For example, the manufacturing cost is affected by the latency to access services: higher latency means that data and command buffers must be larger to avoid stalling tasks. Reducing the latency reduces buffer sizes, which translates to a smaller chip area, and hence lower cost. The next section further elaborates these cost aspects.

3.4   Implementations and the Manufacturing Cost

A design (the blueprint) is manufactured to a device. The manufacturing costs include the bill of materials (e.g. related to the silicon area), cost of testing, and so on. To avoid the explicit distinction between the cost of the device and the cost of the design that led to it, we define the term *manufacturing cost*. The resources a design uses are reflected directly in the cost of the device. Examples are the code size of a program (resulting in embedded or external memory), and memory management (leading to more or less memory). Other examples are power-efficient computation and communication, electromagnetic interference, and number of IO pins of a device. All affect the price of the chip package, and must be taken into account during the design process.

Recall from Table 1 that the manufacturing cost is composed of the cost of the implementation while using the interaction language (the *cost of use of interaction language*), the cost of the implementation of the interaction language itself (the *interaction language implementation cost*), and the cost of using the interaction language in an implementation (the *running cost*).

The *cost of use of interaction language* is basically the cost of the implementation of the required application using the given interaction language. Whereas the the cost of designing measures the effort spent in getting to the design, the cost of use of the interaction language quantifies the end result, ignoring the cost of implementing the interaction language itself. Usually, for an interaction language at a high level of abstraction both the cost of designing (Figure 1) and the cost of the use of the interaction language are low (Figure 2(A)) because, to some extent, the interaction language absorbs application functionality.

The *interaction language implementation cost* depends on the abstraction level of the services it has to offer as well as on the architecture on which it has to be implemented. Implementing an interaction language with few services is always cheaper than implementing an interaction language offering more. However, Figure 1 shows that offering few services raises the cost of designing (i.e. getting to a design takes longer). Offering too many services, and thus raising the interaction language implementation cost, is also to be avoided. An option only open to emulated services is that services that are not used in a design can be omitted from the implementation of the interaction language. The services are tailored to the design, as it were. Examples are Horus [30], x-kernel [18], and Koala [29]. It will not escape attention that offering the service of protocol stripping will not be free. See Figure 2(B) for some possible relationships between the services and their cost of implementation. An emulated implementation (curve 2(B)I-2(B)III) may be cheaper than a native implementation for few services (curve 2(B)II-2(B)IV) but lose when cross-service optimisations kick in (2(B)V).

Another influence on the manufacturing cost is the *running cost* of a interaction language. A first example is memory management. When the average-case and worst-case memory requirements vary in time and throughout the system, global dynamic memory management will use fewer resources than local static memory management. Arachne and STM fall in the first category. C-HEAP, with its local static memory management, has pessimistically sized buffers. In the end, however, its buffer sizes may be comparable to those of Arachne and STM (2(C)II) because its efficient distributed implementation offers services with lower latency [15] (2(C)I), reducing the sizes of its buffers.

A second example is scheduling. Dynamic global (multi-processor) preemptive task scheduling may have minimal running costs (2(C)II) but expensive to achieve (2(B)IV). Dynamic local (per-processor) task scheduling can

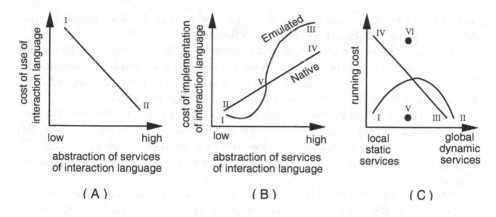

Fig. 2. Services, implementations, and costs.

be pre-emptive, or by explicit hand-over (using synchronisation primitives like setjmp/longjmp, coroutines [19], etc.) at medium implementation cost (2(B)v). Static local task scheduling avoids run-time scheduling altogether and is cheap to implement (2(B)II). It will perform badly when processor loads vary much over time and place (2(C)IV), when dynamic global task scheduling will excel (2(C)III).

A third example is the coherent shared-memory service [7]. A native hardware implementation perhaps costs more than an emulated software implementation (2(B)IV versus 2(B)III) but is more efficient at run-time (2(C)V versus 2(C)VI).

We conclude that for identical services different implementation choices result in different manufacturing costs (i.e. cost of use of interaction language, cost of interaction language implementation, and running cost).

4   Closing Remarks

In this paper we focus on high-volume consumer products for multimedia applications. Multimedia applications are increasingly dynamic and complex. Interaction languages help to contain this complexity by structuring the design process. This includes separating communication and coordination from computation. Furthermore abstraction, composition, and application-specific services (e.g. FIFO-based streaming) are offered.

High-volume consumer products are implemented as embedded systems that are cost driven. Interaction languages impact the cost in two ways: the cost of designing and the manufacturing cost (Table 1). We classify services that an interaction language can offer in coordination services, communication services, and inspection services. The ensemble of services must match the application domain of the interaction language. Offering more services will reduce the cost of designing an embedded system (see Figure 1). Services to enhance re-usability of (parts of) systems may lead to a higher design cost for lead products, but derivative products should be cheaper to design.

Next, we categorise the ways in which services can be implemented. Examples are distributed versus centralised, and native versus embedded implementations. The implementation choices must match the services:- a global service is better implemented centrally than in distributed fashion, for example.

We divide the manufacturing cost into the cost of using the interaction language, the implementation cost of interaction language, and its running cost. An interaction language with more services reduces the cost of use (Figure 2(A)), may reduce the running costs (Figure 2(C)), but is more expensive to implement (Figure 2(B)).

The final cost of a product is made up of a combination of the cost of designing (especially influenced by the time to market) and the manufacturing cost. Defining and using the right interaction language for the application domain amounts to finding the right trade-off between the various costs. These trade-offs can be judged only by the cost of the final products.

References

1. F. Arbab, C. L. Blom, F. J. Burger, and C. T. H. Everaars. Reusable coordinator modules for massively concurrent applications. *Software Practice and Experience*, 28(7):703–735, 1998.
2. F. Arbab, F. S. de Boer, and M. M. Bonsangue. A coordination language for mobile components. In *Proceedings of SAC, ACM press*, pages 166–173, 2000.
3. Farhad Arbab. The IWIM model for coordination of concurrent activities. In *Coordination languages and models*, volume 1061 of *Lecture notes in computer science*, pages 34–56, 1996.
4. M. Boasson. Control systems software. In *IEEE Transactions on Automatic Control*, volume 38, pages 1094–1106, July 1993.
5. R.J. Bril, C. Hentschel, E.F.M. Steffens, M. Gabrani, G. van Loo, and J.H.A. Gelissen. Multimedia QoS in consumer terminals. In *IEEE Workshop on Signal Processing Systems*, pages 332–343, 2001.
6. Paolo Ciancarini and Davide Rossi. Jada - Coordination and Communication for Java Agents. In Jan Vitek and Christian Tschudin, editors, *Mobile Object Systems: Towards the Programmable Internet*, volume 1222, pages 213–228. Springer-Verlag: Heidelberg, Germany, 1997.
7. A. L. Cox, S. Dwarkadas, P. Keleher, H. Lu, R. Rajamony, and W. Zwaenepoel. Software versus hardware shared-memory implementation: A case study. In *Proc. of the 21th Annual International Symposium on Computer Architecture (ISCA'94)*, pages 106–117, 1994.
8. J. D. Day and H. Zimmerman. The OSI reference model. In *Proceedings of the IEEE*, volume 71, pages 1334–1340, 1983.
9. Gjalt G. de Jong, Bill Lin, Carl Verdonck, Sven Wuytack, and Francky Catthoor. Background memory management for dynamic data structure intensive processing systems. In *Proceedings of the international conference on computer-aided design*, pages 515–520, 1995.
10. E.A. de Kock, G. Essink, W.J.M Smits, and P. van der Wolf. YAPI: Application modeling for signal processing systems. In *Proceedings 37th Design Automation Conference*, 2000.

11. S. Edwards, L. Lavagno, E.A. Lee, and A. Sangiovanni-Vincentelli. Design of embedded systems: Formal models, validation, and synthesis. In *Proceedings of the IEEE*, volume 85, pages 366–390, 1997.

12. D. Engler, M. Kaashoek, and J. O'Toole Jr. Exokernel: An operating system architecture for application-level resource management. In *Proceedings of the Fifteenth ACM Symposium on Operating Systems Principles*, 1995.

13. A. Ferrari and A. Sangiovanni-Vincentelli. System design: traditional concepts and new paradigms. In *International Conference on Computer Design*, pages 2–12, 1999.

14. Eric Freeman, Susanne Hupfer, and Ken Arnold. *JavaSpaces: Principles, Patterns and Practice*. Addison-Wesley, 1999.

15. O. P. Gangwal, A. Nieuwland, and P. E. R. Lippens. A scalable and flexible data synchronization scheme for embedded HW-SW shared-memory systems. In *International Symposium on System Synthesis*, pages 1–6, Montréal, October 2001.

16. K. G. W. Goossens. A protocol and memory manager for on-chip communication. In *International Symposium on Circuits and Systems*, volume II, pages 225–228, Sydney, May 2001. IEEE Circuits and Systems Society.

17. Christine R. Hofmeister. *Dynamic Reconfiguration of Distributed Applications*. PhD thesis, Computer Science Department, University of Maryland, College Park, 1993.

18. N. C. Hutchinson and L. L. Peterson. The x-kernel: An architecture for implementing network protocols. *IEEE Transactions on Software Engineering*, 17(1):64–76, 1991.

19. G. Kahn and David M. MacQueen. Coroutines and networks of parallel processes. In B. Gilchrist, editor, *Proceedings of IFIP*, pages 993–998, 1977.

20. Jeffrey Kang, Albert van der Werf, and Paul Lippens. Mapping array communication onto FIFO communication – towards an implementation. In *Proceedings of international symposium on system synthesis*, pages 207–213, 2000.

21. J. Kramer and J. Magee. The evolving philosophers problem: Dynamic change management. *IEEE Transactions on Software Engineering*, 16(11):1293–1306, 1990.

22. Ronaldo Menezes. Experiences with memory management in open Linda systems. In *ACM Symposium on Applied Computing*, pages 187–196, March 2001.

23. Hyunok Oh and Soonhoi Ha. Data memory minimization by sharing large size buffers. In *ASP-DAC*, Tokyo, January 2000.

24. Rafael Peset Llopis, Marcel Oosterhuis, Sethuraman Ramanathan, Paul Lippens, Albert van der Werf, Steffen Maul, and Jim Lin. HW-SW codesign and verification of a multi-standard video and image codec. In *IEEE International Symposium on Quality Electronic Design*, pages 393–398, 2001.

25. Umakishore Ramachandran, Rishiyur S. Nikhil, Nissim Harel, James M. Rehg, and Kathleen Knobe. Space-time memory: a parallel programming abstraction for interactive multimedia applications. In *10th ACM SIGPLAN Symposium on Principles and Practice of Parallel Programming*, May 1999.

26. A. Rowstron and A. Wood. Bonita: a set of tuple space primitives for distributed coordination. In *Proceeding of HICSS30, SW Track*, pages 379–388, Hawaii, 1997. IEEE Computer Society Press.

27. D.B. Stewart, R. A. Volpe, and P. K. Khosla. Design of dynamically reconfigurable real-time software using port-based objects. *IEEE transactions on Software Engineering*, 23(12):759–776, 1997.

28. Marino T.J. Strik, Adwin H. Timmer, Jef L. van Meerbergen, and Gert-Jan Root-selaar. Heterogeneous multi-processor for the management of real-time video & graphics streams. *IEEE Journal of Solid-Sate Circuits*, 35(11):1722–1731, November 2000.
29. Rob van Ommering, Frank van der Linden, Jeff Kramer, and Jeff Magee. The Koala component model for consumer electronics software. In *IEEE Computer*, volume 33, pages 78–85, 2000.
30. Robbert van Renesse, Kenneth P. Birman, and Silvano Maffeis. Horus: A flexible group communication system. *Communications of the ACM*, 39(4):76–83, April 1996.

Operational Semantics for Coordination in Paradigm

Luuk Groenewegen[1] and Erik de Vink[1,2]

[1] LIACS, Leiden University, The Netherlands
luuk@liacs.nl
[2] Department of Mathematics and Computer Science
Technische Universiteit Eindhoven, The Netherlands
evink@win.tue.nl

Abstract. Paradigm is the modeling language of SOCCA regarding communication, coordination and cooperation. A transition system or STD-based operational semantics for Paradigm is proposed and illustrated with basic producer-consumer examples. The proposed semantics for Paradigm, in contrast to other approaches, provides a sound basis for reasoning about system dynamics and system comparison.

1 Introduction

Coordination belongs to the key concepts of computer science. Software systems usually consist of many components, communicating with each other and with their environments. Coordination then is the consistent organization of the communication and its effects, such that required cooperation between all components involved is established.

As this consistent organization is crucial for all software systems, the importance of coordination, although only recently recognized as an issue of its own, is beyond dispute. Equally beyond dispute is coordination is being formulated and studied through an impressively large collection of formalisms, languages, approaches, architectural constructs. Examples thereof are team automata [2], Manifold [1], Statecharts [11], CORBA [3], blackboard architectures [14]. Thus, coordination in highly complex communicative systems is indeed specified, designed and built. And what is more, these highly complex systems are in use, to the perhaps not entire, but at least reasonable satisfaction of their stake holders.

Notwithstanding the substantial success of such systems, it is also clear that the essence of coordination, and of the communication it is based on, is still poorly understood. Concerning coordination one can make the following observation. We specify and build it, but we do not yet sufficiently understand it.

The observation follows for instance from the difficulties one has in object-orientation, formulating a proposal for a correct as well as satisfying semantics of all UML diagrams and diagram parts related to behaviour and coordination thereof. What is even more difficult, is providing some such proposal where in addition the semantics for the separate diagrams and diagram parts are well-integrated, resulting in necessary behavioural and communicative consistency

F. Arbab and C. Talcott (Eds.): COORDINATION 2002, LNCS 2315, pp. 191–206, 2002.

between these parts and diagrams, such that required coordination can be ensured [9].

Among the many object-oriented approaches preceding the UML, there is one taking a somewhat unusual approach toward coordination. It is called SOCCA —Specification Of Coordinated Cooperative Activities, cf. [8]. For the communication, coordination and cooperation it uses a restricted form of Paradigm (PARallelism, its Analysis, Design and Implementation by a General Method) as a sublanguage. Recently, two different formal specifications of SOCCA have appeared, one in Z [12], and one in EER/Gral [16] which is also rather Z-like. Another, recent and independent approach to the formal description of Paradigm is reported in [7].

It is the merit of Paradigm, that a SOCCA model can provide an uncommonly clear insight in the coordination of the multi-threaded objects. The communication on which the coordination is built, thereby can range from synchronous to completely asynchronous, with many gradations of asynchronism in between. In addition, as communication often takes place distributed over a certain time interval, it makes sense to discriminate between communication at the start or at the end or somewhere in the middle of such an interval. It is Paradigm offering the notions to do so in a well-structured and clear way. Hence, a Paradigm modeler (or a SOCCA modeler for that matter) can devise and reason about the coordination he wants to achieve, based on these notions. See for example [10].

In this paper we want to concentrate on Paradigm, without any details as well as restrictions related to object-orientation. Through Paradigm one can reformulate the sequential behaviour within the various STD components (State Transition Diagrams) of a model in a more global, phase-like manner. This way the modeling perspective is lifted from behaviour to behaviour of behaviours.

It is the idea of behaviour of behaviours that is the kernel of Paradigm. Behaviour of (the underlying, original) behaviours is actually a global view on the original behaviours. Moreover, the global view is such, that even during execution the global behaviour as it is viewed as occurring, remains consistent with the original behaviour that is actually occurring on the underlying, more detailed level. To that aim, Paradigm has been constructed such that consecutive phases always have a certain overlap. The larger the overlap, the more asynchronous is the corresponding communication. This allows one to formulate the necessary coordination in terms of these global behaviour descriptions, the phases and their overlaps, thereby providing the cooperation one is after. What makes Paradigm so different from other approaches such as CCS and CSP (cf. [13,6]) and statecharts, is the idea of an overlap between the phases. One can build the same communication by means of other formalisms, but one nearly looses the idea of the phases and one completely looses the idea of the overlaps, thus seriously hampering understanding the coordination achieved through the communication. By relating the two types of behaviour consistently to each other as in Paradigm, one can not only understand the cooperation and coordination one is after, but one can even enforce it.

In the literature Paradigm (without SOCCA) has been presented in an informal manner only [15]. Here we shall give a formal presentation of Paradigm based on STDs. By means of the Paradigm notions, coordination of sequential components (STDs) can be specified as a requirement in a rather clear way. Moreover we add semantic formality to the Paradigm notions by means of operational semantics. This provides the means to transform the coordination requirements straightforwardly into a program that meets the coordination requirements. So the programs for the components indeed behave and communicate sufficiently consistent. Paradigm's STD basis together with its clean operational semantics make formal reasoning about the programs and their interaction relatively straightforward, a goal also underlying motivating the operational semantics of [5] for Manifold.

The paper has the following structure. After Section 1, Section 2 presents Paradigm based on STDs, and introduces the various notions by means of a small example —a producer-consumer variant. The operational semantics is discussed in Section 3, exploiting the running on example. It also illustrates flexibility and clarity of the approach by varying the example. A rather more complicated variant can be found in Section 4, where flexibility and clarity are illustrated with respect to larger numbers of producer and consumer components. Conclusions are formulated in Section 5.

2   Paradigm

In this section we formally introduce Paradigm, and will present the notions on which the behaviour of behaviours and its required consistency with the underlying, more detailed behaviour are based. It seems reasonably straightforward to base the Paradigm notions on transition systems or STDs. Statecharts instead of STDs would have been an alternative, if we could easily prevent their superstates to be overlapping with other superstates. As we actually want to have a special form of overlap, statecharts seem to be less suited for our purpose. So our first definition specifies our notion of an STD and of its behaviours.

Definition 2.1

(a) An STD S is a triple $\langle ST, LB, TS \rangle$. Here ST is called the set of states, or also the state space; LB is a set of transition labels or actions, also called the action space; $TS \subseteq ST \times LB \times ST$ is the set of transitions. We write $x \xrightarrow{a} x'$ in case $(x, a, x') \in TS$. An STD is also referred to as a process.

(b) Given an STD $S = \langle ST, LB, TS \rangle$ and a state $x_0 \in ST$, a behaviour of S starting in x_0 is a finite or infinite sequence $x_0, a_0, x_1, a_1, x_2, \ldots$ such that $x_i \xrightarrow{a_i} x_{i+1}$ for all appropriate indices i.

Based on this concept of an STD, Paradigm introduces two notions which constitute its kernel: the notion of a *subprocess* of an STD and the notion of a *trap* of a subprocess. A subprocess is an STD, restricted to a subset of the state and action spaces of the original STD, with the actions having the same behavioural effect. This means, any behaviour of a subprocess is a subsequence of some behaviour of the original STD. This is the reason we informally refer to a subprocess as a model of a certain phase within the set of possible behaviours of the original STD. The trap, being a subset of a subprocess' state space, models a kind of final stage within such a phase: once entered, it cannot be left within that same phase. It is only through the behaviours of a next phase, i.e. in another subprocess, that a trap can be left. As the trap's states thus belong to the state spaces of two subprocesses, we informally refer to such traps as overlaps between two subprocesses or rather overlaps between two subsequent phases.

Definition 2.2 Let an STD $S = \langle \text{ST}, \text{LB}, \text{TS} \rangle$ be given.

(a) A subprocess of S is an STD $\langle \text{st}, \text{lb}, \text{ts} \rangle$ such that $\text{st} \subseteq \text{ST}$, $\text{lb} \subseteq \text{LB}$, and $\text{ts} = \{ (x, a, x') \in \text{TS} \mid x, x' \in \text{st}, a \in \text{lb} \}$.

(b) A trap t of a subprocess $s = \langle \text{st}, \text{lb}, \text{ts} \rangle$ is a nonempty set of states $t \subseteq \text{st}$ such that $x \in t$ and $x \xrightarrow{a} x' \in \text{ts}$ imply that $x' \in t$. If $t = \text{st}$, the trap is called trivial, otherwise the trap is called nontrivial.

(c) If two traps t and t' of the same subprocess have the property $t \subseteq t'$, these traps are called nested; t is called an inner trap of t', and t' is called an outer trap of t.

(d) Let $s = \langle \text{st}, \text{lb}, \text{ts} \rangle$ and $s' = \langle \text{st}', \text{lb}', \text{ts}' \rangle$ be two subprocesses of the same process. A trap t of s is called a trap from s to s' if either $s = s'$, or the states belonging to the trap t are states in s' as well, i.e., $t \subseteq \text{st}'$.

The fourth part of the above definition actually defines the overlap discussed above as a trap from a first subprocess to a second subprocess. Note that such a trap is, in general, not a trap of the second subprocess.

Based on the two central notions of subprocess and trap, i.e. of phase and overlap, a number of structuring notions are additionally defined. First of all, the framework needs to view the original, detailed behaviours of a process in terms of a high-level but still behaviour-like sequence of subprocess s_0, trap t_0, subprocess s_1, trap t_1, subprocess s_2, etc. In addition, the framework is also geared toward specifying required coordination between different processes (non-subprocesses) in terms of these global behavioral views. Some of these structuring notions are part of the above Definition 2.2, the others are formulated in the definitions below. Before we do so, we clarify the kernel notions by means of an example.

The example is the well-known Producer-Consumer problem, here with buffer capacity 2. Below, Figure 2.1 presents a tentative STD modeling the producer, called *TentProd*. State names refer to the effect of the last action by means of which the state was entered. There are two relevant actions: produce and fill —both of one unit— which speak for themselves. The same figure also contains a slightly more unfolded STD, called *ProdCap₂*, modeling the producer such that its behavioural freedom with respect to the buffer capacity of 2 is certainly less than one full behavioural cycle. State names are less relevant here, but the two same action names still are.

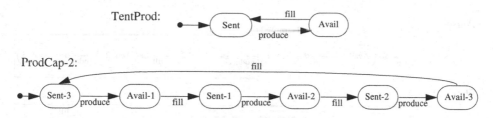

Fig. 2.1. Producer and consumer processes

Figure 2.2 visualizes the relevant subprocesses and traps of $ProdCap_2$. A first phase of the producer is: it may perform three producings and two fillings, because after that the buffer is full, unless the consumer has emptied at least one buffer slot. If indeed so, the phase of the producer slightly shifts from "immediately after its first fill until just before its fourth fill (which is the first because of the behavioural cycle)". Analogously, the producer's third phase shifts again from "immediately after its second fill until just before its fifth (which is its second) fill". The fourth phase then is equal to the first, and so on. In the visualization we use a polygon surrounding states to indicate a nontrivial trap consisting of these states. Circumstances causing such a shift are twofold: the producer has performed one fill, as well as the consumer has performed one empty.

We do not indicate the trivial traps as they are self-evident. As the names of the nontrivial traps suggest, they serve as overlap from subprocess $Phase_1$ to subprocess $Phase_2$, from $Phase_2$ to $Phase_3$ and from $Phase_3$ to $Phase_1$. We could have preferred to indicate an inner trap of the nontrivial traps, being entered by the fill that starts from a state inside the outer nontrivial trap. This would offer a possibility to skip one phase, so to say, but, for the sake of presentation, we leave the example as it is.

It is indeed because of the subprocesses in Figure 2.2 that we prefer the second producer model from Figure 2.1, $ProdCap_2$, above the first, $TentProd$: each subprocess would have covered $2\frac{1}{2}$ cycles of $TentProd$, which frustrates a meaningful choice of nontrivial traps. (For general buffer capacity k the unfolding should be a cycle of $k + 1$ produce-fill pairs, and the subprocesses are all subsequences containing $k + 1$ producings and k fillings: $k + \frac{1}{2}$ cycles of $TentProd$.)

Figure 2.2 shows another very useful property: the three subprocesses together cover the full behaviours of the original STD $ProdCap_2$. Moreover, the nontrivial traps are such that they indeed form an overlap from $Phase_1$ to $Phase_2$, from $Phase_2$ to $Phase_3$ and from $Phase_3$ back to $Phase_1$. This is an example of the kind of structure we want to have for an STD which behaviours are to be viewed more globally in terms of subprocesses and traps: the structuring offers the possibility to order the subprocesses according to their overlaps. This kind of structuring is formalized in the next definition.

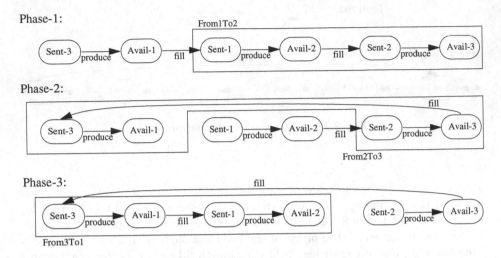

Fig. 2.2. Subprocesses and traps of $ProdCap_2$

Definition 2.3

(a) Let $S = \langle \text{ST}, \text{LB}, \text{TS} \rangle$ be an STD. A set $\text{PT} = \{ s_i \mid i \in I \}$ of subprocesses of S, with $s_i = \langle \text{st}_i, \text{lb}_i, \text{ts}_i \rangle$, is called a partition of S, if $\text{ST} = \bigcup \{ \text{st}_i \mid i \in I \}$, $\text{LB} = \bigcup \{ \text{lb}_i \mid i \in I \}$, and $\text{TS} = \bigcup \{ \text{ts}_i \mid i \in I \}$. We use the notation $\text{st}(s_i)$ to denote st_i.

(b) Let S be an STD with a partitioning $\text{PT} = \{ s_i \mid i \in I \}$. Let, for each $i \in I$, tr_i be a set of traps for the subprocess s_i of S, such that the trivial trap $\text{st}_i \in \text{tr}_i$. Then $\text{TR} = \{ \text{tr}_i \mid i \in I \}$ is called a trap structure for S and PT. We use the notation $\text{tr}(s_i)$ to denote tr_i. For $y \in \text{st}_i$, $trap(y, s_i)$ is the set of all traps of s_i containing y, i.e. $trap(y, s_i) = \{ t \in \text{tr}_i \mid y \in t \}$.

(c) An attainability rule or global transition for an STD S, with respect to a partitioning PT of S and a trap structure TR for S and PT, is a triple of the form $s \xrightarrow{t} s'$ with $s, s' \in \text{PT}$, $t \in \text{tr}(s)$, and $t \subseteq \text{st}(s')$, i.e., s and s' are subprocess of S and t is a trap from s to s'. If $s \xrightarrow{t} s'$ we say that s' is directly attainable from s via t.

(d) An employee or employee process $\mathcal{E}$ is an STD $S = \langle \text{ST}, \text{LB}, TS \rangle$ together with a partitioning PT of S, a trap structure TR for S and PT and a set of attainability rules AT for S with respect to PT and TR. We will write $\mathcal{E} = \langle \text{ST}, \text{LB}, \text{TS}, \text{PT}, \text{TR}, \text{AT} \rangle$.

Based on Definition 2.3 we can say the following concerning Figure 2.2. The three subprocesses together are a partitioning of $ProdCap_2$. The three nontrivial traps together with the three trivial traps are a trap structure. $Phase_2$ is directly attainable from $Phase_1$; so is $Phase_3$ from $Phase_2$, and also $Phase_1$ from $Phase_3$. Finally, $ProdCap_2$ is an employee.

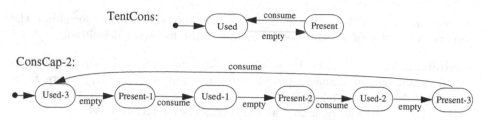

Fig. 2.3. Two STDs as consumer models

Up to here we have said nothing about an STD model for the consumer. But it is the consumer, which by emptying the buffer is supposed to change the freedom of $ProdCap_2$, e.g. it should cause $ProdCap_2$ to change its subprocess $Phase_1$ into the subprocess $Phase_2$ after $ProdCap_2$ has entered its trap $From1to2$. Figure 2.3 presents two such potential consumer STDs. The first, called $TentCons$, consists of the simple behavioural cycle of emptying and consuming. The second STD, called $ConsCap_2$, is an unfolded version of the first. Similar to the unfolded producer, the second STD suits us better than the first as we will point out.

When introducing the subprocesses of the producer by means of Figure 2.2, we already referred to a certain behavioural dependency between the consumer and the producer. This is the heart of the Producer-Consumer problem: in case of a buffer capacity 2, the producer may only continue to fill the buffer once more —one unit at a time— if the consumer has at least emptied the buffer up to, but not necessarily including the last unit put in it; in addition, the consumer may only continue to empty the buffer once —again, one unit at a time— if the producer has at least filled the buffer with a unit not yet taken from it. So, in view of the required coordination, there is a certain consistency needed between the behaviours of $ProdCap_2$ and $ConsCap_2$. As it turns out, this required consistency can be formulated rather elegantly in terms of the above subprocesses and traps of $ProdCap_2$, relating them to the states and to the transitions respectively, of $ConsCap_2$. Figure 2.4 illustrates this, by mirroring $ConsCap_2$'s structure and referring to $ProdCap_2$'s phases and their overlaps.

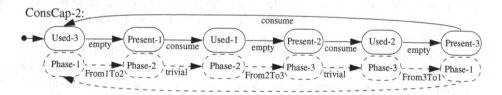

Fig. 2.4. Required consistency between behaviour and behaviour behaviour

This then means that the required behavioural consistency between $ProdCap_2$ and $ConsCap_2$ can be formulated as a required consistency between the detailed behaviours of $ConsCap_2$ and the global behaviours of $ProdCap_2$. In other words, $ConsCap_2$, through its detailed behaviours, models the required behaviour of behaviours of $ProdCap_2$. The formal structure for being able to formulate the required consistency, is expressed by means of the following definition.

Definition 2.4 An STD $M = \langle ST, LB, TS \rangle$, together with a relation γ, is called a manager or manager process with employees $\mathcal{E}_1, \ldots, \mathcal{E}_n$, where $\mathcal{E}_i = \langle ST_i, LB_i, TS_i, PT_i, TR_i, AT_i \rangle$ for $1 \leq i \leq n$, if $\gamma \subseteq TS \times AT_1 \times \cdots \times AT_n$. We will write $\mathcal{M} = (M, \gamma)$ and refer to γ as the consistency relation of $\mathcal{M}$.

Figure 2.4 implicitly suggests the consistency relation for the manager $ConsCap_2$ with respect to employee $ProdCap_2$, viz.

$$\gamma(Used_3 \stackrel{empty}{\to} Present_1, Phase_1 \stackrel{FromOneToTwo}{\to} Phase_2),$$
$$\gamma(Present_1 \stackrel{consume}{\to} Used_1, Phase_2 \stackrel{triv}{\to} Phase_2), \quad \ldots$$

If one, as a modeler, really thinks that the manager expresses the required consistency, this should be enforced upon the combined system of the manager and its employees. By means of the semantic rules to be presented in the next section, we shall indeed be able to guarantee the consistency as desired.

3   Operational Semantics and Basic Examples

In the previous section we have introduced the notions of a manager and of an employee. Now we will consider systems of a manager process and a single or more employee processes, put together in one system as parallel threads.

Definition 3.1 Let $\mathcal{M}$ be a manager of employees $\mathcal{E}_1, \ldots, \mathcal{E}_n$. The statespace of a Paradigm-model $\langle \mathcal{M}, \mathcal{E}_1, \ldots, \mathcal{E}_n \rangle$ of $\mathcal{M}$ and $\mathcal{E}_1, \ldots, \mathcal{E}_n$ are all $n + 1$-tuples of the form $[\![x, (s_i)_{i=1}^n ; (y_i)_{i=1}^n]\!]$ with $x \in st(\mathcal{M}), s_i \in pt(\mathcal{E}_i)$ and $y_i \in st(s_i)$ for $i \in \{1, \ldots, n\}$.

An employee $\mathcal{E}$ consists, according to Definition 2.4, of six components. The underlying STD comprises three of these, viz. states, labels, and transitions. The remaining ones, subprocesses, trap structure and attainability rules, can be grouped together as well. This way an employee represents two STDs, or rather two views on the same STD: a low-level view in terms of states and action-labeled transitions, and, a high-level view in terms of subprocesses and attainability transitions between them that are labeled with traps.

The low-level behaviour is restricted by the subprocesses. The high-level behaviour is triggered by traps. Once a subprocess has reached a trap, it may be transferred to another subprocess by the manager. Therefore, when considering a system of a manager with employees we should distinguish between this two types of dynamics. The low-level operational semantics are the interleavings of the runs of the manager process and the subprocesses of the employees. For the high-level operational semantics one simply restricts to the moves of the manager, i.e. the traces obtained from the low-level model by abstracting away local employees transitions, thus focusing on the steps of the manager. We first give the low-level operational semantics.

Definition 3.2   The low level operational semantics of a Paradigm-model $\mathcal{P} = \langle \mathcal{M}, \mathcal{E}_1, \ldots, \mathcal{E}_n \rangle$, consisting of a manager $\mathcal{M} = (M, \gamma)$ and employees $\mathcal{E}_i = \langle ST_i, LB_i, TS_i, PT_i, TR_i, AT_i \rangle$, is the STD with states as given by Definition 3.1, labels as in $\mathcal{M}$ and $\mathcal{E}_1$ through $\mathcal{E}_n$ and the following transitions:

- *manager transitions* $[\![x, (s_i)_{i=1}^n \, ; \, (y_i)_{i=1}^n]\!] \xrightarrow{a} [\![x', (s_i')_{i=1}^n \, ; \, (y_i)_{i=1}^n]\!]$ iff $\gamma(x \xrightarrow{a} x', s_1 \xrightarrow{t_1} s_1', \ldots, s_n \xrightarrow{t_n} s_n')$ holds for traps $t_i \in trap(y_i, s_i)$ and indices $i \in \{ 1, \ldots, n \}$;
- *employee transitions* $[\![x, (s_i)_{i=1}^n \, ; \, (y_i)_{i=1}^n]\!] \xrightarrow{a} [\![x, (s_i)_{i=1}^n \, ; \, (y_i')_{i=1}^n]\!]$ iff for some index $j \in \{ 1, \ldots, n \}$, $y_j \xrightarrow{a} y_j'$ in s_j and $y_i' = y_i$ for all $i \neq j$, $i \in \{ 1, \ldots, n \}$.

The modeling with Paradigm thus support the factorization of a system in coordination and computational activity. Manager transitions represent coordination steps, employee transitions represent computation steps. As the manager and employees are regarded as autonomous processes, their execution is in parallel, restricted only by the partitioning into subprocesses and the corresponding attainability rules.

In the definitions above, one could also, straightforwardly, have allowed for multiple managers. Since this is at the expense of clarity at this point, we stick in this section to the case of exactly one manager. Hierarchical system are feasible as well, but are beyond the scope of this paper.

Consider again a producer process *Prod* and a consumer process *Cons* sharing a one-place buffer. We plan to have the consumer as the manager and, as discussed in the previous section, find it profitable to enfold the loop of the producer one time. See Figure 3.1. The producer process can be turned into an employee by partitioning it into two subprocesses s_1 and s_2 each with two traps, viz. the trivial trap $triv_i$ (not shown) and an inner trap ok_i, $i = 1, 2$. See Figure 3.2 Furthermore, he producer is endowed with the following attainability rules:

$$s_1 \xrightarrow{triv_1} s_1, \quad s_1 \xrightarrow{ok_1} s_2, \quad s_2 \xrightarrow{triv_2} s_2, \quad s_2 \xrightarrow{ok_2} s_1.$$

The consumer process is viewed as a manager of the employee process above by introducing the consistency relation

$$\gamma(c_1 \xrightarrow{empty} c_2, s_1 \xrightarrow{ok_1} s_2), \quad \gamma(c_1 \xrightarrow{empty} c_2, s_2 \xrightarrow{ok_2} s_1),$$
$$\gamma(c_2 \xrightarrow{cons} c_1, s_1 \xrightarrow{triv_1} s_1), \quad \gamma(c_2 \xrightarrow{cons} c_1, s_2 \xrightarrow{triv_2} s_2).$$

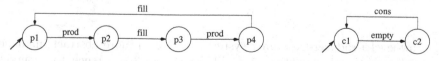

Fig. 3.1. One-place buffer: producer is employee, consumer is manager

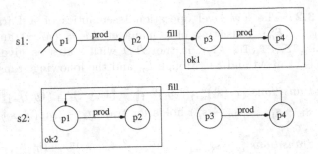

Fig. 3.2. One-place buffer: two producer subprocesses

The operational system semantics as captured by Definition 3.2 enforces a proper interleaving of the fill and empty actions of the producer and consumer, respectively. A *fill*-action can only be done by the producer by entering an inner trap. An *empty*-action will only be performed, according to the consistency relation, by the consumer after the producer has reached such a trap. Conversely, an *empty*-action from the consumer will result in a transfer of the producer to a subprocess which brings the producer out of the inner trap —thereby blocking an *empty*-action for the consumer— and with admits another *fill*-action.

The abstract description in terms of Paradigm results in a low-level system that complies with the behavioural requirements. In the simple case of this producer-consumer it is feasible to provide the complete STD for the whole system. See Figure 3.3.

$$
\begin{array}{cccc}
[1] & [2] & [3] & [4] \\
\downarrow cons & \downarrow cons & \downarrow cons & \downarrow cons \\
\end{array}
$$

$$
[\![c_1, s_1 ; p_1]\!] \overset{prod}{\to} [\![c_1, s_1 ; p_2]\!] \overset{fill}{\to} [\![c_1, s_1 ; p_3]\!] \overset{prod}{\to} [\![c_1, s_1 ; p_4]\!]
$$

$$
\downarrow empty \qquad \downarrow empty
$$

$$
[\![c_2, s_2 ; p_3]\!] \overset{prod}{\to} [\![c_2, s_2 ; p_4]\!] \overset{fill}{\to} [\![c_2, s_2 ; p_1]\!] \overset{prod}{\to} [\![c_2, s_2 ; p_2]\!]
$$

$$
\downarrow cons \qquad \downarrow cons \qquad \downarrow cons \qquad \downarrow cons
$$

$$
[\![c_1, s_2 ; p_3]\!] \overset{prod}{\to} [\![c_1, s_2 ; p_4]\!] \overset{fill}{\to} [\![c_1, s_2 ; p_1]\!] \overset{prod}{\to} [\![c_1, s_2 ; p_2]\!]
$$

$$
\downarrow empty \qquad \downarrow empty
$$

$$
[\![c_2, s_1 ; p_1]\!] \overset{prod}{\to} [\![c_2, s_1 ; p_2]\!] \overset{fill}{\to} [\![c_2, s_1 ; p_3]\!] \overset{prod}{\to} [\![c_2, s_1 ; p_4]\!]
$$

$$
\begin{array}{cccc}
\downarrow cons & \downarrow cons & \downarrow cons & \downarrow cons \\
[1] & [2] & [3] & [4] \\
\end{array}
$$

Fig. 3.3. Low-level STD of the producer-consumer problem with consumer as manager

The low-level Producer-Consumer systems hints at a more abstract, manager-oriented operational semantics; the STD in Figure 3.3 is much too concrete. Instead we might want to focus on the steps of the manager, i.e. on the vertical transitions.

Definition 3.3 The high-level operational semantics of a Paradigm-model $\mathcal{P} = \langle \mathcal{M}, \mathcal{E}_1, \ldots, \mathcal{E}_n \rangle$, consisting of a manager $\mathcal{M} = (M, \gamma)$ and employees $\mathcal{E}_i = \langle \mathrm{ST}_i, \mathrm{LB}_i, \mathrm{TS}_i, \mathrm{PT}_i, \mathrm{TR}_i, \mathrm{AT}_i \rangle$, is an STD with states as given by Definition 3.1, labels from $\mathcal{M}$ together with a fresh label *skip*, and the following transitions:

- *manager transitions* $[\![x, (s_i)_{i=1}^n \,;\, (y_i)_{i=1}^n]\!] \xrightarrow{a} [\![x', (s_i')_{i=1}^n \,;\, (y_i')_{i=1}^n]\!]$ iff
  $\gamma(x \xrightarrow{a} x', s_1 \xrightarrow{t_1} s_1', \ldots, s_n \xrightarrow{t_n} s_n')$ holds for traps $t_i \in trap(y_i, s_i)$ and $y_i \rightarrow^* y_i'$ in s_i for all $i \in \{ 1, \ldots, n \}$;

- *employee transitions* $[\![x, (s_i)_{i=1}^n \,;\, (y_i)_{i=1}^n]\!] \xrightarrow{skip} [\![x, (s_i)_{i=1}^n \,;\, (y_i')_{i=1}^n]\!]$ iff
  $y_i \rightarrow^* y_i'$ in s_i for all $i \in \{ 1, \ldots, n \}$.

A graphical representation of the high-level semantics does not differ that much when compared to its low-level model. In fact, assuming an appropriate transitive closure, only the employee transitions will be relabeled into *skip*. However, the employee steps are now considered internal, the system can now be analyzed e.g. using techniques for weak bisimulation [13,4]. This way systems that may differ in their respective component, in particular in the employee behaviour, can be compared at the system level for equivalence.

Especially in the context of hierarchical Paradigm-models, in which managers on the one level can act as employees at a higher-level, such a notion of system equivalence will prove useful. Safety or liveness properties that are proved with respect to a certain layer, can be starting point for the analysis at a higher layer. E.g., the fact that the number of retrievals from a particular buffer does not exceed the number of deliveries, can be used as assumption in an analysis of a chain in which the producer-consumer system is only one single component.

From the point of view of the high-level semantics, our requirement on traps of Definition 2.3c can be explained once more. It will not matter whether the progress $y_i \rightarrow^* y_i'$ is made with respect to the subprocess s_i or with respect to the subprocess s_i', as long as $t_i \subseteq \mathrm{st}(s_i')$.

The high-level modeling of the producer-consumer example with Paradigm is more clear than the 'brute force' approach of the low-level transition system. At the abstract level it is also easy to switch the role of manager and employee. If we prefer in our example the producer as the manager and the consumer as its employee, we can model this as follows:
Similar to the previous situation the employee is splitted into two subprocesses, each with the trivial and an inner trap. The inner trap signals that the consumer is ready for an empty action. The producer will allow this as soon it has put a new item in the buffer. This is then achieved by the transfer of the consumer from the one subprocess to the other. The corresponding consistency relation is:

$$\gamma(p_1 \xrightarrow{prod} p_2, s_i \xrightarrow{triv} s_i), \quad \gamma(p_2 \xrightarrow{fill} p_1, s_1 \xrightarrow{ok_1} s_2), \quad \gamma(p_2 \xrightarrow{fill} p_1, s_2 \xrightarrow{ok_2} s_1)$$

We next look at a variation of the above setting by considering the producer-consumer problem with a buffer of *infinite* capacity. Clearly, as we need to distinguish the infinitely many loadings of the buffer, it will be handy to start off

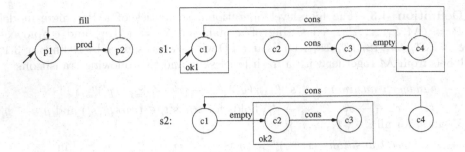

Fig. 3.4. One-place buffer: producer is manager, consumer is employee

with the producer and consumer processes as infinite linear processes. The producer will be the employee; the consumer will be the manager. See Figure 3.5. As consistency relation we now have

$$\gamma(c_1 \overset{empty}{\to} c_2, s \overset{t_1}{\to} s) \quad \gamma(c_3 \overset{empty}{\to} c_4, s \overset{t_2}{\to} s) \quad \gamma(c_5 \overset{empty}{\to} c_6, s \overset{t_3}{\to} s)$$
$$\gamma(c_2 \overset{cons}{\to} c_3, s \overset{triv}{\to} s) \quad \gamma(c_4 \overset{cons}{\to} c_5, s \overset{triv}{\to} s) \quad \cdots$$

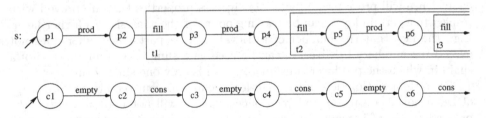

Fig. 3.5. Infinite buffer: producer is employee, consumer is manager

Note that there is a single subprocess for the producer that has an infinite nesting of traps. Intuitively this is obvious: there are no restrictions on the producer, and when the producer fills the buffer with another item, the consumer should be in a position to get this. The consumer can not retrieve more items as there are in the buffer, since the *empty*-transition is coupled with a *fill*-transition of the producer, via the consistency relation.

Dual to the situation above we can have the producer as the manager for the infinite buffer case. See Figure 3.6. As consistency relation for the producer is the following:

$$\gamma(p_1 \overset{prod}{\to} p_2, s_i \overset{triv}{\to} s_i) \quad \gamma(p_3 \overset{prod}{\to} p_4, s_i \overset{triv}{\to} s_i) \quad \gamma(p_5 \overset{prod}{\to} p_6, s_i \overset{triv}{\to} s_i)$$
$$\gamma(p_2 \overset{fill}{\to} p_3, s_1 \overset{triv}{\to} s_2) \quad \gamma(p_4 \overset{fill}{\to} p_5, s_2 \overset{triv}{\to} s_3) \quad \cdots$$

Now we partition the consumer into infinitely many subprocesses: each next subprocess is allowed to retrieve, and also to consume, one item more from the buffer. The producer transfers the consumer to this next process in parallel with

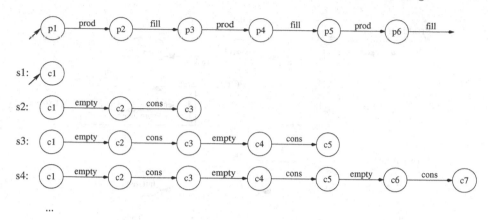

Fig. 3.6. Infinite buffer: producer is manager, consumer is employee

its own fill action. Note that the consumer is not enforced to handle any item from the buffer. However, via the inclusion of the states of the trivial trap of the one process, the local state is preserved, i.e., it is 'memorized' how many items there have been taken from the buffer already.

4   A More Complicated Example

The examples presented so far are relatively easy. However, really complicated examples can be handled in a similar fashion. As it turns out, once a manager has been modeled, together with its employees having suitable subprocesses, traps and attainability rules, a solution implementing this specification is easy to formulate. So the harder part of the problem is, finding a suitable Paradigm model. In our experience, also this is not very difficult, as the notions invite an sufficiently experienced modeler to remain on a level of adequate abstraction. This is, in fact, the main advantage of Paradigm. There seems to be some analogue with the way human managers in organizations actually manage, by checking and controlling not so much each step, but more global phases. Paradigm provides the notions to get the syntax of the solution right, thereby clarifying the consequences of the coordination requirements as specified. The structural operational semantics then guarantee the implementation to be in line with the required coordination.

To give an impression thereof, we present a variant of the producer-consumer problem, where the buffer capacity is 2, and where two producers and three consumers may try to fill and empty one of the two buffer slots. A producer may only do so if the slot is empty, and the consumer may only do so if the slot is full. Moreover, if two slots happen to be full, a consumer asking for emptying a slot, gets the one filled first.

Figure 4.1 visualizes the STD Producer for the two producers and the STD Consumer for the three consumers. In this case we have enlarged the the cycle of the producers and the consumers by the extra step —action, transition— called

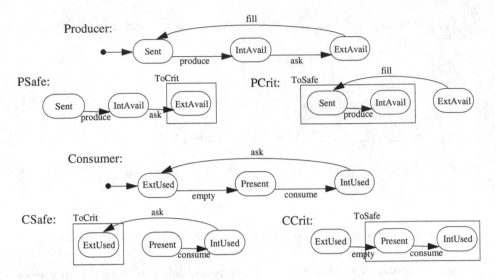

Fig. 4.1. A producer and a consumer, both as employees

ask, meaning the asking for using the buffer once. Having this permission is the critical phase of a full behavioural cycle, modeled as subprocess *PCrit* for the producer and as *CCrit* for the consumer. In the critical phase a producer or consumer may fill or empty one buffer slot, but it may not ask for another permission (as it is having it). The safe phase, modeled as *PSafe* for the producer and as *CSafe* for the consumer, is where filling or emptying are not allowed. Note that producing or consuming are allowed in every subprocess. Asking a permission corresponds to a small trap, in both cases called *ToCrit*: the communication is as synchronous as possible, as the permission should be given only if really needed. The other trap, in both cases called *ToSafe*, is substantially larger, to allow continuing to produce or to consume even if the permission has not yet been withdrawn.

A separate manager, called *Buffer*$_2$ and represented in Figure 5.2, suggests a rather clear solution. Each state name starts with a number indicating how many buffer slots are full; after the colon it either indicates that all producers and consumers are supposed to be in their safe phase —denoted as *AllSafe*— or it indicates how many producers and/or consumers are in their critical phase - denoted as 1*PCrit*, 2*PCrit*, 1*CCrit*, 2*CCrit* or 1*C*&1*PCrit*. Each action name starts with globally mentioning either one (arbitrary or particular) producer or one (arbitrary or particular) consumer; after the colon it mentions the trap this producer or consumer should have reached in order to make this action appropriate.

Manager *Buffer*$_2$ is indeed high-level in the Paradigm sense, as it specifies how to control subprocess combinations of its five employees, based on their traps reached. In addition, *Buffer*$_2$ is even more high level, as it does not specify any order of checking producers and consumers for having entered a nontrivial trap, as it does not discriminate between specific producers or consumers and as it does not indicate which slot has the oldest content. A fully fledged *Buffer*$_2$ should indeed do so, but our *Buffer*$_2$ concentrates on the essential part of the coordination, which is hardest. Moreover, based on this requirement specification also the requirements for buffers with a different capacity and/or different numbers of producers or consumers are rather straightforward to specify; and the producers and consumers do not change at all, which shows how the globalization of the behaviour in terms of subprocesses (as states) and traps (as transitions) supports designing sufficiently flexible components.

For brevity's sake, we omit a full description of the consistency relation, as the reader can easily guess its values from the intuitive state and action names.

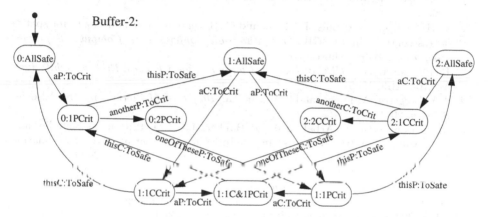

Fig. 4.2. A multi-producer multi-consumer Paradigm-model of a buffer of capacity 2

5   Concluding Remarks

This paper discusses the high-level modeling language Paradigm and proposes an operational semantics for it. Paradigm provides a simple but powerful mechanism for the coordination of processes based on the notion of subprocess, trap and attainability rules.

Using Paradigm one can abstract away from the low-level details of processes by focusing on relevant phases, called subprocesses and on relevant overlaps between phases, called traps. Processes are divided into the manager and employees. An employee is partitioned into subprocesses, prescribing the allowed behaviour. A manager can be triggered to transfer one of its employees from one subprocess to another based on global information expressing which overlap, i.e. trap, has been reached. This is captured by the so-called attainability rules. A transition system-style low-level semantics for Paradigm systems is proposed, that couples the subprocess behaviour and steps of the manager based on the attainability rules. An abstraction of this model focusses on the latter steps, yielding a high-level semantics.

Several experiments in which we implemented our semantics using Prolog have been performed. These experiments provided insight in the trace semantics of the Paradigm-models at hand. Further work will concentrate on extending this and will seek for proof principles for the equivalence of Paradigm systems. It is likely that techniques employed for weak bisimulation will show profitable here. We also plan to address the interplay of the semantics and the accompanying equivalences for hierarchical systems.

References

1. F. Arbab. *Manifold version 2: Language reference manual.* CWI, Amsterdam, 1996.
2. M.H. ter Beek, C.A. Ellis, J. Kleijn, and G. Rozenberg. Team automata for spatial access control. In *ECSCW 2001, European Conference on Computer Supported Cooperative Work.* Kluwer, 2001.
3. R. Ben-Natan. *CORBA, a Guide to Common Object Request Broker Architecture.* McGraw-Hill, 1995.
4. J.A. Bergstra, A. Ponse, and S.A. Smolka. *Handbook of Process Algebra.* Elsevier Science, 2001.
5. M.M. Bonsangue, F. Arbab, J.W. de Bakker, J.J.M.M. Rutten, A. Scutella, and G. Zavattaro. A transition system semantics for the control-driven coordination language MANIFOLD. *Theoretical Computer Science*, 240:3–47, 2000.
6. S.D. Brookes, C.A.R. Hoare, and A.W. Roscoe. A theory of communicating sequential processes. *Journal of the ACM*, 31:560–599, 1984.
7. A. de Bruin and S. van der Made. Introduction to Paradigm. Technical Report ERS-2002-09-LIS, Erasmus University Rotterdam, 2002.
8. G. Engels and L.P.J. Groenewegen. Socca: Specifications of coordinated and cooperative activities. In A. Finkelstein, J. Kramer, and B.A. Nuseibeh, editors, *Software Process Modelling and Technology*, pages 71–102. Research Studies Press, Taunton, 1994.
9. G. Engels and L.P.J. Groenewegen. Object-oriented modeling: A roadmap. In A. Finkelstein, editor, *The Future of Software Engineering, 22nd International Conferenece on Software Engineering*, pages 103–116. ACM Press, 2000.
10. G. Engels, L.P.J. Groenewegen, and G. Kappel. Coordinated collaboration of objects. In M.P. Papazoglou, S. Spaccapietra, and Z. Tari, editors, *Advances in Object-Oriented Data Modeling*, pages 307–331. The MIT Press, 2000.
11. D. Harel. Statecharts: A visual formalism for complex systems. *Science of Computer Programming*, 8:231–274, 1987.
12. P.J. 't Hoen. *Towards Distributed Development of Large Object-Oriented Models.* PhD thesis, LIACS, Leiden University, 2001.
13. R. Milner. *Communication and Concurrency.* Prentice-Hall, 1989.
14. M. Shaw and D. Garlan. *Software Architecture: Perspectives on an Emerging Discipline.* Prentice Hall, 1996.
15. M.R. van Steen, L.P.J. Groenewegen, and G. Oosting. Parallel control processes: Modular parallelism and communication. In L.O. Hertzberger, editor, *Intelligent Autonomous Systems*, pages 562–579. North-Holland, 1987.
16. R. Suettenbach. *Formalisierung visueller Modellierungssprachen Objektorientierter Methoden.* PhD thesis, Dept. of Comp. Sc., Universität Koblenz-Landau, 2001.

Service Provision in Ad Hoc Networks

Radu Handorean and Gruia-Catalin Roman

Department of Computer Science
Washington University
Saint Louis, MO, 63130
{raduh, roman}@cs.wustl.edu

Abstract. The client-server model continues to dominate distributed computing with increasingly more flexible variants being deployed. Many are centered on the notion of discovering services at run time and on allowing any system component to act as a service provider. The result is a growing reliance on the service registration and discovery mechanisms. This paper addresses the issue of facilitating such service provision capabilities in the presence of (logical and physical) mobility exhibited by applications executing over ad hoc networks. The solution being discussed entails a new kind of service model, which we were able to build as an adaptation layer on top of an existing coordination middleware, LIME (Linda in a Mobile Environment).

1. Introduction

As the network infrastructure continues to grow, more and more devices are being attached directly to the network. The opportunity for applications to exploit an ever-increasing range of resources is expanding rapidly. All entities, which must be connected to the network, can provide services advertised over the network, making the network a service repository. The number of such services is expected to grow significantly in the coming years. Given the variety of devices accessing the network and the ever-growing number of services that become available, a high-level approach was needed to allow one to discover services dynamically, as the need arises.

In the client-server model, which continues to dominate distributed computing, the client knows the name of the server that supports the service it needs, has the code necessary to access the server, and knows the communication protocol the server expects. More recent strategies allow one to advertise services, to lookup services and to access them without explicit knowledge of the network structure and communication details. Services offered by servers may be discovered at runtime. They are being used through proxies they provide. A proxy abstracts the network from the client by offering a high-level interface, specialized in service exploitation while the proxy's interface to the server remains unknown to the client. Services are advertised by publishing a profile containing attributes and capabilities useful when searching for a service and proper service invocation. Clients search for services using templates generated according to their momentary needs. These templates must be matched by the advertised profiles. A service profile can include the service's location and a client can use this information in evaluating the suitability of that service.

F. Arbab and C. Talcott (Eds.): COORDINATION 2002, LNCS 2315, pp. 207–219, 2002.

However, in contrast to the classic client-server model, publishing the location of a service it not a requirement for the service model to work, since it does not play a key role in the process of discovery. Services use a service registry to advertise their availability and clients use this registry to search for the services they need. This approach enables a great degree of run time flexibility.

Our model completely eliminates network awareness from the process of discovery and utilization of a service. The client only has to ask for the service it needs and does not have to know how the service will be reached. Our model differs from others by providing a distributed service registry that is guaranteed to reflect the real availability of services at every moment in a mobile ad hoc environment and a communication technique that is not affected by physical or logical mobility. We achieve a consistent representation of the available services by atomically updating the view of the service repository as new connections are established or existing ones break down. A data repository similar to the service registry can be used for communication. This data repository offers both synchronous and asynchronous communication and hides physical host movement or logical agent migration.

We implemented the service model as a veneer on top of LIME [1, 2], a middleware for mobility with strong support for coordination in ad hoc networks. The veneer, a thin adaptation layer, uses LIME tuple spaces to store service advertisements and pattern matching to find services of interest. More significantly, our veneer exploits the transient tuple space sharing feature of LIME to provide consistent views of the available services in the entire ad hoc network in a uniform manner i.e., as if all service advertisements were part of the local registry. This allows us to achieve the deployment of the new service infrastructure in an ad hoc setting with minimal programming effort.

The reminder of the paper is organized as follows: Section 2 presents the motivation for this research. Section 3 introduces an adaptation of the basic service model, for use in ad hoc mobility. Section 4 describes the implementation of the service model in terms of an existing coordination middleware. Section 5 discusses lessons learned and future work.

2. Service Model

The *service model* is composed of three components: services, clients and a discovery technology. Services provide useful functionality to clients. Clients use services. The discovery process enables services to publish their capabilities and clients to find and use needed services. As a result of a successful lookup, a client may receive a piece of code that actually implements the service or facilitates the communication to the server offering the service.

The discovery process differentiates among various existing implementations of the model. Sun Microsystems developed Jini [3, 4, 5, 6, 7] that uses as service registry lookup tables managed by special services called lookup services. These tables may contain executable code in addition to information describing the service. A Jini community cannot work without at least one lookup service *even if services and potential users are co-located* (co-located refers to services and potential clients residing on the same physical host). IETF offers the Service Location Protocol [8, 9, 10, 11] where directory agents implement the service registry. They store service profiles and the location of the service but no executable code. The discovery of services involves first locating these directory agents. If no directory agent is available, clients may multicast requests for services and servers may multicast advertisements for their services. The most common service types use, by default, the service templates standardized by Internet Assigned Numbering Authority (IANA). Microsoft proposed Universal Plug'n'Play (UPnP) [12], which uses the Simple Service Discovery Protocol (SSDP) [13]. This protocol also uses centralized directory services, called proxies, for registration and service lookup. If no such proxy is available, SSDP uses multicast to announce new services or to ask for services. The advertisement contains a Universal Resource Identifier (URI) that eventually leads to an XML description of the service. This description is accessible only after the service has been already discovered through a lookup service. The novelty of this model is the autoconfiguration capability based on DHCP or AutoIP. The Salutation project [14] also uses a relatively centralized service registry called Salutation Manager (SLM). There may be several such managers available, but the clients and servers can establish contact only via these SLMs. The advantage of this approach is the fact that these SLMs can have different transport protocols underneath, unlike the above-mentioned models that all assume an IP transport layer. To realize this, Salutation uses transport-dependent modules, called Transport Managers that broadcast internally, helping SLMs from different transport media interact with each other.

3. Mobility

All these models assume (more or less) a fairly stable network. Nomadic computing takes one step in breaking the wired network rigidity by allowing mobile users to connect to the network via wireless means. It is important to note that the universe in nomadic computing also includes a fixed component. The infrastructure composed of base stations ensures communication in a communication cell. The implementations of the service model may have some limitations in terms of functionality because of the particularities of the new settings. The idea of using the base stations as hosts for service registries is very appealing. However, overloading the base station of a communication cell may lead to a defensive behavior on the part of its software, e.g., terminating advertisement broadcasts or completely ignoring client communication. The failure of a base station leads to a complete lack of communication between the agents in its cell and between clients and services whose communication is routed via this base station, even if they could communicate directly. The similarity to classic networks with centralized service registries is strong. In nomadic networking, reusability of communication frequencies is very important, but introduces a new limitation. In a large cell, the number of devices inside the cell increases, and additional frequencies are needed. Since the range of available frequencies is usually limited, this leads to a limitation in the number of devices in a cell, and implicitly to limitations in terms of service availability. Broadcast discovery is also limited to the current cell, thereby limiting the scope of service advertisements. We can can still leverage off much of the infrastructure used in classic networking, since many of the new problems are solved at a lower level in the stack of communication protocols. In conclusion, even if the nomadic networks bring a certain degree of mobility, as long as there is an infrastructure that *must* be used by the agents to communicate, the differences relative to classic networks are minimal.

A high degree of freedom and a fully decentralized architecture can be obtained in mobile ad hoc networks, at the expense of facing significant new challenges. Mobile ad hoc networks are opportunistically formed structures that change in response to the movement of physically mobile hosts running potentially mobile code. New wireless technologies allow devices to freely join and leave networks, form communities, and exchange data and services at will, without the need for any infrastructure setup and system administration. Frequent disconnections inherent in ad hoc networks lead to inconsistency of data in centralized service directories. Architectures based on centralized lookup directories are no longer suitable. The broadcast implementations need frequent messages in order to preserve consistency. This leads to increased bandwidth consumption. The service model needs to adapt to the new conditions. For example, if the node hosting the service registry suddenly becomes unavailable, the advertising and lookup of services becomes paralyzed even if the pair of nodes representing a service and a potential client remains connected. This scenario is depicted in Figure 1(left).

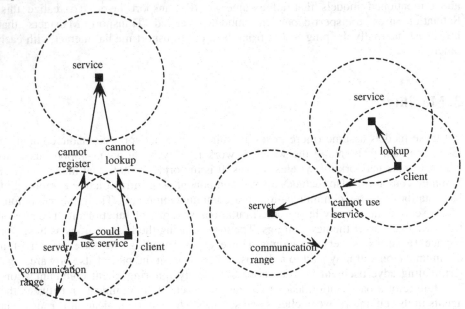

Fig. 1. Left: The client could use the service but it cannot discover it since the service registry is not accessible. Right: A client discovers a service that is no longer reachable

Our aim is to make these two nodes communicate. Furthermore, because of frequent disconnections, the service registry should immediately reflect changes affecting service availability. Services that are no longer reachable should not be available for discovery. In Figure 1 (right) we present a scenario that can happen in Jini, where the advertisement of a service is still available in the lookup table until its lease expires. In a model addressing these issues, all nodes should be simple users or providers of services. However, the system should not depend on the behavior of a single node. Broadcast discovery reduces the timeline to discrete moments when clients can update their knowledge about the available services introducing intervals of inconsistency of duration up to the frequency of broadcasts. In ad hoc networking, frequent disconnections may prevent a client from ever discovering the service it needs, even if the service is present and it periodically announces its availability via broadcast messages. The new challenge is to permit users and programs to be as effective as possible in this environment of uncertain connectivity, without changing their manner of operation (i.e., by preserving the interface). The advertising and lookup of services in this setting need a lightweight model that supports direct communication and offers a higher degree of decoupling. A consistent, distributed, and simple implementation of the service registry is the key to the solution.

4. Service Model Revisited

In this section we put forth a new service provision model well suited for use in ad hoc networks. The model finds its inspiration in the transient tuple space sharing capabilities of LIME.

Each active entity, having the ability to perform some computation will be called an agent. Agents represent application components or devices. An agent can be a client, a server, or both. An agent that can migrate from one host to another will be called a mobile agent. Two agents that reside on the same host are co-located. Hosts are assumed to be mobile, i.e, can move freely through space, and to form ad hoc networks when within communication range.

Services are advertised by publishing a profile that contains the capabilities of the service and attributes describing these capabilities, so the clients can discover and use the services properly. The interface used to access services refers only to capabilities advertised in the profile. Location information is not needed to discover the service requested by the client. The client can use the attributes to decide if the service meets its requirements in terms of quality of service parameters. Along with the profile, the server provides a service proxy. This proxy will represent the service locally to the client.

Clients search for services using a template that defines what the needed service profile must match. If a service profile satisfying all client requirements is available, the service proxy, as part of the profile, is returned to the client. The client will use the proxy to interact with the service as if it were local.

The interface provides primitives for service advertisement and lookup and the proxy offers the service interface. Every agent has its own service registry where it advertises the services it provides. The registries of co-located agents are automatically shared. Thus, an agent requesting a service that is provided by a co-located agent can always access the service. If two hosts are within communication range they form a community and their service registries engage, forming a federated service registry. Upon engagement, the primitives operating on the local service registry are extended automatically to the entire set of service registries present in the ad hoc network. An agent in the community will access this federated registry via the same API, i.e., via its own local registry. The sharing of the service registries is thus completely transparent to agents.

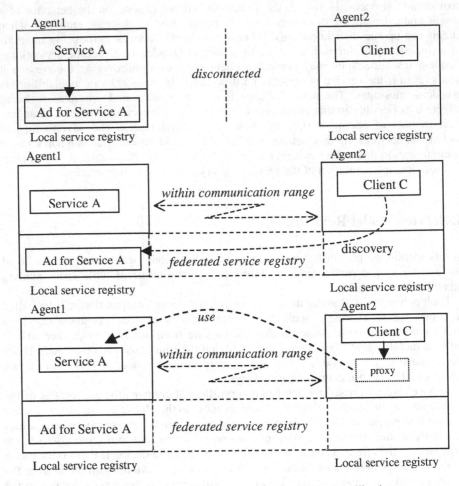

Fig. 2. Local service registry sharing and service proxy utilization

Maintaining the consistency of data in the service registry is a very important issue in such a rapidly changing environment. In our model, an ad for a specific service can be discovered if and only if the service is available. Any update to the contents of the federated service registry occurs atomically, at the moment of individual host engagement or disengagement of each host. Discovery and accessibility of remote servers is scoped by host connectivity. Thus, when the host of the service becomes unreachable (i.e., gets disconnected), the local repository *atomically* becomes unavailable as well and the service cannot be discovered anymore. This helps solve several important problems. First, it eliminates the need for a centralized directory for registration and lookup. Second, it guarantees that two hosts within communication range are able to exchange services. Third, it prevents a client from discovering a service that is not available anymore at the time of the lookup. Figure 2 presents the use of the distributed service registry.

5. Coordination-Based Design Solution

This section provides an overview of the implementation and discusses some of the technical difficulties we encountered during this on-going development effort. The starting point is a brief overview of the LIME coordination middleware. The design of the new service provision model is introduced and a case is made that LIME is particularly well suited to support the development of service provision capabilities for the ad hoc environment.

5.1 LIME Overview

LIME is a middleware supporting applications that involve physical and logical mobility. LIME extends the Linda [15] coordination model by adding support for coordination in ad hoc networks. The global and persistent tuple space of Linda is replaced in LIME by tuple spaces carried by individual agents residing on hosts that can be mobile. These local tuple spaces are automatically shared among co-located agents and transparently shared among all hosts within communication range. The resulting federated tuple space acts as a distributed repository of elementary data units called tuples. Tuples are sequences of typed values and can contain data or code. These tuples can be added to a tuple space using an out(tuple) operation and can be removed by executing an in(template) operation. Tuples can also be read from the tuple space using the rd(template) operation. Tuples are selected using pattern matching between a template and the tuples available in the tuple space. The template can be composed of actuals and formals. Actuals are values, while formals are types that are used as wild cards. Both in and rd are blocking operations. LIME offers an extension to this synchronous communication by providing probe variants for the traditional blocking operations, e.g., rdp(template) and inp(template). If no matching tuple is found, a NULL value is returned. For any of these operations, if several tuples match the pattern, one is selected non-deterministically. LIME also implements several other extensions of the basic Linda primitives designed to handle groups of tuples e.g., outg, rdg and ing.

Another extension to the basic Linda model are the location parameters LIME primitives can use. Hosts and agents store information about their location, information that can be used to define a projection of the transiently shared tuple space. For example, an out operation could specify a destination location for the tuple it writes. This tuple will be written to the local tuple space of the agent issuing the out operation and then it will migrate to the specified destination, if available. The in and rd operations can also use location information to restrict the scope of their actions to a projection of the complete federated tuple space.

Finally, LIME offers mechanisms to react to changes in the contents of tuple spaces i.e., support for reactive programming. A reaction is specified by providing a template and a piece of code that must execute in response to the appearance of a matching tuple in a particular tuple space. Two types of reactions are available in LIME. Strong reactions are executed atomically with the context change that enables them. For practical reasons, these reactions can only be enabled by tuples residing in the local tuple space. Achieving the atomicity of execution in a distributed environment involves transactions across multiple hosts, which are expensive to implement in highly dynamic environments. Another reason for this restriction is the possibility of creating chains of reactions spanning the network, i.e., global transactions whose scope may expand out of control. LIME also offers weak reactions to detect changes in the federated tuple space. If a matching tuple is found, the execution of the code associated with a weak reaction is guaranteed to take place eventually if the connectivity is preserved, but not atomically with the detection of the tuple. For technical reasons, blocking operations are not allowed in the code associated with a reaction.

5.2 Service Representation

Each service is represented by a profile stored in a tuple. This tuple contains fields for a service id, a list of attributes, a list of capabilities, a proxy object, and some information about the communication between the proxy object and the server. When the service registers, the system assigns it a globally unique service id. This id will represent the service as long as it is available, and can be used for rediscovery of the same service. The attributes quantify the capabilities of the service (e.g., "color" and "laser" can be attributes for a service advertising the "print" capability). The client may use attributes when searching for services to filter the results. The proxy object is the front end of any service. The client uses the proxy object to access the service as if the service were implemented locally. The proxy object may have one of two behaviors: it may fully implement the service with no remote communication or it may provide an interface to a remote service provider while hiding the details of the communication protocol from the client. The latter situation is encountered when the service needs a specific piece of hardware to execute the job (e.g., a printer), or other resource that cannot migrate to the client. The protocol used by the server and the proxy for their private communication is arbitrary. It can be a well-known protocol (e.g., Java RMI) or a proprietary protocol that is well suited for the application needs.

   While the proxy hides the network from the client, the proxy must know where the server is located. In the presence of mobility, the location information may change upon migration of the service. For example, if the agent providing the service moves to another host, the IP address changes but the port number may not. Likewise, if the proxy and the server use RMI to communicate, it is very likely for the server to use the same registration string at the new location, even though its IP changed. This led us to a design that splits the location information in two parts. One part represents the physical location of the agent running the server and the other part represents a logical address within the addressing space available at the physical location (e.g., the range of useable ports or the RMI registration strings). While mobility causes physical location to change, this logical address is not likely to change. Since the physical location is unique for all servers run by each mobile agent but the logical address is specific to each server and does not change, we chose to publish them separately. The physical location is published along with the agent's id in a special tuple space, called the location tuple space (ServiceLocationTupleSpace). This tuple space contains one location tuple for each agent, and the content is updated upon agent migration. This way, an agent needs to update only one tuple when it migrates, regardless of the number of services it provides. The logical address is part of the tuple that contains the advertisement of the service. Upon migration, these tuples will follow the agent automatically and unchanged.

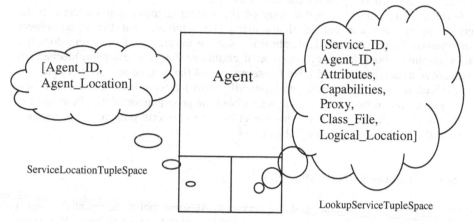

Fig. 3. The agent and the two local tuple spaces storing the service profiles and the agent's physical location

5.3 Service Access

The tuples describing the services an agent wants to publish are written (using the out operation) into a tuple space local to the agent, called the lookup tuple space. By using the same name (LookupTupleSpace) for all local lookup tuple spaces, we are able to take advantage of LIME's transparent sharing of tuple spaces with the same name. Thus, each agent's lookup tuple space is automatically shared with any co-located agents. Upon engagement with a new host or group of hosts, this tuple space is shared with all the agents in the community, forming a federated lookup tuple space. Since engagement and disengagement are atomic operations, each agent sees a consistent and up to date set of services available across the ad hoc network. During migration, the local lookup tuple space of a mobile agent is not accessible to the rest of the community. An agent migration involves unsharing the local tuple space, moving to the new physical location and sharing again the content of the local service registry.

A client searches for services by querying the federated lookup tuple space using a template that describes the desired service. In this template, the client can request a service with a specific id, services that have certain attributes, services that implement certain interfaces, or a combination of the above. A tuple is considered to match the client's requirements if the service it advertises has *all* the properties the client demands. This means the list of capabilities (interfaces) specified by the client in its query template should be a subset of the capabilities advertised for a specific service. In this case, subsetting should be understood including the polymorphism of the Java programming language. The attributes specified in a template also have to be a subset of the attributes published for the matching service. In this latter case, an exact match is performed, i.e., the two attributes compared should match as values, not as types.

For example, if a client wants a color (attribute) printer (interface), a service that only specifies printing as a capability without giving details about the quality of printing will not be returned as a possible match for the query.

Once the client has obtained a copy of the matching tuple, it has access to the service proxy, and can call methods using the interface that the proxy object implements. There is no standardization for service interfaces. If the client does not know anything about the proxy interface, it could use the Java reflection mechanism to discover what a proxy can do, but the semantics of the method and argument names are difficult to correctly interpret automatically. This led us to favor an approach that assumes a common Java interface known to both the programmer of the client and the programmer of the service. This way, the client can correctly prepare the arguments and call the methods on the proxy object.

5.4 Service Continuity upon Migration

Mobile agents run the clients and the services. At some point, an agent running a client or an agent providing a service may decide to migrate to a new host. With tuple space based communication no special measures are required to resume collaboration between the client and the server when migration occurs and if client and server remain within communication range. The tuple spaces (associated with the application and used for client/server coordination) are automatically transferred to the new location, and the respective tuple spaces continue to be uniformly accessed since the location does not influence the process of tuple retrieval.

If the agent running the client decides to move, a private socket protocol between the proxy and its server must reopen the communication channel with the server using the same location information. If RMI is being used for communication, the client will reuse the location information to contact the remote RMI registry and obtain a new proxy object. This is necessary because the RMI implementation embeds the location of both communication ends in the proxy object generated (i.e., an RMI stub object cannot be transferred and reused on a different host from the one where it was - deployed by the RMI infrastructure – the stub is tied to the host where is was first deployed).

If the agent running server code migrates, its physical location tuple must be updated. The clients will need to reconnect to the server using the new location information. In the case of RMI communication, the server also needs to re-register with the new RMI registry at the new location. The client will need to download a new proxy object (RMI stub file) from the RMI registry using the new physical location information.

Agent migration in LIME is supported via μCode. The implementation preserves the memory state, but not the control state. This means that at its destination, the agent restarts execution with the memory initialized to the content present when the migration was triggered. This initialization includes the re-registration of the services. Having the memory content preserved helps implement a *resume* behavior. That is, it can only perform those actions from the registration that are absolutely needed (e.g., it can only update the location tuple). This also allows the client and the server to resume the communication from a certain point without restarting the entire task.

5.5 Discussion

LIME offers support for implementing the service model in the mobile ad hoc networking environment. The transient sharing of the tuple spaces used in LIME enables the atomic update of the service registry, maintaining its consistency across connected hosts. A single interface allows access to the entire federated tuple space as if it were local. However, some changes in the functionality of LIME were required. The initial public release of LIME has typical Linda-style pattern-matching capabilities. The actuals in the template fields must match exactly the type of the corresponding fields in the tuple being examined. It turns out that we needed additional flexibility in our implementation. We changed the matching algorithm to allow polymorphism in pattern matching, i.e., a field containing a formal in a template will match the corresponding field in a tuple if the latter implements the interface, or subclasses the pattern type. This is necessary in order to enable clients to use services they discover for the first time and for which they know only an interface that the service implements. The stricter pattern matching would have required the client to already have the class file of the proxy it receives, thus reducing the usability of the services. Given the particularities of the Java programming language, in order to use an object, the JVM must have access to the class file of which the object is an instance. To use a service that is discovered for the first time, the client needs to obtain the class file of the proxy object, not only an instance of it. In Jini or in simple RMI based applications, the class file is obtained via HTTP download from the host that offers the service. We provide this class file via the registration tuple. This code on demand approach helps keep a small footprint for services on the client side. The code can be downloaded if needed and discarded when no longer useful. The approach also enables dynamic updates to the latest version of the service advertised by a server.

The pattern matching policy used has a big impact on the representation of a service in the tuple space. Because of the Linda-style pattern matching, a tuple can match only templates of the same arity. A service can advertise itself by publishing multiple capabilities and attributes. A client may be interested in only part of service's portfolio. This eventually leads to a situation where the template generated by the client needs to match only part of the service's advertisement. Because of the strict pattern matching implementation currently available, the representation of a service in the tuple space is a group of tuples that covers the cartesian product of the set of attributes and the set of capabilities advertised by the service. We can reduce the number of tuples and, implicitly, the memory usage and the time for service lookup by changing again the pattern-matching algorithm. We plan to adapt the pattern matching policy so that each field contains an element that is a set and a field in the template will match a field in a tuple if the template field represents a subset of the corresponding field in the tuple. The set inclusion should be understood as using the polymorphism mentioned above. This change will allow us to use only one tuple for each advertised service, where the fields representing the attributes and capabilities are sets both in the tuple and in the template. Other changes to the pattern matching process that would be particularly helpful in enabling flexible service discovery may be the evaluation of a predicate over the elements being checked. In our case these elements are corresponding fields from the tuple and the template. In the first step we relaxed the strict Linda-like pattern matching by enabling the object oriented polymorphism in predicate evaluation. Next step is to relax even more the matching algorithm by providing a way to overcome the limitation introduced by the need to match the arity of tuples with that of templates. A template with n fields could match only tuples of arity n. By introducing set inclusion as a matching criterion we relax further the constraints on comparisons among individual fields (e.g., a variable number of attributes for services leads to tuples of different length; using a set as a container of attributes, we need only one field, thus obtaining fixed length tuples). Another useful relaxation of the matching policies is to allow templates to specify a range of values for the data in the tuples or any other type of predicate to be used. Our current plan is to include application-supplied field matching conditions.

The semantics of the lookup operation can vary from implementation to implementation. One could choose to block the client until the lookup operation returns successfully. Another implementation may allow the client to continue execution if an attempt to use a service fails. A third case may allow the client to announce its interest for a service and its desire to be notified when the service becomes available. In some cases, the client may need more than one service of a given type, an implementation of the look up primitive that handles groups of tuples. Other situations may permit a client to use a service whenever the latter becomes available. All these implementations of the lookup primitive are easily constructed on top of LIME.

Current implementation has been built on top of LIME using two different protocols for communication between the proxy object and the server: RMI and a socket communication. We plan a public release of our current version of the software as a veneer on top of LIME.

6. Conclusions

This paper examined the service model (widely used in client-server systems) with respect to its ability to support flexible application development in an ad hoc networking environment. We have been able to show that the complexity of the ad hoc networking can be hidden behind a simple service registry interface that can offer transparent access to both local and remote services in a uniform way. The effects of mobility are completely masked and expressed simply as changes in the contents of a local service registry. This study serves also as a demonstration of expressive power of coordination models in general, and of the LIME middleware, in particular.

Acknowledgements. This research was supported in part by the National Science Foundation under Grant No. CCR-9970939. Any opinions, findings, and conclusions or recommendations expressed in this paper are those of the authors and do not necessarily reflect the views of the National Science Foundation. The authors thank Qingfeng Huang, Christine Julien and Jamie Payton for their thoughtful comments and criticisms of earlier drafts.

References

1. Murphy, A. L., Picco, G. P., and Roman, G.-C., "LIME: A Middleware for Physical and Logical Mobility," *Proceedings of the 21ˢᵗ International Conference on Distributed Computing Systems*, April 2001, pp. 524-533.
2. Picco, G.P., Murphy, A.L., and Roman, G.-C., "Lime: Linda meets Mobility," In *Proceedings of the 21st International Conference on Software Engineering*, May 1999, pp. 368-377.
3. W. K. Edwards: Core Jini. The Sun Microsystems Press. Java Series. 1999
4. J. Newmarch, "Guide to JINI Technologies", APress, November 2000
5. Jini home page http://www.sun.com/jini/
6. Jini specifications http://www.sun.com/jini/specs/
7. The community resource for Jini technology http://www.jini.org/
8. E. Guttman, Service Location Protocol: Automatic Discovery of IP Network Services, *IEEE Internet Computing*, 3(4): 45-53, July 1999
9. C. Renner, Introduction to the SLP Implementation, 2000, http://www.lkn.e-technik.tu-muenchen.de/~chris/slp/IntroSLP.html
10. C. Perkins, White Paper on SLP, 1997. http://playground.sun.com/srvloc/slp_white_paper.html
11. E. Guttman, C. Perkins, RFC 2608: Service Location Protocol, Sun Microsystems, June 1999.
12. Universal Plug and Play Forum. Universal Plug and Play home page. http://www.upnp.org/, 2001
13. Y. Goland, T. Cai, P. Leach, Y. Gu: Simple Service Discovery Protocol http://www.upnp.org/download/draft_cai_ssdp_v1_03.txt Microsoft Corporation, Shivaun Albright, Hewlett-Packard Company, October 1999
14. Salutation Specifications, http://www.salutation.org/, 2001
15. D. Gelernter, N. Carriero, "Coordination Languages and Their Significance", *Communications of the ACM*, vol. 35, no. 2 feb 1992, pp. 96-107

PN^2: An Elementary Model for Design and Analysis of Multi-agent Systems

Kunihiko Hiraishi

School of Information Science,
Japan Advanced Institute of Science and Technology
1-1 Asahidai Tatusnokuchi Ishikawa 923-1292, Japan
hira@jaist.ac.jp

Abstract. Agent technology is widely recognized as a new paradigm for design of concurrent software and systems. The aim of this paper is to give a mathematical foundation for design and analysis of multi-agent systems by means of a Petri-net-based model. The proposed model, called PN^2, is based on place/transition nets (P/T nets), which is one of the simplest classes of Petri nets. The main difference between PN^2s and P/T nets is that each token, representing an agent, is also a P/T net. State equation and invariants are known as standard techniques for the analysis of P/T nets. As the first step of mathematical analysis of PN^2s, we define these for PN^2s, and show how the invariants are computed in an efficient way.

1 Introduction

Agent technology is widely recognized as a new paradigm for design of concurrent software and systems. The aim of this paper is to give a mathematical foundation for design and analysis of multi-agent systems by means of a Petri-net-based model.

Petri nets are a well-known model for concurrent and distributed systems, and there have been many results on the theory, and also on practical applications[14]. A natural way to represent an agent in Petri-net-based models is to introduce notion of *objects*, i.e., a collection of data with methods that give access to them, into attributes of tokens. There have been various Petri-net-based models having this concept[1]-[16]. Since most of these classes of *object Petri nets* are based on high-level Petri nets, i.e., they allow arbitrary transformation functions on data, they are too complex to be analyzed. These high-level object Petri nets aim to describe real applications in an object-oriented manner, and their research directions are different from that of this paper. We aim to propose a model that is sufficiently simple for the analysis, but has enough expressivity for fundamental features of multi-agent systems. Like place/transition nets (P/T nets) in Petri net theory, such an elementary model is useful in early stage of design processes.

Recently, an elementary class of object Petri nets, called *elementary object systems* (EOS), has been proposed[18]. The approach of this paper is similar to

F. Arbab and C. Talcott (Eds.): COORDINATION 2002, LNCS 2315, pp. 220–235, 2002.

that of EOS, i.e., it is to model systems in an object oriented manner, keeping the model as simple as possible. The proposed model, called PN^2 ("Petri Nets in a Petri Net") is based on P/T nets. Intuitively, a PN^2 is a Petri net such that each token, representing an agent, is also a P/T net. This feature is essential to represent autonomous agents. Each agent changes its internal state by firing its transitions, and can move between places.

2 Concept of Multi-agent Systems

We first describe the concept of multi-agent systems to be modeled. We follow the definition in [22]. Agents are assumed to behave as follows:

- *Intelligent and autonomous behavior:* Each agent has its design objective and is capable of autonomous action in some environment. More precisely,
  - Agents are able to perceive their environment, and respond in a timely fashion to changes that occur in it.
  - Agents are able to exhibit goal-directed behavior by taking the initiative.
  - Agents are capable of interacting with other agents.

  Then the key problem facing an agent is that of deciding which of its actions it should perform in order to best satisfy its design objective.
- *Interaction with environment:* Usually, environments are too complex for an agent to observe completely. Therefore, an agent will not have complete control over its environment. It will have at best partial control, in that it can influence it. Not all actions can be performed in all situations. In this sense, an environment restricts the behavior of agents. There are two kinds of environment: *static environment* and *dynamic environment*. A static environment is one that can be assumed to remain unchanged except by the performance of actions by the agent. A dynamic environment is one that has other processes operating on it, and which hence changes in ways beyond the agent's control[1].

Hence, we need a formal method to describe (i) procedures or rules that decide actions of each agent, (ii) static and dynamic environments independently of the description of agents, and (iii) communication among agents.

3 PN^2

3.1 Example of Modeling

To explain the idea of PN^2s, we use a simple mobile agent system[12]. The example concerns mobile phones. There are vehicles on the move, each connected

---

[1] Consider an automated guided vehicle (AGV) systems. For an AGV, possible directions of the movement is constrained by the track, and are also constrained by existence of other AGVs around it. The former is considered as a static environment, and the latter is a dynamic environment.

by a unique wavelength to a single transmitter. The transmitters all have fixed connections to a central control. On some event (e.g., signal fading) a vehicle may be switched to another transmitter.

The following is a description in the π-calculus for the case of one vehicle and two transmitters[12]. Each transmitter has four parameters $talk$, $switch$, $gain$, $lose$ representing current links. The car can talk via the transmitter. The transmitter can be told by the central control to lose the car $(lose(t, s))$. Then the transmitter tell the car to switch the connection $(\overline{switch}\langle t, s\rangle)$.

$$Trans(talk, switch, gain, lose) \equiv talk.\overline{Trans}\langle talk, switch, gain, lose\rangle$$
$$+lose(t, s).\overline{switch}\langle t, s\rangle.Idtrans\langle gain, lose\rangle.$$
$$Idtrans(gain, lose) \equiv gain(t, s).Trans\langle t, s, gain, lose\rangle.$$

The control issues a new channel-pair to transmit to the car to replace its old channel-pair. It also issues the same pair to the other transmitter.

$$Control_1 \equiv \overline{lose_1}\langle talk_2, switch_2\rangle.\overline{gain_2}\langle talk_2, switch_2\rangle.Control_2.$$
$$Control_2 \equiv \overline{lose_2}\langle talk_1, switch_1\rangle.\overline{gain_1}\langle talk_1, switch_1\rangle.Control_1.$$

The car can either talk or switch to a new channel-pair if requested.

$$Car(talk, switch) \equiv \overline{talk}.Car\langle talk, switch\rangle + switch(t, s).Car\langle t, s\rangle.$$

The entire system is

$$System_1 \equiv \mathbf{new}\ talk_1, switch_1, gain_1, lose_1, talk_2, switch_2, gain_2, lose_2$$
$$(Car\langle talk_1, switch_1\rangle|$$
$$Trans\langle talk_1, switch_1, gain_1, lose_1\rangle|Idtrans\langle gain_2, lose_2\rangle|$$
$$Control_1).$$

A PN^2 consists of two layers. The net in the upper layer is called *the environment net* (*the env net*, for short), and the nets in the lower layer are called *agent nets*. Each agent net describes the behavior of an agent. In the above example, the system consists of four agents, a car, two transmitters, and the controller, which are modeled by labeled P/T nets shown in Figure 1.

Representation of the environment has an important role in the modeling of multi-agent systems, because possible actions/interactions of each agent depends on the environment in which it is located. In the modeling by PN^2s, both dynamic and static environments are modeled by the env net independently of agent nets. The env net of the example is shown in Figure 2.

The state transition rule of PN^2s is described as follows. The formal definition will be shown later.

- Every transition of agent nets has a label, and can be synchronized with a transition of the env net if it is enabled in the agent net it belongs to.
- A transition component of the env net is a subset of arcs with a common label, which will be bound to a particular agent net. For each transition component, a label of transitions in agent nets is specified, which is indicated as the inscription on the transition.

- A *transition binding* of the env net is a mapping that assigns to each transition component an agent net having an enabled transition with the same label. If a transition binding occurs, then the transitions of the agent nets bound to the transition components fire, and simultaneously the marking of the env net changes, i.e., agent may move between places of the env net.

In the example, the following transition binding for t_5 with inscription "$x : lose_1, y : \overline{lose_1}$" can occur:

$$x \mapsto lose_1 \text{ in } Trans_1, \, y \mapsto \overline{lose_1} \text{ in } Control.$$

An occurrence of this transition binding does not change the marking of the env net because t_5 composes self-loops. Next the following transition binding for t_3 becomes enabled:

$$x \mapsto switch_1 \text{ in } Car, \, y \mapsto \overline{switch_1} \text{ in } Trans_1.$$

After the occurrence, the marking of the env net changes to

$$p_1 \mapsto Trans_1, \, p_2 \mapsto Car + Trans_2, \, p_3 \mapsto Control.$$

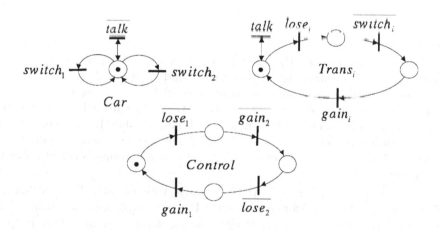

Fig. 1. Agent nets.

3.2 Preliminaries

We describe here notation necessary to define PN^2s. A multi-set over a non-empty set S is a function $M : S \rightarrow \mathbb{N}$, i.e., for each $s \in S$, $M(s)$ denotes the number of occurrences of s in M. Let $\mathcal{M}_S$ denote the family of all multi-sets over S. For $M \in \mathcal{M}_S$, let $|M| = \sum_{s \in S} M(s)$. We usually denote a multi-set M

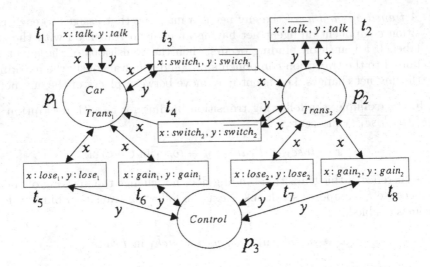

Fig. 2. The env net.

by a formal sum $\sum_{s \in S} M(s)\#s$. For two multi-sets M_1, $M_2 \in \mathcal{M}_S$, we write $M_1 \subseteq M_2$ if $M_1(s) \le M_2(s)$ for every $s \in S$. Moreover, the difference $M_2 - M_1$ is defined only when $M_1 \subseteq M_2$, and is a multi-set $\sum_{s \in S}(M_2(s) - M_1(s))\#s$. We simply write s to denote $1\#s$, and write $\emptyset$ to denote the empty multi-set.

A *place/transition net* (P/T net) is a triple $\Theta = (P, T, A)$, where P is a finite set of places, T is a finite set of transitions, and $A : (P \times T) \cup (T \times P) \to \mathbb{N}$ is a function representing arcs. A *marking* of Θ is a multi-set over P. Let Σ be a finite set of symbols. A P/T net $\Theta = (P, T, A)$ with a labeling function $\ell : T \to \Sigma$ is called *a labeled-P/T net* (ℓ–P/T net, for short), and is denoted by Θ^ℓ. We can identify an ℓ-P/T net with a P/T net if the labeling function ℓ is an injection. A pair $\mu = (\Theta^\ell, m)$ of an ℓ-P/T net and a marking is called *a marked ℓ-P/T net*.

Let $\mu = (\Theta^\ell = (P, T, A)^\ell, m)$ be a marked ℓ-P/T net. A transition t is *enabled* in a marking m if for every $p \in P$: $A(p, t) \le m(p)$. An enabled transition can *fire*. A firing of transition t changes the marking to m' such that $m'(p) = m(p) + A(t, p) - A(p, t)$ ($p \in P$). We write $m \xrightarrow{t} m'$ to denote this situation. Moreover, this notation is extended to finite sequences of transitions, i.e., we write $m \xrightarrow{\sigma} m'$ to denote that firing of a sequence of transitions $\sigma \in T^*$ changes the marking from m to m'. We say that marking m' is *reachable* from marking m if $m \xrightarrow{\sigma} m'$ for some $\sigma \in T^*$. Let $\mathcal{R}(\mu)$ denote the set of all markings reachable from m.

Since marked ℓ-P/T nets will be treated as tokens in PN^2s, we introduce a state transition function δ on the set of all marked ℓ-P/T nets by $\delta(\mu, t) = \mu'$, where $\mu = (\Theta^\ell, m)$, $m \xrightarrow{t} m'$ and $\mu' = (\Theta^\ell, m')$. Let PT_Σ denote the class of all marked ℓ-P/T nets with labeling functions to Σ.

3.3   Definition of PN^2s

A PN^2 is a 9-tuple $PN^2 = (P, \Sigma, T, E, {}^{\bullet}\cdot, \cdot^{\bullet}, \cdot_{\Sigma}, \cdot_T, s_0)$, where

1. P is a finite set of *places*;
2. Σ is a finite set of *symbols*;
3. T is a finite set of *transitions*;
4. E is a finite set of *transition components*;
5. ${}^{\bullet}\cdot : E \to \mathcal{M}_P$ (inputs of each transition component);
6. $\cdot^{\bullet} : E \to \mathcal{M}_P$ (ouputs of each transition component);
7. $\cdot_{\Sigma} : E \to \Sigma$ (the label for specifying transitions of agent nets);
8. $\cdot_T : E \to T$ (the transition each transition component belongs to);
9. s_0 is *the initial configuration*, where a configuration is a mapping $s : P \to \mathcal{M}_{PT_{\Sigma}}$.

Example 1. Figure 3 is a graphical representation of the following $PN^2 = (P, \Sigma, T, E, {}^{\bullet}\cdot, \cdot^{\bullet}, \cdot_{\Sigma}, \cdot_T, s_0)$:

1. $P = \{p_1, p_2, p_3\}$;
2. $\Sigma = \{\lambda, a, b, c, d\}$;
3. $T = \{t_1, t_2, t_3, t_4\}$;
4. $E = \{e_1, e_2, e_3, e_4, e_5, e_6\}$;
5. ${}^{\bullet}e_1 = p_1, {}^{\bullet}e_2 = p_1, {}^{\bullet}e_3 = p_3, {}^{\bullet}e_4 = p_2, {}^{\bullet}e_5 = p_2, {}^{\bullet}e_6 = p_2 \mid p_3$;
6. $e_1^{\bullet} = p_1, e_2^{\bullet} = p_0, e_3^{\bullet} = p_0 + p_0, e_4^{\bullet} = p_1, e_5^{\bullet} = \emptyset, e_6^{\bullet} = p_1 \mid p_3$;
7. $e_{1\Sigma} = \lambda, e_{2\Sigma} = a, e_{3\Sigma} = c, e_{4\Sigma} = b, e_{5\Sigma} = c, e_{6\Sigma} = d$;
8. $e_{1T} = t_1, e_{2T} = t_2, e_{3T} = t_2, e_{4T} = t_3, e_{5T} = t_3, e_{6T} = t_4$;
9. $s_0 : p_1 \mapsto \mu_1$; $p_2 \mapsto \emptyset$; $p_3 \mapsto \mu_2$, where μ_1 and μ_2 are the marked ℓ-P/T nets shown in the figure.

The 6-tuple $(P, T, E, {}^{\bullet}\cdot, \cdot^{\bullet}, \cdot_T)$ defines the env net, and marked ℓ-P/T nets in the configuration are agent nets. Each transition $t \in T$ in the env net consists of a set of transition components $E_t := \{e \in E \mid e_T = t\}$. In the graphical representation, we associate labels $x, y, z, \cdots$ with each arc to distinguish transition components, and write "$x : a, y : b, \cdots$" to indicate that $x_{\Sigma} = a$, $y_{\Sigma} = b$, $\cdots$ for transition components $x, y, \cdots$.

3.4   State Transition Rule

Let T_{Σ} denote the set of all transitions of marked ℓ-P/T nets in PT_{Σ}. Let $t \in T$ be a transition of the env net. *A transition binding* for transition t is a pair of functions $b : E_t \to PT_{\Sigma}$ and $w : E_t \to T_{\Sigma}$ such that for each $e \in E_t$: (i) $w(e)$ is an enabled transition of agent net $b(e)$, and (ii) $w(e)$ has label e_{Σ}.

A transition binding (b, w) is *enabled* in configuration s if for each $p \in P$:

$$\sum_{e \in E_t} ({}^{\bullet}e)(p) \# b(e) \subseteq s(p). \tag{1}$$

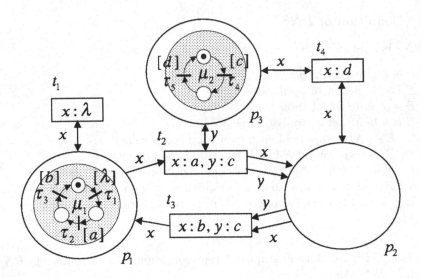

Fig. 3. An example of PN^2s.

A transition binding can *occur* if it is enabled. An occurrence of a transition binding (b, w) changes the configuration to s' such that for each $p \in P$:

$$s'(p) = s(p) - \sum_{e \in E_t} (^\bullet e)(p) \# b(e) + \sum_{e \in E_t} (e^\bullet)(p) \# \delta(b(e), w(e)). \qquad (2)$$

Let B_t denote the set of all possible transition bindings for transition t and let $B = \bigcup_{t \in T} B_t$. We write $s \xrightarrow{(b,w)} s'$ to denote that an occurrence of a transition binding (b, w) changes the configuration from s to s', and this notation is extended to finite sequences of transition bindings. We say that configuration s' is *reachable* from configuration s if $s \xrightarrow{\sigma} s'$ for some $\sigma \in B^*$.

Example 2. We consider a PN^2 in Figure 3. Denoting each configuration s by a vector $[s(p_1), s(p_2), s(p_3)]$, the configuration changes as follows:

$$[\mu_1, \emptyset, \mu_2] \xrightarrow{(b_1, w_1)} [\mu'_1, \emptyset, \mu_2] \xrightarrow{(b_2, w_2)} [\emptyset, \mu''_1 + \mu_2, \mu'_2]$$
$$\xrightarrow{(b_3, w_3)} [\emptyset, \mu''_1 + \mu_2, \mu_2] \xrightarrow{(b_4, w_4)} [\mu_1, \emptyset, \mu_2],$$

where $\mu'_1 = \delta(\mu_1, \tau_1)$, $\mu''_1 = \delta(\mu'_1, \tau_2)$, $\mu'_2 = \delta(\mu_2, \tau_4)$, and (b_i, w_i) $(i = 1, 2, 3)$ are unique transition bindings for transition t_i such that

$$b_1 : e_1 \mapsto \mu_1, \quad w_1 : e_1 \mapsto \tau_1;$$
$$b_2 : e_2 \mapsto \mu'_1, e_3 \mapsto \mu_2, \quad w_2 : e_2 \mapsto \tau_2, e_3 \mapsto \tau_4;$$
$$b_3 : e_6 \mapsto \mu'_2, \quad w_3 : e_6 \mapsto \tau_5;$$
$$b_4 : e_4 \mapsto \mu''_1, e_5 \mapsto \mu_2, \quad w_4 : e_4 \mapsto \tau_3, e_5 \mapsto \tau_4.$$

3.5   Properties of Multi-agent Systems Modeled by PN^2s

The following features of multi-agent systems can be represented by PN^2s.

- *Static/dynamic environment*: In PN^2s, there is no distinction between active objects and passive objects. Some of agent nets can be used for representing agents (active objects), and some for representing local data (passive objects). Static environment is represented by the graph structure of the env net together with passibe objects, and dynamic environment by existence of other active objects.
- *Agent actions/observation*: Possible actions taken by each agent net is restricted by the local environment where it is located. Since in PN^2s observation of the environment is also represented by taking some actions, each agent net can get only partial information about the environment. Note that the static environment is not necessarily a physical location in the real world. It is a collection of constraints that affects the ability for actions taken by agents.
- *Mobility of agents*: By occurrence of transition bindings, each agent net can move from a place to another place. This corresponds to the situation that an agent changes its location.
- *Duplication of agents*: If a transition component has multiple outputs, then agent nets will be duplicated by occurrence of transition bindings.
- *Agent communication*: Each agent net can communicate with other agent nets through occurrence of transition bindings. If a transition of the env net composes self-loops, then the movement of agent nets does not happen. There are two kinds of agent communication: communication in the same place (local communication) and communication among different places (remote communication).
- *Autonomous actions*: Autonomous action of an agent are performed without any interaction with outside. Such an autonomous action can be modeled in PN^2s as follows. (i) We associate the special symbol λ with every autonomous transition of agent nets, and (ii) add the following transition to the env net: it consists of exactly one transition component, and composes a self-loop with the place (see transition t_1 in Figure 3). We can assume every place has such transition for autonomous actions. The reason why PN^2s do not have explicit representation of autonomous actions is just for simplifying the formalism.

3.6   Relationship between P/T Nets and PN^2s

Marked P/T nets can be considered as a special class of PN^2s by treating each token as a marked ℓ-P/T net with one transition and no places, i.e., it has only one state and the transition is always enabled.

A PN^2 is called *finite-sort* if (i) for every transition component e: ${}^\bullet e \neq \emptyset$ and (ii) all marked ℓ-P/T nets contained in the initial configuration are bounded[2].

---

[2] A marked ℓ-P/T net μ is bounded if there exists a nonnegative integer k such that for every $m \in \mathcal{R}(\mu)$ and every $p \in P$: $m(p) \leq k$.

Otherwise, it is called *infinite-sort*. When a PN^2 is finite-sort, there exists a marked P/T net $\widetilde{PN}^2 = (\widetilde{P}, \widetilde{T}, \widetilde{A}, \widetilde{m}_0)$ that simulates the behavior of the PN^2. We show the construction. First we define the following sets.

- $\overline{PT_\Sigma}$ is the set of all marked ℓ-P/T net (Θ^ℓ, m) such that $m \in \mathcal{R}(\mu_0)$ for some $\mu_0 = (\Theta^\ell, m_0)$ in the initial configuration.
- $\overline{B_t}$ is the set of all transition binding (b, w) for transition t such that for all $e \in E_t$: $b(e) \subseteq \overline{PT_\Sigma}$. Let $\overline{B} = \bigcup_{t \in T} \overline{B_t}$.

By the assumption, both $\overline{PT_\Sigma}$ and $\overline{B}$ are finite and effectively computable. In general not all marked ℓ-P/T nets in $\overline{PT_\Sigma}$ appear in reachable configurations.

For each place $p \in P$ and each marked ℓ-P/T net $\mu \in \overline{PT_\Sigma}$, we prepare a place p_μ, and for each transition $t \in T$ and each transition binding $(b, w) \in \overline{B_t}$, we prepare a transition $t_{(b,w)}$, where arcs are connected as follows:

- $\widetilde{A}(p_{b(e)}, t_{(b,w)}) = {}^\bullet e(p)$ and $\widetilde{A}(t_{(b,w)}, p_{\delta(b(e),w(e))}) = e^\bullet(p)$ $(e \in E_t)$;
- Otherwise, $\widetilde{A}(\cdot, t_{(b,w)}) = \widetilde{A}(t_{(b,w)}, \cdot) = 0$.

The initial marking $\widetilde{m}_0$ is defined by $\widetilde{m}_0(p_\mu) = s_0(p)(\mu)$. Then the state transition diagrams of PN^2 and $\widetilde{PN}^2$ are isomorphic to each other. In tis sense, $\widetilde{PN}^2$ simulates the behavior of PN^2.

It was shown that the class of infinite-sort PN^2s has the same level of modeling power as Turing machines[7]. This means that there exists a PN^2 in this class that cannot be simulated by any P/T net.

4   Mathematical Analysis of PN^2s

In this section, we first define incidence matrices of PN^2s, and then show how to define the state equation and invariants. As is well-known, the state equation and invariants gives important information about Petri nets[14].

In what follows, we will use a subclass of PN^2s, called *injective PN^2s*, to simplify the argument. A PN^2 is called injective if every marked ℓ-P/T net in the initial configuration has an injective labeling function, i.e., no two transitions have the same label in every agent nets. Given any PN^2, we can construct an equivalent injective PN^2 by (i) relabeling transitions in agent nets if more than one transitions have the same label, and (ii) duplicating transitions in the env net corresponding to the relabeling.

In injective PN^2s, we can omit the second part of transition bindings, therefore a transition binding for a transition t is defined by a function $b : E_t \to PT_\Sigma$ such that for each $e \in E_t$, the unique transition having label e_Σ is enabled in $b(e)$. Therefore, we will identify a label with the transition having the label.

4.1   State Equation

We show how the state equation of an injective PN^2 is defined. We first define *firing count vectors*. Suppose that $T = \{t_1, \cdots, t_n\}$ and $P = \{p_1, \cdots, p_m\}$. In what follows, we will use an index i to denote transitions, and j to denote places. In addition, we will write just i (j) in subscripts to indicate the transition t_i (place p_j), e.g., we will write E_i instead of E_{t_i}, and B_i instead of B_{t_i}.

A *firing count vector* is a $|T|$-dimensional column vector $x = [x_1, \cdots, x_n]^t$, where each x_i is a multi-set over B_i and indicates how many times each transition binding to occur. For a sequence of transition bindings $\sigma \in B^*$, let $\psi(\sigma) = [x_1, \cdots, x_n]^t$ denotes a firing count vector such that for each transition t_i, x_i is the sum of transition bindings for t_i occurring in σ. The vector $\psi(\sigma)$ has sufficient information to determin the final marking. If $s \xrightarrow{\sigma_1} s'$, $s \xrightarrow{\sigma_2} s''$, and $\psi(\sigma_1) = \psi(\sigma_2)$, then $s' = s''$ holds.

In this formulation of firing count vectors, it is necessary to consider all elements in $\overline{B}$, and $|\overline{B}|$ may increase exponentially in the size of the net. This problem is avoidable by introducing a different representation of firing count vectors. Let $E_i = \{e_i^1, \cdots, e_i^{|E_i|}\}$. We represent each x_i by a $|E_i|$ dimensional vector $\hat{x}_i = [x_i^1, \cdots, x_i^{|E_i|}]$ such that

(i) for each $l = 1, \cdots, |E_i|$: $x_i^k = \sum_{b \in B_i} x_i(b) \# b(e_i^k)$.
(ii) for every $k, k' \in \{1, \cdots, |E_i|\}$, $|x_i^k| = |x_i^{k'}|$.

The second requirement is necessary for the vector to be decomposed into a multi-set over B_i. The reason why this compact representation of firing count vectors is possible is that there is no interference among transition components. The following example shows how we can avoid dealing with the exponential number of transition bindings: Suppose that $E_i = \{e_i^1, \cdots, e_i^h\}$, $e_{i\Sigma}^k = a$ ($k = 1, \cdots, h$), and the input place of t_i contains r marked ℓ-P/T nets having an enabled transition with label a. Then the number of possible transition bindings for t_i is $O(r^h)$. In the different representation, however, the space necessary to represent x_i is $O(rh)$.

Let $\hat{\psi}(\sigma) = [\hat{x}_1, \cdots, \hat{x}_n]^t$ denotes the different representation of $\psi(\sigma)$ described above. Then $\hat{\psi}(\sigma)$ also keeps sufficient information to determine the final marking, i.e., if $s \xrightarrow{\sigma_1} s'$, $s \xrightarrow{\sigma_2} s''$, and $\hat{\psi}(\sigma_1) = \hat{\psi}(\sigma_2)$, then $s' = s''$.

We now define two matrices I^- and I^+, called *the input incidence matrix* and *the output incidence matrix*. Each of these contains a row for each place and a column for each transition. Each component $I^-(p_j, t_i)$ ($I^+(p_j, t_i)$) corresponds to $\bullet e_i^k$ ($e_i^k \bullet$) of $e_i^k \in E_i$, and is defined as follows:

– $I^-(p_j, t_i)$ is a row vector $[w_{j,i,1}^- \# Id, \cdots, w_{j,i,|E_i|}^- \# Id]$, where $w_{j,i,k}^- \in \mathbb{N}$, and Id is the identity function.
– $I^+(p_j, t_i)$ is a row vector $[w_{j,i,1}^+ \# \delta_{e_{i\Sigma}^1}, \cdots, w_{j,i,|E_i|}^+ \# \delta_{e_{i\Sigma}^{|E_i|}}]$, where $w_{j,i,k}^+ \in \mathbb{N}$, and δ_τ is a function on $\mathcal{M}_{PT_\Sigma}$ such that $\delta_\tau(M) = \sum_{\mu \in PT_\Sigma} M(\mu) \# \delta(\mu, \tau)$.

Multiplication between incidence matrices and a firing count vector is defined as follows.

$$I^-(p_j, t_i) \cdot \hat{x}_i := \sum_{k=1}^{|E_i|} w_{j,i,k}^- \# Id(x_i^k) = \sum_{k=1}^{|E_i|} w_{j,i,k}^- \# x_i^k, \qquad (3)$$

$$I^+(p_j, t_i) \cdot \hat{x}_i := \sum_{k=1}^{|E_i|} w^+_{j,i,k} \# \delta_{e^k_{i\Sigma}}(x^k_i). \tag{4}$$

A configuration s is represented by a column vector $[s_1, \cdots, s_m]^t$ such that each s_i is a multi-set over PT_Σ. Hence, we obtain the following state equation.

Theorem 1. *if $s \xrightarrow{\sigma} s'$, then $s' = s + I^+ \hat{\psi}(\sigma) - I^- \hat{\psi}(\sigma)$.*   □

Example 3. The incidence matrices of the PN^2 in Figure 3 are

$$I^- = \begin{bmatrix} [Id] & [Id, \emptyset] & [\emptyset, \emptyset] & [\emptyset] \\ [\emptyset] & [\emptyset, \emptyset] & [Id, Id] & [Id] \\ [\emptyset] & [\emptyset, Id] & [\emptyset, Id] & [Id] \end{bmatrix}, \quad I^+ = \begin{bmatrix} [\delta_\lambda] & [\emptyset, \emptyset] & [\delta_b, \emptyset] & [\emptyset] \\ [\emptyset] & [\delta_a, \delta_c] & [\emptyset, \emptyset] & [\delta_d] \\ [\emptyset] & [\emptyset, \delta_c] & [\emptyset, \emptyset] & [\delta_d] \end{bmatrix}.$$

The firing count vector for the sequence of transition bindings in Example 2 is

$$\hat{x} = [[\mu_1], [\mu'_1, \mu_2], [\mu'_2, \mu'_2], [\mu''_1, \mu_2]]^t.$$

For finite-sort PN^2s, firing count vectors and incidence matrices can be represented by integer vectors/matrices. To evaluate the size of matrices, we will use the following numbers:

$$\#_{all} = |\overline{PT_\Sigma}|, \quad \#_{i,k} = |\overline{PT_\Sigma}(e^k_{i\Sigma})|, \quad \#_{sum} = \sum_{i=1}^{n} \sum_{k=1}^{|E_i|} \#_{i,k},$$

where $\overline{PT_\Sigma}(a)$, $a \in \Sigma$ denotes the set of all marked ℓ-P/T nets of $\overline{PT_\Sigma}$ in which a transition with label a is enabled.

Now we show integer representation of firing count vectors and incidence matrices. Each x^k_i is represented by a $\#_{i,k}$-dimensional nonnegative integer vector each components of which corresponds to a marked ℓ-P/T net in $\overline{PT_\Sigma}(e^k_{i\Sigma})$. Suppose $\overline{PT_\Sigma}(e^k_{i\Sigma}) = \{\mu^1_{i,k}, \cdots, \mu^{\#_{i,k}}_{i,k}\}$. Then the vector is $[x^k_i(\mu^{k,1}_i), \cdots, x^k_i(\mu^{k,\#_{i,k}}_i)]$. Each $w^-_{j,i,k} \# Id$ ($w^+_{j,i,k} \# \delta_{e^k_{i\Sigma}}$) in $I^-(p_j, t_i)$ ($I^+(p_j, t_i)$) is represented by a nonnegative integer matrix having rows corresponding to $\overline{PT_\Sigma}$, and columns corresponding to $\overline{PT_\Sigma}(e^k_{i\Sigma})$. Suppose $\overline{PT_\Sigma} = \{\mu_1, \cdots, \mu_{\#_{all}}\}$ and $\overline{PT_\Sigma}(e^k_{i\Sigma}) = \{\mu^1_{i,k}, \cdots, \mu^{\#_{i,k}}_{i,k}\}$. Then the matrix for $w^-_{j,i,k} \# Id$ is $[v^-_{rl}]$, where

$$v^-_{rl} = \begin{cases} w^-_{j,i,k} & (\mu^l_{i,k} = \mu_r) \\ 0 & \text{(otherwise)} \end{cases}. \tag{5}$$

The matrix for $w^+_{j,i,k} \# \delta_{e^k_{i\Sigma}}$ is $[v^+_{rl}]$, where

$$v^+_{rl} = \begin{cases} w^+_{j,i,k} & (\delta_{e^k_{i\Sigma}}(\mu^l_{i,k}) = \mu_r) \\ 0 & \text{(otherwise)} \end{cases}. \tag{6}$$

The size of the incidence matrices is $m \cdot \#_{all} \times \#_{sum}$.

Example 4. I^- and I^+ of the PN^2 in Figure 3 are represented by the following integer matrices. We omit rows with all zero components.

$$
I^- = \begin{array}{c} \\ \mu_1 \\ \mu_1' \\ \mu_1'' \\ \mu_2 \\ \mu_2' \\ \mu_2 \\ \mu_2' \end{array}
\begin{array}{c} \mu_1\ \mu_1'\ \mu_2\ \mu_1''\ \mu_2\ \mu_2' \\
\left[\begin{array}{cc|cc|cc}
1 & 0 & 0 & 0 & 0 & 0 \\
0 & 1 & 0 & 0 & 0 & 0 \\
0 & 0 & 0 & 1 & 0 & 0 \\
0 & 0 & 0 & 0 & 1 & 0 \\
0 & 0 & 0 & 0 & 0 & 1 \\
0 & 0 & 1 & 0 & 0 & 0 \\
0 & 0 & 0 & 0 & 0 & 1
\end{array}\right]
\end{array}
,\quad
I^+ = \begin{array}{c} \\ \mu_1 \\ \mu_1' \\ \mu_1'' \\ \mu_2 \\ \mu_2' \\ \mu_2 \\ \mu_2' \end{array}
\begin{array}{c} \mu_1\ \mu_1'\ \mu_2\ \mu_1''\ \mu_2\ \mu_2' \\
\left[\begin{array}{cc|cc|cc}
0 & 0 & 0 & 1 & 0 & 0 \\
1 & 0 & 0 & 0 & 0 & 0 \\
0 & 1 & 0 & 0 & 0 & 0 \\
0 & 0 & 0 & 0 & 0 & 1 \\
0 & 0 & 1 & 0 & 0 & 0 \\
0 & 0 & 0 & 0 & 0 & 1 \\
0 & 0 & 1 & 0 & 0 & 0
\end{array}\right]
\end{array}.
$$

Then the state equation for the firing count vector in Example 3 is

$$
\begin{bmatrix} 1 \\ 0 \\ \hline 0 \\ 0 \\ 0 \\ \hline 1 \\ 0 \end{bmatrix}
=
\begin{bmatrix} 1 \\ 0 \\ \hline 0 \\ 0 \\ 0 \\ \hline 1 \\ 0 \end{bmatrix}
+
\begin{bmatrix}
-1 & 0 & 0 & 1 & 0 & 0 \\
1 & -1 & 0 & 0 & 0 & 0 \\
0 & 1 & 0 & -1 & 0 & 0 \\
0 & 0 & 0 & 0 & -1 & 1 \\
0 & 0 & 1 & 0 & 0 & -1 \\
0 & 0 & -1 & 0 & 0 & 1 \\
0 & 0 & 1 & 0 & 0 & -1
\end{bmatrix}
\cdot
\begin{bmatrix} 1 \\ \hline 1 \\ \hline 1 \\ \hline 1 \\ \hline 1 \\ \hline 1 \end{bmatrix}.
$$

4.2 Invariants

Computing invariants is one of important and effective procedures in the analysis of Petri nets[14,8], because existence of invariants is necessary for the system to show stable behavior in the sense of the system theory. In the case of P/T nets, invariants are obtained by solving systems of linear homogeneous equations. Using the integer matrix representation, we can compute invariants of PN^2s by various methods developed for P/T nets.

A *T-invariant* of a PN^2 is a firing count vector x such that any sequence $\sigma \in \overline{B}^*$, $\psi(\sigma) = x$ does not change the configuration. In other words, a T-invariant corresponds to a cycle in the state transition diagram. It was shown that if the set of reachable configurations is finite and the system never terminates, then there always exists a T-invariant.

In the different representation, it is a firing count vector $\hat{x} = [[x_1^1, \cdots, x_1^{|E_1|}], \cdots, [x_n^1, \cdots, x_n^{|E_n|}]]^t$ such that

(i) $I^+\hat{x} = I^-\hat{x}$;

(ii) For each $i \in \{1, \cdots, n\}$, $|x_i^1| = |x_i^2| = \cdots = |x_i^{|E_i|}|$.

In the integer matrix representation, each x_i^k is a nonnegative integer vector $[x_i^{k,1}, \cdots, x_i^{k,\#_{i,k}}]^t$, $x_i^{k,l} \in \mathbb{N}$. Then the condition (ii) is written as follows.

$$
\sum_{l=1}^{\#_{i,1}} x_i^{1,l} = \sum_{l=1}^{\#_{i,2}} x_i^{2,l} = \cdots = \sum_{l=1}^{\#_{i,|E_{t_i}|}} x_i^{|E_{t_i}|,l} \quad (i = 1, \cdots, n). \tag{7}
$$

We can easily construct an integer matrix I_{Tinv} such that $I_{Tinv} \cdot x = \mathbf{0}$ is equivalent to the conditions (i) and (ii). The size of I_{Tinv} is $(m \cdot \#_{all} + \sum_{i=1}^{n} |E_i| - n) \times \#_{sum}$.

Example 5. A T-invariant of the PN^2 in Figure 3 is

$$\hat{x} = [x_1^1 = \mu_1, x_2^1 = \mu_1', x_2^2 = \mu_2, x_3^1 = \mu_1'', x_3^2 = \mu_2, x_4^1 = \mu_2']^t.$$

In the nonnegative integer matrix representation, $\hat{x} = [1 \mid 1, 1 \mid 1, 1 \mid 1]^t$.

In P/T nets, a P-invariant is a vector of weights so that the weighted sum of the number of tokens in each place is constant by any occurrence of transitions. By computing P-invariants, we can verify many dynamic properties such as reachability, boundedness, liveness and fairness[8].

P-invariants of a PN^2 are similarly defined. Let x_b denotes the firing count vector of a single occurrence of transition binding b. *A weight function* C is a function on $\mathcal{M}_{PT_\Sigma}$ in the form

$$C \left(\sum_{\mu \in PT_\Sigma} n_\mu \# \mu \right) := \sum_{\mu \in PT_\Sigma} c_\mu \cdot n_\mu \# \mu, \ (c_\mu \in \mathbb{N}). \tag{8}$$

A P-invariant is a row vector $y = [y_1, \cdots, y_m]$ of weight functions such that for every $b \in \overline{B}$: $y \cdot (I^+ \cdot x_b - I^- \cdot x_b) = \emptyset$. In the integer matrix representation, each y_i is represented by an integer vector $[y_i^1, \cdots, y_i^{\#_{all}}]$, and x_b by a nonnegative integer vector $[[x_1^1, \cdots, x_1^{|E_i|}], \cdots, [x_n^1, \cdots, x_n^{|E_i|}]]^t$ such that each x_i^k is an $\#_{i,k}$-dimensional unit vector, i.e., it has value 1 for one component and 0 for others.

The number of transition bindings in $\overline{B}$ is $\sum_{i=1}^{n} \prod_{k=1}^{|E_i|} \#_{i,k}$. However, it is not necessary to solve the equation for all of the transition bindings. Let I_i^k denote the $\#_{all} \times \#_{i,k}$ submatrix of I corresponding to e_i^k, and let $I_i^{k,l}$ denote the l-th column vector of I_i^k. Then a vector y of weight functions is a P-invariant if and only if:

(i) $y \cdot \sum_{k=1}^{|E_i|} I_i^{k,1} = 0$ $(i = 1, \cdots, n)$;
(ii) $y \cdot I_i^{k,l} = y \cdot I_i^{k,l+1}$ $(i = 1, \cdots, n, \ k = 1, \cdots, |E_i|, \ l = 1, \cdots, \#_{i,k} - 1)$.

We can easily construct an integer matrix I_{Pinv} such that $y \cdot I_{Pinv} = \mathbf{0}$ is equivalent to the conditions (i) and (ii). The size of I_{Pinv} is $m \cdot \#_{all} \times (n + \#_{sum} - \sum_{i=1}^{n} |E_i|)$.

Example 6. A P-invariant of the PN^2 in Figure 3 is $y = [y_1 = [1, 1, 0, 0, 0], y_2 = [0, 0, 1, 0, 0], y_3 = [0, 0, 0, 1, 1]]$, where components in y_i corresponds to the weights for $\mu_1, \mu_1', \mu_1'', \mu_2, \mu_2'$, respectively. Note that the condition (ii) is not considered here since $\#_{i,k} = 1$ for all i, k.

5   Related Work

As written in the introduction, *elementary object systems* (EOS)[18] have been proposed as an elementary class of object Petri nets. EOS also consist of two layers and have a Petri net as a token. We here compare PN^2s and EOS.

- *Modeling power (in the theoretical sense)*: Infinite-sort PN^2s can have infinitely many states, while EOS do not allow to have infinitely many states. Each lower-level nets in EOS is an elementary net system, i.e., it has finitely many reachable markings, and duplication of agents is not allowed.
- *Agent communication*: In PN^2s, communication links are defined by the function $\cdot_\Sigma$, which specifies transition labels of agent nets, and are dynamically generated by occurrence of transition bindings. In EOS, they are given as the interaction relation, which is a binary relation between the set of transitions in the upper-level net and the set of transitions in lower-level nets. Both representations are equivalent except that communication links in EOS are restricted to those between two agents. PN^2s allow links in which more than two agents participate.

  EOS also provide another type of interaction between two objects in the same place, called *object/object interaction*. Communication links for this interaction is defined by a symmetric relation on the set of transitions in lower-level nets. In PN^2s, the same type of interaction can be represented by adding transitions with self loops to the place of the env net.

  In EOS, the object/object interaction relation is universal in all places of the upper-level net, while PN^2s can describe different interaction relation in each place. As a result, PN^2s model the following situation: some agent/agent communication is possible in an environment but is impossible in another environment.
- *Semantics*: PN^2s are based on *the value semantics*[19], whereas many of object Petri nets are based on *the reference semantics*. In the reference semantics, each net as a token is a reference (or a pointer) to the object. Therefore, duplication of tokens does not mean duplication of objects. In the value semantics, each net as a token represents an independent instance of objects, and therefore duplication and vanishing of objects are allowed. EOS are basically based on the reference semantics[3].

  Value semantics may cause the following problem in the implementation level. Suppose that there exists a transition component e such that $|{}^\bullet e| = n > 1$. Then occurrence of transition bindings concerning e requires a procedure to check that n agent nets are identical, i.e., they have the same ℓ-P/T net structure and the same marking. However, this is hard to implement in real situation, because each agents needs to inform other agents of its internal state when it intends to communicate.
- *Mathematical analysis*: The main purpose of proposing EOS is to give formal semantics of object systems, and the research direction is slightly different

---

[3] Relationship between value semantics and reference semantics in EOS is discussed in [19]

from that of PN^2s. On the other hand, PN^2s are designed to enable efficient mathematical analysis such as invariant analysis. In addition, allowing dynamic bindings of transitions may cause a combinatorial number of transition bindings, but it is avoidable in the invariant analysis.

Process algebra is an alternative approach to model concurrent systems. Several models based on process algebra have been proposed to represent mobility of agents, such as π-calculus[12], CHOCS (Calculus of Higher Order Communicating Systems) [17], and ambient calculus[4]. π-calculus realizes the mobility of agents by movement of links between processes. Each process can send link names to other processes, and communication links between agents are dynamically constructed. CHOCS is a higher order process algebra. In CHOCS, each process can send and receive processes. This feature enables to represent mobile codes in a distributed environment. An ambient is a bounded place where agents interact. In ambient calculus, each agent can enter into or exit from an ambient, and can also dissolve an ambient. Communication between agents are described as the movement of messenger agents.

These models are oriented to expressiveness of agent-based systems. In contrast to these models, PN^2s represent the mobility by movement of agents (agent nets) in a virtual environment (the env net), and are oriented to mathematical analysis such as the state equation and invariant anlaysis. There are differences in the representation of agent communication between PN^2s and π-calculus. In π-calculus, each agent keeps communication links, equivalently knows other agents to be communicated. Link names are sent to other agents and are used as new links. In PN^2s, each agent knows only names of links (labels of transitions), and does not know other agents to be communicated. Communication links are dynamically determined by the environment (transition bindings).

6   Conclusion

The proposed formalism of PN^2s is designed as a fundamental model for representing the various features of multi-agent systems. The following topics concerning PN^2s remain as future work: reachability analysis and efficient state space exploration, design of agents in a given environment, precise comparison with π-calculus, and extension of PN^2s to high-level versions. In addition, the incidence matrices are still too large and sparse. We will be able to omit redundant rows and columns which will not participate in the state transition.

References

1. M. Baldassari, An Environment for Object-Oriented Conceptual Programming Based on PROT Nets, Lecture Notes in Computer Science, Vol.340, pp.1–19 (1988).
2. E. Battiston, F. De Cindio, G. Mauri, OBJSA Nets: A Class of High-Level Nets Having Objects as Domains, Lecture Notes in Computer Science, Vol.340, pp.20–43 (1988).

3. O. Biberstein, D. Buchs, and N. Cuelfi, CO-OPN/2 - A Specification Language for Distributed System Engineering, Technical Report 96/167, Software Engineering Laboratory, Swiss Federal Institute of Technology (1996).
4. L. Cardelli and A. D. Gordon, Mobile Ambients, Lecture Notes in Computer Science, vol.1378, pp.140-155, 1998.
5. M. Ceska, V. Janousek, and T. Vojnar, PNTalk - A Computerized Tool for Object Oriented Petri Nets Modelling, Lecture Notes in Computer Science, Vol.1333, pp.591–610 (1994).
6. J. Engelfriet, G. Leih, G. Rozenberg, Net-based Description of Parallel Object-based Systems, Lecture Notes in Computer Science, Vol.489, pp.229–273 (1990).
7. K. Hiraishi, A Petri-net-based Model for the Mathematical Analysis of Multi-agent Systems, to appear in IEICE Trans. Fundamentals.
8. K. Jensen, Coloured Petri Nets: Basic Concepts, Analysis Methods and Practical Use, Volume I, II, III, Springer-Verlag (1992, 1995, 1997).
9. O. Kummar and F. Wienberg, Renew - the Reference Net Workshop, Petri Net Newsletter, No.56, pp.12–16 (1999).
10. C. Lakos and C. Keen, LOOPN++: A New Language for Object-Oriented Petri Nets, Technical Report, R94-4, Department of Computer Science, University of Tasmania (1994).
11. C. Lakos, From Coloured Petri Nets to Object Petri Nets, Lecture Notes in Computer Science, Vol.935, pp.278–297 (1995).
12. R. Milner, Communicating and Mobile Systems: The π-Calculus, Cambridge university press (1999).
13. T. Miyamoto and S. Kumagai, A Multi Agent Net Model of Autonomous Distributed Systems, Proc. CESA'96, Symposium of Discrete Events and Manufacturing Systems, pp.619–623 (1996).
14. T. Murata, Petri Nets: Properties, Analysis and Applications, Proceedings of the IEEE, Vol.77, No.4, (1989).
15. S. Philippi, System Modeling Using Object-Oriented Pr/T-Nets, Research Report No. 25/97, Institute for Computer Science, University Koblenz - Landau (1997).
16. C. Sibertin-Blanc, Cooperative Nets, Lecture Notes in Computer Science, Vol.815, pp.471–490 (1994).
17. B. Thomsen, A Theory of Higher Order Communicating Systems, Information and Computation, vol.116, pp.38-57, 1995.
18. R. Valk, Petri Nets as Token Objects - An Introduction to Elementary Object Nets, Lecture Notes in Computer Science, Vol. 1420, pp.1–25 (1998).
19. R. Valk, Relating Different Semantics for Object Petri Nets, Research Report FBI-HH-B-226/00, Faculty of Informatics, University of Hamburg (2000).
20. J. L. Peterson, Petri Net Theory and the Modeling of Systems, Prentice-hall (1981).
21. P. Ramadge, and W. M. Wonham: The Control of Discrete Event Systems, Proc. IEEE, Vol.77, No.1, pp.81–98 (1989).
22. G. Weiss (ed.), Multiagent systems - A Modern Approach to Distributed Artificial Intelligence: Chapter I, The MIT Press (1999).

A Recovery Technique Using Multi-agent in Distributed Computing Systems[1]

Hwa-Min Lee[1], Kwang-Sik Chung[2], Sang-Chul Shin[1],
Dae-Won Lee[1], Won-Gyu Lee[1], and Heon-Chang Yu [1]

[1] Dept. of Computer Science Education, Korea University,
Seoul, Korea
{zelkova, sangchul, ldw1996, lee, yuhc}@comeud.korea.ac.kr
http://gcomedu.korea.ac.kr
[2] Dept. of Computer Science, University College London,
London, UK
{k.chung}@ucl.ac.uk

Abstract. This paper proposes a new approach to rollback-recovery, using multi-agent in distributed computing system. Previous rollback-recovery protocols were dependent on inherent communication and operating system, which cause a decline of computing performance in distributed computing system. By using multi-agent, we propose rollback-recovery protocol which works independently on operating system. We define three kinds of agent. One is a recovery agent that performs rollback-recovery protocol after a failure. Other is an information agent that constructs domain knowledge as a rule of fault tolerance and information during failure-free operation. The other is the facilitator agent that controls the efficient communication between agents. Also we propose rollback-recovery protocol using multi-agent and simulate the proposed rollback-recovery protocol using JAVA and agent communication language in CORBA environment.

1 Introduction

A distributed computing system is one in which components located at networked computers communicate and coordinates their actions only by passing messages. Recently, distributed computing systems have become increasingly popular to satisfy requirements for increasing computing power. The vast computing potential of these systems are often hampered by their susceptibility to failures, that include individual component failures and network failures. And each process which composes distributed computing system has no shared memory. Especially, if long-running applica-

---

[1] This work was supported by grant No. R01-2001-00354 from the Korea Science & Engineering Foundation.

tions are executed on the systems, the failure probability becomes significant[6]. Thus the systems require protocol for supporting fault-tolerance. Many rollback-recovery techniques have been developed to add high reliability and high availability to distributed computing systems.

The rollback-recovery protocols are classified into the checkpoint-based and the log-based[2], [7], [9]. Checkpoint-based protocols rely solely on checkpointing for system state restoration. Checkpointing can be coordinated, uncoordinated, and communication-induced[1], [2], [9]. Log-based protocols combine checkpointing with logging of nondeterministic events, encoded in tuple called determinants. Depending on how determinants are logged, log-based protocols can be pessimistic, optimistic, and causal[2], [3], [7].

Most of the rollback-recovery protocols have adapted fail-stop model. For this reason, rollback recovery procedure is managed by operating system after a failure. In other words, failed process and other processes which are dependent on failed process must perform synchronization for recovery under each operating system. These approaches decrease the system's computing power. Also previous rollback-recovery protocols are dependent on inherent communication and operating system. To mitigate this problem, we propose rollback-recovery protocol that is independent of operating system using multi-agent. Our multi-agent system consists of recovery agent, information agent and facilitator agent. Through using multi-agent, fault-tolerance functionality is positioned at different layer that is independent of application layer in distributed computing system. Layer of fault-tolerance protocol coincides with concept of micro kernel that is the core of distributed system, and this leads to an increasing portability and expansibility of fault-tolerance.

In this paper, we use pessimistic message logging approach with the independent checkpointing. Independent checkpointing makes the best of agent's autonomy. Also it is reported that message logging approach works well, when integrated with independent checkpointing. Because our rollback-recovery protocol study using agents is still on its early stage, we use pessimistic message logging approach which simplifies recovery procedure of each process.

This paper is organized as follows : In Section 2 we present a system model and system components. In Section 3 we define the ontology for rollback-recovery, KIF for constructing domain knowledge, and KQML for agent communication language. Section 4 discusses rollback-recovery algorithm using agents. Section 5 shows simulation results. Finally, the paper concludes in Section 6.

2   Multi-agent Based Fault-Tolerance System Architecture

2.1   System Model

The distributed computing system consists of n processes executed on hosts, recovery agents, information agents, facilitator agents and communication channel. Processes have no global memory and physical global clock. They communicate via messages sent through reliable first-in-first-out (FIFO) channels. The system is asynchronous : Each process is executed at its own speed and communicates with each other only through messages at finite but arbitrary transmission delays. We assume that the communication network is immune to partitioning and there is a stable storage that every process can always access[3]. Additionally, we assume that if the hosts fail, they would lose contents in their volatile memories and stop their executions, according to the fail-stop model[10]. Events of processes in a failure-free execution are ordered using Lamport's happened before relation[8].

Figure 1 shows fault-tolerant system using agents. In a figure 1, the agents communicate only with the facilitator agent. The facilitator agent routes the messages to the appropriate places such as process or other agents.

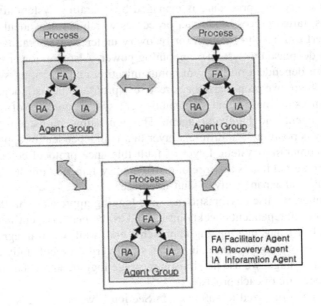

Fig. 1. Fault-tolerance system model using multi-agent

Figure 2 shows modified 3-tier, when multi-agent system is employed in rollback-recovery protocol.

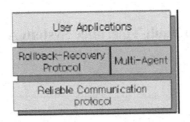

Fig. 2. Modified 3-tier

2.2 System Components

The proposed fault-tolerance system consists of recovery agent, information agent and facilitator agent. Recovery agent performs recovery procedure when process fails. For recovery, recovery agent uses domain knowledge and cooperates with other agents. Information agent constructs domain knowledge using KIF(Knowledge Interchange Format) in the stable storage. Domain knowledge is composed of rules for rollback-recovery and process' event information during a failure-free operation. Upon failure, an information agent infers last checkpoint and event list information and then sends them to a recovery agent. A facilitator agent offers efficient communication between agents as well as processing and an agent. If some agents need cooperation with other agents, they would only send request messages to a facilitator agent. For this reason having a specific capability, facilitator agent must receive the advertise messages from other agents manages the capability information.

3 Agent Communication Language

An agent is a component of communication software through which information is interchanged using an agent communication language(ACL). The power of expression of the ACL is a major factor in determining the overall ability of an agent. An ACL can be thought of three parts : (1) an outer language, called the knowledge query and manipulation language(KQML), (2) an inner language, called the knowledge interchange format(KIF), and (3) an ontology[4], [5].

3.1 Ontology for Rollback-Recovery

In the ACL, the ontology is a set of vocabularies to be used. In this paper, we define the ontology, which is used for rollback-recovery in distributed computing system, called Rollback_Recovery. Table 1 is Rollback_Recovery ontology.

Table 1. Rollback_Recovery ontology

Vocabulary	Semantic
checkpoint	process takes a local checkpoint
send	process sends message to other process
receive	process receives message from other process
before	front event precede rear event
log	process logs received message
rollback	process rollbacks last checkpoint
lastckp	last checkpoint that process takes
eventlist	event list that happened after last checkpoint
broadcast	broadcast message to all agent
replay	replay the events that include broadcasted event list

3.2 KIF for Domain Knowledge

An agent has its own domain knowledge and reasoning ability. The KIF is a computer-oriented language for the interchange of knowledge among disparate programs and a prefix version of first-order predicate calculus with LISP-like syntax. In this paper, we use KIF in order to construct agent's domain knowledge. The KIF BNF grammar for rollback-recovery is given in figure 3.

```
<upper>  ::= A | B | C | ··· | Y | Z
<lower>  ::= a | b | c | ··· | y | z
<digit>  ::= 0 | 1 | 2 | ··· | 8 | 9
<alpha>  ::= ! | $ | % | & | * | + | - | . | / | < | = | > | ? | @ | _ | ~ |
<special> ::= " | # | ' | ( | ) | , | \ | ` | ^ |
<white>  ::= space | tab | return | linefeed | page
<normal> ::= <upper> | <lower> | <digit> | <alpha>
<word>   ::= <normal> | <word>+
<expression> ::= <word> | (<expression>*)
<string> ::= empty | "<normal>
<indvar> ::= <?word>
<seqvar> ::= <@word>
<termop> ::= listof | quote | if
<sentop> ::= = | /= | not | and | or | => | <= | <=> | forall | exists
<defop>  ::= defobject | deffunction | defrelation | deflogical | := | :-> | :<= | :=>
<variable> ::= <indvar> | <seqvar>
<operator> ::= <termop> | <sentop> | <defop>
<constant> ::= <word> - <variable> - <operator>
<funconst> ::= function definition
<logterm> ::= (if <sentence> <term> [<term>]) | (cond (<sentence> <term>) ···
              (<sentence> <term>))
<quoterm> ::= (quote <expression>)
<term>   ::= <indvar> | <constant> | <string> | <funconst> | <logterm> |
             <quoterm>
<sentence> ::= <logconst> | <equation> | <inequality> | <relsent> | <logsent> |
              <quantsent>
<equation> ::= (= <term> <term>)
<inequality> ::= (/= <term> <term>)
<relsent> ::= (<relconst> <term>* [<seqvar>]) | (<funconst> <term>+)
<logsent> ::= (not <sentence>) | (and <sentence>*) | (or <sentence>*) | (=>
              <sentence>* <sentence>) | (<= <sentence> <sentence>+) | (<=>
              <sentence> <sentence>)
<quantsent> ::= (forall <indvar> <sentence>) | (forall (<indvar>+) <sentence>) |
               (exists <indvar> <sentence>) | (exists <indvar>* <sentence>)
```

Fig. 3. KIF BNF grammar for rollback_recovery

3.3 KQML for Agent Communication

The KQML is both a message format, and a message handling protocols for exchanging and sharing knowledge. In the sense that the programs are autonomous and asynchronous, the KQML is most useful for communication among agent-based programs. The KQML complements new approaches to distributed computing system, which focuses on the transport level. The KQML BNF grammar for agent communication is given in figure 4.

```
<performative> ::= (<word> {<whitespace> :<word> <whitespace>
                    <expression>}*)
<expression> ::= <word> | <quotation> | <string> | (<word> { <whitespace>
                    <expression>}*)
<word> ::= <character><character>*
<character> ::= <alphabetic> | <numeric> | <special>
<special> ::= < | > | = | + | - | * | / | & | ^ | ~ | _ | @ | $ | % | : | . | !
                    | ?
<quotation> ::= '<expression> | '<comma-expression>
<comma-expression> ::= <word> | <quotation> | <string> |
                    ,<comma-expression>        (<word>        (<whitespace>
                    <comma-expression>}*)
<string> ::= "<stringchar>*" | #<digit><digit>*"<ascii>*
<stringchar> ::= |<ascii> | <ascii> -+<double-quote>
```

Fig. 4. KQML BNF grammar for agent communication

The KQML represents an attitude (i,e., a query, a request, or a command) with re-spect to content expression. The basic component of KQML messages representing this attitude is called a *performative*, which constitutes the complete KQML messages with other components, and also identifies a type of communication protocol. Table 2 shows reserved performatives used in this paper.

Table 2. KQML performatives

Basic query performatives	ask-if, ask-one, ask-all ...
Generic informational performatives	tell, achieve, cancel, untell ...
Capability-definition performatives	advertise, subscribe, monitor ...
Networking performatives	register, unregister, broadcast ...

The following is a simple example of a KQML message :

```
(ask-one    : send ra1
            : receiver ia1
            : reply-with id1
            : language KIF
            : ontology Rollback_Recovery
            : content (lastckp p1 ?c))
```

Here, the performative name is ask-one, which denotes that the message is a query and that a reply message, such as the following, is requested according to its proto-col :

```
(tell       : send ia1
            : receiver ra1
            : in-reply-to id1
            : language KIF
```

```
: ontology Rollback_Recovery
: content (lastckp p1 c2))
```

The tell performative denotes that the *:content* fact is true. Therefore, the above conversation represents that the recovery agent *ra1* asks information agent *ia1* the last checkpoint of process *p1*, and *ia1* answers that the last checkpoint is *c2*. The *:sender* component refers to the message sender, and the *:receiver* component refers to the receiver. The *:in-reply-to* component of the *tell* message uses an identical identification number, *id1*, asked by the *:reply-with* part of the *ask-one* message. The *:language* parameter shows that the *:content* component is written in KIF. The *:ontology* term denotes the name of the ontology that contains definitions of the rollback-recovery vocabulary.

4 Rollback-Recovery Algorithms Using Agents

We now present the pessimistic message logging scheme using multi-agent for recovery in distributed computing systems. We base on the following assumptions: (1) facilitator agent, information agent, and recovery agent is created with process; (2) an the agent-group always operates during process execution and have no failure. Figure 5 shows data structures using in this paper.

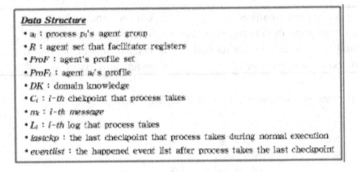

Fig. 5. Data structures

4.1 Basic Algorithm During Failure-Free Operation

An algorithm during failure-free operation consists of multi-agent's registration stage and domain knowledge constructing stage. During failure-free operation, agent group(facilitator agent, information agent, recovery agent) creates with process. And information agent and recovery agent register to facilitator the agent. After registration stage completes, information agent performs to construct domain knowledge by the process' event information. Whenever an event happens at the process stage, facilitator agent monitors it and reports to information agent. Information agent adds the

received event information to domain knowledge using KIF. If more than two events happen, information agent adds their order information to domain knowledge.
Figure 6 shows multi-agent's algorithm during failure-free operation.

```
Facilitator Agent FA;
  Created with process p; ;
    R ← Ø;
    ProF ← Ø;
    if receive register message from a; then
      if ( a; ∉ R ) then
        R ← R ∪ { a; };        ProF ← ProF ∪ { ProF; };
      fi;
      send ack message to a;
    fi;
  Do
    if receive system message from process p; then
      translate system message to KQML;
      send addDK_request message to IA;
    fi;
  oD;

Information Agent IA;
  Created with process p; ;
  Do
    send register message to FA; ;
    receive ack message from FA; ;
    if receive addDK_request message from FA; then
      translate addDK_request message to KIF;
      add KIF to DK;
    fi;
  oD;
```

Fig. 6. Basic algorithm during failure-free operation

4.2 Rollback-Recovery Algorithm after a Failure

When a process p recovers from a failure, multi-agent executes rollback-recovery algorithm as presented in figure 7. Facilitator agent monitors process' recovery and requests to perform recovery procedure to a recovery agent. Recovery agent, which receives recovery request message, requests to find the last checkpoint information to the information agent. Information agent finds last checkpoint information at domain knowledge and returns it to the recovery agent. After receiving the last checkpoint information, the recovering agent requests subsequence events list to information agent. Information agent that received new request extracts events list at domain knowledge and returns the result to the recovery agent. When recovery agent receives events list message from information agent, rollbacks the own process to the last checkpoint and sends request messages to replay events in events list to the other facilitator agents.

4.3 Example

Figure 9 shows the domain knowledge and KQML message contents for the execution
in figure 8.

```
Facilitator Agent FA;
  Do
    if receive recovery_request message from FA; then
      send lastckp_request message to IA;
      if receive lastckp_reply message from IA; then
        send eventlist_request message to IA;
        if receive eventlist_reply message to RA; then
          decide rollback_point;
          send rollback_request to p;
          send replay_request to F;
          receive ack_message to p;
        fi;
      fi;
    fi
  oD;


Recovery Agent RA;
  Do
    if receive recovery_request message from FA; then
      send lastckp_request(msg, IA;) message to FA;
      wait lastckp_reply(msg, RA;) message from FA;
      if receive lastckp_reply(msg, RA;) message from FA; then
        send eventlist_request(msg, IA;) message to FA;
        wait eventlist_reply(msg, RA;) message to FA;
        if receive eventlist_reply(msg, RA;) message to FA; then
          decision rollback_point;
          send rollback_request(msg, p;) to FA;
          send replay_request(msg, F;) to FA;
          wait ack_message(ack, p;) to FA;
          receive ack_message(ack, p;) to FA;
        fi;
      fi;
    fi
  oD;


Information Agent IA;
  Do
    if receive lastckp_request message to IA; then
      find last_checkpoint from DK;
      translate last_checkpoint KIF to KQML;
      send lastckp_reply message to RA;
    fi;
    if receive eventlist_request message to IAl then
      find eventlist after last_checkpoint from DK;
      translate eventlist KIF to KQML;
      send eventlist_reply message to RA;
    fi;
  oD;
```

Fig. 7. Rollback recovery algorithm after a failure

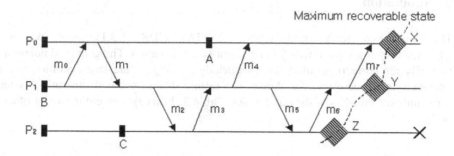

Fig. 8. Example execution

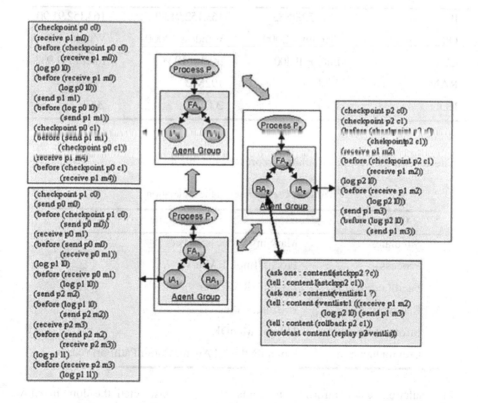

Fig. 9. Domain knowledge and KQML messages example

5 Simulation

The multi-agent code was written in JAVA(JDK 1.3.1). And we used CORBA(VisiBroker for Java 4.5.1) for agent communication. The goal of simulation is to verify the correctness of domain knowledge during failure-free operation and to operate rollback-recovery procedure after a failure. The distributed computing system for simulation consists of the three nodes. Table 3 shows system environment of each node.

Table 3. System environments

	P0	P1	P2
IP	163.152.91.82	163.152.91.89	163.152.91.90
OS	Windows 2000	Windows 2000	Windows 2000
CPU	Intel P-II 400	Intel P-III 900	Intel P-III 933
RAM	256MB	192MB	192MB
HDD	13GB	20GB	20GB

The classes used in the simulation represent in table 4.

Table 4. Used classes in the simulation

Component	Class name
Simulator	ManSim, ProcessServer
Process	ProcessImpl, FAServer
Facilitator Agent	FAImpl, RAServer
Recovery Agent	RAImpl, IAServerl
Information Agent	IAImpl, ManDK
Communication	CommPathWithAgent, CommPathForProcess

In simulation result, information agents correctly constructed the domain knowledge by using the process' event information during failure-free operation. Figure 10 shows domain knowledge that process p2's information agent construct.

After a failure, a recovery agent performed rollback-recovery procedure through cooperating with information agents. Therefore a recovery agent rollbacks to the last checkpoint and requests replaying events, which happens after the last checkpoint, to other facilitator agents. Figure 10 shows recovery agent's replaying request KQML message.

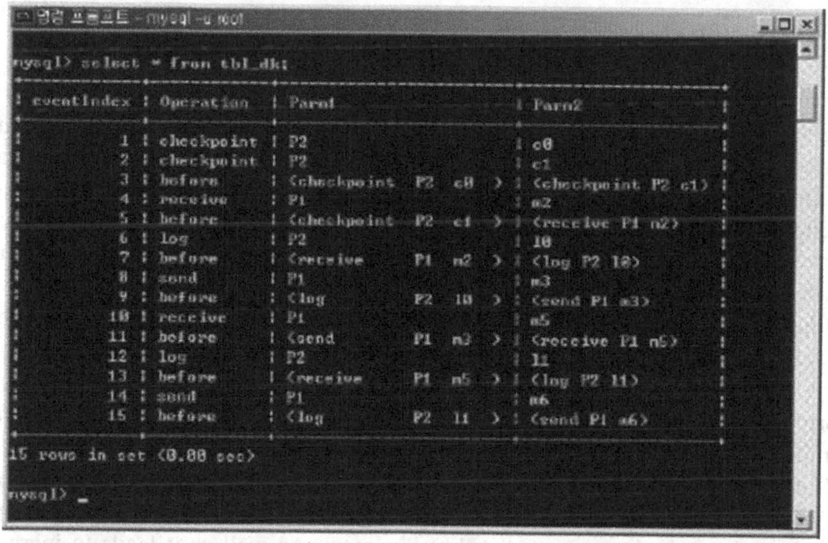

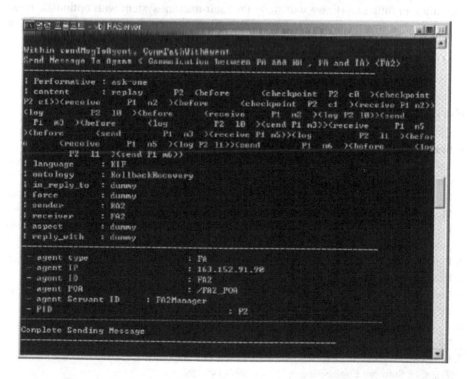

Fig. 10. Domain knowledge constructing by an information agent

Fig. 11. Replaying request KQML message of a recovery agent

6   Conclusion

Previous rollback-recovery protocols depended on inherent communication and operating system, which reduced computing performance in distribute computing system. In order to separate the recovery protocol from inherent communication and operating system we propose rollback-recovery protocol that does not depend on the operating system using multi-agent. In this paper, we defined recovery agent that performs rollback-recovery protocol after a failure, information agent that constructs domain knowledge as a rule of fault tolerance, information during failure-free operation, and a facilitator agent that controls communication of agents. Also we proposed rollback-recovery protocol using multi-agent and simulated rollback-recovery protocol using JAVA and agent communication language in CORBA environment. Rollback-recovery algorithm using agent relieves the reduction of process performance and offers fault-tolerance independent of operating system. Also, fault tolerance functionality is layered at different layer that does not depend on application layer in the distributed computing system. As layer of fault tolerance protocol coincides with the concept of micro kernel that is the core of distributed system. As well as it leads to increasing portability and expansibility of fault-tolerance protocol.

In this paper, we performed rollback-recovery using pessimistic message logging algorithm. In future work, we will study the fault-tolerant system with optimistic message logging protocol or causal message logging protocol based on the multi-agent system.

References

1. B. Bhargava, S. R. Lian : Independent Checkpointing and Concurrent Rollback for Recovery - An Optimistic Approach, In Proceedings of the Symposium on Reliable Distributed Systems (1988) 3-12
2. E. N. Elnozahy, D. B. Johnson, Y. M. Wang, : A Survey of Rollback-Recovery Protocols in Message Passing Systems, CMU Technical Report CMU-CS-99-148 (1999)
3. E. N. Elnozahy : Manetho: Fault tolerance in distributed systems using rollback-recovery and process replication, Ph. D. Thesis, Rice University (1993)
4. Finin T., Fritzson R., Mckay D., McEntire R. : KQML as an agent communication language, Proc. of CIKM '94 (1994) 126-130
5. Genesereth M., Fikes R. : Knowledge interchange format version 3.0 reference manual, Technical Report Logic-92-1, Computer Science Department, Stanford University (1992)
6. L. Alvisi : Understanding the message logging paradigm for masking process crashes, Ph.D. Thesis, Department of Computer Science, Cornell University (1996)
7. L. Alvisi, K. Marzullo : Message Logging: Pessimistic, Optimistic, Causal and Optimal, IEEE Trans. on Software Engineering, Vol. 24 (1998) 149-159
8. L. Lamport : Time, Clocks and the Ordering of Events in a Distributed System, Communications of the ACM, 21 (1978) 558-565

9. R. Koo and S. Toueg : Checkpointing and rollback-recovery for distributed systems, IEEE Trans. on Software Engineering, Vol. SE-13, No. 1 (1987) 23-31
10. R.D. Schlichting and F.B. Schneider : Fail-stop processors: an approach to designing fault-tolerant distributed computing systems", ACM Transactions on Computer Systems 1 (1985) 222-238

An Order-Based, Distributed Algorithm for Implementing Multiparty Interactions

José Antonio Pérez, Rafael Corchuelo, David Ruiz, and Miguel Toro

Universidad de Sevilla, Dpto. de Lenguajes y Sistemas Informáticos
Avda. de la Reina Mercedes, s/n. Sevilla 41.012 (Spain)
jperez@lsi.us.es, www.lsi.us.es/~tdg

Abstract. Multiparty interactions have been paid much attention in recent years because they provide the user with a useful mechanism for coordinating a number of entities that need to cooperate in order to achieve a common goal. In this paper, we present an algorithm for implementing them that is based on the idea of locking resources in a given order. It improves on previous results in that it can be used in a context in which the set of participants in an interaction cannot be known at compile time, and setting up communication links amongst interaction managers is costly or completely impossible.

Keywords: Multiparty interactions, coordination algorithms, open systems, α–core.

1 Introduction

Since Hoare's work on communicating sequential processes [Hoa85], interactions have become a fundamental feature in many languages for distributed computing. Often, they are biparty because they do only involve two entities that need to synchronise before exchanging data, but this concept can be easily extended to an arbitrary number of entities that need to agree and cooperate to achieve a common goal. These interactions are usually said to be multiparty, and they provide a higher level of abstraction because they allow to express complex cooperations as atomic units.

A taxonomy of languages offering linguistic support for multiparty interactions can be found in [JS96], and one of the most recent ones is IP [FF96]. It has also attracted the attention of the designers of the well–known Catalysis method [DW99], which is a next generation approach for the systematic UML–based, business–driven development of component–based systems. Catalysis has been used by Fortune 500 companies in fields including finance, telecommunication, insurance, manufacturing, embedded systems, process control, flight simulation, travel and transportation, or systems management, thus proving the adequacy of this novel interaction model in so different application domains.

In this paper, we present an algorithm that deals with the multiparty synchronisation problem. Our solution improves on others in that it does not require the set of entities participating in an interaction to be defined at compile time,

F. Arbab and C. Talcott (Eds.): COORDINATION 2002, LNCS 2315, pp. 250–257, 2002.

there is no need for communication links amongst interaction managers, and entities are not directly dependent on each other, which makes our solution suited for open contexts.

The organisation of the paper is as follows: the interaction model we deal with is presented in Section 2; the algorithm is presented in Section 3; we glance at other author's work in Section 4, and finally, our main conclusions are drawn in Section 5.

2   The Multiparty Interaction Model in a Nutshell

In this section, we introduce the main features of the multiparty interaction model we deal with. It is quite usual in the languages described in [JS96], being the only difference that the identity of the entities that can participate in an interaction is only known at run time. We think that this feature makes the model more general and introduces a number of problems that have not been addressed by other authors.

In this context, the terms *entity* or *participant* refer to any computing artifact that is able to perform local computations and decides autonomously when it is interested in participating in a number of interactions. Multiparty interactions are usually provided as guards in multi-choice commands, so that an entity may be willing to participate in several interactions at the same time, although only one shall be finally executed. This model is thus well-suited to coordinate processes, threads, objects or components, as well.

Each interaction is identified by an *interaction name*, and has a fixed number of participants referred to as its *cardinality*. Often, we refer to interactions with cardinality n as n–party interactions. In general, n can be assumed to be greater or equal than two, although the results we show work well with single-party interactions. For an n–party interaction to become *enabled*, n participants need to be *offering participation* in it. Once several entities have been coordinated, communication depends completely on the constructs provided by the language under consideration, but most have been designed so that it is relatively easy to determine data communication requirements.

Roughly speaking, a multiparty interaction can be viewed as a set of data exchange actions that need to be executed jointly and coordinatedly by a number of entities, each of which must be ready to execute its own action so that the interaction can occur. An attempt to participate in an interaction delays an entity until all other participants are available, and after an interaction is executed, the participating entities exchange some data and continue their local computations on their own accord.

It is worth noting that an interaction being enabled does not amount to its execution. Figure 1 depicts a simple system composed of four participants, a two–party interaction and a three–party interaction. Notice that participant P_1 is offering participation in I_1, whereas P_3 and P_4 are offering participation in I_2, and P_2 is offering participation in either I_1 or I_2. This means that these interactions cannot be executed simultaneously and they are said to be *conflicting ones.* Thus an election needs to be held to decide which one should be executed. The one that is executed is referred to as the *winner interaction* and the other as the *loser interaction.*

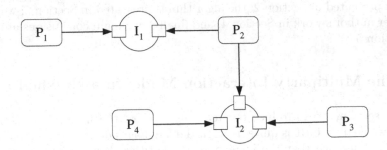

Fig. 1. A system composed of four participants and two conflicting interactions.

3   Our Proposal: α–core

In this section we present a brief description of our algorithm. Its full formal description including correctness proof, as well as a performance analysis and a performance comparison with other proposals can be obtained from the authors.

We call our algorithm α–core, because it is the core of a more general algorithm that we called α. An overview of the α algorithm can be found at [PCRT02]. The α–core algorithm has been devised to detect enabled interactions and select as many as possible amongst conflicting ones in a simple, effective way. It considers an entity that offers participation in more than one interaction as a *shared resource* amongst a number of coordinators responsible for managing those interactions. For an interaction to be executed, its corresponding coordinator must ensure exclusive access to all of its participants, i.e., coordinators must compete for their shared participants so that they can execute the interaction they manage.

We assume that each entity participating in an interaction runs independently from each other, and that each interaction is managed by a different independent *coordinator*. The communication between coordinators and participants is modeled by means of *asynchronous messages* because this communication primitive is available on almost every platform.

The overall picture of the main ideas behind α–core may be sketched by means of a simple example. Figure 2 shows a typical scenario for the system depicted in Figure 1, and Table 1 describes the messages α–core uses. We only need to make three assumptions about the underlying message passing system: (i) every message must be received sooner or later, (ii) messages sent from the same origin to the same destination must be processed in the same order they were sent, and (iii) messages are stored in a FIFO queue until they are processed.

Table 1. Messages used by α–core.

Message	Description
ACKREF	Message sent from a coordinator to acknowledge it has got a REFUSE message from a participant.
LOCK	Message sent from a coordinator to a shared participant to request exclusive access to it.
OFFER	Message sent from a participant to a number of coordinators to offer them participation in the interactions they manage.
OK	Message sent from a participant to a coordinator to notify that it grants it exclusive access. This message is sent as a reply to a LOCK message.
PARTICIPATE	Message sent from a participant to only one coordinator to inform it that it is only interested in the interaction it manages.
REFUSE	Message sent from a participant to a coordinator to cancel an offer.
START	Message sent from a coordinator to a locked participant to notify it that the interaction it manages may start.
UNLOCK	Message sent from a coordinator to a shared participant to release exclusive access.

In this scenario, P_1 is the first entity ready to participate in I_1. Since it is only interested in this interaction, it notifies its offer to coordinator I_1 by means of a *PARTICIPATE* message, and then waits for a *START* message before beginning the execution of this interaction. Assume that P_2 gets then ready to participate in either I_1 or I_2. Since it offers participation to more than one coordinator, it sends two *OFFER* messages by means of which the coordinators that receive them can infer that this participant is shared with others, although they need not know each other directly.

As soon as coordinator I_1 receives the offers from its two participants, it detects that I_1 is enabled and tries to lock P_2 by sending it a *LOCK* message. There is no need to lock P_1 because this participant is interested in only one interaction; thus it is not a shared participant. Assume that P_3 and P_4 decide then to participate in I_2 and send a *PARTICIPATE* message to its coordinator. It then detects that it is also enabled, and tries to lock P_2, too.

Unfortunately, the *LOCK* message sent to P_2 by I_1 is received before the *LOCK* from I_2 arrives. Thus, P_2 notifies I_1 that it accepts to be locked by means of an *OK* message, but it does not acknowledge the lock message received later from coordinator I_2, but records it, just in case I_1 cannot be executed. Coordinator I_2 waits until it gets an answer from P_2 before going on, thus it cannot lock a participant if another lock is still pending. When I_1 receives the *OK* message, it knows that it has exclusive access to its shared participant, and thus sends a *START* message to P_1 and P_2. When the shared participant P_2 receives the *START* message from I_1, it knows that it can execute that

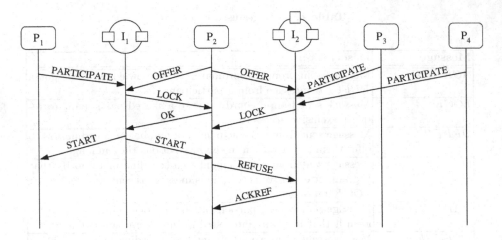

Fig. 2. A possible scenario for the system in Figure 1.

interaction and cancels the offer made to I_2 by sending it a $REFUSE$ message that is acknowledged by means of an $ACKREF$ message.

Therefore, the idea behind α–core consists of locking shared participants, and an interaction may be executed as long as its corresponding coordinator has acquired exclusive access to all of its shared participants. The problem is that locks need to be carried out carefully in order to avoid deadlocks. We use an idea proposed in [EGCS71]: α–core assumes that coordinators may sort their participants according to a given immutable property, e.g., their net address, their Universally Unique Identifier (UUID) [Rog97] or their Universal/Uniform Resource Identifier (URI) [BLFM98], so that lock attempts are made in increasing order. This idea was proven not to produce deadlocks and it is quite effective.

At a first glance, one might think that a solution to the leader-election problem [FF96] suffices to select amongst conflicting coordinators, but it is not enough because the set of conflicting interactions is not static, but changes as new conflicting interactions become enabled. Another key point is that we do not want coordinators to know each other in order to make our solution suitable for open systems, but usual solutions to the leader-election problem, e.g., organising entities in rings, would require neighbouring coordinators to know each other.

4   Related Work

Several solutions to implement multiparty interactions have been proposed. For instance, the simplest one was presented in [FF96], and it consists of using a central manager responsible for all interactions. Each participant sends it a *ready* message when it arrives at a point where it needs to coordinate its activities with others, and the manager uses a counter per interaction to determine when they become enabled on reception of a ready message. If several ones become enabled by the same *ready* message, a random variable may be used to select amongst them. Although this algorithm may be suitable for certain systems, the concerns of performance and reliability argue for a distributed solution.

The first algorithms for distributed coordination were produced in the context of CSP, and were restricted to two–party interactions. Later, the problem of multiparty interactions became of great interest, and Chandy and Misra [CM88] developed two algorithms that became the basis of Bagrodia's algorithm [Bag89]. Currently, this algorithm is one of the most cited in this field.

Bagrodia presented a distributed version of the basic centralised algorithm called EM that uses a number of interaction managers, each one responsible for managing a subset of interactions. When a participant wants to participate in a number of interactions, it sends *ready* messages to the corresponding managers, that have to coordinate in order to achieve mutual exclusion of conflicting interactions. In this case, mutual exclusion is achieved by means of a circulating token that allows the manager having it to execute as many non–conflicting interactions as possible.

Having a circulating token has several drawbacks because it amounts to additional network load, even if no interaction is enabled. The token also needs to circulate amongst managers in a given order, thus organising them in a unidirectional ring, which may lead to a situation in which a manager can never execute one of the interactions it is responsible for because it never gets to have the token at the right time.

In α–core, there is a coordinator, i.e., a manager, per interaction and the exclusion is achieved by looking participants in a given order. In [ECCS71], this idea was proven to be correct and that it does not produce deadlocks. α–core also reduces the possibility of an interaction never being executed because when a participant is in the $LOCKED$ state and it is unlocked by a coordinator, it selects the next prospective winner coordinator randomly, thus introducing some variability in the exclusion problem. In addition, α–core does not require the set of participants to be known in advance, which is an interesting feature because it allows our algorithm to be used in open systems.

A modified version of the basic algorithm was also presented in [Bag89]. It was called MEM, and it combines the synchronisation technique used in EM with the idea of using auxiliary resources to arbitrate between conflicting interactions. The exclusion problem is solved by mapping the multiparty interaction problem onto the well-known dining philosophers problem or onto the drinking philosophers problem [CM84]. In this extension, conflicting managers are considered to be philosophers that need to acquire a single fork placed between them in mutual exclusion. The fork is then a shared resource whose acquisition guarantees mutual exclusion amongst conflicting interactions. A difficulty arises in MEM because between enablement detection and acquisition of forks, a conflicting interaction may have started executing. The complex part of MEM is the way it uses the information communicated during the mutual exclusion to detect that an enablement is no longer current.

MEM has an important drawback because the number of forks a manager has to acquire to guarantee mutual exclusion increases as the number of conflicting interactions increases. This implies that the probability of acquiring all the forks decreases accordingly. In α–core, there is no need for virtual resources. Instead shared processes are considered to be resources that coordinators need to acquire. Thus, the probability of gaining mutual exclusion decreases as the number of shared participants increases, but, in general, this is less problematical because most practical multiparty interactions are three– or four–party. Interactions with a higher cardinality are not usual, but, even in those cases, there is an upper, small bound on the maximum number of shared participants.

Both EM and MEM need managers to know each other, which may be considered a drawback in open systems where new interactions may become available unexpectedly. In [JS98], another algorithm that does not use interaction managers and also deals with fairness concerns was recently presented. Unfortunately, participants also need to know each other at compile time and, thus, that algorithm is not applicable to open systems.

In a chapter of [CRT+99], we presented a previous solution to implement multiparty interactions that also had coordinators, and a central scheduler responsible for selecting amongst conflicting ones. Although this solution was suitable for some problems in the traffic control area, the central conflict resolutor is problematical in the general case.

Currently, we are using α–core to implement a run–time system for supporting the Aspect–Oriented language $\mathcal{CAL}$ [PCRT01,CPT00], which is aimed at increasing the level of abstraction of a program by considering the concurrent behaviour of components as an aspect where multiparty interactions are the sole means for synchronisation and communication.

5   Conclusions and Future Work

The multiparty interaction model captures three main issues in the design of distributed systems: synchronisation, communication and exclusion. In this paper, we have presented a solution to implement this interaction model, but we have not addressed the problem of communication because this feature is tightly coupled with the language we are using.

A variety of solutions exist in the literature, and ours is innovative in the sense that we do not require the set of active entities in a system to be fixed and known in advance. In addition, participating entities or interactions do not depend on each other in our solution, which is an important drawback in other proposals. This way, our solution can be easily applied in open contexts such as Internet applications where multiparty interactions can be used to coordinate an arbitrary number of entities.

The algorithm relies on an idea that was introduced and proven to be correct years ago in the field of operating systems. Although this idea did not work well in this field because resources in an operating system are difficult to sort and usually cannot be requested in increasing order, it has been successfully applied in α–core. Due to the short length of this paper, we could not present our experimental results, but we think that those results are satisfactory, and that our algorithm achieves a good performance.

References

[Bag89]   R. Bagrodia. Process synchronization: Design and performance evaluation
            of distributed algorithms. *IEEE Transactions on Software Engineering*,
            15(9):1053–1065, September 1989.
[BLFM98]   T. Berners-Lee, R. Fielding, and L. Masinter. RFC 2396: Uniform resource
            identifiers (URI): Generic syntax, August 1998.
[CM84]   K.M. Chandy and Jayadev Misra. The drinking philosophers problem.
            ACM Transactions on Programming Languages and Systems, 6(4):632–646,
            October 1984.
[CM88]   K.M. Chandy and J. Misra. *Parallel Program Design: A Foundation.*
            Addison–Wesley, 1988.
[CPT00]   R. Corchuelo, J.A. Pérez, and M. Toro. A Multiparty Coordination Aspect
            Language. *ACM SIGPLAN*, 35(12):24–32, December 2000.
[CRT+99]   R. Corchuelo, D. Ruiz, M. Toro, J.M. Prieto, and J.L. Arjona. *A Dis-
            tributed Solution to Multiparty Interaction*, pages 318–323. World Scientific
            Engineering Society, 1999.
[DW99]   D. F. D'Souza and A.C. Wills. *Objects, Componentes, and Frameworks
            with UML: The Catalysis Approach.* Addison–Wesley, 1 edition, 1999.
[EGCS71]   M.J. Elphick E. G. Coffman and A. Shoshani. System Deadlocks. *Computer
            Surveys*, 3:67–68, June 1971.
[FF96]   N. Francez and I. Forman. *Interacting processes: A multiparty approach to
            coordinated distributed programming.* Addison–Wesley, 1996.
[Hoa85]   C.A.R. Hoare. *Communicating Sequential Processess.* Prentice Hall, 1985.
[JS96]   Y. J. Joung and S. A. Smolka. Strong interaction fairness via randomiza-
            tion. In *Proceedings of the 16th International Conference on Distributed
            Computing Systems*, pages 475–483, Hong Kong, May 1996. IEEE Com-
            puter Society Press.
[JS98]   Y.J. Joung and S.A. Smolka. Strong interaction fairness via randomization.
            IEEE Transactions on Parallel and Distributed Systems, 9(2), February
            1998.
[PCRT01]   J.A. Pérez, R. Corchuelo, D. Ruiz, and M. Toro. A framework for aspect–
            oriented multiparty coordination. In *New Developments in Distributed
            Applications and Interoperable Systems*, pages 161–174. Kluwer Academic
            Publishers, 2001.
[PCRT02]   J.A. Pérez, R. Corchuelo, D. Ruiz, and M. Toro. An enablement detection
            algorithm for open multiparty interactions. In ?, editor, *Proceedings of the
            Symposium on Applied Computing SAC'02*, number ? in ?, page ?, Madrid,
            Spain, March 2002. ?, ? Appearing soon.
[Rog97]   D. Rogerson. *Inside COM.* Microsoft Press, 1997.

Exploiting Transiently Shared Tuple Spaces for Location Transparent Code Mobility

Gian Pietro Picco and Marco L. Buschini

Dipartimento di Elettronica e Informazione, Politecnico di Milano
P.za Leonardo da Vinci, 32, I-20133 Milano, Italy
Phone: +39-02-23993519, Fax: +39-02-23993411
picco@elet.polimi.it, buschini@computer.org

Abstract. Code mobility greatly improves the flexibility of the architecture of a distributed application. However, currently available platforms do not exploit fully the potential of mobile code. For instance, remote dynamic linking of code is often restrained to a well-known site, and applications are prevented from manipulating their own code base.
In this paper, we use the notion of transiently shared tuple space, originally introduced in the LIME coordination model, to overcome these limitations. We allow tuples to contain classes, and tuple spaces become the code base associated to the loading mechanism in the mobile code runtime support. Transient sharing allows for location transparent retrieval of classes, and accommodates changes determined by the reconfiguration of the system, e.g., due to mobility. In doing this, we effectively define a new coordination approach that deals uniformly with code and data.
The presentation is completed by a proof-of-concept prototype, built by extending an existing Java-based mobile code toolkit.

1 Introduction

Code mobility [7] is increasingly considered among the options available to the designer of distributed applications. Mobile code enables run-time component relocation, hence decoupling a component from the location where it is executed. This separation provides several advantages, notably the potential for a better use of communication resources and the enhanced flexibility of the overall system.

Technologies supporting mobile code differ in the mechanisms provided and in the relocation styles supported[1]. However, code mobility is typically exploited to download code from a well-known source, that acts as a code repository, thus providing the ability to extend at run-time a remote executing unit. This solution has proven its validity in several domains, among which the downloading of Web applets from a server to a browser is probably the most popular and best known.

Nevertheless, this solution can be overly limiting in scenarios that are less stable and predictable, like those defined by mobility, and where it is not possible (or not practical) to expect to know statically the location where a code fragment

---

[1] For a survey of technologies, architectures, and applications of code mobility see [7].

F. Arbab and C. Talcott (Eds.): COORDINATION 2002, LNCS 2315, pp. 258–273, 2002.

will be found at run-time. Moreover, most of the middleware exploiting mobile code keeps it behind the scenes. Code relocation happens only as an indirect effect of some system event, like the need to resolve a class that is not found locally. Applications are almost never enabled to manage directly their code base, e.g., by explicitly adding or removing code fragments. Nevertheless, this latter capability is often useful to define code caching schemes.

In this paper, we explore an approach to deal with mobile code that: *i)* does not depend on the presence of one or more code repositories dispersed in the network, rather it enables applications to localize and retrieve code with various degrees of location transparency; *ii)* allows applications to manage explicitly the code fragments that are being relocated within the system.

To achieve this goal, we adopt a coordination perspective rooted in the idea of transiently shared tuple space introduced by LIME [15,13], a middleware that adapts Linda to the domain of physical and logical mobility. In LIME, Linda's notion of a global and persistent tuple space is replaced by a transiently shared tuple space that contains the union of the tuple spaces belonging to the mobile units currently in range, and whose content is dynamically rearranged according to mobility. In this work, we explore the opportunities that arise when the LIME notion of transiently shared tuple space is coupled with mobile code mechanisms. The result is a coordination infrastructure that treats code and data in a uniform way, and enables the coordination of agents not only through the exchange of information, but also by direct manipulation of the agent behavior.

To prove the feasibility of our ideas we implemented a proof of concept prototype that extends the mobile code toolkit μCODE [14] with the ability to dynamically load classes in a location transparent way from a transiently shared tuple space. Nevertheless, it is not our intent to present here a final, full-fledged solution or system. Instead, by eliciting the synergies between coordination models and mobile code, and by showing an implementation path towards their realization, our ultimate goal is to spur further research about this topic.

The paper is structured as follows. Section 2 discusses the motivations of the work we present. Section 3 gives a brief overview of the LIME model. Section 4 discusses the advantages and opportunities disclosed by coupling a transiently shared tuple space with mobile code. Section 5 reports about the design and implementation of our prototype. Section 6 places our paper in the context of related work. Finally, Section 7 discusses ongoing and future work on the topic of this paper, together with some brief concluding remarks.

2   Motivation

Currently available support for mobile code is mostly limited to variations of the well-known class loading mechanism provided by Java[2]. In Java, the class loader is programmable, and allows for redefinition of most of the logic determining

---

[2] Since Java-based mobile code systems are by far the most common, and the systems considered in this paper are Java-based, we often use *class* instead of *code fragment*, although a lot of what follows is applicable also to systems that do not rely on Java.

how a class is retrieved at name resolution time. Systems exploiting mobile code typically specialize the Java class loader by defining alternative ways to retrieve classes, e.g., by downloading them from a specified site. This code on demand [7] approach is the one originally used to support Java applets in Web browsers and is increasingly being exploited also in middleware, e.g., for dynamic downloading of stubs in Java/RMI and Jini. Moreover, it is being exploited in mobile agent platforms, to allow an agent to travel with only a subset of the classes needed, and dynamically download the others on demand.

Unfortunately, in its most common incarnations this approach has at least two relevant drawbacks. First of all, the local *code base*, i.e., the set of classes locally available, is usually accessible only to the run-time support, and hence it remains hidden from the applications. Moreover, remote dynamic linking of code is usually limited to a well-known site acting as a centralized remote code base. In the following, we analyze these two limitations in more detail.

Lack of Dynamic Access to the Code Base. Usually, applications can intervene on the code base only statically, e.g., by specifying the value of the CLASSPATH environment variable. As a consequence, an application cannot query or modify at run-time the set of classes available locally or at a remote site. Nevertheless, this capability turns out to be useful in several situations. For instance, it would open up the ability for dynamic reconfiguration. The current code base could be inspected by a system administrator operating remotely, or even by a mobile agent co-located with the application, and upgraded with code fragments containing new functionality, or replacing obsolete ones.

Moreover, it would enable applications to define code caching schemes. Some amount of caching is already provided in Java-based systems, where the redefined class loader typically maintains a class cache to avoid unnecessary retrieval and definition of class objects already loaded. Nevertheless, the cache is typically filled only at name resolution time, after the bytecode retrieval and class object definition. Again, there is no way to explicitly and dynamically modify the cache content, e.g., by pre-loading classes that are known to be needed in the future.

As an example, imagine a monitoring agent installed on a remote host, e.g., to perform network management. A reasonable design for these systems is to place in the agent the core functionality for reporting data back to a centralized management station and to perform local recovery from some common anomalous situations, and let the agent retrieve on demand the code needed for handling exceptional situations. However, what if the management station determines that network is about to become partitioned, e.g., due to congestion? Access to the agent's code base would allow the management station to upload additional routines on the agent, to cope with the anomalous situation during the period of disconnection, before the latter actually occurs. Similarly, class caching could be beneficial in situations where only weak connectivity is available. For instance, a server communicating with a PDA over an increasingly noisy wireless link may decide to proactively push some of the application classes into the PDA's class cache, instead of letting the PDA download them when needed, and hence possibly during a likely disconnection.

Location-based Dynamic Linking. The other relevant drawback of current approaches to mobile code lies in the pairwise nature of the remote dynamic linking process. As we mentioned, missing classes are usually downloaded from a well-known site. For Web browsers, the site is the Web server from which the page was downloaded. For Java/RMI, it is the Web server whose URL is specified as a code base in the stubs associated to either the source or the target object of a remote method invocation. For mobile agent platforms, it is typically either the source of migration or a centralized code repository like in Aglets [11], Mole [16], or JumpingBeans [6], to cite some among the best known Java-based systems.

Granted, this simple mechanism already allows for unprecented levels of flexibility in deploying the code of a distributed application. Still, it appears to be a limitation in several situations, e.g., when the code repository is not available, when its location cannot be determined in advance, and generally in applications characterized by a high degree of dynamic reconfiguration.

An example is provided by the field of code mobility itself. One of the advantages often claimed in the literature for mobile code is the ability to support disconnected operations [7,9]. In situations where communication with another machine over a network link should be minimized, e.g., because the communication link is noisy, subject to disconnections, expensive, or insecure, mobile code can be exploited to allow the sender to ship application code to the target machine, where it can perform processing on behalf of the sender during disconnection. This idea is brought to an extreme by mobile agents, which allow a whole executing unit (e.g., a thread) to roam autonomously in the network without the need for connectivity towards its sender. Clearly, the aforementioned schemes for dynamic downloading, that are indeed surprisingly a very common choice in mobile code and mobile agent platforms, actually hamper the use of these systems for supporting disconnected operation.

Another setting where location transparent class loading is likely to be key is provided by mobile computing and in particular by mobile ad hoc networks (MANET) [12], which bring network reconfiguration to an extreme by assuming that the fixed infrastructure is totally absent. The fluidity of the MANET environment is such that network functions like routing must be provided by the mobile hosts themselves. Similarly, the application layers usually favor a peer-to-peer architecture over a client-server one, since it is usually difficult to pick a stable spot to place a server. Essentially, the mobile hosts can count only on those resources that are present in the system at a given moment—and code is no exception. As a possible application of location transparent code mobility, imagine a scenario in the automotive application domain, where cars on a highway are part of a MANET. Mobile code could be exploited to propagate in an epidemic way upgrades to car maintenance or monitoring routines, while cars are in range, or even while they are passing in opposite directions.

Nevertheless, even in scenarios where connectivity is permanent and a code repository is always available, alternatives are often preferrable. An application executing at a given site and needing a class to proceed with execution, may actually find it on a site close by or even on the same site, simply because other application components already downloaded it. Similarly, a mobile agent may find out that a needed class is present at a site nearby and either fetch it, or move to that site and link it locally, if fetching is somehow prevented. Linking from a statically determined location is simply too rigid a scheme.

In this work, we provide a way to expose the code base of the executing units belonging to a distributed application, and to couple it with a location transparent class loading mechanism supporting the linking of mobile code. We achieve this goal by building upon an existing coordination model and system called LIME, towards which we now turn our attention before describing in detail our approach in the remainder of the paper.

3   LIME: Linda in a Mobile Environment

The LIME model [15,13] defines a coordination layer for applications that exhibit logical and/or physical mobility, and has been embodied in a middleware available as open source at http://lime.sourceforge.net. LIME borrows and adapts the communication model made popular by Linda [8].

In Linda, processes communicate through a shared *tuple space*, a multiset of tuples accessed concurrently by several processes. Each tuple is a sequence of typed parameters, such as <"foo",9,27.5>, and contains the actual information being communicated. Tuples are added to a tuple space by performing an out(t) operation. Tuples are anonymous, thus their removal by in(p), or read by rd(p), takes place through pattern matching on the tuple content. The argument p is often called a *template*, and its fields contain either *actuals* or *formals*. Actuals are values; the parameters of the previous tuple are all actuals, while the last two parameters of <"foo",?integer,?float> are formals. Formals act like "wild cards" and are matched against actuals when selecting a tuple from the tuple space. For instance, the template above matches the tuple defined earlier. If multiple tuples match a template, selection is non-deterministic.

Linda characteristics resonate with the mobile setting. Communication is implicit, and decoupled in *time* and *space*. This decoupling is of paramount importance in a mobile setting, where the parties involved in communication change dynamically due to migration, and hence the global context for operations is continuously redefined. LIME accomplishes the shift from a fixed context to a dynamically changing one by breaking up the Linda tuple space into many tuple spaces, each permanently associated to a mobile unit, and by introducing rules for transient sharing of the individual tuple spaces based on connectivity.

Transiently Shared Tuple Spaces. A mobile unit accesses the global context only through a so-called *interface tuple space* (ITS), permanently and exclusively attached to the unit itself. The ITS, accessed using Linda primitives, contains tuples that are physically co-located with the unit and defines the only context available to a lone unit. Nevertheless, this tuple space is also *transiently shared* with the ITSs belonging to the mobile units currently accessible. Upon arrival of a new unit, the tuples in its ITS are merged with those, already shared, belonging to the other mobile units, and the result is made accessible through the ITS of each of the units. This sequence of operations, called *engagement*, is performed as a single atomic operation. Similarly, the departure of a mobile unit results in the *disengagement* of the corresponding tuple space, whose tuples are no longer available through the ITS of the other units.

Transient sharing of the ITS is a very powerful abstraction, providing a mobile unit with the illusion of a local tuple space containing tuples coming from all the units currently accessible, without any need to know them explicitly. Moreover, the content perceived through this tuple space changes dynamically according to changes in the system configuration.

The LIME notion of a transiently shared tuple space is applicable to a mobile unit regardless of its nature, as long as a notion of connectivity ruling engagement and disengagement is properly defined. Figure 1 shows how transient sharing may take place among mobile agents co-located on a given host, and among hosts in communication range. Mobile agents are the only active components, and the ones carrying a "concrete" tuple space; mobile hosts are just roaming containers providing connectivity and execution support for agents.

Controlling Context Awareness. The idea of transiently shared tuple space reduces the details of distribution and mobility to changes in what is perceived as a local tuple space. This view is powerful as it relieves the designer from specifically addressing configuration changes, but sometimes applications may need to address explicitly the distributed nature of data for performance or optimization reasons. For this reason, LIME extends Linda operations with location parameters, expressed in terms of agent or host identifiers, that restrict the scope of operations to a given projection of the transiently shared tuple space.

The out$[\lambda](t)$ operation extends out by allowing the programmer to specify that the tuple t must be placed within the tuple space of agent λ. This way, the default policy of keeping the tuple in the caller's context until it is withdrawn can be overridden, and more elaborate schemes for transient communication can be developed. The semantics of out$[\lambda](t)$ involve two steps. First, the tuple t is inserted in the ITS of the agent calling the operation, like in a normal out. If the agent λ is currently connected, t is atomically moved into λ's ITS. Otherwise, the

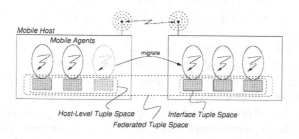

Fig. 1. Transiently shared tuple spaces encompass physical and logical mobility.

"misplaced" tuple t remains within the caller's ITS unless λ becomes connected. In this case, t migrates to λ's ITS as part of the engagement process.

Location parameters are also used to annotate the other operations to allow access to a slice of the current context. For instance, $\mathsf{rd}[\omega, \lambda](p)$ looks for tuples matching p that are currently located at ω but destined to λ.

Reacting to Changes in Context. In the dynamic environment defined by mobility, reacting to changes is a big fraction of application design. Therefore, LIME extends the basic Linda tuple space with a notion of *reaction*. A reaction $\mathcal{R}(s, p)$ is defined by a code fragment s specifying the actions to be performed when a tuple matching the pattern p is found in the tuple space. Details about the semantics of reactions can be found in [15,13]. Here, it suffices to note that two kinds of reactions are provided. *Strong reactions* couple in a single atomic step the detection of a tuple matching p and the execution of s. Instead, *weak reactions* decouple the two by allowing execution to take place eventually after detection. Strong reactions are useful to react locally to a host, while weak reactions are suitable for use across hosts, and hence on the federated tuple space.

4   Transiently Shared Tuple Spaces as Code Bases

Coordination through LIME allows agents to access the global data space provided by the coordinated agents with varying degrees of location transparency, and yet to ignore the details of the system configuration. Nevertheless, similarly to other tuple space approaches, LIME tuple spaces are exploited to contain data, which are typically used either to provide the information necessary for coordination, or to store directly the information of interest for the application.

Instead, in this work we explore a very simple twist to the notion of tuple space. Essentially, we ask ourselves: What can we accomplish by allowing a LIME tuple space to contain classes, and by exploiting it as the code base associated to a class loading mechanism?

While the idea is very simple, its implications are far reaching. To begin with, one of the problems we highlighted in Section 2, namely, the need for abstractions that expose the code base to the application code, finds a natural solution. An agent can now manipulate its own code base through the primitives defined on LIME tuple spaces, since tuples containing classes can be treated just as ordinary data tuples, e.g., allowing class retrieval through pattern matching. Moreover, since a LIME tuple space is permanently and exclusively associated with its agent, when the latter moves its code base migrates along with it. Hence, tuple spaces provide a natural way to represent the code and state associated to a mobile agent, and to deal with the relocation of both in a uniform way.

However, transiently shared tuple spaces push the advantages one step further. Since, as we described, a LIME agent can share its tuple spaces with those belonging to other agents in range, each agent will have access to a code base that is potentially much bigger than its own. Transient sharing effectively stretches the boundaries of an agent code base to an extent possibly covering the whole system at hand. Hence, the agent code base effectively becomes distributed, and its content dynamically and automatically reconfigured according to host connectivity and agent migration, according to the semantics of LIME.

This use of transiently shared tuple spaces solves the other problem mentioned in Section 2. A proper redefinition of the class loader, like the one we describe in Section 5, can operate on the LIME tuple space associated to the agent for which the class needs to be resolved, and query it using the operations provided by LIME. Thus, the class loading mechanism can now resolve class names by leveraging off of the federated code base to retrieve and dynamically link classes in a location transparent fashion, e.g., through a rd, or use location parameters to narrow the scope of searches, e.g, down to a given host or agent.

Nevertheless, the use of transiently shared tuple spaces needs not be confined to the innards of the class loading mechanism. The coordinated agents can be allowed to manipulate directly the tuple spaces holding classes, and representing code bases. In this case, the potential of combining transiently shared tuple spaces and mobile code is fully available for coordination, as LIME operations on the transiently shared tuple space are now available to manipulate the federated code base. Hence, not only can an agent proactively query up to the whole system for a given class, but it can also insert a class tuple into the code base of another agent by using the out[λ] operation, with the semantics of engagement and misplaced tuples even taking care of disconnection and subsequent reconciliation of the federated code base. This new class can then be used by the receiving agent to execute tasks in previously unknown ways, or even to behave according to a new coordination protocol. Blocking operations acquire new uses, allowing agents to synchronize not only on the presence of data needed by the computation, but also on the presence of code needed to perform, or augment, the computation itself. LIME reactive operations add even more degrees of freedom, by allowing agents to monitor the federated code base and react to changes with different atomicity guarantees. Reactions can be exploited straightforwardly to monitor the federated code base for new versions of relevant classes. Replication schemes can be implemented where a new class in an agent's code base is immediately replicated into the code base of all the other agents. The content of an agent's code base can be monitored to be aware of the current "skills" of the agent. The possibilities become endless.

Essentially, by exploiting the notion of transiently shared tuple space for code mobility we are defining an enhanced coordination approach that, besides accommodating reconfiguration due to mobility and providing various degrees of location transparency, enables a new form of coordination no longer limited to data exchange, but encompassing also the exchange of fragments of behavior.

5   Enhancing a Mobile Code Toolkit with Location Transparent Class Loading

To understand what it takes to bring transiently shared tuple spaces into an existing mobile code system, we implemented a proof-of-concept prototype, whose design and implementation[3] is the subject of this section. The prototype extends the functionality of an existing mobile code toolkit by coupling its class loading mechanism with a transiently shared tuple space, and by identifying an appropriate interface for managing the resulting federated code base.

The toolkit we chose to extend is called μCODE [14], and is available at http://mucode.sourceforge.net. The availability of the toolkit as open source was one of the factors driving the choice, together with more pragmatic reasons like the expertise of one of the authors as a developer for both LIME and μCODE, and the fact that the two systems have already been shown to work seamlessly together. Nevertheless, the approach followed here can most likely be adapted to other systems, as discussed later in this section.

We now review briefly the salient characteristics of μCODE, and then discuss how transiently shared tuple spaces holding classes have been integrated into it.

5.1   μCode

μCODE [14] is a lightweight and flexible toolkit for code mobility that, in contrast with most of similar platforms, strives for minimality and places a lot of emphasis on modularity. μCODE revolves around three fundamental concepts: groups, group handlers, and class spaces.

Groups are the unit of mobility, and provide a container that can be filled with arbitrary classes and objects (including thread objects) and shipped to a destination. Classes and objects need not belong to the same thread. Moreover, the programmer may choose to insert in the group only some of the classes needed at the destination, and let the system exploit remote dynamic linking for downloading the missing classes from a target specified at group creation time.

The destination of a group is a μServer, an abstraction of the run-time support. In the destination μServer, the mix of classes and objects must be extracted from the group and used in some coherent way, possibly to generate new threads. This is the task of the *group handler*, an object specified by the programmer at group creation time, which is instantiated in the destination μServer where its operations are automatically invoked. Any object can be a group handler. Programmers can define their own specialized group handlers and, doing so, define their own mobility primitives.

During group reconstruction, the system needs to locate classes and make them available to the group handler. The classes extracted from the group must be placed into a separate name space, to avoid name clashes with classes reconstructed from other groups. This capability is provided by the *class space*. Classes shipped in the same group are placed together in a private class space, associated with that group. However, these classes can later be "published" in a shared class space associated to a μServer, where they become available to all the threads executing in it, as well as to remote ones.

Class spaces play also a role in the resolution of class names. When a class name C needs to be resolved during execution of a thread t managed by a μServer

---

[3] The implementation is included in the public distributions of LIME and μCODE.

S, the redefined class loader of μCODE is invoked to search for C's bytecode by performing the following steps: *i)* check whether C is a *ubiquitous class*, i.e. a class available on every μServer (e.g., system classes); *ii)* search for C in the private class space associated with t in S; *iii)* search for C in the shared class space associated with S; *iv)* if t is allowed to perform dynamic download, retrieve C from the remote μServer specified by the user at migration time, and load C; *v)* if C cannot be found, throw a `ClassNotFoundException`.

Moreover, μCODE provides higher-level abstractions built on the core concepts defined thus far. These abstractions include primitives to remotely clone and spawn threads, ship and fetch classes to and from a remote μServer, and a full-fledged implementation of the mobile agent concept.

5.2   Providing Transiently Shared Class Spaces in μCode

We now discuss in detail the design of our prototype, by highlighting the design choices we made, and the extensions that were required to μCODE. Notably, no modification was required to LIME.

Generalizing the Addressing of Dynamic Link Sources. μCODE supports dynamic linking using a traditional scheme where the address `host:port` of the μServer holding the class is somehow known. Hence, we need to change this address format into one supporting a location transparent scheme. In our prototype, this is achieved by using Uniform Resource Identifiers (URI) [1] instead of arbitrary strings, thus effectively generalizing the way the dynamic link source is specified. The old μCODE format becomes now a URI `mucode://host:port`, while a URI starting with `lime://`, together with the appropriate addressing scheme we describe below, exploits LIME for identifying a location transparent link source, or an appropriate portion of the federated code base.

Incidentally, this effectively decouples the mechanism used to retrieve the missing classes, and thus opens up additional possibilities for dynamic class loading, e.g., loading it from an HTTP connection, or through coordination infrastructures other than LIME.

Generalizing μCODE Class Spaces. Class spaces were introduced in μCODE with the intent of providing the programmer with more flexibility in dealing directly with mobile code, inspired by considerations similar to those presented in Section 2 and 4. By leveraging off transiently shared tuple spaces, we essentially provide a generalization of the class space concept by stretching its boundaries to cover potentially the whole system.

The private class space is unchanged in our prototype, as it is necessary for providing a separate name space for loading classes during group reconstruction. Instead, the shared class space is now defined by a LIME transiently shared tuple space whose tuples may contain classes, in bytecode form, and hence represents a sort of *class tuple space*. By borrowing ideas from the LIME model, we can define the following kinds of class tuple spaces, capturing varying degrees of sharing:

- *Agent class tuple space* (`lime://<lime agent id>/<tuple space name>`). Classes are searched only in the class tuple space of the agent whose LIME identifier is provided. Note that it is different from the private class space, that is not a tuple space and remains hidden from the rest of the system.
- *μServer class tuple space* (`lime://<lime host id>/<tuple space name>`). Classes are searched only in the transiently shared tuple space generated by the agents currently hosted by the μServer.
- *Federated class tuple space* (`lime://*/<tuple space name>`). Classes are searched in the whole transiently shared tuple space.

In the classification above, the format of the URI for each kind of class tuple space is provided. This address can be used to restrict the scope of searches when a class resolution needs to retrieve a missing class through remote dynamic linking. Alternatively, applications may query and manipulate the class tuple space by using LIME operations, by treating class tuples as normal data tuples.

Storing Classes in a μServer. The shared class space of μCODE provided a way to "publish" to the rest of the system some of the classes belonging to a group, and originally in its private space. We now provide this functionality in a much more powerful fashion by using transiently shared tuple spaces.

Nevertheless, shared class spaces also provided a persistency root for classes that was useful in several situations, e.g., to implement class caching schemes. This capability would now be lost, due to the transient nature of the shared tuple space containing the classes: only those classes associated to a running LIME agent would remain available. The solution is to associate a transiently shared tuple space to the μServer. The semantics of LIME forces the `LimeTupleSpace` object representing a transiently shared tuple space to be permanently and exclusively associated to the agent that created it. The μServer must then become also a LIME agent. This is achieved straightforwardly by letting the class `MuServer` implement the `lime.ILimeAgent` interface.

Placing Classes into Tuples. In our scheme, mobile code is transferred by retrieving a tuple containing the class bytecode. A design issue is then how to embed code into a tuple. A straightforward solution is simply to place the byte array containing the bytecode in one of the tuple fields, and use the others to provide information used to match the tuple (i.e., at least the class name), like in `<String name, byte[] bc>`[4]. Different applications may associate different information to the class bytecode, e.g., a version number, certificates, or application-dependent information, and hence define different tuple formats.

Redefining the Class Loader. Last but not least, the loading strategy of the class loader embedded in μCODE must be changed to encompass searches in the transiently shared tuple space.

---

[4] The API of the prototype actually defines a `MarshalledClass` helper class, to overcome the Java limitation about using scalar types (like `byte[]`) in tuple fields.

```
public class DistributedClassSpace extends ClassSpace {
    public boolean containsClass(String className, String uri);
    public void removeClass(String className, String uri);
    public Class getClass(String className, String uri);
    public void getClassByteCode(String className, String uri);
    public void putClassByteCode(String className, String uri);
    public int addClassListener(String name, String uri,
                                ClassListener listener, short mode);
    public void removeClassListener(int id);
}
```

Fig. 2. The class `DistributedClassSpace`. Exception declarations and overloaded methods are omitted for the sake of clarity.

The strategy we adopted is similar to the original one, in that ubiquitous classes are searched first, followed by classes in the private space. Nevertheless, the steps of searching into the shared class space and possibly attempting a remote dynamic linking are now collapsed into a single one. In fact, the shared class space is now stretched to encompass possibly the whole system, and the dynamic link source parameter specifies a scope for searching the class that ranges from the class tuple space of a single agent, finer-grained than the original shared class space, up to the whole federated tuple space[5].

The actual implementation of class retrieval is straightforward, and relies on parsing the URI to determine the parameters to be passed to the LIME operations performing the actual query on the class tuple space.

5.3 Hiding LIME

As we mentioned earlier, the possibility for coordinated agents to access directly the tuple spaces containing the classes is the alternative that leaves more degrees of freedom to the application, and that leverages the most of the uniform access provided by the coordination infrastructure to the application code and state.

Nevertheless, for other applications it might be reasonable to shield the co-ordination infrastructure behind a set of interfaces that hide the details of how classes are retrieved. This latter alternative is surely more constrained. On the other hand, it decouples the API used to access the federated code base from the coordination infrastructure that enables it.

In our prototype, we leveraged off of the class space concept already provided by μCODE. The class `DistributedClassSpace`, shown in Figure 2, specializes `mucode.ClassSpace` and redefines the methods that originally allowed to query the local class space (e.g., `getClass`) to perform the same query on the federated code base using the URI scheme we defined previously. This is the class that holds a reference to the actual transiently shared tuple space containing the code base.

---

[5] Searches can also be restricted to the hosting μServer (i.e., without considering the spaces of co-located agents), by specifying a URI containing the LIME agent identifier associated to the μServer.

Moreover, `DistributedClassSpace` is equipped also with the ability to react to the insertion of a class in the class space. This is accomplished by registering a class listener, implemented using a LIME (weak) reaction. The `mode` parameter allows to specify whether the listener should fire only once, or remain registered to detect the appearance of other classes, until explicitly deregistered.

5.4   Other Considerations

The approach we followed for coupling transiently shared tuple spaces with μCODE was to specialize some of μCODE classes. The task was simplified by the fact that all of the relevant classes, including the class loader, were already publicly accessible—a condition unlikely to hold true in the majority of mobile code systems. Nevertheless, a small number of minor changes, e.g., to allow access to class features originally declared as `final`, indeed required access to the source code.

In principle, the approach we followed can be applied also to other systems, e.g., mobile agent platforms. Several are available, and many are also open source. For instance, this is the case of the Aglets system, whose latest release actually provides a `CacheManager` class as part of the run-time support, that could be exposed to the user to provide functionality similar to μCODE class spaces, and extended with a design similar to the one described in Section 5.3. For applications that do not rely on mobile agents, a custom class loader containing an application-specific loading strategy could also be developed.

As for LIME, no modification was required but a couple of points need further elaboration. First, we relied on an extension of LIME, contained in the current public distribution, that provides the ability to invoke probe operations like `inp` and `rdp` on the whole federated tuple space. In the original LIME model, the use of probes was limited only to the transiently shared tuple space of a given host or agent, in the attempt to retain the atomicity guarantees of probe invocation and yet allow for a practical and efficient implementation. The aforementioned extension strikes a different balance between the two aspects, by lifting the atomicity requirement. Hence, a probe may now execute on the whole federated tuple space, but its (distributed) execution is not atomic, and is then allowed to miss some tuples that might have appeared in the tuple space while the probe was executing. This extension is actually the initial step of a broader ongoing effort by the authors of LIME to weaken the atomicity requirements of the model.

Moreover, the LIME implementation currently requires that threads accessing a tuple space must implement an `ILimeAgent` interface. This means that application threads that want to exploit the mechanisms described here must comply to this requirement, e.g., by subclassing from `StationaryAgent` or `MobileAgent`, or by directly implementing the interface. This is not likely to be a big obstacle for most applications, and surely it was not for the simple applications we used to test our proof-of-concept prototype. However, further experience with our approach may lead us in a different direction, e.g., requiring modifications to the LIME implementation to lift this constraint during accesses to a class loader.

6 Discussion and Related Work

The idea of placing code in a tuple space is already present in the Linda model, where the eval primitive allows for a code fragment to be inserted in the tuple space, and eventually evaluated to produce a new tuple. Other approaches, e.g., PoliS [5] allow tuple spaces to contain rules that, when fired, can modify the tuple space. However, these and other approaches enhance the coordination infrastructure by introducing behavior into it, under the form of tuples containing some form of *"active"* code that is able to modify the tuple space by itself.

Instead, our work takes a different viewpoint where the tuples contain *"passive"* code that cannot be activated by itself and modify the tuple space, rather it is exploited directly by the applications, or indirectly through the class loading mechanism, to augment the functionality of the coordinated agents. Interestingly, in principle the two perspectives are complementary and could be rejoined. Thus, for instance, it could be conceivable to have eval tuples or PoliS rules contain only a subset of the code specifying the active behavior, and let the missing portion be linked dynamically into the tuple by retrieving it from the current content of the tuple space, be it transiently (like in LIME) or permanently shared (like in Linda, PoliS, and other existing approaches).

Existing Java-based tuple space systems surprisingly do not leverage much of mobile code, although they allow Java objects to be contained in tuple fields. For instance, both TSpaces [10] and JavaSpaces [17] allow the coordinated agents to access a remote tuple space using a client-server paradigm. However, TSpaces assumes that the classes for the objects contained in a tuple being transferred between an agent and the tuple space server are found at the latter, thus essentially relying on the default loading strategy of Java[6]. Instead, JavaSpaces provides a more elaborate scheme that is nonetheless location-based. Classes are annotated with the URL of a codebase, usually constituted by a Web server hosted by each JavaSpaces client. This latter mechanism is exploited by Jini [18] to implement a discovery and lookup service, by storing in the tuple space objects representing service proxies. Upon a service request, a reference to these service objects is passed to the client, which can access the service remotely. Since this mechanism is implemented on top of RMI, dynamic linking is triggered when some of the stubs needed for remote invocation are missing on either the client or the server.

With our approach, we are able to provide a similar functionality—and more. First of all, we are able to relocate code separately from objects, and also independently from the immediate need of remote dynamic linking due to name resolution. Moreover, transiently shared spaces eliminate the need to know the location of a lookup server, by allowing queries that are intrinsically location transparent. Actually, the peer-to-peer perspective adopted by LIME, opposed to the client-server architecture exploited by Jini, allows any client to host its own code base and services without the need to register with a lookup server or to rely on a centralized code base, and thus yields an architecture that is inherently more amenable to reconfiguration.

---

[6] A location-based scheme similar to the one described later for JavaSpaces was posted in the TSpaces mailing list, but apparently never made it into the official distribution.

In this presentation, we did not consider security issues, since our focus is in examining the potential of the novel idea of coupling transiently shared tuple spaces and mobile code. In our approach security issues are potentially exacerbated by the fact that now agents are allowed to manipulate each others' code base, and can potentially do this on a system-wide basis. Nevertheless, the mechanisms commonly used for sandboxing in Java-based systems, coupled with well-known techniques based on certificates and public keys should cover most of the needs. Moreover, recent proposals of secure extensions for LIME [4] or other tuple space models [2] are likely to be adaptable to our approach.

Similarly, in this paper we did not address scalability issues. The ability to issue class retrieval requests potentially spanning the whole system surely adds expressive power, but may lead to poor performance. Again, we expect these problems to be dealt with at another level, i.e., by modifying the underlying model and system supporting transiently shared tuple spaces, LIME in this case. As we briefly mentioned earlier, ongoing work by the authors of LIME and by other researchers (e.g., [4,3]) aims at lifting some of the atomicity assumptions of the model, in an attempt to provide a more efficient and scalable implementation.

7   Conclusions and Future Work

Currently available systems do not explore fully the potential of code mobility, in that they support linking schemes where code is dynamically retrieved from a well-known location, and they do not expose the code base to applications. In general, the expressiveness of the abstractions currently available to deal with mobile code is poor if compared to the potential that code mobility may unleash.

In this paper, we presented a different perspective by coupling the idea of transiently shared tuple space, originally introduced in the LIME model, with the mechanisms supporting mobile code. The result is an enhanced model of coordination where the code base, that is indeed exposed to applications, is virtually shared across the whole system and where mobile code is dealt with both in a location aware and location transparent fashion. The fact that code can be treated as data enables the use of the existing coordination primitives and supports a unified treatment of the code and state necessary to coordination.

Future work on this topic will focus on the development of applications and middleware based on the concepts described in this paper, to assess the implications of this model. In particular, an ongoing effort is currently aiming at implementing a Jini-like discovery and lookup service that leverages off of the peculiarity of our coordination infrastructure.

Acknowledgments. The authors wish to thank Amy Murphy for her insightful comments on an early draft of this paper.

References

1. T. Berners-Lee, R. Fielding, and L. Masinter. Uniform Resource Identifiers (URI): Generic Syntax. IETF Network Working Group, RFC 2396, August 1998.

2. C. Bryce, M. Oriol, and J. Vitek. Secure object spaces: A coordination model for agents. In *Proc. of COORDINATION'99*, LNCS 1594, pages 4–20. Springer, 1999.
3. N. Busi and G. Zavattaro. Some Thoughts on Transiently Shared Tuple Spaces. In *Proc. of Workshop on Software Engineering and Mobility, co-located with the 23rd Int. Conf. on Software Engineering (ICSE01)*, May 2001.
4. B. Carbunar, M.T. Valente, and J. Vitek. Lime Revisited—Reverse Engineering an Agent Communication Model. In *Proc. of the 5th Int. Conf. on Mobile Agents (MA 2001)*, LNCS 2240, pages 54–69. Springer, December 2001.
5. P. Ciancarini, F. Franzè, and C. Mascolo. Using a Coordination Language to Specify and Analyze Systems Containing Mobile Components. *ACM Trans. on Software Engineering and Methodology*, 9(2):167–198, April 2000.
6. Ad Astra Engineering. Jumping Beans Web page. http://www.jumpingbeans.com.
7. A. Fuggetta, G.P. Picco, and G. Vigna. Understanding Code Mobility. *IEEE Transactions on Software Engineering*, 24(5):342–361, May 1998.
8. D. Gelernter. Generative Communication in Linda. *ACM Computing Surveys*, 7(1):80–112, Jan. 1985.
9. C.G. Harrison, D.M. Chess, and A. Kershenbaum. Mobile Agents: Are they a good idea? In J. Vitek and C. Tschudin, editors, *Mobile Object Systems: Towards the Programmable Internet*, LNCS 1222, pages 25–47. Springer, April 1997.
10. IBM Research. TSpaces Web page. http://www.almaden.ibm.com/cs/TSpaces.
11. D.B. Lange and M. Oshima, editors. *Programming and Deploying Java Mobile Agents with Aglets*. Addison-Wesley, 1998.
12. M.Corson, J.Macker, and G.Cinciarone. Internet-Based Mobile Ad Hoc Networking. *Internet Computing*, 3(4), 1999.
13. A.L. Murphy, G.P. Picco, and G.-C. Roman. LIME: A Middleware for Physical and Logical Mobility. In *Proc. of the 21st Int. Conf. on Distributed Computing Systems (ICDCS-21)*, pages 524–533, May 2001.
14. G.P. Picco. μCODE: A Lightweight and Flexible Mobile Code Toolkit. In *Proc. of Mobile Agents: 2nd Int. Workshop MA'98*, LNCS 1477, pages 160–171. Springer, September 1998.
15. G.P. Picco, A.L. Murphy, and G.-C. Roman. LIME: Linda Meets Mobility. In *Proc. of the 21st Int. Conf. on Software Engineering (ICSE'99)*, pages 368–377, May 1999.
16. M. Straßer, J. Baumann, and F. Hohl. Mole—A Java Based Mobile Agent System. In M. Mühläuser, editor, *Special Issues in Object-Oriented Programming: Workshop Reader of the 10th European Conf. on Object-Oriented Programming ECOOP'96*, pages 327–334. dpunkt, July 1996.
17. Sun Microsystems. JavaSpaces Web page. http://java.sun.com/products/javaspaces.
18. Sun Microsystems. Jini Web page. http://www.sun.com/jini.

Formal Specification of JavaSpaces™ Architecture Using μCRL*

Jaco van de Pol and Miguel Valero Espada

Centrum voor Wiskunde en Informatica,
P.O. Box 94079, 1090 GB Amsterdam, The Netherlands
{Jaco.van.de.Pol, Miguel.Valero.Espada}@cwi.nl

Abstract. We study a formal specification of the shared data space architecture, JavaSpaces. This Java technology provides a virtual space for entities, like clients and servers, to communicate by sharing objects. We use μCRL, a language that combines abstract data types with process algebra, to model an abstraction of this coordination architecture. Besides the basic primitives write, read and take, our model captures transactions and leasing. The main purpose of the proposed formalism is to allow the verification of distributed applications built under the JavaSpaces model. A simple case study is analyzed and automatically model checked using the μCRL and CADP tool sets.

1 Introduction

It is well known that the design of reliable distributed systems can be an extremely arduous task. The parallel composition of processes with a simple behavior can even produce a wildly complicated system. A distributed application has to face some important challenges: it has to facilitate communication and synchronization between processes across heterogeneous networks, dealing with latencies, partial failures and system incompatibilities. The use of coordination architectures is a suitable way to manage the complexity of specifying and programming large distributed applications.

Re-usability is one of the most important issues of coordination architectures. Once the architecture has been implemented on a distributed network, different applications can be built according to the requirements without any extra adaptation. Programmers implement their systems using the interface provided by the architecture, which consists of a set of primitives or operators.

In this paper we study the JavaSpaces™ [14] technology that is a Sun Microsystems, Inc. architecture based on the Linda coordination language [6]. JavaSpaces is a Jini™ [15] service that provides a platform for designing distributed computing systems. It gives support to the communication and synchronization of external processes by setting up a common shared space. JavaSpaces

---

* Partially supported by PROGRESS, the embedded systems research program of the Dutch organisation for Scientific Research NWO, the Dutch Ministry of Economic Affairs and the Technology Foundation STW, grant CES.5009.

F. Arbab and C. Talcott (Eds.): COORDINATION 2002, LNCS 2315, pp. 274–290, 2002.

is both an application program interface (API) and a distributed programming model. The coordination of applications built under this technology is modeled as a flow of objects. The communication is different from traditional paradigms based on message passing or method invocation models. Several remote processes can interact simultaneously with the shared repository, the space handles the details of concurrent access. The interface provided by JavaSpaces is essentially composed by insertion and lookup primitives. In the following section we present some details of the technology specification.

The goal of our research is to verify the correctness of applications built using JavaSpaces services. Therefore we propose a formal model of the architecture which will allow to prototype these distributed applications. We use the language μCRL [11] to create an operational and algebraic definition of the technology. μCRL is a language based on the process algebra ACP [9], extended with equational abstract data types. Its tool set [1] combined with the CÆSAR ALDÉBARAN DEVELOPMENT PACKAGE (CADP) [8] allows the automatic analysis of finite systems.

This paper is structured as follows. After this introduction, we complete the description of JavaSpaces and we present the μCRL language. We continue with the study of a model of JavaSpaces in the formal language μCRL. Then we present a simple case study showing the main features of the proposed specification and the model checker. Before the conclusions, we provide pointers to some related work. The formal specification and some examples can be found at: "http://www.cwi.nl/~miguel/JavaSpaces/".

2   JavaSpaces

Components of applications built under the JavaSpaces model are "loosely coupled", they do not communicate with each other directly but by sharing information via the common repository. They execute primitives to exchange data with the shared space. Figure 1 presents an overview of the JavaSpaces architecture.

A *write* operation places a copy of an entry into the space. Entries can be located by "associative lookup" implemented by *templates*. Processes find the entries they are interested in by expressing constraints about their contents without having any information about the object identification, owner or location. A *read* request returns a copy of an object from the space that matches the provided *template*, or *null* if no object has been found. If no matching entries are in the space, then *read* may wait a user-specified amount of time (*timeout*) until a matching entry arrives in the space. *ReadIfExists* performs exactly like *read*, but it only blocks if there are matching objects in the space but they have conflicting locks from one or more other transactions. *Take* and *takeIfExists* are the *destructive* versions of *read* and *readIfExists*: once an object is returned, it is removed from the space.

JavaSpaces also provides support to distributed events, leasing and transactions, from the Jini architecture [15]:

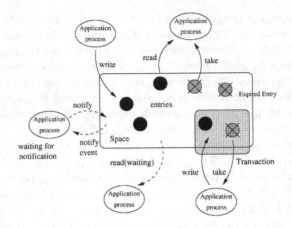

Fig. 1. JavaSpaces architecture overview

JavaSpaces supports a transactional model ensuring that a set of grouped operations are performed on the space atomically, in such a way that either all of them complete or none are executed. Transactions affect the behavior of the primitives, e.g. an object written within a transaction is not externally accessible until the transaction commits, the insertion will never be visible if the transactions aborts. Transactions provide a means for enforcing consistency. Transactions on JavaSpaces preserve the ACID properties: Atomicity, Consistency, Isolation and Durability.

JavaSpaces allocates resources for a fixed period of time, by associating a lease to the resource. The lease model is beneficial in distributed systems where partial failures can produce waste of resources. The space determines the time during which an object can be stored in the repository before being automatically removed. Also transactions are subject to leasing, an exception is sent when the lease of a transaction has been expired. Leases can always be renewed or canceled.

The space manages some distributed events, in particular: a process can inform the space its interest in future incoming objects, by using the *notify* primitive. The space will notify by an event when a matching object arrives to the space. Notification will not be studied in this paper.

To know more about JavaSpaces, please consult the references [10,14].

3   Introduction to µCRL

A µCRL specification is composed by two parts. First, the definition of the data types, called **sorts**. A sort consists of a signature in which a set of function symbols, and a list of axioms are declared. For example, the specification of the booleans (*Bool*) with the conjunction operator (*and*) is defined as follows:

sort   Bool
func   T,F:→Bool

```
map   and: Bool×Bool→Bool
var   b: Bool
rew   and(T, b) = b
      and(F, b) = F
```

The keyword **func** denotes the *constructor* function symbols and **map** is used to declare additional functions for a sort. We can add equations using variables (declared after **rew** and **var**) to specify the function symbols.

The second part of the specification consists of the process definition. The basic expressions are actions and process variables. *Actions* represent events in the system, are declared using the keyword **act** followed by an action name and the sorts of data with which they are parameterized. Actions in μCRL are considered atomic. There are two predefined constants: δ which represents deadlock, and τ which is a hidden action. *Process variables* abbreviate processes, and are used for recursive specifications. *Process operators* define how the process terms are combined. We can use:

- The sequential, alternative and parallel composition (.,+,∥) process operators.
- **sum** ($\sum$) to express the possibility of infinite choice of one element of a sort.
- The conditional expression "if-then-else" denoted $p \lhd b \rhd q$, where b is a boolean expression, p and q process terms. If b is true then the system behaves as p otherwise it behaves like q.

They keyword **comm** specifies that two actions may synchronize. If two actions are able to synchronize we can force that they occur always in communication using the operator ∂_H. The operator τ_I hides enclosed actions by renaming into τ actions. The initial behavior of the system can be specified with the keyword **init** followed by a process term:

System = $\tau_I \partial_H (p_0 \parallel p_1 \parallel ...)$
init System

4   Formal Specification

The μCRL model we propose supports the main features of the JavaSpaces specification introduced in previous sections. The choices made on the implementation of the model try to keep it as compliant as possible with the specification. However, some concepts have been abstracted away trying to keep the model simple and suitable to do model checking.

First we present the architecture from the application point of view focusing on the API, going later into specific details of the implementation.

4.1   Application Point of View

The space is modeled as a single process called *javaspace* (we have not experimented with using multiple spaces). User applications are implemented as external processes executed in parallel with the space. External applications exchange data between them by transferring entries through the shared space. The communication between the *javaspace* process and the external applications is done by means of a set of synchronous actions, derived from the JavaSpaces API. A JavaSpaces system is specified in μCRL as follows:

$$\text{System} = \tau_I \partial_H (javaspace(...) \parallel external\_P_0(id_0 : Nat, ...)$$
$$\parallel external\_P_1(id_1 : Nat, ...) \parallel ...)$$

The arguments of the *javaspace* process represent the current state of the space. They are composed by: stored objects, active transactions, the current time, et cetera... These arguments are explained in detail in the following section.

External processes have unique identification number. They have to add it as parameter to every invocation of a primitive. The space uses this *id* to control the access to the common repository.

Processes use the sort *Entry* to encapsulate the shared data. In the JavaSpaces specification, an entry corresponds to a serializable Java^{TM} object which implements the public interface Entry (with some other restrictions). In our model, entries are represented by a **sort**. Users can define their own data structure according to the application requirements. Data fields, from standard sorts (naturals, booleans,...) or new sorts, and operators can be included. The sort must include the equality (*eq*) function, and the constructor *entryNull* because they are necessary to perform the look up actions. The following code presents the definition of a simple counter:

```
sort    Entry
func    entryNull:→Entry
        counter: Nat→Entry
map     eq: Entry×Entry→Bool
        value:Entry→Nat
        inc:Entry→Entry
var     n,n': Nat
rew     eq(entryNull, entryNull) = T
        eq(counter(n), counter(n')) = eq(n, n')
        eq(entryNull, counter(n)) = F
        eq(counter(n), entryNull) = F
        value(counter(n)) = n
        inc(counter(n)) = counter(S(n))
```

The insertion of an entry into the space is done by means of the *write* action. This primitive is defined as follows:

```
sort    Nat, Entry
act     write: Nat×Entry×Nat×Nat
```

The arguments of the action *write* are: the process identification number, the entry, the transaction identifier and the requested lease. The behavior of the action depends on whether it is executed under a transaction or not. If it is not joined to any transaction, the *transaction id* parameter is equal to 0 or *NULL*, then the insertion is instantaneously updated in the space. In our model there are no possible exceptions thrown during the operation. It means that when a *write* has been executed the entry is successfully inserted. Different *write* invocations will place different objects in the repository, even if the data values are equal. The use of transactions is explained further in the present section.

When a user performs a *write*, he can associate a lease to the entry. An entry is automatically removed from the space when its lease expires. A lease is a natural number from 0 to *FOREVER*. The null value (0) means that the entry is deleted at the same unit of time that it is placed in the space. The *FOREVER* value says the entry will never be removed. Our model differs from the JavaSpaces specification because the lease requested is always granted by the space and it cannot be canceled or renewed.

An example of *write* invocation in which the application process inserts a null counter in the space without transaction and leased for one time tick, is defined as follows:

proc   p(id:Nat) =
        ...
        .write(id, counter(0), NULL, S(0))
        ...

Look up primitives could be classified not destructive and non destructive, depending on whether the item is removed or not after the execution of the action, and in *blocking* and *non-blocking* depending on whether the process waits until it receives the requested item. We can invoke destructive look ups (*take*) or non-destructive (*read*), setting up the time during which the action blocks.

The JavaSpaces specification says that a look up request searches in the space for an Entry that matches the template provided in the action. If the match is found, a reference to a copy of the matching entry is returned. If no match is found, *null* is returned. We don't use templates to model the matching operation but by adding to every invocation one predicate, as argument, which determines if an Entry matches or not the action. This predicate belongs to the **sort** *Query*, defined by the user according to the specification of the *Entry*. The sort must include the operator *test* used to perform the matching.

Let's see an example of Query **sort** that has two possible queries: *any* that will match any entry in the space and *equal* that match any entry with a data field, accessed via the operator *value*, is equal to a given parameter:

sort   Query
func   any: →Query
          equal: Nat→Query
map   test: Query×Entry→Bool
var   e: Entry
          n: Nat
rew   test(any, e) = T
          test(equal(n), e) = eq(n, value(e))

An entry of the space will match a look up action if it satisfies the associated query, as indicated by the *test* predicate.

There are implemented four look up primitives: *read*, *take*, *readIfExists* and *takeIfExists*. All of them take the following arguments: process identification number, transaction identification number, timeout and query.

The execution of a look up primitive is done by means of two atomic actions. First the external process invokes the primitive (*read*, *take*, ...), then the space communicates the result of the request by returning a matching entry if the operation was successfully performed or an *entryNull* if the timeout has expired and no objects satisfied the query.

The μCRL specification of the actions is:

sort Nat, Entry, Query
act   read, take, readIfExists,takeIfExists: Nat×Nat×Nat×Query
         Return:Nat×Entry

Let's see an example program using the *take* operation, which request any entry of the space and blocks for one time step:

proc p(id:Nat) =
         ...
         .take(id, NULL, S(0), any)
         .($\sum_{e:Entry}$ Return(id, e)
             .(...◁ not(eq(e, entryNull)) ▷...))
         ...

The behavior of the four primitives depends on how the space is updated after the action (whether the entry is removed or not), and whether the action performs a test of presence (if there are matching objects with conflicting locks). The behavior is different if the actions are executed under a transaction.

In our model the instantiation of a transaction is done by the action *create*, which has the arguments: process identification number, transaction identification number (assigned by the space), and lease. The space allocates a new resource and returns to the user the identification number of the created transaction. Once the transaction has been created, operations join to it by passing its *id* number to the primitives.

A transaction can complete by the explicit actions *commit* and *abort*, or by being automatically aborted when its lease expires. If the last case happens the space informs to the creator of the transaction the expiration of the transaction by "sending an exception". We model the exceptions by a communication action called *Exception* parameterized with the *id* of the transaction and the *id* of the process to whom the exception is directed to. If a process creates a transaction it has to add the possibility of receiving an exception on all the actions executed until the commitment of the transaction.

In our model, we restrict to the case that a transaction can only be used by a single process. Only the creator can join primitives and receives the timeout exception. The following example shows how the transaction model can be used in external processes:

act   create: Nat×Nat×Nat

        commit, abort, Exception:Nat×Nat

proc p(id:Nat) =

    ...

    $\sum_{trc:Nat}$ (create(id, trc, S(0))

    .(write(id, ..., trc, ...) + Exception(id, trc).*handle_actions*)

    .(take(id, ..., trc, ...) + Exception(id, trc).*handle_actions*)

    .(commit(id,trc) + Exception(id, trc).*handle_actions*))

      or

    .(abort(id, trc) + Exception(id, trc).*handle_actions*))

    ...

The Jini's transaction model has been simplified, for example our model doesn't support nested transactions or transactions over multiple processes.

Transactions make changes on the semantics of the primitives, e.g. when a *write* action is performed under a transaction, the entry will be externally visible only after the transaction commits, if the transaction is aborted no changes will be updated in the space. If a process inserts an entry under a transaction, and meanwhile another process executes a *readIfExists*, the second process blocks waiting for the commitment of the transaction (or for the timeout), if the entry is the only in the space that satisfies the query.

We have introduced the main features of the specification. Although all the JavaSpaces services have not been implemented, the proposed framework is suitable to model and verify many interesting JavaSpaces applications. Now let's present some details about the space implementation.

4.2   Implementation Point of View

The *javaspace* process handles the concurrent access of the external applications to the common repository. It manages a data base storing the shared entries, the active transactions, and other data structures like pending actions. The process has also to manage some timeouts of leased resources.

To support leasing and the timeouts, the space has to deal with the notion of "time". We propose the implementation of a centralized clock. This is appropriate, because in reality a Javaspace server has a centralized implementation, in multiple JavaSpaces each space would have its own clock. There is no clock synchronization between the space process and the external applications, so we have not made any assumption about the relative speed of the processes.

The clock is implemented by a discrete counter. More than one service can be processed in the same time unit. So between two units the *javaspace* process can treat several communication primitives. Externally we can say several actions are performed in parallel (in the sense of interleaving).

The *javaspace* process increments arbitrarily a counter that determines the duration of time from the startup of the system to the present state. The μCRL tool set can only analyze finite instances of the specification so we have to limit the time duration of the system. For this reason we use a constant which indicates after how many time steps the system must halt. The process will run from 0 to *FOREVER* clock ticks.

map FOREVER:→Nat
rew FOREVER = S(...S(0))

Now, we are going to analyze the most important issues of the specification of *javaspaces*.

In the first part of the specification we define a number of standard data types which will allow us to define more complex structures. We can find at the top of the specification the sorts: booleans (*Bool*) and naturals numbers (*Nat*) with their usual operations. The declaration of the sort *Bool* must be included in every μCRL specification because booleans are used for modeling the guards in the "if-then-else" construction. The *Bool* specification has been presented in Section 3. Naturals have two constructors: *0* for the null value and *S(n)*, for the successor of a natural.

Entries are internally encapsulated in the *Object* sort, which includes the entry, the requested lease and an identification number. The space automatically assigns a fresh *id* to every new entry. The signature of the *Object* sort is defined as follows:

sort   Object
func   object: Nat×Entry×Nat→Object
map   eq: Object×Object→Bool
           id:Object→Nat
           entry:Object→Entry
           lease:Object→Nat

Objects are stored in a data base that has the structure of a set. The *javaspace* process manages this data base by inserting, removing and looking up entries. The entries are organized without any order, so when the space executes a search action, all of the matching entries have the same possibility to be selected.

The data base is defined by the *ObjectSet* sort. It has two constructors the *emO* that creates a new empty set and *in* that inserts an object in a set. It has other operators to locate entries, remove, compare et cetera...

When the space receives an external invocation of a *write*, it creates a new *object* and it inserts it in the set. The following fragment of code corresponds to a *write* action without transaction.

proc   javaspace(t:Nat, M:ObjectSet,..., objectsIDs:Nat,...) =
           ...
           +
           $\sum_{processID:Nat}(\sum_{e:Entry}(\sum_{trcID:Nat}(\sum_{lease:Nat}($
           Write(processID, e, trcID, lease)
           .javaspace(t, in(object(objectIDs, e, plus(lease,t)),M),..., S(objectIDs),...)
           ◁
           and(eq(trcID, NULL),...)
           ▷ δ))))
           + ...

In the code, M represents the object set, t is the current time, and *objectIDs* is a counter used to assign a fresh *id* to every new entry.

Regarding the look up primitives: when the space receives a search request first it creates a *pending action*. A *pending action* includes: the *id* of the process that executed the primitive, the type (*read, take, ...*), the transaction *id*, the time the process wants to block and the query. The *pending actions* are stored in a set of the sort *ActionSet* whose definition is similar to the object set's one.

If there is an object that matches one of the pending actions then the space returns the entry to the corresponding external process by means of the *return* action. An entry matches an action if the execution of the *test* operation of the associated query returns true. If there is a pending action with an expired timeout the space returns the *entryNull* Figure 2 shows how this mechanism works.

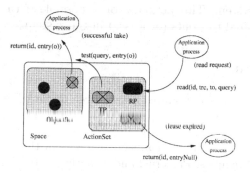

Fig. 2. Look up mechanism

We can see below the sort that defines a transaction:

sort   Transaction
func   transaction: Nat×Nat×ObjectSet×ObjectSet×ObjectSet→Transaction
map   eq: Transaction×Transaction→Bool
       id:Transaction→Nat
       timeout:Transaction→Nat
       Wset, Rset, Tset:Transaction→ObjectSet

Every new transaction receives a fresh identification number, 0 is reserved for the *NULL* transaction. Transactions have three object sets. The sets are used to trace the changes performed by the operations joined to the transaction:

- *Wset*: stores the entries written under a transaction. After a commit the objects are placed in the space set.
- *Tset*: after a *take* the object is removed from the space and is placed in the transaction set. If the transaction commits the *Tset* is deleted, if it aborts the objects are put back in the space.

- *Rset*: stores the entries read under the transaction. When an object is in a *Rset* it cannot be taken outside the transaction.

When a process executes a *readIfExists* or *takeIfExists* and there is no matching object in the space, we check in the *Wsets* and *Tsets* of the other transactions to decide if the process has to block or not. When the lease of a transaction expires the space aborts it and informs the user by executing the action *Exception*.

In summary, the *javaspace* process can ever:

- Receive request of services: look ups or insertions.
- Match entries with pending actions, sending the result to the external processes.
- Perform actions related to the lease or timeout expirations: to remove old entries, abort expired transactions, unblock process waiting for an entry.
- Increment the clock by one unit until the time limit, leaving unchanged the state of the system. This action is only possible if there are no matched actions or expired timeouts (or leases) in the system.

5   Verification

We are going to formalize a simple JavaSpaces application to show the possibilities of the μCRL tool set for system verification. The system is inspired by the classical arcade game Ping-Pong, in which two players throw one ball from one to the other. This example has been taken from the chapter 5 of the book "JavaSpaces™ Principles, Patterns, and Practice" [10]. The players are modeled by two processes called Ping and Pong which communicate by means of an entry that encapsulates the ball. In the first section we propose a very simple version of the game, in the second we did some small changes to the game rules, that allow us to use more functionality of the specification.

5.1   Simple Ping-Pong

In this version, players can only catch and throw the ball. The system halts when players have sent the ball a fixed number of rows or when the space life time expires.

The Entry **sort** (ball) is defined as follows:

```
sort   Entry
func   entryNull:→Entry
       ball: Name→Entry
map    eq: Entry×Entry→Bool
       receiver:Entry→Name
var    e: Entry
       n,n': Name
rew    eq(...,...)
       receiver(ball(n)) = n
```

The only field the entry has is the name of the player whom the ball is directed to. The name is from the sort *Name*, that has two constructors *Ping* and *Pong*, and one function (*other*) used to switch from one to the other (*other(Ping)* = *Pong*). To get the ball from the space, a player uses a query:

sort Query
func forMe: Name→Query
map   test: Query×Entry→Bool
var   e: Entry
          n,n': Name
rew   test(forMe(n), e) = eq(n, receiver(e))

The code of both players is the same. It has as arguments: the given name, the identification number, and the number of player rows:

proc player(id:Nat,name:Name,round:Nat) =
          take(id, NULL, FOREVER, forMe(name))
          $\cdot \sum_{e:Entry}$ (Return(id,e)
            .print(name)
            .write(id, ball(other(name)), NULL, FOREVER))
          .player(id,name,S(round))
          ◁ lt(round, maxRounds) ▷ δ

Print is an external action used to communicate to the environment that a player has catched the ball and is going to throw it back. In the initial state the space includes a ball directed to *Ping*. The values of the other main data structures (TransactionSet, PendingActionSet,...) are initialized to empty. The system instantiation is as follows:

$$System = \tau_{\{W,E,Rt\}} \partial_{\{write,Write,take,Take,return,Return\}}$$
$$(javaspace(0, in(object(0, ball(Ping), FOREVER), emO),$$
$$emT, emA, S(NULL), S(0), 0)$$
$$\| player(0, Ping, 0) \| player(S(0), Pong, 0))$$

To each μCRL specification belongs a labeled transition system (LTS) being a directed graph, in which the nodes represent states and the edges are labeled with actions. If this transition system has a finite number of states the μCRL tool set can automatically generate this graph. Subsequently, the CÆSAR ALDÉBARAN DEVELOPMENT PACKAGE (CADP) can be used to visualise and to analyse this transition system. Figure 3 shows the generated LTS of a two rows game reduced by tau equivalence.

The fair execution of the game is 0-3-1-2-4. If the time reaches the bound the system halts, and it's possible that the system stops before all the rows have been completed, this behavior corresponds to the transitions 0-4, 3-4 and 1-4.

Some properties can be automatically verified by the Evaluator tool from the CADP package. These properties are expressed in temporal logic. We used the regular alternation-free μ-calculus formulas [13]. For example, a safety property expresses the prohibition of "bad" execution sequences. The following formula means that the player *Ping* cannot throw the ball twice in a row:

[true* . ”*print(Ping)*” . (not ”*print(Pong)*”)* .”*print(Ping)*”] false

The tool set verifies if the formula holds or not. In the same way we can verify invariants, liveness or fairness properties et cetera. . .

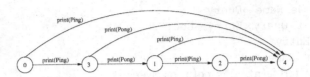

Fig. 3. External behavior of 2 rows simple Ping-Pong game

5.2 More Complex Ping-Pong

We introduce a small change in the rules of the game. In this version, once a player catched the ball, he has one time unit to put it back in the space, otherwise he looses the game. We model this approach by using transactions. After a player has performed the *take*, he creates a transaction leased for one second. Once the *write* operation is done, the transaction can commit. Let's see the process code:

```
proc   player(id:Nat,name:Name,round:Nat) =
          take(id, NULL, FOREVER, forMe(name))
           ·∑_{e:Entry} (Return(id,e)
              ·∑_{trc:Nat} (create(id, trc, S(0))
                .(write(id, ball(other(name)), trc, FOREVER)
                   + Exception(id, trc).looser(name))
                .(print(name) + Exception(id, trc).looser(name))
                .(commit(id, trc)) + Exception(id, trc).looser(name)))
           .player(id,name,S(round))
           ◁ lt(round, maxRounds) ▷ δ

proc   looser(name:Name) = I_am_the_looser(name).δ
```

Figure 4 shows the reduced LTS associated to the system. In the state number 6 the game has finished. The system can halt due to the end of the match or because one of the players has lost or the time has expired.

From the state 0 there are 5 possible transitions:

- *print(Ping)* to the state 3. The player Ping has taken the ball and the transaction expires. Ping looses.
- *print(Ping)* to the state 6. The player displays the message and the system halts (because $t = FOREVER$). Nobody looses.
- *I_am_the_looser(Ping)* to the state 6. The player takes the ball but the transaction expires before printing. *Ping* looses.

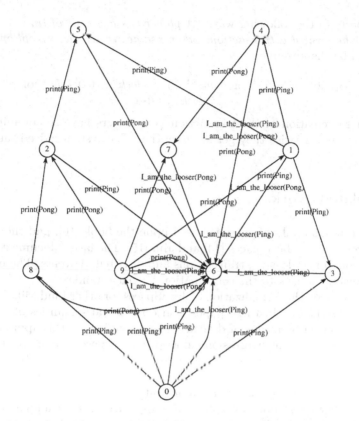

Fig. 4. External behavior of 2 rows complex Ping-Pong game

- $print(Ping)$ to the state 9. Normal execution, player has catched and thrown the ball. The fair game execution path is 0-9-1-4-6.
- $print(Ping)$ to the state 8. The player throws the ball correctly but in the last time step of the system so the transaction can not expire anymore. In the states 8, 2 and 5 the transactions timeouts are always greater than *FOREVER*. Following this path nobody can loose.

We can see that the property *"A player has one unit of time to throw the ball after he catched it"* doesn't hold, because after the return of the *take* action the player can wait as long as he wants before creating the transaction. We prove this by showing that the following formula doesn't hold for the system (without hiding internal actions):

[true* . 'T.*'.(not ('E.*' or 'print.*')*) . "clock" . (not ('E.*' or 'print.*')*) .
"clock"] false

The formula says that after a take communication (*T*), we can not have two consecutive clock ticks without an intermediate exception (*E*) or a *print*. The model checker gives a path that doesn't satisfy the formula. Next, we rewrite the property in the following way: *"A player has one unit of time to throw the ball after he created a transaction, otherwise he receives an exception".* This is expressed by the formula:

[true* . '*C(. *)*'.(not ('*E. *'* or '*Cm. *'*)*) . *"clock"* . (not ('*E. *'* or '*Cm. *'*)*) . *"clock"*] false

After the creation of the transaction (*C*), players have to commit (*Cm*) in one time step otherwise they get an exception. The system indeed satisfies this formula.

6   Related Work

Our information on JavaSpaces is based upon the book [10], and the documentation from Sun on JavaSpaces [14] and Jini [15]. The latter document describes a.o. the concepts of leasing, transactions and distributed events. The basic ideas of JavaSpaces go back to the coordination language Linda [6].

Some work on the formalization of JavaSpaces (or other Linda-like languages) exist, notably [3,4,5]. In these papers, an operational semantics of JavaSpaces programs is given by means of derivation rules. In fact, in this approach JavaSpaces programs become expressions in a special purpose process algebra. Those authors aim at general results, i.e. comparison with other coordination languages, expressiveness, and results on serializability of transactions. Verification of individual JavaSpaces programs wasn't aimed at.

Although we also take an operational approach, our technique is quite different. We model the Javaspace system, and the JavaSpaces programs as expressions in the well-known, general-purpose process algebra, μCRL [11]. This allows us to use the existing μCRL tool set [1] and the CADP tool set [8] for the verification of individual JavaSpaces programs. In our model, the JavaSpaces programs communicate with the JavaSpaces system synchronously.

Our technical approach is similar to the research in [7,12]. In these papers, programs written under the Splice architecture [2] are verified. Both papers give an operational model of Splice in μCRL, and use the μCRL and CADP tool sets to analyse Splice programs. One of the main purposes of the Splice architecture is to have a fast data distribution of volatile data. To this end, the data storage is distributed, as opposed to the central storage in JavaSpaces. In Splice, data items are distributed by a publish/subscribe mechanism. Newer data items simply overwrite outdated items.

7   Conclusion

In this paper, we provide a framework to verify distributed applications built using the JavaSpaces architecture. We have modeled in μCRL a formal specification of the main features of the coordination architecture that allow to prototype and analyse JavaSpaces applications. The language μCRL is expressive enough to support all the functionality of JavaSpaces. The main features have been implemented: primitives, leases, timeouts, transactions and events. We foresee no major problems in the specification of the remaining services.

The last part of the paper is dedicated to the study of a very simple JavaSpaces application. Although we cannot verify the correctness of the proposed specification, we can see in small examples, that the behavior corresponds to the JavaSpaces specification. Together with the μCRL simulator this provides some validation of the model. We also present some ideas of how to verify properties of applications. In the same way of the example we can study more complex problems.

There are many possibilities for future work. First we can extend the specification by including the remaining features: notify primitive, lease renewal, nested transactions, multiple spaces, etc. We can also analyse properties of the formal specification or the transactional model, do formal comparision with other approaches [4,5], or to go further in the verification of applications by studying real world applications.

References

[1] S.C.C. Blom, W.J. Fokkink, J.F. Groote, I.A. Langevelde, B. Lisser, and J.C. van de Pol. μCRL: a toolset for analysing algebraic specifications. In *Proc. of CAV*, LNCS 2102, pages 250–254. Springer, 2001.

[2] M. Dougherty. Control systems software. *IEEE Trans. on Automatic Control*, 38(7):1094–1106, July 1993.

[3] M.M. Bonsangue, J.N. Kok, and G. Zavattaro. Comparing coordination models based on shared distributed replicated data. In *Proc. of SAC*, pages 146–155. ACM, 1999.

[4] N. Busi, R. Gorrieri, and G. Zavattaro. Process calculi for coordination: From Linda to JavaSpaces. In *Proc. of AMAST*, LNCS 1816, pages 198–212. Springer, 2000.

[5] N. Busi and G. Zavattaro. On the serializability of transactions in JavaSpaces. In U. Montanari and V. Sassone, editors, *Electronic Notes in Theoretical Computer Science*, volume 54. Elsevier Science Publishers, 2001.

[6] N. Carriero and D. Gelernter. *How to Write Parallel Programs: A First Course*. MIT Press, 1990.

[7] P.F.G. Dechering and I.A. van Langevelde. The verification of coordination. In *Proc. of COORDINATION*, LNCS 1906, pages 335–340. Springer, 2000.

[8] J.-C. Fernandez, H. Garavel, A. Kerbrat, L. Mounier, R. Mateescu, and M. Sighireanu. CADP – a protocol validation and verification toolbox. In *Proc. of CAV*, LNCS 1102, pages 437–440. Springer, 1996.

[9] W. J. Fokkink. *Introduction to Process Algebra*. Texts in Theoretical Computer Science. Springer-Verlag, 2000.

[10] E. Freeman, S. Hupfer, and K. Arnold. *JavaSpaces principles, patterns, and practice*. Addison-Wesley, Reading, MA, USA, 1999.

[11] J.F. Groote and M.A. Reniers. Algebraic process verification. In J.A. Bergstra et al., editor, *Handbook of Process Algebra*, chapter 17. Elsevier, 2001.

[12] J.M.M. Hooman and J.C. van de Pol. Formal verification of replication on a distributed data space architecture. In *Proceedings ACM SAC, Coordination Models, Languages and Applications*, page (to appear), Madrid, 2002. ACM press.

[13] R. Mateescu. *Verification des proprietes temporelles des programmes paralleles.* PhD thesis, Institut National Polytechnique de Grenoble, 1998.

[14] SUN Microsystems. *JavaSpaces*[tm] *Service Specification*, 1.1 edition, October 2000. See http://java.sun.com/products/javaspaces/.

[15] SUN Microsystems. *Jini*[tm] *Technology Core Platform Specification*, 1.1 edition, October 2000. See http://www.sun.com/jini/specs/.

Objective vs. Subjective Coordination in Agent-Based Systems: A Case Study*

Alessandro Ricci[1], Andrea Omicini[2], and Enrico Denti[3]

[1] DEIS - Università degli Studi di Bologna
Via Rasi e Spinelli, 176   47023 – Cesena (FC), Italy
aricci@deis.unibo.it
[2] DEIS - Università degli Studi di Bologna
Via Rasi e Spinelli, 176   47023 – Cesena (FC), Italy
aomicini@deis.unibo.it
[3] DEIS - Università degli Studi di Bologna
Viale Risorgimento, 2   40136 – Bologna, Italy
edenti@deis.unibo.it

Abstract. This paper aims at showing the benefits of objective coordination in the design and development of agent-based distributed applications. We compare the subjective and objective coordination approaches in the engineering of a simple case study – a distributed MP3 encoding application – pointing out the benefits of the objective ones. In particular, we discuss the design and development of the sample application using three different solutions according to such approaches: a subjective solution, based on conversation and middle-agents, as often found in Distributed Artificial Intelligence and in Multi-Agent Systems; JavaSpaces, as a notable example of loosely-objective approach, not expressive enough to gain all the advantages of objective coordination; and TuCSoN as a fully-objective approach, providing a hybrid coordination model able to exploit the full potential of objective coordination.

1   The Case Study

The case study presented here is taken from an article of the Jiniology series in the *JavaWorld* electronic magazine [4]: there, the author shows how to develop a simple distributed MP3 encoding application using the JavaSpaces technology. Despite its simplicity, this application involves some typical coordination issues about resource sharing, task scheduling, synchronisation, and communication.

A typical way [4] of producing an MP3 file is to compress some digital audio data (e.g., a WAV file): to do so, we may submit the WAV file to an online MP3 encoding service. Since a single-server architecture would cause delays in case of multiple simultaneous requests, we may think of parallelising the process, given that tasks are mutually independent. However, guaranteeing fairness in a distributed application is not obvious: building the application upon a bag of

---

* This work has been partially supported by MIUR, and by Nokia Research Center, Burlington, MA, USA.

F. Arbab and C. Talcott (Eds.): COORDINATION 2002, LNCS 2315, pp. 291–299, 2002.

MP3 requests (deposited by clients and picked up by servers) and a bag of MP3 results (deposited by servers and picked up by clients) gives no assurance that some newer encoding requests won't be serviced before older requests. If a key requirement is that requests are serviced according to a FIFO policy, a total order among client requests must be enforced.

Two kinds of dependencies can be identified: *task assignment dependencies* and *transfer and usability dependencies*. Assigning tasks to MP3 encoders so as to satisfy MP3 requests is an example of the first kind, while ensuring a coherent information flow between MP3 clients and servers calls for coordination, which is an example of the second kind of dependencies.

Here the social task can be identified in the *fairness provision* of the service. This task is *social* since it is not a specific agent's goal, but involves the specification of the correct behaviour of the system as an agent society. According to the SODA [7] agent-oriented design methodology, a social task is assigned to a *group*: *social roles* are then responsible of specific tasks within a social task. Here, two such roles can be identified – *MP3Requester*s and *MP3Worker*s.

Individual usability dependencies are managed defining, for each social role, an interaction protocol suitable for the role's task: the *MP3Requester*'s protocol consists of asking for the service and getting result, while the *MP3Worker*'s protocol is supposed to collect the new requests and provide the converted files. An *interaction rule* assigned to the group specifies how to manage the dependencies among its social roles: in our application, the interaction rule must *(i)* force *MP3Requester*s' requests to be sorted according the channel policy, *(ii)* dispatch requests to free *MP3Worker*s, and *(iii)* act as a mediator between the protocol and the communication language used by *MP3Requester*s and *MP3Worker*s.

2   Design and Development: Objective vs. Subjective Coordination

The distinction between subjective and objective coordination plays a fundamental role in the engineering of multiagent sytems (MAS) [11]. In subjective approaches, coordination is the result of the attitudes of each individual towards the organisation / society it belongs to. Objective approaches, instead, promote the separation between the individual perception of coordination and the global coordination issues, enabling the modelling and shaping of the interaction space independently of the interacting entities.

For the design and development of the case study, we consider three different solutions: *(i)* a subjective approach, mainly focused on negotiation, ACL protocols and mediator agents – some of the subjective coordination mechanisms typically used for MAS coordination [1,6]; *(ii)* a loosely-objective approach, based on an objective coordination model (JavaSpaces) which turns out not to be expressive enough to take full advantage of objective coordination; *(iii)* a fully-objective approach, based on a coordination model (TuCSoN [9]) that is expressive enough to capture and manage all the objective dependencies of the multi-agent system.

2.1 The Subjective Approach

Since the notion of agent is the only available concept, each element identified in the analysis stage can be mapped uniquely onto agents, including the the group abstraction and the related social task. So, there must be agents embodying the *MP3requester* and *MP3worker* roles, which we will call MP3requester and MP3worker, respectively. To map the group abstraction, we exploit the concept of *middle-agent* [2]: a set of such agents is charged of the coordination activities related to the social task of the group. As stated in [6], middle-agents provide a means for meaningfully coordinating activities among agent providers and requesters (information, goods, or expertise) on the Internet, locating and connecting agents in open environments. The engineering properties of this solution vary considerably when using 0, 1 or n middle-agents.

Situation A: No middle agents. This situation is typical of the DAI context, where coordination and cooperation activities are completely distributed among the coordinated / coordinating agents. Coordination is mainly achieved either via ACL-structured interaction protocols (called *conversations*), or driven by the semantics of the adopted agent communication language (such as the BDI semantics in the case of FIPA ACL). Since there are no mediators, MP3requester and MP3worker agents are responsible themselves for the coordination activities: in particular, MP3requesters must coordinate so as to enforce a total ordering of the encoding requests and guarantee the required fairness property with FIFO service policy (see Fig.1 – left picture – for an overview of the solution).

Situation B: One single middle-agent. Here, the group abstraction and related coordination tasks are mapped onto a single mediator agent, which acts as *the* coordinator managing all objective dependencies (see Fig.1 – on the right). The coordinator collects the requests from MP3requesters and sorts them according to the FIFO policy, chooses a ready MP3worker (for instance, via an auction) for each request to be served, and dispatches requests to the selected agents. The coordinator can assume either a *broker* behaviour or a *match-maker* behaviour. As a broker, it sends the results received from MP3workers back to MP3requesters; as a match-maker, it simply mediates the request stage, since result are sent directly from the MP3worker to the proper MP3requester.

Situation C: Multiple middle-agents. Here, the group abstraction and the social task are mapped onto a multiplicity of middle-agents, acting as cooperating coordinators. This case is much more complex than the previous one, because it is necessary to *coordinate coordinators*. Since no inter-coordinator protocols can be specified to establish a total request ordering, either a "main coordinator" is elected to take care of sorting requests, or – as in the solution with no mediators – part of the coordination burden must be put onto MP3requests.

2.2 The JavaSpaces Approach

JavaSpaces [5] is a Java technology based on an extension of the Linda coordination model: the coordination media (*javaspaces*) are blackboards where Java

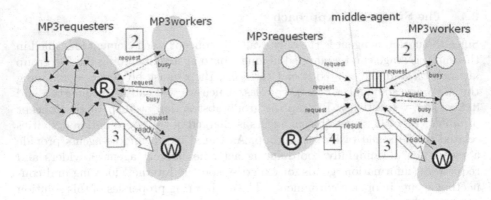

Fig. 1. Subjective approach solutions. *On the left*: no middle-agent are used, the coordination is completely spread among requesters and workers agents; the main interaction stages involve: *1* – MP3requesters coordinate themselves to elect the next requester (tagged with R) that can ask for the service; *2* – the elected agent selects the worker (W) available for the encoding service, by means of a contract-net-like protocol; *3* – an interaction protocol is finally entailed between requester and worker agents to accomplish the service. *On the right*: a middle-agent mediates between requesters and workers; the main phases are: *1* – MP3requesters issue the service request to the middle-agent coordinator (tagged with C), which keeps a sorted list of the requests and establishes the next requester (tagged with R) to serve, according to the turn; *2* – the coordinator selects the worker (W) available for the encoding service, by means of a contract-net-like protocol; *3* – an interaction protocol is entailed between coordinator and worker to get the result of the service; *4* – the coordinator provides the result to the requester agent.

objects can be placed / retrieved via a Linda-like coordination language. In this case, the group abstraction and related social task can be *partially* mapped onto the coordination medium (a JavaSpace), which is used for agent communication / synchronisation and for storing the distributed data involved in the coordination activities. The control part of the coordination must still be mapped onto MP3requester and MP3worker agents. More precisely, MP3requester and MP3worker are responsible for specifying and enacting the coordination policy via suitable interaction protocols, used to access and manage a queue-based repository, called *channel*, stored in the shared space. Table 1 (top part) shows the core of the solution, expressed in pseudocode (more details can be found in [4]). As a result, while part of the agents' behaviour is actually devoted to their real goals, some other is devoted to actually implementing and enforcing the channel coordination policy.

Table 1. JavaSpaces *(top)* and TuCSoN *(bottom)* solutions. For both, MP3requester *(left)* and MP3worker *(right)* agents behaviour description in pseudo-code is provided. The TuCSoN part also shows the coordination laws coded in ReSpecT, below agents' pseudocode. For the sake of simplicity, agents are supposed to have only one single thread of control, therefore operating sequentially. **Java solution:** MP3requester agent follows the channel coordination policy placing a request with an index that reflects the current channel tail: first, the current index is retrieved (line 4), its value is updated (lines 5–6), and used in the request (line 7) as appropriate. Then, the agent waits for the result (line 8). To fulfill the channel coordination policy, a MP3worker agent must serve the request at the head of the queue. To check for pending requests, the head and tail indexes are retrieved (lines 2–3): if the queue is empty, the agent restores the original head index (line 5), since no requests are present. If, instead, there are requests, the head index is updated (lines 7–8), the request at the head of the queue is removed (line 9), and the result is computed and output into the space (lines 10–11). **TuCSoN solution:** Agents' behaviour is completely focused on agents' goals: MP3worker (left) just manifests its needs (line 4) and waits for the result in which it is interested (line 5); MP3worker (right) just manifests its attitude to provide a service (line 2), and then provides the service (lines 3–4). The coordination policy is totally expressed by the ReSpecT code: When a new request is placed by means of an out(mp3request(FileName,RawData,myId) operation, reactions 1 and 2 are triggered. If there are available workers, the request is not queued (reaction 1 succeeds, reaction 2 one fails): rather, it is immediately served by an available MP3worker, whose in pending query becomes satisfiable (line 2 of the MP3worker behaviour). If, instead, no MP3workers are available, the request is queued by removing the mp3request tuple, placing a now suitable tuple req_queue(T1,Name,Data,From), and updating the tail index accordingly. When an MP3worker manifests his/her availability by placing the request in(mp3request(Name,Data,From)) reactions 3, 4 and 5 are triggered. Reaction 5 is always successful, and updates the number of the available workers as appropriate. The coordination flow depends on the presence / absence of queued requests to be served. If the queue is empty, reaction 3 succeeds (while reaction 4 fails) and no other action is taken; otherwise, reaction 4 succeeds (while reaction 3 fails), retrieves the head index of the queue and updates it accordingly. Then, it retrieves the first request req_queue(H,N1,D1,F1) to be served, and outputs a suitable tuple, that makes the worker request satisfiable (line 2 of the MP3worker behaviour). So, when a worker gets a new task, leading the in operation at line 2 of the MP3worker behaviour to be served, reaction 6 is successfully triggered, and the number of available workers is updated accordingly. For the correct behaviour of reactions, tuples tail(0), head(1), and workers_available(0) are supposed to be stored in the tuple centre at the start-up.

```
1 while (true) {                                  1 while (true) {
2    acquireFromGUI(FileName)                      2    rd(tail(T))
3    readRawData(FileName,RawData)                 3    in(head(H))
4    in(tail(T))                                   4    if (T<H) {
5    T1 ← T + 1                                     5       out(head(H))
6    out(tail(T1))                                 6    } else {
7    out(mp3request(T1,FileName,RawData,myId))     7       H1 ← H + 1
8    in(mp3result(FileName,ResultData,myId))       8       out(head(H1))
9 }                                                9       in(mp3request(H,FileName,Data,FromWho))
                                                  10       MP3Data ←from_raw_to_mp3(Data)
                                                  11       out(mp3result(FileName,MP3Data,FromWho))
                                                  12 }}
```

```
1 while (true) {                          1 while (true) {
2   acquireFromGUI(FileName)              2   in(mp3request(FileName,Data,FromWho))
3   readRawData(FileName,RawData)         3   MP3Data <- from_raw_to_mp3(Data)
4   out(mp3request(FileName,RawData,myId))4   out(mp3result(FileName,MP3Data,FromWho))
5   in(mp3result(Name,Data,myId)          5 }
6 }
```

```
1 reaction(out(mp3request(_,_,_)),(       4 reaction(in(mp3request(Name,Data,From)),(pre,
    rd_r(workers_available(N)),               in_r(head(H)),rd_r(tail(T)),
    N>0)).                                     T >= H,
2 reaction(out(mp3request(Name,Data,From)),(  H1 is H + 1, out_r(head(H1)),
    rd_r(workers_available(N)),               in_r(req_queue(H,N1,D1,F1)),
    N == 0,                                    out_r(mp3request(N1,D1,F1)))).
    in_r(tail(T)),T1 is T + 1,out_r(tail(T1)) 5 reaction(in(mp3request(_,_,_)),(pre,
    in_r(mp3request(Name,Data,From)),         in_r(workers_available(N)),
    out_r(req_queue(T1,Name,Data,From)))).    N1 is N + 1,out_r(workers_available(N1)))).
3 reaction(in(mp3request(Name,Data,From)),(pre, 6 reaction(in(mp3request(_,_,_)),( post,
    rd_r(head(H)),rd_r(tail(T)),             in_r(workers_available(N)),
    T < H)).                                  N1 is N - 1,out_r(workers_available(N1)))).
```

2.3   The TuCSoN Approach

The hybrid coordination model of TuCSoN [9], exploiting tuple centres as programmable tuple spaces [8], provides the expressiveness required to fully support the objective coordination activities involved by our case study. The group abstraction and the related social task can then be mapped onto a tuple centre: the interaction rules defined in the analysis stage are mapped directly onto the coordination laws that specify the medium behaviour, and then coded in ReSpecT [8] in the development stage. Table 1 (bottom part) shows the agents' behaviour in pseudo-code and the ReSpecT code implementing the channel coordination policy. As in the JavaSpaces case, the tuple centre acts as an associative blackboard, storing information about the distributed data of the coordination activities. The key feature of the TuCSoN approach is that, unlike JavaSpaces, the tuple centre embeds also the control needed to enforce the coordination activities and manage channel data structures: the algorithm encoded in ReSpecT takes care of managing task assignment and the producer/consumer dependencies that characterise the channel coordination policy. These dependencies are mapped onto events that trigger reactions: these, in turn, compute by taking/placing tuples, manipulating the tuple centre's current communication and coordination states. As a result, all interactions and computations of both MP3requesters and MP3workers are now devoted to the agents' goals only: the control issues of the coordination activities are completed charged upon the coordination medium.

3   Discussion

Some important remarks emerge from the comparison of the engineering impact of subjective and objective approaches, from both the individual agents' and the society's viewpoints.

Agent interaction protocols. Objective approaches promote lighter interaction protocols than subjective approaches, where protocols are necessarily more complex, since agents must engage a greater amount of interactions and exchange more (coordination-related) information. For purely subjective approaches this typically means engaging negotiation protocols (such as contract net protocols): in the case study, a sort of election/sorting protocol has been used to establish a total ordering among MP3requesters, using an auction to select a ready MPworker. Objective coordination approaches typically allow the communications and negotiation interactions to be minimised, making the whole coordination process simpler and automated: the intricacies of coordination are transferred onto the *infrastructure*, avoiding that agent interaction protocols are concerned with details which are irrelevant for the agents' goals.

Openness and heterogeneity. In fully objective approaches, agents can take part to coordination even if unable to participate actively to the coordination process or just unaware of it. This is not the case in purely subjective and in loosely-objective approaches, where the coordination is open only to agents that know its logic and are able to execute its computations and interactions.

Scalability. A related issue concerns scalability in coordination [3]: How does the model support increasingly complex coordination activities? Models and architectures fully supporting objective coordination offer a way to realize more heterogeneous and articulated solutions, where coordination activities can be distributed to agents and media, according to both the application goals and the environment characteristics (in terms of available resources). Using a subjective approach, everything must be placed inside agents: so, the more complex the coordination activities are, the more complex the interaction protocols become, making it harder to pursue the global goals.

From the viewpoint of societies – that is, focusing on the coordination activities concerning the *ensemble* of agents – the objective approaches provide two key advantages: encapsulation and prescriptive coordination.

Encapsulation. A fully objective approach promotes the encapsulation of the logic of coordination and the specification/execution/enforcement of the related laws / activities inside suitable abstractions, outside the coordinated agents. In purely subjective approaches, instead, the computations about coordination are mangled with the computational (and interactive) behaviour of the coordinated agents. This happens also for the objective approach if the expressiveness of the coordination model is inadequate, as shown in the management of tail and head indexes by MP3requester and MP3worker agents in the JavaSpaces approach. Instead, the features of subjective approaches explicitly using middle-agents are more similar to the objective case, since the coordination policy can be embedded inside specialised agents. Encapsulation provides the typical benefits well known in the context of programming languages and software engineering:

– *Reuse.* The ReSpecT coordination specification can be designed so as to be reused in different contexts, which share the same conceptual coordination problem. For instance, by slightly modifying the example, we can define a ReSpecT code realising the channel coordination pattern useful anywhere a FIFO master-worker coordination policy is needed. This could be a valuable tool to build effectively libraries of executable coordination patterns.

– *Maintenance, Evolution, Dynamism.* The encapsulation of coordination inside suitable abstractions supports the evolution / changing / replacement of coordination policies without changing agents. In the TuCSoN approach of the case study, for instance, changing the task scheduling policy from FIFO to LIFO amounts just to changing the ReSpecT behaviour specification of the involved tuple centre, with no impact on agents. In purely subjective case and the JavaSpaces approach, instead, changing the coordination policy involves changing the code / behaviour of all the agents involved in the activity, since they are all fully or partially responsible of its specification and execution.

– *Design/Development uncoupling.* Fully objective approach promotes uncoupled design and development of agents and global coordination activities. This separation of concerns greatly facilitates the debugging and testing of individual agents' behaviour and the behaviour of the society as a whole.

Prescriptive coordination. In objective approaches, coordination laws are enforced by the medium, which guarantees that coordination activity is carried on in spite of failure/mistakes or malicious behaviour of participating agents: in fact, a careful design of the behaviour of coordination medium makes it possible to exclude from the coordination activities the agents behaving differently with respect to their social role, without compromising the social task of the agent society. Instead, in the subjective case, a mistake or failure or a malicious interaction of an agents participating the coordination compromises the entire activity. Loosely-objective approaches such as JavaSpaces suffer the same problem, too. In the case study, for instance, a failure of the MP3requester agent immediately after the in(tail(T)) (line 4) causes the blocking of the global coordination activity. As an other example, a malicious MP3request agent could read the head index and use it in the request placed in the space, in order to be served immediately.

In short, the case study has provided some glances about the effectiveness of objective coordination in the design and development of multiagent systems, in particular for the engineering of the social issues concerning the management of inter-agent aspects, agent-environment interaction, organisation of the agent society and of the environment. Of course, there are contexts where subjective coordination can be more effective: typical examples are scenarios where the coordination activities are not-well defined or with a lower degree of automation, involving the interaction of few (intelligent) agents, whose ability to observe their interaction context, reason and act upon it overcomes the vagueness of the social relationships.

References

1. S. R. Cost, Y. Labrou, and T. Finin. Coordinating agents using agent communication languages conversations. In Omicini et al. [10], chapter 7, pages 183–196.

2. K. Decker, K. Sycara, and M. Williamson. Middle-agents for the internet. In *Proceedings of the 15th International Joint Conference on Artificial Intelligence*, Nagoya, Japan, 1997.
3. E. H. Durfee. Scaling up agent coordination strategies. *IEEE Computer*, 34(7), July 2001.
4. S. Hupfer. Make room for JavaSpaces, part 6. In *Java World*, Jiniology. Springer-Verlag, Oct. 2000. Electronic Magazine, http://www.javaworld.com/javaworld/jw-10-2000/jw-1002-jiniology.html.
5. JavaSpaces Home Page. http://java.sun.com/products/javaspaces/.
6. M. Klusch and K. Sycara. Brokering and matchmaking for coordination of agent societies: A survey. In Omicini et al. [10], chapter 8, pages 197–224.
7. A. Omicini. SODA: Societies and infrastructures in the analysis and design of agent-based systems. In P. Ciancarini and M. J. Wooldridge, editors, *Agent-Oriented Software Engineering*, volume 1957 of *LNCS*, pages 185–193. Springer-Verlag, 2001. 1st International Workshop (AOSE 2000), Limerick (Ireland), 10 June 2000, Revised Papers.
8. A. Omicini and E. Denti. From tuple spaces to tuple centres. *Science of Computer Programming*, 41(3):277–294, Nov. 2001.
9. A. Omicini and F. Zambonelli. Coordination for Internet application development. *Journal of Autonomous Agents and Multi-Agent Systems*, 2(3):251–269, September 1999. Special Issue: Coordination Mechanisms for Web Agents.
10. A. Omicini, F. Zambonelli, M. Klusch, and R. Tolksdorf, editors. *Coordination of Internet Agents: Models, Technologies, and Applications*. Springer-Verlag, Mar. 2001.
11. M. Schumacher. *Objective Coordination in Multi-Agent System Engineering – Design and Implementation*, volume 2039 of *LNAI*. Springer-Verlag, Apr. 2001.

Scheduling under Uncertainty: Planning for the Ubiquitous Grid

Neal Sample, Pedram Keyani, and Gio Wiederhold

Computer Science Department
Stanford University, Stanford CA 94305
{nsample, pkeyani, gio}@cs.stanford.edu

Abstract. Computational Grid projects are ushering in an environment where clients make use of resources and services that are far too expensive for single clients to manage or maintain. Clients compose a megaprogram with services offered by outside organizations. However, the benefits of this paradigm come with a loss of control over job execution with added uncertainty about job completion. Current techniques for scheduling distributed services do not simultaneously account for autonomous service providers whose performance, reliability, and cost are not controlled by the service user. We propose an approach to scheduling that compensates for this uncertainty. Our approach builds initial schedules based on cost estimates from service providers and during program execution monitors job progress to determine if future deadlines will be met. This approach enables early hazard detection and facilitates schedule repairs to compensate for delays.

1 Introduction

Advances in the speed and reliability of computer networks in combination with distribution protocols (such as CORBA and Java RMI) allow clients to abstract away heterogeneities in the network, platform, language, etc., and make use of distributed services and resources that were previously unavailable. Remote services and resources can be utilized as if they were locally available. There are still complications that arise from geographic distance, security concerns, service autonomy, and compensation. In order to complete the abstraction to transparently use remote services and resources, it is necessary to have a mechanism to deal with the uncertainties introduced by scheduling services not under local control.

The development of Grid computing has enabled a model where organizations can develop services and charge a fee for their use to clients. Fee-based computing models are gaining success in both cooperative and commercial computing environments [3,5,7,8,11]. In these grids, service providers charge fees or trade resources for the use of their service. The value of the service offered is a combination of the software itself and the execution of the software. This is an attractive opportunity for service providers because they can amortize their development and maintenance costs and share these expenses with clients, while protecting their proprietary interests in the

F. Arbab and C. Talcott (Eds.): COORDINATION 2002, LNCS 2315, pp. 300-316, 2002.

service. Also, under the CHAIMS model, service updates can be performed in a central location and not need to be propagated to end-users.

Clients also gain from this model in that they can access services that they don't have to develop or maintain [12]. Many clients do not have the resources to develop sophisticated software or purchase the high-end machinery necessary to accomplish their tasks. For example, suppose a small university's genomic research lab had a digitized DNA sequence from which they wanted to isolate a certain gene. Instead of developing the necessary software "in house" they hire a service provider that has the computational power and appropriate genomic software to analyze their data and give them the result they seek. Contracting for the service has the same result as purchasing the computational hardware and proprietary software, but at a fraction of the cost. In an open market, valuable software services may have multiple service providers competing for the same pool of customers. A natural pricing structure would evolve based on the time to completion and the surety of the service providers. (Surety is the probability that a job will finish execution within a deadline window forecast by the service provider.) Quick executing services with a high surety would of course be more valuable than the same services that have longer running times or a low surety. A customer's choice of service providers would depend on what value they place on time, cost, and surety, simultaneously. Until now, schedulers have treated the remote service problem as a multivariate optimization involving only two variables: cost and time [2,4,13]. We extend the worldview by accounting for the uncertainty introduced when services are not under the client's control.

Access to an array of services provides many opportunities for service composition. The ability to compose services is an especially powerful tool for multi-disciplinary projects where no single client has expertise in all sub-problem areas [12]. By allowing for composition of existing modules, researchers can devote less effort to software development and more time to central research questions. But there is a pitfall: distributed services are not under the control of the client. This means that estimates for job completion time may be inaccurate and clients cannot control resource allocation to recover from hazards. An inaccurate estimate in the completion time of single service is undesirable; in a program comprised of multiple services this can quickly become untenable.

The main research problem we address in this paper is the decreased level of scheduling surety that comes from composing a program from multiple distributed services [12,14]. By making programs composed of distributed services more reliable, these compositions become an increasingly viable solution for a wide range of problems, and become an appropriate solution for a larger class of clients.

At a finer resolution, the goal of this project is to take a program composed of multiple services and complete it within a soft deadline and cost budget, while guaranteeing a client-specified minimum level of surety. The scheduling process begins with the selection of an initial schedule based on service provider estimates for completion time and fee [35]. The initial schedule is driven by dependencies (data, control, etc.) between service invocations and estimates from service providers. At runtime, job monitoring detects misbehaving services that can jeopardize the completion of the entire program. During the monitoring phase, surety is recalculated whenever progress is made (or not made, but time has advanced). If surety drops below the minimum threshold determined by the client, the scheduler takes action to recover from the delay and increase surety to an acceptable level. Any measures taken require finding alternative schedules for the remainder of the program that restore surety without exceeding the program's budget. Monitoring coupled with reactive rescheduling is key to providing clients with the surety of distributed job completion, as they would expect from a program running solely on local resources.

Systems such as CHAIMS (Compiling High-level Access Interfaces for Multi-site Software) allow clients to abstract away heterogeneity and service autonomy while simultaneously compensating for pitfalls associated with both [15]. We focus on scheduling with CHAIMS because its preferred development language (CLAM – Composition Language for Autonomous Megamodules) provides key language primitives that enable dynamic scheduling with the possibility of recovery from hazards. CLAM contains a primitive to get estimates of the job completion time and cost from a service provider (ESTIMATE), and a primitive to examine job progress from a service provider (EXAMINE)[16]. These two capabilities used in concert allow for scheduling a program with more confidence in execution time. Other coordination languages such as MANIFOLD are appropriate for this type of composition, but lack the EXAMINE and ESTIMATE primitives found in CLAM [17,18].

The current supported runtime system for CHAIMS is known CPAM (CHAIMS Protocol for Autonomous Megamodules) [19]. The protocol removes the barriers imposed by different programming languages and distribution protocols, while providing support for the scheduling primitives in CLAM. Programs written in CLAM are known as megaprograms, though the class of programs is known by myriad names in other scheduling literature (ensembles, compositions, grid programs, workflows, etc.) [5,19,22,23]. Within CHAIMS, megaprograms are composed from megamodules. Megamodules are what we have referred to simply as services; they are assumed to possibly come from multiple programming languages, distinct hosts, and have different native distribution protocols [16].

An initial objective of CHAIMS was to simply develop a language and runtime support for the programs composed from distributed modules. The focus of this work is to add a dynamic scheduler to the system that can deal with the issues that arise in an unreliable environment. We build on their prior efforts because the language and runtime support overlap well with the requirements of runtime testing and surety monitoring. However, our work is broadly applicable to any system where estimates may be gathered a priori and where clients may monitor runtime progress.

Current distributed service scheduling research has not presented a complete solution that incorporates uncertainty. Most distributed computation schedules assume a cooperative environment where delays are rare, and that initial estimates come from oracles. The foundation of this work is that distributed systems (in practice) are rife with uncertainty that affects the reliability of schedules generated a priori. Section 2 discusses the characteristics of autonomous service providers and the attributes central to the scheduling task. Section 3 gives a brief description of CHAIMS and how it enables composition and coordination of distributed services. Section 4 explains the scheduling techniques and job monitoring that we advocate. Section 5 covers related work and explains how our techniques may be leveraged in distributed architectures other than CHAIMS. This research has opened further questions, detailed in section 6.

2 Autonomous Service Providers

The Internet has made distributed services a reality and opened up a completely new scheduling problem area to explore [1,4,21,24,25]. Without careful consideration, as computations are moved farther and farther from client control, it is increasingly likely that hazards will slow or halt progress. These hazards may arise from hardware or software failures, to power outages, to resource mismanagement by a service provider. Additionally, in competitive markets, service providers try to maximize profits. A greedy service provider could mistakenly take on more jobs than it can handle and delay the finishing time of all jobs. Alternately, an unscrupulous service provider might stop the execution of a low-paying job, however unfair it may seem, for more lucrative jobs that arise. Running into delays for a single service can be costly, but when programs are composed from multiple distributed services, delays in one service can have an undesirable cascade effect that destroys scheduling commitments for the entire client program. One aid to avoid such problems comes in the form of contracts [11, 34]. In the simplest contracts, clients use initial estimates of job completion time to bind service providers. This still does not guarantee that service providers will be able to meet the deadline of their contract. As such, it is also necessary to monitor job progress during execution to determine if the contract will be met (and to react swiftly and appropriately to recover if it is not).

In this uncertain environment it is necessary to leverage contracts to motivate clients and service providers to meet their mutual obligations. At its core, the contract enables two parties who do not trust each other to enter into a mutually beneficial agreement. While contracts are a tool to promote accountability, they do not enforce it. In this paper we do not discuss contracts negotiation or enforcement, as they are implementation details that each distribution model must decide on. However, more information on contracts and negotiations within distributed systems can be found in [2,20,23]. We expect contracts to consider:

- *Cost* – what a service provider will charge for the service.
- *Completion time* - the estimated length of time to complete the job.
- *Variance* - the amount of time before or after the completion time that the job may finish. (It is assumed no service provider can be completely accurate in job estimation.) Variance may be presented symmetrically or asymmetrically. In this paper, we assume symmetric variance in the examples, but provide equations to handle asymmetric variance.
- *Late fee* – a credit the service provider returns to the client per unit of time that the job is not finished after completion time plus variance.

- *Cancellation fee* - a set amount that the service provider will return to the client if the client breaks the contract. This value may be zero, but is of utility to both client and service provider.
- *Reservation* – an amount the client pays after negotiating the contract to hold resources until it exercises the contract and invokes the service. This reservation fee guarantees that the client will be given access to the service provider's resources, and confidence that the client can have some control over job start time. Reservations are a complicated issue themselves, and are further discussed in [11,23]. We assume "American options", which allow a client to start a service at any point until expiry.

This distributed computational model for accessing services closely parallels traditional economical models. Significant detail on how grid computing relates to (and can leverage) various economic mechanisms can also be found in [2,4,11,23]. We do not make assumptions about the trading or cash economies that will lubricate the grid; we simply examine the general considerations that economic factors place on scheduling under uncertainty.

3 CHAIMS

Technological advancements and social change have made grid computing a feasible option for computation. We have chosen the CHAIMS platform as a test bed for our investigations for the reasons mentioned in section 1. Specifically, we leverage its compositional programming language (CLAM) and the runtime support system (CPAM) to enable composition and coordination of distributed services. In the future we expect to plug our scheduler into other compositional and grid platforms. In this section, we give more detail about CHAIMS.

3.1 CLAM

CLAM is a declarative language intended for large-scale module composition that lacks constructs for complicated computation [16]. Motivating the absence of computational primitives in CLAM was a desire to create a simple language for non-programmer domain experts to accomplish their desired tasks [19]. The premise rests on the idea that there is a collection of service providers who will offer some services that may be used with other distributed services, or perhaps with modules locally controlled by domain experts.

CLAM is designed for a large-scale environment where parallelism is important. Unlike many languages for distributed or parallel computing (e.g., HPF (High Performance Fortran) [26]), CLAM does not specify what resources a service invocation uses. This permits service instances to be scheduled identically, regardless of the capabilities and resources of the service's backing system. Breaking free from resource specification enables freedom in choosing service providers at runtime, rather than compile time, thus selecting providers based on costs at runtime. This late binding time is similar to the tactic introduced in [11,13].

While CLAM is simply a declarative compositional language, it makes heavy use of the coordination capabilities supported by CPAM to achieve good performance. CPAM enables asynchronous service invocation and parallel execution. The key facilities that CPAM offers are the ability to get estimates on job completion and to examine job progress during service execution. These two CPAM capabilities are mirrored in the ESTIMATE and EXAMINE primitives of CLAM. Further discussion in Section 4 will show how ESTIMATE and EXAMINE provide the capabilities for building an intelligent scheduler. Note that enabling these primitives in any distributed framework provides a generic framework for scheduling under uncertainty.

3.2 CPAM

CPAM is a generic high-level protocol for remote service invocation. CPAM compensates for language and platform differences by representing data as ASN.1 structures [19]. Data is transmitted from clients to services (and between services) opaquely, with no alteration possible during transit. Services must be wrapped to unpack data type locally. CPAM has been implemented above many transport protocols such as DCOM, Java RMI and CORBA. There is also a "native" transport mechanism for CPAM.

CPAM breaks service invocation into a multi-step process to enable asynchrony and parallelism. The steps of invocation are SETUP, SETPARAM (parameter setting), ESTIMATE (partial cost estimation), INVOKE, EXAMINE (monitor program), EXTRACT and TERMINATE [16]. An extended discussion of each is available in [16]. These functions are exposed to programmers in CLAM. However, with an automated scheduler, ESTIMATE and EXAMINE are not required in the language, just as part of the runtime. ESTIMATE and EXAMINE are necessary for scheduling because they allow the construction of an initial schedule and allow for monitoring during runtime. Calling ESTIMATE from a service provider returns an estimate of job completion time and a variance related to that value. Because the runtime of a service is often dependent on its input, SETPARAM is used to give the service provider enough information to make an informed estimate. Once a service is executing, EXAMINE can be called to view the progress of the job. The ultimate goal is to deprecate the EXAMINE and EXTRACT primitive in CLAM by leveraging them in a scheduler built directly on top of CPAM. Runtime support provided by mature grid implementations such as Legion are also appropriate [27,28].

4 Scheduling in an Uncertain Environment

In order to deal with an uncertain environment it is necessary to consider surety when scheduling. A surety threshold is set before a program is started, and is monitored throughout the execution lifetime of the program. When progress information indicates that the surety threshold has been breached, dynamic repair and rescheduling operations are triggered. As mentioned previously, the scheduler will make use of the ESTIMATE and EXAMINE capabilities to build initial schedules and to monitor progress.

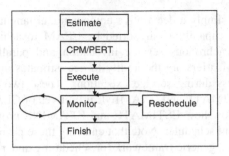

Fig. 1. The scheduling process

Before scheduling can start, the client determines a budget for the program. A budget is made up of (1) the deadline that the program must be finished by, (2) the amount of consideration (money, credits, bartered resources, etc. depending on the economic model) that can be spent on the program execution, and (3) the minimum level of surety that must be met by the scheduler. Individual clients determine the amount of time and consideration available for a specific program's execution. The surety is a limit on the risk the client will tolerate in meeting their budget. Once the constraints of the budget are determined, the client can select to optimize or balance these three budgetary concerns (time, cost, surety). Figure 1 shows a simplified view of the scheduling process; steps not central to this work are omitted. We will discuss each of these steps in detail. In this section, we present an overview of the process steps.

First, estimates are collected for each service from potentially many service providers and used in the program to build possible schedules. In our current naïve implementation, we exhaustively enumerate all schedules and select one from the pool of best choices. Before discussing which schedules are "best", we will clarify our underlying schedule evaluation techniques.

Once a candidate schedule is created, the shortest expected running time of that schedule can be determined using CPM (Critical Path Method)[29]. With this information it is trivial to test whether a schedule meets the minimum time and budget criteria, however nothing is known at this point about surety. The longest path (in terms of expected execution time) in the program determines the runtime of the program. This longest path is called the "critical path" because any delay along the critical path will affect the running time of the entire program. To determine surety it is necessary to extend the CPM analysis to a probabilistic PERT (Program Evaluation and Review Techniques) analysis [29,30,31]. PERT extends CPM by accounting for the uncertainty in each estimated service duration to compute the surety of the entire program. We will discuss our use of PERT in significant detail in the next section.

Once a schedule is selected and contracts are finalized, the scheduler may invoke any ready services in the program. As services execute, their progress is monitored to ensure that completion times are met; if the overall surety of program completion drops below the predetermined threshold, the scheduler begins the repair and reschedule phase. In the repair phase there are many options. New service providers may be found to replace the service module that is delaying overall progress. Or other services along the critical path may be substituted for alternative services that have shorter runtimes (though at an increased cost). Once repair and rescheduling is complete, the scheduler returns to monitoring the execution.

4.1 Simple Planning

The first step in scheduling is program analysis to discover any dependencies among component services and construct a dependency graph for the workflow. The very simple program in Figure 2 shows implicit data dependencies between services. For instance, service3 takes A and B as input. A and B are outputs of service1 and service2, respectively. These dependencies are mapped into the workflow of Figure 3 where nodes represent services and dependencies are shown as arcs between nodes with the arrow pointing to the dependent node. These workflows consist of paths that are created by dependencies between nodes. Once the dependencies are mapped, the scheduler requests bids from service providers in order to fill in cost values for the proposed schedule.

The scheduler contacts a repository or directory service that returns a list of service providers that perform a specific service. Based on this list, the scheduler contacts the service providers and requests bids. The *bid request* is based on the service needed, the expected start time for the service, and information about the size and complexity of the input parameters to the service. For some services, the inputs cannot be known at runtime because they are the outputs of other services; in these cases information about the size and complexity of parameters is currently based on heuristics that the Service provider uses to make best estimates. Service providers collate this information and calculate a possible bid. The client receives a collection of bids and will either accept one or more bids for the schedule, or attempt to renegotiate with the service providers [2,20,23]. The deciding factor in which bids are accepted is based on the Pareto optimality [32] of the "best" schedules. For a bid to be Pareto optimal, there can be no other bid with an absolute advantage in terms of price, time and surety. The Pareto curve in this case is weighted by the optimization strategy presented by the client, for instance in soft real-time applications surety will have a high weighting. All decisions are based simultaneously on cost, time, and surety.

```
// begin program
A = service1();
B = service2();
C = service3(A,B);
D = service4(C);
E = service5(C);
// end of program
```

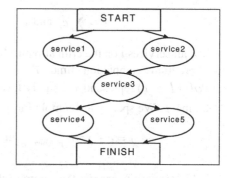

Fig. 2. Sample program   **Fig. 3.** Dependency graph of sample program

Using CPM gives the scheduler the critical path and the expected runtime of the program. This information allows the schedule to select candidate schedules that meet the client's budget and to further optimize and refine the schedule. For instance, CPM indicates positions of "slack" in the schedule, where cheaper, longer running processes may be used because they're not along the critical path [29]. By choosing slower services in these non-critical paths, the scheduler can possibly decrease the overall cost of the program, thus saving resources that may be necessary for repairs at a later time. The total price cost for all services executed plus the cost of any reservations not kept is the total cost of the program.

The PERT method extends CPM to account for uncertainty of individual service completion times and determines the probability of completing a complete program by an expected time [29].   PERT analysis forms the basis for our rescheduling decisions. To perform the initial analysis, the scheduler uses three time estimates for each service: most likely(m), optimistic(a) and pessimistic(b) completion times. "Optimistic" and "pessimistic" times are derived from the expected time coupled with the variance. With this information, the *expected duration* e_i of a single service can be determined by a weighted combination of the most likely duration m_i and the midpoint of the distribution $\dfrac{(a_i + b_i)}{2}$ for each service i:

$$e_i = \frac{2m_i + \dfrac{a_i + b_i}{2}}{3} \tag{1}$$

There is a spread of about 6 standard deviations from a_i to b_i thus:

$$\sigma_i = \frac{b_i - a_i}{6} \tag{2}$$

Activity durations are independent; hence the sum of the independent random expected functions e_i is normally distributed. From the expected completion time and standard deviation of each service on the critical path, we construct the expected completion time and standard deviation of the entire program as:

$$\bar{e} = \sum e_i \text{ and } \sigma_{program} = \sqrt{\sum \sigma_i^2} \tag{3}$$

for all services i on the critical path. With this we can calculate the probability that the program completion time T is less than the deadline of time t.   This $prob\ (T \leq t)$ represents the surety level of the program completing execution by its deadline, t. We specify the completion time as:

$$t = \bar{e} + x * \sigma_{program} \quad \text{giving us} \quad x = \frac{t - \bar{e}}{\sigma_{program}} \tag{4}$$

which is used to express the surety of the program as:

$$prob\,(T \le t) = \left[\frac{T - \bar{e}}{\sigma_{program}} \le \frac{t - \bar{e}}{\sigma_{program}} \right] \tag{5}$$

This is the same as the probability of a random variable from N(0, 1) distribution being less than or equal to $\dfrac{t - \bar{e}}{\sigma_{program}}$.

Using CPM and PERT, the scheduler can evaluate the bids that form the final schedules. What follows now is an example of the complete repair and scheduling activity.

In this example, Table 1 shows a set of bids produced for the sample program in Figure 2. In some cases, multiple service providers bid for a service, giving the scheduler some flexibility. In the case of service3, only one service provider has replied with a bid, thus it will have to be used.

Table 1. Bids received for each service

Service	Cost	Time
service1	8	8 +/- 2
	9	10 +/- 1
	11	6 +/- 0
service2	10	5 +/- 2
	12	4 +/- 1
service3	8	8 +/- 0
service4	15	2 +/- 0
	10	4 +/- 2
service5	20	1 +/- 0
	10	2 +/- 2
	5	3 +/- 1

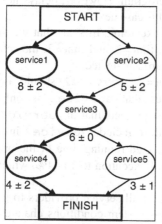

Fig. 4. Sample Schedule

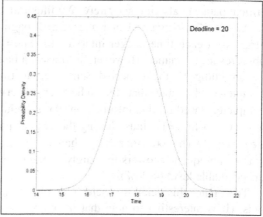

Fig. 5. Probability distribution of original program schedule

After all bids have been received, the scheduler searches for an optimal schedule, based on the client's budget. Assume the client has given a deadline of 20 units of time, a budget of ¥65 and a minimum surety requirement of 90%. (We use the "¥" symbol simply to distinguish the cost numbers from the time numbers, and make no implication about any particular specie or economic model.) The bids from table 1 are used to construct the schedule in Figure 4. In Figure 4, the critical path to consist of nodes service1, service3, and service4. By application of CPM, this schedule has an expected finishing time of 18, an earliest finishing time of 14, and latest finishing time of 22 assuming no hazards. The total budget estimated for this program is ¥38, allowing a reserve of ¥27, which can be used to repair the schedule in case of delay or hazard. Figure 5 shows the probability distribution of this program's completion time. The surety for the program is determined via PERT to be 98.31%, an acceptable level (≥90%). Please note that these values for cost, time, and surety are from an *a priori* analysis based solely on service provider estimates. In the next section, we explain surety based monitoring and repair strategy.

4.2 Monitoring and Repairing Schedules

Once the initial planning stage is complete and contracts have been drawn, execution starts. For our running example, we assign this start time a convenient value of time=0. The schedule for our example (shown in Figure 4) is very "tight" in terms of cost. There are alternative assignments of service instances that would give a lower overall cost. This trades off with overall runtime of the schedule to some extent, but the tradeoff is considered acceptable because the schedule does not fall below the surety threshold.

Of course delays along the critical path are likely to be the most damaging since they extend the run time of the entire program. Constant monitoring is required to ensure that single delays do not affect the entire program. However, delays not in the critical path can also impact surety. We illustrate this case next.

At time=0, service1 and service2 begin execution. Imagine that we monitor progress at each time integer interval. At time=1, time=2, and time=3, the scheduler observes no anomalies. However, at time=4, a hazard is detected.

According to the expected schedule, at time=4, service2 should be 80% completed. Imagine that the scheduler observes that service2 is only 50% complete. Based on this information, the scheduler projects that the service2 will complete at time=11, thus altering the critical path to include service2 instead of service1. This potential delay changes the expected running time of the program, which subsequently lowers the surety of the overall execution to 14.44%, which is an unacceptable level (< 90%).

To counter this delay, the scheduler first contacts all service providers to get new bids. (It is interesting to note that in our model as system conditions change, initial estimates become moot. This is especially true when scheduling long-running services.) The scheduler determines that the most effective strategy is to accept a bid to attempt to finish service2 at an earlier time. At time=4, a bid for an instance of service2 that will cost ¥10 and complete in 5 units of time (with a variance of 2 (5±2)) is found and accepted. Immediately, this second service provider for service2 begins work in parallel with the delayed instance. This repair strategy has increased the surety of the complete program, but we now expect the program to finish somewhere between time=15 and time=23 with a mean expectation of time=19. This repair increases the surety to 85.56%, and reduces the reserve budget to ¥17. A surety of 85.56% is below the threshold. This schedule requires further repair.

After the delay is caught and an alternative found, the surety remains below the 90% threshold. To further increase surety, it is necessary to select a node along the critical path and either find alternate service providers that can perform the same service in less time, or contract with multiple service providers to execute the same service in parallel, thus increasing the probability that at least one of them will deliver results in time. The method used to increase surety depends on how much budget is left over, and if alternative service providers can be found with the required performance capabilities. In this example, assume that we discover another service provider that offers `service4` for ¥10 with a completion time of 3, and variance of 2. Using this service provider increases overall surety to 95.83%, which is above the threshold for this execution.

Surety represents the risk of a client program not meeting its deadline that the client will accept. Monitoring job execution at runtime allows our CHAIMS scheduler to compare current surety to the limit established by the client. Falling below the surety threshold triggers the scheduler to repair or reschedule to counteract the effects of hazard. This is achieved primarily by finding alternative or duplicate services increase surety. If surety is set too high (e.g., 100%) or the budget too low, the space of acceptable schedules is radically reduced, and the likelihood of successful schedules decreases as well.

4.3 Initial Results

Initial results are promising but difficult to quantify. The prototype scheduler generates Pareto optimal schedules and selects a schedule based on the client-specified criteria. However, this does not address the central performance question: *how effective is the scheduler at working around delays and hazards?* Our initial evaluation strategy was to simulate network conditions and service providers and allow the scheduler to make its best attempt at scheduling a set of randomly generated programs. Various delays plagued the scheduler during simulation, and we determined a metric for comparison. Using dynamic programming, we simulated all schedules and compared the optimal overall costs and completion times to our scheduler's performance.

This analysis technique does not produce meaningful results. For instance, we tested a program in which its last required service would become permanently unavailable shortly after its execution began. It turns out that the "ideal" schedule is counter-intuitive and would not be selected by any rational scheduler. For instance, if a schedule had only very long running, inexpensive services, then it would fail because it exceeded its time budget long before reaching the final service that was designed to go offline. In those cases, the schedule that had no chance to finish on time wasted less of the client's resources during a futile attempt to solve the problem. This edge case shows the extreme flaw in straightforward quantitative analysis: if a schedule cannot be completed, the worst scheduling policies are rewarded. In this particular case, a scheduler that constantly returned "failure to find any satisfying schedules" would performance best. We are exploring alternative ways to quantify our results.

5 Related Work

There is significant work in the area of scheduling, though the missing ingredient to move from laboratory conditions to real world systems has been surety. Our approach differs from previous research operating under closed world assumptions where a) *a priori* estimates are provided by infallible oracles, or b) *a priori* estimates of cost will be valid at time=n, where n is potentially far in the future after the estimate was given. Finally, we see scheduling techniques for time and cost simultaneously, and repair strategies under the oracular estimates assumption, but we have not seen these techniques in conjunction with surety analysis.

5.1 Mariposa

Mariposa is a scheduler for operations over large distributed databases. Entities negotiate with each other for services such as queries, data transmission, and storage [11,13]. Entities act through agents to process their requests. A key assumption is that estimates will be met, without exception. This assumption only holds if a central administrator manages all entities and the administrator ensures that each entity behaves properly. Our scheduler could provide Mariposa the intelligence to handle issues that arise when there is no resource overseer, as expected in a truly distributed environment.

5.2 NOW (Networks of Workstations)

The premise of NoW [33] is that collections of desktops working together have a much better price-performance ratio than mainframes and supercomputers of the same power. Applications considered highly suitable for NoW range from cooperative file caching to parallel computing within a network. Specific projects such as POPCORN [5] seek to take concepts of NoW and extend them to work on the entire Internet. POPCORN is providing programmers with a virtual parallel computer by utilizing processors that participate in this system. POPCORN is based on the notion of a market where buyers and sellers come together and barter for resources.

POPCORN assumes that nodes will fail, and that it is easier to repeat work on backup nodes if a worker misses a deadline. Our scheduling system could account for this uncertainty by monitoring job progress and rapidly migrating computation to alternative nodes if delays are detected.

5.3 Grid Computing

Many computational grid projects are being developed simultaneously (ecogrid, DataGrid, power grid, etc.) [9,10,22]. Contributions to this field are coming from many different projects, each with tailored goals for grid computing. An overarching goal is to allow for resource sharing and services spread over large geographic, political, and economic distances. Projects like the European DataGrid currently focus significant attention on developing a network infrastructure that supports the rapid transport of multi-PetaByte datasets between different locations [1].

Other projects such as Globus provides tools to bridge the gap between heterogeneous grid participants [6]. Globus provides a low level toolkit to handle issues of network communication, authentication and data access. These tools can be used to create high-level services such as intelligent schedulers that can be inserted into a computational grid. Thus, Globus makes it possible to insert our scheduler into a grid infrastructure and provide surety to clients. The resulting increase in schedule dependability will extend the power and use of grid computing.

5.4 ePert and Extensions

This work extends workflow management systems to include time management [30,31]. ePert determines internal deadlines in the workflow and monitors progress at run-time. If deadlines are not met, alternate schedules are chosen. However, these alternative schedules must be known at runtime, and fully available during execution time. ePert extends the PERT method to include with it alternate execution paths a process can take. These extensions allow for some level of pro-active scheduling by detecting time failures and recovering from them. Our scheduling techniques can contribute dynamic components to their work. However, the closed-world assumptions are more likely to hold with workflow schedulers since there is often a strong command and control structure responsible for the workflow (e.g., workflows within a single corporation).

6 Future Work

This project has produced tools that allow us to develop and test advanced scheduling techniques. We are currently working on two parallel tracks. First, we are testing various scheduling heuristics that should improve our repair tactics. Second, we are investigating techniques to quantify performance of our scheduler. We have considered various multivariate analysis evaluation metrics but since they neglect the notion of surety in their cost models, reasonable and rational schedules have demonstrably poor performance compared to the most irrational schedulers in certain cases. We reiterate that the usefulness of our scheduler is not limited to the CHAIMS system, but we are eager to fulfill this claim by inserting our scheduler into a standard grid component.

7 Conclusions

We present a scheduling technique that uses surety to overcome much of the uncertainty naturally present in distributed computing environments. We take a program composed of multiple distributed services and complete it within a client-specified soft deadline by guaranteeing that a minimum level of surety is maintained throughout the program execution. The scheduling tactics demonstrated here make initial schedules, monitor runtime progress, and then repair the schedule if surety drops below a threshold value. This work is broadly applicable to systems whose distributed nature is impacted by uncertainty.

References

1. F. Berman, High Performance Schedulers in Building a Computational Grid, I. Foster and C. Kesselman, editors, Morgan Kaufmann, 1998.
2. R. Buyya, J. Giddy, D. Abramson, "An Evaluation of Economy-based Resource Trading and Scheduling on Computational Power Grids for Parameter Sweep Applications," The Second Workshop on Active Middleware Services (AMS 2000), August 1, 2000.
3. S. Lohr, "I.B.M. Making a Commitment to Next Phase of the Internet" New York Times 2001, http://www.nytimes.com/2001/08/02/technology/02BLUE.html.
4. D. Marinescu, L. Bölöni, R. Hao, and K. Jun, "An Alternative Model for Scheduling on a Computational Grid," Proceedings of ISCIS'98, the Thirteenth International Symposium on Computer and Information Sciences, Antalya, pp. 473-480, IOP Press, 1998.
5. N. Nisan, S. London, O. Regev, and N. Camiel, "Globally distributed computation over the internet-the popcorn project," In Proceedings for the 18th Int'l Conference on Distributed Computing Systems, 1998.
6. I. Foster and C. Kesselman, "Globus: A Metacomputing Infrastructure Toolkit," Proceedings of the Workshop on Environments and Tools for Parallel Scientific Computing, SIAM, Lyon, France, Aug. 1996.
7. Juno, "Juno Announces Virtual Supercomputer Project," Juno Press Release, February 1, 2001), http://www.juno.com/corp/news/supercomputer.html.
8. United Devices "Edge Distributed Computing with the MetaProcessor(TM) Platform," White paper, 2001, https://www.ud.com/customers/met.pdf.asp.
9. UDDI, Technical White Paper, September 6, 2000 http://www.uddi.org/pubs/Iru_UDDI_Technical_White_Paper.pdf.
10. C. Kurt, "UDDI Version 2.0 Operator's Specification", UDDI Open Draft Specification 8, June 2001 (Draft K) , http://www.uddi.org/pubs/Operators-V2.00-Open-20010608.pdf
11. M. Stonebraker, R. Devine, M. Kornacker, W. Litwin, A. Pfeffer, A. Sah, and C. Staelin. "An economic paradigm for query processing and data migration in Mariposa," In Proceedings of the Third International Conference on Parallel and Distributed Information Systems, Austin, TX, September 1994.
12. Carl Bartlett, Neal Sample, and Matt Haines "Pipeline Expansion in Coordinated Applications", 1999 International Conference on Parallel and Distributed Processing Techniques and Applications (PDPTA'99), Las Vegas, Nevada, June 28 - July 1, 1999.
13. J.Sidell, "Performance of Adaptive Query Processing in the Mariposa Distributed Database Management System," unpublished manuscript, June 1997.

14. W. K. Shih, J. W. S. Liu, and J. Y. Chung. "Algorithms for scheduling imprecise computations with timing constraints," In Proc. IEEE Real Time Systems Symposium, 1989.

15. G. Wiederhold, P. Wegner, S. Ceri, "Towards Megaprogramming", CACM, Nov.1992.

16. N. Sample, D. Beringer, L. Melloul and G. Wiederhold, "CLAM: Composition Language for Autonomous Megamodules," 3rd Int'l Conference on Coordination Models and Languages, Amsterdam, Apr. 1999.

17. F. Seredynski, P. Bouvry, and F. Arbab, "Parallel and distributed evolutionary computation with Manifold," In V. Malyshkin, editor, Proceedings of PaCT-97, volume 1277 of Lecture Notes in Computer Science, pages 94--108. Springer-Verlag, September 1997.

18. F. Arbab, "The IWIM Model for Coordination of Concurrent Activities," First International Conference on Coordination Models, Languages and Applications (Coordination'96), Cesena, Italy, April 15-17 1996.   (Also appears in LNCS 1061, Springer-Verlag, pp. 3456.)

19. L. Melloul, D. Beringer, N. Sample and G. Wiederhold, "CPAM, A Protocol for Software Composition," CAiSE'99, Heidelberg, Germany, June 1999 (Springer LNCS).

20. A. Garvey, K. Decker, and V. Lesser, "A Negotiation-based Interface Between a Real-time Scheduler and a Decision-Maker," Tech. Rep. 94-08, U. of Massachusetts Department of Computer Science, March 1994.

21. A. Garvey and V. Lesser. "Design-to-time scheduling with uncertainty," CS Technical Report 95--03, University of Massachusetts, 1995.

22. F. Berman, "High-performance schedulers," The Grid: Blueprint for a New Computing Infrastructure, 1999.

23. R. Buyya, J. Giddy, D. Abramson, "A Case for Economy Grid Architecture for Service-Oriented Grid Computing," 10th IEEE International Heterogeneous Computing Workshop (HCW 2001), In conjunction with IPDPS 2001, San Francisco, CA, April 2001.

24. A. Geppert, M. Kradolfer, and D. Tombros. "Market-Based Workflow Management," Int'l Journal on Cooperative Information Systems (IJCIS), 7(4):297--314, December 1998.

25. M.J. Atallah et al, "Models and Algorithms for Coscheduling Compute-Intensive Tasks on a Network of Workstations," Journal of Parallel and Distributed Computing, Vol. 16, 1992.

26. High Performance Fortran Forum (HPFF), "HPF Language Specification", Version 2.0, January 31, 1997.

27. A. Grimshaw and W. Wulf. "Legion - a View from 50,000 Feet," Proc. 5th IEEE Symp. on High Performance Distributed Computing, pp. 89-99, IEEE Press, 1996.

28. N. Sample, C. Bartlett, M. Haines, "Mars: Runtime Support for Coordinated Applications," Proceedings of the ACM Symposium on Applied Computing, San Antonio, TX, February 28- March 2, 1999.

29. P. Lawrence, editor, Workflow handbook 1997, John Wiley 1997.

30. H. Pozewaunig, J. Eder, and W. Liebhart. "ePERT: Extending PERT for Workflow Management Systems," In First EastEuropean Symposium on Advances in Database and Information Systems ADBIS ' 97, St. Petersburg, Russia, September 1997.

31. J. Eder, E. Panagos, H. Pezewaunig, and M. Rabinovich, "Time Management in Workflow Systems," In 3rd Int. Conf. on Business Information Systems, 1999.

32. J. Doyle, "Reasoned assumptions and Pareto optimality," Proc. Ninth International Joint Conference on Artificial Intelligence, 1985.

33. T. Anderson, D. Culler, and D. Patterson, "A Case for Networks of Workstations: NOW," IEEE Micro, February 1995.

34. R. G. Smith, "The CONTRACT NET: A formalism for the control of distributed problem solving," In Proceedings of the 5th Intl. Joint Conference on Artificial Intelligence (IJCAI-77), Cambridge, MA, 1977.
35. R. Balzer and K. Narayanaswamy, "Mechanisms for generic process support," In Proc. First ACM SIGSOFT Symp. Foundations Software Engineering, pages 21--32. ACM Software Engineering Notes, Vol. 18(5), December 1993

Using Logical Operators as an Extended Coordination Mechanism in Linda

Jim Snyder and Ronaldo Menezes*

Florida Institute of Technology
Department of Computer Sciences
Melbourne, Florida, USA
jsnyder@cfl.rr.com,rmenezes@cs.fit.edu

Abstract. In the last 20 years of research in coordination, researchers were able to demonstrate that distributed languages are made of two distinct parts: a computation and a coordination language. Among a plethora of coordination models (the basis of a coordination language) available today, LINDA is perhaps the most successful. LINDA advocates that processes should interact solely via associative shared memories called tuple spaces. LINDA has developed from a single-tuple-space into a multiple-tuple-space model but the coordination mechanism used was never extended to express the multiple-tuple-space model full potential. This paper describes an extension of the LINDA model, called LOGOP, where primitives can use logical operators to combine tuple spaces on-the-fly. It is argued that LOGOP provides a simpler and more elegant coordination mechanism than LINDA. An implementation of LOGOP is also described and initial results indicate that LOGOP implementations are efficient when dealing with multiple tuple spaces.

1   Introduction

Coordination is a fast-growing research area. Emerging fields such as mobile computation and mobile computing, amorphous computing [1], and large scale Internet applications require non-trivial coordination patterns.

LINDA [3] is arguably the most important coordination model. LINDA has suffered a series of extensions. Among these, the extension from a single tuple space to a multiple tuple space model [4] can be said to be of prime importance for it made the model a better abstraction for open distributed systems.

Despite all research in LINDA, little has been done to improve the suitability of the model to areas of computer science that require advanced coordination patterns. There are a few good specialized extensions of LINDA for a variety of fields but none has looked into exploring the full potential of features already provided in LINDA such as multiple tuple spaces. This paper argues that the potential of the multiple-tuple-spaces abstraction is yet to be explored because the LINDA primitives provide a very basic coordination mechanism when it comes to using multiple tuple spaces.

---

* Corresponding author

F. Arbab and C. Talcott (Eds.): COORDINATION 2002, LNCS 2315, pp. 317–331, 2002.

This paper introduces LogOp, a Linda-based model that uses logical operators at the primitive level to provide an extended coordination mechanism, which is better suited to the multiple tuple space abstraction.

This paper is divided as follows: Section 2 describes the Linda model; Section 3 describes LogOp model and the semantics of its primitives when used with logical operators; Section 4 describes a LogOp implementation; Section 5 describes some preliminary results that demonstrate that the expressiveness of LogOp has some influence on the performance of the implementation; Section 6 identifies other works that are related to the expressiveness of Linda; and Section 7 discusses future work and present the conclusion.

2   Background

Linda provides primitives to processes enabling them to store and retrieve tuples from tuple spaces. Although the names of the primitives vary slightly in different implementations, the functionalities are normally very similar. Processes use the primitive out to store tuples. They retrieve tuples using the primitives in and rd. These primitives take a template (a definition of a tuple) and use associative matching to retrieve the desired tuple — while in removes a matching tuple, rd takes a copy of the tuple. Both in and rd are blocking primitives, that is, if a matching tuple is not found in the tuple space, the process executing the primitive blocks until a matching tuple can be retrieved. The blocking nature of these primitives and the fact that they can only deal with one tuple space at a time motivated the proposal of LogOp

In addition to the primitives above some Linda implementations provide non-blocking versions of in and rd, called inp and rdp respectively. These primitives have the same semantics of their blocking counterparts when a matching tuple is can be found in the tuple space. However, they behave significantly different if a matching tuple cannot be found — they fail instead of blocking.

The standard Linda assumes a single tuple space. In the multiple tuple-spaces variants, these spaces are disjoint. In other words, processes can only access one tuple space at a time — processes that require access to several tuple spaces have to do so by serializing the access. Although this serialization is reasonable in many cases, it limits the ability of Linda to express coordination where the contents of different tuple spaces need to be considered as a whole.

For instance, in producer-consumer architectures the type of coordination described in Figure 1 appears frequently. In the scenario depicted in Figure 1 a process X is waiting for a tuple to appear in *either* of the tuple spaces so it can proceed. This situation is also commonplace in other areas such as job scheduling. In job scheduling Figure 1 could be used to represent a process X that depends on the termination of either process A or B. Despite the simplicity of this scenario, Linda is unable to properly express it if ordering is *not* important. Due to its blocking nature, in cannot be used to implement the scenario. This paper proposes to extend the primitives so that they can deal with more than one tuple space at a time, thus allowing simple scenarios such as the one depicted in Figure 1 to be elegantly expressed.

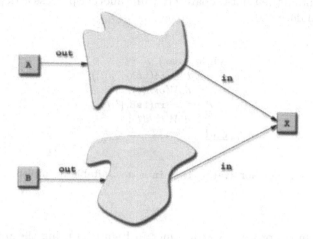

Fig. 1. Process X wants access to both tuple spaces but *does not* want to impose any ordering in the access.

3 LogOp Linda

LogOp is a coordination model which aims at improving the expressiveness and efficiency of Linda primitives. Linda is widely acceptable in the coordination community due to its elegance and simplicity but it lacks the ability to maintain its elegance in problems such as the one described in Section 2.

Efficiency is also a concern for LogOp. Some could argue that models are not directly linked to efficiency. However, a good, well-thought, model is likely to produce better implementations — the model's characteristics are embedded into their implementations.

Very few models have looked into improving the efficiency of their implementations by modifying the model characteristics. Rowstron's work on efficiency of open Linda systems has produced two interesting models whose implementation were shown to be more efficient than implementations of the standard Linda model. Rowstron's models assume that tuple spaces are organized in a hierarchy[12], and add the concept of asynchronous primitives [13].

LogOp primary concern is expressiveness but it tries to achieve good performance at the implementation level as a consequence of expressiveness. This approach is different from Rowstron's approaches where performance is the main focus — implementations should be efficient even if expressiveness is lost.

Section 2 described a simple situation where two independent processes are producing data to a consumer using different tuple spaces. While in some cases it may be possible to use a single tuple space to store the produced data, this assumption, besides restrictive, is not always true. It is not uncommon for processes to maintain their data separately while another process is dependent upon the generated data.

```
while (true)
    t := in(tsA, [?int]);
    doWork(t);
    t := in(tsB, [?int]);
    doWork(t);
end
```

Fig. 2. Pseudo-code demonstrating that **in** is not suitable to implement process X in Figure 1.

Figure 2 shows process X (consumer in Figure 1) using the primitive **in**. It is clear that this example does not express the consumer process X correctly; the process will block on tuple space **tsA** first and then on **tsB**. This solution is incorrect because the data produced in **tsB** would never be consumed unless data is also produced in **tsA**. In fact, the number of elements produced in both tuple spaces must always be the same. Thus, **in** is not the appropriate primitive to be used in this case.

```
while (true)
    t := inp(tsA, [?int]);
    if (!isEmpty(t))
        doWork(t);
    end
    t := inp(tsB, [?int]);
    if (!isEmpty(t))
        doWork(t);
    end
end
```

Fig. 3. Possible solution using **inp**.

One may be tempted to solve the problem using **inp** instead of **in** since **inp** is not a blocking primitive. Figure 3 shows such a solution. Although this solution will correctly produce the desired results, it is also extremely inefficient. The polling caused by the execution of the process may make it prohibitive. At each loop iteration the process will make up to N requests where N is the number of tuple spaces involved in the operation. It is not difficult to see that if several process constantly rely on this solution to get data from tuple spaces, the LINDA kernel may quickly become a bottleneck given the number of requests it has to process.

LOGOP was developed to tackle problems as the one described above. It is easy to observe that the required associations amongst the tuple spaces relate to basic logical operators such as AND, OR and NOT. These operators are used in LOGOP primitives making them more suited to deal with multiple tuple spaces.

$$< \text{PRIMITIVE} > (< \text{EXP} >, < \text{TUPLE} >)$$

where
```
<EXP>  ::= <OP>(<ARGS>)
<ARGS> ::= <ARG> | <ARG>,<ARGS>
<ARG>  ::= handle | <EXP>
<OP>   ::= AND | OR | NOT
<PRIMITIVE> ::= in | rd | out
<TUPLE> := tuple | template
```

Fig. 4. BNF of LOGOP primitives.

The BNF in Figure 4 describes the general form of LOGOP primitives. LO-GOP adds the feature of combining tuple spaces with logical operators. The logical operators may be used in conjunction with most primitives. However, this paper describes the semantics only for the standard blocking and non-blocking primitives (in, rd and out). The BNF is meant to show what type of expression can be used in the LOGOP model. For instance the grammar recognizes an expression such as in (OR (ts1,ts2,ts3),[?int]).

Another issue that had to be addressed was the subset of logical operators being considered. As shown in Figure 4 this paper describes only the operators AND, OR and NOT. The choice for working with these operators does not make LOGOP any less general. It is known that logical expressions involving other operators can be reduced to an equivalent one using AND, OR and NOT. Yet, the explicit use of other logical operators improves expressiveness and will be considered in future work.

In the sections to follow, the semantics of each logical operator is described in the context of all three primitives.

3.1 The OR Operator

The OR operator has the effect of combining tuple spaces so that processes can store and retrieve tuples from any of the tuple spaces from a list without having to impose an order on the way the tuple spaces are accessed. For instance, consider once again the scenario in Figure 1. It may be necessary for a process (say a consumer) to read tuples from any of several tuple spaces. The OR operator, when used to combine tuple spaces, allows processes to express this scenario. When storing tuples the use of the OR operator adds another level of non-determinism to the model. The informal semantics of each of LOGOP primitive is as follows:

out : The use of an out along side with the OR operator causes a tuple to be placed in any of the tuple spaces defined in the primitive. The tuple space is chosen non-deterministically. For instance, out (OR (ts1,ts2),[''Hello'']) will store the tuple [''Hello''] in either ts1 or ts2. The choice of which one is made non-deterministically. The semantics of a conditional OR was used here. Due to the fact that an out operation always succeeds, the use of an logical OR would make the it similar to the out using the AND operator.

in, rd : The use of an in and rd along side with the OR operator will make LOGOP search for a tuple matching the given template in the tuple spaces defined in the operation. If none of the tuple spaces contain a matching tuple the process blocks until a tuple is placed in any of the tuple spaces and can be retrieved. For the primitive to succeed (not block) a tuple must be found in one or more of tuple spaces in the list. These primitives return a list of tuples found. If the OR operator takes n tuple spaces, the result is a list containing at most n tuples and at least 1 (one) — since 0 (zero) makes the process block.

For instance, when a process executes in (OR (ts1,ts2,ts3),[?string]) it blocks if tuples matching the template [?string] cannot be found in any of the tuple spaces listed. If a matching tuple can be found in one of these tuple spaces the process will not block and the tuple is returned. One other case is when a matching tuple is found in more than one tuple space. In this case a list of tuples will be returned. This list contains one tuple from each tuple space where a matching tuple could be found.

The semantics tries to follow the exact definition of a logical OR (as opposed to the concept of a conditional OR). At the implementation level it may be possible to implement both variants so as to maximize parallelism or/and improve efficiency. It is clear that this definition is not symmetric to the given definition of the OR when used with an out.

inp, rdp : These primitives are failing versions of the primitives above. inp and rdp behave exactly like the primitives above when a matching tuple can be found in at least one tuple space. The difference in this case is when a matching tuple cannot be found in any of the tuple spaces. While the primitives in and rd block, inp and rdp would fail returning an *empty* list of tuples to the process.

Figure 5 shows the solution for the producer consumer problem described earlier. Observe that LOGOP is able to express the solution in a very elegant way. This simple example already shows a case where LOGOP expressiveness has an impact in the solution.

The idea that primitives may return a list of tuples instead of a single tuple is also a consequence of the extension of the primitives to the multiple tuple space model. The decision to make the *getter* primitives (in, inp, rd, rdp) return a list of tuple spaces is based on the logic behind the operator OR. If one assumes that there is a true or false value associated with a tuple space (depending on whether the tuple space contains a matching tuple), one could use boolean logic to find out the action that results from the execution of a getter primitive. Since several false values combined with OR result in false, the primitive fails — in

while (*true*)
  $t := $ **in**(OR(**tsA**, **tsB**), $[?int]$);
  doWork(*t*);
end

Fig. 5. Process in LOGOP representing a consumer in the scenario depicted in Figure 1.

the case of **in** and **rd** this causes the process to block. On the other hand, if at least one tuple space has the value **true** the result of the OR operator will also be **true** meaning that primitive succeeded in getting a tuple (or more).

Table 1 summarizes the action in all cases involving two tuple spaces. Note that **true** means that a tuple space has a matching tuple and **false** means that a matching tuple cannot be found.

Table 1. Summary of the action upon the execution of *getter* primitives along with OR.

ts1	ts2	Action
false	false	Fail
true	false	One tuple is returned
false	true	One tuple is returned
true	true	Two tuples are returned

3.2   The AND Operator

The AND operator allows processes to consider *all* tuple spaces in a list. The use of AND to combine tuple spaces ranges from event notification to broadcast of information. The semantics of this operator is not as obvious as the semantics of OR and need a more detailed description:

out : The use of AND with an **out** allows processes to store a tuple in a list of tuple spaces in just one step. Although broadcast operations are not easily expressed in LINDA, the LOGOP version of this primitive is more elegant and is likely to generate a more efficient implementation — if n tuple spaces are involved in the operation, LINDA would have to execute the **out** primitive n times. This operation could be very expensive due to the overhead associated with sending n messages separately to the kernel. In LOGOP only one message is sent to the kernel. Once the message is in the kernel, it is stored in the individual tuple spaces.

in, rd : The AND operator can also be used in blocking primitives. The semantics of these primitives is such that the process will block if one ore more tuple spaces in the list fail to contain a tuple matching the template given in the primitive.

Similar to the OR case, the decision on whether the primitive fails (block) is made based on the concept that tuple spaces have the `true` or `false` values associated with them. For an AND to produce `true` all tuple spaces that are considered in the primitive must have value `true` — they all must have a matching tuple.

The primitive returns a list containing n tuples — one from each tuple space, where n is the number of tuple spaces considered in the operation.

inp, rdp : These primitives are failing versions of the ones above; thus they never block. When used with an AND to combine tuple spaces, these primitives either return a list containing n tuples, where n is the number of tuple spaces defined in the primitive, or return an empty list.

It should be noticed that a naive implementation of the operator AND with getter primitives may cause deadlock. Suppose a process executes an `in` combining two tuple spaces, `ts1` and `ts2`, using an AND. If the implementation is such that a matching tuple is retrieved from tuple space `ts1` before knowing whether tuple space `ts2` also has matching tuple, a deadlock may happen if these operations are performed while another process grabs a matching tuple from `ts2` and blocks on `ts1`. This situation is not uncommon but it is not a problem introduced by LOGOP. In fact, LOGOP may actually be a better solution than using the original primitives in series when it comes to avoiding deadlocks of this kind. Using standard primitives the programmers would have to control these situations. In LOGOP, in some cases, the kernel may be able to identify a possible deadlock situation and use a deadlock avoidance mechanism to deal with the problem.

LOGOP kernel should implement the blocking primitives as atomic operations. This may be achieved using transactions — a process either get all tuples it requires or none. The control of the blocked process by the kernel has to be done with care. The kernel may maintain a list of blocked process and keep track of tuples being stored or retrieved using a tuple-monitoring sub-system [8] so as to be able to unblock process whenever possible.

3.3   The NOT Operator

Before describing this operator, it is important to explain the concept of *a complement of a tuple space* that is used in the semantics of the NOT operator in LOGOP. In any implementation of LINDA it is possible for the kernel to keep track of the tuple spaces that a particular process knows. This idea has been implemented already in a few LINDA systems [11,7]. In LOGOP the complement of a tuple space `tsA` (or NOT (`tsA`)), represents the set of all tuple spaces that a process has knowledge of beside `tsA`.

Note that the complement of a tuple space may differ from process to process. This is the case because the universe set used to compute the complement depends on the process executing the operation. The complement is *not* based on the total number of tuple spaces available in the system because this would generate security concerns such as a process accessing a tuple space private to another process. Additionally, since the universe set used is independent for each process, the creation of a tuple space by another process does not side effect the execution of NOT.

There is an equivalence between the NOT operator and the OR operator. The execution of a primitive using a NOT (tsA) by process P1 is the same as the execution of the same primitive along with an OR in the complement of tsA from the point of view of P1. However, LOGOP includes this operator to improve the expressiveness of the system — instead of writing a long list of tuple spaces combined by OR except for one, the programmer could just use the NOT.

The specific semantics of NOT when used in conjunction to the each of the primitives are:

out   : The semantics of NOT with out is quite straightforward. The tuple will be non-deterministically stored in any of the tuple spaces that form the complement of the tuple spaces defined in the operator. Since it has been shown that there is a relationship between NOT and OR the semantics here is similar to the semantics for the operator OR.

in, rd   : Here also the semantics is equivalent to the use of OR in the complement of the tuple spaces defined in the NOT operator. The process will block if a matching tuple cannot be found in any of the tuple spaces that form the complement of the tuple spaces. This primitive returns n tuples where n is the number of tuple spaces that contain a matching tuple.

inp, rdp   : These primitives are failing versions of the primitives above. If a tuple cannot be found in any of the tuple spaces forming the complement of the tuple spaces defined in the operation the primitive fails and returns an empty list.

Figure 6 shows a process in LOGOP making use of the NOT operator. If one assumes that this process currently knows about three tuple spaces: ts1, ts2 and ts3, the execution of the primitive in Figure 6 is the same as executing out (OR (ts2,ts3),[45,''Hello'']).

$$out(\text{NOT}(\text{ts1}), [45," Hello"]);$$

Fig. 6. Using the NOT operator applied to tuple space ts1.

It should be noticed that deadlock may also occur if the NOT operator is used incorrectly. Suppose for instance that a process only knows about one tuple space, say ts1. If a process contains the execution of an in or a rd on NOT (ts1) the process will go into a deadlock situation. Because the process is blocked, it cannot acquire knowledge of other tuple spaces. Consequently, NOT (ts1) will always be an empty list.

In these situations it may be desirable to have the LOGOP kernel reject the primitive. Since the kernel can find out that the complement of a tuple space is an empty list, it could generate some exception or make the primitive fail. Either solution will affect the known semantics of the blocking primitives as failing is not part of the expected behavior of an in or a rd.

4 Implementation

A LOGOP prototype has been implemented using Java. LOGOP uses an open client-server architecture where the number of servers and clients is not pre-determined at compile time. In order to avoid bottlenecks, multi-threading is extensively used. Each LOGOP server has four threads: two dealing with server requests and two dealing with client requests. A pair of threads is used to connect servers and clients in order to make the task of receiving objects and sending objects concurrent. On the client side, each LOGOP primitive has its own thread as this improves performance when large quantities of primitives need to be processed.

A list of LOGOP servers available in the system is statically kept in file. This file is loaded by the servers when they start. New servers can start at any time and if they were not originally listed in the file they add their names to the file and broadcast to other servers the information that they are now available in the system. Currently, the client tries to connect to a server in the same machine (same IP address) and if one is not available a server is chosen randomly from the list of servers available in the system. After the connection is established, the server chosen becomes the *default server* for this client.

LOGOP uses the concept of distributed central servers, where the tuple spaces contents are not distributed across several servers — each tuple space is entirely stored in one server. When a server receives a request to create a tuple space, it creates the tuple space locally. One of the properties of a tuple space is its location (IP number of the server where the tuple space is stored). This property is used to route requests that processes make to different tuple spaces.

When a client executes a getter primitive, the request is sent to the process default server. In the LOGOP server, the operation is broken into smaller operations by a server component named the *decomposer* and the list of tuple space analyzed. The decomposer takes the list of tuple spaces and groups them by IP addresses. After they are grouped each server involved in the primitive is contacted. The server receives its list of tuple spaces, the primitive being executed, and the logical operator used to combine the tuple spaces. Then, the default server waits for an answer from all the other servers involved. As responses come back from other servers, their tuples (if any) are placed into a list object that will be returned to the client process. When all responses are received, the object is sent back to the client.

When a client executes a *setter* primitive such as an out, the request is sent directly to the client's default server. Again the decomposer analyzes the list of tuple spaces and groups them based on their IP addresses. The tuple is then sent to each server involved in the operation so that they, in turn, can store the tuple in the tuple spaces. This process is slightly different when OR is the operator being used since the default server chooses one of the tuple spaces in the list to send the tuple. After the default server acknowledge that the message was received, the client is allowed to proceed (the primitive returns).

It should be noted that the above does not mean to say the an out is a blocking primitive. The need for an acknowledgment is mainly due to the out-ordering requirement [2].

4.1   Using Wrapper Functions

It is important to discuss the issue of using wrapper functions to implement the LogOp logical operators. The name wrapper functions refers to the fact that they combine existing functions into a new function that achieves the desired functionality.

In the case of LogOp it is true to say that wrapper functions could be used to provide the same expressiveness as LogOp operators. However, LogOp is a coordination model and should not rely on artifacts of computation languages to achieve advanced coordination mechanisms.

Additionally, wrapper functions are normally implemented just as a mere translation from one function call to the (several) original function calls. In other words, the expressiveness of a possible solution using wrapper functions would be achieved using the standard primitives. Therefore all the problems already described, such as polling, would still be present in the system.

5   Preliminary Results

This section covers some preliminary results on the performance of LogOp's primitive in. Three machines on the same subnet running Sun's Solaris 8 were involved for testing purposes. The first system (machine X) contains four CPUs and 1Gb of memory. The other two systems (machines A and B) are Sparc 5 with 256Mb of memory.

The goal of the experiment is to demonstrate the advantages (in terms of execution time) of LogOp's primitives when compared to Linda's. Four tuple spaces were created in the systems: two tuple spaces, ts1 and ts2, held in machine A and the other two, ts3 and ts4, held in machine B.

Three processes were implemented. Two of them (in machine A and B) created the tuple spaces and stored a number of tuples in each tuple spaces. The third process was placed on machine X and had the job of retrieving all the tuples stored in all four tuple spaces. The test sample consists of six different counts of tuples: 100, 500, 1000, 5000, 10000 and 15000. The number of tuples were divided equally amongst all four tuple spaces.

In LogOp, due to the existence of the AND operator, the producer processes (in machine A and B) store the tuples using the code shown in Figure 7. In fact, the producer processes differ slightly since they deal with different tuple spaces. Figure 7 shows the code for producer in machine A.

The code for the consumer process has to consider all four tuple spaces at the same time. This is shown in Figure 8 where the consumer also make use of the AND operator.

The traditional way to implement this idea in LINDA is by serializing the primitives which diminishes the degree of parallelism of the implementation. The code for the standard LINDA does not use the AND operator. Therefore, the producers will have two primitives out, one after the other, whereas the consumer will have four primitives in.

> **while** *(index < maxTuples)* **do**
>   out(AND(**ts1, ts2**), *new Integer(index)*);
>   *index* + +;
> **end**

Fig. 7. Code for producer process in LOGOP.

> **while** *(index < maxTuples)* **do**
>   in(AND(**ts1, ts2, ts3, ts4**), *new Formal(*"**Integer**"*)*);
>   *index* + +;
> **end**

Fig. 8. Code for the consumer process in LOGOP.

Table 2 shows a comparison of the times taken to retrieve all the tuples in all tuple spaces using LINDA and using LOGOP. This table does not account for the cost of the out primitive, only the time taken to perform the in primitives is measured.

Table 2. Comparison of LINDA and LOGOP of the time taken to retrieve tuples based using in.

No. Tuples	Time in LINDA	Time in LOGOP
100	21.634	11.522
500	106.072	55.796
1000	210.882	113.380
5000	1043.950	554.677
10000	2083.667	1111.477
15000	3185.943	1666.896

It can be seen in Table 2 that in average LINDA took approximately 50% more time than LOGOP to perform the operations. In a similar experiment with the primitive out, it was also found that LOGOP performed a little better. However, the gain is not too significant due to the fact the out is normally an efficient primitive.

When compared against a series of inp primitives, instead of in, the results were similar to the results described in Table 2. This outcome was expected since the tuples were placed in the tuple spaces before the execution of the consumer and the semantics of inp and in are the same when a matching tuple is found.

6   Related Work

Merrick and Wood [9] have proposed to replace the idea of tuple spaces with the concept of SCOPES. In their model tuples can belong to multiple scopes. Scopes are created either empty (no tuples) or by combining other existing scopes. In terms of expressiveness, SCOPES is better than LINDA and it can indeed model more coordination patterns than LINDA. However, in order to solve problems as the one depicted in Figure 1, a new scope will have to be created combining the two existing ones. While this assumption is not a problem in small systems, the creation of these scopes in large dynamic systems may force many extra structures to be created. Furthermore, a scope is a "permanent" structure that need to be explicitly created. In LOGOP the model (LINDA) is not changed nor any extra structure needs to be created — tuple spaces are combined on-the-fly and only from the point of view of the process executing the primitive.

Another solution that aims at modeling the examples described in this paper are the event-driven coordination models such as Lime [10] and TSpaces [5]. In these models, processes can register for events in the kernel. Once processes are registered, the kernel notifies them every time the event takes place. For instance, a process could register with two tuple spaces to receive any tuples that match the template [?int]. From the moment processes register onwards, if a tuple arrives in any of the two tuple spaces and this tuple matches the given template, the tuple is immediately sent to the process.

Event-driven coordination models are very powerful and are able to express diverse coordination patterns. Yet, these models are aimed at avoiding blocking of processes. Processes normally register for an event but carry on with their execution. Event-driven models are analogous to the idea of subscribing to a mailing list for instance; once you say you want to receive messages, the messages will keep arriving in your mailbox until you cancel your subscription (cancel the event).

Jacquet and De Bosschere describe an extension of the μLog model where relations between blackboards can be defined [6]. However, the relations are normally defined as rules of pertinence of tuples in the blackboards. For instance, they are able to express with these rules that *if a tuple t is placed in blackboard A it should also be placed in blackboard B*. Surely this is somewhat similar to an AND; the difference in LOGOP is that rules are not created *per se* and no relation between tuple spaces is created in the context of the entire system. LOGOP offers more flexibility as it allows users to define the scope of the primitive on-the-fly.

LOGOP primary concern is with blocking primitives. It extends the model to allow a process to *wait* on several tuple spaces at the same time, without imposing any ordering. Another difference between LOGOP and event-driven models is that events (normally tuples) are sent one at a time from the kernel to the process, while LOGOP allows for several tuples to be retrieved at the same time. For instance the use of AND forces the kernel to return either N tuples or none. In a event-driven model this would be difficult to achieve since tuples would be sent to the process as they appear in the tuple space.

7   Conclusion and Future Work

This paper described an extension for the LINDA model that makes better use of multiple tuple spaces. It has been argued that the extensions provided in LOGOP allow for more elaborate synchronization architectures when compared to the standard primitives of LINDA.

It has been demonstrated that for a class of problems where simultaneous access to several tuple spaces is required, LINDA is not able to express a reasonable solution. LOGOP allows the programmer to combine tuple spaces using the abstraction provided by logical operators. It is believed that such abstraction is quite natural when dealing with tuple spaces.

A LOGOP prototype has been implemented and the experiments look promising. This confirms the expectation that changes in the model level would affect the performance of implementations.

Future work in LOGOP involves implementing a fully functional system where logical operators besides AND, OR and NOT are not available. It is also desirable to have a module in the kernel that can apply simplification rules to the expressions involving tuple spaces. This on itself is a difficult task but should allow the implementation to work with more elaborate expressions.

Further work is still required on the semantics of LOGOP primitives. It is unclear what should be the behavior of the processes when faced with more elaborate expressions such as in (OR (ts1,NOT (ts2),AND (ts1,ts3)),[?int]). Again, the implementation of a logical expression evaluator should shed some light on the semantics on LOGOP.

Finally, it would be interesting to see how logical operators could be applied to templates. This would create a LOGOP implementation with two levels of logical operators. In this system, one would be able to express: *retrieve a tuple matching either template A or template B which is stored in either tuple space X or tuple space Z*. This extension is being planned to be added to LOGOP after the implementation of a more elaborate logical expression evaluator.

References

1. H. Abelson, D. Allen, D. Coore, C. Hanson, G. Homsy, T. F. Knight, R. Nagpal, E. Rauch, G. J. Sussman, and R. Weiss. Amorphous computing. *Communications of the ACM*, 43(5):74–82, May 2000.
2. A. Douglas, A. Wood, and A. Rowstron. LINDA Implementation Revisited. In P. Nixon, editor, *Proc. of the 18th World Occam and Transputer User Group*, pages 125–138. IOS Press, April 1995.
3. D. Gelernter. Generative Communication in LINDA. *ACM transactions in programming languages and systems*, 1:80–112, 1985.

4. D. Gelernter. Multiple Tuple Spaces in LINDA. In *Proc. of PARLE 89*, pages 20–27. Springer-Verlag, 1989.
5. IBM Corporation. *T Spaces Programmer's Guide*, 1998. Eletronic version only. http://www.almaden.ibm.com/cs/TSpaces/.
6. J. Jacquet and K. DeBosschere. On Relating Blackboards in the mLog Coordination Model. In *Proc. HICSS30, Sw Track*, pages 359–368, Hawaii, 1997. IEEE Computer Society Press.
7. R. Menezes. Experience with Memory Management in Open Linda Systems. In *Proceedings of the 16th ACM Symposium on Applied Computing*, pages 187–196. ACM, March 2001.
8. R. Menezes and A. Wood. Garbage Collection in Linda using Tuple Monitoring and Process Registration. In *Proc. of the 10th International Conference on Parallel and Distributed Computing and Systems*, pages 490–495, Las Vegas, Nevada, USA, 1998. Acta Press.
9. I. Merrick and A. Wood. Coordination with scopes. In *Proceedings of the 2000 ACM symposium on Applied computing 2000*, volume 1, pages 210–217, Como, Italy, March 2000. ACM.
10. G. P. Picco, A. L. Murphy, and G.-C. Roman. LIME: Linda Meets Mobility. In D. Garlan, editor, *Proceedings of the 21st International Conference on Software Engineering (ICSE'99)*, pages 368–377, Los Angeles, CA, USA, May 1999. ACM Press.
11. A. Rowstron. WCL: A co-ordination Language for geographically distributed agents. *World Wide Web*, 1:167–179, 1998.
12. A. Rowstron and A. Wood An Efficient Distributed Tuple Space Implementation for Networks of Workstations. In L. Bougé, P. Fraigniaud, A. Mignotte, and Y. Robert, editors, *Euro-Par'96*, volume 1123 of *Lecture Notes in Computer Science*, pages 510–513. Springer-Verlag, 1996.
13. A. Rowstron and A. Wood. BONITA: A Set of Tuple Space Primitives for Distributed Coordination. In H. El-Rewini and Y. N. Patt, editors, *Proc. of the 30th Hawaii International Conference on System Sciences*, volume 1, pages 379 388. IEEE Computer Society Press, January 1997.

A Framework for Coordinating Parallel Branch and Bound Algorithms

Andries Stam[1,2]

[1] LIACS, Leiden University, The Netherlands
[2] Ordina Institute for Research and Innovation, Gouda, The Netherlands
andries.stam@ordina.nl

Abstract. Branch and bound algorithms can be used for a variety of optimization problems. They are known to be very well suited for parallelization, which is a useful property to investigate in the light of coordination. This paper presents a general framework for parallel branch and bound algorithms, implemented using the coordination language MANIFOLD. Within this framework, the code for the optimization problem is separated from the generic branch and bound algorithm and the coordination strategy is separated from the coordinated components. The framework is an example of how the use of a coordination language can lead to a clean, comprehensible and flexible software architecture for complex parallel systems.

1 Introduction

Branch and bound algorithms are known to be very well suited for parallelization, a property which we found useful to investigate in the light of coordination. We have done so by building a general framework for parallel branch and bound algorithms, which can be parameterized with a specific optimization problem and a specific *coordination strategy*. The coordination strategy determines which framework components are used and how they are interconnected.

The framework is built using the coordination language MANIFOLD [2]. Though the framework could also be implemented by using a data-driven coordination language such as Linda [1], we have chosen to use the (control-driven) MANIFOLD, in order to gain experience with its direct and rigid separation of coordination strategy and computational code. The MANIFOLD language has been used in several other complex parallel or distributed settings [5,4].

In this paper we present the results of our investigation, thereby focusing on coordination issues. We provide an introduction to branch and bound algorithms, their rules and their parallelization in Section 2. An overview of MANIFOLD is given in Section 3. In Section 4 we show which generic components we have identified and implemented thus far. In Section 5 we briefly mention some existing frameworks and their differences with the one described in this paper. Finally, conclusions are drawn in Section 6.

F. Arbab and C. Talcott (Eds.): COORDINATION 2002, LNCS 2315, pp. 332–339, 2002.

2   Branch and Bound Algorithms

In this section we give an overview of a generic branch and bound algorithm, explain its basic rules and discuss how such an algorithm can be parallelized.

2.1   Overview

Branch and bound algorithms [8] partition the problem space by reducing a known problem to a set of smaller problems (branch). They also try to reduce the search tree as far as possible, by computing *lower bounds* on problems (bound), maintaining a global *upper bound* and eliminating problems with lower bounds that exceed the global upper bound. Important optimization problems for which branch and bound implementations exist, are the Traveling Salesman Problem and the Knapsack Problem.

A simple example of a problem which can be solved with a branch and bound technique is the *Eight Puzzle* problem ([9], pp. 339–342). In this problem, a 3x3 board contains eight tiles which have to be rearranged in row-major order by repeatedly moving a tile to the single hole on the board. The bound of a problem, in this case a specific board configuration, can be computed by taking the sum of the Manhattan distance between each tile and its correct location and adding the number of moves made so far. A branch can be done by considering all board configurations obtained by performing a single move. A board configuration can be eliminated when its lower bound exceeds the global upper bound. This upper bound on its turn can be taken equal to the lower bound of the best solution to the problem found so far.

In general, a branch and bound algorithm works with the following rules, which are specific to the problem to be solved:

- A *Branch Rule* which specifies how a problem is divided into subproblems;
- A *Bound Rule* which states how a lower bound on a problem is computed;
- A *Selection Rule* which determines the order for branching subproblems;
- An *Elimination Rule* which states if a subproblem is feasible or not.

2.2   Parallelization

A branch and bound algorithm can be parallelized at *two* levels [11]: A *low* level parallelization which parallelizes the *basic actions* of the algorithm like branching, computing the lower bound, checking for feasibility and selecting a subproblem, and a *high* level parallelization which parallelizes *subproblem investigation*. In this framework we have implemented high level parallelization.

In high level parallel branch and bound algorithms, multiple subproblems are visited in parallel by a set of computational entities: *Workers*. These Workers select unvisited problems from a global *Subproblem Pool*, calculate their lower bound, check their feasibility and take a branch if applicable. Care has to be taken to inform all Workers about available global information, for example the global upper bound. The distribution of this global information over the entire pool of Workers in a parallel setting introduces a fair amount of communication which is not easy to reduce. Another important issue is termination of the algorithm. The algorithm terminates when there are no unvisited subproblems left and all Workers are idle, something which can only be determined by use of global information.

3   Manifold

MANIFOLD [2] is a coordination language for managing complex, dynamically changing interconnections among sets of independent, concurrent, cooperating processes, which is based on the IWIM model, described in [3]. Communication between processes is done via asynchronous channels, called *streams*.

In MANIFOLD, the atomic Workers of the IWIM model are called atomic processes. Atomic processes can only produce and consume units through their ports, generate and receive events, and compute.

Coordination processes are written in the MANIFOLD language and are called manifolds. Each manifold consists of a finite number of states. Transition to a state occurs when certain events have been received that match the event pattern given in the header of that state. The body of a state defines the set of actions that are to be performed (in a non-deterministic order) upon transition to that state. Examples of actions are creating and activating processes, generating event occurrences, and connecting streams to ports.

In MANIFOLD, the asynchronous IWIM channels are called streams. A stream is a communication link that transports variable-length units of data and represents a reliable and directed flow of information from its *source* to its *sink*. The constructor of a stream between two processes is, in general, a third process. Once a stream is established between a producer process and a consumer process, it operates autonomously. The sink of a stream is suspended only if no units are available in the stream. It is resumed as soon as the next unit becomes available for its consumption. The source of a stream is never suspended because the infinite buffer capacity of a stream is never filled.

In MANIFOLD, once an event is *raised* by a process, this process can continue with its activities, while the event occurrence propagates through the environment independently. Any receiver process that is interested in such an event occurrence will automatically receive it in its *event memory*. The observed event occurrences in the event memory of a process can be examined and reacted upon by this process at its own leisure.

The only control structure in the MANIFOLD language is an event-driven state transition mechanism, out of which more familiar control structures can be built.

4   The Coordination Framework

We have implemented a framework for parallel branch and bound algorithms as follows: First, there is a set of generic components, implemented as atomic manifolds in the C language. Second, we have implemented a set of coordination modules in **MANIFOLD**. Next to these, a set of interfaces for problem specific parts is implemented, which is not discussed in this article since it does not contribute to the issue of coordination.

4.1   Components

In Figure 4.1 the generic components of the framework are depicted. Some of these components must be parameterized with a problem specific part, which is indicated with a small hole in the component.

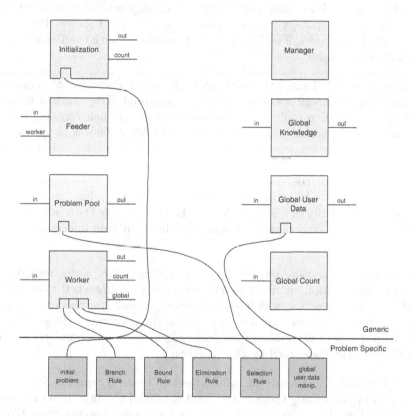

Fig. 4.1. Interfaces of the generic components of the framework.

Initialization. The *Initialization* manifold creates one working unit and puts it to its output port. The created unit represents the problem that has to be solved. Creation of this unit is done by an external problem specific C function. The manifold terminates after it has finished creating and sending the unit.

Selection. The *Feeder* manifold gets working units and distributes them over several Worker manifolds. The inner side of its own input port is permanently connected to a *Problem Pool* manifold, which represents the pool of unvisited subproblems and which is parameterized with the Selection Rule. Once a Worker sits idle, it sends a reference to itself to a special port of the Feeder. The incoming reference is dereferenced by the Feeder and the input port of the obtained Worker is connected to the output port of the Problem Pool in order to fetch an unvisited subproblem. After having done so, the Worker raises an event, whereafter the Worker is decoupled from the Problem Pool and the Feeder waits for the next Worker reference to come in.

Processing. The *Worker* manifold continuously fetches unvisited subproblems from the Problem Pool, processes them and creates several new subproblems when a branch occurs. New subproblems are sent to the Problem Pool via the input port of the Feeder. The Worker is parameterized with the Branch, Bound and Elimination Rules.

Global Information. There are two manifolds for maintaining global information: a *Global Knowledge* and a *Global User Data* manifold. Their task is to continuously get information units from Workers and convert their contents to global information, if applicable. For example, when a Global Knowledge process gets a unit with information about a solution just found with a lower bound that is smaller than the current upper bound, it will update the global upper bound. The output ports of the Global Knowledge and Global User Data manifolds work like variables, which can be read by every Worker when needed (e.g. for checking the feasibility of a subproblem). The Global User Data manifold is parameterized with C functions with which problem specific information can be manipulated.

Termination. The *Global Count* manifold gets special *count units* from Workers, containing information about units fetched, processed, branched from or eliminated. This process acts as a global *termination* process: it shuts down the entire program when it detects that no work can be done anymore. This is the case when there are no unvisited subproblems left in the Feeder and there are no subproblems being processed by the Workers.

Overall Control. The *Manager* manifold has two tasks: it *registers* Workers into the system by connecting them to the Feeder, Global Count, Global Knowledge and Global User Data. Next to that, it receives *request* events from Workers, which denote that a Worker is waiting for a new working unit. For each incoming request, it sends an event source reference to the Feeder, which will provide a working unit.

4.2   Coordination

In Figure 4.2 a standard configuration for the branch and bound algorithm is depicted. This configuration consists of a global Problem Pool and a set of local

Workers. The configuration is created dynamically and can be changed over time. Within the overview, forward and backward connections are depicted separately for convenience.

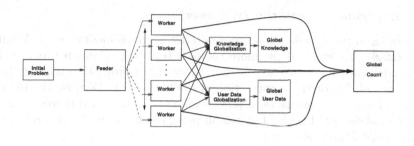

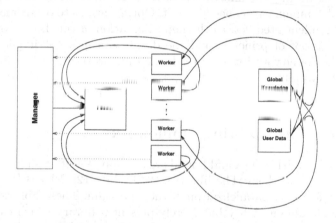

Fig. 4.2. Overview of processes and streams in a standard configuration

The Initial Problem manifold starts the algorithm by sending the initial problem to be solved to the Feeder. Continuously, Workers ask the Feeder for unvisited (sub)problems and are able to use of the information from the Global Knowledge and Global User Data manifold. Workers produce three types of units:

1. If the subproblem at hand is branched, a Worker produces new unvisited subproblems which are sent back to the Feeder (which sends them to its internal Problem Pool); if the subproblem can be solved directly, the global upper bound is updated by sending a unit to the Global Knowledge manifold.
2. If a Worker produces globally interesting information (for example, certain heuristic information derived while calculating a bound for a subproblem) it sends this information to the Global User Data manifold, as to make this information available to the entire set of Workers.

3. The third kind of unit contains information necessary for the Global Count manifold, which determines when to terminate the algorithm. This information consists of the number of units created in a branch.

4.3 Experiments with the Framework

We have used the coordination framework for an implementation of the simple eight puzzle problem and the more complex traveling salesman problem. Both the componentization and the localization of the coordination strategy turned out to be helpful for the construction of the framework. Because the interfaces of the various components were very clean and the data structures needed for communication could be held uncomplicated, the individual components could be easily developed separately.

Within the current implementation however, Workers treat each subproblem as a single unit of work, so that they are often more concerned with communicating than with computing; the unit of computation is too small in comparison with the amount of communication needed for it. Optimizations to overcome this drawback are not implemented yet, as the implementation of this framework is rather meant as a proof of principle and the disadvantage is not implied by the structure of the framework itself. Instead, the framework merely facilitates experimenting with various processing strategies and various types of Workers with different units of computation working on the same problem.

5   Comparison with Existing Frameworks

Several libraries for parallel branch and bound are developed. In this short paper we briefly mention four of them. The libraries PPBB-Lib [12], PUBB [10] and BoB [6] have their focus on parallelization of the algorithm. These libraries do not have the ease of configurability but merely present a library which can be used to implement entire branch and bound algorithms with an *endogenous* coordination style, which makes it more difficult to change or reuse the chosen coordination strategy. PICO (Parallel Integer and Combinatorial Optimizer) [7] is an object-oriented framework for parallel branch and bound algorithms. It does not have the centralized coordination strategy as represented by the MANIFOLD coordination modules.

6   Conclusions and Further Research

The branch and bound framework presented in this article shows an interesting application of coordination languages for achieving comprehensibility and configurational flexibility. From the perspective of software development, the use of coordination languages leads to a set of generic components which have a plain, simple interface. Next to this, the coordination modules, which determine the behaviour of the algorithm, are reusable and reduce the time needed to modify the coordination strategy.

Though current implementation has some performance disadvantages, the framework facilitates optimizations to overcome this drawback. Working out these optimizations has not been done; implementation of the framework was primarily meant as a proof of principle. In our opinion, the coordination framework presented in this short paper is an example of how the use of coordination languages for creating complex parallel systems can lead to software architectures which are well understandable and easy to configure or modify.

Acknowledgements. The author would like to thank Farhad Arbab and Kees Everaars for their kind help and support during experimentation with the MANIFOLD language.

References

1. S. Ahuja, N. Carriero, and D. Gelernter. Linda and friends. *IEEE Computer*, 19(8):26–34, 1986.
2. F. Arbab. Manifold version 2: Language reference manual. Technical report, Centrum voor Wiskunde en Informatica, Kruislaan 413, 1098 SJ Amsterdam, The Netherlands, 1995.
3. F. Arbab. The IWIM model for coordination of concurrent activities. In *Coordination '96*, Lecture Notes in Computer Science. Springer-Verlag, 1996.
4. F. Arbab and E.B.G. Monfroy. Distributed splitting of constraint satisfaction problems. In *Coordination 2000*, Lecture Notes in Computer Science. Springer-Verlag, 2000.
5. C.L. Blom, F. Arbab, S. Hummel, and I.J.P. Elshof. Coordination of a heterogeneous coastal hydrodynamics application in manifold. Technical Report SEN–R9833, Centrum voor Wiskunde en Informatica, Kruislaan 413, 1098 SJ Amsterdam, The Netherlands, 1998.
6. B. Le Cun and C. Roucairol et al. BoB: a unified platform for implementing branch-and-bound like algorithms. Technical Report 95/16, Laboratoire PRiSM, Université de Versailles, Saint Quentin en Yvelines, 1995.
7. J. Eckstein, C.A. Phillips, and W.E. Hart. PICO: An object-oriented framework for parallel branch and bound. Technical report, Rutgers Center for Operations Research, Rutgers University, New Jersey, 2000.
8. L.G. Mitten. Branch-and-bound methods: General formulation and properties. In *Operations Research 18*, pages 25–35, 1970.
9. Michael J. Quinn. *Parallel Computing - Theory and Practice*. McGraw Hill, inc., 1994.
10. Y. Shinano, M. Higaki, and R. Hirabayashi. A generalized utility for parallel branch and bound algorithms. Technical report, Department of Management Science, Science University of Tokyo, 1994.
11. H.W.J.M. Trienekens and A. de Bruin. Towards a taxonomy of parallel branch and bound algorithms. Technical Report EUR-CS-92-01, Erasmus University Rotterdam, Dept. of Computer Science, 1992.
12. S. Tschöke and T. Polzer. Portable parallel branch-and-bound library PPBB-Lib user manual, library version 2.0. Technical report, Department of Computer Science, University of Paderborn, 1996.

Policies for Cooperative Virtual Teams

Samir Tata

UMR n°7503 LORIA - Université Henri Poincaré
Campus Scientifique, BP 239
54506 Vandœuvre-lès-Nancy Cedex - FRANCE
Samir.Tata@loria.fr

Abstract. The work we propose here is principally concerned with co-operative interaction control in virtual teams. The objective is to allow members of a virtual team to describe in a simple way cooperative interactions in term of cooperation policies. Policies is described by access and synchronization contracts established between members of the virtual team. Indeed, cooperative interactions in virtual teams occur in the more common case through role managing and activity synchronisation. Policies can be combined to support different types of cooperatives interactions even the complex ones.

1   Introduction

Cooperative applications have seen, in the last few years, a very important development and a real improvement of their underling technologies. Among others, the particular class of cooperative applications dedicated to support cooperative virtual team is actually emerging, but still need effective concepts and mechanisms to enter a real development stage. A virtual team is a group of partners distributed in time, in space, over organisations, and gathered around a common project. Thus, partners with complementary competencies and knowledges can be gathered to carry out a project which is not with the range of only one person: the cooperation allows the team members to benefit from knowledge of each other. With this intention, partner activities are not carried out in an isolated manner, but interact during their execution while sharing common data in a coordinated way. Coordination brings a synergy that contributes to the improvement of each participant work performances.

On one hand, interactions can be relevant and constructive if they complement each other and converge the work towards the objective of the virtual team. On the other hand, they can cause adverse effects if they are not well coordinated or if participants don't follow their roles in the cooperation. An action effect can unintentionally remove the effect of an other action. The effective result of the cooperation and the desired objective are then likely to diverge.

To prevent this type of undesirable interaction behaviours, we think that it is important to manage three cooperation aspect: the management of the participants' roles during data sharing, the coordination of their activities and the interaction unpredictability. Indeed, the presence of users, with multiple levels of

F. Arbab and C. Talcott (Eds.): COORDINATION 2002, LNCS 2315, pp. 340–347, 2002.

experiment introduces a certain degree of unpredictability in cooperation. The objective of this paper is to control interactions in the cooperative virtual teams. For this reason, we aim at the definition of an interaction model to support these three cooperation aspects. Section 2 describes the inadequacies of access control and coordination models to support interactions in virtual teams. We presents in Section 3 a model that expresses cooperatives interactions in term of policies. The problem of policy consistency and composition is studied. Section 5 presents a framework that we developed to support cooperative interactions. Finally, Section 6 concludes this paper and presents some future work.

2   Related Work

To describe cooperative interactions, several models were presented. We can classify them into two categories. The first category is concerned by the management of roles. As in many works, in this category roles are defined as access rights. This category gathers consequently the access control models. The second category gory includes the coordination model developed in order to allow the application components to interact by following some fixed rules.

Firstly, the cooperative systems based on access models like Cruiser [1] or Montage [2] have used models which authorize or refuse for all users the access to shared data. And then systems like Duplex [3] or Grove [4] came. They have introduced the concepts of users and groups. The models of these systems have defined how one grants rights to users and groups. They have defined traditional rights, like the rights of reading and writing, as well as new rights, like the right of sharing a view [5]. Currently, the access control models (*e.g.* [6], [7]...) are presented to control roles of users sharing some common data. The concept of role considered as a means of organising the cooperation. It is considered that each user has a role (possibly many). For each common data, we associate with each role an access right. The combination role/access right defines for each user the set of operations which s/he can carry out on the common data.

To control interactions, coordination models, including workflow models [8, 9] and models based on processes theories [10,11], are based on the explicit knowledge of all activities and their dependencies. In general, they prescribe all the activities and their interaction in advance. Consequently, we think that these models are not appropriate to describe interactions in the cooperative applications. In addition to their weak support of data sharing, they cannot describe the cooperative interactions since these ones are unpredictable.

Generally, neither a model of coordination only nor a model of access control only is enough to support interactions in virtual teams. It is in fact necessary to define a model which integrates at the same time the coordination and the management of roles.

3   Interaction Model

The interaction model we propose in this paper integrates the role management, the activity coordination and supports the interaction unpredictability. Given a set of team members and a set of objects, the interaction model describes cooperative interactions the members can perform while they share common objects. Actions performed by a team member may be encapsulated into activities. But s/he can perform action outside activities. These interactions are defined in term of a list of cooperation policies. An activity is a finite sequence of actions with a name, a beginning and an end. A participant is a team member or an activity.

Formally the model is represented by $(Part, Obj, PL, AccessInf, SyncInf)$ where $Part$ is the set of participants, Obj is the set of shared objects and PL (Policy List) is the set of cooperation policies. Each one is composed by access and synchronisation contracts.

A cooperation policy is a set of rules defined between participants sharing some common objects. These rules are defined in terms of access and synchronisation contracts. The access contracts represent rights the participants have on shared objects and describe roles the they play when they share objects. The synchronisation contracts represent coordination rules the participant activities have to follow. Each policy has a set of administrators who have the right to perform operations on the policy to support the dynamics of work rules.

Formally the model is represented by $(PolAdmins, PolParts, PolObjects, Po-lAccess, PolSync, PolOperations)$. $PolAdmins$ is the administrators, $PolParts$ is the participants including the team members involving in the policy and their activities, $PolObjects$ is the set of shared objects, $PolAccess$ is a set of access contracts, $PolSync$ is a set of synchronisation contracts, and $PolOperations$ are operation executed by $PolAdmins$.

3.1   Access Contracts

We define an access contract as the association of a participant, an access right and an object. Formally, an access contract, noted $Access$, is a function from $Part \times Obj \times Right$ to $\{true, false\}$. An access right expresses alloowed operations on a shared object when it is positive. Whereas, it expresses unauthorised operations when it is negative.

Given a cooperation policy, we grant the right $+r$ to the participant p on the object o, if the set $PolAccess$ contains $(p, o, +r)$. If it contains the $(p, o, -r)$, then the right is refused.

3.2   Synchronization Contracts

We define a synchronization contract as the association of two activities, an object and a type of synchronization [12]. Formally a contract of synchronization, noted $Sync$, is a function from $Act \times Act \times Obj \times SyncType$ to $\{true, false\}$. To check if there is a synchronization (A, B, O, s), the set $PolSync$ is firstly consulted. If it contains (A, B, O, s) then the synchronization is valid and A and

B must follow it along their life cycle. In order to present the set $Sync\,Type$ (the different types of synchronization) we define in the following the notions of state and view sequences.

We call the *state sequence* of an object O, noted S^o, the ordered set of the states of O. We can define S^o as $S^o = \{S^o_0, S^o_1, \ldots\}$, where S^o_0 is the initial state of the object and S^o_1, S^o_2, ... are the successive states of O. An object can change its state when an activity performs an operation that changes the value of one of its attributes. An activity can observe a state of the object if it performs an operation which returns a value reflecting the state of this object. Note that no assumptions are made on the granularity of a state change. Depending on the context and of the application being specified, this may vary from one single character in a textual document to a CAD object.

We call *view sequence* of an activity A on an object O, noted S^o/A, the ordered subset of S^o restricted to the states observed by A.

Given an object, a synchronisation contract binds two activities to express the fact that there is a constraint on the some states observed by these activities. The synchronisation is a *activity synchronisation*, if it expresses constraints on the sequence of states observed by one or the other of the two activities. It is a *state synchronisation*, if it expresses constraints on only one state observed by one or the other of the two activities.

For a given object O, the activity A is synchronised to the activity B on O when S^o/A is included s^0_B. We mark this synchronisation type $ActSync$ (i.e. $sync(A, B, O, ActSync) \overset{\text{def}}{=} s^0_A \subset s^0_B$).

A and B are state synchronised if there exists a state $s^o_{a,i}$ observed by A and a state $s^o_{b,j}$ observed by B that are identical. We note this synchronisation type S_Sync $(Sync(A,\ B,\ o,\ S\_Sync) \overset{\text{def}}{=} \exists i \in \{0..n\},\ \exists j \in \{0..m\}\ e^o_{A,i} = e^o_{B,j})$ where n (respectively m) denotes the number of states observed by A (respectively B). This type of synchronisation can be used to specify the more general case of two activities synchronised on an arbitrary state. However, there is a lot of situations in which such synchronisation occurs at the beginning or at the end of one or both of the synchronised activities. For this reason, we provide specialised synchronisation types corresponding to the synchronisation of

- an activity initial state and an activity:$sync(A, B, O, IS\_Sync) \overset{\text{def}}{=} s^0_{A,0} \in S^0_B$
- the initial states of two activities: $sync(A, B, O, SIS\_Sync) \overset{\text{def}}{=} s^0_{A,0} = S^0_{B,0}$
- an activity final state and an activity:$sync(A, B, O, FS\_Sync) \overset{\text{def}}{=} s^0_{A,n} \in S^0_B$
- the final states of two activities: $sync(A, B, O, SFS\_Sync) \overset{\text{def}}{=} s^0_{A,n} = s^0_{B,m}$
- a final state with an initial state: $sync(A, B, O, Sq\_Sync) \overset{\text{def}}{=} s^0_{A,n} = s^0_{B,0}$
- two state sequences of two activities:

$$sync(A, B, O, TotSync) \overset{\text{def}}{=} n = m \wedge \forall i \in \{0..n\}, s^0_{A,i} = s^0_{B,i}$$

From these definitions, we can define a partial order on the set $Sync\,Type$: Let s_1 and s_2 be two synchronisation types, then $s_1 \to s_2 \overset{\text{def}}{=} \forall A, B \in Act, \forall o \in Obj$ $sync(A, B, O, s_1) \Rightarrow sync(A, B, O, s_2)$

3.3 Examples

Assume that in a given architectural design project there are three cooperating partners: an architect, an engineer, and an economist. The architect is the person responsible for the production of the final plan of the building and all of the related documents. However, the engineer can be in charge of some parts of this plan or of some technical details. Thus, they both modify the plan in parallel, and the last version produced by the engineer will be reviewed and included by the architect in the final documents. This situation is captured by the a policy with the following synchronization and access contracts:

$$Sync(engineer, architect, plan, FS\_Sync) \wedge \; Access(architect, plan, write) \wedge$$
$$Access(engineer, plan, write)$$

Their work is constrained by the workplan provided by the contracting authority. In general, this authority produces several successive versions of the workplan. Thus, the architect and the engineer both read the workplan, but do not modify it. In addition, it seems desirable to impose that the architect also accesses all the versions accessed by the engineer, but the reverse is not mandatory: the architect may work alone without reporting to the engineer. This situation is captured by a policy with the following contracts:

$$Sync(engineer, architect, program, ActSync)$$
$$\wedge Access(architect, program, read) \; \wedge Access(engineer, program, read)$$

All along the design process, the economist of the team produces cost estimations corresponding to the current version of the plan. These cost estimations may be read by the architect in order to check the compatibility of the project with the budget conditions. While it seems unnecessary to ensure that the architect has read all the successive estimations, a useful policy is to render mandatory that s/he reads the final one. This situation is captured by the a policy with the following contracts:

$$sync(architect, economist, estimation, SFS\_Sync)$$
$$\wedge Access(architect, estimation, read) \wedge \; Access(economist, estimation, write)$$

4   Consistency and Composition of Cooperation Policies

The access contracts define access rights on shared objects. Each positive right authorizes its holder to execute a set of operations on the object. For example, the right *write* on a directory authorizes its holder to create, to move or remove entries of the directory. However, a negative access right on an object unauthorises its holder to execute a set of operations on this object. To follow son synchronization contracts, participants in a cooperation policy must observe some states of the shared objects. Indeed, if there is a synchronization contract $Sync(p, p_2, o, s)$ then p must observe at least once the object o. With this intention, s/he must execute at least an operation that allows him to observe a state of o. If there is a synchronization contract $Sync(p_2, p, o, s)$ then p must observe at least one state of o if the synchronization type s belongs to $\{SIS\_Sync, SFS\_Sync, TotSync, Sq\_Sync\}$. So a synchronization contract defines a set of obligatory operations the policy participants must execute.

A participant p can follow a policy if for any object of this policy, all the obligatory operations are allowed (positive rights) and all the obligatory operations are not refused (negative rights).

A cooperation policy is consistent if all its participants can follow it.

$consistent(P) \overset{\text{def}}{=} \forall p \in P.PolParts, \forall o \in P.PolObjects$

$(ObligatoryOp(P,p,o) \cap RefusedOp(P,p,o) = \emptyset) \wedge$

$ObligatoryOp(P,p,o) \subset PermittedOp(P,p,o))$

If a user (or an activity) participates in two cooperation policies then s/he must follow both of them. To do that, s/he must execute their obligatory operations, should not execute any refused operation and all permitted operations by one policy are not refused by the other one. Consequently the composition of two policies P_1 and P_2 constitutes a composite policy P such that the participants of P are the participants of P_1 and P_2, the objects of P are the objects of P_1 and P_2 and for a given participant and for a given object:

- the permitted operations of P are the operations permitted by P_1 or P_2.
- the obligatory operations of P are the obligatory operations of P_1 or P_2,
- the refused operations of P are the operations refused by P_1 or P_2.

5   Motu : A Framework for Virtual Teams

Our objective is to develop a framework to control, using various cooperation policies, interactions within a virtual team application. For that, It is necessary for us to be able to store data, to define cooperation policies, then to apply these policies to control the interactions between virtual team participants.

The policies we propose are independent of the object granularity as well as its state changes. To validate our model, we propose to implement it on the Motu infrastructure[13]. Motu keeps the various shared object states as successive versions, organised according acyclic graphs.

As shows in the figure 1, Motu proposes a repository organised in two components: a cooperation space accessible by all users (with some access rights) in which are stored the shared objects and a workspace (one for each user) on which the user can work to achieve his/her task. In fact, s/he will have to transfer documents on which s/he wants to work from the cooperation space to his/her workspace (*checkout*). When s/he considers his/her work completed, s/he will publish its new version (*checkin*) in the cooperation space. From this moment, this document could be imported by other users. Commands provided by Motu mainly handle versioned object (*checkin, checkout...*). In order to control interactions, we have developed a set of new commands to handle the policies. A client can send these commands to the server which is the responsible for their execution if they don't introduce any inconsistency in data or in policies.

The interaction manager supervises the various commands sent by the client of Motu. It is divided into two parts: the policy controller and the interaction controller. The policy controller checks if commands for policy handling sent by the client don't introduce inconsistencies. For each command aiming to define

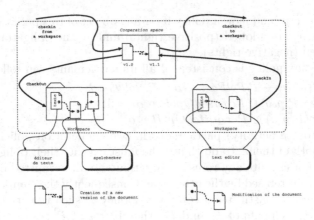

Fig. 1. Architecture of the object manager

or to update a policy, the policy controller calculates the permitted, refused and obligatory operations. It doesn't authorise the command executions that lead to inconsistencies. The interactions controller checks if commands for object handling sent by clients follow the established policies.

6   Conclusion and Future Work

In this work we have identified needs for cooperation support in the virtual teams. Mainly, the management of roles coordination of activities and interaction unpredictability support. Indeed, the management of roles allows to each participant to benefit from the results of other participants and allows the team to carry out objectives which are not with the range of only one participant. In addition, the activity coordination is concerned with the way in which participants must synchronise their activities with an aim of bringing synergistic effects that improve the performances of each participant.

To take into account these dimensions and interaction unpredictability, we have proposed a model of interactions which defines the roles in term of access contracts. It describes relationships between participants manipulating shared objects in term of synchronisation contracts.

Currently, we foresee two possible evolutions for our work: the support of the awareness in virtual teams and the definition of a interaction language.

The support of the awareness allows participants to coordinate their actions in an informal way and to work in an autonomous way while being aware of what occurs in the virtual team. This support notifies changes to the participants and the actions which occur within the team (creation of a new version of a resource by an activity, departure of a participant ...). The notifications must be filtered and structured. In fact, it is necessary to know how to extract relevant information to notify and it is necessary to determine the participants concerned with this information. Since the cooperation policies describe the work rules within a team, they can in our view be adapted to be used as framework for the extraction and the structuring of useful information for the awareness of the team. Indeed, by the means of the policies we can know whom shares what and by what it is interested: the policies gather the participants having an interest and a common history within a project.

In addition we aim at the definition of an interaction language which will constitute a concreted operational tool for the interaction model. This language will enable us to specify policies of cooperation. It must address the problems of power of expression and flexibility the current coordination languages suffer. It must be able to support the unpredictable interactions and the dynamics of work rules.

References

1. Root, R.W.: Design of a multi-media vehicle for social browsing. In: Proceedings of the ACM Conference on Computer-Supported Cooperative Work. Remote Communications, ACM Press (1988) 25–38
2. Tang, J.C., Isaacs, E.A., Rua, M.: Supporting distributed groups with a montage of lightweight interactions. In: Proceedings of ACM Conference on Computer-Supported Cooperative Work. From Video Phoning to Video Interacting, ACM Press (1994) 23–34
3. Proull, F., Sandoz, A., Schiper, A.: Duplex: A distibuted collaborative editing environment in large scale. In: Proceedings of the ACM Conference on Computer Supported Cooperative Work, Chapel Hill, NC, USA, ACM Press (1994) 165–173
4. Ellis, C., Gibbs, S., Rein, G.: Groupware: some Issues and Experiences. In: Communications of the ACM, 34 (1). (1994) 38–58
5. Dewan, P.: An inheritance model for supporting flexible displays of data structures. Software Practice and Experience **21** (1991) 719–738
6. Shen, H., Dewan, P.: Access control for collaborative environments. In: Proceedings of the Conference on Computer Supported Cooperative Work, Toronto, Canada, ACM Press (1992)
7. Dewan, P., Shen, H.: Flexible meta access-control for collaborative applications. In: Proceedings of ACM Conference on Computer-Supported Cooperative Work. Primitives for Building Flexibile Groupware Systems, ACM Press (1998) 247–256
8. Alonso, G., Agrawal, D., Abbadi, A.E., Mohan, C.: Functionality and limitations of current workflow management systems. IEEE Expert Journal (1996)
9. Coalition, W.M.: Terminology & Glossary. Technical Report WFMC-TC-1011, Issue 2.0, Workflow Management Coalition (1997)
10. Hoare, C.: Communicating sequential processes. Communications of the ACM **21** (1978) 666–677
11. Bergstra, J., Klop, J.: Process algebra of synchronous communication. Information and control **30** (1984) 109–137
12. Tata, S., Canals, G., Godart, C.: Specifying interactions in Cooperative applications. In: Eleventh International Conference on Software Engineering and Knowledge Engineering (SEKE'99), Kaiserslautern , Germany (1999)
13. Canals, G., Bouthier, C., Godart, C., Molli, P.: Tuamotu : Une infrastructure distribuée pour le support des entreprise-projets. In: Actes du Colloque International sur les Nouvelles Technologies de la Répartition (NOTERE'98), Montréal, Québec, Canada (1998)

The SPACETUB Models and Framework

Robert Tolksdorf[1] and Gregor Rojec-Goldmann[2]

[1] TU Berlin, Fakultät IV Informatik, FLP/KIT, Sekr. FR 6–10, Franklinstr. 28/29,
D-10587 Berlin, Germany, research@robert-tolksdorf.de,
http://www.robert-tolksdorf.de
[2] TU Berlin Fakultät IV Informatik, iVS, Sekr. EN6, Einsteinufer 17, D-10587 Berlin,
Germany, gr@ivs.tu-berlin.de

Abstract. SPACETUB is a framework to model a variety of coordination languages
from the LINDA family and a testbed for experimentation with them. We describe
the design of the framework derived from a comparative analysis of a set of
language, its structure and its initial implementation.

Coordination languages are studied since the middle of the eighties. A plethora of languages, systems and models has been proposed and explored. In this work, we analyse a set of coordination languages wrt. several criteria and try to detect similarities and differences. Our specific interest is on coordination languages suited for open distributed systems. Table 1 shows the set of languages selected for this study.

Table 1. Languages studied

Language	Ref	Language	Ref	Language	Ref
BAUHAUS	[11]	BONITA	[25]	JAVASPACES	[28]
EXT. JOYCE-LINDA	[22]	LAW-GOVERNED LINDA	[20]	LIME	[21]
LINDA	[10]	MARS	[9]	OBJECTIVE LINDA	[17]
OPENSPACES	[13]	PARADISE	[26]	PLINDA	[5]
RESPECT	[12]	SCOPES	[19]	SECOS	[6]
SONIA	[2]	TSPACES	[30]	WCL	[23]

The goal of our work is an implemented object-oriented framework in which coordination languages from the Linda-family can be expressed and implemented. Such a testbed is rooted in a set of basic concepts common to the languages. The first part of this paper surveys the named languages to to explore that set of concepts. From this, we design the SPACETUB framework. In experimenting with SPACETUB one then can implement the concepts found and try variations of them.

We use an object-oriented approach for the study and the UML ([3]) as the modeling language. A coordination language can be modeled as a class with the primitives as methods of the class. An object of that class then is an interpreter for the language under consideration. Note that we do not consider the behavior of that interpreter here, but only

F. Arbab and C. Talcott (Eds.): COORDINATION 2002, LNCS 2315, pp. 348–363, 2002.

the interface. We derive similarities amongst coordination languages by looking at the interface and the informal description of its semantics. We use inheritance to identify extensions of one language to another. As the languages tend to be related in various aspects, a class diagram including all aspects and all relations would be too complex to be useful. Thus, we structure our analysis into several *aspects* and provide UML models for each of them.

The models presented in section 1 are the basis for the framework presented in section 2. SPACETUB is implemented as a collection of Java classes and intended to serve as a testbed for the experimental implementation of coordination languages.

1   Analysis and Classification

The SPACETUB framework is based on the analysis and classification of various coordination languages wrt. the aspects supported primitives, tuple space model, handling of time, security, activity creation, typing and fault tolerance. We omit the last two aspects in this paper for brevity.

The class diagram in figure 1 is the top level classification used. The central class is *TupleSpace* which is extended by all coordination languages. It consists of many *Entry* objects which are usually *Tuple*s. In some coordination languages *Entry* can also be some sort of *Activity* or nested *TupleSpace*s. *Template*s are used to identify *Tuple*s in a *TupleSpace*. *Agent*s operate on a *TupleSpace* through *TupleSpaceOperation*s.

While most choices are obvious, we do not relate *Tuple* and *Template* by subclassing in our model. There are several views on their relation. For one, a *Tuple* could be a special kind of *Template*, namely one that uses no bottom-elements for fields. Also, a *Template* could be a *Tuple* specialized with a *matches* method and additional constructors that allow for formals in fields. TSPACES follows a different view. Here, there is no distinction of *Tuple*s from *Template*s. Both carry a *matches* method and the *usage* of that method classifies a *Tuple* to be temporarily a *Template*. We simply relate both in our top-level model but do not specify whether they are in some super-/subclass relation.

To model tuple space operations as first class entities, we make them objects while they actually are methods of the *TupleSpace* class. Since they are modeled as objects, they can be aggregated into languages. As an object of a class that represents a language actually implements an interpreter for that language, the objects representing operations model the respective parts of that interpreter. Most *TupleSpaceOperation* objects are either *TupleInsertionOperation* or *TupleRetrievalOperation*. In this study, we will not take care of renamed primitives etc., like *take*, *waitToTake*, *pick* for the LINDA *in*.

1.1   Primitives

LINDA has a minimal set of primitives for exchanging tuples, which was sufficient for parallel computing in closed systems. For open systems, new tuple space primitives were introduced. Three major sets of additional tuple space primitives were proposed: (a) predicate operations for asynchronous tuple retrieval, (b) bulk operations to manipulate more than one tuple at a time, and (c) streaming operations where an agent places a request for tuples in a tuple space and the tuple space delivers a stream of matches.

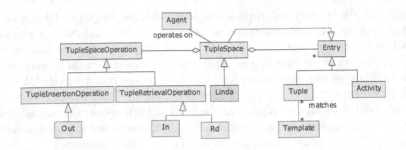

Fig. 1. Top level model

Predicate operations. The predicate operations *inp* and *rdp* were introduced with LINDA and return *true* if a matching tuple is present, *false* otherwise. The operations were later dropped because their semantics was unclear. [15] proposes a precise semantics for *inp* which can also be implemented for open distributed tuple space systems.

Many languages incorporate some kind of a predicate operation with vague semantic descriptions. Such operations are supported by PLINDA, PARADISE, JAVASPACES, OPEN-SPACES and TSPACES. Their tuple space implementations often run on one machine which makes it easier to take a snapshot of the tuple space.

Bulk operations. With the non-deterministic *rd* operation, it is not possible to look at all matching tuples with repeated operations, as the same tuple could be chosen twice.[24] addresses this issue and proposes the new tuple space primitive *copy-collect(ts1, ts2, template)*. It copies tuples that match *template* from tuple space *ts1* to another tuple space *ts2* and returns the number of tuples copied. [8] also proposes a *collect* primitive which moves all tuples from one tuple space to another tuple space and returns the number of moved tuples.

MARS, OPENSPACES and TSPACES support similar operations for retrieving multiple tuples. They all pass the matched set of tuples directly to the agent and not to another tuple space. There are different representations of a set of tuples on the agent side. MARS bulk operation returns the set as a *Vector* object, OPENSPACES as an array and TSPACES as a tuple where each field holds one retrieved tuple.

Streaming operations. BONITA ([25]) proposes a different solution for predicate and bulk operations, which is suited for distributed systems. The LINDA primitives are replaced by the two primitives *dispatch* and *dispatch_bulk*. The basic idea is to perform a non-blocking operation on a tuple space and then check locally if the result of the operation was delivered by the tuple space.

dispatch is an overloaded primitive which can be used to insert tuples to or retrieve them from the tuple space, depending on the arguments. If a tuple is passed as an argument then it is inserted into the tuple space. When a template is passed as an argument then a tuple is retrieved from the tuple space and an extra field is used to indicate if the tuple should be removed from the tuple space (*destructive*) or copied (*nondestructive*). The primitive is *non-blocking* and returns a request identifier (*rqid*) which is used with other primitives to retrieve the matched tuple. *dispatch_bulk* copies or moves tuples that match *template* from *ts1* to *ts2*. *obtain(rqid)* is the only blocking primitive which waits for the result associated with *rqid* to arrive.

The WCL coordination language ([23]) was influenced by BONITA and provides a rich set of tuple access with synchronous *and* asynchronous versions of all primitives. It introduces a new primitive called *monitor(ts, template)* which streams all tuples to the agent that match the template and also all tuples that are subsequently inserted. The primitive creates a continuous stream of tuples to the agent. Another new primitive is *touch* which inserts a tuple in the tuple space and then tries to remove it. This is useful in the combination with *monitor*, because by invoking the *touch* primitive, the tuple will be sent to all agents that registered a monitor with a template that matches the tuple.

Atomic synchronization. TSPACES implements a new primitive called *rhonda*. The primitive takes a tuple and a template as arguments and swaps the tuple with another agent that also executed *rhonda* if the template of the first agent matches the tuple of the second agent and the template of the second agent matches the tuple of the first agent. An agent could use this primitive to enforce that the tuple will only be passed to an agent with a certain key. Also, a client can obtain a service request with rhonda which could be later used to retrieve the result of the service.

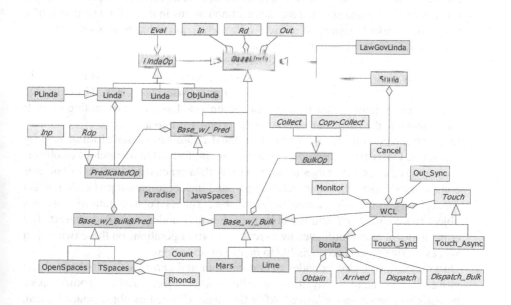

Fig. 2. Data-exchange operations

Modeling tuple space primitives. In the model in figure 2 we classified the coordination languages according to operations for inserting and retrieving tuples. There are three major groups of operations, basic operations (*in*, *out*, *rd*), predicate operations and bulk operations. Some of them also incorporate the *eval* primitive. All languages have basic operations, and there are several combinations of the other groups.

1.2 Tuple Space Models

In LINDA, all processes share a single global tuple space. There is no mechanism to group tuples or to partition the tuple space. [18] notices that a single tuple space is too restrictive for open systems because it creates an intolerable bottleneck it is impossible to isolate distinct process groups. Several proposals extend the single tuple space mode. The structure, creation and naming issues are discussed in this section.

Hierarchical tuple spaces. LINDA, BAUHAUS and OBJECTIVE LINDA support hierarchical tuple spaces. They differ in the mechanisms used to access tuple spaces.

– In LINDA3 ([14]), a new type *ts*, a new operation *tsc* and a naming scheme are introduced. Tuple spaces are first-class objects, thus the flat structure of a single global tuple space is replaced by a hierarchy of tuple spaces. By executing *eval(tsc(S))* an empty tuple space is created and can be referenced by the name *S*. LINDA operations can be prefixed by a name that references a tuple space. In *S*, another tuple space can be created by *S.eval(tsc(T))*. To access nested tuple spaces, tuple space names can be combined with /, and names can be relative to the current space or absolute to some root. Nested tuple spaces are also represented as tuples and LINDA operations can be applied to them. If *space* is a *ts* variable, then *in(?space)* will match a tuple space, withdraw it and suspend all active computations in it and bind an image of it to the local variable *space*. To reinsert *space*, *eval(space)* has to be executed. This will also reactivate all suspended computations.
– BAUHAUS ([11]) doesn't differentiate between tuples, tuple spaces, templates, active and passive tuples. Instead, a single structure called multiset (mset) is used for all. In multisets, there is no order of fields like in tuples. Msets are matched by existence of elements in them. A BAUHAUS agent can only address the surrounding mset. It has to move to the particular mset with the primitives *into* and *outof*.
– OBJECTIVE LINDA ([17]) is an object oriented coordination model influenced by BAUHAUS. OBJECTIVE LINDA computations are performed in hierarchies of objects containing other objects. Objects can be passive data or active entities. Active objects consist of two parts, the computational part and the coordination part called *object space*. Every active object knows only two object spaces it can operate with, its own object space called *self* and the object space it is included in, called *context*. The computational part coordinates by executing LINDA operations on these two object spaces. Active objects are invisible to *in* and *rd* operations.
   OBJECTIVE LINDA also provides operations *join* and *enter*, with which an object moves through the hierarchy. An object allows other objects to enter its object space by outing an *object space logical*. After the object *G* outed its object space logical, the object *H* could match it by executing *join* and move to its object space. *enter* operates exactly as *join* with the exception that it consumes the matched logical.

Multiple disjoint tuple spaces. In more recent systems the simpler flat model of multiple disjoint tuple spaces has proved more popular ([19]). These models provide multiple tuple spaces that are explicitly created, referenced and destroyed. These models use a handle *(name, reference)* such as a URL for referencing a tuple space. It is possible to set access rights to tuple spaces, allowing only certain agents access to a space and to tuples in it. Agents use tuple space creation operations to create new tuple spaces.

Handles can be duplicated, published or passed to other agents via a tuple space. This way, a hierarchical structure can be designed. In contrast to hierarchical spaces, however, the lifetime of tuple spaces is independent from each other. If a tuple space containing a handle to another tuple space is destroyed, the other space is not affected.

Tuple space models for mobile agents. In MARS ([9]) mobile agents automatically access their default tuple space, depending on their position. Each execution environment on the network contains a tuple space, and when a mobile agents moves to that node, a tuple space of that node is bound to the agent. The only way a mobile agent can access a remote tuple space is by explicitly migrating to that node. When the agent leaves the node, the connection to the tuple space also gets lost.

LIME ([21]) is another coordination language for mobile agents. It is based on *transiently shared tuple space*. The basic idea of LIME is that agents carry their private tuple space with them as they move through the network and this is the only tuple space they can access. As they arrive to a node, their private tuple space merges with the tuple space associated with the execution environment. An agent has then access to the entire tuple space of the node, consisting of all private tuple spaces of agents currently located on that node. When *out*ing a tuple to a tuple space, it is possible to define where it should be placed- its own tuple space or the private tuple space of another agent. It is also possible to restrict the *in* operation to the tuple space of a single agent. As an agent leaves the node, its private space with all the tuples is removed from the shared space.

Overlapping tuple spaces [19] proposes a generalized idea of nested tuple spaces by allowing, amongst other things, *overlapping* tuple spaces. Tuple spaces are replaced by SCOPES. A scope is a viewpoint through which certain tuples can be seen. Scopes are first-class values that can be combined to produce other scopes using scope expressions. Scopes can be thought of as sets of atomic names. If two scopes overlap, they are said to match. Two scopes match if they have an atomic name in common. A tuple in a "space" has a scope associated to it (the scope it is outed to). When an operation $in(s,t)$ is performed, a tuple must be matched by the template t and its scope must be matched by s. *in* returns a tuple *and* its original scope. When a tuple is retrieved an agent can modify its original scope with scope expressions and insert it into the new scope.

Modeling tuple space models. In the model in figure 3 we focus on the tuple space structure. Agents coordinate via a *SingleTupleSpace* in LINDA, MARS and LIME. Note that in LINDA the single space really exists, in MARS it is the one at the current location and in LIME it is the one formed by joining those of colocated agents.

HierarchicalTupleSpace consists of further *HierarchicalTupleSpace*s which belong to only one tuple space. Composition is chosen here because with the destruction of a tuple space the subspaces are also destroyed. The model shows also that *BauhausAgent*s only operate on one *HierarchicalTupleSpace* (one level). *ObjectiveLindaAgent* operates on two tuple spaces, its own and on the surrounding one. LINDA3 is also a *HierarchicalTupleSpace* but its agents (*MultipleSpaceAgent*) can access different tuple spaces regardless of their location.

DisjointTupleSpaces have a flat structure where tuple spaces are independent but can contain references to other tuple spaces. Many tuple spaces can contain a reference to one tuple space. Agents can have access to many *DisjointTupleSpaces*.

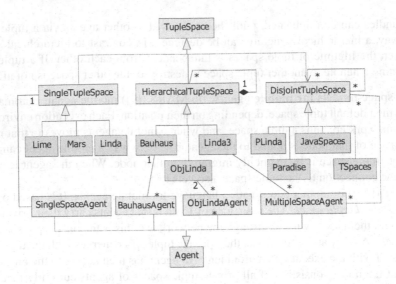

Fig. 3. Tuple space models

1.3   Time

Several coordination languages support the notion of time. Time can either be associated with tuples defining their lifetime or with operations defining timeouts.

Time with operations. The most common way of incorporating time with tuple space operations is to define timeouts on blocking tuple retrieval operations. This mechanism is supported by SONIA, JAVASPACES, TSPACES and OBJECTIVE LINDA. This way an agent can define how long it is going to wait for a tuple to occur. OBJECTIVE LINDA adds a timeout to all tuple space operations. This way, *out* and *eval* fail and return *false* if they could not be completed within a specified timeout.

Time with tuples. In some coordination languages agents can define a lifetime of a tuple. This is an important property in open systems because tuple spaces might exist over a long period of time. Since the behavior of agents is not predictable as in closed systems, tuples could wait for ever to get collected.

JAVASPACES, TSPACES and SONIA agents can add an expiry time to the tuple. A sophisticated mechanism is supported by JAVASPACES with Jini's ([1]) leasing model by which a tuple space controls the lifetime of tuples inserted into the tuple space.

1.4   Security

In LINDA one cannot prohibit agents access to certain tuples or tuple spaces. [29] discusses that extending the LINDA model with a security mechanism will change the semantics of the underlying model. When an agent performs an *out*, how is the situation handled, when it doesn't have the right to out a tuple into a particular tuple space? LINDA *out* is nonblocking and it is assumed that it will be successful at some time.

Access control on a tuple space level. To define access policies on tuple spaces, one defines operations that a certain agent can invoke on a certain tuple space. PARADISE, TSPACES and OBJECTIVE LINDA protect tuples on a tuple space level.

In PARADISE one can allow or prohibit reading, writing and removing tuples, creating or destroying a tuple space and removing all elements from the tuple space. Permissions are associated with a tuple space handle. When an agent wants to access a particular tuple space, it first has to retrieve a handle for it which gives then the agent certain access to the tuple space.

TSPACES provides a more sophisticated mechanism for establishing security policies. Agents have identities. They use their user id and password to connect to a tuple space. Agents can be members of (nestable) groups. This way hierarchies can be built by combining groups and user ids to new groups. Permissions that are granted to a group are passed to all the groups and users that are members.

In OBJECTIVE LINDA an agent needs a *tuple space logical* to operate on the space. It is a key with which an agent can enter a certain space. There are special tuple space primitives for retrieving tuple space logicals and connecting to a tuple space.

Access control on a tuple level. When access control is defined on a tuple level, then every tuple holds the information, who can do what with it. To change a policy of a group of tuples, all tuples must be retrieved and inserted again.

MARS provides access control on a tuple level. Every tuple has an Access Control List (ACL) associated with it. The security policy is based on *roles* which leads to a better uncoupling between the agent system and MARS ([9]). The administrator of a site defines roles like *reader*, *writer* or *manager* and maps agent identities to them.

Tuples can also be protected by using *cryptography*. The SECOS ([6]) is a LINDA based coordination language that provides secure access to tuple spaces via explicit cryptographic techniques. Agents can retrieve encrypted entries but have to use the corresponding key to reveal the data of the entry. The serious limitation of the model is that any agent can *in* a tuple even when it doesn't have the corresponding key. Another problem is that agents have to distribute the keys themselves.

EXTENDED JOYCE-LINDA ([22]) uses a public and a private key for enabling directed communication in LINDA where the tuple space checks if the provided key is correct. Pinakis also addresses the issues of key creation and key distribution. If an agent creates a key itself, then another agent might be using the same key. Another approach would be to have a central entity that generates unique keys.

Access control on tuple class level. Tuples could also be protected by defining security policies on tuple classes. A tuple class could be defined by a template. All tuples that match a certain template are treated the same.

LAW-GOVERNED LINDA's security mechanism allows it to define security policies on tuple classes. For every tuple space operation rules can be defined to allow only certain agents to invoke the operation with certain arguments. Agents have identities which can be checked when an agent invokes an operation on a tuple space.

In OPENSPACES a configuration policy is defined for every class of objects that are exchanged through a space. A space checks the argument of an operation and can reject the operation. But there is no authentication. OPENSPACES configuration policies are discussed in section 1.5.

1.5 Activity

Coordination languages supporting some kind of activity creation can be classified into three groups: (a) The *eval* approach, which was introduced by LINDA, (b) the *event notification* mechanism where a tuple space can inform an agent that there was a certain change of state in the tuple space, and (c) the *definition of reactions* which are executed in the tuple space on the occurance of a certain event such as a tuple space operation with a certain argument.

Eval starts a parallel activity which is then independent of the process that invoked it.

Passing a function to eval. One class of coordination languages implementing *eval* pass a reference to *a function* as an argument. In LINDA, *eval(f(x))* starts *f(x)* in parallel with other activities and replaces the function-reference with the result upon termination.

BAUHAUS creates parallel activity by outing a process: *out process W = f(x).* The process is visible to *in* and *rd*. When reading a process, the reader acquires a suspended copy of the process image. *in* operation acquires the active process itself. Neither *in* nor *rd* change the number of active processes in the system.

Passing an executable to eval. The second class of coordination languages use an operating system level executable file as the unit of parallelism an invoke a process to execute it. This allows the runtime system to exploit the process management facility provided by the underlying OS instead of providing customized mechanism.

PLINDA provides the *pl_proc_eval* operation which, like LINDA, takes a series of expressions to be converted to a tuple (called argument tuple). The first field of the argument tuple must be the name of the executable file. *pl_proc_eval* creates a child process, which can read an argument tuple by a special read operation *pl_arg_rdp* and runs the specified executable.

PARADISE provides the similar *spawn* which attempts to run the command on the specified computer system. Command output and status tuple will be outed to a given tuplespace. The agent explicitly defines the location of the executio of the process.

Passing an object to eval. The third class of languages are object-oriented languages. Here, the object that is passed to *eval* has to implement a certain interface with a method like *evaluate* as in OBJECTIVE LINDA. These objects can be passed to data exchange operations and to *eval*. When an object is passed to *eval*, its *evaluate* method is invoked.

Reactions. LINDA provides a basic mechanism for coping with events. An agent could use a separate process with an *in* or *rd* followed by some code that handles the event. The schema can be generalized to reactions which are pairs (Reaction Condition, Action) where Action will be executed when the Reaction Condition is satisfied.

Reactions on the client side. In LINDA, agents have to "pull" out tuples from the tuple space ([21]). With event notification mechanisms agents can register to be notified of events as they happen in a tuple space.

JAVASPACES has a simple event notification mechanism. An agent registers a template and an event-listener object with the *JavaSpace.notify()* method on the specified JAVASPACES server. When an entry that matches the template is inserted, tuple space informs the agent by invoking the *notify()* method on agents event-listener object.

TSPACES event notification can be used for monitoring the insertion or the removal of a tuple in a tuple space. An agent uses the *TupleSpace.eventRegister()* method to specify the TSpace server, the operation (write or delete), and an object that implements the *Callback* interface. When an event occurs, the system calls the *call()* method of the callback object. A copy of the tuple that triggered the event is passed to the agent.

Reactions in the space. By shifting the event handling actions from agents to the tuple space the behavior of the tuple space can be dynamically programmed.

RESPECT ([12]) distinguishes between tuple space operations invoked by an agent and tuple space operations invoked from a reaction. In reactions only special tuple space operations are allowed, such as *out_r*, to avoid recursions.

Reactions can change the argument of the result of the tuple space operation that triggered it. Such reactions are *synchronous* to the operation and directly change the semantic of the tuple space operation. *Asynchronous* reactions do not change the argument or the result and can be seen as events in the tuple space. They do not change the semantics of the tuple space operation.

In LAW-GOVERNED LINDA rules prescribe the effect of tuple space operations invoked by an agent. The operation can be carried out with the argument passed to the operation or some other argument. A rule can additionally *out* some other tuple. *rd* and *in* are not allowed in the ruling of the law because the controller should not stall. This way, tuple space can be programmed to change the results of the tuple space operations and trigger additional *out*s with arbitrary arguments.

LIME introduces a reactive statement having the form *TS.react(s, t)*, where *s* is a code containing non-reactive statements that is to be executed when a tuple matched by template *t* is found in the tuple space *TS*. After every *out*, all reactive statements that match the outed tuple are executed in a non-deterministic order. All reactions are executed before any other statement of the co-located agents. Blocking operations are not allowed in *s* and the tuple outed is not modified. A second reactive statement, *upon* reacts asynchronously to the availability of tuples and can be used to monitor the tuples in a geographically remote tuple space. It would be impractical to use synchronous reactions on remote tuple spaces because it is difficult to maintain the atomicity and serialization imposed by reactive statements.

MARS extends the LIME reactive model by representing reactions via quadruples of the form: *(Rct, T, Op, I)*. This tuple describes that the *reaction* method of the *Rct* object will be executed when an agent with the identity *I* invokes the operation *Op* on the tuple matching *T*. By using wildcards (null) for *T*, *Op* or *I*, reactions to any operations with a certain tuple class as a parameter can be defined. The result of the tuple space operation is then passed through the reaction it triggers and the result can be modified. If there are more than one reaction triggered, then they are executed in a pipeline, and the result tuple is passed through them in a serialized order.

OPENSPACES extends the idea of triggering a reaction after a tuple space operation. It also allows to define a reaction that is executed before the tuple space operation that triggered it. This way, the parameter to the tuple space operation can also be checked, modified or rejected and any other operation can be triggered. Every tuple class has an instance of the *ConfigurationPolicy* object associated with it. *ConfigurationPolicy* defines operations such as *preWriteCheck* and *postWriteCheck*. There are also similar operations for *read* and *take*. The precheck tests the parameter to the operation and can modify it, the postcheck is then executed with the result of the operation which can also be modified. Any action can be triggered.

TSPACES doesn't provide a mechanism to register reactions in the space, but it allows agents to dynamically define new tuple space operations or replace the existing ones. The semantics of the space can be easily changed. This can only be done by agents with administrative rights on the space.

2   The SPACETUB Framework

We use the knowledge gathered in the analysis to design a framework for experimenting with coordination languages. This is similar to BERLINDA ([27]) but without providing the underlying infrastructure such as a tuple space management and tuples. While BERLINDA tried to integrate Linda and other coordination approaches like KQML, SPACETUB aims exclusively at Linda-like languages. We do not address any semantic issues with this work – this is left to the respective formal comparisons of expressibilty of Linda-like languages like [4,7,16].

2.1   Design

Our framework was inspired by MARS' meta-level tuples of the form *(Rct, T, Op, I)* which are used for the definition of reactions. *Rct* will be executed when an agent *I* invokes the operation *Op* with an argument that matches *T*. Another motivation were LAW-GOVERNED LINDA's rules for the definition of security policies.

We define a coordination language with a set of rules. When a set is inserted into a tuple space, the tuple space is programmed to behave according to the desired coordination language. Rules are quadruples of the form *(Operation op, Reaction rct, Template t, Agent a)*. *op* defines an operation that can be executed when an agent whose id is matched by *a* invokes an operation that is matched by *op* with an argument tuple that is matched by the template *t*. In addition, a reaction *rct* will be executed.

There are two types of reactions, *pre* and *post*. Pre reactions are executed before the operation and post after the operation. Reactions can be synchronous or asynchronous. Synchronous reactions can change the argument passed to the operation or they can change the result of the operation. Asynchronous reactions can be seen as reactions to events which happen in the tuple space. They are evaluated concurrently and don't directly influence the result of the operation.

There is only one operation which can be directly invoked on a tuple space, the *evaluate(Operation op, Tuple argt)* operation. When an agent performs the *evaluate* operation, it tries to invoke the operation defined by the *op* object with the *argt* tuple as an argument. The tuple space then decides according to rules if the operation can actually be invoked. Performing *evaluate* leads to the execution of the following steps:

1. A matching mechanism gets all rules that match the arguments *(op, argt)* and agents identity. To match a rule, the operation fields have to match, the template has to match the argument, and the invoking agent must match the agent field in the rule.

2. If there is at least one match, then the agent has the right to perform this operation and continues with 3, otherwise the operation is aborted.
3. Every asynchronous reaction from the matched set of rules is evaluated concurrently with *argt* as argument. If there is a synchronous reaction in the matched set of rules, it is evaluated with *argt* and its result is passed to the operation *op*.
4. The result of *op* is used for new matching of rules with a post reaction. All asynchronous reactions are executed concurrently with the result of *op* and at most one synchronous reaction is executed with the result of *op*.

Our operations are objects with the method called *operate()* which is invoked after a successful matching of a rule. Reactions are objects with the method *react()* which is invoked on all reaction object from the matched rules. The *AgentID* object holds the information about the identity of the agent. The *AgentID* object in the rule is used as a template to decide if an agent invoking an operation is allowed to perform this action. It has a method *equals()* which decides if the agents identity matches the identity requirements defined by the template.

A Linda-like matching functionality identifies reactions and enforces the security mechanisms. A rule has three formal fields, the operation, an argument template and an agentID. These have to match the corresponding objects when an agent performs the *evaluate* operation. Our matching is implemented with TSpaces matching mechanism.

Our framework provides four tuple space operations: *out*, *in*, *rd* and *copy-collect* which operate on the underlying coordination system. All operations are implemented blocking since the *operate* method of the operation object is blocking, but they don't block agents that invoke them. They are started in a separate thread. In the spirit of BONITA, the *evaluate* primitive returns a request object on which two methods can be invoked, *arrived* and *obtain*. Tuple space delivers the result of the operation to the agent which then uses the non-blocking predicate *arrived* to check the availability of the result and the blocking primitive *obtain* to wait for the result.

We used Java as a programming language and the TSpaces coordination system for the underlying infrastructure to implement SPACETUB. Package *tub.spacetub* is a collection of interfaces which define our framework. The following interfaces are defined: *Space*, *Operation*, *Request* and *AgentID*. There are also several *Reaction* interfaces. Figure 4 shows relationships between classes that implement these interfaces.

2.2 Usage

SPACETUB can be used directly as a coordination language or it can be used for exploring and implementing LINDA based coordination languages. A coordination language can be defined as a class with methods as coordination primitives. A Space can be defined as a private attribute of the coordination language class. SPACETUB can also be used as a coordination language. Agents could coordinate by directly invoking its *evaluate* primitive, or a class similar to a coordination language could be defined which fulfills the requirements of a particular application.

As an example, we want to define a tuplespace which is able of doing *out* and *in* (but not *rd*) and which is "typed" in that it accepts only tuples and templates that consist of one float and one string field.

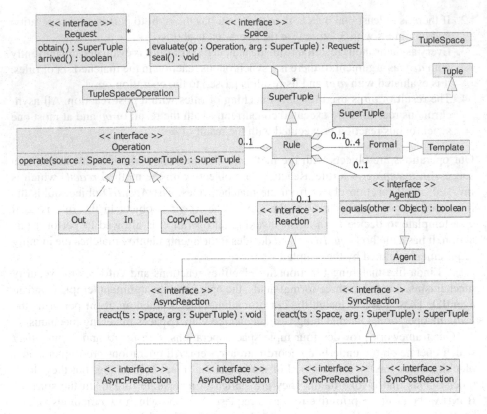

Fig. 4. Structure of SPACETUB

Figure 5 shows the constructor of a class that set up such a space. The array *rules* contains the rules that define supported operations and their types. The first rule allows an *out*-operation which is preceded by an example prereaction and which takes only tuples of the form defined in *floatStringTuple*. The second rule enables *in* which always triggers a postreaction and takes only the respective two-fielded tuples.

Now *ts* is initialized with a new SPACETUB. The rules are entered into that spaces with *evaluate*. To make insertion of multiple rules simple, a special operation, *InitSet*, is defined that takes an array of rules. After the asynchronous operation is really finished as indicated by the termination of *obtain*, the example space is set up. In order to prevent further changes to the set of rules, we *seal* it.

Figure 6 shows the reactions associated with operations by the rules. The first, applied for *out*, increases the float value in every first tuple field by ten percent. After that, it is entered to our example space. The post reaction, associated with every *in* copies the tuple retrieved to some other tuple space, in this case one named sold_items.

Figure 7 shows the rules for a simple Linda with *in*, *rd* and *out*. All three operations work on all kinds of tuples, thus the rules include the bottom element of tuples.

Advanced rule can transform tuples by some encryption mechanisms or wrap it into some active objects to implement timeouts etc.

```
package tub.spacetub.tspacetub.example;
import tub.spacetub.*;          import tub.spacetub.tspacetub.*;
import com.ibm.tspaces.*;
public class ExampleSpace {
  private Space ts;
  ExampleSpace() throws TupleSpaceException {
    Tuple fSTuple = new Tuple(new Field(Float.class),
                             new Field(String.class));
    Rule[] rules={   // Out with <Float,String> and prereaction
      new Rule(new OutOp(), new ExamplePreReaction(),fSTuple),
      // In with  <Float,String> and postreaction
      new Rule(new InOp(),new ExamplePostReaction("sold_items"),fSTuple)
    };
    ts= new TSSpace("ExampleSpace");
    // out all rules into the ExampleSpace
    Request req=ts.evaluate(new InitSet(), new Tuple(rules));
    req.obtain();
    ts.seal(); // Only operations allowed by rules possible
  }
}
```

Fig. 5. An example space

```
package tub.spacetub.tspacetub.example;
import tub.spacetub.*;          import tub.spacetub.tspacetub.*;
import com.ibm.tspaces.*;
/** Synchronous pre reaction increasing the float field */
public class ExamplePreReaction implements SyncPreReaction {
  public  SuperTuple react(Space ts, SuperTuple arg)
          throws TupleSpaceException {
    arg.setField(0,new Field(new Float(price*1.1))); // set new price
    return arg;
  }
}

package tub.spacetub.tspacetub.example;
import tub.spacetub.*;          import tub.spacetub.tspacetub.*;
import com.ibm.tspaces.*;
public class ExamplePostReaction implements AsyncPostReaction {
  String name;
  public ExamplePostReaction(String n){ name=n; }
  public void react(Space ts,SuperTuple arg) throws TupleSpaceException{
    Space sold = new TSSpace(name);
    (sold.evaluate(new OutOp(), arg)).obtain();
  }
}
```

Fig. 6. Example reactions

```
Rule[] lindaRules = {
  new Rule(new OutOp(),new Tuple()),
  new Rule(new InOp(),new Tuple()),
  new Rule(new RdOp(),new Tuple())
};
```

Fig. 7. Rules for LINDA in SPACETUB

3 Conclusions

We have analyzed a set of coordination languages wrt. the aspects supported primitives, tuple space model, handling of time, security and activity creation. The analysis has led to a structured overview on the family of Linda-like languages.

The survey showed the variety of concepts used. SPACETUB is a framework based on the analysis which can serve as a testbed for experimenting with coordination languages. It turned out that reactions provide the most flexible way to describe coordination operations. SPACETUB allows it to define reactions that type a tuplespace wrt. the set and typing of operations permitted. The reactions themselves are represented as tuples and kept in a tuplespace. SPACETUB is implemented as an object-oriented framework in Java. The initial version is implemented on top of TSPACES.

References

1. K. Arnold, A. Wollrath, B. O'Sullivan, R. Scheifler, and J. Waldo. *The Jini specification.* Addison-Wesley, Reading, MA, USA, 1999.
2. M. Banville. SONIA: an Adaptation of Linda for Coordination of Activities in Organizations. In P. Ciancarini and C. Hankin, editors, *Coordination Languages and Models*, volume 1061 of *LNCS*, pages 57–74. Springer-Verlag, Berlin, Germany, 1996.
3. G. Booch, J. Rumbaugh, and I. Jacobson. *The Unified Modeling Language User Guide.* Addison-Wesley, Reading, Massachusetts, USA, 1st edition, 1999.
4. A. Brogi and J. Jacquet. On the expressiveness of Coordination Models. In P. Ciancarini and A. Wolf, editors, *Proc. 3rd Int. Conf. on Coordination Models and Languages*, volume 1594 of *Lecture Notes in Computer Science*, pages 134–149, Amsterdam, Apr. 1999. Springer.
5. T. Brown, K. Jeong, B. Li, S. Talla, P. Wyckoff, and D. Shasha. PLinda User Manual. Technical Report TR1996-729, New York University, Dec., 1996.
6. C. Bryce, M. Oriol, and J. Vitek. A Coordination Model for Agents Based on Secure Spaces. *Lecture Notes in Computer Science*, 1594:4–20, 1999.
7. N. Busi, R. Gorrieri, and G. Zavattaro. Comparing three semantics for Linda-like languages. *Theoretical Computer Science*, 240(1):49–90, June 2000.
8. P. Butcher, A. Wood, and M. Atkins. Global synchronisation in Linda. *Concurrency: Practice and Experience*, 6(6):505–516, 1994.
9. G. Cabri, L. Leonardi, and F. Zambonelli. MARS: A Programmable Coordination Architecture for Mobile Agents. *IEEE Internet Computing*, 4(4):26–35, July/Aug. 2000.
10. N. Carriero and D. Gelernter. Linda in context. *Communications of the ACM*, 32(4):444–458, Apr. 1989.
11. N. Carriero, D. Gelernter, and L. Zuck. Bauhaus-Linda. In *Workshop on Languages and Models for Coordination, European Conference on Object Oriented Programming*, 1994.

12. E. Denti, A. Natali, and A. Omicini. On the Expressive Power of a Language for Programming Coordination Media. In J. Carroll et al., editors, *Proc. ACM/SIGAPP Symp. on Applied Computing (SAC 98)*, pages 169–177. ACM Press, 1998.

13. S. Ducasse, T. Hofmann, and O. Nierstrasz. OpenSpaces: An Object-Oriented Framework For Reconfigurable Coordination Spaces. In A. Porto and G.-C. Roman, editors, *Coordination Languages and Models*, LNCS 1906, pages 1–19, Limassol, Cyprus, Sept. 2000.

14. D. Gelernter. Multiple Tuple Spaces in Linda. In E. Odijk, M. Rem, and J.-C. Syre, editors, *Proceedings of the Conference on Parallel Architectures and Languages Europe : Vol. 2*, volume 366 of *LNCS*, pages 20–27, Berlin, June 1989. Springer.

15. J. L. Jacob and A. M. Wood. A Principled Semantics for inp. In A. Porto and G.-C. Roman, editors, *Coordination Languages and Models, 4th International Conference, COORDINATION 2000, Limassol, Cyprus, September 11-13, 2000, Proceedings*, volume 1906 of *Lecture Notes in Computer Science*, pages 51–65. Springer, 2000.

16. J.-M. Jacquet, K. D. Bosschere, and A. Brogi. On Timed Coordination Languages. In A. Porto and G.-C. Roman, editors, *Proc. 4th Int. Conf. on Coordination Models and LanguagesCoordination Models and Languages*, volume 1906 of *LNCS*, pages 81–98, 2000.

17. T. Kielmann. Designing a Coordination Model for Open Systems. In P. Ciancarini and C. Hankin, editors, *Coordination Languages and Models*, volume 1061 of *LNCS*, pages 267–284. Springer-Verlag, 1996.

18. R. Menezes, R. Tolksdorf, and A. M. Wood. Scalability in Linda-like Coordination Systems. In A. Omicini, F. Zambonelli, M. Klusch, and R. Tolksdorf, editors, *Coordination of Internet Agents: Models, Technologies, and Applications*, chapter 12, pages 299–319. Springer-Verlag, Mar. 2001.

19. I. Merrick and A. Wood. Coordination with scopes. In *Proceedings of the 2000 ACM symposium on Applied computing, Como Italy*, volume 1, pages 210–217, 2000.

20. N. Minsky and J. Leichter, Law-Governed Linda as a Coordination Model. In P. Ciancarini, O. Nierstrasz, and A. Yonezawa, editors, *Object-Based Models and Languages for Concurrent Systems*, LNCS 924, pages 125–146. Springer-Verlag, 1995.

21. G. P. Picco, A. L. Murphy, and G.-C. Roman. LIME: Linda Meets Mobility. In D. Garlan, editor, *Proceedings of the 21st International Conference on Software Engineering (ICSE'99)*, pages 368–377, Los Angeles, CA, USA, May 1999. ACM Press.

22. J. Pinakis. Providing Directed Communication in Linda. Technical report, Department of Computer Science, University of Western Australia, 1991.

23. A. Rowstron. WCL: A co-ordination language for geographically distributed agents. *World Wide Web*, 1(3):167–179, 1998.

24. A. Rowstron and A. Wood. Solving the Linda Multiple rd Problem. In P. Ciancarini and C. Hankin, editors, *Proc. 1st Int. Conf. on Coordination Models and Languages*, volume 1061, pages 357–367, Cesena, Italy, 1996. Springer-Verlag, Berlin.

25. A. Rowstron and A. Wood. Bonita: a set of tuple space primitives for distributed coordination. In *Proc. HICSS30*, pages 379–388, Hawaii, 1997. IEEE Computer Society Press.

26. Scientific Computing Associates, Inc., New Haven, CT. *Paradise 4. Reference Manual*, 1996.

27. R. Tolksdorf. Berlinda: An object oriented platform for implementing coordination languages in Java. In D. Garlan and D. LeMetayer, editors, *Proc. 2nd Int. Conf. on Coordination Models and Languages*, volume 1282 of *Lecture Notes in Computer Science*, pages 430–434, Berlin, Germany, Sept. 1997. Springer-Verlag, Berlin.

28. J. Waldo et al. JavaSpaces Specification - 1.0. Technical report, Sun Microsystems, 1998.

29. A. Wood. Coordination with Attributes. In P. Ciancarini and A. Wolf, editors, *Proc. 3rd Int. Conf. on Coordination Models and Languages*, volume 1594 of *Lecture Notes in Computer Science*, pages 21–36, Amsterdam, Netherland, Apr. 1999. Springer-Verlag, Berlin.

30. P. Wyckoff, S. McLaughry, T. Lehman, and D. Ford. T Spaces. *IBM Systems Journal*, 37(3):454–474, 1998.

Tuple-Based Models in the Observation Framework*

Mirko Viroli and Andrea Omicini

DEIS, Università degli Studi di Bologna
via Rasi e Spinelli 176
47023 Cesena (FC), Italy
{mviroli,aomicini}@deis.unibo.it

Abstract. In this paper, we elaborate on modelling tuple-based coordination media in terms of observable sources providing coordination as a service. Only the medium's part directly affecting its observable behaviour is explicitly represented, while its inner activity is represented only as a source for proactive behaviour, thus abstracting away from its details. As an example of this methodology, we formalise JavaSpaces' time passing and leasing mechanisms, which are both modelled in terms of the medium's inner activity. Then, the formalisation of tuple centres is also shown that emphasises the ability of our approach to deal with the explicit representation of complex coordination services.

1 Introduction

1.1 Classes of Formal Frameworks for Coordination

Many approaches have been proposed and developed to provide a formal specification for coordination models. We classify these approaches according to the way in which they model coordination media, and divide them in two classes: the *holistic* and the *reductionistic* approaches.

In the holistic approach, a coordination model's semantics is generally given by representing (coordinated) systems as the composition of the coordinated entities and the coordination medium altogether. System's evolution over time is characterised through the interactions between coordinated entities and coordination medium – the latter typically not representable independently of the former. Examples of this approach are those based on process algebras for tuple-based coordination models [5] – such as that of Busi, Ciancarini, Gorrieri, and Zavattaro (see [2] for a survey and more references), or the one shown in De Nicola and Pugliese's [6] – as well as other formalisations for channel-based coordination models – e.g. the formal model of Manifold [1].

In the reductionistic approach, on the other hand, the focus is put on the coordination medium, which is seen as a clearly characterised abstraction / software

---

* This work has been partially supported by MIUR, and by Nokia Research Center, Burlington, MA, USA.

F. Arbab and C. Talcott (Eds.): COORDINATION 2002, LNCS 2315, pp. 364–379, 2002.

component interacting with its environment through a communication language, by sending and receiving communication messages. Several modellisation styles exist for this approach, which differ for their different degrees of completeness of the medium's description.

In the *white-box* approach, the coordination medium's behaviour is completely modelled, for instance as described in [10]. There, coordination media are seen as a purely reactive components, characterised at any time by a global state, and whose behaviour is defined in terms of the input message received, the corresponding state changes, and the output messages produced. For instance, this technique has been exploited for modelling ReSpecT tuple centres [11].

On the other hand, the *black-box* approach studies a coordination medium's behaviour by precisely characterising its admissible interaction histories. An example of its application to Linda is presented in [16]. The interaction histories of an Abstract Linda System (ALS) – there called ALS's traces – are defined as sequences of messages sent from and received by a Linda tuple space. Various properties are defined on traces that also describe Linda's features, such as locality, safety, and liveness. One of the main goals of this approach is to evaluate the correctness of an implementation by observing its interaction histories through suitable tests.

In between the black-box and the white-box approach, a *grey-box* approach can be defined which is based on the idea of partially modelling the coordination medium's behaviour. In order to decide which part has to modelled and which has to be abstracted away, and correspondingly giving a semantics to the modelled part's behaviour, we rely on an ontology for the *observation* issue in computer systems that we previously introduced in [13]. This ontology is based on the idea of modelling the ways in which software components allows their inner status and its dynamics to be observed by external entities. Here, we exploit such an ontology as a means for defining a model for coordination media, interpreting them as observable sources. According to this model, coordination media are conceptually divided in an observable part, devoted to managing the medium's interactions with the coordinated entities, and an inner activity, which is abstracted away and is represented only as far as it affects the observable part.

On the one hand, the key advantage of this approach over the black-box ones, is that it provides for a more detailed characterisation of a coordination medium's observable behaviour, which is now not only related to its communication events, but also to the status of a smaller yet relevant subpart of it. In general, this allows for a better understanding of a communication event's semantics, which can be expressed in terms of how the event influences or it is caused by the coordination medium's dynamics.

On other hand, unlike white-box approaches, our framework provides a tool for specifying complex coordination media with the desired level of abstraction. Firstly, a coordination medium is often characterised by some sort of proactive behaviour responsible for sending messages in a decoupled way with respect to message receiving. Such an activity is typically implemented through a non-trivial machinery, so, the only way to provide a compact characterisation of the overall medium's behaviour is to exploit a grey-box approach, abstracting away from unnecessary details. An example of proactiveness in coordination medium presented in this paper is time passing in JavaSpaces [8], whose effects on the medium's behaviour are represented here in terms of the medium's inner activity. Secondly, the inner activity's abstraction can also be exploited to deal with a coordination medium's complex features whose details are better to be abstracted away. For instance we adopt this approach to model lease management in JavaSpaces – represented as the medium's proactive behaviour even though it does not actually express any form of proactiveness.

Overall, the holistic and reductionistic approaches feature different properties and advantages. Holistic approaches generally interpret a coordinated system as a whole. Since medium and coordinated entities are represented altogether it is generally simpler to prove global properties of interest. For instance, Busi *et al.* proved Turing-equivalence of Linda coordination primitives [2], and precisely characterised the expressiveness of other features related to JavaSpaces [3]. On the other hand, the reductionistic approach better captures the feeling of a coordinated application as clearly divided into the coordinated entities and coordination medium. Formalising a coordination medium as a self-contained software component promotes a notion of *coordination as a service*, provided to applications by a *coordination infrastructure*. As a result, this approach seems to better support a systematic engineering methodology for coordinated applications, supporting a coordination infrastructure's specification, design, implementation, and validation. Even more, the grey-box approach seems the most reasonable one for harnessing the most complex aspects of current and future coordination infrastructures.

The remainder of the paper is organised as follows. The rest of this section is devoted to an informal presentation of the observation approach to the modellisation of a component's interactions. Section 2 formally introduces the observation framework and elaborates on its applicability to the specification of coordination media. Section 3 puts the framework to test in the simple case where the coordination medium is a Linda tuple space – here acting as an introductory application example of our methodology. Section 4 applies the observation approach to the JavaSpaces model, providing a formalisation mostly equivalent to the one described in [3]. While this section emphasises the usefulness of the inner activity's abstraction, Section 5 shows the expressiveness of the model in the explicitly representation of complex coordination services. This is done by modelling the tuple centre coordination model [11], whose internal reactions' mechanism has been shown to be Turing-equivalent [7]. Section 6 reports on related works and presents some perspectives on future works.

1.2   The Observation Approach

The ontology for observation presented in [13] interprets computer systems as made of three kinds of entity: *(observable) sources*, *observers*, and *coordinators*. Sources are able to provide their knowledge and services to interested observers by *manifesting* an observable behaviour through chunks of information delivered in form of messages. Coordinators are entities which can configure sources so as to produce particular kinds of manifestation to observers, namely by *conditioning* the sources' observable behaviour. Observers and coordinators can be considered as the ends of the observation patterns, so they can be easily modelled as black-box entities represented in terms of their outputs – coordinators producing conditionings – and inputs – observers receiving manifestations. On the other hand, sources are the core of the observation pattern, so a source's inner state and dynamics are worth to be explicitly represented, at least as far as they affect the way in which the source participates to the observation pattern. As a result, the core idea of the observation approach is to represent components' interactions in terms of the observation patterns. In particular, since sources are the core entities involving in this pattern, here components are modelled in terms of (observable) sources. So, on top of the ontology the following model for sources is built.

A source is modelled in terms of its *(observable) core*, that is, the source's part that both affects the way the source is perceivable from and can be influenced by the environment – namely, the part responsible for the source's *observable behaviour*. Source's core itself is conceptually composed by two subparts, the source's *place* and the source's *configuration*. Place models the source's part of the status directly affecting its observable behaviour. Configuration determines the dynamics of manifestations over time, by keeping track of the pending observation requests coming from outside, as well as representing which kinds of proactive behaviour the source manifests.

The source dynamics can be described as follows. The source is said to be in *equilibrium* while its core remains unchanged, modelling the source's inner activity not perceivable by the environment. While in equilibrium, a source's status is characterised by a *position*, that is, by a place and a configuration. Equilibrium can be broken in one of two ways. On the one hand, a coordinator can *condition* the source by changing its configuration, modelling the coordinator willing to alter the source's observable behaviour – e.g., by issuing an observation request. On the other hand, a *spontaneous move* can occur within the source, represented by a place change, and modelling a source's proactive event affecting the observable behaviour. In general the ability of manifesting a proactive behaviour hides some kind of complex machinery – a local control, some intelligent behaviour or an event fired due to some particular inner management strategy. Spontaneous moves are introduced as a means for dealing with this case: the inner activity is abstracted away, only its observable effect is represented – namely, as place changes occurring in an unpredictable way.

As a result of one of these two events, the source is said to leave equilibrium and enter a *motion* state. While in motion, the source's state is characterised by (i) the place's *move* – namely a pair of places representing the old one and new one – and by the current configuration. After leaving equilibrium, the source moves across a sequence of motion states defining a *trajectory*. At each step, an *evaluation* process takes the current motion state and yields a new motion state and a set of *manifestations*, representing output messages sent towards observers. The evaluation process can eventually terminate, so the source comes back to equilibrium and waits for either a new conditioning or a spontaneous move.

2   Formal Framework

2.1   Notation

Throughout this paper, variables written starting with an uppercase letter denote sets, while the corresponding variables written starting with a lowercase letter denote their elements. So, when the set X is defined, variables x and its variations $(x', x'', .., x_1, x_2, ..)$ are automatically defined that range over X.

Given any set X, the special symbol $\perp_X$ is used to denote an exception value in the set $X_\perp$ defined as $X \cup \{\perp_X\}$, while the variable $\hat{x}$ is supposed to range over $X_\perp$. The set of multisets over X is denoted by $\overline{X}$, and its elements by the variable $\overline{x}$ and its variations $(\overline{x}', \overline{x}'', ..)$. The content of a multiset can be specified by enumerating its elements through the symbol $\{\}_M$ – e.g. writing $\overline{x} = \{x', x', x'', x''', ...\}_M$ – or by the union of two multisets through the binary operator $|$, as in $\overline{x} = \overline{x}'|\overline{x}''$. The void multiset is denoted by the symbol $\bullet$. With an abuse of notation, sometimes x denotes a singleton element either in a multiset $\{x\}_M$ or in a set $\{x\}$, so expression $x|\overline{x}$ denotes a multiset containing the element x. Equation $\perp_X |\overline{x} = \overline{x}$ is always supposed to hold. A finite sequence of elements $x_1, \ldots, x_n$ is denoted by the symbol $\langle x_1, \ldots, x_n \rangle$ and is considered as an element of the cartesian product $X_1 \times \ldots \times X_n$.

2.2   The Operational Semantics of an Observable Source

The observable behaviour of a source – or rather of a class of sources – is defined as a quartet $\langle P, C, M, J \rangle$. P is the set of *places* of the source system – representing the possible states for the source's place. C is the set of *configuration atoms*, or *c-atoms* for short. The set of possible states for the source's configuration is defined as the set $\overline{C}$ of multisets of c-atoms.

The state of a source system in *equilibrium* is given in terms of the set $P \times \overline{C}$, which is called the set of *positions* of the source, providing the pair: current place, current configuration. The position $\langle p, \overline{c} \rangle$ is denoted by the symbol $p[\overline{c}]$. *Moves* are element in the set $P \times P$. *Conditionings* are characterised by a c-atom, and their effect on a configuration is to add the c-atom on it. *Motion* states are triplets of the kind $\langle p, p', c \rangle$ – where p is the old place, p' is the new one, and c is the new configuration – denoted by symbol $\langle p, p' \rangle [c]$.

The third element of an observable source's specification is the set of messages M, defining the *manifestations* that a source can produce, which in this paper are expressed as terms $\underline{o}\, v$, where $o \in \mathcal{O}$ is the receiver's identifier, and v is the content of the message – which can be of any sort.

The fourth component J determines how spontaneous moves and conditionings lead to a certain *trajectory*, resulting to a core's dynamics and to manifestations. Formally, J is a couple of relations $\langle select, eval \rangle$ called *selection* and *evaluation*, respectively.[1] Selection is a relation $select \subseteq (P \times P \times \overline{C}) \times \overline{C}$: the proposition $\langle p, p', \overline{c}, \overline{c}' \rangle \in select$, which is denoted by the syntax $\langle p, p' \rangle[\overline{c}] \hookrightarrow_\sigma \overline{c}'$, represents the fact that in the motion state $\langle p, p' \rangle[\overline{c}]$ the multiset of c-atoms $\overline{c}'$ can be selected. The following well-formedness properties are supposed to hold:

$$\langle p, p' \rangle[\overline{c}] \hookrightarrow_\sigma \overline{c}' \Rightarrow \overline{c}' \subseteq \overline{c} \qquad \forall p, p', \overline{c}: \ \exists \overline{c}': \ \langle p, p' \rangle[\overline{c}] \hookrightarrow_\sigma \overline{c}'$$

In particular, when the rules one defines for giving semantics to selection do not satisfy the latter property, then *select* is supposed to be automatically completed with the minimum set of tuples of the kind $\langle p, p', \overline{c}, \bullet \rangle$ so that such a property is made hold.

When selected, a multiset of c-atoms is then evaluated. First of all, the evaluation of a single c-atom is specified by the relation *eval*, which is of the kind $eval \subseteq C \times (P \times P) \times (C_\perp \times P_\perp \times \overline{M})$. The proposition $\langle c, p, p', \langle \widehat{c}, \widehat{p}, \overline{m} \rangle \rangle \in eval$, which here is denoted by the syntax $c : \langle p, p' \rangle \hookrightarrow_c \langle \widehat{c}, \widehat{p}, \overline{m} \rangle$, means that under the current move $\langle p, p' \rangle$, the evaluation of c causes:

- $\widehat{c}$ to be written in the configuration replacing c. In case $\widehat{c} = \perp_C$, no c-atoms has to replace c (i.e., c is simply dropped from the configuration after its evaluation);
- the place moving to $\widehat{p}$. In case $\widehat{p} = \perp_P$, no changes are applied to the current move. This is supported by the operator $\langle p, p' \rangle :> \widehat{p}$, accepting the move $\langle p, p' \rangle$ and the new place $\widehat{p}$, and yielding the move defined as:

$$\langle p, p' \rangle :> p'' = \langle p', p'' \rangle \qquad \langle p, p' \rangle :> \perp_P = \langle p, p' \rangle$$

- the multiset of messages $\overline{m}$ to be sent out.

The effects of evaluating each c-atom are then joined together as specified by a relation $mEval \subseteq \overline{C} \times (P \times P) \times (\overline{C} \times P_\perp \times \overline{M})$. The tuple $\langle \overline{c}, p, p', \langle \overline{c}', \widehat{p}, m \rangle \rangle$ occurring in $mEval$ represents $mEval$ assigning to the current motion state $\langle p, p' \rangle[\overline{c}]$ the triple $\langle \overline{c}', \widehat{p}, m \rangle$ orderly representing (i) the new configuration, (ii) the new move (obtained through the operator :>), and (iii) the manifestations to produce. The semantics of $mEval$ can be given in terms of the relation *eval* through the following rules:

$$mEval(\bullet, p, p', \langle \bullet, \perp_P, \bullet \rangle)$$

$$\frac{eval(c_0, p_0, p_0', \langle c, \widehat{p}, \overline{m} \rangle) \qquad mEval(\overline{c}_0, p_0, p_0', \langle \overline{c}, \widehat{p}', \overline{m}' \rangle)}{mEval(c_0|\overline{c}_0, p_0, p_0', \langle c|\overline{c}, \widehat{p}, \overline{m}|\overline{m}' \rangle)}$$

that is, (i) each configuration is evaluated on the same initial move $\langle p_0, p_0' \rangle$, (ii) the manifestations produced by each c-atom are joined, (iii) each c-atom

---

[1] Selection is modelled in terms of a relation and not simply a function from motion states to multisets of c-atoms so as to naturally take into account non-determinism.

is updated according to its local evaluation, (iii) the new move is chosen in a non-deterministic way from those obtained from each evaluation.

It is useful sometimes to express *select* in terms of *eval*, in particular in order to define when a c-atom has to be selected depending on how (and if) it evaluates. To this end, a new predicate is introduced relating a c-atom c to the moves $\langle p, p' \rangle$ on which it defines an evaluation, denoted by the symbol $\langle p, p' \rangle \leftrightarrow_\gamma c$ and called *guard predicate*. This is defined as:

$$\frac{\exists \langle \widehat{c}, \widehat{p}, \overline{m} \rangle, \; c : \langle p, p' \rangle \leftrightarrow_\epsilon \langle \widehat{c}, \widehat{p}, \overline{m} \rangle}{\langle p, p' \rangle \leftrightarrow_\gamma c}$$

In the move $\langle p, p' \rangle$, c is said to apply if $\langle p, p' \rangle \leftrightarrow_\gamma c$ holds.

The operational semantics of a source is formally described by means of a labeled transition system with four kinds of transitions: *move* ($\longrightarrow_M$), *conditioning* ($\longrightarrow_C$), *evaluation* ($\longrightarrow_E$), and *stop* $\longrightarrow_S$, defined as

$$\begin{aligned}
\longrightarrow_M &\subseteq (P \times \overline{C}) \times (P \times P \times \overline{C}) \\
\longrightarrow_C &\subseteq (P \times \overline{C}) \times C \times (P \times P \times \overline{C}) \\
\longrightarrow_E &\subseteq (P \times P \times \overline{C}) \times \overline{M} \times (P \times P \times \overline{C}) \\
\longrightarrow_S &\subseteq (P \times P \times \overline{C}) \times (P \times \overline{C})
\end{aligned}$$

In equilibrium either a spontaneous move ($\longrightarrow_M$) or a conditioning ($\longrightarrow_C$) can occur, causing the source's motion. During motion, a sequence of evaluations ($\longrightarrow_E$) occurs, each time selecting a multiset of c-atoms from the configuration, applying the relation *mEval*, and producing a new motion state as well as some manifestations. When a void multiset is selected, the source returns on equilibrium ($\longrightarrow_S$). This behaviour can be expressed by the four rules:

$$p[\overline{c}] \longrightarrow_M \langle p, p' \rangle [\overline{c}] \qquad p[\overline{c}] \xrightarrow{c}_C \langle p, p \rangle [c|\overline{c}] \qquad \frac{\langle p, p' \rangle [\overline{c}] \leftrightarrow_\sigma \bullet}{\langle p, p' \rangle [\overline{c}] \longrightarrow_S p'[\overline{c}]}$$

$$\frac{\langle p_0, p_0' \rangle [\overline{c}_0] \leftrightarrow_\sigma c'|\overline{c}' \qquad mEval(c'|\overline{c}', p_0, p_0', \langle \overline{c}, \widehat{p}, \overline{m} \rangle) \qquad \langle p_0, p_0' \rangle :> \widehat{p} = \langle p, p' \rangle}{\langle p_0, p_0' \rangle [\overline{c}_0] \xrightarrow{\overline{m}}_E \langle p, p' \rangle [\overline{c}]}$$

2.3   Modelling a Coordination Medium

In order to apply this formal framework to the specification of a coordination model, we first need to distinguish coordinated entities and coordination media. While coordinated entities are the entities subject to coordination, the coordination medium is the abstraction ruling the interaction among coordinated entities. According to [10], the coordination language generally expresses the syntax used by coordinated entities for communication operations, and its semantics in terms the related communication events. By adopting the viewpoint of coordination media, input communication events are messages from coordinated entities to the media, and output communication events are messages from the media to coordinated entities.

In our approach, a coordination medium is modelled as a source. As a result, input communication events are represented as conditionings of its observable behaviour, while output coomunication events are represented as manifestations. Coordinated entities are seen as coordinators when they are about to produce input communication events for the medium, and are seen as observers when they receive output communication events from the medium.

Choosing what part of a coordination medium has to be represented in terms of a source's core, and what instead has to be astracted away and handled as the source's inner activity generally introduces a trade-off, basically depending on which coordination medium's aspects has to be promoted to a first-class level and put in the core part. In this paper only the coordination medium's proactive features are considered as part of the inner activity, while the aspects such as the tuple space content, the pending queries waiting to be served, and the synchronisation policy are explicitly represented in the medium's core.

3   Modelling Linda Tuple Spaces

As an introductory application example of the observation framework described in previous section, here the Linda coordination model [9] is analised.

At a given time a Linda space is completely defined by the multiset of tuples $t \in T$ it contains, represented as an element $T \vdash \overline{T}$. Operations for querying the space are based on the tuple matching mechanism, which here is modelled through a predicate $matches \subseteq Tm \times T$, associating tuple templates $tm \in Tm$ to tuples. In this paper we abstract away from details on the structure of tuples, tuple templates, and matching mechanism. Then, in order to shorten the notation, the predicate $\mu \subseteq Tm \times \overline{T} \times T_{\perp}$ is also introduced that models a non-deterministic choice of a tuple into a tuple multiset that matches a given tuple template:

$$matches(tm, t) \Rightarrow \mu(tm, t | \overline{t}, t) \qquad (\nexists t \in \overline{t}, \; matches(tm, t)) \Rightarrow \mu(tm, \overline{t}, \perp_T)$$

Five kinds of operation allowed on a Linda tuple space: rd, in, rdp, inp, and out.[2] rd(tm) waits for a tuple that matches tm occurring in the space; when this happens such a tuple is returned to the requestor. in(tm) behaves in a similar way, but the tuple returned is also dropped from the space. rdp(tm) and inp(tm) are the asynchronous versions of rd(tm) and in(tm). If at the time their request arrives in the space a tuple matching tm occurs, then they behave as rd(tm) and in(tm); otherwise an exception message is immediately returned to the requestor. Finally, out(t) simply puts the tuple t in the space.

The observable behaviour of the class of Linda spaces can be defined through the tuple $\langle P, C, M, J \rangle$ as follows. The set of places is the set of tuple multisets, that is $P = \overline{T}$. In fact, the tuples currently stored in the space represent the part of the space's state that somehow affects its observable behaviour. Then,

---

[2] In this paper we don't consider the primitive eval.

$$\frac{matches(tm, t)}{crd(tm)^\circ : \langle \overline{t}, t | \overline{t'} \rangle \leftrightarrow_\epsilon \langle \bot_c, t | \overline{t'}, \underline{o}\, t \rangle} \tag{L-RD}$$

$$\frac{matches(tm, t)}{cin(tm)^\circ : \langle \overline{t}, t | \overline{t'} \rangle \leftrightarrow_\epsilon \langle \bot_c, \overline{t'}, \underline{o}\, t \rangle} \tag{L-IN}$$

$$\frac{\mu(tm, \overline{t}, \widehat{t})}{crdp(tm)^\circ : \langle \overline{t}, \overline{t} \rangle \leftrightarrow_\epsilon \langle \bot_c, \overline{t}, \underline{o}\, \widehat{t} \rangle} \tag{L-RDP}$$

$$\frac{\mu(tm, \overline{t}, \widehat{t})}{cinp(tm)^\circ : \langle t | \overline{t}, \widehat{t} | \overline{t} \rangle \leftrightarrow_\epsilon \langle \bot_c, \overline{t}, \underline{o}\, \widehat{t} \rangle} \tag{L-INP}$$

$$cout(t) : \langle \overline{t}, \overline{t} \rangle \leftrightarrow_\epsilon \langle \bot_c, t | \overline{t}, \bullet \rangle \tag{L-OUT}$$

Fig. 1. Evaluation rules for the Linda specification

the set of c-atoms corresponds to the set of operations the space can handle, that is, to the set of incoming messages it processes. This can be defined as:

$$C = \{crd(tm)^\circ, cin(tm)^\circ, crdp(tm)^\circ, cinp(tm)^\circ, cout(t)\}$$

For operations implying a reply, the corresponding c-atom also specifies a reference $o \in \mathcal{O}$ to the requesting agent, which the space has to keep track of in order to properly send the message reply. Notice that in the case of Linda, the set of c-atoms directly corresponds to the set of operations allowed. This happens because Linda is a purely reactive model, so the configuration simply keeps track of the pending requests.

Messages are generally of the kind $\underline{o}\, \widehat{t}$, carrying one tuple representing a query result or $\bot_T$, which denotes some kind of exception. In particular, this is used as reply when **inp** and **rdp** fail to find a tuple.

The semantics of c-atoms, that is, their effects on the tuple space, is given by means of relations *eval* and *select*. Evaluation of c-atoms is defined by the rules shown in Figure 1. The c-atoms $crd(tm)^\circ$ and $cin(tm)^\circ$ apply in the move $\langle \overline{t}, \overline{t'} \rangle$ when one tuple matching tm occurs in the updated place $\overline{t'}$. In fact, the guard predicate obtained by their evaluation semantics is defined by rules:

$$\frac{\mu(tm, \overline{t'}, t)}{\langle \overline{t}, \overline{t'} \rangle \leftrightarrow_\gamma crd(tm)^\circ} \qquad\qquad \frac{\mu(tm, \overline{t'}, t)}{\langle \overline{t}, \overline{t'} \rangle \leftrightarrow_\gamma cin(tm)^\circ}$$

Then, rules (L-RD) and (L-IN) specify the effects of evaluating $crd(tm)^\circ$ and $cin(tm)^\circ$, that is: (i) *crd* leaves the space unchanged while *cin* extracts the tuple matching the template, (ii) they both send a message to the observer o specifying the tuple, and (iii) they are both dropped from the configuration after evaluation. On the other hand, c-atoms $crdp(tm)^\circ$ and $cinp(tm)^\circ$ are to be evaluated as soon as they are conditioned in the space. Their semantics rules (C-INP) and (C-RDP) are built so as to make them apply only in the move $\langle \overline{t}, \overline{t} \rangle$ – that is due to a conditioning. Their evaluation is similar to that of c-atoms $crd(tm)^\circ$ and $cin(tm)^\circ$, but the manifestation they produce can possibly carry symbol $\perp_T$, meaning that the tuple searched is not present in the space. Analogously, c-atom $cout(t)$ is evaluated when it is conditioned, it adds t to the space, produces no messages and is then dropped from the configuration.

Finally, selection relation has to be defined that specifies the c-atoms to evaluate in the case many of them apply. Consider the straightforward rules

$$\frac{\langle p, p' \rangle \hookrightarrow_\gamma c}{\langle p, p' \rangle [c | \overline{c}] \hookrightarrow_\sigma \{c\}_M} \qquad \frac{\nexists c \in \overline{c}, \langle p, p' \rangle \hookrightarrow_\gamma c}{\langle p, p' \rangle [\overline{c}] \hookrightarrow_\sigma \bullet}$$

selecting at a given time one of the c-atoms that apply in the current move[3]. This selection causes the asynchronous c-atoms $cinp(tm)^o$, $crdp(tm)^o$, and $cout(t)$ to be evaluated when they are conditioned. Then, as a result of the latter c-atom a tuple can be inserted in the space that triggers a new selection.

In general, a number of **rd** and **in** operations may be pending on a tuple template matching the tuple just inserted. As a result, these c-atoms are selected and evaluated until a **in** is evaluated which drops the tuple and makes the space return in equilibrium. In general, a specific ordering semantics is not specified for Linda that prevents this behaviour. However, it may be the case to rely on a different selection relation that chooses all the **rd** operations and just one **in**, which can be defined as:

$$\frac{c \neq cin(tm)^o \qquad \langle p, p' \rangle \hookrightarrow_\gamma c}{\langle p, p' \rangle [c | \overline{c}] \hookrightarrow_\sigma \{o\}_M}$$

$$\frac{cin(tm')^{o'} \notin \overline{c} \qquad \langle p, p' \rangle \hookrightarrow_\gamma cin(tm)^o}{\langle p, p' \rangle [cin(tm)^o | \overline{c}] \hookrightarrow_\sigma \{cin(tm)^o\}_M}$$

The former rule gives priority to all the c-atoms different from cin, and only when they are all evaluated a cin is selected which drops the tuple.

The formalisation presented in this section provides some flavour about the applicability of the observation framework to the modellisation of a coordination medium. However, it does not emphasise the property of being a grey-box approach. This holds since Linda is a simple reactive coordination model, so there is no need for isolating an inner activity and representing its effects on interactions through spontaneous moves.

4 Modelling JavaSpaces

JavaSpaces [8] is a non-academic coordination medium based on Linda, which comprises a number of additional features enhancing its general expressiveness and power, such as: the management of transactions, expiring data, time-out, notification, lease mechanism, and so on. The lack of a precise understanding of JavaSpaces's behaviour has being recently overcame thanks to the research

---

[3] Notice that the latter rule is implicitly defined as mentioned in Section 2.2, so in the remainder of the paper it will be generally omitted.

done by Busi et al., describing the semantics of notification [4], timeout, leasing, and transactions (see e.g. [3]), which are both a reference and inspiration to the formalisation we provide here. In order to show how the observation approach makes it possible to easily represent proactive coordination media, here we concentrate on modelling a subset of JavaSpaces' behaviour, which is mostly similar to that modelled in [3].

As for Linda, details on tuples, templates, and matching is abstracted away, so the mathematical structures T, Tm, *matches*, and μ, are used here with same semantics as in previous section. Increasing time is modelled through the set of natural numbers $\mathcal{N}$, ranged over by variable τ. We omit the whole management of transactions. So, our specification focuses on the following operations:

- readIfExists(tm) and takeIfExists(tm) which has similar behaviour to rdp(tm) and inp(tm) in Linda.
- read(tm, τ) and take(tm, τ) correspond to rd(tm) and in(tm), where τ specifies the operation time-out. When this is expired the operation returns an exception, here modelled as a message $\varrho \perp_T$. The case where $\tau = 0$ gives to these operations same semantics as readIfExists(tm) and takeIfExists(tm), while $\tau = \infty$ corresponds to the semantics of operations rd and in in Linda.
- notify(tm, o) registers the listener o for being notified each time a tuple that matches tm is inserted in the space. For simplicity, we suppose not to model any lease mechanism for notification, which in JavaSpaces is exploited to associate an expiration time to notify operations.
- write(t, τ) is a request for putting tuple t in the space proposing a lease time τ for its duration. In JavaSpaces an object of class Lease is returned that can be used to get the assigned lease time, and to renew and cancel the lease request. Here we abstract away from lease renewing and cancelling, and simply suppose a message is returned to the requestor, specifying the actual lease time assigned to the tuple.

The space content is modelled as a multiset of pairs $\langle t, \tau \rangle$ called *entries*. Each entry represents tuple t expiring at the space's time τ, and is denoted by the syntax t_τ. We let variable e range over the set of entries $E = \langle T, \mathcal{N} \rangle$. Given the multiset of entries $\overline{t_\tau}$, the corresponding multiset of tuples is denoted by $\overline{t}$. The lease management is represented through a function $\lambda \in \Lambda = \mathcal{N} \mapsto \mathcal{N}$, accepting a lease time request τ and yielding the time granted by the space according to the current policy.

The observable behaviour of the class of JavaSpaces is modelled through the tuple $\langle P, C, M, J \rangle$ as follows. In our model for JavaSpaces, the details of time passing and lease management are supposed to be part of the inner activity the observation framework intentionally neglects. As a result, the set of places is defined as $P = \mathcal{N} \times \overline{E} \times \Lambda$. The three components orderly represent (i) the current space's time, (ii) the multiset of entries, and (iii) the current leasing policy represented by function $\lambda \in \Lambda$.

Two spontaneous moves are supposed to be allowed for the space[4], representing the two kinds of inner activity we consider. Moves of the kind $\langle\langle\tau,\overline{e},\lambda\rangle,\langle\tau',\overline{e},\lambda\rangle\rangle$ with $\tau < \tau'$ model time passing – which in this paper is supposed to be synchronous according to the definition in [3]. Moves of the kind $\langle\langle\tau,\overline{e},\lambda\rangle,\langle\tau,\overline{e},\lambda'\rangle\rangle$ model the space's leasing policy changing – whose actual cause and characteristics we abstract away according to our grey-box approach.

The set of c-atoms is defined as:

$$C = \{jsrd(tm,\tau)^o, jstk(tm,\tau)^o, jsntf(tm)^o, jswr(t,\tau)^o, jscollect\}$$

A JavaSpaces' operation executed at the space's time τ_0 from an agent o is modelled through the conditioning of a c-atom as follows:

$$\begin{array}{ll}
\mathbf{readIfEx}.(tm) \mapsto jsrd(tm,\tau_0)^o & \mathbf{takeIfEx}.(tm) \mapsto jstk(tm,\tau_0)^o \\
\mathbf{read}(tm,\tau) \mapsto jsrd(tm,\tau_0+\tau)^o & \mathbf{take}(tm,\tau) \mapsto jstk(tm,\tau_0+\tau)^o \\
\mathbf{notify}(tm,list) \mapsto jsntf(tm)^{list} & \mathbf{write}(tm,\tau) \mapsto jswr(t,\tau)^o
\end{array}$$

The c-atom $jscollect$ is not used to represent a pending request, but the proactive behaviour responsible for dropping expired tuples from the space. Other c-atoms that are evaluated through spontaneous moves exist as well which are then responsible for a proactive behaviour, namely $jsrd(tm,\tau)^o$ and $jstk(tm,\tau)^o$ which send an exception message $o \perp_T$ when their time-out expires.

The set of manifestations is defined as $M ::= o \, l | o \, \tau$. The former kind is used for messages containing tuples, or the notification of an absence of $\mathbf{readIfExists}$ and $\mathbf{takeIfExists}$, or a time-out expiration in $\mathbf{take}$ and $\mathbf{read}$ – through symbol $\perp_T$. The latter kind is used as a response for $\mathbf{write}$, providing the actual lease time granted by the space. Figure 2 shows semantics rules for C-atoms.

The semantics of operation $\mathbf{read}$ is defined by two rules, one managing the case where a tuple matching the template is found – similarly to the case of Linda –, the other dealing with time-out and reacting to spontaneous moves modelling time passing. Operation $\mathbf{take}$ has a similar semantics.

The rule for operation $\mathbf{notify}$ is similar to the rule for tuple-matching in $\mathbf{read}$, with the only difference that the generic c-atom $jsntf(tm)^o$ is always re-iterated and is never dropped from the configuration. Write operation gets the granted lease time from leasing function λ, puts the tuple in the space, and replies the lease time to the requestor. C-atom $jscollect$ reacts to time passing by dropping expired tuples. Given a move $\langle p,p'\rangle[\overline{c}]$ we define

$$\langle p,p'\rangle[\overline{c}]_\beta = \{c \in \overline{c}: (c \neq jstk(tm,\tau)^o) \wedge (\langle p,p'\rangle \leftrightarrow_\gamma c)\}_M$$

as the multiset of c-atoms which can be concurrently evaluated, that is, all the applying c-atoms not representing a $\mathbf{take}$ operation. Based on this definition,

---

[4] In this version of the observation framework, the spontaneous moves actually allowed are not generally comprised in the source's specification. However, as shown in [15] this can be done without great impact on the formal model, and here it is avoided for simplicity.

$$\frac{matches(tm, t')}{jsrd(tm, \tau)^\circ : \langle p, \langle \tau_0, t'_{\tau'} | \bar{e}, \lambda \rangle \rangle \hookrightarrow_\epsilon \langle \bot_c, \langle \tau_0, t'_{\tau'} | \bar{e}, \lambda \rangle, \varrho \, t' \rangle} \qquad \text{(JS-RD)}$$

$$\frac{\tau_1 > \tau > \tau_0 \qquad \nexists t'_{\tau'} \in \bar{e} : matches(tm, t')}{jsrd(tm, \tau)^\circ : \langle \langle \tau_0, \bar{e}, \lambda \rangle, \langle \tau_1, \bar{e}, \lambda \rangle \rangle \hookrightarrow_\epsilon \langle \bot_c, \langle \tau_1, \bar{e}, \lambda \rangle, \varrho \perp_T \rangle} \qquad \text{(JS-RDE)}$$

$$\frac{matches(tm, t')}{jstk(tm, \tau)^\circ : \langle p, \langle \tau_0, t'_{\tau'} | \bar{e}, \lambda \rangle \rangle \hookrightarrow_\epsilon \langle \bot_c, \langle \tau_0, \bar{e}, \lambda \rangle, \varrho \, t' \rangle} \qquad \text{(JS-TK)}$$

$$\frac{\tau_1 > \tau > \tau_0 \qquad \nexists t'_{\tau'} \in \bar{e} : matches(tm, t')}{jstk(tm, \tau)^\circ : \langle \langle \tau_0, \bar{e}, \lambda \rangle, \langle \tau_1, \bar{e}, \lambda \rangle \rangle \hookrightarrow_\epsilon \langle \bot_c, \langle \tau_1, \bar{e}, \lambda \rangle, \varrho \perp_T \rangle} \qquad \text{(JS-TKE)}$$

$$\frac{matches(tm, t)}{jsntf(tm)^\circ : \langle \langle \tau, \bar{e}, \lambda \rangle, \langle \tau, t_{\tau'} | \bar{e}, \lambda \rangle \rangle \hookrightarrow_\epsilon \langle jsntf(tm)^\circ, \langle \tau, t_{\tau'} | \bar{e}, \lambda \rangle, \varrho \, t \rangle} \qquad \text{(JS-NTF)}$$

$$\frac{\tau' = \lambda(\tau_0)}{jswr(t_0, \tau_0)^\circ : \langle \langle \tau, \bar{e}, \lambda \rangle, \langle \tau, \bar{e}, \lambda \rangle \rangle \hookrightarrow_\epsilon \langle \bot_C, \langle \tau, t_{\tau+\tau'} | \bar{e}, \lambda \rangle, \varrho \, \tau' \rangle} \qquad \text{(JS-WR)}$$

$$\frac{\tau' > \tau \qquad \bar{e}' = \bar{e} \setminus \{t_{\tau_0} \in \bar{e}, \tau_0 < \tau'\}_M}{jscollect : \langle \langle \tau, \bar{e}, \lambda \rangle, \langle \tau', \bar{e}, \lambda \rangle \rangle \hookrightarrow_\epsilon \langle jscollect, \bar{e}', \bullet \rangle} \qquad \text{(JS-LEA)}$$

Fig. 2. Evaluation rules for the JavaSpaces specification

the following selection relation gives priority to **read** and **notify** with respect to **take**, analogously to the case of Linda:

$$\frac{\bar{c}' = \langle p, p' \rangle [\bar{c}]_\beta \neq \bullet}{\langle p, p' \rangle [\bar{c}] \hookrightarrow_\sigma \bar{c}'} \qquad \frac{\langle p, p' \rangle [c|\bar{c}]_\beta = \bullet \qquad \langle p, p' \rangle \hookrightarrow_\gamma c}{\langle p, p' \rangle [c|\bar{c}] \hookrightarrow_\sigma \{c\}_M}$$

The formalisation provided in this section is meant to emphasise the applicability of the observation framework as a grey-box approach for modelling coordination media. Traditional aspects related to tuple-based coordination models such as tuple reading and consuming, synchrony / asynchrony, and also notification, can be easily represented as reactive behaviours, that is, handled through a medium's trajectory fired by an input message conditioning. In general, the framework provides a good support for their complete and explicit representation as the medium's core. On the other hand, the observation approach promotes modelling more complex behaviours – such as JavaSpaces' time passing and lease mechanism – as part of the medium's inner activity. Correspondingly, their actual effect on the medium's observable behaviour are represented as proactive behaviours, fired by the medium's spontaneous moves.

5   Modelling Tuple Centres

In this section, a formalisation of tuple centres coordination media is provided based on the observation framework, which is based on the specification reported in [11].

A tuple centre is a tuple space equipped by a behaviour specification. This specification defines *reaction* activities that are associated to communication events and alter the tuple centre's behaviour. Formally, a tuple centre can be viewed as a 6-tuple $\langle T, Oe, Ie, Z, trig, react \rangle$. T is the set of tuples, Oe is a set of output messages the centre can emit, while Ie is the set of incoming communication events. The tuple centre's behaviour at a given time is determined by one or more reactions $z \in Z$ occurring in it, representing computation activities possibly altering the centre's content and producing output messages. The centre's state is characterised by a triplet $\langle \bar{t}, \overline{ie}, \bar{z} \rangle$ containing the multiset of tuples inserted in the space $\bar{t}$, the multiset of incoming messages waiting to be served $\overline{ie}$, and the multiset of reactions waiting to be executed $\bar{z}$.

When an input or output communication event occurs in the space, relation $trig \subseteq (Ie \cup Oe) \times \overline{Z}$ is used to non-deterministically associate a multiset of reactions $\bar{z} \in \overline{Z}$ to it, whose computational activity's execution is modelled by relation $react$ defined as $react \subseteq Z \times \overline{T} \times \overline{Ie} \times \overline{Z} \times \overline{Oe} \times \overline{T} \times \overline{Ie} \times \overline{Z}$. In particular, when reaction z is evaluated in the centre's state $\langle \bar{t}, \bar{z}, \overline{ie} \rangle$, this moves to $\langle \bar{t}', \bar{z}', \overline{ie}' \rangle$ and the output messages $\overline{oe}$ are sent out, according to the occurrence of $\langle z, \bar{t}, \overline{ie}, \bar{z}, \overline{oe}, \bar{t}', \overline{ie}', \bar{z}' \rangle$ in $react$. At a given time, reactions are non-deterministically selected and evaluated until none occurs in the space.

The whole behaviour can be formally represented through the observation framework as follows. First of all, to each $ie \in Ie$ two transition systems $\langle \overline{T}, \longrightarrow_{L,ie}, Ie_\perp \rangle$ and $\langle \overline{T}, \longrightarrow_{S,ie}, Oe \rangle$ are defined that describe, respectively, its incoming and outgoing effect on the tuple centre. In particular, $\bar{t} \xrightarrow{\widehat{ie}}_{L,ie} \bar{t}'$ means that when ie arrives on a centre with tuples $\bar{t}$, the centre moves to t' and $\widehat{ie}$ is eventually added to the set of pending queries (if any). On the other hand, $\bar{t} \xrightarrow{oe}_{S,ie} \bar{t}'$ means that when pending query ie is served on a centre with tuples $\bar{t}$, the centre moves to $\bar{t}'$ and oe is sent out. As an example, the semantics of incoming communication events $rd(tm)^o$ and $out(t)$ is described by the rules:

$$\bar{t} \xrightarrow{rd(tm)^o}_{L,rd(tm)^o} \bar{t} \qquad \frac{matches(tm, t)}{t|\bar{t} \xrightarrow{o\,t}_{S,rd(tm)^o} \bar{t}} \qquad \bar{t} \xrightarrow{\perp_{Ie}}_{S,out(t)} t|\bar{t}$$

The set of places is defined as $P = \overline{T} \times \overline{Ie} \times \overline{Z}$ respectively representing the tuples occurring, the pending queries, and the pending reactions. C-atoms can be either of the kind $listen(ie)$, $evaluator$, or $speaker$, orderly modelling: (i) the c-atom representing the conditioning of incoming message ie, (ii) the c-atom responsible for evaluating reactions, and the c-atom responsible for executing satisifiable pending queries. The set of messages is Oe. The rules giving semantics to c-atoms are as follows:

$$\frac{\bar{t} \xrightarrow{\widehat{ie}}_{L,ie} \bar{t}' \qquad trig(ie, \bar{z})}{listen(ie) : \langle p, \langle \bar{t}, \overline{ie}, \bullet \rangle \rangle \hookleftarrow_\epsilon \langle \perp_C, \langle \bar{t}', \widehat{ie}|\overline{ie}, \bar{z} \rangle, \bullet \rangle}$$

$$\frac{\bar{t} \xrightarrow{oe}_{S,ie} \bar{t}' \qquad trig(oe, \bar{z})}{speaker : \langle p, \langle \bar{t}, ie|\overline{ie}, \bullet \rangle \rangle \hookleftarrow_\epsilon \langle speaker, \langle \bar{t}', \overline{ie}, \bar{z} \rangle, oe \rangle}$$

$$\frac{react(z, \bar{t}, \overline{ie}, \bar{z}, \overline{oe}, \bar{t}', \overline{ie}', \bar{z}')}{evaluator : \langle p, \langle \bar{t}, \overline{ie}, z|\bar{z} \rangle \rangle \hookleftarrow_\epsilon \langle evaluator, \langle \bar{t}', \overline{ie}', \bar{z}' \rangle, \overline{oe} \rangle}$$

In previous section, the flavour of the observation approach as a suitable support for the modellisation of proactive behaviours have been discussed. In this section, instead, we showed how the medium's dynamics – represented through source's trajectories – can be easily adapted to represent reactive behaviours independently of their complexity. To this end, we formalised the behaviour of tuple centres. In fact, ReSpecT tuple centres [7] have been showed to allow the definition of any computable input/output behaviour through very simple forms of reactions [11]. The observation framework supports a direct formalisation of this approach, emphasising its flavours as a support for the modellisations of complex reactive behaviours as well.

6   Related Works and Conclusions

In [13] we started discussing the observation issue in computer systems in general, providing an ontology for comparing features of seemingly diverse software entities and components coming from different areas – such as agent-based systems, distributed systems, programming languages, and databases. On top of this ontology, a formal framework has been built with the goal of clearly characterising, classifying, and specifying the most commonly-occurring interactions patterns related to a component's state observation. Here, the framework of [13] has been exploited to develop an operational semantics for software components modelled in terms of observable sources. The resulting formal model is significantly changed: in particular, the operational semantics we defined here is sensibly simpler yet more expressive, and is exploited to describe any source's interaction with the environment, not only those involving an observation.

The applicability of our approach to proactive components – here put to test on some aspects of the JavaSpaces coordination medium – has been discussed in [14] as well, where it is applied to agent-based systems. In particular, the key aspect of separating a component's interactive behaviour from its inner activity seems particularly appealing for agents, which are often characterised by intelligent behaviours making impossible to provide for full modellisations. So, the observation approach presented in this paper has the potential of unifying very diverse coordination approaches coming from different research areas and academic communities. While here we elaborated on its applicability to coordination models and infrastructures, other coordination approaches such as those based on mediator agents [12] – providing coordination by means of intelligent and proactive behaviours – can be taken into account as well. A systematic comparison between these two approaches, however, deserves further studies and is likely to be subject of future research.

Other current and future works are devoted to inspecting the usefulness of our approach to the engineering of software components, both at the specification, design, implementation, and validation levels. Then, we believe it also worth studying theoretical aspects of the grey-box approach, fostering comparisons with classical studies on interactive computing, such as those on the observation equivalence issue.

References

1. M. M. Bonsangue, F. Arbab, J. W. de Bakker, J. J. M. M. Rutten, A. Scutella, and G. Zavattaro. A transition system semantics for the control-driven coordination language MANIFOLD. *Theoretical Computer Science*, 240(1):3–47, June 2000.
2. N. Busi, R. Gorrieri, and G. Zavattaro. On the expressiveness of Linda coordination primitives. *Information and Computation*, 156(1-2):90–121, Jan. 2000.
3. N. Busi, R. Gorrieri, and G. Zavattaro. Process calculi for Coordination: From Linda to JavaSpaces. In T. Rus, editor, *8th International Conference, AMAST 2000*, volume 1816 of *LNCS*, pages 198–212. Springer-Verlag, 2000.
4. N. Busi and G. Zavattaro. On the expressiveness of event notification in data-driven coordination languages. In *9th European Symposium on Programming*, volume 1782 of *LNCS*, pages 41–55. Springer-Verlag, 2000.
5. P. Ciancarini, K. K. Jensen, and D. Yankelevich. On the operational sematics of a coordination language. In P. Ciancarini, O. Nierstrask, and O. Yonezawa, editors, *Object-Based Models and Languages for Concurrent Systems*, volume 924 of *LNCS*, pages 77–106. Springer-Verlag, 1994.
6. R. De Nicola and R. Pugliese. A process algebra based on LINDA. In P. Cincarini and C. Hankin, editors, *Coordination Languages and Models*, volume 1061 of *LNCS*, pages 160–178. Springer-Verlag, 1996.
7. E. Denti, A. Natali, and A. Omicini. On the expressive power of a language for programming coordination media. In *1998 ACM Symposium on Applied Computing (SAC'98)*, pages 169–177, Atlanta (GA), 27 Feb. – 1 Mar. 1998. ACM. Track on Coordination Models, Languages and Applications.
8. E. Freeman, S. Hupfer, and K. Arnold. *JavaSpaces. Principles, Patterns, and Practice*. The Jini Technology Series. Addison-Wesley, 1999.
9. D. Gelernter. Generative communication in Linda. *ACM Transactions on Programming Languages and Systems*, 7(1):80–112, January 1985.
10. A. Omicini. On the semantics of tuple-based coordination models. In *1999 ACM Symposium on Applied Computing (SAC'99)*, pages 175–182, San Antonio (TX), 28 Feb. – 2 Mar. 1999. ACM. Track on Coordination Models, Languages and Applications.
11. A. Omicini and E. Denti. From tuple spaces to tuple centres. *Science of Computer Programming*, 41(3):277–294, Nov. 2001.
12. K. Sycara. Multi-agent infrastructure, agent discovery, middle agents for Web services. In M. Luck, V. Mařík, O. Štěpánková, and R. Trappl, editors, *Multi-Agent Systems and Applications*, volume 2086 of *LNAI*, pages 17–49. Springer-Verlag, 2001.
13. M. Viroli, G. Moro, and A. Omicini. On observation as a coordination pattern: An ontology and a formal framework. In *16th ACM Symposium on Applied Computing (SAC 2001)*, pages 166–175, Las Vegas (NV), 11–14 Mar. 2001. ACM.
14. M. Viroli and A. Omicini. Multi-agent systems as composition of observable systems. In *WOA 2001 – Dagli oggetti agli agenti: tendenze evolutive dei sistemi software*, Modena, Italy, 4–5 Sept. 2001. Pitagora Editrice Bologna.
15. M. Viroli and A. Omicini. Specifying agents' observable behaviour. In *1st International Joint Conference on Autonomous Agents and Multi-Agent Systems (AAMAS 2002)*, Bologna, Italy, 15–19 July 2002. ACM.
16. L. D. Zuch and D. Gelernter. On what Linda is: Formal description of Linda as a reactive system. In D. Garlan and D. Le Métayer, editors, *Coordination Languages and Models*, volume 1282 of *LNCS*, pages 187–204. Springer-Verlag, 1997.

Extending the Matching Facilities of Linda

George Wells[1], Alan Chalmers[2], and Peter Clayton[1]

[1] Department of Computer Science, Rhodes University,
Grahamstown, 6140, South Africa
{G.Wells, P.Clayton}@ru.ac.za
[2] Department of Computer Science, University of Bristol,
Bristol BS8 1UB, U.K.
alan@compsci.bristol.ac.uk

Abstract. This paper discusses the associative matching mechanism used in the Linda coordination language for the retrieval of data. There are a number of problems with this mechanism which are discussed in the light of the requirements of applications using Linda. A number of solutions to these problems have been proposed. These are discussed and compared with a new approach to solving these problems. The benefits and the limitations of the new approach are considered, showing how it provides a considerable improvement in this area.

1 Introduction

The Linda[1] coordination language for distributed and parallel programming was first proposed by David Gelernter in the mid-1980's[1]. In recent years it has become a popular approach for handling the coordination of distributed processes in Java[2] programs, with a number of commercial products and research projects based on the Linda model[2,3,4,5,6,7,8,9,10,11,12,13,14,15,16]. Many of these systems have attempted to address a number of problems arising from the simple associative matching mechanism that is used by Linda for the retrieval of data.

The first section of this paper presents a brief discussion of the problems related to the use of the associative matching mechanisms in Linda (full details of the Linda programming model may be found in [17]). This is followed by a survey of Java implementations of Linda which have embodied various solutions to the matching problems. It then describes our work on an extended version of the Linda model called *eLinda*. The eLinda system contains a number of extensions, including the *Programmable Matching Engine*, intended to help overcome the deficiencies of the conventional Linda associative matching technique.

---

[1] Linda is a registered trademark of Scientific Computing Associates.
[2] Java is a registered trademark of Sun Microsystems, Inc.

F. Arbab and C. Talcott (Eds.): COORDINATION 2002, LNCS 2315, pp. 380–388, 2002.

2   Problems with the Associative Matching Mechanism

The associative matching mechanism used for the retrieval of tuples in Linda works very well in many situations, such as simple one-to-one communication, one-to-many communication, implementing semaphores, barrier synchronisation, etc. However there are situations where this simple matching is not adequate.

As a simple example, consider a set of tuples, where an application needs to locate the tuple with the maximum value of some field. Using Linda to solve this problem is possible, but is not efficient. The application would need to retrieve *all* of the tuples, search through them for the one with the maximum value, and then return the tuples to the tuple space. During this procedure the tuples are not available for other processes to make use of, potentially restricting the degree of parallelism possible. Furthermore, in a distributed implementation, there is a large amount of unnecessary network traffic generated by this application.

While this is a simple example, it illustrates a general problem, namely that applications may need a "global view" of the tuples in tuple space. Other examples include finding tuples with with values "close to" some specified value, or lying within a specified range of values. These types of problems cannot be solved efficiently using the standard associative matching technique.

3   Extended Linda Systems

In an attempt to address the problem described in the preceding section (and others) a number of different extensions to the basic Linda approach have been proposed. This section outlines some of these projects.

3.1   TSpaces

TSpaces is a Linda-like system developed by IBM's alphaWorks research division[2,3]. It is considerably extended from the original Linda model, particularly in terms of support for commercial applications. More importantly from our perspective, it includes several new operations, and provides a mechanism that allows applications to add new operations to the tuple space server dynamically. Each of these aspects is relevant to our discussion and will be covered in more detail in the following sections.

New Operations. TSpaces provides new operations for the input and output of multiple tuples, and a number of operations that specify tuples by means of a "tuple ID" rather than the usual associative matching mechanisms. There is also the **rhonda** operator, which performs an atomic synchronisation and data exchange operation between two processes. Lastly, there is an "event registration" mechanism. This allows a process to request notification when a specified tuple is written to the tuple space or deleted from it.

Matching tuples in TSpaces can be done using so-called "indexed tuples". In this case the fields of tuples may be named, ranges of values may be included in the matching process, and AND and OR operations may be specified. These features may all be used in combination. It is also possible to perform matching on XML[3] data contained in tuples.

Extending the Server. New commands can be added to the TSpaces system relatively easily. The implementation of TSpaces makes use of a number of layers of software. At the lowest level the tuples themselves are stored in a form of database. This may be an actual DBMS product, or a data structure in memory. Above this is the tuple management layer, which handles the retrieval of tuples from the database. Above this layer, accessed through a well-defined programming interface, is the operator management level. This is comprised of a number of "factory" objects arranged in a list. The factories are responsible for creating "tuple handlers" for each command that is passed to the tuple space. If a factory does not recognise a particular command then it is passed down to the next factory in the list.

Users with administrator permission levels can add new factories and handlers to the system dynamically, providing a great deal of flexibility. However, this is a complex process from a programmer's perspective, as has also been noted by Foster et al[13].

Application of the Extensions. The extended features of TSpaces provide for a somewhat better solution to the "maximum" matching problem outlined in Section 2. In this case either the scan or the consumingScan operation provided by TSpaces can be used to retrieve all of the tuples in one step. The application can locate the required tuple, and then return the tuples to tuple space if necessary. While the end effect is exactly the same as in the original Linda model, the application is simplified through the use of these new operations.

The extended matching facilities in TSpaces (allowing ranges of values, XML-matching, etc.) may be useful in that they cover a number of common situations. However, they do not provide a general solution for the matching requirements of all applications. Notably, they do not address the "maximum" problem described in Section 2.

The possibility of extending the TSpaces server to include specialised matching commands also exists. For our example problem, this would entail writing a new command handler to search through the tuple space and return the one with the maximum value. However, there are a number of drawbacks to this approach:

– The users of applications requiring new matching operations will need to be granted administrator rights (or the system administrator must install all new matchers).

---

[3] Extensible Markup Language, a specification for structured documents produced by the World Wide Web Consortium[18].

- From a system design perspective, modifying the server in order to support specific applications may be undesirable. Ensuring that different new commands do not interfere with each other in unintended ways may also be problematic.
- The new commands are awkward to use.
- As already noted, the process of adding new command handlers is not simple.

3.2   XMLSpaces

With the wide adoption of XML in the computer industry, it is increasingly useful for XML support to be provided by a Linda system. XMLSpaces was designed as an extension of TSpaces to address the limited facilities that it has for matching XML-formatted data[4]. As such, XMLSpaces does not attempt to provide a general solution to the matching problem, but one that is aimed at a specific application area.

The XML support in XMLSpaces is provided through the object-oriented features of the Java programming language. The `Field` class used by TSpaces for the fields in tuples is subclassed to create a new class called `XMLDocField`. This class overrides the matching method used by TSpaces to provide matching on the basis of the XML content of the field. The matching is performed by a method of the anti-tuple that can be provided by the application programmer. This results in a great deal of flexibility for XML matching operations. A number of matching operations are currently supported, including the use of XML query languages, such as XPath[19].

3.3   The Work of the York Coordination Group

The coordination research group at the University of York has been actively researching in the area of Linda systems for some time. One of their major projects has been to extend the Linda operations with `collect` and `copy-collect`[5,6]. These *bulk operations* may be used to move or copy multiple tuples from one tuple space to another. This provides similar functionality to the `scan` and related operations of TSpaces. While these do not directly affect the matching mechanisms, they may be used to simplify applications that need a "global view" of tuple space, such as the maximum example discussed above.

3.4   Liam

Liam is a Linda system, based on the *Chemical Abstract Machine*, or *CHAM*[7]. This is an unusual programming model, in which systems are expressed as "solutions of molecules" (multisets, describing the state of the system), and subjected to "chemical reactions" (rewriting of the multisets, subject to "reaction rules"). Programs in this model consist of sets of reaction pairs, composed of a condition, specifying when the rule may be applied, and an action, which is a function that produces new molecules from the reactants. This model is ideally suited to parallel implementation, as independent reactions may take place simultaneously.

Liam allows the matching algorithm for tuples to be provided in CHAM form. This has the drawback that programmers must become familiar with the syntax used by the Chemical Abstract Machine. This is not a simple notation for the average application programmer to learn and use.

3.5   Objective Linda

Objective Linda is a model for object-oriented implementations of Linda[8,9]. All aspects of an application (i.e. data, active agents and the tuple spaces) are modelled as objects. Tuple spaces form a strongly encapsulated hierarchy of objects, containing passive objects (i.e. tuples), active objects (i.e. agents) and other tuple spaces.

Of particular iterest are the extensions to the usual Linda matching mechanism. The objects that are to be used as tuples in Objective Linda are required to provide a `match` method. This method is then called when performing an input operation. This means that the programmer writing the classes to be used as tuples in an application can define the precise meaning of a "match".

This feature of Objective Linda provides a restricted form of extended matching similar to that in the eLinda system. The strengths and weaknesses of this approach will be discussed at the end of the next section.

3.6   CO^{3}PS

CO^{3}PS stands for "Computation, Coordination and Composition with Petri net Specifications"[10,11]. The coordination model used in CO^{3}PS is based closely on that of Objective Linda. The main application of extended matching in CO^{3}PS is to support the introduction of *non-functional requirements* into the design of a system. Examples of such requirements are efficiency, load-balancing and security.

In order to support this design technique, CO^{3}PS makes use of a *reflective architecture*. This is an architecture that permits the designer to reflect on the behaviour of the system, and to adapt it, without affecting the interaction with clients. The developers of CO^{3}PS emphasize that this should be done without impacting on the semantics of the coordination operations.

Discussion of Objective Linda and CO^{3}PS. Both Objective Linda and CO^{3}PS allow the matching method for tuples to be overridden. This is rather counter-intuitive, in that the matching is effectively provided by the *tuple*, rather than the anti-tuple. This has the implication that programmers writing classes for tuples need to consider how they may be retrieved, while it is the anti-tuples that are used for input operations in Linda. Furthermore, this makes it extremely difficult to apply different matching criteria to a single type of tuple at different times (or in different applications). Associating the matching logic with the anti-tuples is thus a more natural approach.

Matching is also constrained to a one-to-one situation: the `match` method is called to determine whether the tuple matches a single anti-tuple. Thus there is no way of providing operations that aggregate tuples to form a result.

In CO^3PS this approach has been adopted for the reflective architecture, providing for the non-functional requirements of an application. The key to this philosophy is that the semantics of the coordination operations may not be altered by the imposition of non-functional requirements. However, in many situations it is very useful to be able to relax or alter the semantics of the matching operations (such as aggregating multiple tuples to form a result).

3.7 ELLIS

ELLIS (EuLisp LInda System) is a Linda system developed in EuLisp[12]. Of particular interest is that matching is performed by a method in the tuple space class. This allows the matching method to be overridden, but the mechanism seems clumsy: new classes of tuple spaces must be created to support new matching algorithms. Few details of this process are given in the description of ELLIS, but the programming interfaces for new matchers appear to be complex and to involve dealing with the pool of tuples at a very low level of abstraction.

3.8 Summary

What all of these projects indicate is an underlying weakness in the basic Linda associative matching technique. While each of these systems has addressed this problem in one way or another, they each have their own deficiencies. The next section presents the eLinda system and the extensions to the associative matching procedure, which overcomes these problems.

4 eLinda

The eLinda system is based closely on the standard Linda model. It uses a fully-distributed tuple space model where any tuple may reside on any node. This poses particular problems for matching, in that many processing nodes may be required to participate in a matching operation. Testing has shown that the performance of eLinda is on a par with that of other Java Linda systems (such as TSpaces and JavaSpaces[20]), but that Java is currently not a viable platform for parallel processing applications[21].

The eLinda system contains three extensions to the Linda programming model: a "broadcast" output operation, multimedia support and the *Programmable Matching Engine*. The focus of this paper is on the last of these. Further details of the other features can be found in [22].

4.1 The Programmable Matching Engine

The Programmable Matching Engine (or *PME*) allows the use of more flexible criteria for the associative addressing of tuples. This is useful in situations such as that exemplified by finding the tuple with the maxiumum value for some field. As has already been noted, such queries can be expressed using the standard Linda associative matching methods, but will generally be quite inefficient. If the tuple space is distributed, searching for a tuple may involve accessing the sections held on all the processors in parallel. This problem is handled efficiently in eLinda by distributing the matching engine so that network traffic is minimised, and moving the necessary computation out of the application and into the matcher. For example, in searching for the maximum tuple, each section of the tuple space would be searched locally for the largest tuple and that returned to the matcher running in the originating process, which would then select the largest of all the replies received. This process is completely transparent to the application, which simply inputs a tuple, using a specialised matcher. From the application programmer's perspective this could be expressed simply as `in.maximum(?field1, ?=field2)`. The notation that is used is to follow the Linda input operation with the name of the matcher to be used. The field (or fields) to be used by the matcher is denoted by `?=`.

In addition to this simple usage, matchers may also perform *aggregated operations* where a tuple is returned that in some way summarises or aggregates information from a number of tuples. For example, a matcher might calculate the total of numeric fields in some subset of the tuples in tuple space. It is also possible to write matchers that return multiple tuples, similar to the TSpaces "scan" operations, or the York bulk operations.

New matchers are written as Java classes. They can make use of a simple library that provides controlled access to tuple space, communication mechanisms, etc.

4.2   Limitations and Applications of the Programmable Matching Engine

There are some limitations to the kinds of matching operations that are supported by the PME. Notably, some matching operations may require a complete global view of the tuple space (e.g. where a tuple is required that has the *median* value of some field). In such situations the use of the PME may not be ideal, as all the tuples need to be gathered together in order to find the result. However, it is important to note that such problems are handled no less efficiently than if the application were to handle them directly, using a conventional Linda system. Furthermore, the PME approach minimises the network traffic in such cases.

Most of the examples of matchers given above have been in the domain of numeric applications. However, it would be incorrect to believe that the PME is limited to these—it is just as applicable to textual, XML or other problem domains.

5   Conclusions

The significant number of projects that have, in one way or another, extended the functionality of the matching operations in Linda points to the weakness that is embodied in the original programming model. The nature of the extensions ranges from those exemplified by TSpaces, where the tuple space server itself is reconfigured to support new operations, to systems like XMLSpaces, Objective Linda and Liam where the matching process is specified by overriding the matching method used, in some cases for very specific purposes.

What is found in comparing these proposals with the eLinda PME is that the PME proposal can emulate all of these alternative approaches. Furthermore, the PME approach allows for a range of tuple space implementation techniques, ranging from fully distributed to centralised, whereas most of the other systems are implemented only for centralised configurations.

In many cases the PME approach is more intuitive and elegant than the alternatives. The approach adopted in Objective Linda and CO^3PS, where the matching method in an object/tuple can be overridden, fits well with the object-oriented philosophy of Java. However, it limits matching operations to one-to-one situations, and fixes the matching possibilities at the time that the tuple class is written. By providing the matcher as an independent object, the PME approach opens up the possibilities of aggregating operations, and provides the flexibility of being able to apply many matchers to a single type of tuple. The approach used for adding new commands in TSpaces, while providing a high degree of flexibility, effectively requires the reconfiguration of the tuple space server to support new operations. This is complex and potentially dangerous in a multi-user situation.

5.1   Future Work

A number of Linda systems have made extensions in the area of *output* and *update* operations, similar in some respects to those described above for input operations. [2,13,14]. This again points to a weakness in the Linda programming model, and it appears that an approach analagous to that of the Programmable Matching Engine may be beneficial in such situations too.

Acknowledgments. This work was supported by the Distributed Multimedia Centre of Excellence in the Department of Computer Science at Rhodes University, with funding from Telkom SA, Lucent Technologies, Dimension Data and THRIP.

References

1. Gelernter, D.: Generative communication in Linda. ACM Trans. Programming Languages and Systems **7** (1985) 80–112
2. IBM: TSpaces. (URL: http://www.almaden.ibm.com/cs/TSpaces/index.html)
3. Wyckoff, P., McLaughry, S.W., Lehman, T.J., Ford, D.A.: T Spaces. IBM Systems Journal **37** (1998) 454—474
4. Tolksdorf, R., Glaubitz, D.:   Coordinating web-based systems with documents in XMLSpaces. URL: http://flp.cs.tu-berlin.de/~tolk/xmlspaces/-webxmlspaces.pdf (2001)

5. Butcher, P., Wood, A., Atkins, M.: Global synchronisation in Linda. Concurrency: Practice and Experience **6** (1994) 505–516
6. Rowstron, A., Wood, A.: Solving the Linda multiple rd problem. In Ciancarini, P., Hankin, C., eds.: Coordination Languages and Models, Proc. Coordination '96. Volume 1061 of Lecture Notes in Computer Science., Springer-Verlag (1996) 357–367
7. Campbell., D.: Constraint matching retrieval in Linda: extending retrieval functionality and distributing query processing. Technical Report YCS 285, University of York (1997)
8. Kielmann, T.: Objective Linda: A Coordination Model for Object-Oriented Parallel Programming. PhD thesis, University of Siegen, Germany (1997)
9. Kielmann, T.: Object-Oriented Distributed Programming with Objective Linda. In: First International Workshop on High Speed Networks and Open Distributed Platforms, St. Petersburg, Russia (1995)
10. Holvoet, T., Berbers, Y.: Reflective programmable coordination media. [23] 1236–1242
11. Holvoet, T.: An Approach for Open Concurrent Software Development. PhD thesis, Department of Computer Science, K.U.Leuven (1997)
12. Broadbery, P., Playford, K.: Using object-oriented mechanisms to describe Linda. In Wilson, G., ed.: Linda-Like Systems and Their Implementation. Technical Report 91-13. Edinburgh Parallel Computing Centre (1991) 14–26
13. Foster, M., Matloff, N., Pandey, R., Standring, D., Sweeney, R.: I-Tuples: A programmer-controllable performance enhancement for the Linda environment. [23] 357–361
14. Rowstron, A.: Mobile co-ordination: Providing fault tolerance in tuple space based co-ordination languages. URL: http://www.research.microsoft.com/~antr/-papers/mobile.ps.gz (1999)
15. Sudell, A.: Design and implementation of a tuple-space server for Java. URL: http://www.op.net/~asudell/is/linda/linda.html (1998)
16. Smith, A.: Towards wide-area network Piranha: Implementing Java-Linda. (URL: http://www.cs.yale.edu/homes/asmith/cs690/cs690.html)
17. Carriero, N., Gelernter, D.: How to Write Parallel Programs: A First Course. The MIT Press (1990)
18. World Wide Web Consortium: Extensible markup language (XML). (URL: http://www.w3.org/XML)
19. World Wide Web Consortium: XML Path language (XPath) version 1.0. W3C Recommendation, URL: http://www.w3.org/TR/xpath.html (1999)
20. Freeman, E., Hupfer, S., Arnold, K.: JavaSpaces Principles, Patterns, and Practice. Addison-Wesley (1999)
21. Wells, G., Chalmers, A., Clayton, P.: A comparison of Linda implementations in Java. In Welch, P., Bakkers, A., eds.: Communicating Process Architectures 2000. Volume 58 of Concurrent Systems Engineering Series. IOS Press (2000) 63–75
22. Wells, G.: A Programmable Matching Engine for Application Development in Linda. PhD thesis, University of Bristol, U.K. (2001)
23. Arabnia, H., ed.: Proc. International Conference on Parallel and Distributed Processing Techniques and Applications (PDPTA'2001). CSREA Press (2001)

Semantics of Protocol Modules Composition and Interaction

Paweł T. Wojciechowski, Sergio Mena, and André Schiper

EPFL, School of Computer and Communication Sciences, 1015 Lausanne, Switzerland
{First.Last}@epfl.ch

Abstract. This paper studies the semantics of protocol modules composition and interaction in configurable communication systems. We present a semantic model describing Cactus and Appia — two frameworks that are used for implementing modular systems. The model covers protocol graph, session and channel creation, and inter-module communication of events and messages. To build the model, we defined a source-code-validated specification of a large fragment of the programming interface provided by the frameworks; we developed an operational semantics describing the behaviour of the operations through state transitions, making explicit interactions between modules. Developing the model and a small example implementing a configurable multicast helped us to better understand the design choices in these frameworks. The work reported in this paper is a first step towards reasoning about systems composed from collections of modules.

1 Introduction

Modularization is a well-known technique for simplifying complex communication systems. Here, we describe an approach which is based on implementing an application's individual properties as separate protocols, and then combining selected protocols using a software framework. This approach helps to clarify the dependencies among properties required by a given communication system, and makes it possible to construct systems that are customized to the specific needs of the application or underlying network environment. We are particularly interested in implementations of group communication infrastructure (or middleware), as configurability of protocols should be clearly required here; for example, different applications may demand very different properties and guarantees as far as the quality of service and failure semantics are concerned.

In this paper, we are primarily interested in the programming abstractions provided by Cactus [10] (which subsumes the x-kernel model [3]), and Appia [4]. We have described an operational semantics of the programming interface offered by each framework, covering enough abstractions for expressing interactions between modules composed into a protocol graph. The frameworks also support primitives that can simplify the construction of protocols, such as support for processing messages, marshalling messages to the network format, and

F. Arbab and C. Talcott (Eds.): COORDINATION 2002, LNCS 2315, pp. 389–404, 2002.
© Springer-Verlag Berlin Heidelberg 2002

timeouts, but they are not covered here. We illustrate the model with a small program, implemented in Cactus and Appia.

We have chosen Cactus and Appia for two reasons. Firstly, each of the frameworks implements a very different approach to building configurable software, with a different range of programming abstractions. Therefore, it is interesting to look at each framework in turn. More importantly, we want a model that is general enough for building any kind of communication service, not just group communication. For example, Cactus has been used to implement many configurable protocols and services in distributed systems, such as Group RPC, real-time channels, secure communication service, and QoS components for CORBA. Appia has been used for the development of group communication and real-time protocols. On the other hand, systems such as Horus and Ensemble [1] have been designed to support modular and reconfigurable group communication, however the protocol stack can only be configured from selected protocols that use pre-defined event types.

The frameworks for building configurable services are highly concurrent with complex programming interfaces. This complexity makes it hard to achieve a clear understanding of the framework's behaviour based only on informal descriptions, in turn making it hard to build robust configurable systems. To the best of our knowledge, there exist only informal natural-language documents describing Cactus and Appia, covering the general architecture of each design and the programming interface but not precise enough or free from ambiguities; for example, we had to inspect source code on several occasions since the documentation was not clear enough.

Our work aims at precise understanding of the behaviour of programs that are implemented using these frameworks. An important question is about the sense in which the semantics of network subsystems composed from collections of protocol modules will relate to the behaviour of the actual implementation. This is an area that is often a secondary priority for the developers of practical module composition frameworks, yet is crucial to the long-term acceptance of this approach. While the work described here has not quite reached the point of reasoning about composition, it makes the important first step in this direction.

2   Architecture

Figure 1 presents the architecture of Cactus and Appia. The protocol names are taken from our small example, which is described in Section 5. It can be noticed that the frameworks differ considerably in the way protocol modules (represented by boxes) are composed. The dynamically created instances of modules are called *sessions*. The protocol sessions (ovals) communicate using messages or events, which are sent along communication paths (arrows).

The composition of protocols is defined by a directed acyclic graph, in which edges define communication channels. The protocols in Cactus communicating using messages are internally structured as collections of microprotocols. The microprotocols communicate using events and shared data such as messages, with

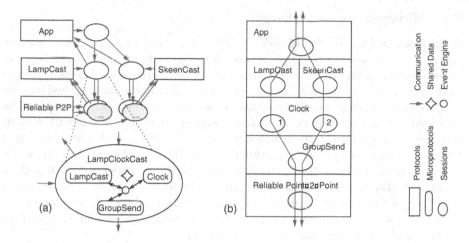

Fig. 1. Example Protocol Composition in (a) Cactus, and (b) Appia

the events dispatching actions defined by event handlers; messages coming from outside the protocol session normally trigger an event. A protocol in Cactus can create a new session dynamically, e.g. when a message arrives from a new participant. In Appia, all sessions must be created before a relevant communication channel is established (usually at the time when a protocol stack is configured).

The sessions (or protocols) in Cactus decide themselves which other sessions are to receive a message — in the case of messages incoming from the network this information is usually extracted from the message. The message is forwarded to a next session by invoking an interface method. The message arrival to a session causes appropriate event handlers (within the session) to be invoked. In Appia, there is a scheduler which forwards events to sessions in the order which is defined by a communication channel; the channel name is extracted from the event.

In the following sections, we describe each framework in turn, giving semantics of the most important operations. We do not require from the reader knowledge of the formal semantics methods, but instead we use algebraic objects that should be also well known for non-theoreticians, such as sets, lists, tuples, maps, and relations. We introduce our notation when it is first used. Due to lack of space, some rules have been omitted (they are included in [8]).

3 Cactus

Cactus extends the x-kernel hierarchical composition of protocols with fine-grain parallel composition. The Cactus protocols can be composed of semi-independent microprotocols, each of which implements a well-defined property or function of the protocol. Below we focus on Cactus/J, which is one of the prototype implementations of Cactus.

3.1   Microprotocols and Events

A *microprotocol* is a section of code, structured as a collection of *event handlers*, where an event handler is simply a procedure invoked with every occurrence of the event. We define *Microprotocol* as the set of microprotocol names, ranged over by x, y. The set *Handler* is the set of event handler names, ranged over by h. An *event* defines an occurrence that causes one or more microprotocols to be executed. For example, an event such as message arrival might trigger the event handlers of a microprotocol which detects host failures, and a microprotocol which is responsible for message ordering, etc. The events not only drive the flow of control, by executing event handler procedures associated with a given event, but also pass data from the trigger point to the handler. The set *Event* is the set of valid event names (or types), ranged over by e, e'. We denote the *occurrence* of an event e as a triple (x, e, v), where x is the caller which raised event e, and v is a value passed with the event.

In order to describe behaviour of the operations supported by the programming interface (represented as functions), we use a transition relation of the form $S, p \vdash op(n) \triangleright S'$, which means that the execution of operation op initiated or invoked by p in some state (or context) S leads to state S'; op has parameters n. The state is represented by relevant set(s) of elements. In our case, the context of every transition relation is always a single protocol stack, i.e. S always describes (part of) the state of a local runtime system only. To express and maintain the internal state, we will need maps storing bindings from keywords of type T to values of type T'. We represent maps using a set $\mathcal{M}(T \mapsto T')$ of all mappings from elements in T to elements in T', together with operations for adding and removing bindings from a map, and looking up an element. We also use lists of elements in T; $\mathcal{L}(T)$ is to denote all possible lists of elements such that each element is in T.

In order to associate a handler with a particular event, a microprotocol invokes an operation

$$\text{bind} : Event \times Handler \times Int \rightarrow ()$$

specifying the event name, the handler name, an integer which is used to determine an *order* in which handlers will be executed, and a static argument (omitted here) which is passed to the handler when an event occurs (this can be used to parameterize a handler and allow its use with more than one event types). Below a microprotocol x binds an event handler h to event e.

$$\frac{hl = E[e]}{E, x \vdash \text{bind}(e, h, i) \triangleright E \oplus (e \mapsto sort_{\leq}((h, i) :: hl))}$$

This registers a handler h of event e in a map $E \in \mathcal{M}(Event \mapsto \mathcal{L}(Handler \times Int))$, which is part of the Cactus/J state of a composite protocol that contains x. The map E stores bindings from an event name to a list of event handlers which are to handle the event, where each handler name is paired with the order argument i; the list is ordered with increased i. The value i does not need to be unique for each handler; handler names with the same order argument are placed in an indeterminate order. With every occurrence of e, the handlers will be executed in sequence as they appear in the list $E[e]$. We use the following notation: $E[e]$ looks up e in map E and returns the list of handlers bound to e, :: is a concatenation symbol to append a new element to a list, $sort_\leq(l)$ returns a list l sorted by partial order relation $\leq$, and $E \oplus (e \mapsto l)$ returns map E with a new binding of e to l; if e was already bound in E, its previous binding disappears.

3.2 Event Raising and Handling

An event can be raised by calling

$$\text{raise} : Event \times \{\text{SYNC}, \text{ASYNC}\} \times \mathcal{T} \to ()$$

specifying the name of the event, the calling mode, and a dynamic argument, such as a message that is associated with the event. When an event is raised, handlers bound to this event execute sequentially in the specified order. Each handler is passed both the static argument defined at binding time and the dynamic argument. The calling mode μ is either SYNC, which invokes handlers immediately and blocks the caller until the last handler is executed, or ASYNC, which allows the caller to proceed concurrently with the handlers (the handlers can be executed after a specified delay, omitted here).

Below we define the behaviour of raise, assuming that a microprotocol x raises an event e with a dynamic argument v.

$$
\begin{array}{l}
\boxed{\text{raise}(e,\mu,v):} \\[4pt]
\mu = \text{SYNC} \vee \mu = \text{ASYNC} \\
\quad\quad\quad E[e] = (h_1, \_) :: ... :: (h_n, \_) :: nil \\
\hline
E, x \vdash invoke(h_1, v), ..., invoke(h_n, v) \rhd E \wedge (x, e, v)_\mu \; \textit{raised}
\end{array}
$$

This looks up in map E a list of handlers of event e and executes the handlers, passing v to each handler. The event raising is modelled by relation *raised*.

The caller x is either blocked until the last handler returns, or not, depending on mode μ. While the handlers of a particular event occurrence execute sequentially, it is important to note that they can execute concurrently with other occurrences of the same event or with other microprotocol code. Therefore access to any shared data should be synchronised.

3.3 Messages

Protocols in Cactus communicate using *messages*; a message is created by the application or a protocol session, and can travel through several layers of protocol sessions and across a network. Messages contain data stored in *attributes*, which can be accessed and modified by microprotocols. Message creation raises a predefined event *NewMessage*.

Below, we use the set *Session* of session names, ranged over by s, and the set *Message* of message names (or references), ranged over by m, n. A message m is modelled as a triple of message attributes a, a message type T, and send votes V^m (the last two parameters are local to a session and never transmitted), i.e.

$$m = (a, T, V^m)$$

where each named attribute in a record a has a defined scope; it can be visible only in the current session, in the current stack, or within peer sessions only; otherwise it is discarded or concealed. The message type T is equal $\uparrow$ if the message arrived from a session below, or $\downarrow$ if from above. The message type $\diamond$ is for a temporary message local to a session. The send votes are described in §3.4.

A protocol can send a message to a Cactus session below or above using

$$\mathsf{sendDown} : [Session \times] Message \to ()$$
$$\mathsf{sendUp} : [Session \times] Message \to ()$$

where the first (optional) parameter is the name of a session to which the message is to be sent. If a message is sent to a non-Cactus session, e.g. to an x-kernel session, message attributes are converted into message headers by using a user-defined procedure (see also the push and demux operations in [8]). Below we define the default behaviour of sendDown, assuming that a protocol session s sends a message m downward to a session s', created by Cactus/J.

$$s \vdash \boxed{\mathsf{sendDown}(s',m)\text{:}}$$

$$\text{DOWN} \quad \frac{s \vdash s'.\mathsf{fromAbove}(m)}{M, s' \vdash \mathsf{raise}(MsgFromUser, \text{Async}, m) \rhd M \oplus (m \mapsto s')}$$

The session s invokes an operation fromAbove of the lower-level session s', passing m as the parameter. The execution of fromAbove raises asynchronously an event *MsgFromUser* which carries the message m. The message migration is recorded in map $M \in \mathcal{M}(Message \mapsto Session)$ of active messages bound to their current sessions. Microprotocols which are interested in receiving messages from sessions above could handle the *MsgFromUser* event. Note, however, that any subsequent invocation of sendDown will also raise this event. Therefore, if the protocol requires to receive messages in a first-in-first-out order, some synchronisation is necessary so that the microprotocol handlers will be invoked in a sequence (e.g., in our example program, we have overwritten the operation fromAbove so that it executes a synchronous operation raise($MsgFromUser$, Sync, m)).

The semantics of message flow in the opposite direction is similar. The main difference is that sendUp calls either fromBelow of a specified higher-level session (inside which an event *MsgFromNet* is raised), or an operation demux of a higher level protocol, if no session has been specified.

3.4   Message Events

An event can be associated with a particular message type ($\downarrow$,$\uparrow$). This event is triggered by a collective action of all microprotocols that have registered an interest, providing a way for microprotocols to agree upon event raising. To declare the interest, a microprotocol invokes

$$\text{register} : \{\downarrow, \uparrow\} \times \textit{Event} \to ()$$

passing a message type and an event name. Every subsequent message creation of that type has the potential of triggering the event. (If the event is to be caught, a bind call is also necessary.)

$$\overline{R_e^T, x \vdash \text{register}(T, e) \triangleright R_e^T \oplus (x \mapsto \textit{false}) \wedge (x, e, T) \textit{ registered}}$$

The invocation of register adds a new entry in a map R_e^T for message type T and event e. We mark registration by relation *registered*. The map $R_e^T \in \mathcal{M}(\textit{Microprotocol} \mapsto \textit{Boolean})$ is created dynamically and updated each time when some microprotocol executes operation register; it is a map from names of microprotocols to Boolean values (initially *false*) that represent the microprotocol "votes" signalling readiness of the event e to be raised for message type T (where T not equal $\diamond$).

For each message m, whenever message type T is assigned, Cactus/J uses maps R_e^T to build a (local to m) map V^m. For each event e that has been associated with the message type T, map V^m stores a copy of corresponding map R_e^T, i.e. $V^m[e] = \textit{copyOf}(R_e^T)$. Each event e can be raised only once per message; that occurrence of e will pass name m to event handlers bound to e

For each message, the message event is raised as soon as all of the interested microprotocols have called

$$\text{signal} : \textit{Message} \times \textit{Event} \to () \ .$$

The signal operation requires to pass as arguments the names m of the message and e of the event which will carry the message. The behaviour of signal invoked by microprotocol x is below; the execution of signal should be atomic.

$$m = (a, T, V^m)$$
$$\frac{V^m[e][x] = \textit{false} \wedge \forall y \neq x \ V^m[e][y] = \textit{true}}{E, V^m[e], x \vdash \text{signal}(m, e) \triangleright E, V^m[e] \oplus (x \mapsto \textit{true}) \wedge (x, e, m)_{\text{ASYNC}} \textit{ raised}} \quad (1)$$

$$m = (a, T, V^m)$$
$$\frac{\exists y \neq x \mid V^m[e][y] = \textit{false}}{E, V^m[e], x \vdash \text{signal}(m, e) \triangleright E, V^m[e] \oplus (x \mapsto \textit{true}) \wedge (x, e, m) \textit{ signalled}} \quad (2)$$

Rule (1) checks if x signals e for the first time and if all other microprotocols set their "vote" to raise event e associated with the message. If so, the event is raised asynchronously and all event handlers which have been bound to this event will receive the name of the message (see §3.2 for details). Otherwise (2), event e cannot be raised and we only set in V^m the message readiness as far as microprotocol x is concerned (and mark that the relation *signalled* holds).

For example, we can use this mechanism to implement a collective sending by several microprotocols. Below, we have two microprotocols x and y which share a message m and want to agree when to invoke an event carrying this message.

$$\frac{\begin{array}{l}(x, e, \downarrow) \; registered \\ (y, e, \downarrow) \; registered \\ m = (a, \downarrow, V^m) \\ (y, e, m) \; signalled\end{array}}{E, x \vdash \mathsf{signal}(m, e) \rhd E \wedge (x, e, m)_{\mathrm{ASYNC}} \; raised}$$

We assume that microprotocols x and y registered their interest in raising an event e when a message of type $\downarrow$ will be received from above by the composite protocol. We also assume that some message m of this type eventually appeared and was handled and signalled by microprotocols x and y. Since x is the last microprotocol which signalled the readiness of message m, therefore it causes event e to be raised. A microprotocol (more precisely one of its event handlers) which has been bound to event e can now be invoked and, e.g., it might send the message out of the composite protocol.

4   Appia

A *protocol* in Appia consists of two static parts, one is called *layer* and the other one is called *session* (not to be confused with a session in Cactus). Protocols interact using one or more coordinated channels. A *channel* defines routing of events across protocols, and is defined by a set of instances of sessions (i.e. objects of class "Session").

4.1   Layers and Sessions

A *layer* declares types of events which are either generated, required, or accepted by the protocol. Appia uses the event declarations to verify partial correctness of QoS definitions (we describe this verification below). A layer is also used to create instances of its session. A *session* implements the actual protocol code, in particular it generates and handles events which have been declared by the corresponding layer. An event may carry a message. Messages can be marshalled and communicated in a network.

The set *Layer* is a set of layer names, ranged over by l. The set *Session* is a set of session names, ranged over by s. The name of a layer identifies unambiguously a protocol whose definition the layer is part of (so we may sometimes use terms "layer" and "protocol" interchangeably). A layer can use an operation

$$\mathsf{createSession} : Layer \rightarrow Session$$

to create many instances of its session (the name of the layer is passed as the operation argument).

Below we use a set $P \in \mathcal{S}(Layer)$ of names of all protocols/layers which are used to form a given protocol stack ($\mathcal{S}(Layer)$ denotes all possible subsets of the set $Layer$, i.e. $\mathcal{S}(\mathcal{T})$ is the powerset of $\mathcal{T}$, usually denoted $2^{\mathcal{T}}$). In the context of P, we define the following three maps E_g, E_r, and E_a, which store bindings from layer names to, respectively, a set of types of events which are generated by a protocol, types of events which are required by the protocol, and types of events which are accepted by the protocol (that includes the former set), i.e.

$$E_g, E_r, E_a \in \mathcal{M}(P \mapsto \mathcal{S}(EventType)), \quad \forall l \in P \; E_r[l] \subseteq E_a[l]$$

where $EventType$ is a set of abstract event types. A protocol l declares some event type T to be in $E_a[l]$ but not in $E_r[l]$ if the absence of events of this type is not critical for the protocol execution; therefore we could use protocol l to build protocol stacks which are meaningful even if events of type T are never generated in these stacks.

The Appia state contains set P of layers which are used to form a single protocol stack, together with a map $S \in \mathcal{M}(P \mapsto \mathcal{S}(Session))$ from layer names to sessions created by the layers. New sessions are created as follows.

$$\frac{l \in P}{P, S, l \vdash s := \mathsf{createSession}(l) \triangleright P, S \oplus (l \mapsto S[l] \cup \{s\})}$$

This transforms the state at a time when the protocol stack is initiated, recording a new session s created by layer l in map S.

4.2   QoS Definitions and Channels

A *QoS definition* is simply a static list of layers, which is used to create a communication *channel*. The Appia framework partially verifies each QoS definition, checking if events that the layers declared as required are also declared as generated. The verified QoS definition is used to build a channel with blank slots; the slots can be filled as appropriate with sessions that are created by the layers.

A channel defines the flow of events through the sessions. Each channel maps layers from the QoS definition into concrete sessions which have been created by the layers. By selecting appropriate channels for routing different events through the protocol stack, an application can obtain a requested *quality of service* (QoS).

We model a QoS definition as a list of names of layers which are used to build a single protocol stack. A QoS definition $qos \in \mathcal{L}(P)$ constructed using protocols from P is *well formed* if for each event type T required by each protocol l from set L (of all elements from list qos) there exists some protocol l' in L which generates event e. This verification is usually done before any session is created. The set $Q \in \mathcal{S}(\mathcal{L}(P))$ of QoS definitions, such that each definition is well formed can be used by Appia to create channels.

A set $Channel = \mathcal{L}(Session \times Layer)$ is a set of channels, ranged over by c. Let $C \in \mathcal{M}(Id \mapsto Channel)$ be a mapping from channel identifiers to channels in a given protocol stack, where a single channel c in map C is modelled as a list of session names paired with names of the corresponding layers in the protocol stack, i.e.

$$c = (s, l) :: t \quad \text{where } l \in P, \ s \in S[l] \ .$$

The channel identifiers are unique per protocol stack; they are used by messages to identify a (corresponding) channel on a remote site that should be chosen to deliver the messages to peers. Here is how a new channel is created and bound to sessions (first by user-defined binding and then automatic binding).

$$\frac{c := \mathsf{createUnboundChannel}(ID, qos) \wedge qos \ \textit{well-formed}}{P, S, C \vdash c = defaultBind(userBind(c)) \triangleright P, S, C \oplus (ID \mapsto c)}$$

This first creates a new channel c from a well formed QoS definition qos using an Appia operation $\mathsf{createUnboundChannel} : Id \times \mathcal{L}(Layer) \to Channel$. The channel is identified by a fresh name $ID \in Id$. The new channel is initially $unbound$, i.e. each element (s, l) of c has a session name s equal $null$. After the channel is filled with sessions, a mapping of ID to the channel is recorded in map C.

In order to bind the free slots of an unbound channel to sessions that are created by corresponding layers (of the qos definition), the following two procedures are used. The first procedure must be set up by the protocol programmer, who can specify in this way which channels should share a common session.

$$\boxed{userBind(c):}$$
$$c = (null, l) :: t \quad \text{where } l \in P$$
$$\frac{\exists s \in S[l] \mid s \ \textit{required-by} \ c}{P, S, C \vdash return((s, l) :: userBind(t)) \triangleright P, S, C}$$

This binds free slots in channel c to some existing sessions s, which are selected by a programmer from set $S[l]$. They have been created before with $\mathsf{createSession}$. The sessions s are likely to be bound already to some other channels, so that they can process different types of events which originate from different channels. The choice of sessions is application-dependent; here modelled by relation $required\text{-}by$. If the relation does not hold, $null$ slot is left.

The free slots that have not been bound explicitly by $userBind$ are bound automatically by a default procedure below.

$$\boxed{defaultBind(c):}$$
$$c = (null, l) :: t \quad \text{where } l \in P$$
$$\frac{s := \mathsf{createSession}(l)}{P, S, C \vdash return((s, l) :: defaultBind(t)) \triangleright P, S \oplus (l \mapsto S[l] \cup \{s\}), C} \quad (1)$$

$$\frac{c = (s, l) :: t \wedge s \neq null}{P, S, C \vdash return((s, l) :: defaultBind(t)) \triangleright P, S, C} \quad (2)$$

This creates a new session s for each session-free layer l in a channel c and returns the channel with free slots filled with the session names.

A *protocol stack* is a composition of all protocols that share (transitively) some communication channels. We define F to be a *well formed* set of channels where well-formedness means that each channel in F (built from a well-formed QoS definition) shares at least one session (selected by the user) with some other channel in the protocol stack. We represent a protocol stack as a map C from channel identifiers to channels which are taken from set F.

4.3   Routing Table

After channels have been created, Appia can use information about the channels and events declared by protocols to construct an optimal routing path for each event type that is associated with a given channel.

We model a *routing table* as a map $R \in \mathcal{M}(Id \times EventType \mapsto \mathcal{L}(Session))$ from channel identifiers paired with types of events to routing paths, where a *routing path* is a list of sessions (ordered from top to bottom) which accept these events. A session *accepts* an event of type T if the session was created by a protocol which declared T in its set of accepted events (in map E_a, which has been defined in §4.1).

The map R is created from *all* routing paths which are well formed. A routing path $r \in \mathcal{L}(Session)$ of events of type T that are to travel in a channel identified by ID is *well formed* if r is a list of sessions constructed from a superset of sessions taken from channel c identified by ID, so that each session in r accepts events of type T and the order of sessions in r is the same as order of sessions in c. Routing paths are kept unchanged during system lifetime.

4.4   Events and Messages

Events are the only mean which can be used by protocol sessions (including the application session) to communicate with other sessions in the protocol stack. Messages are specialised events which can be marshalled and sent over network to remote sites; they contain headers with protocol-dependent data. The set *Event* is the set of valid event (and message) names, ranged over by e.

An *event* (or *message*) $e \in Event$ is represented as a tuple (T, ID, r, n), where T is the event type, ID is the name of the channel carrying events of type T, r is the list of sessions to be visited by e (which is built from the channel), and n is the event content. We say that a channel l *carries* (or *accepts*) events of type T if the QoS definition used to create the channel contains at least one layer l, such that $T \in E_a[l]$. The event content n has two components *attrs* and m (denoted $n = attrs + m$), where *attrs* is the record (with named fields) of event attributes, and m is the list of message headers (attached to e by visited protocols). The m fragment is marshalled and sent over network together with T and ID. If e is not a message then m is empty; if e is a message then two attributes s and d of *attrs* are predefined and should contain the source and destination of the message.

Before a message of type T which arrived from a network can be injected into a local channel c identified by ID, it must be first verified (by a user-defined procedure) and then "wrapped" by one of the event tuples below

$$e^{\downarrow} := (T, ID, R[(ID, T)], n)$$
$$e^{\uparrow} := (T, ID, reverse(R[(ID, T)]), n) \ .$$

The event tuples contain local routing data, which is found in R. The routing data will not change during e's lifetime. The choice between tuples $e^{\downarrow}$ and $e^{\uparrow}$ depends on if the event/message uses channel ID to travel downward, or upward ($reverse(l)$ returns a reversed list l). The verification procedure should check if T is accepted by channel ID.

4.5   Event Scheduling and Routing

Below we confuse events and messages for simplicity, and describe the flow of messages in a channel, modelled by modifications to a map of events $E \in \mathcal{M}(Session \times Id \mapsto Event)$ from channel sessions to events.

A session s holding an event $e = (T, ID, r, n)$ can pass it along a channel identified by ID by invoking an operation $\mathsf{go}(e)$.

$$\text{DOWN/UP} \quad \frac{E[(s, ID)] = e = (T, ID, r, n)}{C, E, \Phi, s \vdash \mathsf{go}(e) \rhd C, E \ominus (s, ID), \Phi \cup \{(s, e)\}} \quad (1)$$

This transfers control to a (default or user-defined) scheduler ϕ, modelled as a set Φ of events paired with their last visited session, together with a function $takeEvent$, which returns one element from the set. We record the change of state by modifying the map of events and the scheduler set ($E \ominus e$ returns map E without a binding of e). The scheduler ϕ selects an event e from Φ (the choice depends on the implemented scheduling algorithm), and passes e to the next session to be visited by the event.

$$(s, e) = takeEvent(\Phi)$$
$$e = (T, ID, r, n)$$

$$\text{DOWN/UP} \quad \frac{s' = next(s, r)}{C, E, \Phi, \phi \vdash s'.\mathsf{handle}(e) \rhd C, E \oplus ((s', ID) \mapsto e), \Phi \setminus (s, e)} \quad (2)$$

This selects an event e together with its last visited session s from Φ, and uses s to find out which is the next session s' to visit by e according to the routing path r (which has been extracted from the event tuple). It then invokes an operation handle of session s' to handle event e. We record the change of state by modifying a map of events, and removing (s, e) from the scheduler set. The handle operation will recognise a type of e and invoke a user-defined procedure to handle e. For simplicity, we assume in the rule above that a session can only hold one event at a time. The scheduling of events depends on the event scheduler. The default policy is such that each two events which are initially processed by some session in a certain order (e.g. defined when the events are injected into a protocol stack by an application, or received from the network) will never be processed in the opposite order by any other session in the protocol stack. This implies that the whole protocol stack (i.e. all channels) behaves like a distributed queue which holds a first-in-first-out property.

5   Example Protocol Decomposition

To experiment with Appia and Cactus/J we have implemented in each of these frameworks a small example application that uses two communication services. The first service (AB) sends a message atomically to all processes in a distributed system and guarantees Atomic Broadcast. The second service is an Atomic Multicast (AM), which sends only to a specified group of processes. We have decomposed each service into several modules, each implementing a small protocol, so that some modules in the protocol graph can be shared by the two services (in a given system). The modules are presented in Figure 1. The Atomic Broadcast algorithm and pseudocode of an example modular implementation in Appia and Cactus are described in [8]. In Cactus/J, we have decided to place modules *LampCast* and *Clock* in one composite protocol so that they can share a clock variable C_i, which both modules need to read (see Figure 1a); we did the same for modules *SkeenCast* and *Clock* (not shown in Figure). We might experiment with even finer grain protocols; e.g. the *LampCast* module could be further decomposed into two "microprotocols", one for receiving an application message, and the second one for receiving an acknowledgement message.

The clock variable in module *Clock* of the Appia implementation is not shared by other protocols. Therefore, we need to send a specialised event *ClockEvent* (1) in order to propagate the current clock value to *SkeenCast*, each time a new message arrives from the network. Also, we need to send another specialised event *TimeEvent* (2) with a timestamp of the message which is required by *LampCast*. The events are illustrated in Figure 2. Notice that both events must be propagated upward *before* the event of type *Msg* carrying the message (types *AppMsg*, *AckMsg*, and *GroupMsg*

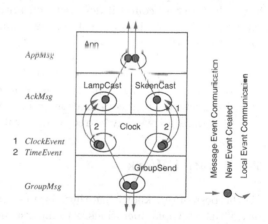

Fig. 2. Example Decomposition in Appia

are all subtypes of *Msg*). Unfortunately, we cannot pass the clock and timestamp values between modules using network messages since the message headers can only be accessed at the level on which they have been created by a peer participant (e.g. a header which contains the timestamp required by *LampCast* is stripped by layer *Clock*). Also, for sanity reasons, attributes should not be used for this either since, e.g. the current clock value is required only by *SkeenCast* — it does not seem reasonable to extend the message format to include this value because we want to be able to remove or replace module *SkeenCast* at any time, however the format of network messages should not change so often (the same for the timestamp value and *LampCast*).

6   Brief Comparison

Cactus supports fine-grain composition of microprotocols, which communicate using events or shared data. A composite protocol (built from a collection of microprotocols) can also be composed with other (composite) protocols, forming a protocol graph. This two-level architecture allows to decompose a given service in an arbitrary way. Appia offers less flexibility of the composition — modules are composed into a graph, and the pattern of communication between modules is restricted by the communication channels. The channels are static, optimised routing paths in the protocol stack. In Cactus, the idea is that each well-defined property or function of a protocol could be implemented as a microprotocol. However, we need more experience to attain confidence when such fine-grain composition would be justified. In particular, increasing the number of concurrent microprotocols per composite protocol (which have to share resources) may increase the number of mutual dependences, in turn making it harder to notice possible deadlocks.

Appia supports partial evaluation of the protocol composition — for each communication channel it can verify if events declared as required are also generated. This helps to reject protocol compositions which are clearly not meaningful, however, of course it does not guarantee correctness (see [8]). This simple evaluation could be improved if a programmer was able to specify some additional (application-dependent) constraints when defining a module, e.g. a requirement that *all* modules below in the communication channel should declare some event(s) as accepted, or required. In the context of Cactus, Hiltunen [2] developed a methodology which is based on identifying relations between modules that dictate which combinations are correct; a configuration tool based on these relations allows only correct configurations to be created.

7   Related Work

To the best of our knowledge there is no other work that models the behaviour of Cactus or Appia operations. An understanding of the behaviour is critical for actually programming with these frameworks. In the Ensemble project, formalisation using the Nuprl theorem prover provided insight into the structure of the layered protocols and their optimization [1], however the framework itself has not been described formally. There has been work on formalisation of modules composition, e.g. [7], however it further abstracts away from programming frameworks.

The approach of Serjantov *et al.* [5] is similar to ours in that they aim to model the behaviour of partial systems, making explicit the interactions that the infrastructure offers to applications. They constructed an experimentally-validated specification of the standard UDP/ICMP sockets interface, including loss and failure, and integrated the above with semantics for an executable fragment of a programming language (OCaml) with OS library primitives. In our case, the "infrastructure" and "application" correspond in turn to the protocol framework and communicating protocols, with correspondingly more complex dependencies and mutual interactions. However, unlike them we do not need to deal with the distributed phenomena and complex failure semantics.

The goals put forth in [6] in the area of the location-independent communication for mobile agents are also related to the approach described here in the sense that the choice or design of protocols must be somewhat application-specific. However, unlike the Nomadic Pict programming language [9] which has been implemented and used to design many different communication infrastructures, provided as encodings of the high-level language primitives, the frameworks described in this paper use standard language facilities and support multi-level protocol composition.

8   Conclusion

8.1   Contribution

We have given a mathematically precise and experimentally validated model of protocol modules composition and interaction in Appia and Cactus (which subsumes the x-kernel model). It has been illustrated with a simple example application that uses two (idealised) group communication algorithms. The model consists of a set of inference rules defining operations and state transitions. The contribution of the formalisation is twofold. It provides a clear and concise description of a fragment of the programming interface provided by each frame work. Moreover, we think that this specification is at the right level of abstraction to help reasoning about the design differences — it describes the frameworks' behaviour (sufficiently accurately) but without going into too many implementation details. The specification is also precise enough to give some useful hints for the designers and implementors of such systems. However, the model is not complete — our primary goal was to understand the design features of the example frameworks, instead of developing concrete reasoning tools that could be applied for programs in Cactus or Appia. Nevertheless, it might be interesting to see how we could express and verify certain properties in this model, like for instance deadlock freedom. Due to lack of time, we also did not cover the whole programming interface and some operations are missing, e.g. for dealing with timeouts and dynamic microprotocol loading; also the description of threads, error situations, and event scheduling should be sufficiently covered. Developing and refining a small example application identified a bug in one of the frameworks, which has been fixed up in a newer release of the system.

8.2   Further Research

The work described in this paper is a step towards a better understanding of protocol modules composition and interaction. However, it provides only a starting point — much additional work is required on algorithms decomposition, semantics, and implementation. We hope to address some of this within our Crystall project, that aims at the design of group communication services with solid semantics foundations. In our future work, we would like to design a language with clean abstractions for module composition and interaction in the context of fault-tolerant computing. One way of making an application tolerant to partial failures, is to replicate its services on different machines using group communication algorithms. The goal is to decompose the algorithms into configurable modules in such a way that module dependencies are reduced, and the (internal) communication between modules is optimised. The language should adopt a model which allows an application to specify its requirements so that they can be adequately reflected by a protocol suite built from modules. The language should also support a type system that can be used to verify certain properties of the protocol suite. Eventually, it should be possible to integrate the language abstractions with standard frameworks that are used to build component based software, in order to increase the applicability of the method.

Acknowledgements. We would like to thank Rick Schlichting and anonymous reviewers for useful comments that helped us to improve the paper. We also thank Luis Rodrigues for explaining some details of the Appia implementation. The project is supported by EPFL grant "Semantics-Guided Design and Implementation of Group Communication Middleware".

References

1. Mark Hayden. The Ensemble system. Technical Report TR98-1662, Department of Computer Science, Cornell University, January 1998.
2. Matti A. Hiltunen. Configuration management for highly-customizable software. *IEE Proceedings: Software*, 145(5):180–188, October 1998.
3. Norman C. Hutchinson and Larry L. Peterson. The x-kernel: An architecture for implementing network protocols. *IEEE Transactions on Software Engineering*, 17(1):64–76, January 1991.
4. Hugo Miranda, Alexandre Pinto, and Luís Rodrigues. Appia, a flexible protocol kernel supporting multiple coordinated channels. In *ICDCS'01*, 2001.
5. Andrei Serjantov, Peter Sewell, and Keith Wansbrough. The UDP calculus: Rigorous semantics for real networking. In *TACS'01 (Sendai)*, October 2001.
6. Peter Sewell, Paweł T. Wojciechowski, and Benjamin C. Pierce. Location-independent communication for mobile agents: A two-level architecture. In *Internet Programming Languages*, LNCS 1686, pages 1–31, 1999.
7. Purnendu Sinha and Neeraj Suri. On simplifying modular specification and verification of distributed protocols. In *HASE'01*, October 2001.
8. Paweł T. Wojciechowski, Sergio Mena, and André Schiper. Semantics of protocol modules composition and interaction. Technical report, School of Computer and Communication Sciences, EPFL, February 2002.
9. Paweł T. Wojciechowski and Peter Sewell. Nomadic Pict: Language and infrastructure design for mobile agents. *IEEE Concurrency*, 8(2):42–52, April-June 2000.
10. Gary T. Wong, Matti A. Hiltunen, and Richard D. Schlichting. A configurable and extensible transport protocol. In *INFOCOM'01*, April 2001.

Author Index

Lecture Notes in Computer Science

For information about Vols. 1–2228
please contact your bookseller or Springer-Verlag

Vol. 2266: S. Reich, M.T. Tzagarakis, P.M.E. De Bra (Eds.), Hypermedia: Openness, Structural Awareness, and Adaptivity. Proceedings, 2001. X, 335 pages. 2002.

Vol. 2267: M. Cerioli, G. Reggio (Eds.), Recent Trends in Algebraic Development Techniques. Proceedings, 2001. X, 345 pages. 2001.

Vol. 2268: E.F. Deprettere, J. Teich, S. Vassiliadis (Eds.), Embedded Processor Design Challenges. VIII, 327 pages. 2002.

Vol. 2269: S. Diehl (Ed.), Software Visualization. Proceedings, 2001. VIII, 405 pages. 2002.

Vol. 2270: M. Pflanz, On-line Error Detection and Fast Recover Techniques for Dependable Embedded Processors. XII, 126 pages. 2002.

Vol. 2271: B. Preneel (Ed.), Topics in Cryptology – CT-RSA 2002. Proceedings, 2002. X, 311 pages. 2002.

Vol. 2272: D. Bert, J.P. Bowen, M.C. Henson, K. Robinson (Eds.), ZB 2002: Formal Specification and Development in Z and B. Proceedings, 2002. XII, 535 pages. 2002.

Vol. 2273: A.R. Coden, E.W. Brown, S. Srinivasan (Eds.), Information Retrieval Techniques for Speech Applications. XI, 109 pages. 2002.

Vol. 2274: D. Naccache, P. Paillier (Eds.), Public Key Cryptography. Proceedings, 2002. XI, 385 pages. 2002.

Vol. 2275: N.R. Pal, M. Sugeno (Eds.), Advances in Soft Computing – AFSS 2002. Proceedings, 2002. XVI, 536 pages. 2002. (Subseries LNAI).

Vol. 2276: A. Gelbukh (Ed.), Computational Linguistics and Intelligent Text Processing. Proceedings, 2002. XIII, 444 pages. 2002.

Vol. 2277: P. Callaghan, Z. Luo, J. McKinna, R. Pollack (Eds.), Types for Proofs and Programs. Proceedings, 2000. VIII, 243 pages. 2002.

Vol. 2278: J.A. Foster, E. Lutton, J. Miller, C. Ryan, A.G.B. Tettamanzi (Eds.), Genetic Programming. Proceedings, 2002. XI, 337 pages. 2002.

Vol. 2279: S. Cagnoni, J. Gottlieb, E. Hart, M. Middendorf, G.R. Raidl (Eds.), Applications of Evolutionary Computing. Proceedings, 2002. XIII, 344 pages. 2002.

Vol. 2280: J.P. Katoen, P. Stevens (Eds.), Tools and Algorithms for the Construction and Analysis of Systems. Proceedings, 2002. XIII, 482 pages. 2002.

Vol. 2281: S. Arikawa, A. Shinohara (Eds.), Progress in Discovery Science. XIV, 684 pages. 2002. (Subseries LNAI).

Vol. 2282: D. Ursino, Extraction and Exploitation of Intensional Knowledge from Heterogeneous Information Sources. XXVI, 289 pages. 2002.

Vol. 2283: T. Nipkow, L.C. Paulson, M. Wenzel, Isabelle/HOL. XIII, 218 pages. 2002.

Vol. 2284: T. Eiter, K.-D. Schewe (Eds.), Foundations of Information and Knowledge Systems. Proceedings, 2002. X, 289 pages. 2002.

Vol. 2285: H. Alt, A. Ferreira (Eds.), STACS 2002. Proceedings, 2002. XIV, 660 pages. 2002.

Vol. 2286: S. Rajsbaum (Ed.), LATIN 2002: Theoretical Informatics. Proceedings, 2002. XIII, 630 pages. 2002.

Vol. 2287: C.S. Jensen, K.G. Jeffery, J. Pokorny, Saltenis, E. Bertino, K. Böhm, M. Jarke (Eds.), Advances in Database Technology – EDBT 2002. Proceedings, 2002. XVI, 776 pages. 2002.

Vol. 2288: K. Kim (Ed.), Information Security and Cryptology – ICISC 2001. Proceedings, 2001. XIII, 457 pages. 2002.

Vol. 2289: C.J. Tomlin, M.R. Greenstreet (Eds.), Hybrid Systems: Computation and Control. Proceedings, 2002. XIII, 480 pages. 2002.

Vol. 2291: F. Crestani, M. Girolami, C.J. van Rijsbergen (Eds.), Advances in Information Retrieval. Proceedings, 2002. XIII, 363 pages. 2002.

Vol. 2292: G.B. Khosrovshahi, A. Shokoufandeh, A. Shokrollahi (Eds.), Theoretical Aspects of Computer Science. IX, 221 pages. 2002.

Vol. 2293: J. Renz, Qualitative Spatial Reasoning with Topological Information. XVI, 207 pages. 2002. (Subseries LNAI).

Vol. 2296: B. Dunin-Kęplicz, E. Nawarecki (Eds.), From Theory to Practice in Multi-Agent Systems. Proceedings, 2001. IX, 341 pages. 2002. (Subseries LNAI).

Vol. 2299: H. Schmeck, T. Ungerer, L. Wolf (Eds.), Trends in Network and Pervasive Computing – ARCS 2002. Proceedings, 2002. XIV, 287 pages. 2002.

Vol. 2300: W. Brauer, H. Ehrig, J. Karhumäki, A. Salomaa (Eds.), Formal and Natural Computing. XXXVI, 431 pages. 2002.

Vol. 2301: A. Braquelaire, J.-O. Lachaud, A. Vialard (Eds.), Discrete Geometry for Computer Imagery. Proceedings, 2002. XI, 439 pages. 2002.

Vol. 2302: C. Schulte, Programming Constraint Services. XII, 176 pages. 2002. (Subseries LNAI).

Vol. 2303: M. Nielsen, U. Engberg (Eds.), Foundations of Software Science and Computation Structures. Proceedings, 2002. XIII, 435 pages. 2002.

Vol. 2304: R.N. Horspool (Ed.), Compiler Construction. Proceedings, 2002. XI, 343 pages. 2002.

Vol. 2305: D. Le Métayer (Ed.), Programming Languages and Systems. Proceedings, 2002. XII, 331 pages. 2002.

Vol. 2306: R.-D. Kutsche, H. Weber (Eds.), Fundamental Approaches to Software Engineering. Proceedings, 2002. XIII, 341 pages. 2002.

Vol. 2308: I.P. Vlahavas, C.D. Spyropoulos (Eds.), Methods and Applications of Artificial Intelligence. Proceedings, 2002. XIV, 514 pages. 2002. (Subseries LNAI).

Vol. 2309: A. Armando (Ed.), Frontiers of Combining Systems. Proceedings, 2002. VIII, 255 pages. 2002. (Subseries LNAI).

Vol. 2314: S.-K. Chang, Z. Chen, S.-Y. Lee (Eds.), Recent Advances in Visual Information Systems. Proceedings, 2002. XI, 323 pages. 2002.

Vol. 2315: F. Arhab, C. Talcott (Eds.), Coordination Models and Languages. Proceedings, 2002. XI, 406 pages. 2002.

Vol. 2322: V. Mařík, O. Stěpánková, H. Krautwurmová, M. Luck (Eds.), Multi-Agent Systems and Applications II. Proceedings, 2001. XII, 377 pages. 2002. (Subseries LNAI).